Non-Governmental Organisations and International Law

Prahlad Rai

Non-Governmental Organisations and International Law

Springer

Prahlad Rai
Department of Law
University of Rajasthan
Jaipur, Rajasthan, India

ISBN 978-981-97-5468-7 ISBN 978-981-97-5469-4 (eBook)
https://doi.org/10.1007/978-981-97-5469-4

This Springer imprint is published by the registered company Springer Nature Singapore Pte Ltd.
The registered company address is: 152 Beach Road, #21-01/04 Gateway East, Singapore 189721, Singapore

Preface

The purpose of this book is to understand non-governmental organisations through the lens of international law. This book primarily addresses NGO community and students of law, political science, sociology, masters of social work and management studies. It is a ready reference for activists, officials and also corporate social responsibility department of various corporations. I have presented the past 200 years of NGOs' story in a very simple and readable manner in diverse issue areas.

The term non-governmental organisation explicitly entered the United Nations Charter and the corpus of international law, in mid-twentieth century. This opened an opportunity for NGOs to work with other international actors like States, intergovernmental organisations (IGOs) and corporations, who enjoy sovereign powers, authorisation and economic clout, respectively. NGOs have none of these powers; they simply have altruism and activism. However, their influence and expertise has grown over the years.

I have highlighted the performance and achievements of NGOs in this book as well as their possibilities and limitations. NGOs have played a very constructive role in the making of international law and global governance. I have referred to some peaceful methods and techniques that have been employed by NGOs over the years, innovating them further as per changing needs and contexts.

NGOs have engaged with some of the most crucial issue areas of our time-human rights, environment and business ethics. I have looked for insights in these issue areas to identify the role of NGOs, besides States, IGOs and corporations. Based on this, I have provided indications towards better use of public space and mutual learning for furthering their NGOs' activities in democratic, authoritarian and mixed governments.

The protection of human rights defenders, environmentalists and activists is vital. NGOs have already received a legal identity, and maintaining their accountability and transparency certainly enhances their global standing.

In this book, I have covered all the core areas and themes involving the functioning, funding and other concerns of NGOs. I wish the best to the readers about to embark on a journey to make a positive change in the world and to those already working to address global challenges that humanity faces. I hope that this book will be instrumental in developing and evolving newer perspectives for the way forward.

Jaipur, India Prahlad Rai

Acknowledgements

I am grateful to the Indian Council for Social Science Research, New Delhi, for awarding me with the Senior Fellowship to study non-governmental organisations.

I am highly indebted to all the scholars and activists I could consult and who provided guidance, inspiration and feedback on the subject. Also all those who researched and created reference material that enlightened my understanding of the subject and helped me in shaping the structure of this book.

My sincere acknowledgement to the three anonymous reviewers who took the time and effort to take a closer look at the manuscript and provided me with constructive suggestions to further improve the content and its relevance.

I am grateful to Dr. Nupoor Singh for reviewing my book proposal and for accepting my manuscript for publication.

I am also thankful to Springer Nature and their editorial team for their care, co-operation and diligence during the entire publishing process.

I am especially thankful to Dr. Vinai K. Singh of Indian Society of International Law, New Delhi, for his constant support and encouragement to carry on this project with enthusiasm. I also express my sincere thanks to Ms. Lalitha Ravindran for her valuable suggestions.

Last but not least, I would like to thank my wife, Manju, for her unwavering support and for bearing with me during the years this has taken to complete and for being my pillar of strength. I'm also thankful to my sons, Mudit and Mohneesh, for their optimism and support.

About The Book

Point 1

Non-Governmental Organisations and International Law

Point 2

In the last few decades, Non-Governmental Organisations worldwide have been working on various critical areas affecting people's lives and expectations to facilitate a more humanising international law. Their sphere of influence is within the State and beyond. They embrace the spirit of *Vasudhaiva Kuthumbhkam*—the whole world is one family.

The Author delves into how NGOs enrich the international community. The book provides ideas, highlights issues, and identifies actors, actions, and the scope of NGOs in international law. It charts the possibilities and limitations of NGOs within the legal framework of a State and its evolution over the years. NGOs have obtained 'consultative status' from the UN Economic and Social Council and extended their access to inter-governmental organisations, international courts and tribunals. The book spotlights NGOs' influence on these international actors.

NGOs have played an important role in the making of human rights, protection of environment and business ethics. The book is an overview of their performance.

Point 3

NGOs are governed by a set of national and international law. This book highlights their accountability under the international legal framework and provides them guidance to influence international actors and engage in protection of human rights, environment and business ethics. The book provides legal insights for NGOs efficacy and how their contribution can strengthen international law. Today the NGO activism in the sinking public sphere is an enthusiasm.

Contents

Part I Status of NGOs

1 Introduction 3
- 1 What is an NGO? 3
- 2 Salient Features of an NGO 5
- 3 Classification of NGOs 9
- 4 The Idea of Civil Society 11
- 5 The Public Sphere and NGOs 16
- 6 Possibilities for NGOs 21
- References 24

2 A Short History of NGOs 29
- 1 Introduction 29
- 2 Origins of Non-governmental Organisations: 1775–1914 31
- 3 Time of Engagement and Disengagement: 1914–1945 38
- 4 Expanded Horizons: 1945–Present Day 47
- 5 Conclusion 51
- References 51

3 Legal Personality 55
- 1 Introduction 55
- 2 Evolution of Legal Personality in International Law 57
- 3 Legal Personality of State 59
- 4 Legal Personality of Non-state Entities 60
- 5 Legal Personality in Europe 68
- 6 Observer Status in Africa 73
- 7 Rights and Responsibilities of NGOs 74
- 8 Right to Freedom of Association 76
- 9 Conclusion 79
- References 80

4 Consultative Status 85
1 Introduction 85
2 The United Nations System 86
3 Article 71 of the UN Charter 89
4 Process of Consultative Status 93
5 The Cardoso Report 97
6 NGOs and the General Assembly 100
7 NGOs and the Security Council 102
8 Conclusion 105
References 105

Part II NGOs Relation with International Actors

5 Operative Methods 111
1 Introduction 111
2 Agenda-Setting 113
3 Fact-Finding 116
4 Coalition, Campaigning and Networking 120
5 Protection of Human Rights Defenders 125
6 Conclusion 129
References 131

6 NGO Relations with Inter-Governmental Organisations 135
1 Introduction 135
2 Development of NGO-IGO Relationship 137
3 Institutionalisation of NGOs-IGOs Relationship 139
4 NGOs and the World Trade Organisation 143
5 B. NGO's Strive for Hearing People's Voice 144
6 NGOs and the United Nations Educational, Scientific and Cultural Organisation 149
7 NGOs and the World Bank 153
8 Conclusion 158
References 158

7 NGOs Before International Courts and Tribunals 161
1 Introduction 161
2 Permanent Court of Arbitration 164
3 International Court of Justice 164
4 International Criminal Court 167
5 The International Tribunal for the Law of the Sea 172
6 WTO Adjudicative Body 175
7 International Centre for Settlement of Investment Disputes 180
8 World Bank Inspection Panel 185
9 Conclusion 187
References 188

Part III Role of NGOs in Making of International Law

8 NGOs in the Making of Human Rights 195
1 Introduction 195
2 Precursor of International Human Rights Law 197
3 Universal Declaration of Human Rights (UDHR) 1948 199
4 International Covenants 1966 202
5 Specific Rights 209
6 Groups Rights 212
7 Conclusion 217
References 218

9 Enforcement of Human Rights 223
1 Introduction 223
2 Charter-Based Bodies 225
3 Communication Procedure 229
4 Universal Periodic Review (UPR) 231
5 United Nations Special Procedure 233
6 Treaty-Based Bodies 236
7 Performance of NGOs in Treaty Bodies 239
8 Conclusion 242
References 243

10 Regional Machinery 247
1 Introduction 247
2 Evaluation of Regional Human Rights 249
3 European Machinery 251
4 Inter-American Machinery 257
5 African Machinery 262
6 Conclusion 266
References 267

11 Protection of the Environment 271
1 Introduction 271
2 The Development of International Environmental Law 272
3 Conservation of Nature 276
4 Protection of the Atmosphere 285
5 Protection of the Marine Environment 291
6 Nuclear Risk 296
7 Conclusion 297
References 299

12 Business Ethics ... 305
1 Introduction ... 305
2 International Trade Law ... 309
3 Trade Linkages ... 314
4 International Investment Law ... 320
5 Protection of NGOs Cross-Border Funding ... 325
6 Conclusion ... 329
References ... 331

Part IV Recent Developments

13 NGO Accountability ... 339
1 Introduction ... 339
2 Concept of Accountability ... 341
3 NGOs' Accountability Discourse ... 343
4 Accountability Mechanisms ... 347
5 Codes, Standards and Watchdogs ... 355
6 Conclusion ... 359
References ... 360

14 Case Study ... 363
1 Introduction ... 363
2 The Institute of International Law ... 365
3 Permanent International Peace Bureau ... 366
4 The Quakers ... 367
5 Amnesty International ... 368
6 International Physicians for the Prevention of Nuclear War ... 372
7 International Campaign to Ban Landmines ... 373
8 Mėdicines Sans Frontiėrs (MSF) ... 375
9 Tunisian National Dialogue Quartet ... 379
10 International Campaign to Abolish Nuclear Weapons ... 381
11 Ales Bialiatski, and Memorial, and Centre for Civil Liberties ... 384
12 Conclusion ... 386
References ... 387

About the Author

Prahlad Rai is former Professor and Head, Department of Law, University of Rajasthan, Jaipur, India. He was a Senior Fellow of Indian Council of Social Science Research (ICSSR) from 2016–18. He obtained his Ph.D. from Jawaharlal Nehru University (JNU), New Delhi, India; and was awarded doctoral fellowship from The Hague Academy of International Law, Netherlands in 1988. His areas of research interest are international law, constitutional law, and human rights; and he has conducted University Grants Commission (UGC) research projects on construction labour and on shipping in international law; and a National Commission of Women's research project on domestic violence.

Part I
Status of NGOs

Chapter 1
Introduction

1 What is an NGO?

The 'Non-governmental organisations' (NGOs) term was employed by the Charter of the United Nations in 1945 and has formed an integral part of the international law lexicon. The term 'NGOs' has very wide connotations. In order to understand ideas of NGOs in the proper perspective, a precise definition and conceptual framework is needed. Peter Willets in his study: "*What is a Non-Governmental Organisation?*" (2002) has explained that.

> an NGO is defined as an independent voluntary association of people acting together on a continuous basis, for some common purpose, other than achieving government office, making money or illegal activities.[1]

Kerstin Martens published her popular research paper, "*Mission Impossible? Defining Non-Governmental Organisations*", in 2002. She observed: NGOs have become recognised actors in international affairs, particularly over the last decade. It has not yet been clearly defined what the term NGO encompasses.[2]

In the early twentieth century, D.W. Bowett referred to NGOs as private international unions.[3] In order to co-ordinate NGOs' activities and to maintain their records, the Union of International Association (UIA) was founded in 1907. Then the UIA published Yearbook of International Organisations with content information about non-governmental and inter-governmental organisations (IGOs). But the Yearbook did not define NGOs. The Private International Union term was no more used in international law. But legal literature used the term NGO with more frequency in comparison with other terms, starting 1945.

An NGO is said to be a private person's initiative with public interest; they have a motivation to serve people without the personal gain of any of its members. This

---

[1] Willets (2002).

[2] Martens (2002).

[3] Bowett (2009).

P. Rai, *Non-Governmental Organisations and International Law*,
https://doi.org/10.1007/978-981-97-5469-4_1

is a voluntary association for common cause. The NGO is an institution that has permanent structure and durability. They have independent identity from the state, inter-governmental organisations and corporations. These are social organisations that are distinct from social movements, because social movements deal with the specific assertion of people at large for the time being, while NGOs are transboundary activists with a durable set structure and a legal identity.

NGOs have emerged from ideas of charity, philanthropy and not-for-profit but they have their own features and characteristics under the umbrella of non-governmental entity or non-business agency. They are engaged in developing alternatives, law-making and enforcement of rules, but are not involved directly in power politics. Therefore, they steer clear of political parties and aren't engaged with the replacement of government or its takeover.

Pierre-Marie Dupuy observed:

> We are led back to the role of legal scholars faced with the paradox of NGOs; de jure, these entities have no existence or a very narrowly defined one, if any; but de facto they do a lot, especially in the functioning of international institutions and the implementation of the law created in their midst.[4]

NGOs do not have a legal definition because there is no specific international agreement unlike inter-governmental organisations. The legal framework of NGOs was first ever provided in Article 71 of the UN Charter and followed by the ECOSOC Resolution 1996/31. The United Nations Economic and Social Council (ECOSOC) Resolution lays down a workable definition of NGO:

> Any such organisation that is not established by a governmental entity or intergovernmental agreement shall be considered a non-governmental organisation for the purpose of these arrangements, including organisations that accept members designated by government authorities, provided that such membership does not interfere with the free expression of views of the organisation.[5]

The ECOSOC Resolution emphasised on NGOs not being created either by government or inter-governmental agreements but rather by a private person's collective institution. NGOs enjoy independence in expression and action outside the orbit of government and business. The resolution further laid down certain conditions for granting consultative status to NGOs, inter alia: NGOs' aims and purposes shall be in conformity with the spirit, purposes and principles of the UN Charter; recognised standing within the particular field of its competence; a representative character; headquarters with an executive officer; a democratically adopted constitution; and appropriate mechanism of accountability.[6] These are some of the essential elements for obtaining consultative status.

The Institute of International Law made attempts to define NGOs in 1910 and consolidate the definition of NGOs on the basis of certain criteria. The institute used

---

[4] Dupuy (2008).

[5] *Consultative relationship between the United Nations and non-governmental organisations*, ECOSOC Resolution E/RES/1996/31 (25 July 1996), para 12.

[6] Ibid., paras 2, 9–12.

the term private international organisations instead of NGOs. Private international organisations or NGOs are private initiatives, non-profit making and performing activities at the international level. NGOs are further defined by the Council of Europe in 1951 and subsequently 1986, the Organization of American States (OAS) in 1999 and African Union in 1963, in their respective legal documents.

Apart from the UN Charter, the ECOSOC Resolution, specialised agencies, Council of Europe, Organization of American States, African Union and a number of writers such as Boli and Thomas,[7] Schermers and Blokker,[8] Willets,[9] White,[10] Hermann H.K. Rechenberg,[11] Lador-Lederer,[12] Anna-Karin Lindblom[13] and Steve Charnovitz[14] have defined NGOs as well. These writers and institutions identified a set of salient features. By and large, they have argued upon them.

2 Salient Features of an NGO

NGOs, as institutions, possess some salient features that distinguish them from other international actors. NGOs are primarily a private person's initiatives, known as not-for-profit organisations. They are actively engaged in peoples' interests and are generally good at national and international level. Moreover, they are not supposed to earn profit for the distribution among its members or promoters. NGOs are autonomous bodies that can take independent decisions on international affairs unlike the representatives of nations. They express their opinion freely and carry out missions in their chosen issue areas.

NGOs essentially fall outside the orbit of state and market. They seek their permission or registration, income tax exemption, receive funds and undertake compliance of government regulations without losing their functional autonomy and integrity. NGOs encounter market place, interface business and interact with corporations but they remain away from any profit or trading interests. They shall keep away from any kinds of violence. NGOs pursue their objectives and transnational boundary activism by peaceful and democratic means. Their operative methods are globally accepted, like peaceful assembly and protest, campaign and networking, spreading of awareness and educating people on contemporary issues, building public opinion and suggesting alternate policy framework. Generally, NGOs do not indulge in direct politics, either to replace or to take over the government. They are essentially societal organisations and refrain from power politics and business earnings.

---

[7] Boli and Thomas (1999).

[8] Schermers and Blokker (2018).

[9] Willets (1966).

[10] White (1951).

[11] Rechenberg (1997).

[12] Lador-Lederer (1963).

[13] Lindblom (2005).

[14] Charnovitz (2006).

NGOs' aims and purposes are: public interest and the promotion of peoples' well-being. They have their objectives and means in conformity with the spirit, principles and purposes of the United Nations. Hopefully, they think beyond 'self-interest' and work selflessly, inculcating the altruistic behaviour within themselves. Ever since their inception, NGOs have been inherently operationalised in their envisaged objectives with the spirit of voluntarism.

NGOs are located within any given country and carry out activities inside their national boundary and beyond. They have to think globally, have international orientation and are not confined to nationalistic ideas. NGOs are not essentially state representatives in international conferences and world summits. They participate as autonomous entities and represent voices of the voiceless in national and international conferences.

'Non-governmental entities' is thereby a very broad term. A number of synonymous terms are used in the fraternity[15] like civil society, non-state actors, social movements, not-for-profit organisations, voluntary associations, charity, philanthropy, foundations, public trusts and so on.

Each term has its own meaning, connotation and implications. Indeed, they are interrelated in the broadest sense and sometimes overlap, but they are not interchangeable and synonymous with each other. For instance, the term 'civil society' is broader than the term, NGOs. Apart from NGOs, civil society includes political parties, trade unions, foundations, religious organisations, academia, voluntary associations, clubs, professional organisations and every kind of non-governmental entity. Even in the broadest sense, civil society encompasses freedom of speech, rule of law and independent judiciary and democracy. However, the idea of civil society is closely related to the idea of NGOs. The history and theory of NGOs and civil society intersect through the ages. In short, civil society is an idea, while NGOs is an activism from outside the realm of family, state and the world of business.

The concept of civil society emerged at the time of Aristotle in the third century BC. The ideas of civil society continue to this day. Civil society ideas, civic values, ethos and norms are also inseparably shared by NGOs. These theoretical tools and methods are applied to the NGOs' conceptual discourse.[16]

NGOs function as societal actors and have a close connection to social movements. Social movements are a collective endeavour of private individuals who wish to protest, to resist, to demonstrate against powerful regimes and raise a voice for oppressed populations. Social movements are engaged with social change and exist to transform the political system in democracy. For instance, the Civil Rights movement in America of the 1960s, Arab Spring in 2011 and the Me Too movement in 2017 have focussed on the cherished human values of equal treatment, democratic rights and gender justice respectively.

These movements were the collective challenge to powerful individuals and regimes alike; that nobody is above the law and standards of civic behaviour. Therefore, social movement ethos with the NGOs coalition and their network come for

---

[15] Woodward (2010).

[16] Ehrenberg (2007) and Whaites (1998).

advocacy. The NGOs coalition ban on Anti-personnel Mines, 1997, and the Prohibition of Nuclear Weapons, 2017, appeared like social movements. NGOs are rooted in social movement, ever since the latter's resurgence in the eighteenth century. Since NGOs organised movements against anti-slavery, prostitution, opium and armament, they have been overlapping with civil society and social movements.

However, NGOs are distinct from social movements because they have infrastructure and durability in comparison with the social movements. Social movements are spontaneous, issue-based and time-specific. Their purpose may or may not be achieved. For example, the Arab Spring of 2011 resulted in success for Tunisia, but not elsewhere.[17] Being institutions, NGOs can therefore sustain and remain engaged in transboundary activism.

Of late, the term 'non-state actors' (NSA) is used in academic literature. Likewise, civil society and non-state actors having broader connotations encompass corporations, media, the national liberation movement, NGOs, people's movements, religious groups and even violent groups and business magnates. NGOs are different from NSAs because NGOs' working is based on the principle of non-violence, whereas some NSAs are said to be involved in insurgent and disruptive activities. But those NSA that do not believe in violent means are approximately interlinked to NGOs, civil society and social movements.[18]

The Cotonou Agreement between the European Union and African, Caribbean and Pacific countries was concluded in 2000, and the term non-state actors included civil society, trade unions and the private sectors under Article 6 Clause 3 of this agreement.[19]

Voluntary associations are also closely related to NGOs because the idea of voluntarism is one of the core values of the NGO community. Volunteer associations are also a private citizen's creation and represent non-profit sectors. The volunteers have a common cause, such as trade unions and professional associations. 'Volunteer association' is a very wide term covering all sort of groups including residential welfare associations and business associations. Volunteer associations differ from NGOs because they do not require to be registered in their country while NGOs are generally registered civic associations.

Every non-profit organisation is not an NGO. For instance, any business entity that does not engage in profit earnings is certainly close to an NGO. In India, a non-profit company registered under section 8 of the Company Act, 2013, is a charitable organisation that receives tax exemptions. This type of company is a business organisation and also carries out commercial activities, but strictly, it cannot distribute its earnings or benefits among its members, shareholders and promoters. A non-profit company has a social cause as per the choice of its shareholders.[20]

Charities, public trusts, foundations and philanthropic associations/organisations come under the ambit of non-profit activities. They fall broadly within the confines

---

[17] Diani and McAdam (2003), Tilly (2008), and Staggenborg (2008).

[18] Wagner (2010), Keck and Sikkin (1998), and Arts and Reinalda (2001).

[19] The Cotonou Agreement (2000).

[20] Anheier (2006) and Hartigan (2006).

of civil society and NGOs. Charities, foundations, public trusts and philanthropic organisations are primarily donors or funders in the interest of general and common causes.

Historically, charity is rooted in religion and rich persons' generosity. Out of their fortune, they distribute money or kind to the poor, needy and distressed people. In 1601, charity organisations were engaged in health, housing, education and the amelioration of living prisoners.

In the era of enlightenment, charity became a secular and cultural practice and law also promoted it through tax exemptions. Charity provided funds to social movements and campaigns. For instance, the anti-slavery movement in the nineteenth century and the anti-nuclear weapons campaign in the twenty-first century received donation from charities. In the era of a flowing globalised economy and free market, charity became more relevant to the areas of poverty, health, housing, education, environment, human rights, food security and community development.[21]

Public trust was incorporated to institutionalise charitable work and received tax exemptions. These charitable trusts generated goodwill through their work and donations in the alleviation of poverty, promotion of education, health, environment and community life. They played a significant role in Iran, India, the United Kingdom and the United States.[22]

The public foundation is a non-profit organisation. They provide funds to NGOs or individuals for charitable purposes.[23] In the same way as a trust, the foundation is also public or private in nature. Private foundations and trusts are endowed by individuals or families. It has very restricted tax exemptions in comparison to public trusts and foundations. Private foundations and trusts are generally controlled by a donor, an individual or a family.

Philanthropy is a private initiative for public interest. It focusses mainly on the improvement of human life. Philanthropy in its broad sense stands for the love for humanity. Individuals engaged in philanthropy are known as philanthropists. Examples of these are Andrew Carnegie, John D Rockefeller, Ford, Tata, Warren Buffet, Bill and Melinda Gates and many more. They have contributed most of their fortunes to charity. Charity and philanthropy both dedicate their funds and resources for public good. Charity is spontaneous and can be undertaken by any individual. It may be a one-time affair. Philanthropy, on the other hand, may be a long-term solution. Philanthropic foundations provide funds to NGOs and civil societies. Generally, they do not engage in field activities.[24]

---

[21] Chisolum (1988–1989).

[22] Edwards and Stockwell (2013).

[23] Poelofs (2003).

[24] Adam (2004), Ilchman et al. (1998), Kinger (2008).

3 Classification of NGOs

Jurgen Habermas described non-governmental entities as the public sphere. It is a sphere of national and domestic social interaction.[25] Associational life of civil society is a basic human instinct. There are two broad areas, governmental and non-governmental institutions. Non-governmental organisations have the basic unity in their essential features: non-governmental, non-profit, non-uni-national and non-violent. These NGOs' criteria differentiate themselves from governmental and inter-governmental organisations (IGOs).

Civil society, in the broader sense, encompasses all social, economic, cultural and political relations, but the emphasis is usually on political aspects of these relations.[26] Civil society is outside the governmental apparatus but it is not necessarily against the government. Although they are almost always against authoritarian regimes.[27] The United Nations has included business and civil society in its 'back page site' for providing information. For instance, the UN Department of Economic and Social Affairs has integrated all kinds of civil society organisations with a single unified system.[28] This was protested against because corporations' economic monopoly had pushed civil society to the fringe of the world affairs.

NGOs practice non-violence, hence criminal mafia, gangsters, terrorists and insurgents are beyond the purview of this inclusive study. However, are trade unions included in the realm of NGOs? Steve Charnovitz proposed to incorporate labour unions and professional associations within the NGO fold.[29] Charnovitz's ideas were a reflection of the United Nations' past practice. The UN endowed consultative status to labour unions via ECOSOC accreditation procedure in 1946, in the category of NGOs.

There are no specific provisions to register or to regulate NGOs under international law, except when it comes to consultative status accorded by the UN Economic and Social Council. NGOs are first registered under their own country's legal system. Subsequently, they obtain consultative status in the UN system.

The legal system of NGOs around the world is obviously different. Hence, the creation of NGOs overall differs from one another. In democratic nations, it is very easy for NGOs to obtain registration. While in authoritative nations, NGOs' registration or permission is a hard nut to crack. In case they get permission, they might be pushed back. For instance, in China, NGOs are looked upon as anti-government as opposed to non-governmental entities.[30] The core idea of civil society has remained intact despite their origins in diverse legal systems.[31]

---

[25] Habermas (1974).

[26] Peter Willetts, *supra note* 9, p. 14.

[27] Edward (2009).

[28] http://www.un.org/esa/coordination/ngo.

[29] Steve Charmovitz, *supra note 14*, p. 350.

[30] Ashley and He (2008).

[31] Cohen and Arato (1994).

The journey of modern NGOs began from Western Europe and Northern America, with most NGO headquarters being located in the northern hemisphere. The office bearers and chief executives are from western countries.[32] The winds of change began to blow in the last quarter of the twentieth century, when the office bearers' and chief executives' posts were shared between developing and developed nations.

Diversification in the NGO community is inevitable due to their growing number, reach, size, issue areas and activities. NGOs have differences in their cultures, ideologies, legal status, orientation and locations. In spite of their diversity, the community has unique characteristics with regard to its members, objectives, headquarters, constitution or articles of association, governance, registration, tax exemptions and permissions for receiving foreign funding.

The classification of NGOs is based on their legal status, membership, level of operation, issue areas and their accreditation status within the UN system. NGOs' legal status is divided into four categories: (1) un-incorporated voluntary association, for example club or any similar groups; (2) incorporated voluntary association registered under registration and taxation law, for example Amnesty International and other NGOs; (3) charity, foundation and public trust, for example Ford Foundation, Tata Trust and Worldwide Fund for Nature (WWF), etc.; and (4) companies, not-for-profit under Company Act, for example Give Directly—a non-profit company.[33]

Peter Willets classified international organisations into three categories, i.e. (1) inter-governmental organisations (IGOs), for example the African Union, the UN, UNESCO, World Bank and others; (2) hybrid international organisations, for example ILO and IUCN and ICRC; and (3) international non-governmental organisations, for example Amnesty International, Transparency International, Doctors Without Borders (MSF), Human Rights Watch and numerous others.

Willets further divided NGOs on the basis of membership and funds. First, NGOs have only government employees as members, for instance International Union of Police Federation. Second, members of NGOs are private persons and welcome government funds, for example International Planned Parenthood Federation. Some NGOs do not prefer government funds, for instance Amnesty International.[34]

On the operation level, NGOs are classified as local, national, regional and international. They are broadly divided into two categories: national and international. Those NGOs operating in two or more countries are known as international NGOs, for example Doctors Without Borders (MSF). As far as UN consultative status goes, after 1996, no such classification exists, but they are categorised by ECOSOC as general, specialised and roster NGOs.[35] The World Bank divided NGOs into the categories of operational and advocacy.[36]

[32] Chandok (2005).

[33] Stillman (2007).

[34] Peter Willets, *supra note 9*, p. 8.

[35] ECOSOC Resolution 1996/31.

[36] Malena (1995).

Kerstin Martens has classified NGOs on the basis of structure and functions.[37] The base structure of NGO is either to be federative or centralist. A federative NGO is an umbrella organisation that functions along with or is loosely connected to other NGOs. It is a coalition of NGOs, in a sense. Oxfam International and Friends of the Earth International are cases in point of the above. A centralist NGO, on the other hand, has strong headquarters. They operationalise projects and plans from their central offices' directives. Affiliated NGOs or branches are not allowed to take independent projects, plans or other initiatives from their own end. Amnesty International, Human Rights Watch, Green Peace International, CARE International, Save the Children International, etc. are examples of these.

The functional basis of NGOs is also classified into two categories, i.e. service NGO[38] and advocacy NGO. Service NGOs are engaged in relief work and humanitarian actions, for example CARE, Oxfam and Plan International. Advocacy NGOs are actively involved in policy-making, influence government decisions, create public debate and build public opinion; they are more than simply lobbyist and pressure groups. For instance, Green Peace International, Transparency International, the International Campaign to Ban Landmines (ICBL) and the International Campaign to Abolish Nuclear Weapons (ICAN).

4 The Idea of Civil Society

NGOs form one of the components of the dense network that is civil society. The word civil society denotes an aggregate of some of the non-governmental entities. They are located outside the state apparatus and intimate family systems. Therefore, all civic organisations, institutions, movements and processes are an integral part of civil society. In the broadest sense, civil society could be understood in the context of freedom, individual initiatives, group activism and the community's creativity. Civil society is not just an institute but a living idea of human civilisation. The idea of civil society has been the central theme of political thinkers through the ages.[39] It refers to a description of a certain type of social structure, behaviour, a set of ideals and movements. It is a possibility to revive social institutions like the trade union, NGOs and the associational life of a community. This idea was rooted in classical civilisation, deeply discussed in the time of enlightenment and again, has been well received in the globalised world.[40]

The idea of civil society can be understood in three ways: firstly, it is opposite to natural society, where there is a lack of organised political community on the basis of reason, civilisation and law. Secondly, it is against the state because civil society is an autonomous body that is rooted in the private sphere. And thirdly, it is against

[37] Martens (2005).

[38] Coston (1998), Beigbeder (1991), and Weiss (1998).

[39] Jen L. Cohen and Andre Arata, *supra note 31*.

[40] Kaviraj and Khilnani (2001); John Ehrenberg, *supra note 16*.

selfishness and social isolation because it emphasised on associational life.[41] Civil society is essentially an idea, and that idea is very much useful to our time.[42]

NGOs are inseparable to civil society. Both are intertwined concepts. Therefore, their historical background and theoretical aspect are unified. Alan Whaites rightly observed:

> NGOs were identified as a possible point of contact with the building blocks of civil society: namely civil associations.[43]

A. **Classical Heritage**

The NGO as an institute, a movement and a legal entity has shared the theoretical evolution of civil society down the centuries.

In the classical era, third century BC, people organised themselves into different associations or organisations. The first and foremost organisation was Greek polis or city states. Apart from city states, people also lived in different associations to achieve their own specific and varied objectives.[44] These diverse organisations were known as civil societies or in Aristotle's words: *Komonia politike* (polis or political community).

According to John Ehrenberg, Roman philosopher Marcus Tullius Cicero, in the first century BC, enriched the classical ideas of civil society. He introduced the term, *Societas Civilis,* and further expanded it from the political community level to the societal level. The term 'civil society' is directly inherited from Cicero's term: *Societas Civilis.*

In classical civilisation, Greek philosophers Plato, Aristotle and others had grounded civil society on moral reasons and justice. These ideas were further enriched by stoic thinkers. They promoted the idea of universal civil society on the basis of virtue and the unity of the material world. With the decline of Greek city states in the second century BC, the idea of civil society was further developed in the ancient Roman civilisation.

Cicero in the first century BC was the most important thinker of the classical era. Greek ideas were inherited by Roman thinkers. They found them useful for Roman society and grounded civil society on the people's common good. Civil society is a social bonding of community. Human beings desire inherently to live and to sustain community life. The laws and institutions were necessitated by the Romans for sustainability of their community life outside of social constraints.[45]

Gradually, Rome became the epicentre in the fourth century and, in collaboration with the church, consolidated state power. The idea of civil societies was spread by the church and theologians across Europe and beyond.

---

[41] Sudipta Kaviraj and Sunil Khilnani, Ibid., p. 288.

[42] Kumar (1993).

[43] Whaites (1996).

[44] John Ehrenberg *supra note 40*, pp. 20–21.

[45] Ibid., p. 35.

In the fifth century, Saint Augustine observed that 'civil society' was not based only on human reasons and virtues but also on faith, scripture and the church.[46] Classical Greek and Roman ideas of civil society were based on political theory and rationality, while Augustine overshadowed them with religious faith and the church. Augustine's religious ideas were modified by Thomas Aquinas in the thirteen century. He emphasised on Aristotle's approach to political community and human nature in order to live an associational life. God gifted human beings with rationality and guidance to take righteous decisions. "Civil society is now a necessary condition for freedom."[47]

B. The Era of Enlightenment

The notions of religiosity in the Middle Ages were replaced by state sovereignty. The paramountcy of modern states was firmly established in society in the seventeenth century. Europe witnessed renaissance, in other words, enlightenment. Civilisation was organised around family, economy, morality and political power. States were responsible to provide security and to promote human creativity.

Thomas Hobbes wrote his famous treaty, *Leviathan*, in 1651. He included civil society in the realm of state sovereignty, emphasising that civil society was only possible within the bounds of state supremacy. However, civil society existed before modern states. In the classical and Middle Ages, they were considered a space for collective community life.

The ideas of modern states and their sovereignty were also subscribed to by John Locke. However, he opposed state interference in the private affairs of individuals as well as the creativity of community. In his famous book, *Two Treatises of Government* (1689), he propounded the concept of individual right to life, liberty and property. Locke's concept of freedom prescribed that anyone has the power to do what he wants to do or perform any particular action. Hobbes and Locke rooted their ideas of state and civil society in the social contract theory. According to them, civil society was a space of private activities under the purview of state sovereignty.

Adam Ferguson, in his famous book, *An Essay on the History of Civil Society* (1767), gave new horizons to the all-important subject. He rooted civil society in moral sentiments and the love for humanity. He had the highest estimation about human kindness and affection and thus concluded that civil society had progressed in moral values.[48] These ideas were further developed by Adam Smith in his classic work, *The Wealth of Nations* (1776). Smith propounded the notion of free market in the book. In his view, free market is indispensable to the prosperity of society and people's happiness. Smith visualised private interest with public welfare through free market and division of labour .

[46] Ibid., p. 43.
[47] Ibid., p. 61.
[48] Hill (1997).

C. **Modernity**

Aristotle, Cicero and Ferguson had indicated that civil society was the moral progress of humanity. These moral views were further elaborated by Immanuel Kant in the ground breaking work, *Metaphysics of Morals* (1785),[49] *Critique of Pure Region* (1781)[50] and *Critique of Practical Region* (1788).[51] Kant was influenced by Thomas Hobbes and Jean-Jacques Rousseau.[52] Kant's views on civil society were an outcome of human nature. According to him, human nature was the reflection of free will. The state ought to make it possible to create free will in civil society.

Freedom plays an important role to transform natural life into civil life. Every man bears virtues of humanity. The state of nature was not a favourable condition for each other.[53] The state ought to protect the individual's security, property, freedom and justice. A human is a rational being, can cultivate virtues and has the power of free choice. They conduct themselves in society by reason as opposed to desire. However, the states' authority is imperative to protect individual autonomy and freedom. The state protects individuals' rights by enforcing a legal framework within their jurisdiction.[54]

GWF Hegel's civil society is located between family and the state. Civil society is distinct from the state and family and rested in the realm of economy. Hegel elaborated on civil society in his well-known book, *Philosophy of Rights* (1821).[55] Hegel is a great admirer of civil society, and he said that civil society is an achievement of the modern world that can be helpful to resolve contemporary social problems like poverty, ignorance and many more.[56] Moreover, civil society promotes an individual's ethical life and freedom. In the world of Hegel, the main role of civil society is to educate people. It spreads awareness among individuals to hold intellectual ideas, universal approaches and objectivity of actions.

Civil society makes individuals into rational human beings and conscious keeper citizens. It endeavours to transform the individual into an ethical person, effectively upgrading them from nobody to somebody. A person who conducts himself, engages in work and carries out activities in an ethical and universal way. Hegel's main focus lays on an individual's central aspect of life, his recognition by himself and by society. In addition, every human being wants satisfaction from their life. Civil society puts its efforts into a rational order that contains institutions that are responsible for attaining the said satisfaction. For instance, business agency and corporations generate employment and products and remove the fear of unemployment and scarcity of goods.[57]

---

[49] Kant (1998).

[50] Kant (1999).

[51] Kant (2004).

[52] Suprenant (2010).

[53] Ibid., p. 83.

[54] Ibid., p. 92.

[55] Hegel (1968).

[56] Stillman (1980).

[57] Ibid., p. 635.

Apart from individuals, civil society is also indispensable to the sustainability of the state. According to Hegel, the ancient Greek polis or city state was lacking in civil society institutions. Due to the lack of civil society, the Greek polis was distracted. Indeed, civil society encouraged the people to participate directly in politics and live an ethical life.[58] State, civil society and family are interconnected and interdependent on each other. The state and society benefitted immensely from a family that cultivated ethical values and virtues in children. But family does not suffice, and that's why the state opened schools and people formed civic society organisations. These engage in educating and awakening people for participation in the workforce, livelihood and happiness.

Hegel's civil society is mediated between family and state. Civil society is the site for the proper understanding of the right to freedom, private property and the discourse surrounding public policy. Civil society stimulated individuals for self-determination, self-consciousness and rational choices. An individual engaging in work is liberated from the status of nature, and it gives him satisfaction and recognition.[59] Hegel imagined civil society to be a mediating institution to resolve the issues of selfishness and responsibility towards people. Hegel's main contribution was a theoretical analysis of origin, nature and function of this mediating institution, i.e. civil society.[60]

The idea of civil society in the nineteenth century was re-shaped as a distinct sphere that was not synonymous with private property or free market or moral sentiments. The nineteenth-century thinkers conceptualised civil society as an autonomous body located beyond the intimate relations of family and the state apparatus.

Karl Marx revisited Hegelian civil society. Marx described civil society as a social organisation evolving directly around production and commercial activities, and it formed the basis of the state.[61] Marx's civil society was a sphere of the higher economic strata of society. He did not see them apart from the state apparatus.

Civil society has varied origins and diverse theoretical explanations but it remains a group action in the general interest of people. Moreover, civil society educated citizens and stimulated people to participate in the political arena of the state. It cultivated a sense of civic participation, development of individual personality and voluntarily solution of social problems. That is a third path besides the state and market. In its broadest sense, civil society was the sphere of culture 'where values and meaning are established', "where they are debated, contested and changed."[62]

---

[58] Ibid., p. 641.

[59] Ibid., p. 626.

[60] Church (2010).

[61] Krishan Kumar, *supra note* 42, p. 377.

[62] Ibid., p. 383.

5 The Public Sphere and NGOs

In the sphere of culture, civil society represents an uneven field where not everyone stands on equal footing. Antonio Gramsci described it as a site of culture hegemony, where without employee coercing, hegemony was established by the capital class. They received consent from the lower strata or working class through civil society under their subordination. Gramsci called it 'spontaneously' or 'willingly' receiving consent from the deprived people of society.[63]

Gramsci's theory of culture hegemony is a modality of power to continue domination in society over marginalised people. By the culture hegemony theory, Gramsci exposed the capitalistic society's claims of democracy. In his view, the civil society and the state were integrated with each other. Civil society comprises cultural, social and economic institutions, whereas the state is a political society.[64] Whenever the state stumbled, a strong structure of civil society immediately swung into action to support the state apparatus. "The communist ideal is destroying itself on the eve of the twentieth century because it could not create the 'fortress and earth works' of civil society, nor accommodate them."[65]

Gramsci did not subscribe to those traditional ideas of socialists who opposed laissez faire in the economic sphere. Indeed, they wanted to install an omnipotent state that could suppress the private sphere, civil society and freedom.[66] Gramsci supported the free market regime and was opposed to the protectionist policy of the state. Moreover, Gramsci also defended privacy and freedom of the individual.

Gramsci views that civil society does not comprise neutral institutions because it protects, primarily, the privileged class. As a consequence, it loses its universal characteristic. The state and dominant class co-opted civil society in order to maintain their hegemony through a non-coercive way. Some NGOs play a more active role in the existing hegemony block.[67] NGOs like the International Chamber of Commerce (ICC) and the World Business Council for Sustainable Development (WCSS)[68] and others in the same bracket are in deep collaboration with state and corporations.

Gramsci's civil society is not a static institute, rather a creative sphere where marginalised peoples could be mobilised for the creation of counter hegemony. For this purpose, a successful movement is needed that could be backed up by trichology: organisation, ideology and action.[69] Change takes place only after the re-negotiation of unequal power relations between deprived people and the rich class. The political consciousness of deprived people makes a difference to strengthen their position in society. Deprived people can frame a broader coalition or historical block by

---

[63] Gremsci (2011).

[64] Buttigieg (1995).

[65] Lewis (1989), cited by Joseph A. Buttigieg, Ibid., p. 3.

[66] Ibid., p. 6.

[67] https://iccwbo.org (founded in 1919 in Paris, France).

[68] www.wbcsd.org (founded in 1995 in Geneva, Switzerland).

[69] Katz (2006).

including various civil society organs such as the peace movement, women empowerment groups, environmentalists, religious groups, ethical organisations and others in the same vein. Single-minded groups are a broad-based network of civil associations and NGOs. Civil society is a continuously evolving process of social relations.[70]

Civil society is not just an idea but also an action. Hannah Arendt indicated civil society as political action.[71] Arendt gives deep insight into the polis of Greece, the republic of Rome and the declaration of independence and the drafting of the constitution of the United States. There is space for individual freedom, family and economic life. Moreover, there is also space for conduct politics. The public space of action is a place for debating and negotiating people's well-being.[72] Personal life is at stake in the realm of private space but national and international life is at stake in public place.

In the Middle Ages, public space was occupied by the Church and religion. It was only in the sixteenth century that Machiavelli rediscovered antiquity and the classical ideas of governance. Arendt gives Machiavelli credit for enduring secular body politics.[73] Subsequently, secular body politics was adopted on both of sides of the Atlantic Ocean. The United States adopted constitutional democracy that was full of freedom, politics and action.

Thomas Jefferson, the President of the United States (1801–1809), proposed regular Town Meetings at the local level for American citizens. That was a practical workout of the expansion of freedom and action within the realm of constitutional democracy. Citizens assembled to debate, protest and demonstrate peacefully as well. According to Arendt, people are the origin and repository of power in each and every state.[74] People's actions make history, like India's Freedom Movement, United States' Civil Rights Movement, the Eastern European struggle against totalitarianism, the Arab spring and many others have left indelible footprints on human civilisation.

Spontaneous political action was welcomed by Arendt. She defended the opposition to the Vietnam War in the 1960s because the movement was primarily political and did not affect economic and social aims much. In spite of political action for peoples' well-being, we cannot ignore the state, because it is identical to the common interest. Moreover, collective life is possible, and it succeeded within state power.[75] Deliberations and diversity are essential to exercise state power judiciously.

Arendt recognised that public policy was a matter capable of being contested. Anyone who wishes can participate or even initiate public debate or discussion.[76] She emphasised on voluntary participation. In democracy, the election of representatives and the formation of institutes are necessary. Besides, Arendt stresses on political

---

[70] Ibid., pp. 336–337.

[71] Arendlt (2009) and Arendt (1998, 2006).

[72] Betz (1992).

[73] Ibid., pp. 386, 389.

[74] Wolin (1983).

[75] Ibid., p. 17.

[76] Issac (1994).

space and grassroot-volunteerism in order to manifest the people's participation in the democratic process. Creative minds like novelist Albert Camus and poet Rene Char had participated actively in the resistance movement against abuse and misuse of powers.[77] Civil societies act as 'Oases in the Desert' or 'Islands in the Ocean' when it comes to civic initiatives and the participation and networking of like-minded persons and groups.

Arendt's civil society is a political notion that makes possible a public sphere for sociability and human interaction. Citizens' common concerns motivated them towards political action. These political actions are contingent, spontaneous and creative, and their beauty and greatness lies in plurality, voluntary participation and does not adhere to its outcome. Arendt talks in the similar vein as *Shrimad Bhagwat Gita's* Second Chapter: Do not let the fruits of your actions be your motive for doing them.[78] Hannah Arendt's founding moment of public sphere was a political action of civil society. It facilitated the plurality of opinion. Thus, civil society collectively searches the meaning of terms such as common cause, national interest and general good and tries to build consensus in their midst.

The concept of public sphere was expounded greatly by Jurgen Habermas in 1998.[79] Habermas defined public sphere as "a realm of our social life in which some public opinion can be formed. Access is guaranteed to all citizens."[80] He further said: it is a guarantee of freedom of assembly; association; and expression to the citizens when they behave as a public body and use these public spaces seamlessly.[81] Newspapers, magazines, TV, radio and the internet are the public sphere in our life. Thus, the public sphere is a space or arena where civil society mediates between community and state.

The concept of public sphere originated in eighteenth-century Europe. The public sphere was located beyond the private sphere of family, church and religious affairs. It was recognised as an independent domain from the state. It originated when the first ever state budget was separated between private and public expenditure. Thus, the idea of public expenditure was borne from the state exchequers.

The concept was further developed in the coffee houses of London and elsewhere in the eighteenth century. Literate individuals and intellectuals gathered in coffee houses and had discussions on important public issues of the day.[82] Each and every person who wanted to participate in civic life and be involved in ongoing discussions had easy access to coffee houses. They exercised their reasons on any public issues and expressed their views.[83] Participants collectively read newspapers and magazines. The coffee houses created the locale of publicness, an ideal public space for the manifestation of political culture. It led to the strengthening of democracy and

[77] Ibid., p. 162.

[78] Yildirim (2015).

[79] Habermas (1998).

[80] Jürgen Hebermas, *supra note* 25, p. 49.

[81] Ibid.

[82] Cown (2004).

[83] Ibid., p. 346.

exhibited the fairness of public opinion. Moreover, it facilitated literary activities.[84] A coffee house was an urban sociable life space within industrial society. And a popular saying at the time was, "If anyone asks for me John, to the coffee house I have gone."

In France, parallel to the British coffee houses, there were the salons where people organised discussions on literature, science and politics. In the eighteenth century, they were a symbol of civility or *civicness*, a network of citizenship and egalitarian participation.[85] They engaged in debate on public issues and other common causes. In these places—either coffee houses or salons—the citizenry exercised their freedom and creativities. It was a definite moment of citizenship, the right to vote and participate in the democratic process and civil society.[86]

Indeed, the public sphere and civil society bind together in this locale. Coffee houses, salons and the Town Hall were historic sites of public sphere where communication among people took place in a meaningful manner. The public sphere could shape political action; governments watched the site of public sphere such as the streets, newspapers, magazines, coffee houses, primetime TV, the internet and social media, keenly. The state-regulated public sphere is a matter related to individual privacy, public decency, defamation, hate speech, fraudulent advertisement, suggestive material at work places and speeches in sensitive areas like airports, railway stations, schools, colleges and hospitals. Civil society is visible at public places and is involved in the process of communication and publicity.[87]

The public sphere crystallised the idea of public opinion through critical discussion and the exchange of views.[88] Sometimes, it possessed the ability to revitalise social, economic and political change in public life. It had played the catalyst in the French resistance in World War II, the American Civil Rights Movement, the Budapest Revolution in Hungry and the Arab Spring. It was remarkable because individuals had come together and constituted themselves into public space for a common cause.[89]

Throughout the eighteenth and nineteenth centuries, urban life was vibrant but the same ethos could not be maintained in the twentieth century because contemporary life was occupied by radio, TV and the Internet. These virtual sites have fundamentally changed the landscape of the public sphere.[90] In olden times, the Greek polis and republic of Rome encouraged strangers to get involved in social life. Public spaces such as streets, marketplaces, theatres and squares offered great value. These public arenas manifested dialogue, discussion, conversation and creativity among people whose common cause centred on general good and people's well-being.

[84] Ibid., p. 349.

[85] Adut (2012).

[86] Ibid., p. 240.

[87] Ibid., p. 251.

[88] Bernstein (2012).

[89] Ibid., p. 773.

[90] Calhoun (2011).

Public space anchors face-to-face interaction between people with diverse backgrounds. These public areas differ from country to country, for instance in the US, it's the Town Hall, coffee houses in the UK, salons in France, the railways in India and so on. Any kind of physical site or virtual space facilitated communication and public discussion, raising the awareness of citizens in the process. Sometimes, it resulted in monumental achievements like the French Revolution and the United States Declaration of Independence that adopted a constitution and democracy. In this series, India's national movement and the drawing up of the constitution are also significant events. These were giant steps in the history of mankind.

The idea of public sphere, down the years, has spread worldwide. Initially, the public sphere was a routine source of entertainment, subsequently evolving into and gaining ground in the field of humanitarian assistance, human rights law, environmental protection and business ethics. Public sphere is the lifeline for NGOs. Without it, they can neither carry out their mission and philanthropic activities in an effective way nor can they engage in transboundary activism and public action.

In the core public sphere, a matter of communication may either be real or virtual, facilitating peoples' conversations on national and international issues. These conversations differ from intimate family discussions that happen in the private sphere. The public sphere is publicness open to all, participated in by anyone who can freely express their views. It is a genuine public product. Cyberspace has expanded the public sphere to a global level. It makes the approach to people, ideas, content and problems easy across nations. It aids in the seamless organisation of collective actions as well. Transboundary communication has facilitated new alliances, for instance Reporters Without Boarders—an NGO of media persons, which came into existence in 1985.[91] The BBC World Service (1932), CNN International (1985) and Al Jazira (1996) were founded in the same vein. The aforementioned electronic media globalised news and views rapidly. It is far from easy to monitor and control websites and the internet. NGOs such as Action Work[92] and Digital Freedom Network[93] have maintained independent news portals to cover torture and the violation of human rights.[94]

The global public sphere is about advancing and sharing common values of humanity.[95] NGOs also give voice to international public opinion, manifesting contributory global dialogue on the key issue of international law.[96] For instance, NGOs' parallel conversations on social networking sites, on the UNFCCC, conferences (of parties) about climate change and biodiversity have been held. They have emphasised that state representatives do more in the protection of biodiversity and climate. The primary objective of NGOs is to educate people at large to change their lifestyle and consumption habits in a sustainable way.

[91] http://rsf.org.

[92] www.action-works.org.

[93] http://digitalfreedom.ph.

[94] Volkmer (2003).

[95] Vasconcelas (2011).

[96] Ibid., p. 6.

The state might drift from its subject, without an effective civil society which is capable of structuring and channelising citizen debate over diverse ideas and conflicting interests.[97] The public sphere is a site of interaction between state, citizens and NGOs, where an exchange of constructive dialogue and communication takes place in order to maintain a balance between change and stability. In the public arena, all international players—states, multinational companies, world religious bodies, NGOs, cultural groups and intellectuals, participate and present their viewpoints. They initiate debate and conversation beyond the traditional notion of state sovereignty. NGOs and other stakeholders highlight everyday reality—globalisation and its discontents.[98] Globalisation includes within its fold not only globalised economy and ecology but also human rights, environmental protection, business ethics, security against weapons of mass destruction and terrorism. Globalisation has cast its lasting influence on each and every individual throughout the world.

Francis Fukuyama observed:

> Globalisation has been the bearer not just of capital but ideas and culture as well. Everyone is well aware of ways in which globalisation injures indigenous cultures and threatens long-standing traditions. But it also leaves new ideas, habits and practices in its wake, from accounting standards of management practice to NGO activities.[99]

6 Possibilities for NGOs

In this era of globalisation, states, IGOs, NGOs and corporations form the major players in the world order of governance. However, states remain the primary players in the national and international arena and have remained as such since the treaty of Westphalia of 1648.

T. Mathew said:

> The end of the Cold War has brought no more adjustment among states but a novel redistribution of power between the market and civil society. National governments are not simply losing autonomy in a globalised economy. They are sharing powers including political, social, and security roles at the core of sovereignty with business, with international organisations, and a multitude of citizens groups known as non-governmental organisations.[100]

Today, it is a reality that states and markets have not fulfilled the expectations of the people in providing goods, services and quality of life.[101] Therefore, it has facilitated a more active role for civil society, NGOs, IGOs and private sectors. Teegen, Doh and Vachani have narrated the NGOs' role in value creation as far as business and good governance are concerned.[102] The UN and its specialised agencies

---

[97] Castelis (2008).

[98] Ibid., p. 80.

[99] Fukuyama (2001).

[100] Mathew (1997).

[101] Florini (2003).

[102] Teegen et al. (2004).

have established partnerships and co-operations with NGOs on a large-scale for the purposes of mutual benefit and also for promoting people's well-being.

P.C. Simmons in his famous piece of writing, 'Learning to live with NGOs', observed:

> The question facing national governments, multinational institutions and national and international corporations is not whether to include NGOs in their deliberations and activities. Although many traditional centres of power are fighting a rear-guard action against these new players, there is no real way to keep them out. Instead, the real challenge is figuring out how to incorporate NGOs into the international system in a way that takes into account their diversity and scope, their various strengths and weaknesses, and their capacity to disrupt as to create.[103]

Presently, NGOs have proliferated around the world. They are engaged in multiple issues in international law. Jessica T. Mathews denoted it in 'Powershift' while P.G. Simmons suggested it in 'Learning to live with NGOs'. But in reality, the private sector isn't a substitute for state powers,[104] even today. States must remain sovereign powers within their country and primary movers and shakers in the international arena.

NGOs have a limited role in global governance because states are not losing their capacity of power-wielding. The state reoriented itself, using information technology, networking and co-ordinating to resolve transnational issues such as terrorism, organised crime, environmental degradation, money laundering, bank failure and security fraud. They increase inter-governance learning through adopting judicial decisions, creating institutions and finding out more responsive ways to address people's concerns. Anne-Marie Slaughter said:

> Many pressing international and domestic problems result from the state's insufficient power to establish order, build infrastructure and provide maximum social services. Private actors may take up some slack, but there is no substitute for the state.[105]
>
> She further said, "Doing away with the state, however, is hardly the answer."[106]

Apart from the state, NGOs could establish meaningful relationships with corporations. Traditionally, corporations are engaged in the interest of shareholders and busy in profit-earning through value creation. Since the 1980s, corporations have shifted focus from shareholders to stakeholders.[107] The management pays attention to all stakeholders. These stakeholders are those who happen to be affected by corporate activities. In order to address stakeholders' concerns, corporations adopted the theory of Corporate Social Responsibility (CSR) and social audit. In spite of different kinds of organisation, setup, goals and work culture in corporations, NGOs can effectively collaborate with them to achieve mutual benefit.[108]

---

103 Simmons (1997).

104 Slaughter (1997).

105 Ibid., p. 184.

106 Ibid., p. 195.

107 Freedman and Reed (1983) and Freeman (1984).

108 Lindenberg (2019).

Corporations have emerged as major players in the international community. In a globalised economy and free market, the state often failed to exert control over big companies.[109] The globalised economy and free market are deemed necessary to maintain economic growth and the society's prosperity. In the prevailing scenario, NGOs are best placed to engage in transboundary activism. They amplify the voice of the people, highlight contemporary global problems and make the state and market forces more responsive.

Both NGOs and corporations are non-governmental actors, one is closely related to business and the other is deeply involved in civic society and social movements. They both have their legal status and accountability. Corporations are responsible primarily for all stakeholders while NGOs are accountable to the community alone.[110] NGOs are one of the stakeholders of corporations, in addition to other shareholders such as consumers, employees and community. NGOs may be secondary stakeholders as opposed to primary stakeholders.[111] The shareholders and a company have a direct relationship; and they are direct stakeholders both ways, whereas NGOs are loose and indirect stakeholders of a company.

NGOs claim and represent the cosmopolitan, transnational justice and global civil society. That's why NGOs have assumed the role of a watch dog, advocacy and a rule-maker in the interest of the public. They are engaged in the protection of human rights, environment and inclusive economic development. NGOs claim to represent the current to future generations, and the poor and marginalised who lack financial, technological and educational resources to make themselves to be heard. NGOs raise the voice of the voiceless at the international level as well as on national forums. They highlight contemporary global issues, emphasising more responsible behaviour from the state and market forces.

NGOs' relationship with corporations may be understood into two ways: they either target corporations for degradation of the environment that adversely affects the local community, exploitation of working class, the violation of human rights and lack of business ethics. Contrary to this aforementioned point, NGOs and corporations ought to establish an understanding for social transformation and economic growth.[112] The interaction between NGOs and corporations may be helpful in the promotion of general good. NGOs have negligible economic resources at their disposal when compared to that of corporations. They are unequal partners in the context of corporations' economic power. But NGOs are in a strong position to engage in discourse on public issues through meetings, leaflets, research, demonstrations, campaigns and networking. When corporations harm the environment, NGOs can raise the issue first at the community level, which then mobilises the consumer to be aware and discourage them from buying products.[113]

---

[109] Yazil and Doh (2009).

[110] Ibid.

[111] Goodstein and Wicks (2007).

[112] Arenas et al. (2009).

[113] Spar and La Mure (2003).

A majority of prominent NGOs, with visible influence globally, are based in the developed countries of North America and Western Europe. Their policy programmes and agenda are framed as per the cultural lineage of located areas. Developing countries in need of representation are not adequately accommodated. Neera Chandoke said:

> And when we realise that INGOs hardly ever came face to face with the people whose interests and problems they represent, or that they are not accountable to the people they represent, the matter becomes even more troublesome.[114]

The most prominent NGOs are located in the Northern Hemisphere but they are without borders. An NGO is an idea, an imagination and an activism of private persons. They collectively represent volunteerism and philanthropic ideas. Since their inception, NGOs have been engaged to humanise international law. Today, NGOs actively participate in the making and working of international legal framework.

According to Monica Hakimi:

> As the scope of international law has expanded, the world has become more integrated. The number and range of actors who engage on global governance issues have grown, and their interactions have become more frequent.

She goes on to say:

> So, we should assess and treat it as such. Rather than persistently trying to curb, curtail, or defuse it, we should, at times preserve or even cultivate it.[115]

References

Adam T (2004) Philanthropy patronage and civil society: experience from Germany, Great Britain and North America. Indiana University Press, Bloomington, USA

Adut A (2012) A theory of the public sphere. Sociol Theory 30(4):238–262 at 239

Anheier HK (2004) Non-profit organisations: an introduction. Routledge, New York

Arenas D, Lozano JM, Albard L (2009) Role of NGOs in CSR: mutual perceptions among stakeholders. J Bus Ethics 88(1):175–197 at 175–179

Arendlt H (2009) The origins of totalitarianism, a harvest book. HarCourt, Inc., Orlando, 2009 (first edition, 1951)

Arendt H (1998) The human condition 1958, 2nd edn. Chicago University Press

Arendt H (2006) On revolution 1963. Penguin, New York

Arts B, Reinalda B (eds) (2001) Non-state actors in international relations. Ashgate, Aldershot, UK

Ashley JS, He P (2008) Opening of one eye and closing the other: the legal and regulatory environment for "grassroots" NGOs in China Today. Boston Univ Int LJ 26:29–68 at 55–64

Beigbeder Y (1991) The role and status of international humanitarian volunteers and organisation: the rights and duties to humanitarian assistance. Martinus Nijhoff, Dordrecht

Bernstein RJ (2012) The normative core of public sphere. Polit Theory 40(6):767–778 at 769

[114] Neera Chandhoke, *supra note* 32, p. 363.

[115] Hakimi (2017).

Betz J (1992) An introduction of the thought of Hannah Arendt. Trans Charts S Peirce Soc 28(3):379–422 at 385
Boli J, Thomas GM (eds) (1999) Constructing world culture: international non-governmental organizations since 1875. Stanford University Press, California, USA, p 20
Bowett DW (2009) Law of international institutions, Sands P, Klein P (eds), 6th edn, Sweet & Maxwell, London, p 4
Buttigieg JA (1995) Gramsci on civil society. Bound 2 22(3):1–32 at 4
Calhoun C (2011) Civil society and the public sphere. In: Edward M (ed) Oxford handbook on the civil society. Oxford University Press, Chapter 25. Available at: LSE Research Online, December 2014. http://eprints.lse.ac.uk/42621/
Castelis M (2008) The new public sphere: global civil society, communication network, and global governance. Ann Am Acad of Political & Social Sci 616(1):78–93 at 78
Chandok N (2005) How global is global civil society. J World System Res 11(2):355–371
Charnovitz S (2006) Non-governmental organisations and international law. Am J Int L 100(2):348–372 at 350–351
Chisolum LB (1988–1989) What is charity: introduction. Case West Reserve L Rev 39(3):653–662
Church J (2010) The freedom of desire: Hegel's response to Rousseau on the problem of civil society. Am J Pol Sci 54(I):125–139 at 133
Cohen J, Arato A (1994) Civil society and political theory. MIT Press, Cambridge, MA
Coston JM (1998) A model and typology of government—NGO relationship. Non-profit Volunt Sect 27(3):358–382
Cown B (2004) Mr. Spectator and the coffee house public sphere. Eighteenth Cent Stud 37(3):345–366 at 361
Diani M, McAdam D (2003) Social movement and network. Oxford University Press
Dupuy PM (2008) Conclusion: written on the legal status of NGOs and on the methodological problems which arise for legal scholarship. In: Dupuy PM, Vierucci L (eds) NGOs in international law. Edward Elgar, Cheltenham, UK, p 214
Edward M (2009) Civil society, 2nd edn. Policy Press, Bristol, UK
Edwards R, Stockwell N (2013) Trust and equity, 11th edn. Pearson Longman, London
Ehrenberg J (2007) *Civil society: The critical history of an idea*, 2nd edn. New York University Press (first edition, 1999)
Florini A (2003) The coming democracy: the new rules for running a new world, 2nd edn. Brooking Institute Press, Washington, DC
Freeman RE (1984) Strategic management: a stakeholder approach. Pitman Publications, Boston, USA
Freedman RE, Reed DL (1983) Stock holders to stake holders: a perspective on corporate governance. California Manag Rev 25(3):88–106
Fukuyama F (2001) Social capital, civil society and development. Third World Q 22(1):7–20 at 19
Goodstein JD, Wicks AC (2007) Corporation and stakeholders responsibility: making business ethics a two-way conversation. Bus Ethics Q 17(3):375–398 at 377
Gremsci (2011) Prisoness botebook 1929–1935, Vols 1, 2 & 3, Buttigieg JA et al (trans and eds). Colombia University Press, New York
Habermas J (1974) Public sphere: an encyclopedia article. New German Critique 3:49–55
Habermas J (1998) The structural transformation of public sphere, Burger T, Lowrence F (trans). MIT Press, Cambridge, MA
Hakimi M (2017) Constructing an international community. Am J Int L 111(2):317–356 at 356
Hartigan P (2006) It's about people, not profits. Bus Strateg Rev 17(4):42–45
Hegel GWF (1968) Philosophy of rights, trans. with notes by Knox TM. Oxford University Press (first edition, 1821).
Hill L (1997) Adam Ferguson and the paradox of progress and decline. History Polit Thought 18(4):677–706
Ilchman WF et al (eds) (1998) Philanthropy in world traditions. Indiana University Press, Bloomington, US

Issac JC (1994) Oasis in the desert: Hannah Arendt on democratic politics. Am Political Sci Rev 88(1):156–168, at 157
Kant I (1998) Ground work of the metaphysics of morals, Gregar M, Timmecrmam J (trans and eds), Intro. by Christine M. Koresgaard. Cambridge University Press (first edition, 1785)
Kant I (1999) Critique of pure region, Guger P, Wood AW (trans and eds). Cambridge University Press (first edition, 1781)
Kant I (2004) Critique of practical region, Abbott KT (trans). Dover Publications, New York (first edition, 1788)
Katz H (2006) Gramsci, hegemony, and global civil society networks. Voluntas 17(4):333–348 at 336
Kaviraj S, Khilnani S (eds) (2001) Civil society: history and possibilities. Cambridge University Press
Keck ME, Sikkin K (1998) Activists beyond borders: advocacy networks in international politics. Cornell University Press, London
Kinger JC (2017) Philanthropists and foundation globalization. Routledge, UK (first edition 2008)
Kumar K (1993) Civil society: an inquiry into the usefulness of an historical term. British J Sociol 41(3):375–395 at 375
Lador-Lederer JJ (1963) International non-governmental organisations and economic: a study of autonomous organisations and Jus Gentuim. A.W. Sijthof, Leiden, p 60
Lewis F (1989) The rise of civil society. New York Times, 25 June (article)
Lindblom A-K (2005) Non-governmental organisations in international law. Cambridge University Press, p 42
Lindenberg M (2019) Reaching beyond the family: new nongovernmental organisation alliance for global poverty allevation and emergency response. Non-profit Volunt Sect Q 30(3):603–615
Malena C (1995) Working with NGOs, operation policy department. World Bank Publication, Washington, DC, pp 13–14
Martens K (2002) Mission impossible? defining non-governmental organisations. Voluntas 13(3):271–285 at 271
Martens K (2005) NGOs and the United Nations. Palgrave Macmillan, New York
Mathew JT (1997) Power shift. Foreign Aff 76(1):50–66 at 50
Poelofs J (2003) Foundations and public policy: the mask of pluralism. New York University Press
Rechenberg HHK (1997) Non-governmental organisations. In: Bernhardt R (ed) Encyclopedia of public international law, vol 3. North-Holland, Amsterdam, pp 612–618
Schermers HG, Blokker NM (2018) International institutional law: unity within diversity, 6th edn. Martinus Nijhoff, The Hague, p 32 (first edition 1972)
Simmons J (1997) Learning to live with NGOs'. Foreign Pol 16(5):183–197 at 184
Slaughter A-M (1997) The real new world order. Foreign Aff 76(5):83–197 at 195
Spar DL, La Mure IT (2003) The power of activism: assessing the impact of global business. California Management Rev 45(3):78–101
Staggenborg S (2008) Social movement. Oxford University Press
Stillman PG (1980) Hegel's civil society: a locus of freedom. Polity 12(4):622–646 at 623
Stillman GB (2007) Global standard NGOs: the essential element of good practice. Lulu, Geneva, pp 13–14
Suprenant CW (2010) Liberty, autonomy and Kant's civil society. History Phil Q 27(1):79–94 at 79
Teegen H, Doh JP, Vachani S (2004) The importance of non-governmental organisations (NGOs) in global governance and value creation: an international business research agenda. J Int Bus Stud 35(6):463–483 at 468
The Cotonou Agreement (2000) https://www.eods>eu.literary>EU_cotonouAgreementPDF
Tilly C (2004) Social movement, 1768–2004. Boulder & Co., USA
Vasconcelas A (2011) Introduction: civil society and the global public sphere. EUISS, Paris, pp 5–11 at 5. Available at http://www.jstor.org/stable/resrep36298.3

Volkmer I (2003) The global network society and the global public sphere. J Develop 46(7):9–16 at 13

Wagner M (2010) "Non-state actors," Max plank encyclopedia of public international law. Oxford University Press

Weiss TG (ed) (1998) Beyond UN subcontracting-task sharing with regional security arrangements and service-providing NGOs. Palagrave Macmillan, London

Whaites A (1998) NGOs, civil society and the state: avoiding theoretical externs in real world issues. Dev Pract 8(3):343–349

Whaites A (1996) Let's get civil society straight: NGOs and political theory. Develop Pract 6(30):240–249 at 240

White LC (1951) International non-governmental organisations: their purposes, methods and accomplishment. Rutgers University Press, New Brunswick, p 7

Willets P (ed) (1966) The conscience of the world: influence of non-governmental organisations in the UN system. Hurst & Co., London, pp 3–5

Willets P (2002) What is a non-governmental organisation? In: The UNESCO encyclopedia of life support system. City University, London, pp 1–18 at 4. http://www.staff.city.ac.uk.p.willetts

Wolin SS (1983) Hannah Arendt: democracy and the political. Salmagundi 60:3–19 at 13

Woodward BK (2010) Global civil society in international law making and global governance. Martinus Nijhoff, Leiden, p 9

Yazil YM, Doh JP (2009). NGOs and corporations: conflict and collaborations. Cambridge University Press

Yildirim S (2015) Arendt's promise to civil society: bridging the social and the political. The European Leg 19(7):869–882 at 870, 874

Chapter 2
A Short History of NGOs

1 Introduction

History is a story of the past. It helps to understand and learn from previous experience to find out the roots of present ideas and institutions. Writing on history is to stick to what the possible sources are, which may be accepted and used to narrate the story of NGOs.

The story of NGOs could potentially have three reasons. Firstly, the narration becomes more enjoyable and interesting; secondly, studying history necessarily involves taking oneself out of one's present context and exploring an alternative world; and thirdly, to think differently about oneself to gather something of how we would come about as individual human beings if made aware of the possibility of doing things differently.[1]

Writing on history is required to periodise the origin, growth and development of NGOs. Next up is the identification of sources available, how to utilise them and what method is to be employed. As far as periodisation goes, the history of international law is broadly divided into antiquity, Middle Ages and modern times. The historians of NGOs started their journey in the last quarter of the eighteenth century. To narrate the era of NGOs, writers divided time frame as per their understanding. Steve Charnovitz has divided the history of NGOs into seven parts. These are:

First, Emergence: 1775–1918; Second, Engagement: 1919–1934; Third, Disengagement: 1935–1944; Fourth, Formalisation: 1945–1949; Fifth, Underachievement: 1950–1971; Sixth, Intensification: 1972–1991; and Seventh, Empowerment: 1992 onwards.[2]

---

[1] Arnold (2001).

[2] Charnovitz (1997).

P. Rai, *Non-Governmental Organisations and International Law*,
https://doi.org/10.1007/978-981-97-5469-4_2

Thomas Davies divided the entire period of NGO history into three phases, i.e. First phase: 1767–1914; Second phase: 1914–1939; and the Third phase: 1939 to the present day.[3]

In the writings of history of international law, two methods were employed. The first one focussed on the development of ideas, and the second focussed on state practices and treaties.[4] The history of international law is indeed the history of European international law. The Asian, African and Latin American era, ideas and state practices were not taken into account properly nor were they given adequate coverage. C.H. Alexandrowicz, R.P. Anand and T.O. Elias have sought to consider Asian-African history within the Euro-centric confines of world history.[5]

Human civilisation began its journey five millennia ago, in Mesopotamia, in India, in Greece and ancient Rome, with it eventually flourishing in the northern parts of the World.[6]

In the ancient world, charity, missions, humanitarian assistance and relief were carried out by religious institutes, missionaries and some individuals. Human civilisation and culture are based on certain common and unique factors of life such as birth, sex and death. Down the years, human values, compassion, tolerance and solidarity were grounded in society. Holy and sacred treaties illustrated morality and spirituality as universal values for humans' survival.

In the fifth century BC, Buddhist monasteries were established in India. They served the people with great dedication and inculcated human values in the society, without any gain. Earlier, Christianity in the Middle East and Europe engaged in missionary work and set up hospitals and extended humanitarian assistance to the people. Similarly, the religious traditions of Islam and Hinduism also put forward their charitable and missionary efforts to promote the human cause. In ancient times, selfless service and kindness were grounded in the religious scriptures and cultural traditions.

For instance, *Bhagwata Gita* lays down:

> Charity given to a worthy person simply because it is right to give, without consideration of anything in return, at the proper time and in the proper place, is stated to be in the mode of goodness. (Chapter 17, Verse 20)

The narratives, terminology and tools were entirely different from modern times. However, the fundamental tenet of the NGO—unconditional love for humanity—remains unaltered. In Europe, this concept was expanded further.

In the fourth century, the Roman Empire embraced Christianity. Since then, the religion began its organised charity and missionary work. The Sovereign Order of Malta was founded in Jerusalem in the eleventh century. The Malta Order survives to this day.[7]

---

[3] Davies (2014).

[4] Nussbaum (1954) and Parry (1965).

[5] Koskemieni (2012), Alexandrowicz (1967), Anand (1987, 2005), and Elias (1972).

[6] Naff (2018).

[7] Thomas Davies, *supra note* 3, p. 20.

In the Middle Ages, in addition to religious organisations, merchant, social and performing arts organisations came into existence as well. However, authentic records are available only from the sixteenth century.[8]

In the seventeenth century, Europe witnessed enlightenment and came up with the idea of building institutions. The term 'Societe' was introduced to the French language and discourse in the final decade of the sixteenth century. 'Societe' or 'Society' advanced in meaning in voluntary connotations in the seventeenth century. Thus, the concept of civil society came into being in the beginning of enlightenment in Europe. Thinkers of the seventeenth century secularised the very idea of society; they emphasised that society was the free invention of human beings.[9]

The Roman Catholic Church liked to remain independent from the state in the Middle Ages. They subscribed to the idea of different domains (spiritual and temporal) to serve their purpose of autonomy for the betterment of the church, institutes and missions.[10]

2 Origins of Non-governmental Organisations: 1775–1914

By the mid-seventeenth century, modern states came into being. Down the centuries, non-governmental organisations (NGOs), transnational corporations (corporations) and inter-governmental organisations (IGOs) were formed. In the initial stages, the states were localised to specific geographical areas, bearing the religious tenets of either Hinduism, Buddhism, Christianity or Islam. The foundations of the states' secularisation process were laid down by India's thought of *Sarv Dharam Sumbhav*, Greek philosophers, Roman jurists and pragmatic rulers. They supported the idea of human reason and its resultant application in the legal realm. Similar to states, NGOs also secularised their activities. They demanded a change in the legal framework on the basis of human reason and conscience.

A. **Abolition of Slavery and the Slave Trade**

Initially, NGOs started their work on single issues[11] and have expanded their horizons over the years. NGOs' first targets were slavery and the slave trade in eighteenth-century United States. The Pennsylvania Society for Prompting the Abolition of Slavery was founded in 1775. At the same time, across the Atlantic in Britain in 1787[12] and France in 1788 the same was done. Abolition of slavery and the slave trade

---

[8] Baker (2001).

[9] Ibid., p. 94.

[10] Ghils (1992).

[11] Demark (2005).

[12] Steve Charnovitz, *supra note* 2, p. 192.

movement became more popular and supported than any other reform movements in Britain for the next half century."[13]

Steve Charnovitz said:

> At the advent of the Congress of Vienna in 1815, 800 petitions were presented to the British House of Commons to stop the international slave trade. This public pressure spurred the British government to press for action at Vienna. Yet, the only agreement that could be achieved was a declaration condemning the slave trade.[14]

The Anti-Slavery Society was established in 1839 and further steps had been under taken to mobilise public opinion in favour of abolition of slavery and the slave trade. In the nineteenth century, the increasing of infrastructure in European waterways, railways, publication of newspapers and books on a large-scale was enabled to strengthen the public discourse against slavery and the slave trade.

In 1839, a conference was called, and finally the Anti-Slavery Society came into existence. The Anti-Slavery Society was the first important NGO and a landmark in the annals of human civilisation. Presently, it is working with a new name, i.e. Anti-Slavery Society International, and is engaged with abolishing all forms of slavery and the slave trade across nations.[15] The Anti-Slavery Conference for the Prohibition of Slavery and the Slave Trade was widely attended by volunteers across the United States, France, Britain and the British colonies. This was the first landmark marking the solidarity of volunteers, campaigns and conscious citizens. They utilised this successful experience and furthered new issue areas such as the peace movement.

B. **Peace Movement**

Peace NGOs began their work for peace and social harmony in 1850. They organised peace movement against the war mongering nations. It is to be noted here that the classical writers of international law focussed mainly on maintenance of peace among states.[16]

In the eighteenth century, Immanuel Kant emphasised peace on the basis of ethical reasoning by enlightened people in the mutual interest of the world.[17] The London Peace Society was founded in 1816 under William Allen. Similarly, under the leadership of William Ladd, three peace societies were founded in 1827. These peace NGOs engaged in the peace movement and mobilised public opinion in Europe and the Unites States. They organised the International Peace Conference in 1840.

The Crimean War broke out in Europe in 1853, slowing the peace movement down in Britain and other countries. The peace movement picked up steam internationally, again. The first International Peace Conference was held in 1899 and the

[13] Seymour Drescher and Paul Finkelman, "Slavery", in *The Oxford Handbook of the History of International Law*, *supra note* 5, p. 901.

[14] Steve Charnovitz, *supra note* 12, p. 192.

[15] Drescher (2009).

[16] Stephen C Neff, *supra note* 6, pp. 8–11.

[17] Cecelia Lynch, "Peace Movements Civil Society and the Development of International Law," in *The Oxford History of International Law*, *supra note* 5, p. 199.

second in 1907 in the Hague. The conference was attended by 425 peace movements and peace societies from around the world.[18] As a result of being excluded from participation in the Hague conference alongside government representatives, these non-governmental entities and individuals took the initiative to organise a separate conference in the Hague. This parallel conference was arranged by peace activists and supporters of the peace movement. This model of a parallel conference in the Hague is followed to this day.

C. **Humanitarian Assistance**

Apart from anti-slavery and the peace movement, the third issue area was undertaken on humanitarian assistance and relief. In the event of war, armed conflicts and natural calamity, NGOs were actively engaged in humanitarian assistance and relief work. It resulted in the creation of monumental institutions, i.e. the International Committee for Red Cross (ICRC) in 1863. Henri Dunant persuaded the Geneva Public Welfare Society to set up a committee to address the problems of wounded soldiers' relief and humanitarian assistance.[19]

The Geneva Conference was called in 1864 for the amelioration of conditions of wounded soldiers of armies in the field. This conference was participated by governmental and non-governmental organisations' representatives, in addition to military and medical officers. A resolution was adapted to set up voluntary societies, to undertake humanitarian relief work during the situation of armed conflicts. The initial set up of these Relief Committees is now referred to as the ICRC, and it was accorded the first Nobel Peace Prize along with its initiator, Henry Dunant, in 1900. The ICRC rigorously perused the humanistic cause of the war-wounded and war prisoners to be addressed. In the twentieth century, the Hague Peace Conferences of 1899 and 1907 were held by states for codification of the law of war on land and maritime warfare. The conference had adopted a comprehensive treaty on the law of war. The belligerents and inhabitants had been provided protection as per the principles and customs established by civilised nations, the law of humanity and as dictated by public consciousness.[20]

D. **Labour Welfare**

In the nineteenth century, Europe witnessed the industrial revolution; the workforce was engaged at a large scale but their work conditions, payments and welfare were ignored by the capitalists. In 1864, an international working-class association, popularly known as the *First International*, was formed to protect and emancipate the working class. The labour cause was undertaken by the workers' association, and trade unions were connected transitionally.

In the last decade of the nineteenth century, several labour conferences were held by mixed delegations of workers and governments. These conferences passed many resolutions that addressed labour issues like, Sunday holiday, emancipation

[18] Cortright (2008).

[19] Best (1980).

[20] Schindler and Toman (2004).

of women and child labour. It resulted in May 1st of every year being declared as Labour Day. Another achievement of the conferences was the formation of the International Association of Labour in 1900. These labour conferences, resolutions and their collective efforts were the precursors of the International Labour Organisation (ILO) and international labour law.

E. **Conservation of Nature**

NGOs, scientists and conservationists conceived the idea to protect nature because man forms one of the components in the entire ecosystem. The survival of the human species depends on flora, fauna and biodiversity. The first International Congress of Society (NGOs) for the protection of animals was held in 1860 at Dresden. The next step taken by the International Congress Society was to put their efforts into safeguarding birds. The first International Ornithological Congress was held in 1884. It started to work for future conferences pertaining to the protection of birds. Governments held a conference to draft a treaty on the protection of birds in 1895. Governments appointed seventeen delegates in this congress to participate on behalf of their states. However, this draft did not come into force. Subsequently, another conference re-drafted this treaty in 1902, and it came into force and ended up becoming a law.[21]

Further to this, the International Ornithological Congress was held in 1910 and emphasised to prohibit the trade of birds and feathers. Meantime, the Association of International Forest Research Station was set up in 1882. The International Friends of Nature was established with the motive to conserve forests.

The World League for Protection of Animals formed in Germany in 1898. This NGO is one of the world's oldest international animal welfare organisations that survives to this day.[22]

Apart from forests, animals and birds, NGOs focussed on the conservation of marine life and fisheries. In 1892, North Fisheries Protection Association raised the issue of the conservation of fisheries with the British Government. This resulted in the North Sea Fisheries Convention being adopted by European Nations. Simultaneously, the North America Fish and Game Protective Association was formed in 1902. The Association urged the legislatures of New York and Ontario to make laws on prohibiting the shooting of wildfowl in the spring.[23] Moreover, they further perused the conservation of marine mammal and seal fish in 1907.

F. **Education and Enlightenment**

In the later part of the eighteenth century, Europe attained enlightenment, proliferating beyond the offshore with missionaries and merchants in Asia and Africa alike. For instance, the Asiatic Society was created in Kolkata in 1784. It established a bridge between Indian and European ideas and cultural traditions.

Dadabhai Naoroji, the first MP of South Asian origin in the British Parliament, founded the East India Association in London in 1866. It consisted of Indians and

[21] Steve Charnovitz, *supra note* 14, p. 206.

[22] Thomas Davies, *supra note* 3, p. 49.

[23] Steve Charnovitz, *supra note* 21, p. 206.

English people. Its main purpose was advocacy for the promotion of interests and welfare of Indians by all legitimate means. The Association published a journal—*Journal of the East India Association*—in 1867. Subsequently, this was subjoined by the *Asiatic Quarterly Review*.[24]

In the beginning of the nineteenth century, the Society of Encyclopaedic (1801) was formed in Paris. The main purpose of this Society was to centralise knowledge from all fields. Unifying this knowledge, the Royal Society in London was established in 1893. The Society formed an International Catalogue Committee to develop a bibliography encompassing all natural sciences.[25]

This networking of knowledge was further taken up by Belgium and thus led to the establishment of the International Institute of Bibliography in 1895 in Brussels. The Institute had developed "Universal bibliographic repertory catalogue card system". The catalogue card system of Bibliography designed the technique for finding information on any areas of learning and human activity. According to Thomas Davies, this may be considered a precursor to the aspects of today's internet search engine.[26]

Charity and religious missions were a precursor to the NGO's engagement towards enlightenment and community empowerment. In the last quarter of the nineteenth century, interfaith and multireligions dialogue were resumed and a number of religious NGOs were established to serve the people. Swami Vivekananda, who spoke on Hinduism at the World Parliament of Religions in Chicago in 1893, also established the Ramakrishna Mission in 1897—an international religious organisation based in India[27]—with a small group of people.

The Roman Catholic religious order was reorganised again, expanding its outreach to the continents of Africa, Asia and the Americas. The Theosophical Society, an organisation was set up in New York in 1875 and it expanded its work further outside United States. Annie Besant established the Theosophical Society in India in 1890. She did very significant work in India through this famed institution and actively participated in the country's freedom struggle. The main focus areas of these religious societies and orders were to propagate religious tenets and to oppose materialism. They engaged with people to strengthen spiritual powers.

In order to counter these religious dogmas, the World Union of Free Thinkers was formulated in 1878, for the propagation of rationalist ideas. The propagation of rationality in society was necessitated for the freedom of conscience and humanity. It took initiatives in the promotion of international trade among nations.

G. **Promotion of Business**

The International Association for Custom Reforms was established in 1846. In 1850, the organisation pursued the governments to arrange world fair and exhibitions. The result was that the first World Fair Trade and Exhibition was held at London in 1850. In fact, the good experience helped to replicate it in other fields too. Like commodity

[24] Asiatic Society (2014).

[25] Wagner (2004).

[26] Thomas Davies, *supra note* 22, p. 46.

[27] Smith (1976).

and products, people's mobility was also increased due to the availability of transportation facilities in this era. To facilitate travellers, businessmen, missionaries and adventurists, the International Hotel Association was formed in 1860, which now goes by the name of the International Hoteliers Alliance.

H. **Intellectual Property**

Nascent industry and business needed the protection of intellectual property at the international level.[28] The French government organised an international conference on industry property that was attended by both private and public institutions and individuals. It set up a commission to draft a convention for the protection of industry property. This drafted convention on industry property was approved by an official conference in 1883.

Similarly, NGOs, activists and writers took initiatives for the establishment of the copyrights regime. Victor Hugo and other eminent writers formed the International Literary and Artistic Association in 1878 during the International Literary Congress. Authors, artists and jurists had proposed a draft to institutionalise the protection of intellectual property. An International Conference of the states had approved the intellectual property rights, as proposed by the International Union for Protection of Literary and Artistic Works.[29]

I. **International Standards**

A uniform system of weight, measures and money is a prerequisite for the promotion of international business. An international association for obtaining a uniform decimal system of measures, weights and coins was formed along with British, French and American branches. This was a private initiative in the development of business.[30]

The practice of uniformity was replicated in other fields as well. For instance, the International Meteorological Organisation was formed in 1891. This consisted of governments and private meteorologists. This is now the World Meteorological Organisation (WMO), a specialised agency of the UN. The WMO is now an IGO, not a mixed organisation of government and private persons. The standardisation further extended into statistics, maths, actuarial and testing material. The International Statistical Institute in 1885; International Maths Congress in 1895; International Actuarial Association in 1893; and the International Association for Testing Materials in 1895 were formed by non-governmental initiatives.

J. **Transportation**

NGOs did the groundwork to facilitate and expedite the transportation network in the railways, roadways and waterways. In 1890, the International Railway Transport was

---

[28] Steve Charnovitz, *supra note* 23, p. 201; Thomas Davies, *supra note* 26, p. 46; Anne Peter and Simone Peter, "International Organizations: Between Technocracy and Democracy," in *The Oxford Hand Book of the History of International Law*, *supra note* 17, p. 186.

[29] Khan (2005).

[30] Yats (1856).

set up as an IGO. In a short span of time, it had received affiliation of over 400 railway companies and nearly 50 governments across the European, Asian, African and American continents. In addition, the International Association of Public Transport and International Association of Navigation were also created and affiliated too.[31]

K. **Social Welfare**

In the last quarter of nineteenth century, Christian religious NGOs undertook community welfare activities. In 1870, the Anglo Oriental Society was formed for the suppression of the opium trade. They were also engaged in prohibiting the illegal trafficking of women and children.

L. **Women Rights**

Women's issues were also visible before the turn of the nineteenth century. NGOs put their efforts into removing hardships being faced by women and overall inequality rife in the society. Pandita Ramabai established the Ramabai Association in 1887 to provide shelter for child widows in India. To arrest the degradation of females in the East, the Society for Promoting Female Education was established in 1834. Its main objectives were to increase learning among the female population. For the protection of young girls, the International Union of Friends of Young Women was set up in 1877.

They emphasised that every adult girl had the right to earn and leave home in search of a livelihood and so, deserved to be protected. They made efforts in the furtherance of the women's movement and demanded female suffrage in all democratic countries. In 1833, the World Women Christian Temperance Union was created in the United States and connected with other parts of the world. Their demand was entertained by New Zealand, and, as a result New Zealand became the first democracy in the world to provide women the right to vote.[32] This was a watershed moment for democracy and women empowerment.

M. **Law-Making**

The progressive development and codification of international law was undertaken before the turn of the nineteenth century. Legally conscious organisations were constituted by private persons, writers and jurists. The two most significant professional bodies, i.e. the International Law Association and the Institute de Droit International were created in 1873.[33] This process was further extended to a national level. In Japan, the Japanese Society of International Law was formed in 1897. This was the oldest international law forum at the national level. NGOs vowed to create the international arbitration forum for an amicable settlement of disputes.

The nineteenth century appeared very long and the most creative in human history. All gains of enlightenment, inventions, discoveries, encounters of north and south, great ideas, experiments and the churning of societies were witnessed. These new

---

[31] Thomas Davies, *supra note* 26, p. 53.

[32] Dalay and Nolan (1994).

[33] Stephen C. Naff, *supra note* 16, p. 15.

challenges and opportunities were well taken by NGOs, and they put forward rigorously their ideas and organised campaigns, advocacy, formed international institutions and networking. They stood up to participate along with the states, IGOs, corporations and faith-based organisations in world affairs.

The tendencies of the nineteenth century lingered on up to the first quarter of the subsequent century. Law-making and adjudication was strengthened further as the American Society of International Law, formed in 1906 by jurists, academics and activists of the United States. The Hague Conference, 1907, created the Permanent Court of Arbitration (PCA)—an inter-governmental body. The PCA, situated in The Hague, is often misunderstood as a permanent court, but in popular terminology, it is not. Its primary function is to maintain a list of arbitrators (judges) that parties in dispute can readily consult and select from for the purpose of achieving amicable settlements. Despite this, it has been successfully resolving international disputes. NGOs have been consistently pursuing world peace and the amicable settlement of disputes. They participate in the dispute-settlement procedure as amicus curiae or friends of the adjudicative forum.

3 Time of Engagement and Disengagement: 1914–1945

One of the landmark events before the outbreak of the First World War (WWI) in 1914 was the establishment of the Union of International Association (UIA) in Brussels (1907).[34] The UIA had facilitated international organisations to connect with each other and published a yearbook. At the time, the yearbook did not categorise organisations. All sort of organisations, whether public or private, IGOs or NGOs, business or religious, issue-based or specialised, advocacy or services organisations, were all referred to as international organisations or associations.[35]

The early part of the twentieth century was rife with warmongering and overcharged nationalism, hindering NGOs and their activities. Their engagement had slowed down. NGOS focussed more on peace and disarmament. During the Hague Peace Conference, a parallel conference was held. That parallel conference had 450 representatives of NGOs, civil society and individuals, and it was a great success.[36]

The First World War (WWI) broke out in 1914 and continued all the way up to 1919. NGOs provided humanitarian assistance and relief to victims of this man-made disaster.

A. **Stimulation of Economic Life**

WWI came to a close in 1919. Everyday life in and around Europe gradually crawled back to normal. But there were some noticeable changes in world affairs. Paramountcy of European powers had undergone a shift from Europe to the United

---

[34] https://uia.org; Bawett (2009).

[35] White (2016).

[36] Cortright (2008) and Beales (1931).

States of America. During the war, the significance of humanitarian assistance and relief was accumulated. After the conclusion of WWI, the normal associational life resumed. Apart from humanitarian action and diplomatic relations, national business, world trade also found new avenues. The non-governmental entities—national business chambers and NGO's had acquired a significant role in promotion of international commerce and intercourse.

After the conclusion of WWI, NGOs took initiatives along with governments to promote world trade through national business chambers. They facilitated a better connectivity of smooth custom duties, easy transportation and communication. In order to further expand business activities, the International Chamber of Commerce (ICC) was founded in Paris in 1919. The ICC had actively participated in humanitarian assistance and relief work that was carried out by the League of Nations and the United Nations, in addition to commercial activities. The main issue areas of the ICC are: promoting business, policy advocacy, resolving business disputes and framing of business rules. It made remarkable contributions in the aforesaid issue areas. That's why the ICC was accorded consultative status in 1945 and subsequently observer status[37] by the United Nations in 2016.

Another legacy of WWI was the creation of new international institutions such as: the League of Nations, the International Labour Organisation (ILO), the Permanent Court of International Justice (PCIJ), regional organisations—the European community and others. Apart from these inter-government institutions, a good number of NGOs were formulated in the United States and Europe. NGOs resumed their activities again. They had the opportunity to work with newly set up inter-governmental organisations (IGOs). NGOs were engaged mainly in the philanthropic, scientific, religious, commercial and labour fields[38] during 1914–1945. NGOs then got some roles in the League of Nations. According to Steve Charnovitz: "The position of assessor was created to obtain private expertise within the League of Nations' framework".

ICRC and ICC were well-known NGOs in the field of humanitarian action and promotion of world trade, respectively. The League of Nations worked with NGOs through legal instruments or membership in the advisory committees. Being a specialised NGO in the field of economy and business, the ICC was associated with ongoing negotiations in the newfound issue areas of finance, trade, transit and tariff in international law.

Besides, Article 25 of the covenant of the League of Nations provides "The establishment and co-operation of duly authorised national Red Cross organisations". Article 25 of the covenant referred only to 'Red Cross' societies and remained silent on other NGOs to be dealt with. Although the number of NGOs had increased, the first decade (1922–1932) of the League of Nations was the most fertile period in which NGOs proliferated and touched new horizons.[39]

---

[37] http://www.iccwbo.org; United Nations General Assembly Resolution (UNGA Res) 156 (13 December 2016) Session 71, 62nd Planary Meeting.

[38] Lagua (2011).

[39] Thomas Davies, *supra note* 31, p. 92.

It is quite clear that the covenant of the League of Nations was silenced about the relationships of NGO's with the League, but the League of Nations heard the voice of silence as per se, consonant with its objective and activities. The League had limited resources and experience in comparison with worldwide expectations. Therefore it became an imperative to seek co-operation from non-governmental institutions. Douglas Williams said: "Under the informal relationship with the League of Nations, NGOs were endowed with greater participatory privileges than they enjoy today with the United Nations."[40]

Apart from the spread of NGOs, their activities within the League of Nations or outside the League have a wide spectrum. Eminent writer Steve Charnovitz has presented a glimpse of NGOs in a very lucid way to narrate their expanded areas and issues during the said period.[41]

The League of Nations and NGOs moved to meet the pressing issues during times of war and the post-war setting. The fundamental task facing the NGOs was to actively participate in the initiatives for revitalising the European economy and societal coherence. ICRC undertook the issue of prisoners of war. There was a desperate need to get them released mutually to exchange and facilitate their safe return to respective countries. There was the repatriation of 425,000 prisoners of war in Europe.[42]

ICRC was engaged not only in man-made disasters like war but also in natural calamities such as earthquakes, floods, cyclones, etc. A special NGO, the International Relief Union, was formed in 1927 to coordinate relief work with various NGOs.

Another pressing issue was health. Hence, the League of Nations called a conference to plan for a health organisation. The health organisation was formulated, and doctors rendered their services to Red Cross societies as and when needed because contemporary diseases like T.B., venereal illnesses and blindness were to be tackled immediately.

The ICRC and ICC have played an important role through their creative involvement with the League of Nations in designing, planning and policy-making to rejuvenate the European economy and aid in the development of international trade and finance. The ICC has been associated with the League of Nations as consultant. It was closely attached to the League's Economic Section of the secretariat of as the business association's representative.[43]

The ICC created in Paris an International Court of Arbitration in 1923 for the settlement of commercial disputes. Ever since its inception, the performance of the Court of Arbitration has been tremendously successful. In 2023, the court will commemorate its centenary. It continues to be at the forefront of resolving financial and trade disputes on a global scale. Over 27,000 cases have been successfully handled by the ICC court so far.

---

[40] Williams (1987).

[41] Steve Charnovitz, *supra note* 28, pp. 212–237.

[42] Walters (1965).

[43] Ridgeway (1959).

Whenever the League of Nations attempted to smooth the custom and tariff among countries, the ICC was directly or indirectly involved in the preparation of groundwork to create drafts for negotiation of the final outcome. In 1927, the World Economic Conference was held under the auspices of the League of Nations with the active involvement of ICC, IFTU and other NGOs. The conference discussed the economic scenario of Europe and beyond. Deliberations were also made about the rejuvenation of global economy. The Davos Plan was designed. The plan indicated the hardship of war and urgent need to reconstruct the European economy. The Plan outcome was adopted by the European governments' respective representatives. The World Economic Conference's initiatives, design and draft were undertaken by the ICC. This was the most significant contribution of an NGO for the world economy[44] of the day, i.e. the ICC.

The Maritime Committee of the League of Nations held a meeting with the ICC, International Chamber of Shipping and International Shipping Conference in 1923. Simultaneously, the International Union of Railway Administration also participated in the conference. In the meantime, the International Air Traffic Association was created by six airlines at The Hague.[45]

The League coordinated with these business associations to develop airways, roadways, railways and maritime routes in a holistic manner. The League established an organisation for communication and transportation in 1927. This was closely associated with representatives, business chambers and NGOs.

The *Handbook of International Organizations* was published in 1929 by the League of Nations. The League collected information about various international organisations, including IGOs, NGOs, businesses and mixed associations. The total listed international organisations were 478 at the time.[46] Out of 478 international organisations, there were more than four hundred private international organisations too. It appears that in 1930 there was no clear-cut demarcation between IGOs, NGOs, corporations and representatives of business organisations; they were all bracketed under common organisations, associations or unions.

Minority identity and protection were among the key issues of the early twentieth century. The League of Nations recognised minority rights and thus received petitions from individuals and NGOs. Then the matter to be resolved was brought under the notice of governments concerned for the redressal of the petitioners' grievances.[47] The matter could be further considered in the council of the League of Nations, if deemed fit, to be referred to PCIJ's advisory opinion. Generally, governments concerned co-operated to resolve the matter. For example, four girls imprisoned

---

[44] George L. Ridgeway, Ibid., p. 244; White (1951); Steve Charnovitz, *supra note* 41, pp. 223–224; Thomas Davies, *supra note* 39, pp. 101–102.

[45] Allaz (2004).

[46] League of Nations: *Handbook of International Organisations*, League of Nations Publication, Geneva 1921–1938.

[47] Burgers (1992).

by the Romanian government were freed following a petition from a Hungarian woman.[48]

B. **Protection of Children**

Save the Children International is a prominent NGO of our time. It was established in 1919 in London. From the very beginning, Save the Children has been engaged in child protection, child rights and child development. It proposed a declaration for the rights of children that was approved in 1924 by the League Assembly. The League formulated the Child Welfare Committee that included government representatives and NGOs. The committee also included child education in addition to child protection and welfare. Those were the joint efforts of the governmental and non-governmental sectors under the aegis of the League of Nations for the welfare and protection of children.

The International Federation for Human Rights (FIDH) was formed in 1922 for the promotion of human values, including justice, liberty, equality and sovereignty of the people. Initially, it expanded to twenty-two countries and tried to disseminate information and promote human values and rights. The FIDH did not much succeed in its efforts when compared to ICRC, Save the Children and the ICC in their issue areas at the time.

C. **Assertion of Labour Rights**

The International Labour Organization, ILO, was established along with League of Nations in 1922, for the welfare of working class. It has remained with us as a specialised agency of the United Nations, the ILO is a tri-party body that includes governments, employers and employees. It has done remarkable work in the development and enforcement of international labour law. The ILO has also established co-operation and consensus among governments, industrialists and workers. The International Federation of Trade Unions (IFTU) was formed in 1920 and it has fought for labour welfare. It has extended active support for peace, disarmament and democracy. IFTU coordinated with the Labour and Socialist International (LSI) for pursuing labour welfare, peace and democratic causes in Europe.[49]

D. **Strive for Peace and Disarmament**

It is interesting to remember that in the eighteenth century, NGOs started their engagement with the peace and anti-slavery movement. They expanded upon the idea of peace attached with disarmament. Thus, it became the Peace and Disarmament Movement. The labour' unions, Inter-Parliamentary Union, human rights groups and the women's movement were also associated with this campaign. In 1922, the World Peace Congress was held in The Hague and the congress adopted resolutions on disarmament and world peace.

The League concluded that the Locarno Agreement of 1925 and undertook preparatory work prevalent in the pacific settlement of international disputes. As

---

[48] Steve Charnovitz, *supra note* 44, p. 230; Molley (2009).

[49] Silver (2003).

per the prevailing conditions in European nations, international women's organisations involved themselves collectively to the peace and disarmament movement. They were engaged at the national level as well as with the League of Nations.[50]

The Disarmament Conference was held in Paris in 1931 and attended by government official and others. Women's NGOs requested the League to discourage the participation of the armed industry and arms traders. A research journal on disarmament was published in 1932 to disseminate information and ideas to the public at large. Steve Charmovitz observed:

> When the Disarmament Conference commenced in February 1932, a session was held to hear presentations from individuals representing women's organisations, religious organisations, League of Nations associations, peace societies, student groups, trade unions and the International League for the Rights of Man and Citizenship. The session was packed![51]

As an outcome of this historical event, international groups for peace and disarmament were formed to coordinate with NGOs' activities. The NGO network had collected twelve million people's signatures for peace and disarmament. Thus, it spanned in excess of 50 nation across the world. Women's NGOs were at the forefront to get signed and spread the message of world peace.[52]

In the 1930s, Europe was facing new challenges. In 1932, the recession hit and resulted in the decline of income and employment opportunities. This adversely affected the funding and financial resources of the NGOs. European nations were witnessing dictatorships in Italy, Germany, Russia and Spain. Nationalism was rising, finding its way to Japan, in the Far East. In such a situation, it was very hard for NGOs to engage with the League of Nations and to pursue public issues. Steve Charnovitz's nomenclature for this timeframe, i.e. 1935–1945 was the "Disengagement of NGOS."[53]

The League of Nations became ineffective, resulting in NGOs becoming dormant at the time. However, NGOs did not cease to exist. They remained in the public arena and made every effort to carry on with their mission. The League of Nations slowly restricted its functions and activities. The Economic Consultative Committee of the League was discontinued in 1930. Moreover, the League did not prefer to facilitate NGOs but they subscribed to their views, and that resulted in putting an additional workload on the officials, staff and finances of the League.

As indicated in the *Handbook of International Organisations*, the number of NGOs increased sizably from 1920 to 1930. NGOs sharpened their knowledge in specific issue areas; for instance, ICC in business and women's organisations in peace. In the joint conferences and meetings, the government representatives and the League officials were facing unpleasant situations. Thus, NGOs' activities and engagements within the League of Nations slowed down. However, outside the League of Nations, they never forgot the people's cause.

---

[50] Walter (1952) and Knudson (1938).

[51] Steve Chartovitz, *supra note* 48, p. 232.

[52] Foster (1989).

[53] Steve Charnovitz, *supra note* 51, pp. 246–249.

In 1930, fascist danger and national jingoism was looming large in Europe. The NGOs' peace and disarmament movement had great appeal, support and moral values, but even the liberal democracies were unable to support them because they had to face the reality of the rise in fascism and dictatorship. Therefore, liberal democracies abandoned the cherished values of peace and non-violence and indulged unwillingly in the race for armament.

E. **Promotion of Cultural Values**

NGOs shifted their strategies and priorities and engaged in social and cultural activities outside the ambit Europe. The International Institute of Social History was established in the Netherlands to safeguard the working class and social science literature.[54]

Outside Europe in the 1930s, NGOs were engaged in forming cultural institutions such as the Academy of Arabic Language in Cairo, in 1932; the Sino-International Library in Shanghai, in 1933; and the International Academy of Indian Culture in New Delhi, in 1935. The Academy of Indian Culture was established by Professor Raghvira.[55] Another Institute of Oriental Classics was established in Tokyo, in 1938. The United Women of America was formed in Latin America in 1935 as well. These cultural and literary institutions awakened the people in Asia and Latin America. This was ultimately germinating the feeling of liberation and self-reliance.

Yet, the freedom of media, the free flow of ideas and movement of people were restricted and even controlled by the governments of the day in Europe. The League of Nations became a non-operative vehicle. Armed conflicts became an imminent danger. Ultimately, the Second World War broke out in 1939, and humanity suffered unprecedentedly up to 1945.

The war spread rapidly throughout Europe, and all resources were engaged to win the battle. In such a grave scenario, the peace and disarmament movement were relegated to the background. For all practical purposes, the League of Nations was completely defunct. NGOs were facing the entirely new situation to readjust their programmes, areas and issues. Most pressing issues included humanitarian assistance and relief to war victims and sufferers. Refugees and displaced persons were increasing by the day. The gravest situation arose in Germany, and that was how to save the Jewish people from the Holocaust. The outbreak of war suddenly posed the challenge against internationalism, and most NGOs were restricted to operating within their countries to support nationalism.

Many NGOs reduced their activities and limited their scope of operation. The International Alliances of Women, for instance, had to abandon its London headquarters for financial reasons and had to postpone several of its meetings and publications. In addition, several volunteers of the women alliance were killed by the Nazis.[56]

WW II was far away from the United States, so American society was not directly in the grip of all the warmongering and suffering. There was space to resume

[54] Linden (2003).

[55] Bakshi and Sharma (1995).

[56] Whittick (1979).

NGOs' work, which would lead to some growth in civil society. In 1940, the Inter-American War Association, the Inter-American Statistical Institute and the Chamber of Commerce of Latin America were formulated. In 1944, the Pan American Liaison Committee of Women's Organizations was created. The aforesaid NGOs were collaborating with North America, Central America, the Caribbean and South America. This was a new phenomenon that cultivated regionalism over internationalism. It also appeared that NGOs growth had slowed down, but it kept taking shape outside Europe. People endeavoured continuously to make the world a better place to live in.

Apart from America, NGOs' movement growth was taking shape in the countries of Asia and Africa. The Indian Institute of World Culture was established in Bangalore in 1945. The Arab Feminist Union was founded in 1944 in Cairo. These were the initial steps taken during times of war and developed on further in due course.[57]

F. **Humanitarian Action**

The Oxford Committee for Famine Relief was formed in Britain in 1942. There was a desperate need for it in Greece to provide human assistance and relief to the victims of war. In order to respond to this calamity, Oxfam was established to coordinate and strengthen the relief effort. Oxfam extended its relief services across the world. Today, it is one of the most significant NGOs in the field of relief, especially in the areas of famine and calamity. It expanded its scope to reduce poverty and injustice.[58]

In 1945, CARE was formed to distribute food and relief material to war victims. CARE was initially a Christian religious organisation, but over the passage of time it morphed into relief activities across nations.[59]

Some initiatives were taken in the field of literature and learning between East and West. In 1941, Pulitzer-Winning Author, Pearl S Buck, founded the Institute of Pacific Relations with the association of like-minded people. Its main purpose was to exchange activities between the United States and Asian countries. In the same year, the Institute of Intercultural Studies was also established in the United States. This institute was meant for the cross-country exchange of culture between east and west.[60]

During the duration of wartime, the decay in internationalism took place in Europe and elsewhere. Widespread jingoism arose in European countries for the war effort. Asian and African countries used these circumstances to strengthen their national liberation movement. In order to come out of this parochial thinking, in 1940, the World Government Association was founded in United States. It aimed to promote a world government on democratic principles.

Citizens Conference on International Economic Union was held in 1943. The main objectives of the Economic Union were to promote free trade, stabilise currencies

---

[57] For Information and Data about NGOs and IGOs See, *Year Book of Union International Associations*, Brussels, Belgium.

[58] http://www.oxfam.org/en.

[59] http://www.care-international.org.

[60] Barnett (2011).

and establish international economic institutes. In a nutshell, it was a dream project of globalising the world economy. Even more ambitious dreams were visualised in 1945. In Chicago, a committee was set up to frame a world constitution for the promotion of world governance. These were the positive approaches and wish lists of most dreamers and thinkers at the time of war and post-war situations.[61]

G. **Post-war Planning**

Post-war planning was one of the important issues during the later years of WWII. NGOs and government institutions were thinking about the post-war reconstruction of Europe, the maintenance of peace and justice and the strengthening of international relations without losing one's sovereignty. These activities and initiatives were mainly undertaken by the United States and the United Kingdom. These were precursors of existing international institutions. Issues relating to economic and financial institutes were visualised by NGOs and citizen groups in 1942. Later on, they were discussed by government representatives at the Britton Woods Conference in 1944. This ultimately resulted in the International Monetary Fund (IMF) and World Bank in 1945.[62]

Apart from post-war financial stability, NGOs took the lead in creating international institutions to maintain world peace and justice. The British Association of the League of Nations had commissioned a study on the organisation of peace. It had made an indispensable contribution to the creation of the United Nations.[63]

NGOs were not directly involved in the negotiation process but they gave their briefs and consultations to the government representatives. These were reflected in the contents of the UN Charter, with provisions of human rights, socio-economic development and consultative status of NGOs. The protection of human rights and basic freedoms become so vital and indispensable owing to the grave situation and Holocaust orchestrated by Germany, that it could not be ignored by the UN Charter. In 1939, the Inter-Movement Evacuees Committee (CIMADE) was established for the direct assistance of those fleeing from prosecution. Another NGO, the International League for Right of Man (ILRM) was established in 1941, in New York. ILRM carried the great legacy of the French Revolution, which established the declaration of rights of man and of the citizens in 1789. NGOs, trade unions, universities and, ultimately, government representatives pushed for the prescription of basic rights and freedoms in the UN Charter in 1945 and the Universal Declaration of Human Rights in 1948.[64]

---

[61] Thomas Davies, *supra note* 44, p. 128.

[62] Ikenbery (1992).

[63] Schlesinger (2004).

[64] Burgers (1992).

4 Expanded Horizons: 1945–Present Day

World War II was over in 1945, and NGOs were engaged again in their issue areas. Indeed, the world was not the same as before. It had been divided into three blocks: first, the United States and Western Europe; second, Russia and Eastern Europe; and third, Asia, Africa and Latin America. The division was based on ideology and level development. They had their own different priorities and projects.

A. Fragmentation of International Community

Despite this, the movement of NGOs was adversely affected by the aforementioned compartmentalised structure of the world. The Cold War the spread between the East and West, whereas the demand for self-determination and equal opportunity of development from Asian and African nations further divided the world between north and south. This led to some tendencies occurring across the world that impacted NGO movement and the working of IGOs. NGOs faced two problems: first, they had primarily restricted their activities to the national level and, up to some extent, the regional level. Another problem was that NGOs split into the Eastern and Western block. Earlier, NGOs thought globally about anti-slavery and word peace. Now they were confined to their blocks. In this divided world, the first causality was the labour. For example, ICFTU was replaced by WFTU in 1949. Thus, the Trade union movement was divided into communist and liberal ideologies.[65]

The second casualty was journalism. For example, the International Organisation of Journalists and International Federation of Journalists were divided into East and West. Likewise, law associations such as the International Association of Democratic Lawyers and International Commission of Jurists were formed by the Eastern and the Western block, respectively. Such tendencies were further extended to the fields of youth, women's organisations and students.

Apart from this, regionalism also spread across the world. The Afro-Asians People Solidarity Organization was formed in 1957, in Cairo, and it focussed on decolonisation. India had taken initiatives in 1947 and established the Indian Council of World Affairs in New Delhi for the promotion of Asian relations.[66]

NGOs managed to persuade world leaders and mobilise public support and participated in drafting of the UN Charter in 1945.[67] They received consultative status under Article 71 of the UN Charter. Moreover, the Universal Declaration of Human Rights (UDHR) in 1948[68] and the Prohibition of Genocide Convention in 1949[69] were adopted by the General Assembly of the United Nations. The General Assembly has also supported and coordinated the decolonisation process throughout Asia and Africa. India got independence under the Indian National Congress led by Mahatma Gandhi through the Non-Violence Movement in 1947. This peace and

---

[65] Shane (1992).

[66] Mansergh (1947).

[67] Russell (1958).

[68] Lador-Lederer (1968) and Korey (2001).

[69] Akhavan (2012).

non-violence experiment spread across the world and was embraced by Nkrumah, Kaunda, Nyerere, Nelson Mandela and Martin Luther King Jr. These were great leaders of the decolonisation and anti-racism movement worldwide.[70]

The decolonisation process thus enabled Asian and African nations to participate in the international system on an equal footing. Five NGOs' headquarters in 1938 were located in Asia but none was from Africa, while in 1951, ten NGOs' headquarters were located in Asia and four in Africa.[71] The International Union for the Conservation of Nature (IUCN) was formed in 1948 for nature conservation. IUCN was the outcome of work done by nature lovers, individuals and associations in the nineteenth and early twentieth century.[72]

In 1945, the nuclear bomb was dropped on Hiroshima and Nagasaki by the United States. This posed a grave challenge to world peace and security. The campaign for nuclear disarmament was launched in 1957 with the help of NGOs' initiatives.[73]

The conservation of nature, peace and nuclear disarmament were persistent issues before NGOs. These needed to be dealt with in the years to come.

In the 1960s, the number and growth of NGOs increased, despite of the prevalence of the Cold War. The Cold War raised tensions between United States and Russia and its allied nations. Side by side, the East and West became closer to their groups, integrating their economies, information and strategy. Meanwhile, Asia, Africa and Latin America were enthusiastic in their development and preservation of their sovereignty over natural resources. The East and West both reached out to these Asia and African countries and offered them technology, capital and information. That facilitated not only the states, but NGOs to interact and learn from each other too.

The United Kingdom constituted a separate ministry for development aid, being a donor country in 1960. Later on, other countries followed this trend to expedite the use of funds. Several NGOs were founded across the world, viz., the Aga Khan Foundation was created in 1967. In order to coordinate with NGOs worldwide, the International Council of Voluntary Agencies (ICVA) was established in 1962.[74]

Amnesty International was created in 1961, in London. It mobilised public opinion in defence of those men and women who were imprisoned because their ideas were unacceptable to the governments of the day.[75] Amnesty International's objectives were laid down in its first report of 1962. The organisation continuously fought against the "imprisonment of conscience" through its volunteers spread across the world. Amnesty has done tremendous work in protecting the dissenting opinion holder, having likely saved many persons who have disappeared.

From the Vietnam War in 1960 to the Cuban Missile Crisis in 1962, it highlighted the dangers of unwarranted armed struggle and the dangers of atomic warfare. Hence,

---

[70] Randle (1944).

[71] *Supra note* 46, pp. 470–491.

[72] Union of International Associations, *Year Book of International Organizations* 1951–1952, Union of International Associations Publications, Brussels, Belgium 1952; Birnie et al.(2021).

[73] Wittner (2009).

[74] Tong (2009).

[75] http://www.amnesty.org.

NGOs united and become active for peace and nuclear disarmament. They succeeded in building public opinion, which resulted in the Nuclear Non-Proliferation Treaty of 1968.[76]

Environmentalists came to know through scientific research that environmental pollution had increased and natural resources were depleting rapidly. To meet out the situation and make for the availability of funds, the World Wide Fund for Nature (WWF) was created in 1961. WWF made funds available for research, the dissemination of information and awareness among people about protecting the environment.[77]

A prominent health NGO—Medicines Sans Frontiers (MSF) or "Doctors Without Borders", was established in 1971 in Paris. MSF was engaged in humanitarian assistance in armed conflict zones and in the prevention of endemic diseases. It was brave enough to be involved in many critical situations over the years, including Biafra, the former Yugoslavia, South Sudan and Rwanda. MSF's work has been greatly appreciated, being awarded the Nobel Peace Prize in 1999.[78]

Human Rights Watch (HRW), earlier known as the Helsinki Human Rights Watch, was founded in 1978 and adopted a new name in 1988. HRW's headquarters were located in New York. Its main objectives were the promotion and protection of human rights, particularly in Russia and Eastern Europe. Meanwhile, it has expanded its engagement worldwide.[79]

Over the years, NGOs were engaged in humanitarian assistance and relief, anti-slavery, human rights, women and child rights, peace and disarmament, environmental protection and developmental aid. NGOs further expanded their engagement to the areas of business ethics, senior citizens, the disabled and migrants. They formed the International Organization of Consumer Union (IOCU), HelpAge International in 1983, Disabled People International in 1981 and LGBT rights groups.

In the first quarter of twenty-first century corporations and internet were the two global phenomena that had to adjust, utilise and to be regulated for benefit of the people. Corporations played a critical role in international trade, investment and marketing and actively participated in world affairs. In 1970, the Nestle corporation launched 'breast feed milk' as a baby food in market. This move was opposed by the NGOs. They published material against the 'baby killer' product[80] and made people aware of its dangers.

The question of corporate social responsibilities (CSR) arose, and NGOs stressed on this to lay down some framework on corporate culture.[81]

Computers and the internet enabled NGOs to disseminate information and to establish a worldwide network. They launched successfully campaigns. For instance, the campaign against land mines, nuclear disarmament and, most recently, "Me Too"

---

[76] Lowrence Whittner, *supra note* 73, p. 259.

[77] Wapner (1996).

[78] http://www.msf.org; Fox (2014).

[79] http://www.hrw.org; Neier (2012).

[80] Chetley (1986).

[81] United Nations Centre on Transnational Corporations (1988).

to combat sexual harassment of women at the workplace. The Internet and Internet corporation for Assigned Name and Numbers (ICANN) was created in 1988 by the Internet Society.

B. **Winds of Change**

The 1989 marked the fall of the German Wall and the starting of the collapse of the Soviet Union (1989–1992). Third world countries acquired some standing in international relations which made it possible for NGOs to engage globally on pressing issues. They actively participated in the Grandmothers and Mothers March in search of their nearest and dearest who had undergone forceful disappearances in Argentina. NGOs launched campaigns that resulted in the UN Convention for the Protection of All Persons from Enforced Disappearance, 2006. NGOs gave new horizons to the anti-slavery movement, discouraging goods produced through forced labour, slavery and child labourers.

The World Social Forum was created in 2001 in Brazil. This was an attempt by the social movement to tame capital, markets and consumerism and to safeguard human values and community life. NGOs highlighted economic inequalities between few rich and large populations of the world. Transparency International, an anti-corruption NGO, was formed in Germany, in 1993. The Global Reporting Initiative and Social Accountability International NGOs were formed in 1997. Their main objectives are social development and social responsibility.

In the twentieth and twenty-first centuries, NGOs' growth, reach and influence increased in many folds in comparison to the nineteenth century. In the first quarter of the twentieth century, NGOs witnessed financial crises that resulted in the reduction of their budget and functions. At the start of the twenty-first century, the World Social Forum began as a dream project of a better world but lost its brightness due to a lack of comprehensive vision, organisational structure and collective activity. WSF's legacy has been relevance and enormous optimism for millions of grassroots workers around the world.

In the second decade of the twenty-first century, the Arab Spring was a significant event against dictatorial rule in Arabic countries. Tunisia's NGOs were awarded the Nobel Peace Prize for their successful role in the promotion of democracy and human rights. The influence of the Arab Spring had far-reaching consequences for NGOs across the Middle East.[82]

Social media such as Instagram, Facebook, Twitter and WhatsApp have played a great role in sustaining NGOs' campaigns without any funds and contributions. For instance, NGOs made online petitions on contemporary issues like climate change, inequality, gender justice, etc.[83]

---

[82] http://www.globalreporting.org; http://www.transparency.org.

[83] http://www.sa-intl.org.

5 Conclusion

The origin of modern NGOs could be traced back to the eighteenth century. In olden times, NGOs were known as charitable, philanthropic, humanitarian groups and relief providers. Their activities were mainly undertaken by religious persons, missionaries, traders and conscience-keepers. In the nineteenth century, NGOs were engaged in the abolition of slavery and the slave trade, the promotion of peace, the standardisation of business and scientific measurement, labour welfare, women's suffrage, humanitarian relief, protecting nature and the upgradation of the means of transportation and communication. The NGO movement was geographically started in European nations and the United States in the nineteenth century, and over the years, it has expanded throughout the world.

Two world wars: WWI (1914–1919) and WWII (1939–1945) were fought in the twentieth century. The League of Nations (1919) and the United Nations (1945) were established by states. Corporations also became prominent participants in international affairs. Another two tendencies of the aforesaid period are to be noted here: first, the Cold War between East and West; and second, the decolonisation of African and Asian countries.

In the last three centuries, NGOs' engagement, growth and horizons have expanded exponentially. The number of NGOs in the eighteenth century was few but that increased in nineteenth and twentieth. This was recorded in the Yearbook of International Organisation, published by the Union of International Association and the UN.[84] In the twenty-first century, NGOs continue to carry on their legacy and evolve as per the needs of the international community.

Inclusive economic growth and prosperity, sustainable development, dangerous atomic weapons, climate change, problems of urbanisation and globalisation are the key issue areas that lie before NGOs in the years to come.

References

Akhavan P (2012) Reducing genocide to law: definition, meaning and the ultimate crime. Cambridge University Press

Alexandrowicz CH (1967) An introduction to the history of the law of nations in the East Indies (16th, 17th and 18th century). Clarendon Press, Oxford

Allaz C (2004) History of air cargo and airmail from the 18th century. Christopher Foyle Publishing, London

Anand RP (ed) (1987) Studies in international law history—an Asian perspective. Nijhoff, Dordrecht

Anand RP (2005) Development of modern international law and India Nomos, Baden–Baden

Arnold JH (2001) History—a very short introduction. Oxford University Press, p 122

Asiatic Society (2014) Time past and time present: two hundred and twenty five years of the Asiatic Society. Asiatic Society Publications, Kolkata (first edition, 2008)

[84] http://uia.org>yearbook.

Baker KM (2001) Enlightenment and the institution of society: note for a conceptual history. In: Kaviraj S, Khilnani S (eds) Civil society-history and possibilities. Cambridge University Press, p 86
Bakshi SR, Sharma SK (eds) (1995) Delhi through ages. Anmol Publications, New Delhi, p 249
Barnett MN (2011) Empire of humanity: a history of humanitarianism. Cornel University Press, Ithaca, New York
Bawett (2009) Law of international institution, Sands P, Klain P (eds), 6th edn. Sweet & Maxwell, London, Chapter 1
Beales ACF (1931) The history of peace: a short account of the organised movement for international peace. G. Bell, London
Best G (1980) Humanity in warfare: the modern history of international law of armed conflict. Weidenfield & Nicolson Ltd., London
Birnie PW, Bolye AE, Redgwell C (2021) International law and the environment, 4th edn. Oxford University Press
Burgers JH (1992) The road of San Francisco: the revival of human ideas in the twentieth century. Hum Rights Q 14(4):447–477 at 447, 464
Charnovitz S (1997) Two centuries of participation: NGOs and international governance. Michigan J Int L 18(3):184–236
Chetley A (1986) The politics of baby food: successful challenges to an international marketing strategy. Frances Pinter, London, pp 44–46
Cortright D (2008) Peace: a history of movement and ideas. Cambridge University Press
Dalay C, Nolan M (eds) (1994) Suffrage and beyond: international feminist perspectives. New York University Press, p 13
Davies T (2014) NGOs—a new history of transnational civil society. Oxford University Press, p VII
Demark WE (2005) NGOs and transnational network. Pluto Press, London, p 66
Drescher S (2009) Abolition: a history of slavery and anti-slavery. Cambridge University Press
Elias TO (1972) Africa and development of international law. Oceana Publications, Leiden
Foster C (1989) Women for all sessions: the story of women's international league for peace and freedom. University of Georgia Press, Athens, GA
Fox RC (2014) Doctors without borders: humanitarian quests, impossible dreams of mėdicines Sans Frontiėrs. John Hopkins University Press, Baltimore, USA
Ghils P (1992) International civil society: international non-governmental organisations in the international system. Int Soc Sci J 44(3):417–431 at 428
Ikenbery GJ (1992) A world economy restored: expert consensus and Anglo-American post war settlement. Int Org 46(1):289–321 at 301
Khan BZ (2005) The democratization of invention: patents and copy rights in American economic development 1790–1920. Cambridge University Press, p 302
Knudson JI (1938) A history of the league of nations. T.E. Smith Company, West-Virginia, USA
Korey W (2001) NGOs and the universal declaration of human rights: a curious grapevine. Palgrave, USA, p 7
Koskemieni M (2012) A history of international law histories. In: Farsbender B, Peters A (eds) Oxford handbook of the history of international law. Oxford University Press, p 963
Lador-Lederer JJ (1968) International group protection: aims and methods in human rights. AW Sijhoff, Leiden, p 396
Lagua D (ed) (2011) Internationalism reconfigured: transnational ideas and movement between the world wars. I.B. Tauris, London
Linden MVD (2003) The transnational labour history: explorations. Routledge, London
Mansergh N (1947) The Asian conference. Int Aff 23(3):295–306 at 303
Molley C (2009) The woman who saved the children: a biography of Eglontyne Jebb. Founder of the Save the Children, One World Publications, UK
Naff SC (2010) A short history of international law. In: Evans MD (ed) International law, 5th edn, Oxford University Press, p 4 (first edition, 2010)

Neier A (2012) The international human rights movement: a history. Princeton University Press
Nussbaum AN (1954) A concise history of law of nations, 2nd edn. Macmillan, New York, p viii (first edition, 1947)
Parry (1965) The sources and evidence of international law. Manchester University Press, pp 34–38
Randle M (1944) Civil resistance. Fontana, London, pp 54–55
Ridgeway GL (1959) Merchant of peace: twenty years of business diplomacy through the international chamber of commerce: 1919–1938. Little, Brown & Co., Boston, Massachusetts, USA
Russell R (1958) A history of United Nations charter. The Brookings Institution, Washington, DC
Schindler D, Toman J (eds) (2004) The law of armed conflict: a collection of conventions resolutions and other documents. Martinus Nijhoff, Leiden, p 55
Schlesinger SC (2004) Act of creation: the founding of United Nations. Basic Books, New York
Shane DM (1992) International labor and its origin of cold war. Clarendon Press, Oxford
Silver (2003) Forces of labour: worker's movement and globalization since 1870. Cambridge University Press
Smith BL (ed) (1976) Hinduism: new essays in the history of religion. Brill, Leiden, pp 108–110
Tong J (2009) ICVA at forty-something: the life and times of a middle-aged NGOs consortium. International Council of Voluntary Agencies Publication, Geneva, p 9
United Nations Centre on Transnational Corporations (1988) Transnational corporations in world development: trends and prospects. UN Publications, New York, p 24
Wagner P (eds) (2004) Transnational intellectual network: forums of academic knowledge and search of cultural identity, campus. Frankfurt, Germany, p 172
Walter FP (1952) History of the league of Nations. Oxford University Press
Walters FP (1965) A history of league of nations. Oxford University Press, p 100
Wapner P (1996) Environment activism and world civil politics. New York University Press
White LC (1951) International non-governmental organizations: their process, method and accomplishment, Rutgers University Press. Brunswick, p 23
White ND (2016) The international organizations, 3rd edn. Manchester University Press, UK (first edition, 1996)
Whittick A (1979) Women into citizen. A Fredrick Miller, London, pp 147–151
Williams D (1987) The special agencies and the United Nations: the system in crisis. Hurst & Co., London, p 260
Wittner LS (2009) Confronting the bomb: a short history of the world nuclear disarmament movement. Stanford University Press
Yats J (1856) Narratives of the origin and formation of the international association for obtaining an uniform decimal system of measures, weight and coins. Bell & Daldy, London

Chapter 3
Legal Personality

1 Introduction

Understanding the legal personality of NGOs in international law requires a background in history as well as theory.[1] Its debate goes to the heart of legal philosophy in one direction and the rules and practice of the international legal system in the other.[2] GW Paton said:

> Hence, personality may mean, either in a philosophic sense, the rational substratum of a human being, or in a legal sense, the capacity of being a rights and duties bearing unit.[3]

Legal personality is an artificial creation of law drawn from the ancient Greek actor's 'mask', which was used in plays to represent certain characters. People perceived the mask-bearing actor as a real character or persona. This was the beginning of the concept of legal personality.

The Roman classical civil law faced issues in trying to portray *corpora, collegia, universitas, personarum* and a group of persons as legal persons. Upon drawing this idea from ancient Greek mask-bearing characters, they arrived upon the legal personification of corporate entities. Thus, in Roman civil law, legal persons began to be constructed on the basis of fiction or abstraction in order to solve contemporary problems in convenient ways.

Human beings are not simply individuals. They are also deemed to be legal persons. Only a legal entity has rights, duties and the capacity to enter into complex legal relations within society.[4] This can be confirmed by sovereign powers or judges assuming to clothe inanimate objects.[5] The assumption of legal personality is a useful device in conducting legal transactions at the national and international levels.

---

[1] Nijman (2004).

[2] Higgins (1994).

[3] Paton and Derham (1972).

[4] Geldart (1911).

[5] Smith (1928).

P. Rai, *Non-Governmental Organisations and International Law*,
https://doi.org/10.1007/978-981-97-5469-4_3

Legal personality is synonymous with the capacity to enter legal relationships. For example, in early times, slaves and aliens did not have the capacity to engage in legal transactions freely and could not file their claims in court, either. But a Hindu idol was considered a legal person,[6] because it had been accorded fictitious legal personality.[7]

Likewise, ships, corporations and unborn children are also bestowed with legal personality in their social actions and thus, bear the due rights, duties and capacities. Teleology of legal personality is surrounded by rights, duties and the capacity of an entity with regard to protection of interest, serving contemporary purposes, and giving stability to legal relations so that anarchy is avoided in society.[8] It protects interests and liberty, and regulates their conduct.

The concept of legal personality was popularised in Roman civil law by Pope Innocent IV in the thirteenth century. Pope Innocent IV was regarded as the father of the dogma of purely fictitious and intellectual characters of juridical persons—which is still relevant.[9] Legal personality was first explained theoretically by Otto Gierke and further popularised in British Common Law by Frederic W. Maitland in 1890.[10]

The collegiate and ecclesiastic institutions endowed[11] with fictitious legal personalities acquired capacity and stability in Roman civil law, while in the common law tradition, the legal personality of a corporate body was not fictional but a juristic reality, with practical purposes like charity and trust. Fictitious or real, they used these ideas in their own ways to protect the interests and serve the purposes of legal transactions. A.V. Dicey observed: 'When a body of twenty or two thousand or two hundred thousand men bind themselves together to act in a particular way for some common purpose, they create a body which by no fiction of law, but by the very nature, differs from the individuals of whom it is composed of.'[12]

Regardless of whether a legal personality is based on abstraction or reality, it has a will, its own interests and purposes to protect, the ability to enter into contracts, preserve property and identity, interact with other actors, provide continuity, and be capable of making claims and fulfilling obligations. The legal personality is firmly grounded in municipal law and international law.[13]

There are questions raised by Fleur Johns about legal personalities in international law, which are broadly concerned with who or what may play a distinct role in legal life. That is, who or what may enjoy the privilege of acting and being recognised as distinct bearers of international legal rights and duties; why particular entities, groups or agents might aspire to wear these masks of legal personality, and the implications

[6] Mullick and Mullick (1925).

[7] Duff (1927).

[8] Salmond (2010).

[9] Dewey (1926).

[10] von Gierke (1987) and Maitland (1900).

[11] Bryant Smith, *supra note* 5, at 293.

[12] Ibid., p. 295.

[13] Brölmann and Nijman (2016).

for the legal order of their doings therein.[14] These questions raised by Fleur Johns are fundamental to the nature of international legal personality.

To examine these questions with respect to non-governmental organisations in the international legal system, this chapter firstly identifies international legal personalities or the international actors in international law. Secondly, it focusses on the historical lobbying of NGOs for legal personality within international law. And thirdly, it analyses the extent to which NGOs enjoy recognition as international legal personalities.

Authors of international law have employed four terms to denote an international legal personality in the past: subject, persons, participants and actors. These terms are interchangeable in contemporary legal literature and international law. Traditionally, the state used to be the sole subject within the framework of international law. Over the years, the scope of international legal persons expanded from the state to intergovernmental organisations (IGOs), individuals, NGOs, corporations, faith-based organisations, indigenous people and non-state groups who participate in armed conflicts.[15] However, this is a non-exclusive list. It can be extended further in keeping with the need of the hour.

2 Evolution of Legal Personality in International Law

The development of international legal personality in international law can be broadly classified into three phases, which are—(1) The Peace of Westphalia (1648), (2) The Reparation for Injuries Case (1949), and (3) The Fall of The German Wall (1989). The history, theories, writings of international law, decisions of courts and tribunals, formation of institutions, world events and internet access have all played a significant role in the development of international legal personality of state and non-state entities.

A. **Peace of Westphalia 1648**

At the end of the thirty-year war in Europe, the peace treaty of Westphalia was signed. It was a turning point in the history of the international legal system. The Peace of Westphalia was the end of an epoch and the beginning of the next. Europe's transition from feudalism to a modern sovereign State resulted in the decline of the Holy Roman Empire and ecclesiastical hegemony.[16]

The idea of state sovereignty originated as a long-term project. It has sustained through the ages and remained with us. Another legacy of Westphalia was the Renaissance in Europe, which gave rise to the modern State, acted as the origin of classical international law and the birth of an international community.[17] The idea of the

[14] Johns (2010).

[15] Worster (2016) and Cassese (2005).

[16] Farr (2005).

[17] Gross (1948).

Middle Ages being personified by emperors and ecclesiastical institutions began to be deconstructed in the secular realm.[18] The classical international law writings of F. Vitoria, F. Suarez and A. Gentili[19] resurfaced during Westphalia. In the beginning of the seventeenth century, Hugo Grotius wrote his famous book, *On the Law of War and Peace* (1625).[20] This book did extremely well in the modern European states. Henceforth, international law developed even further in the hands of writers throughout the seventeenth, eighteenth and nineteenth centuries.[21]

These writers firmly believed that man, by nature, is committed to living a community life, and therefore, an international community is inevitable. They further believed that man, by habit, is obedient to the law. The foundation of international law is consent of the state, either explicit, via conventions, or implied, via customs and state practices. Thus, being binding on states, international law must also govern interstate relations in the benefit of mankind.

The concept of legal personality in international law was introduced by G.W. Leibniz in 1693.[22] Leibniz embraced the '*persona jus gentium*' or personality in international law, because German emperors and princes had claimed recognition in the European community as a sovereign state.[23] Leibniz believed that the sovereignty of a nation was an essential element of its international legal personality. But he did not subscribe to the contemporary idea of unlimited sovereignty for the state.[24]

Thomas Hobbes (1588–1679) viewed absolute sovereignty of the state as a tool to establish order in society as well as the security of a nation. Viewing human nature as selfish, violent and anarchist, Hobbes emphasised on the sovereign power of the state as a means to avoid chaos and anarchy in society.[25] International law originated in the seventeenth century, and it was expected that its global subjects of international legal personality—that is, the states—would only exercise their sovereign powers in international communities within the realms of international law. Thus, the legal personality of a sovereign state was grounded in international law. In the eighteenth century, these ideas and institutions were further developed. Emmerich de Vattel wrote one of the most important books, *The Law of Nations* (1758) published a century after Hugo Grotius's first book on international law.[26] Vattel supported state sovereignty and positivism. He was the product of new beginnings and had witnessed enlightenment in Europe. Therefore, he rejected slavery and supported the theory of inalienable rights.[27]

---

[18] Ibid., p. 38.

[19] Nussbaum (1954).

[20] Ibid., pp. 96–112.

[21] Ibid., Chapters 4–6; Neff (2018).

[22] Verziil (1969); Janne E. Nijman, *supra note* 1, pp. 59 and 77; Altwicker (2019)

[23] Janne E. Nijman, Ibid., pp. 59–60.

[24] Riley (1988).

[25] Hobbes (1981).

[26] de Vattel (2011).

[27] Cavallar (2004).

As far as the idea of international legal personality was concerned, he simply put it aside and directly dealt with the notion of state as a subject of international law. Vattel described the state as a moral person who has consciousness and enjoys sovereignty. Vattel treatise was considered the standard in the United States, United Kingdom and other European countries till Lassa F.L. Oppenheim's monumental treatise, *International Law*, appeared in 1905.[28]

B. **Long Nineteenth Century**

Writers deemed that the long nineteenth century began from the independence of America in 1776 and continued all the way up till the outbreak of the First World War in 1914. Independent America gave the message that legal personality could be created instantly by attaining independence and sovereignty in an international society. One decade hence, the French revolution commenced in 1789. It clarified that sovereignty resided not only with the king or the crown but was inherent to the state on behalf of its people. Individuals adhere to inalienable rights, which must be protected. Notwithstanding, the states are personified as subjects in international law and enjoy absolute sovereignty. These ideas were further strengthened by German philosopher GWF Hegel (1770–1831)[29] and British Jurist John Austin (1790–1859).[30] Austin was a great positivist thinker who designated international law as a form of "positive morality", because it does not command the will of the sovereign. The state obeys international law by habit and through common consent.

3 Legal Personality of State

The essential elements of the state are easy to identify[31] and the United Nations has laid down guidelines for the rights and duties of states.[32] In addition, states exclusively possess legal personality or the full capacity to defend their rights by bringing forth international claims, and being responsible for any breaches of obligations within international law.[33]

The states have changed in several ways over the centuries but their basic elements—identity, continuity and legal personality remain intact. Personification of the state or its construction as a legal person does not make it a human being. On the contrary, being a legal person, the State retains the ability to act, to think and to

---

[28] Jennings and Watts (1996).

[29] Hegel (1991).

[30] Austin (1995).

[31] *Montevideo Convention* of 1933 lays down essential elements of state: permanent population, a definite territory, government and an ability to enter into agreements with other states, 165 LNTS 19, (26 December 1933); Crawford (2006).

[32] UN General Assembly, *Draft Declaration on Rights and Duties of States*. (6 December 1949), UNGA Res. A/RES/375.

[33] Crawford (2019).

preserve herself.[34] The state, like a corporation, is an expression of the spirit of the people.[35] However, in committing crimes against humanity or in warfare, individuals are the ones responsible.[36] They are not allowed to hide behind the shield of state sovereignty.

States have remained permanent legal personalities in international law for the past three centuries. But in the twentieth and twenty-first centuries, the state as a sole subject of international law is an outdated idea. This is because non-state entities have emerged as new legal personalities or subjects of the international legal system.[37]

4 Legal Personality of Non-state Entities

The revival of natural law and the arrival of the individual in the international legal regime was witnessed in the twentieth century. New ideas began gaining the support of courts and the public because positive philosophy had lost much of its assurance and arrangements since the last World War.[38] During the interwar period, existing institutions and concepts of international law were revisited and they came out with new imaginations and fresh ideas. Hans Kelsen, H Lauterpacht, G. Scelle[39] and Verdross[40] were legal philosophers of the twentieth century, who reconstructed the international community to encompass individuals, associations, corporations, and groups, along with states.

Today, there is a long catalogue of non-state legal personalities in international law[41] that relate and resemble states, IGOs, individuals NGOs and corporations. The Sovereign Order of Malta and ICRC are examples of the above.

A. Inter-Governmental Organisations

In the latter half of the nineteenth century, Postmaster General, corporations and citizens took initiatives for the formation of the International Telegraph Union (ITU) and the Universal Postal Union (UPU). Presently, these are specialised agencies under the UN. In the early twentieth century, the League of Nations was founded in Geneva in 1920. The League had working arrangements with the government of Switzerland.[42] It had a separate legal identity from its member states. A couple of decades later, after World War II, the United Nations was established in 1945.[43]

[34] *Supra* note 32.

[35] von Savigny (2020).

[36] von Bernstorff (2014) and Kelsen (2005).

[37] Cassese (2005) and Orakhelashvili (2019).

[38] Wilkin (1949) and Pound (1942).

[39] Kasirer (1987) and Scelle (1953).

[40] Simma (1995).

[41] Worster (2016).

[42] Corbett (1924).

[43] UN (2017) and Higgins et al. (2017).

C.W. Jenks examined the legal personality of the United Nations. He derived this from its constitutive instrument or constitution.[44] The United Nations possesses legal identity, capacity, powers and obligations. In the *Reparation for Injuries* case of 1949, the International Court of Justice (ICJ) declared that the UN has legal personality as part of its seminal advisory opinions. The UN Charter lays down its objectives and purposes to be achieved. It carries out various functions through its organs, specialised agencies, programmes, projects and funds with the partnership of IGOs, NGOs and corporations. In addition, Article 104 of the UN Charter clarifies its legal capacity while Article 105 prescribes the immunities and privileges of officials of the organisation. Finn Seyessted observed:

> The International Court of Justice has taken cognizance of the fact that the capacity of the United Nations is not confined to those specified in its constitution.[45]

Essentially, the Court has not restricted itself to the constituent instrument or the UN Charter to determine the legal personality of the UN. It has gone further to liberally construct Charters and give meaningful life to the UN in the realm of international law. Now, the United Nations has a 'functional' legal personality striving to achieve the envisaged objectives of the UN Charter.[46] ICJ, in its other advisory opinion, has confirmed these inherent powers of the United Nations.[47]

In the *WHO Agreement* case of 1980, the ICJ expanded the legal capacity, or rather, the international legal personality to encompass the specialised agencies of the UN.[48] It was submitted that all IGOs must have legal personality based on its constituent documents, inherent powers, purposes, functions and developed practices.[49] Side by side, the UN and IGOs are responsible for their wrongful acts. For instance, the UN has allegedly failed to stop the genocide in Srebrenica and Rwanda, whereas the World Bank has been accused of undermining human and environmental rights in its projects.[50]

B. **Individual**

International law does not deny individuals as legal persons.[51] But traditionally, legal personality has revolved around state-alone conceptions.[52] According to Frederick Dunn, this fossilised view of the legal frameworks is highly misleading, and, to a large degree, false in nature.[53] The origin of international law was much more concerned

---

[44] Jenks (1945), Schermers and Blokker (2018), and White (2016).

[45] Seyersted (1964).

[46] Rama-Montaldo (1970).

[47] Certain Expenses of the United Nations, Advisory Opinion, ICJ Reports 1962, p. 151.

[48] Interpretation of the Agreement of 25 March 1951 between the WHO and Egypt, Advisory Opinion, ICJ Reports 1980, p. 173.

[49] C.F. Amerasinghe, "International Legal Personality Revisited," in *International Legal Personality, supra note* 14, Chapter 8.

[50] Reinisch (2015).

[51] Parlett (2011).

[52] Portmann (2010).

[53] Dunn and Freeman (1941).

with feelings of need and the interests of human beings in society, when compared to promoting the sovereignty of the states. In 1532, Francisco de Vitoria emphasised the protection of the indigenous people of South America, which was their lawful claim under international law.[54]

Later on, international law became the tool of state sovereignty and free enterprises of capital, leaving aside private citizens' rights. Individuals' welfare and voices greatly deserve to be accommodated within the international legal system. States are still the normal subject of international law but the validity of rules concerning individuals cannot be excluded.[55] Individuals' crimes like sea piracy[56] and slave trading[57] are prosecuted under international law, for the purpose of suppressing crimes against humanity. Thus, individuals get treated as legal persons in international law. Their legal identity is revived in this system.

According to Hersch Lauterpacht, the time is ripe for assessing the significance of changes in substantive law, and the functioning of organised international societies.[58] Similar views were expressed by P.C. Jessup, who was a contemporary of H. Lauterpacht.[59] The legal personality of individuals in international law is foregrounded by international criminal justice.[60] War criminals were prosecuted by international tribunals and hence, as individuals, could not be allowed to hide behind the state. These decisions made it appear as if the individual legal personality was developing as a matter of customary international law.[61]

Individuals are gaining a foothold in the proceedings of courts and tribunals at the international level. The Permanent Court of International Justice (PCIJ) observed that individual cases could be heard against the state as per the treaty in question.[62] The PCIJ further upheld that individual rights and obligations created by the state could also be enforced by the national courts.[63] Individuals' financial claims were accepted in the *Iran-United States Claims Tribunal* case.[64]

Human rights are conferred to individuals across nations and people have direct access to the specialised UN human rights bodies for compliance of envisaged rights under international human rights law (IHRL).[65]

C. **Corporations**

---

[54] Arthur Nussbaum, *supra note 19*, pp. 58–64.

[55] Hans Aufricht, "The Personality in International Law," in *International Legal Personality*, *supra note* 49, Chapter 2.

[56] Kraska (2011).

[57] Thomas (1997).

[58] Lauterpacht (1947).

[59] Jessup (1947).

[60] Taylor (2013), Boister and Cryer (2008), and Schabas (2006).

[61] Gallant (2010).

[62] Steiner and Gross v. Polish State, 4 AD 291 (1928).

[63] Danzig Railway Officials Case, PCIJ, Series B, No. 15 (1928), 4 AD, p. 287.

[64] Caron (1990).

[65] Shelton (2015).

International legal personality covers only states, IGOs and individuals, but also relates to transnational corporations (corporations). In the era of globalisation, companies expanded their commercial activities worldwide. According to JJ Lador-Lederer, "The growth, influence and participation of corporates cannot be ignored in the international legal system. Therefore, their economic powers and resources had to be brought under the international legal regime."[66]

The corporate sectors have witnessed unprecedented growth through the nineteenth and twentieth centuries. But the issue of their legal personality has not settled down so far. The legal personality of corporations is evolving similar to that of NGOs. They have limited rights, duties and capabilities in international law.[67] Corporations are quite visible in the laws of international trade and international investment. Multinational corporations have played a key role in the adoption of intellectual property rights and WTO dispute settlement procedures.[68] They interact regularly with the WTO, World Bank and World Intellectual Property Organization (WIPO). They have access to the International Centre for Settlement of Investment Disputes (ICSID), International Chamber of Commerce (ICC) and other similar adjudicative bodies.

D. **The Sovereign Order of Malta**

The Order of Malta was created in the eleventh century and continues to carry out its mission in the twenty-first century. It is a humanitarian organisation, similar to NGOs. The location of the Order of Malta has changed from time to time, being situated in Jerusalem between the eleventh to thirteenth century; the Island of Rhodes between the thirteenth to fifteenth century; Malta, in the fifteenth to eighteenth century; and finally moving to Rome in 1834.[69] The Order does not have any territory or permanently-settled population.

But they have thousands of volunteers and millions of associate members. The legal personality of the Order of Malta is *sui generis* and its international personality should therefore continue undiminished.[70] It has engaged with international legal actors, maintaining diplomatic relations with almost a hundred nations. The legal personality of the Order is further clarified in the *Association of Italian Knights of the Order of Malta* v. *Piccoli* case of 1984,[71] by the national court of Italy. Moreover, a decade later in 1994, the UN General Assembly also granted 'Observer Status' to the sovereign order of Malta.[72]

The order of Malta illustrates how legal personality can potentially be expanded for non-state entities within international law. Thus, the legal personality of Malta itself has been derived from the national court of Italy, the states' practice, UN

---

[66] Lador-Lederer (1966).

[67] Lindblom (2009).

[68] Nowrot (2006).

[69] Sire (1996).

[70] Farran (1954).

[71] Association of Italian Knights of the Order of Malta v. Piccoli, 65 ILR (1984) pp. 308–312.

[72] Observer Status for the Sovereign Military Order of Malta in the General Assembly (24 August 1994), UN document A/RES/48/265.

endorsement, and the participation of the Order of Malta in the international legal system.

E. International Committee of the Red Cross

Henry Dunant's book, *A Memory of Solferino,* was published in the year 1862. It is a vivid narrative of the dreadful experiences of thousands of wounded soldiers in the battle of Solferino in northern Italy, during the struggle for Italian independence.[73] In 1863, Henry Dunant engaged with like-minded citizens of Switzerland and established the International Committee of the Red Cross (ICRC) in Geneva, to provide aid to wounded soldiers. Subsequently, it became the International Red Cross and Red Crescent Movement.[74]

The ICRC, over the years, has made remarkable contributions in the making and application of international humanitarian law (IHL). The task of monitoring has been mandated to the ICRC. In keeping with its eminent role in humanitarian action during armed conflicts, the Geneva Conventions have also endowed the ICRC with international legal personality.[75] Els Debuf has identified a number of provisions within the 1949 Geneva Conventions, which revolve around the ICRC.[76] Article 5 of the statute of the International Red Cross and Red Crescent Movement also emphasises the legal personality of the ICRC.

The ICRC was established by private persons or individuals and then registered under the Swiss law, which accorded it with full legal capacity. An agreement was reached upon by the ICRC and the government of Switzerland, determining the legal status of the ICRC. The headquarters or Status agreement came into force on 19 March, 1993.

The ICRC retained its consultative status for a long time before being upgraded by the UN General Assembly to observer status in 1990.[77] The General Assembly adopted the resolution unanimously. On this specific occasion, the member states were happy to appreciate the commendable role played by the ICRC. The ICRC enjoys certain privileges and immunities in exchange for the fulfilment of its envisaged objectives. The privileges and immunities of the ICRC are either confirmed through agreements between the State and ICRC or through domestic legislation of the concerned state. These steps are parallel to those of IGOs.

F. Non-governmental Organisations

Legal personalities of non-state entities can be further extended to encompass NGOs. Even at a time when states were deemed as the sole subject of international law, NGOs

---

73 Dunant (2000).

74 Nanda (1998).

75 The 25th International Conference of the Red Cross at Geneva in 1986, adopted the statute of the International Red Cross and Red Crescent Movement at Geneva in 1986, entered into force in November 1986, and amended in 1995 and 1996, ICRC, *Handbook of the International Red Cross and Red Crescent Movement*, 14 edn, ICRC and IFRC Publications, Geneva 2008, pp. 518–548.

76 Debuf (2015).

77 UN Document, A/RES/45/16 (10 October 1990).

actively engaged in the creation, development and enforcement of international law in association with other international actors. As Pierre-Marie Dupuy observed:

> We are laid back to the role of legal scholars faced with the paradox of NGOs. These entities have no existence or a very narrowly defined one, if any; but de-facto, they do a lot, especially in functioning of international institutions and the implementation of the law created in their midst.[78]

The recognition of the legal personality of NGOs is crucial not only for them, but also for the world community. It provides legitimacy, efficacy and a space for these NGOs to move and interact with other international actors. Anna-Karin Lindblom concluded that the international legal status of NGOs is the sum product of all rules and practices laid down by the states and IGOs for their interactions with NGOs on an international plane—and many other general norms which can be inferred from the same.[79]

Another writer, Kerstin Martens, said, "This non-status, however, also creates various problems. Most importantly, in the light of the increasing participation of NGOs in the international political process, this lack of regulation raises questions about NGO representation and legitimacy."[80] The legal personality of NGOs is a significant aspect in the international legal system because it explicitly establishes the legal identity and capacity of NGOs to participate with other international actors.

1. Sources of NGOs' Legal Personality

The legal personality of NGOs has been derived from historical processes and legal literature in which they acquire legal identity and capacity. James E. Hickey Jr. found six sources of legal personality, which he lists as: (1) decolonisation, (2) end of the Cold War and the integration of global economy, (3) the expansion of democracy and free market economy, (4) the increase of computer and internet facilities, (5) enhanced international co-operation in the fields of energy, environment, human rights, intellectual property, trade, finance, natural resources and criminal justice, and (6) the active involvement of non-state entities in the aforesaid global issues.[81] These global tendencies surfaced after the fall of the Berlin Wall (1989) and gave a new horizon to the international legal system.

Eduardo Szazi explained the legal personality of NGOs on the basis of the role they played in the contemporary world.[82] Meanwhile, Raphael H. Ben-Ari traced the legal personality of NGOs to their self-assertion they display via historical processes.[83]

2. Emerging Rules on the NGO's Legal Personality

NGOs began to take initiatives for the promotion of their legal personalities in international law. Towards the end of the nineteenth century, the Hague Peace Conference

---

[78] Dupuy and Vierucci (2008).

[79] Anna-Karin Lindblom, *supra note* 67, p. 514.

[80] Martens (2003).

[81] Hickey (1977).

[82] Szazi (2012).

[83] Ben-Ari (2012).

was held in 1899. The organisers issued very few invitations and did not maintain any transparency regarding the proceedings at the conference.[84] Peace societies, social movements and humanitarian organisations were thus very concerned about the outcome of this Peace Conference.[85] They expected the organisers to listen to them and take their ideas seriously but this did not happen. Therefore, the NGOs organised their own conference outside the official venue. They also published *War Against War,* a short-lived periodical edited by W.T. Stead, to strengthen their campaign for international peace. Non-governmental, non-profit campaigns are still relevant, even one century later, because world peace cannot be dispensed with.[86]

Non-governmental entities collectively established the Union of International Associations (UIA), in Brussels, Belgium.[87] Subsequently, UIA organised its first World Congress of International Associations in 1910, and during this congress, resolutions on the legal identity and status of NGOs were adopted. That was a turning point in the annals of the discourse surrounding the legal personality of NGOs.[88]

Two prominent international institutions, namely the Institute of International Law (IIL), and the International Law Association (ILA), which were established in 1873, endorsed the resolutions passed by the First World Congress of UIA. In addition to this, the IIL and ILA made their own recommendations for the legal personality of NGOs in the early twentieth century.[89] It was submitted therein that the recommendations and resolutions of these three forums i.e. the UIA, the IIL and the ILA, are a reflection of the aspirations of NGOs, and not legal in nature, per se. Which is to say, they are not legally binding. However, these resolutions and recommendations incited a meaningful dialogue among all stakeholders regarding the legal personality of NGOs.

When the League of Nations was established in 1919, the issue of the legal status of non-governmental bodies surfaced again. But the League of Nations could not accomplish a solution. Only Article 25 of the covenant mentioned the Red Cross organisations in order to seek their cooperation for the purposes of public health improvement and the prevention of suffering all over the world.[90]

NGOs were informally associated with the League of Nations. The International Chamber of Commerce (ICC) made particularly significant contributions in the organised conferences surrounding international economic issues under the aegis of the League of Nations. Working relations between NGOs and the League during the interwar period of 1919–1939 were cordial and cooperative. This NGO-League relationship further strengthened the historical movement towards the creation of legal personalities of NGOs.

3. **Consultative Status**

---

[84] Barcroft (1989).

[85] Aldrich and Chinkin (2000).

[86] Best (1999).

[87] www.uia.org (UIA was establishment in 1907).

[88] Ben-Ari (2014).

[89] Rodgers (1960).

[90] Davies (2012).

Article 71 of the United Nations Charter lays down provisions for the consultative status of NGOs. It states: the economic and social council may make suitable arrangements to provide consultative status to non-governmental organisations which are concerned with the matters that come under its purview. Such arrangements may be made with international organisations and, wherever appropriate, with national organisations after consultation with the concerned member of the United Nations.[91]

Article 71, for the first time ever, explicitly employs the term 'non-governmental organisations' in the Charter for the consultative arrangement between the UN and concerned NGOs.

Consultative arrangements with the UN are possible at three different levels—ECOSOC, international organisations, and national organisations. The consultative status of NGOs provides them with the opportunity to engage in the fields of economic, social, cultural and educational development, health, and human and fundamental rights for all.[92]

The consultative status has been in practice for the last 75 years; it has become a part of customary international law. Thus, the UN, the IGOs and the states are under obligation to provide accreditation to the NGOs as long as their aims and purposes are in line with the spirit and principles of the Charter of the United Nations.[93] In 1946, there were merely 41 NGOs which held consultative status in the eyes of the UN, whereas by the end of the twentieth century, this number grew to 6000.

IGOs have extended accreditation facilities to NGOs in their respective issue areas. According to an empirical study, NGOs sought this consultative status for the objectives of visibility, credibility in fundraising, networking with other NGOs and IGOs, and contributing to the UN.[94] Similarly, the existence of consultative status allows the NGOs to provide feedback, expert information and field knowledge to the UN and IGOs.

However, the consultative status arrangement with the UN does not confirm the legal personality of NGOs,[95] albeit giving them a legal identity, status and recognition.

Rama-Montaldo observes that the functional capacity of any actor is to determine its legal status in the world community. This is the inherent capacity of any institution which is reflected in its everyday functions, carried out in order to achieve the envisaged objectives.[96] NGOs resemble IGOs in their constituent instruments, implied powers, objectives and functions, but the basic difference is that while IGOs are the creations of inter-state agreements, NGOs are formed by individuals and private persons. Therefore, in the *Reparation for Injuries* case,[97] the advisory opinion of the

---

[91] Article 71 of the *Charter of the United Nations* (UN Charter), UN Department of Public Information, New York 2014.

[92] UN Charter, Articles 62, 67 & 71; Edwards (2021).

[93] Ibid., p. 333.

[94] Mowell (2020).

[95] Akehurst, *supra note* 37, p. 116.

[96] Manuel Rama-Montaldo, *supra note* 46, p. 126.

[97] Reparation for Injuries case, Advisory Opinion, ICJ Reports 1949, p. 174.

ICJ about the legal personalities of IGOs could not be extended to NGOs. But the principles laid down by the court in this opinion are valuable in the discourse on the legal personality of NGOs.

The Institute of International Law made a draft convention on the legal status of international associations and foundations in its 44th session in 1950.[98] However, the proposed draft convention did not see the light of day because the states' approvals have not been received till date. The draft convention defines the NGOs' requirement of constitutive instruments and recognition under the national law system by one of the contracting parties.

The proposed convention laid down certain rights and duties of NGOs and contracting state parties. It also stated that any association whose activities go against public policy or morality can be denied their legal status. The most important provision was the adjudication of disputes by means of diplomatic negotiation, arbitration or by the International Court of Justice. However, the draft proposal stimulated the Council of Europe (CoE).

5 Legal Personality in Europe

The legal personality of NGOs was developed further by the Council of Europe (CoE), a regional organisation which adopted the European Convention on the Recognition of the Legal Personality of International Non-Governmental Organisations.[99] This is referred to as Convention 124/1986. It provides for the general recognition of the legal personality of an NGO in any state that is a party to the convention.

A. Preparatory Work of the 1986 Convention

At the regional level, European nations took the initiative for the recognition of NGOs' legal personality among their member states. In the last hundred years, the number of NGOs has increased multi-fold, which indicates the State's growing tolerance of non-governmental entities. Western Europe witnessed the enlightenment and democratic tradition from the seventeenth to the nineteenth century. This resulted in individuals utilising their time in meaningful ways and using their money for philanthropic purposes. The national laws for the registration and promotion of NGOs in Europe were liberal. The Belgian Act of 1919, the French Decree of 1939, the Swiss civil code of 1907, and the Togo Protocol of 1983 were cited by the Union of International Associations.[100]

---

[98] Bastid (1950).

[99] European Convention on the Recognition of the Legal Personality of International Non-Governmental Organisations, CETS No. 124, Treaty opened for signature by member states on 24 April, 1986, entered into force 1 January 1991.

[100] Marcel Merle Report, *Colloquy on the Role of International Non-Governmental Organisations (NGOs) in Contemporary Society* (1983), https://uia.org/archive/legal-status-3-5.

The Council of Europe had started working on a regional convention from the early 1980s.[101] Marcel Merle prepared a background report and submitted it to the CoE. The preparatory work on the European Convention on the Recognition of Legal Personality of International NGOs was further undertaken by the CoE Parliamentary Assembly. The Assembly assigned this task to its Legal Affairs Committee, which on the basis of which, Dudley Smith, prepared another report in 1985.[102] A number of NGOs had already obtained consultative status with the CoE, contributing to the purposes of the Council in the process.[103]

Nicole Fontaine prepared a subsequent report in 1986, on behalf of the Committee on Legal Affairs and Citizens' Rights on Non-Profit-Making Associations in the European Communities.[104] She recommended that the concept of 'association' be exclusively reserved for non-profit making organisations, with commercial companies being excluded. Moreover, political parties should also be kept out of this term. However, foundations ought to be viewed as a part of NGOs because their objectives were of philanthropy and common interest. Nicole Fontaine surveyed the national laws of European countries and came to the conclusion that there were numerous points in common—in particular, the freedom of association which was guaranteed by all the said constitutions. But the distinction lay in the right to form associations—registration or merely declaration, tax exemptions or state regulations.

In order to frame a common legal basis for NGOs within European communities, certain interrelated issues like "their head office, their capacity to acquire assets, to seek bank assistance, to open accounts and to transfer capital", need to be settled."[105] NGOs are non-profit, but they directly or indirectly generate employment, and, therefore need freedom of movement, services and capital.

There is also a great need to harmonise diverse legislations and regulations concerning NGOs.[106] For their identity and legal personality, a certificate is required for mobility across countries in Europe. They can mobilise volunteers, funds for public sponsorship of community work, and contribute to development. In order to remove these obstacles, the European parliamentary-assembly moved a timely resolution and adopted the European Convention for the Legal Personality of NGOs.

B. **Provisions of the 1986 Convention**

Article 1 explains the nature of NGOs which includes associations, foundations and other private institutions. An NGO has its own legal personality and also a separate identity from its members. It has the capacity to hold property, enter into contracts and take legal action. An NGO is not for profit-making purposes and must

[101] Status of International Associations under Belgium, French, Swiss and Togo national laws; https://uia.org/archive/legal-status-6-1; https://uia.org/archive-status-6-2; https://uia.org/archive/legal-status-6-3; https://uia.org/archive-status-6-4.

[102] Raphael Ben-Ari, *supra note* 88, p. 26.

[103] *Dudley Smith Report on European Convention on the Recognition of Legal Personality of International NGOs* (1985), http://uia.org/archive/legal-status-3-6.

[104] Fontaine (1986).

[105] Ibid., p. 6.

[106] Ibid., p. 7.

be of international utility. It works for certain groups or for the entire international community. It is established, being governed by the domestic laws of the state. An NGO carries out its activities in at least two states of the CoE. It is also necessary for an NGO to have a statutory office and be based on a constituent instrument or memorandum, and articles of association.

Legal personality is obtained firstly in the parent country, and subsequently in Europe. Obtaining legal personality involves the registration of an NGO, publicity and authorisation. It is also expected that NGOs refrain from contravening in matters of national security, public safety and the protection of health and morals. Moreover, the NGO should maintain friendly relations with other states and preserve international peace and security.[107] Article 9 of the 1986 Convention, lays down that no reservation may be allowed to state parties on this legal instrument.

The committee of ministers of the CoE has adopted recommendations on the legal status of NGOs in Europe.[108] The recommendations have enhanced the performance of NGOs in the development of democracy, the realisation of human rights, and the contributions made in securing transparency and accountability of public authority. NGOs operate through participation in public life, engagement in advocacy, and being vocally active in the framing of laws and public policy. They also monitor the compliance of the concerned states with the due national and international obligations.[109]

NGOs must be free in order to pursue their objectives of awareness, education and research on contemporary issues that are vital to the well-being of people. NGOs are allowed to engage in lawful economic activities by the European community in order to mete out the expenditure for their non-profit activities.[110] The recommendations have prescribed guidelines for the statutes of NGOs, which mirror the Institute of International Law's Draft Convention of 1950.

The legal personality of NGOs should be distinct from that of its members.[111] The legal personality acquired by an NGO is an automatic consequence of its establishment. It reflects the objectivity and activities of the NGO and, therefore, it should not be subject to the discretion of state authority. The rules for acquiring legal personality should be widely published.[112] Resolutions adopted by the NGO suffice for the legal personality accorded to it, and officials can charge a nominal fee for the NGO's approval within a reasonable time limit.[113]

---

[107] CoE Treaty Series—Explanatory Report: European Convention on the Recognition of the Legal Personality of International Non-Governmental Organisations (ETS No. 124/1986), www.worldii.org/int/other/treaties/COETSER/1986/2.html.

[108] Council of Europe, *Committee of Minister on the Legal Status of Non-governmental Organisations in Europe, Recommendation CM/Rec (2007) 14 (10 October 2007).*

[109] Opening Statement of Recommendation of Committee of Ministers of the CoE, HDIM.IO/59/08 (30 September 2008).

[110] Ibid., para 14.

[111] Ibid., para 26.

[112] Ibid., paras 28, 29.

[113] Ibid., paras 32, 33, 34, 37.

The legal personality of an NGO is not periodic, and hence, it need not be renewed.[114] Financial matters and funds are separate issues that cannot be attached to the process of acquiring a legal personality.[115] Foreign NGOs can also obtain legal personality as per the aforementioned.[116]

The management of NGOs is carried out according to their statutes or memorandum of articles. Their decision-making mechanisms are conducted in their own democratic way without any interference from outside.[117] NGOs are free to receive funds in cash, kind, donations from public bodies, philanthropists and international donors, subject only to customs regulation, foreign exchange regulation and anti-money laundering measures.[118] NGOs have access to banking facilities, allowing them to acquire property and receive tax exemptions. They may also make the payments to their staff and volunteers. Moreover, they can transfer their property to another NGO or legal person that shares similar objectives.[119]

The accountability of an NGO is paramount for its credibility and legitimacy, mobilising of volunteers and funds, and garnering media attention and public support. Therefore, a robust system of transparency, reporting and account auditing is indispensable.[120] Prevailing as a legal personality, NGOs have a separate identity from its members for their mission, but they are expected to engage within the boundaries of the national legal system. They are personally liable in the event of a breach of criminal law.[121] However, they are not personally liable to debts, obligations and liabilities.[122] NGOs should not be subjected to search and seizure without objective grounds or appropriate judicial authorisation.[123]

C. **Civic Space in Europe**

In Europe, particularly in the east, the civic spaces of NGOs are sinking. This situation has arisen because of the issues of refugees, displaced persons and migrants, and the rights of the LGBT community which have been raised by NGOs. The governments of the day do not acknowledge the contributions made by NGOs, and instead, choose to undermine their right to freedom of association. This poses a dangerous situation for activists and defenders of human rights. To prevent this shrinking of civic space, the CoE parliamentary-assembly adopted a resolution in 2018[124] called the 'New restrictions on NGO activities in CoE member states'.

---

[114] Ibid., para 41.

[115] Ibid., para 39.

[116] Ibid., para 45.

[117] Ibid., paras 46, 47.

[118] Ibid., para 50.

[119] Ibid. paras 51–56.

[120] Ibid., paras 62, 63 & 65.

[121] Ibid., para, 72.

[122] Ibid., para, 75.

[123] Ibid., para, 69.

[124] Parliamentary Assembly of the Council of Europe Resolution 2226 (2018) 27 June 2018; Restrictions on NGO activities in Council of Europe Member States, Rapporteur: Alexandra Louis, pp. 1–16.

East European countries such as Russia, Turkey, Ukraine, Hungary, Azerbaijan and Romania have made changes in their legislation to create hurdles for NGOs carrying out their activities or those acquiring funds from overseas. They also frequently attack and harass activists and human rights defenders.[125]

Russia enacted a controversial legislation in 2012 which was only amended in 2018. By the provisions of this legislation, they could register NGOs as 'foreign agents' on account of their having received donations from foreign countries. The Russian government could also refuse to register NGOs by stating them to be undesirable for the nation's funds. NGOs filed petitions before the European Court of Human Rights against Russia's Foreign Agent Act, which was claimed to contravene the ECHR and the 1986 Convention on the Legal Personality of NGOs.[126]

Turkey does not lag behind Russia in suppressing NGOs. Turkey dissolved over 1419 NGOs and 145 foundations under its emergency decree. This was also the reason for the failed coup attempt in July, 2016, even though the NGOs did not have any connection with the said episode.[127] In the *Kavala* v. *Turkey* case,[128] the European Court of Human Rights held that the pre-trial detention of NGO activist, Osman Kavala, was illegal, and therefore, he should be relieved immediately. Turkey's action was in compliance with paragraph 4 of Article 5 of ECHR which guaranteed lawful detention and a speedy trial. The constitutional court of Turkey showed little interest in the enforcement of the decision made by the European Court of Human Rights.

On the other side, Croatia, Estonia, Moldova, and Slovenia have been trying to maintain a conducive environment for NGO activities. They are extending support to them and have also improved their national legal system.[129] The civic space in Europe has still remained wide and open with the exception of some states like Russia and Turkey. Otherwise, there is ample scope for NGO activities. Advanced technology has made states capable of enforcing surveillance on NGOs and invading their privacy. Therefore, there is a need for organised efforts to protect their freedom as individuals and as NGOs too.

---

[125] Ibid., p. 9.

[126] Ecodefence and others v. Russia, Application No. 9988/13 and 48 other applicants (cited by A. Louis, Ibid., p. 6).

[127] Turkey: A Perpetual Emergency—Attacks on Freedom of Assembly in Turkey and Repercussions for Civil Society, July 2020, p. 9, http://ihd.org.tr/en/wp-content/uploads/2020/07/202000728_FIDH-OMCTIHD_TurkeyReport.pdf.

[128] Kavala v. Turkey (Application No. 28749/18), E Ct HR Judgement on 10 December 2019, paras 231–232.

[129] Alexandra Louis, *supra note* 124, p. 14.

6 Observer Status in Africa

The legal position of NGOs was further strengthened when the African Commission on Human and Peoples' Rights (African Commission) granted observer status to NGOs in 1987. The African Commission adopted Resolution 361/2016 and laid down certain criteria for this status.[130]

The Commission recognises "the contribution made by African NGOs to the promotion and protection of human and peoples' rights in Africa." The commission calls upon its member states and regional institutions to protect these NGOs and encourage the participation of civil society in the decision-making process, with the aim of consolidating both participatory democracy and sustainable development.[131]

For obtaining observer status within the African Commission, an NGO is required to submit an application to the commission's Secretariat. The criteria for granting observer status are as follows: (1) objectives and activities of the NGO must be in consonance with the fundamental principles of the African Union (AU) Constitutive Act, the preamble to the African Charter of Human and Peoples' Rights, and the Protocol to the Rights of Women in Africa (The Maputo Protocol); (2) the NGO should be working in the field of human and peoples' rights in Africa; and (3) they must declare their financial resources.[132]

NGOs play a significant role in the activities of the Commission. They draw the attention of the Commission to instances of violation of rights and freedoms of the people in African countries. They help individuals communicate with the Commission. NGOs continuously monitor the states' compliance with that of the African Charter of Human and Peoples' Rights. They spread awareness amongst people by organising conferences and so on. In addition, they also highlight the work done by the Commission across the African continent.

NGOs holding observer status are invited to be present at the Commission's meetings. They receive documents in advance and are expected to respond to questions which are proposed to them during the session. Every two years, they must submit a report of their activities to the Commission. NGOs with an observer status have the opportunity to establish a partnership with the Commission in order to engage in the promotion and protection of human rights and sustainable development.

Furthermore, NGOs with observer status can submit human rights violation cases before the African Court of Human and Peoples' Rights.[133] Article 5 of the African Court's Protocol, 1998, states: "the court may entitle relevant non-governmental

---

[130] ACHPR/Res 361 (LIX) 2016, 59th Session held in Banjul, Islamic Republic of the Gambia (21 October–4 November 2016).

[131] Ibid., the Preamble of the Banjul Protocol, 2016.

[132] Banjul Protocol, Article 2.

[133] *Protocol to the African Charter on Human and Peoples' Rights on the Establishment of an African Court on Human and Peoples' Rights.* Addis Ababa, 10 June 1998 entered into force 25 January 2004 (1998 Protocol). In July 2008, that Court became the African Court of Justice and Human Rights after merger of *African Court of Justice and African Court of Human Rights* (2008 Protocol).

organisations with observer status before the commission, and individuals to institute cases directly before it. …" These provisions have been modified and shifted to Article 30(f) in the 2008 Protocol on the statutes of the African Court of Justice and Human Rights. Now, it is necessary that the concerned state makes a separate declaration accepting the competence of the Court to receive the cases of NGOs.[134]

In addition, the cases brought directly by the NGOs before the African Court must be "urgent, serious or systematic violations of human rights." Admissibility of the case is decided by the African Court after seeking the opinion of the African Commission.[135] The two essential things for submitting a case by NGO before the African Court are that the concerned NGO must have observer status and that the state concerned must explicitly declare or accept the protocol to allow NGOs to file cases against themselves. So far, only eight African states out of the fifty-five members of the African Union have made declarations.[136] Only thirty African states have ratified the Protocol.[137] Côte d'Ivoire announced its withdrawal from the special declaration of the jurisdiction of the African Court which provided access to NGOs in 2020.[138] Similarly, Tanzania also withdrew from the jurisdiction of the African Court in matters pertaining to direct access to individuals and NGOs.[139]

The attitude of African states towards the NGOs fighting for LGBT rights is not that stimulative. For example, in 2018, the African Commission removed the observer status of the Coalition of African Lesbians (CAL), following the directions of the member states of the African Union. They viewed the CAL's activities as being against African values.[140]

7 Rights and Responsibilities of NGOs

The United Nations Declaration on the Right and Responsibility of Individuals, Groups and Organs of Society to Promote and Protect Universally Recognised Human Rights and Fundamental Freedoms, 1998,[141] provides the following rights to everyone, be it individually or collectively:

---

[134] https://www.africa-union.org/root/au/Documents/Treaties/treaties.htm; 1998 Protocol, Article 34(6) and 2008 Protocol, Article para 3.

[135] Elsheikh (1997) and Kane and Motala (2008).

[136] These states are Burkina Faso, Malawi, Mali, Tanzania, Ghana, Rwanda, Benin, Zambia, Côte d'Ivoire. https://perma.cc/SE79-XNN8.

[137] Ibid.

[138] Goyal (2020).

[139] Silva (2019).

[140] Jedele (2020).

[141] Declaration on the Right and Responsibility of Individuals, Groups and Organs of Society to Promote and Protect Universally Recognised Human Rights and Fundamental Freedoms, 1998, Adopted by the General Assembly, Resolution 53/144, on 9 December 1998 (UN Declaration 1998).

(1) to meet or assemble peacefully (Article 5a);
(2) to form, join and participate in *non-governmental organisations*, associations or groups (Article 5b);
(3) to communicate with non-governmental or inter-governmental organisations (Article 5c);
(4) to know, seek, obtain, receive and hold information about all human rights and fundamental freedoms (Article 6a);
(5) to disclose information about human rights freely in the public domain (Article 6b);
(6) to develop, discuss new human rights ideas and principles and to *advocate* their acceptance (Article 7);
(7) to have effective access, on a non-discriminatory basis, to *participation* in the government of his or her country and in the conduct of public affairs (Article 8 clause 1);
(8) to submit petitions for the compliance of human rights and fundamental freedoms (Article 8 clause 2);
(9) to benefit from an *effective remedy* and to be protected in the event of the violation of those rights. (Article 9 clause 1);
(10) to offer and provide legal assistance in defending human rights and fundamental freedoms (article 9 clause 3c); and
(11) to lawfully exercise his or her occupation or profession (Article 11).

Simultaneously, the Declaration lays down the responsibilities of individuals, groups and other organs of the society[142] such as: (1) to make the public more aware of questions relating to human rights and fundamental freedoms through activities such as education, training and research[143]; (2) everyone has duties towards and within communities, in which alone the free and full development of his or her personality is possible[144]; and (3) to safeguard democracy, promote human rights and fundamental freedoms, and to contribute in the advancement of institutions and processes.[145]

The Declaration may not be legally binding, per se, but it possesses a corpus of soft international law and has great moral value. Therefore, states observe it in dealing with non-governmental players within their jurisdiction. Naturally, the 1998 Declaration has further developed the legal personality of NGOs.

---

[142] Knox (2008).

[143] UN Declaration 1998, Article 16.

[144] Ibid., Article 18 para 1.

[145] Ibid., Article 18; Clapham (2006).

8 Right to Freedom of Association

Associate rights of individuals and private citizens are inherent to all legal systems across the globe and are also provided in international law.[146] The Universal Declaration of Human Rights (UDHR) has provided freedom of association under Articles 20 and 23.[147] This has further been endorsed by a number of international legal instruments. First of all, the ILO Convention No.87 recognised the right to association or trade unions,[148] on June 17th, 1948.

Article 22 of the International Covenant on Civil and Political Rights (ICCPR),[149] and Article 8 of the International Covenant on Economic, Social and Cultural Rights (ICESCR),[150] elaborately describes this freedom of association. Both being treaty obligations of the state parties, they are legally binding upon the states. Moreover, they are accepted worldwide. Regional instruments i.e. Article 11 of the European Convention of Human Rights,[151] Article 16 of the American Convention on Human Rights,[152] and Article 10 of the African Charter on Human and Peoples' Rights,[153] also provide the right to association and peaceful assembly in their respective continents.

However, ICCPR's guarantee of freedom of association is more elaborate and encompasses all related possibilities of liberal understanding. Associative rights are explicitly endowed to the NGOs under Article 5 of the Declaration on the Right and Responsibility of Individuals, Groups and Organs of the Society, 1998.[154]

Individuals have the right to associate with or to form an NGO. There is no need to seek prior approval or register with the concerned state. This is well protected under international law.[155] An organisation needs objectives which resonate with the purposes, principles and spirit of the UN. In addition, it also needs durability and an organisational setup to engage in the envisaged objectives.[156]

A. **Digital Age**

Information technology is integral to the exercise of the right to peaceful assembly and association.[157] Therefore, information technology has certainly impacted the

[146] Preub (2013).

[147] Brownlie and Goodwin-Gill (2010).

[148] Ibid., p. 573.

[149] Ibid., pp. 388, 395.

[150] Ibid., pp. 370, 373.

[151] Ibid., pp. 681, 686.

[152] Ibid., pp. 955, 960.

[153] Ibid., pp. 1025, 1028.

[154] UN Declaration 1998, *supra note* 141.

[155] Rutzen and Zenn (2011).

[156] McBride (2005).

[157] *Report of the Special Rapporteur on the Rights to Freedom of Peaceful Assembly and of Association*, Rapporteur: N Voule, 2019, pp. 1–20 at 4, United Nations, A/HRC/41/41 (17 May 2019).

legal personality of NGOs in international law. Information technology has created civic space for virtual assembly and to establish a transnational network. It permits NGOs to use digital platforms such as Twitter, Facebook, YouTube, etc. for pursuing its activities on a global scale. It is also relatively cost-effective, rapid and convenient for everyone.

In the digital age, the participation, role and influence of NGOs have been increasing in the international legal system. Karsten Nowrot said that:

> NGOs, also, should be recognised as subjects under international law.[158]

K. Nowrot explained the legal personality of NGOs on the basis of their participation, role and influence in international law.[159] The transboundary advocacy of NGOs has substantially changed in this digital era. Nina Hall observed: "In the digital age, technology is no longer just a means to distribute advocacy messages, but also enables NGOs to orchestrate supporter-led digital networks for online and offline mobilisation."[160] For instance, NGOs have successfully launched online campaigns such as the Arab Spring, #MeToo, Black Lives Matter, #CrowdFunding, Fridays for Future, etc. by using digital technology effectively.

The UN Special Rapporteur referred to a number of successful online campaigns in his report, and in particular, #Verificado19s at the time of the 2018 earthquake in Mexico for credible information and relief. Oy ve Ötesi in Turkey's election had mobilised a large number of virtual volunteers to keep watch on ballot boxes in 2015. To overcome the restrictions imposed by the Russian government on foreign funding of NGOs, OVD-Info, the organisation working to stop political prosecution, has successfully mobilised small-scale funding from domestic sources.[161]

Information technology is changing the allocation of power in the international system. For the last three centuries, power was primarily exercised by the states, but now it is shared between non-state players.[162] Post the invention of print, the digital era is a massive game-changer in international life. People are connected seamlessly as they exchange ideas, culture and ethos while collectively engaging with complex issues for the purpose of resolution. NGOs are gathering information, analysing, exchanging and disseminating data and viewpoints a lot easier than before. Information empowers NGOs to share their inputs in international conferences and platforms, creating new norms in compliance with international law.[163]

B. **Global Civic Space**

An expanse where people individually or collectively express their views freely is known as civic space. It is universally accepted. It is a place where people share their social, economic and political concerns and interests. Civic space is protected

---

[158] Nowrot (1999).

[159] Ibid., pp. 601–636.

[160] Hall et al. (2020).

[161] Report of the UN Special Rapporteur, *supra note* 157, para 7.

[162] Gamble and Ku (2000).

[163] Ibid., p. 225.

under international law as well as in the national legal system.[164] NGOs need civic space for transboundary advocacy and humanitarian action. Civic space has expanded worldwide after the end of colonial rule and the Cold War.

Democracy advocates civic space because it guarantees peoples' rights and freedoms, which are enforceable by the independent judiciary.

The world has witnessed traditional democracies, nascent democracies and the lack and decay of democracies through the centuries. Simultaneously, authoritative governments also exist in many countries. Opponents and dissenters are necessary for the survival of democracies.[165] Democracy provides a nurturing environment for NGOs. But a state with an authoritative government does not refrain from imposing restrictions on NGO activities within their jurisdiction. They often employ multiple measures and tactics such as laying down cumbersome procedures for registration,[166] imposing restrictions on funding,[167] the denying of tax incentives,[168] closing the cyberspace,[169] and abusing the state's criminal law against NGOs and activists.[170]

Issues related to the rights of LGBT persons, migrants, indigenous people, women, refugees and other marginalised groups are raised by NGOs. The advocacy of NGOs for the aforesaid groups might not subscribe to the state they operate in. Hence, over 60 countries have either passed or drafted laws curtailing the activities of NGOs and similar civil society organisations.[171] Overall, a total of 98 countries have taken policy decisions to discourage NGO operations.[172]

C. **Defunding NGOs**

According to an estimate, 65 nations from 1993 to 2016, either enacted laws or adopted policy measures which restricted foreign funding to NGOs.[173] For instance, Ethiopia fixed a 10 per cent limit on direct foreign funding to NGOs in 2009. Such regressive measures soon spread throughout Africa and beyond like wildfire. The Indian parliament passed the Foreign Contribution Regulation Act, 2010, subsequently implementing it even more regressively than envisioned. This resulted in the substantial decline of foreign funding for NGOs in the country.

In 2012, Russia adopted the 'Foreign Agent' law in order to discourage the flow of foreign funds to NGOs within their jurisdiction. This step was quickly replicated by Central Asia and Eastern European nations. Additionally, Russian law become a

164 Khlok (2020).

165 Levistsky and Way (2002).

166 Jenkins (2012).

167 Christensen and Weinstein (2013) and Bromley and Schofer (2019).

168 Bönke et al. (2013).

169 Sandvik (2016).

170 Ferstman (2019).

171 Van De Velde (2019).

172 Carothers and Brechenmacher (2014).

173 Reddy (2018).

model for China. China prescribed that a native NGO's sponsorship had to be the prerequisite for foreign NGOs working and transferring funds to China.[174]

It has been perceived that NGOs played some role in the democratic movement of the former Soviet Union, the Arab Spring, people's uprising in Hong Kong and other countries. Authoritative regimes have taken steps to defame NGOs and reduce their funding, functions and influence.

In some countries, faith-based NGOs are becoming a part of the sectarianism tenet of religion.[175] To overcome these obstacles, NGOs need to become more creative and innovative. In the nineteenth century, trade unions made a change in labourers' lives, succeeding against the industry and states in Europe for using civic space. According to a study, NGOs at the grassroots level are surviving through China's authoritative regime because they refrain from making democratic claims and fail to address social needs that might fuel grievances against the state."[176]

NGOs play a catalytic role in society but they have their set of limitations. NGOs engaged in the women's movement and demilitarisation in Russia succeeded only in the prevention of domestic violence rather than achieving feminism or gender justice, and have only managed to protect military rights rather than stopping militarisation altogether.[177]

9 Conclusion

The legal personality of NGOs in international law has been gaining traction ever since the beginning of the twentieth century. Till date, no international agreement or treaty has been signed. Legal personality has been revolving around the state for the last three hundred years. The Peace Treaty of Westphalia in 1648 is a keystone in the annals of international legal personality. The United Nations Charter was the first instance in which the term 'non-governmental organisations' was used in international law. Article 71 of the Charter endowed NGOs with consultative status. It gave legal identity and standing to NGOs in the international context.

Meanwhile, the ICJ, in the *Reparation for Injuries* case, declared the legal personality of the UN, and by virtue of that decision, encompassed all IGOs. In customary international law, individual legal personality was recognised for limited purposes of prosecution, such as maritime pirates, slave traffickers and war criminals. Human rights law strengthened the status of NGOs' legal identity in international law.

The legal personality of NGOs is the sum of theoretical discourse, state practices, NGOs' participation, partnership with other international actors, and their role and influence in the creation, development and enforcement of international law for the past two centuries. Furthermore, NGOs use global civic space. In the present time,

[174] Patricia Bromley and Evan Schofer, *supra note* 167.

[175] Sogge (2020).

[176] Spires (2011).

[177] Sundstrom (2005).

civic space has become a cyberspace. The cyber age has provided NGOs with an opportunity to increase their access in transboundary advocacy and humanitarian action, but that has not been appreciated by authoritative regimes. These governments often impose domestic restrictions, defund NGOs, and, in the name of combating terrorism, tend to harass NGOs and activists.

The legal personality of NGOs is protected under international law, as Article 22 of the ICCPR guarantees individuals' right to association. Besides ILO conventions, regional conventions, the UN declaration of 1998, the national legal system is also endowed with facilitating the legal standing of NGOs. The UN Special Rapporteurs on Peaceful Assembly and Association, Universal Periodic Review Mechanism of the UN Human Rights Council and the Committee on Civil and Political Rights are there to monitor the compliance of state obligations relating to freedom of association and assembly.

It is submitted that the inter-state procedure, which has never been used before the Committee on Civil and Political Rights, should be invoked in favour of the legal personality of NGOs.

NGOs with legal capacity are better protected against domestic restrictions over their funds and functions. It is imperative for NGOs to be more creative and innovative to overcome hindrances in their global operations.

References

Aldrich GH, Chinkin CM (2000) A century of achievement and unfinished work. Am J Int L 94(1):90–98 at 98

Altwicker T (2019) International law in the best of all possible worlds: an introduction to G.W. Leibniz's "theory of international law." Eur J Int L 30(1):137–158

Austin J (1995) The province of jurisprudence determined, Rumble WE (ed). Cambridge University Press (first edition, 1832)

Barcroft S (1989) The Hague peace conference of 1899. Irish Studies Int Aff 3(1):55–68 at 56

Bastid S (1950) UIA: International Associations statutes series. Report on the proposal of the Institute of International Law. http://uia.org/archive/legal-status-3-4

Ben-Ari RH (2012) The normative position of international non-governmental organisations under international law—an analytical framework. Martinus Nijhoff, Leiden

Ben-Ari RH (2014) The international legal status of international non-governmental organisations: the century-long normative debate and its future prospects. Cardozo J Int Comp Pol Ethics L 23:1–62

Best G (1999) Peace conferences and the century of total war: the 1899 Hague conference and what came after. Int Aff 75(3):pp.619–634 at 623

Boister N, Cryer R (2008) The Tokyo international military tribunal—a reappraisal. Oxford University Press

Bönke T et al (2013) Charitable giving in the Germany welfare state: fiscal incentives and crowding out. Public Choice 154:39–58

Brölmann CM, Nijman JE (2016) Legal personality as a fundamental concept for international law. Amsterdam Law School Research Paper No. 2016-43, pp 1–18 at 3. https://doi.org/10.2139/ssrn.2845222

Bromley P, Schofer E (2019) Contentions over world culture: the rise of legal restrictions on foreign funding of NGOs, 1994–2015. Soc Forces 99(1):281–304

Brownlie I, GoodwinGS (2010) Brownlie's documents on human rights, 6th edn. Oxford University Press, p 39

Caron DD (1990) The nature of the Iran-United States claims tribunal and the evolving of structure of international dispute resolution. Am J Intl 84(1):104–156

Carothers T, Brechenmacher S (2014) Closing space: democracy and human rights support under fire. Carnegie Endowment for International Peace, Washington, DC, p 7

Cassese A (2005) International law, 2nd edn. Oxford University Press, chapter 7

Cavallar G (2004) The law of nations in the age of enlightenment: moral and legal principles. Annual Rev. L Ethics 12:213–229

Christensen D, Weinstein JM (2013) Defunding dissent: restrictions on aid to NGOs. J Democracy 24(2):77–91

Clapham A (2006) Human rights obligations for non-state actors. Oxford University Press

Corbett P (1924) What is the league of nations? British YB Int L 5:119–148

Crawford J (2006) The creation of states in international law, 2nd edn. Clarendon Press, Oxford

Crawford J (ed) (2019) Brownlie's principles of public international law, 9th edn. Oxford University Press, p 115

Davies TR (2012) A 'great experiment' of the league of nations era: international non-governmental organisations, global governance, and democracy beyond the state. Global Govern 18(4):405–423, at 406

De Silva N (2019) Individual and NGO access to the African court on human and peoples' rights: the latest blow from Tanzania. European J Int L: Talk, 16 December available online

Debuf E (2015) Tools to do the job: the ICRC's legal status, priviledges and immunities. Int Rev Red Cross 97:319–344 at 321

de Vattel E (2011) The law of nations, Chitty J (ed). Cambridge University Press (first edition, transl. by Charles G Fenwick 1758)

Dewey J (1926) The historic background of corporate legal personality. Yale LJ 35(6):655–673 at 665

Duff PW (1927) The personality of an idol. Columbia LJ 3(1):42–48

Dunant H (2000) A memory of Solferino. ICRC Publications, Geneva (first edition, 1862)

Dunn FS, Freeman AV (1941) The international rights of individuals. Proc Am Soc Int L 35:14–22 at 14

Dupuy P-M, Vierucci L (eds) (2008) NGOs in international law: efficiency in flexibility? Cheltenham Publishers, UK, p 14

Edwards GE (2021) The United Nations and human rights non-governmental organisations (NGOs)—seventy-five years of consultations, collaboration, and contributions (1945–2000). Pace Int L Rev 33(2):327–340 at 332

Elsheikh IAB (1997) Draft protocol to the African charter on human and peoples' rights on establishment of an African court on human and peoples' rights-introductory note. African J Int Comp L 9(4):943–952 at 945

Farr J (2005) Point: the Westphalia legacy and the modern nation-state. Int Social Sci Rev 80(3–4):156–159

Farran CD (1954) The sovereign order of Malta in international law. Int Comp LQ 3(2):217–234 at 222

Ferstman C (2019) Using criminal law to restrict the work of NGOs supporting refugees and other migrants in council of Europe member states, December, pp 1–50, Expert Council on NGO Law CONF/EXP (2019) 1

Fontaine N (1986) Report on non-profit-making associations in the European Communities, pp 1–13. https://uia.org/archive/legal-status-4-12

Gallant KS (2010) Criminal defence and the international legal personality of the individual. Rev Québécoise de Droit Int 23:75–90 at 82

Gamble JK, Ku C (2000) International law-new actors and new technologies: centre stage for NGOs. L Pol Int Bus 31(2):221–262 at 222

Geldart WM (1911) Legal personality. LQ Rev 27:90–108 at 92

von Gierke O (1987) Political theories of the middle age, (trans. with introduction by Frederic W. Maitland in 1890), reprint. Cambridge University Press
Goyal R (2020) Côtexit from access to the African court on human and peoples' rights. Jurist, 15 June
Gross L (1948) The peace of Westphalia, 1648–1948. Am J Int L 42(1):20–41 at 29–30
Hall N et al (2020) Transnational advocacy and NGOs in the digital era: new forms of networked power. Int Study Q 64(1):159–167 at 61
Hegel GWF (1991) Element of the philosophy of right Nisbet HB (trans and ed). Allen W. Wood, Cambridge University Press (first edition, 1820)
Hickey JE Jr (1977) The source of international legal personality in the 21st century. Hofstra L Pol Symp 2(1):1–18 at 2
Higgins R et al (eds) (2017) Oppenheim's international law: United Nations. Oxford University Press, 2 vols
Higgins R (1994) Problems and process: international law and how we use it. Oxford University Press, p 50
Hobbes T (1981) Leviathan, Macpherson CB (ed). Penguin, UK (first edition, 1651)
Jedele C (2020) Domestic restrictions on non-governmental organisations and potential protections through legal personality: time for a change? Chicago J Int L 21(1):118–148 at 143
Jenkins GW (2012) Non-governmental organisations and the forces against them: lessons on the anti-NGO movement. Brooklyn J Int L 37(2):459–527 at 493
Jenks CW (1945) Legal personality of international organisations. British YB Int L 22:267–275
Jennings R, Watts A (eds) (1996) Oppenhiem's international law, vol 1: Peace, 9th edn. Pearson Education, London (first edition, 1905)
Jessup PC (1947) The subjects of a modern law of nations. Michigan L Rev 45(4):383–408
Johns F (ed) (2010) International legal personality. Routledge, Abingdon UK, p xi
Kane I, Motala AC (2008) The creation of a new African court of justice and human rights. In: Evans M, Murray R (eds) The African charter on human and peoples' rights: the system in practice 1986–2006, 2nd edn. Cambridge University Press, chapter 12
Kasirer N (1987) A reading of Georges Scelle. Canadian Y B Int L 24:372–385
Kelsen H (2005) General theory of law and state, Wedberg A (trans). Routledge, Abingdon, UK (first edition, 1945)
Khlok D (2020) A study on legal system of non-governmental organisations in Cambodia. Lap Lambert Academic Publishing, Moldova
Knox JH (2008) Horizontal human rights law. Am J Int'l L 102(1):1–47
Kraska J (2011) Contemporary maritime piracy. Praeger Publishers, USA
Lador-Lederer JJ (1966) The international corporation—its status in international law. Israel L Rev 1(4):593–615 at 595
Lauterpacht H (1947) Subject of the law of nations. LQ Rev 63:438–460 at 439
Levistsky S, Way LA (2002) The rise of competitive authoritarianism. J Democracy 13(2):51–65 at 60
Lindblom AK (2009) Non-governmental organisations in international law. Cambridge University Press, p 106
Maitland W (1900) The corporation sole. LQ Rev 16:1–14
Martens K (2003) Examining the (non-) status of NGOs in international law. Indiana J Global Legal Stud 10(2):1–24 at 2
McBride J (2005) Freedom of association, the essentials of human rights. Hodder Arnold, London
Mowell B (2020) NGO goal-setting attainment and perceptions of benefits derived within the framework of the UN-ECOSOC consultative status program. Open Polit Sci 3:97–116 at 106
Mullick PN, Mullick PK (1925) LR 52 Indian Appeal, p 245
Nanda VP (1998) Non-governmental organisations and international humanitarian law. Int L Stud 7:337–358 at 339
Neff SC (2018) A short history of international law. In: Evans MD (ed) International law, 5th edn. Oxford University Press, chapter I

Nijman EJ (2004) The concept of international legal personality: an inquiry into the history and theory of international law. TMC Asser Press, The Hague
Nowrot K (1999) Legal consequences of globalisation: the status of non-governmental organisations under international law. Indiana J Global Legal Stud 6(2):579–645 at 601
Nowrot K (2006) Reconceptualising international legal personality of influential non-state actors: towards a rebuttable presumption of normative responsibilities. Philippines LJ 80(4):563–586 at 564
Nussbaum A (1954) A concise history of the law of nations. Macmillan Company, New York, chapter 3
Orakhelashvili A (ed) (2019) Akehurst's modern introduction to international law, 8th edn. Routledge, New York, chapter 6
Parlett K (2011) The individual in the international legal system. Oxford University Press, chapter 2
Paton GW, Derham DP (1973) A textbook of jurisprudence, 4th edn. Oxford University Press, p 249 (first edition, 1946)
Portmann R (2010) Legal personality in international law. Oxford University Press, chapter 5
Pound R (1942) Revival of natural law. Notre Dame L Rev 17(4):287–372
Preub UK (2013) Associative rights. In: Rosenfeld M, Sajó A (eds) The Oxford handbook of comparative constitutional law. Oxford University Press, p 957
Rama-Montaldo M (1970) International legal personality and implied powers of international organisations. British YB Int L 44:111–156
Reddy M (2018) Do good fences make good neighbours? neighbourhood effects of foreign funding restrictions to NGOs. St Antonys' Int Rev 13(2):109–141 at 117
Reinisch R (2015) General reflections on international organisations adopting to a rapidly changing world. Proc Am Soc Int L 109: 283–286 at 285
Riley P (transl. and ed) (1988) Leibniz political writings. Cambridge University Press (first edition, 1693)
Rodgers (1960) Facilitation problems of international associations: the legal, fiscal and administrative facilities of international non-governmental organisations—an international and comparative law, organization, and policy study. Stanford University Press, California, USA. http://www.uia.org/legal/index.htm
Rutzen D, Zenn J (2011) Partnership for human rights: association and assembly in the digital age. Int J Not-for-Profit L 13(4): 1–21 at 4
Salmond JW (2010) On jurisprudence, Fitzgerad EJ (ed), 12th edn. Universal Law Publishing, New Delhi, Chapter 10 (first edition, 1902)
Sandvik KB (2016) The humanitarian cyberspace: shrinking space or an expanding frontier. Third World Q 37(1):1–16
Scelle G (1953) Some reflections on juridical personality in international law and politics in the world community, Lipsky GA (compiled and ed). University California Press, Berkeley, chapter 4
Schabas WA (2006) The UN international criminal tribunals: the former Yugoslavia, Rwanda and Sierra Leone. Oxford University Press
Schermers HG, Blokker NM (2018) International institutional law, 6th edn. Brill, The Hague, chapter 11
Seyersted F (1964) International personality of intergovernmental organisations: do their capacity really depend upon their constitution? Indian J Int L 4(1):1–72 at 20
Shelton D (1999) Remedies in international human rights law, 3rd edn. Oxford University Press, chapter 6 (first edition, 1999)
Simma B (1995) The contribution of Alfred Verdross to the theory of international law. European J Int L 6(1): 33–54, http://www.ejil.org.pdfs
Sire HJA (1996) The knights of Malta. Yale University Press, New Haven
Smith B (1928) Legal personality. Yale LJ 37(3):283–299 at 295
Sogge D (2020) Civic space: shrinking from outside in? Ibero-American J Devt Stud 9(1):74–98 at 81–82

Spires AJ (2011) Contingent symbiosis and civil society in an authoritarian state: understanding the survival of China's grassroots NGOs. Am J Sociol 117(1):1–45 at 1
Sundstrom LM (2005) Foreign assistance, international norms and NGO development: lessons from the Russian campaign. Int Org 59(2):419–449 at 431, 436
Szazi E (2012) NGOs: Legitimate subjects of international law. Leiden University Press, Netherlands
Taylor T (2013) The anatomy of the Nuremberg trials. Skyhorse Publishing, New York (first edition, 1992)
Thomas H (1997) The slave trade—the story of Atlantic slave trade: 1440–1870. Simon & Schuster, USA
UN (2017) Basic facts about the United Nations, 42nd edn. UN Publication, New York
Van De Velde J (2019) The 'foreign agent problem': an international legal solution to domestic restrictions on non-governmental organisations. Cardozo L Rev 42(2):687–747 at 691
Verziil JHW (1969) International law in historical perspective, vol. 2: subjects of international law. Sijhoff Publishing, The Hague, p 2
von Bernstorff J (2014) The public international law theory of Hans Kelsen. Cambridge University Press
von Savigny FC (2020) System of the modern Roman law, William H (trans and ed). Hard Press, Saskatoon, Canada (first edition, 1867)
White ND (1995) The law of international organisations, 3rd edn. Manchester University Press, UK, chapter 3 (first edition, 1995)
Wilkin RN (1949) Natural law: its robust revival defies the positivists. Am Bar Association J 35(3):192–194 at 193
Worster WT (2016) Relative international legal personality of non-state actors. Brooklyn J Int L 42(1):207–273 at 207

Chapter 4
Consultative Status

1 Introduction

The idea of uniting the world and everlasting peace has been a dream of mankind. Since the beginning of human civilisation, people have united as a city state in Greece and as *Janpadas* in ancient India. In the Middle Ages, the catholic theology proposed some form of universal governance and interaction among all people. In the age of Enlightenment in Europe, eminent writers pursued the idea for a union of nations. German philosopher Immanuel Kant wrote *Perpetual Peace* in 1795 and conceptualised the idea of world unity and peace.[1]

In the nineteenth century, Europe witnessed the free flow of ideas, goods, people and the origin of new institutions. European countries were engaged with each other in the battled-field. For peaceful redressal from the scourge of war, nations set up the concert of Europe in 1815. In order to promote communication among nations and people, the International Telegraphic Union (ITU), 1865, Universal Postal Union (UPU), 1875, and the Permanent Court of Arbitration (PCA), 1899, were established. Besides these, Inter-Governmental Organisations (IGOs) and some NGOs like the International Committee of Red Cross (ICRC), 1863 and the Anti-slavery Society, 1839, were also formed by private citizens. European states managed their international relations from 1870 to 1914, somehow. But the First World War (WWI) broke out in 1914, and continued all the way up to 1919. A great loss of human life and economy ensued during the said period.[2]

European powers assembled once more and established the League of Nations in 1919. This was the first monumental step to unite the world. In addition to European countries, United States and Japan were also responsible for the formation of the League. But unfortunately, the United States could not become a member. The League was a failed experience; it did not succeed in stopping the bloody war in Europe.

[1] Kennedy (2006).

[2] Claude (1988).

P. Rai, *Non-Governmental Organisations and International Law*,
https://doi.org/10.1007/978-981-97-5469-4_4

The Second World War (WWII) broke out in 1939 and continued till 1945. It was more severe than WWI and spread throughout the world. The estimated civilian and military casualties of the Second World War were as high as 72 million. The deeper impact of the war was felt in the areas of national economy and global polity.[3] The world lay totally transformed.

In the last phase of WWII, in August 1944, delegates of China, the Soviet Union, Britain and the United States, met at Dumbarton Oaks to draw up a blueprint for the United Nations (UN). They wanted to achieve world peace and security through the UN. They also came to learn that world peace and security was not a viable option in the absence of socio-economic development. The economic crisis and recession in Europe were perhaps responsible for the extreme nationalist and dictatorial regimes in the continent. These adverse conditions precipitated war mongering and the armament race across the region.

Allied powers—the United States, United Kingdom and Soviet Union, France and China—knew the reality of world polity and economy…that all nations were not equal in their population, territory, resources and capacity. They resolved this puzzle through the veto power of five nations in the Security Council and equal vote to all nations in the General Assembly. In addition, they agreed to establish the Economic and Social Council (ECOSOC) for economic, social, cultural, health, environmental and human rights development across the nations. To expedite and realise these goals, specialised agencies, funds and programmes were formed. For financial stability, the Bretton Woods institutions—World Bank and IMF—were created. International Non-Governmental Organisations' (NGOs) relations with the UN system were visualised.

The UN came into existence on October 24th, 1945, with its headquarters in New York. Existing IGOs—ILO, ITU, UPU and PCA were retained because they had done appreciable work in the field of labour, communication and the pacific settlement of disputes.

For the first time, NGOs were acknowledged in the UN Charter and accorded consultative status. Thus, NGOs endowed international personality and were provided an opportunity to become partners in the advancement of social and cultural life of the international community. Ever since the inception of the UN Charter, NGOs were engaged with the UN system, actively participating in the envisaged purposes and principles of the charter.

2 The United Nations System

The UN system includes six principal organs,[4] fifteen specialised agencies, a number of programmes and funds, research and training institutions, subsidiary bodies, and missions and associate organisations. They deal with specific areas and subjects

[3] Hanhimaki (2015) and United Nations (2017).

[4] *Charter of the United Nations* (UN Charter) (2014).

within the realm of the UN Charter. The UN also expanded its reach to IGOs, NGOs, the private sector, parliamentarians and institutions, and for furtherance of its purposes and principles as per the mandate laid down by the Charter.

The principal organs are: (1) the General Assembly; (2) the Security Council; (3) the Economic and Social Council (ECOSOC); (4) the Trusteeship Council; (5) the International Court of Justice; and (6) the Secretariat.

1. **General Assembly**

General Assembly is a universal body with 193 member nations of the world. All member nations are equal in vote, the expression of views and participation. It approves the UN budget, adopts resolutions, makes declarations, debates on issues, discusses reports of specialised agencies, funds and programmes. The Assembly has six committees to systematise its work. The assembly convenes international conferences and meetings. NGOs are not formally associated with the General Assembly.[5]

2. **The Security Council**

The Security Council is an executive body of the United Nations. There are fifteen member nations in the Council. Five nations are permanent members—the United States, the United Kingdom, France, Russia and China. The remaining ten members are temporary, elected by the Assembly for a term of two years. Permanent members have veto power (Article 27). The main task assigned to the Security Council is to maintain world peace and security. This is a primary responsibility of the Security Council (Article 24). All member states of the UN are under obligation to extend support to the Security Council for world peace and security (Article 25). The Security Council has the power to take decisions when world peace and security are under threat. Depending on the situation, it can take diplomatic and military action under Chaps. 6 and 7 of the UN Charter. The Council of the League of Nations was not endowed with this power. The Security Council has been given the said power since 1945 for peacekeeping, peace-building and peace-making missions worldwide. This is exclusively the member states' domain, and these powers are exercised by P-5.[6]

3. **The Economic and Social Council**

The ECOSOC has been assigned the power for economic and social development, within chapter X of the UN Charter. It consists of fifty-four member nations elected by the Assembly for a three-year term. They represent all geographical regions including Asia, Africa and Latin America. ECOSOC fulfils socioeconomic and humanitarian tasks. It coordinates with the General Assembly, specialised agencies, funds and programmes, and NGOs. It also takes initiatives to conduct research studies on socioeconomic issues and report these to the General Assembly. The ECOSOC has special responsibilities for the promotion of human rights. Matters relating to finance

---

[5] UN Charter, Chapter IV, Articles 9–22 and Peterson (2005).

[6] Malone (2004) and Thakur (2016).

and trade are specifically dealt with by the World Bank, the International Monetary Fund (IMF) and the World Trade Organisation (WTO).[7]

The unfortunate experience of two world wars and the failure of the League of Nations make it clear that global economic, social and cultural development are prerequisites to preserve world peace.

4. **Trusteeship**

The Trusteeship Council took over the mandate areas from the League of Nations and colonies from the axis powers of Germany, Italy, Spain and Japan, to govern and develop self-reliance. Since 1994, the Trusteeship Council has ceased to serve any practical purpose as the trusteeship areas it oversaw have achieved self-rule.[8]

5. **Secretariat and Secretary General**

The Secretariat is a permanent body in which international civil servants are recruited from all over the world. They are predominantly committed towards the UN as opposed to their nations. The body is headed by the Secretary General, who is recommended by the Security Council and elected by the General Assembly. The Secretary General is the chief functionary to lead officials and seek the cooperation of 193 countries. According to Jussi M. Hanhimaki: "The job of Secretary General is the most difficult on earth."[9] The tenure of Dag Hammarskjöld, of Sweden (1953–1961), was greatly acclaimed because the Secretary General overcame the shadow of the Cold War and effectively organised impartial peacekeeping in the Congo.

Hammarskjold was killed in an airplane crash in 1961 and thus achieved the martyr status in the middle of the Congo crisis. The UN was conferred the Nobel Peace Prize in the tenure of Kofi Annan (1997–2006), Secretary General. Kofi Annan expanded the UN Mission's outreach beyond the member states to include NGOs, corporations, civil societies, intellectuals, the media and endowment funds, thereby successfully leading the millennium transformation of the UN family.[10]

6. **International Court of Justice**

The International Court of Justice (ICJ) is another principal organ which settles peaceful disputes among nations. Specialised agencies, funds, programmes, and associate organisations are directly engaged in socioeconomic development throughout the world. NGOs are partners in their specific missions.

---

[7] Bowett (2009) and Sharp (1969).

[8] Bowett, Ibid., 7, p. 63; Toussaint (1956).

[9] Jussi M. Hanhimaki, *supra note* 3, p. 36.

[10] Leon (2005) and Mingst and Margaret (2006).

3 Article 71 of the UN Charter

Independent states established the United Nations and they possess voting rights and decision-making powers.[11] NGOs successfully lobbied at the San Francisco Conference in 1945 to obtain their association and participation in the UN system.[12] They were accorded with "Consultative Status" under Article 71 of the UN Charter. Article 71 lays down:

> The Economic and Social Council may make suitable arrangements for consultation with non-governmental organisations which are concerned with matters within its competence. Such arrangements may be made with international organisations, and, wherever appropriate, with national organisations after consultation with the concerned Member of the United Nations.[13]

Article 71 is the only Article which deals with NGOs. It facilitates NGOs to participate in the United Nations system. The scope of this Article is to be understood with the consonant of other provisions and subsequent resolutions adopted by the ECOSOC. The practices of NGOs within the UN system are also relevant to understand the nature and scope of their consultative status.

The scope of consultative status is within the realm of purposes and principles of the United Nations as envisaged in Articles 1 and 2 of the Charter. The purposes are as follows: first, to maintain world peace and security; second, to reaffirm faith in human rights and basic freedoms; third, to uphold respect for international law; and fourth, to promote economic and social progress and better standard of living. In addition, the opening words of the UN Charter, 'we the peoples', perhaps includes states as well as people across the world.[14]

NGOs carry out activities within the gamut of envisaged ideas of the UN Charter. Their consultative status is a promise for the commitment of the people's well-being. Moreover, NGOs have undertaken the work in the available space, as provided by the states and in the UN system. States are still the major actors in world affairs and NGOs have a limited role in the UN system.

Rainner Lagoni and Munich Eleni have observed that: "the charter distinguishes between the rights of members (Art. 69) of specialised agencies (Art. 70) to participate, without vote, in the deliberations of ECOSOC and on the other hand, the consultative relationship of non-governmental organisations established under Article 71."[15]

When states or specialised agencies of the UN are invited to participate in any deliberations of the ECOSOC, they are endowed with observer status without voting rights under Art. 69 and 70. The observer status is broader in comparison to the consultative status of NGOs. Observers keenly watch the deliberations in their own

[11] Wapner (2007).

[12] Willetts (2000).

[13] UN Charter, Article 71.

[14] Mazower (2012).

[15] Lagon and Eleni (2012).

interest, while consultants deliver advice in the interest of ECOSOC. Thus, the consultant status of NGOs is of a restricted nature, facilitated by the participation in the deliberations and associated with ongoing policies and programmes of the ECOSOC.

A. **ECOSOC Resolutions**

In realisation of Article 71 of the UN Charter, the ECOSOC adopted three resolutions: first in 1950[16]; second in 1968[17]; and the third in 1996.[18] NGOs have been active participants since the inception of the United Nations. The first conference of the General Assembly was held in 1946 in London. In this very first session, 41 NGOs were present[19] and were keenly interested to carry forward the ideas and momentum of the United Nations. Over the years, the participation of NGOs within the UN system has increased multifold.

NGOs' participation in the UN system was reviewed in 1950.[20] The ECOSOC adopted the resolution for the accreditation of NGOs as consultative status. In order to systematise relations between NGOs and the UN, ECOSOC further adopted a resolution in 1968.[21] Three categories of NGOs remained there with the change of nomenclature. In 1950, they were categorised in alphabetical order—A, B, C. while in 1968 they were categorised in numerical order i.e. I, II, III. Earlier, there was a committee for NGOs, now that had become the Committee on NGOs.[22]

The writers, generally, preferred the term: NGOs committee. Firstly, the criteria for the granting of consultative status was needed. Secondly, the tackling of NGOs concerned with ECOSOC matters. Thirdly, NGOs' aim of conformity with the UN purposes and principles, and the representation of the larger population through its membership and activities.[23]

In 1968, Category I NGOs made sustainable contributions in the achievement of UN objectives. They were involved closely in the social life of the people. They were allowed to relatively large NGOs working across the nations. They submitted their written statements in 2,000 words. They could be assigned to conduct, study, investigate and prepare papers. Category II NGOs had special competence in specified issue areas covered by the ECOSOC. These NGOs could submit written statements up to

---

[16] *Review of Consultative arrangement with non-governmental organisations*, United Nations Economic and Social Council Resolution (ECOSOC) Res. 288 B(X), 27 February, 1950.

[17] *Arrangement for Consultation with non-governmental organisations*, ECOSOC Res. 1296 (SLIV), 23 May, 1968.

[18] *Consultative relationship between the United Nations and non-governmental organisations*, ECOSOC Res. 1996/31, 25 July, 1996.

[19] Missoni (2013).

[20] *Supra note* 16.

[21] *Supra note* 17.

[22] ECOSOC Res. 1/4, February 16, 1946; *Yearbook of the United Nations* 1946–1947, United Nations Publication, New York 1947, p. 551; Out of 19 member-states of the NGOs Committee; 5 from Africa, 4 Asia, 2 Eastern Europe, 4 Latin America and Carribian, 4 from Western Europe and others; NGOs Committee has been constituted on a geographically equitable basis.

[23] Willets (1996).

500 words. Category III NGOs were placed in the "Roster" list. Roster NGOs were entitled to participate only in public meetings of the ECOSOC and its subsidiary bodies. They were allowed to submit only oral statements.[24]

An NGOs Committee was set up in 1946 to recommend consultative status to the ECOSOC for a final decision. The committee composed of a president and five members, further enlarging membership. Presently, it has a president and eighteen members. The NGOs committee lays down the procedure for arrangement of consultative status of NGOs with the ECOSOC and its subsidiary bodies. Most of the NGOs have their headquarters in the developed world. NGOs of developing countries were not accorded consultative status owing to their population and geographical location.

The UN membership increased substantially after 1960 thanks to the decolonisation of Asian and African countries. In addition to human rights, the environment, trade and investment, peace and nuclear disarmament and the UN began dealing with the issue of land mines. NGO growth was witnessed across nations, which appeared in the annual publication of the Union of International Association (UIA), Yearbook of International Organisations (www.via.org).

B. **Resolution 1996/31**

The ECOSOC adopted a Resolution in 1996 known as 1996/31 and replaced ECOSOC Resolution 1968/1296. The 1996/31 resolution was a comprehensive document that laid down procedures and contents related to NGOs' consultative status. For the purpose of consultative status, the ECOSOC defined an organisation that was not established as a government entity or by an inter-governmental body. Those organisations had autonomy and enjoyed the freedom of expression.[25] Governmental or inter-governmental organisations were not qualified for consultative status.

International NGOs' requirements for consultative status in the ECOSOC Resolution of 1950 and 1968 were dropped in ECOSOC Resolution 1996/31. Local, regional, national and international NGOs were equal as far as consultative status criteria went.[26] NGOs' eligibility for consultative status is further required in:

> their recognised standing within a particular field, representative nature, appropriate mechanism for accountability, transparency in the decision-making process, constitution or article of association, headquarters and executive body. Moreover, the source of funds should not be heavily dependent on government grants.

It is better to have private donors because the over-dependency on government funds reduces the free voice of NGOs.[27]

NGOs are generally registered in their own country, engaged in community activities, therein. When they submit their application, their own states sometimes uphold their consent for consultative status. These objections are forwarded by the NGOs

---

[24] Cassese (1979).

[25] *ECOSOC Res.* 1996/31 25 July, 1996, Para, 12.

[26] ECOSOC Res. 288B(10), 27 February, 1950, Para 8; ECOSOC Res. 1296 (XLIV), 23 May, 1968, Para 7; ECOSOC Res. 1996/31, Para 12.

[27] Ruinner Lagoni and Munich Eleni, *supra note* 15, p. 1072.

concerned to submit a response to the ECOSOC through the NGO Committee.[28] Ruth Alice Hougton said:

> The history of participation by NGOs at the UN highlights a tensional relationship between state and non-state actors... Access to the United Nations is predominantly managed through the UN Economic and Social Council (ECOSOC) Resolution 1996/31.[29]

NGOs attempted to obtain consultative status because they had established their partnership with the UN system. They had gained credibility, exposure, networking with other NGOs, access to headquarters and officials of the UN, participated in meetings and conferences, expressed their views and concerns globally, and defended human rights in compliance bodies. In other ways, NGOs' engagement with the UN also enhanced the UN outreach at the grassroots level, gained a greater foothold in global governance efforts and use of their expert knowledge and services for furtherance of global body policy and programmes.[30]

C. **Categories of Consultative Status**

NGOs are divided into three categories: the first category is general status, the second is specialised status and the third is roster status. NGOs in Category I are concerned with activities of ECOSOC and its subsidiaries.[31] They have a larger membership and operate at an international level in more than three countries, they have a longer engagement in the economic and social life of the people. These NGOs are related to economic, social, labour, women, legal, standardisation, development, health, education, culture, environment and human rights issues. They are capable, well-established and have a proven track record in their respective fields. For example—the International Chamber of Commerce (ICC), International Social Security Association (ISSA), World Federation of Trade Union (WFTU), International Centre for Research on Women (ICRW), Inter-Parliamentary Union (IPU), International Organisation for Standardisation (ISO), Society for International Development (SID), Medicines Sans Frontiers (MSF), World Federation of United Nations Associations (WFUNA) and World Wide Fund for Nature (WWF), etc.

NGOs in Category II have special knowledge and expertise in their chosen fields.[32] They are especially interested in engaging in specific issue areas under international human rights law; for example, Amnesty International, Human Rights Watch (HRW), International Commission of Jurists, etc.. The International Law Association, Institute of International Law, and others have assisted in researching and developing potential areas of international law. Whereas, the International Chamber of Commerce and International Chamber of Shipping work in trade and investment. Some NGOs like Green Peace, IUCN and WWF are fighting for the protection of environmental and sustainable development.

---

[28] ECOSOC Res. 1996/31, Para 8.

[29] Hougton (2014).

[30] Veromen (2017); Paul Wapner, *supra note*, 11, p. 257.

[31] ECOSOC Res. 1996/31 Paras 22, 23, 24.

[32] ECOSOC Res. 1996/31 Para 23.

NGOs in Category III make useful contributions to the work of ECOSOC and its subsidiary bodies, occasionally.[33] 'Roster' NGOs, from time to time, participate in the meetings of ECOSOC, its subsidiaries and specialised agencies as per their competency and issue areas.

4 Process of Consultative Status

A. NGOs Committee

Such a committee undertakes the applications of NGOs for granting consultative status and also discusses the suspension and withdrawal of this status. The NGOs Committee is only a recommendatory authority, with the final decision being taken by the ECOSOC. The Committee was institutionalised in 1950/288B(x) and further endorsed in the 1968/1296 and 1996/31 ECOSOC Resolutions. Its working, practices and provisions of the ECOSOC Resolution 1996/31 was reflected in the partnership with NGOs and the UN framework.[34]

The NGOs Committee organises sessions each year in which it considers applications of NGOs for the consideration of consultative status as well as making recommendations to the ECOSOC. It examines the activities reports of NGOs every four years. In exceptional cases, the Committee may ask for reports from NGOs between regular sessions. On the basis of these reports, the NGOs Committee can recommend for the suspension or withdrawal of any NGOs' consultative status.

B. Criteria of Accreditation

Certain criteria have been laid down in the ECOSOC Resolution 1996/31 for obtaining consultative status under Article 71 of the UN Charter. These criteria are inter alia. The NGO must be concerned with matters within the competency of the ECOSOC, conforming to the spirit, purposes and principles of the UN Charter and supporting the work of the UN system.

In other ways, the formation and governance of NGOs must be transparent, representative and accountable in nature.[35] The NGOs Committee can deprive the consultative status to "servile society", government originated NGOs, business interests NGOs and domesticated NGOs. It can also discourage NGOs which covertly and overtly depend on government funds and diminish their freedom of expression and autonomy.[36]

The NGOs Committee discusses issues related to NGOs' suspension and the withdrawal of their status under Article 71 of the UN Charter, as required under resolution 1996/31 which states that an NGO must submit their quadrennial report to the NGOs

---

[33] ECOSOC REs. 1996/31, Para 24.

[34] Simone Vromen, *supra note*, 30, p. 85.

[35] ECOSOC Res. 1996/31, Paras 1–3; 8–13.

[36] Frouville (2008).

Committee. The report contains activities, funds, functionaries and performance with respect to ECOSOC matters and competence, and is also related to the UN's spirit, principles, purposes and work. NGOs' failure to submit the report within four years of the stipulated timeframe may evoke suspension and the withdrawal of consultative status.[37] The NGOs Committee may send reminders for the submission of the report. If the NGO fails to respond, then it is suspended by the ECOSOC on the recommendation of the NGOs Committee.

NGO should not be in conflict with the law and/or involved in criminal activities such as money laundering, arms and drug trafficking, and in contravention of the purposes and principles of the United Nations. NGOs cannot receive any secret funds or become domesticated. Additionally, if NGOs do not perform in a positive and effective manner or contribute to the work of UN,[38] grounds may be brought, wherein, any member state can call for the suspension or withdrawal of an NGO's consultative status.

The aforesaid points come under the legal framework, where the committee is authorised to accord, suspend or withdraw the consultative status. The provisions of Resolution 1996/31 are not all that clear because of the ambiguous language. The member states primarily oversee their national interest and politics. They observe keenly NGOs' role in the universal periodic review (UPR) report of the UN Human Rights Council. Member states get hostile or uncomfortable with the exposing of human rights violations and the non-compliance with environmental obligations within their shores. To counter, states highlight the delay in submission of the NGOs report and try finding loopholes to invoke the procedure of suspension or withdrawal.

C. **Deprivation of Consultative Status**

The NGOs Committee employs four ways to deprive NGOs consultative status. These are: to deny, to defer, to suspend, and to withdraw. The consultative status of NGOs under the UN Charter has been facing controversy since inception. For instance, the consultative status of the International Chamber of Commerce (ICC) was opposed in 1946 because it had its branch in Spain. The nation was ruled by a dictator back then, and hence, was not allowed to join the UN.[39] In the Cold War period (1950–1990), the United States and Western European countries denied consultative status to NGOs based out of the USSR, Eastern Europe, China and Cuba. As a consequence, the Soviet Union and its a allies repaid the favour.

Western countries tried to deny the World Federation of Trade Unions (WFTU) its consultative status. But they did not succeed because the WFTU was very strong and possessed a good track record. Therefore, the status came through despite the protest by the western world. In the rejoinder, the United States block created a separate organisation—the International Confederation of Free Trade Unions (ICFTU). Just like the WFTU, its admission took place in Category A: General Status.[40]

---

[37] ECOSOC Res. 1996/31, Para 61.

[38] Martens (2005).

[39] *UN Yearbook*, 1948–1949, pp. 709–711.

[40] *UN Yearbook*, 1967, pp. 564–570.

Despite, the East–West rivalry, NGOs' consultative status underwent an increase. Before the origin of the UN, NGOs working over the years were well established. They had to overcome the hurdles of the Cold War. NGOs also faced staunch objection from undemocratic nations and violators of human rights.[41] This fact, notwithstanding, they continue to remain a part of the UN system. In 1948, there were 40 NGOs,[42] while in 1990, there were nearly 1000 NGOs dealing with the ECOSOC.[43] At present, more than 6,000 NGOs possess consultative status.[44]

The NGOs Committee processed the applications of NGOs for consultative status annually. Member states of the NGOs Committee sometimes took decisions, either politically or prejudicially, rather than on merit of the case and spirit of the Charter and Resolution 1996/31. According to studies of 2005 and 2015, the NGOs Committee recommended not granting consultative status to seventeen NGOs.[45] Out of seventeen, nine related to the rights of the LGBT community. In 2006, the NGOs Committee member states alleged that these NGOs supported, and had ties to, pedophilia. The Committee did not process their applications, deferring them all the way to 2011. They used two methods: either recommend denying to the ECOSOC or to merely defer by not processing the applications in a timely manner. In 2011, the regular session of the NGOs Committee deferred 216 applications to subsequent sessions.

Between 2005 and 2010, the Committee suspended the consultative status of four NGOs and withdrew the said status of seven.[46] In 2009, the NGOs Committee suspended The Arab Commission for Human Rights (ACHR). Algeria complained that the ACHR had allowed a criminal absconder who was being investigated by the INTERPOL to speak on behalf of ACHR during a UN Human Rights Council session.[47]

China alleged that Liberal International's behaviour was contrary to the purposes and principles of the UN Charter and Resolution 1996/31. Liberal International representatives had previously challenged the "One China" policy. Despite the Committee's recommendation for the consultative status of the NGO in 2007,[48] Pei-heng Chaing concluded:

There is a tendency for the UN to attempt to "control the character and activities" of NGOs by threatening to withdraw the consultative status of those whose activities outside the UN, it does not approve, as well as those NGOs that criticise certain

[41] Peter Willets, *supra note* 23, p. 37.

[42] Kertin Martens, *supra note* 38, p. 129.

[43] Peter Willets, *supra note* 41, p. 37.

[44] ECOSOC Council, E/2022/INF/5/(31 December 2022) List of NGOs in Consultative Status with ECOSOC as of 31 December 2022.

[45] Simone Vromen, *supra note* 34, p. 90.

[46] Ibid., p. 93.

[47] ECOSOC Res. 1996/31, Para 57.

[48] ECOSOC Res. 1996/31, Paras 47–61.

decisions or actions of the UN or certain governments, threatening to reject those NGOs.[49]

D. **Domesticating of NGOs**

Because of the increasing number, sphere and influence of NGOs within and outside the UN system, governments and business communities formed their own organisations and associations so as to counter the collective free voice of NGOs. They tried to manage consultative status for them in the ECOSOC and ensure their participation in international platforms.[50] Business setup-NGOs are active in the World Trade Organisation (WTO),[51] International Monetary Fund (IMF) and World Bank to serve business and industry interests. The general behaviour and participation in international forums made it amply clear of their real nature and motives, and whom they served.

Indeed, "servile society" are illegal entities. Their main purpose is to serve states and counter genuine NGOs before the ECOSOC, WTO, World Bank and IGOs. They try to acquire consultative status through the NGOs Committee. The NGOs Committee is exclusively constituted by member states and is elected for a term of four years. There is no ban on re-election, therefore, undemocratic and ideologically overbearing states try hard to continue their membership in the NGOs Committee.

In order to discourage and block domesticating NGOs, membership of the NGOs committee should be restricted for one term at a time only so that the other member states of the UN could get elected from the ECOSOC. This leads to the injection of fresh ideas and representation as well the expansion of its global reach.

Oliver de Frouville conducted a study on the domestication of NGOs from 1990 to 2006[52] by analysing the NGOs Committee's annual reports. He narrated various case studies wherein Cuba, China, Argentina, India, Pakistan, Tunisia and the United States were eagerly locking horns with one another to deny the opponents' NGOs and promote their own. The NGOs Committee essentially observes those countries where the constitution does not guarantee freedom of expression, association and assembly, and lacks an independent judiciary.

India and Pakistan have locked horns over the Kashmir conflict for a long time. They have made the United Nations and the NGOs Committee their battleground. They favour NGOs who put forth their cause to the UN Human Rights Council. For example, the All Pakistan Women's-Association is de-facto linked to the government of Pakistan and receives indirect funding and support from it. Its primary role is to defend Pakistan's position on Kashmir and to denounce India's possession on the territory, thereby raising the voice against India's purported genocide against the

[49] Chiang (1981).

[50] Oliver de Frouville, *supra note* 36, pp. 71–115.

[51] Marceau and Pedersen (1999).

[52] Oliver de Frouville, *supra note* 50, p. 72.

Kashmiri population. India's NGOs denounced these false allegations and defended the Indian position in Kashmir.[53]

The United States, as a member of the NGOs Committee, opposed the infiltration of Cuba-based NGOs but promoted Cuban NGOs located beyond the country's borders. The Cuban NGOs countered by heavily criticising the United States for their intervention in the third world and their overall imperialist design. United States' NGOs expressed their anger against Cuba for their lack of freedom, democracy and atrocities against their own people.

Those societies that are closed and have democratic deficiencies tend to push their NGOs before the NGOs Committee to in order to receive consultative status from the ECOSOC. China promoted the All-China Women's Federation, China's Society for Human Rights and even the United Nations Association of China to define China's position on the promotion of human rights and to counter the allegations of NGOs and the UN rapporteurs. It is interesting to note that the United States, China and Cuba have managed their membership continuity within the NGOs Committee. Those countries having hostile relations with other countries with maximum human rights violation cases, lack of freedom, and confined to specific dogmas, are more interested to find a place in the NGOs Committee.

5 The Cardoso Report

Kofi Annan, Secretary General of the United Nations (1997–2006), introduced reforms in the relations between NGOs and the UN. In 2003, he appointed a twelve-member panel on the United Nations–Civil Society relations. The Committee was headed by its chairman, former Brazilian President, Fernando Henrique Cardoso, and the remaining eleven members were equitably distributed from all regions. The members comprised eminent persons, academics, diplomats, government officials and NGOs activists in the fields of environment, socioeconomic development and human rights. The panel is popularly called the Cardoso panel in public parlance, named after its Chairman. The Cardoso Panel submitted its report, "We the Peoples: Civil Society, the United Nations and Global Governance," to the Secretary General in 2004.[54]

A. **Assessment of the Report**

The Cardoso Report, 2004, was not much appreciated by the Secretary General, member states, NGOs and writers of international law and world affairs. Peter Willets

---

[53] These NGOs are: International Institute of Peace; Himalayan Research and Cultural Foundations; and Indian Council of Educations.

[54] *Secretary General Report, Reviewing the United Nations: A Programme for Reform*, UN Doc. A/51/950 (14 July, 1997); Strengthening the United Nations: An Agenda for Further Change, UN Doc. A/57/387 (9 September, 2002).

observed: The Cardoso Report was a mix of ideas such as functionalism, global corporatism and global democracy.[55] He further stated:

> There are three normative arguments for enhancing NGOs' partnership in policy-making: the functionalist appeal for the use of expertise; the corporatist desire to involve the affected interests; and the pluralist belief in democratic policy–making.[56]

The partnership of NGOs with the United Nations was dealt with by the ECOSOC resolutions of 1950, 1968 and 1996. However, the Cardoso Panel neither analysed in depth the existing consultative status nor the working of the NGOs Committee nor the outcome of ECOSOC decisions. The panel report preferred the use of the term 'civil society' rather than 'NGOs'. The term NGO was employed in Article 71 of the UN Charter, gaining popularity over the last seventy years, while the term civil society has not been crystallised yet.

Besides, these entities involve private sectors and other stakeholders. The private sector mainly engages in profiteering and its objective is lobbying for extending business opportunities. This is far removed from the issues of poverty, human rights and environmental issues. The mixing of community interests with business interests and NGOs with corporations was highly objectionable from the non-profit sectors' standpoint. The enhancing of partnership between civil society and the UN resulted in ambiguity.

The Cardoso Report recommended a stronger relationship between NGOs and the UN in so far as policymaking was concerned, but it was not endorsed by the member states. Even larger democratic countries like the United States, India and France were not particularly enthusiastic about the implementation of these ideas.[57] The report recommended the building up of civil society across the southern hemisphere. It ignored the existing Non-Governmental Liaison Services (NGLS) based in Geneva. NGLS had already been engaged to assist the NGOs of developing countries. This was funded mainly by private donors. It is a semi-autonomous body related to the UN. The Cardoso Report proposed to integrate NGLS with the UN, ignoring the availability of private donors and funds.[58]

Some important issues still remain to strengthen the relationship between NGOs and the UN system. But the Cardoso Report did not come out with workable suggestions that could be implemented. For instance, the NGOs Committee is an expensive affair and its work is politicised by member states. Additionally, it delays applications from NGOs and issues warnings by requesting interim reports in between quarterly reports.

The NGOs Committee's recommendations for consultative status of NGOs was finalised by the ECOSOC. NGOs' consultative status, as accorded by the ECOSOC on the basis of the NGOs Committee's recommendations, was not made accessible

---

[55] Willets (2006).

[56] Ibid., p. 306; Further explore the conceptual framework of the functionalism, corporatism and democracy, See Burton (1972), Clarkson (1998), Hutton (1995).

[57] Martens and James (2004).

[58] www.globalpolicy.org.

to anyone. Participation of NGOs with respect to the General Assembly, Security Council, WTO, World Bank and IMF is not covered by a nod by the ECOSOC.

Therefore, it is imperative for the consultative status procedure to be shifted from the ECOSOC to the UN Secretariat, with final approval coming from the General Assembly. The accessibility of NGOs to the entire United Nations system, comprising principal organs, funds, programs, specialised agencies, associated, affiliated, and attached intergovernmental organisations and institutions, is facilitated. Another grey area was the categorisation of NGOs—general, special and roster. In the general category, single-nation NGOs were included without examining their capability and reality. This resulted in the origin of government, domesticated NGOs. The general category should be restricted only to international NGOs that possess vast experience and have a good track record. But this has been totally undermined by the Cardoso Report.

The said report unnecessarily created confusion by referring to the private sectors.[59] Article 71 does not include private sectors; it provides, exclusively, the consultative status to NGOs. The International Chamber of Commerce (ICC) has been associated with the League of Nations since 1922 and the UN since 1946, as an NGO, and not as a business interests group.

B. **Private Sector and the UN**

The 1990s gave birth to a transformed world. The Soviet Union disintegrated. Russia, Eastern Europe and the countries of Central Asia came out as separate states. The world economy globalised, resulting in the free flow of capital and goods with technological advancement taking place at unprecedented pace. Democracy expanded worldwide. The growth of NGOs and corporations was witnessed side by side.

The Earth Summit in 1992 in Rio de Janeiro was attended by a large number of NGOs. This was an indication of their number, strength and influence in the UN Conference: Earth Summit on Environment and Development. The UN Conference, 1992 introduced the idea of "major groups", "multiple stakeholders' dialogue that might include business and industry". The Commission of Sustainable Development was created by the UN Conference, 1992. Apart from the state, the industry and business, IGOs and NGOs were also associated with the commission. This idea was further developed in the Millennium Development Goal (MDG) and World Summit on the Information Society, when they were again called "multiple stakeholders". This was the first conference jointly organised by the states, IGOs, NGOs and corporations.[60]

The private sector's economic power and influence became a reality in contemporary life. A study conducted on behalf of the UNDP by Inge Kaul and Conceica Pedro, concluded that "400 global public–private partnerships were in existence worldwide" currently.[61] In 2005, an interactive session was organised on the relationship between the UN and civil society. In this session, the Secretary General said: the contribution

---

59 Jens Martens and James Paul, *supra note* 57.

60 Martens (2007).

61 Kaul and Pedro (2006).

from the private sector and civil society (including NGOs) in the promotion and implementation of the development programme, was welcome.[62]

The private sector's participation with the UN system, policy and programmes was endorsed by the Secretary General in the meeting of the General Assembly. It seemed that the amendment of the Charter and the formal legal nod were not required in case of the private sector association with the UN and its programmes. In such a situation, NGOs continuously lobbied to extend their formal participation in the General Assembly, Security Council, World Trade Organisation, IMF and World Bank, and in the entire UN system.[63]

6 NGOs and the General Assembly

The consultative status of NGOs was dealt with only by the ECOSOC, explicitly in its competence and matters. Article 71 of the UN Charter was silent about the other principal organs. Since the very beginning, confusion prevailed as to whether NGOs could be involved in the socioeconomic issues of the General Assembly and to access in matters and information from the committees of the General Assembly.[64] States opposed the participation of NGOs in this high-profile universal body, which built up public opinion worldwide.[65] The General Assembly is a barometer of public opinion because it deliberates, discusses and adopts resolutions and recommendations. Any global issues not pending in the Security Council could be undertaken by the General Assembly. (Article 12(1) of the UN Charter).

NGOs were taking part in Committees No. 1 and 4 of the General Assembly, concerned with matters related to development, disarmament, drugs, decolonisation and apartheid. However, NGOs could not participate directly in the meetings and proceedings of the General Assembly. They were lobbying via committees and member states. In the 1970s, NGOs took initiatives against apartheid and the peaceful use of outer space.

They went on to participate in the Population and Development Conference in Cairo in 1993. The sub-committee of outer space formally granted observer status to the International Astronautical Federation, an NGO having special category status.[66] Another NGO, the International Planned Parenthood Federation, with general category status, was extended formal participation to make a presentation before the

[62] *World Summit Outcome*, UN Doc.A/Res./60/1/2005 (16 September, 2005).

[63] Woodward (2010).

[64] ECOSOC Res. 288(X)B (27 Feb. 1950) Para 40(f) *Review of Consultative arrangements with non-governmental organisations*; ECOSOC Res. 1296 (XLIV) (23 May, 1968) Para 46(f), ECOSOC relations with NGOs; ECOSOC Res. 1996/31, Para 67(f), 22 July, 1996, *Consultative relationship between the UN and NGOs*; Above paras (40(f), 46(f) & 67(f)) are dealt with GA and NGOs relationship.

[65] Peter Willet, *supra note* 12, p. 196.

[66] *Yearbook of the United Nations* 1971, UN Publications, 1974, p. 56.

second committee of the General Assembly.[67] Peter Willets observed that, "the facilities for access are sufficient to make lobbying possible." NGOs having expert knowledge and experience make it possible to use the available space and facilities for lobbying in the General Assembly.

The Earth Summit in Rio in 1992 was the turning point for NGOs' relationship with the UN. An unprecedented number of NGOs participated in the UN Conference on Environment and Development (The Earth Summit) and contributed substantively to its outcome. Following the Earth Summit deliberations in the General Assembly, the Secretary General allowed the sub-committees to make formal arrangements with the NGOs.[68]

A. **NGOs' Observer Status**

The International Committee of the Red Cross (ICRC) formed as an NGO in the last quarter of the nineteenth century and was formally granted observer status in 1990 by the General Assembly. Another sui generis actor, the Sovereign Order of Malta, was also endowed observer status in the same vein as ICRC, in 1994. The member states stopped this process for NGOs to be accorded observer status in the General Assembly in 1995.[69]

The main reason was to stop NGOs from being further included in the General Assembly as they were not in a position to deny the consultative status in the Security Council. NGOs then reached out in critical matters like conflict and hostility, and peacekeeping and disarmament. These were very sensitive areas for the United States, in particular. Hence, the United States insisted on not granting consultative status to NGOs similar to that of the ECOSOC status. When the ECOSOC Resolution 1996/31 was adopted, the resolutions of 1950 and 1968 were withdrawn and the consultative status was restricted up to ECOSOC, and did not extend to cover the General Assembly and Security Council.

The legal framework under Article 71 of the UN Charter and resolution 1996/31 were not covered in the General Assembly and Security Council. Therefore, the relations between NGOs and the General Assembly were based on mutual practices and experience. Both the ECOSOC and General Assembly are principal organs but deal with NGOs differently.

B. **NGOs' Participation in the UN Conferences**

In the UN Conferences, Earth Summit, 1992; World Conference on Human Rights, 1993; Global Conference on Small Islands of Developing Countries, 1994; International Conference on Population and Development, 1994; World Social Summit, 1995; World Conference on Women, 1995; and Habitat II, 1996, were attended by NGOs wholeheartedly. But when the outcome and enforcement review of meetings and conferences were held in the General Assembly, NGOs were not allowed to participate at length.

---

[67] UN Doc. A/c 2/48/SR.25 (5 November, 1993).

[68] UN Doc. E/AC 70/1994/5 (26 May, 1994) p. 42.

[69] UN General Assembly Res. 49/2 (19 October, 1994).

Commissions of the aforesaid conferences allowed NGOs to become partners in the enforcement of the outcomes of conferences. The General Assembly in its resolutions in 1995 appreciated the role played by NGOs in the enforcement of the outcomes of the conferences. The General Assembly agreed so far to make necessary arrangements for NGOs to participate in the conferences, meetings and preliminaries of the Assembly. Developing countries did not extend enthusiastic support to NGOs' consultative status in the General Assembly and Security Council. One of the reasons was NGOs' clamour for human rights and environmental issues, making states inconvenient at the international fora. Another reason pertained to their own status as a state; they could not see non-state actor–NGOs as equals on the glamorous world stage.[70]

However, the winds of change appeared when the International Chamber of Commerce, an NGO founded in the early twentieth century, was accorded observer status courtesy the General Assembly in 2016.

7 NGOs and the Security Council

NGOs' consultative status does not cover the Security Council in the same way it does the General Assembly. The Security Council is engaged in peacekeeping operations, whenever situations of conflict arise. It takes decisions that are independent of NGOs. Humanitarian NGOs only participate in assistance and relief programmes during times of armed conflict and peacekeeping operations.

However, the provisional rules of procedure of the Security Council already provide for the possibilities of NGOs' relations with it. As Rule 39 lays down:

> the security council may invite other persons, whom it considers competent for the purpose, to supply it with information or give other assistance in examining matters within its competence.[71]

Rule 39 further clarifies the written statement receipt from NGOs and private individuals. The permanent members—(P-5) do not prefer to take assistance from powerless actors like NGOs. The Security Council is a small executive body, and a symbol of power, privilege and glory.

The Council appeared more active after the end of the Cold War in 1990. Its actions in maintaining world peace and security further increased the issue areas of monitoring of elections, economic sanctions, policing, peacekeeping and peace-building. The sheer number of NGOs, their influence, prestige and scale has also upped. They enhanced their experience and expertise in security, peace, disarmament, humanitarian assistance and relief work. NGOs were willing to participate in the Security Council and appraise the ground-level situation in conflict zones and other tense areas.

---

[70] Peter Willets, *supra note* 55, p. 202.

[71] Bailey (1975), Provisional Rules of Procedure of the Security Council, S/96/Rev. 7 (1983), Rule 39.

The Security Council has a very limited membership i.e. out of a total of 193 only fifteen are members—five permanent and ten non-permanent. Unlike the General Assembly, other member states of the UN do not have membership.[72] When non-member states do not participate in the Security Council directly, why would they promote NGOs to participate there? Article 71 of the UN Charter, Consultative Status Resolution, 1950/288B, 1968/1296(XLIV) 1996/31 did not include the Security Council. Moreover, the Cardoso Report, 2004,[73] and the subsequent response to it by the Secretary General did not endorse NGOs' relationship with the Security Council to be formalised like ECOSOC.[74]

A. **Arria Formula**

The relationship between NGOs and the Security Council work on an informal mechanism through the Arria Formula. Diego Arria of Venezuela was a diplomatic representative in the UN Security Council. In 1992, during the Yugoslavia Crisis, a Bosnian priest came to New York and met Ambassador Arria at the UN headquarters. Ambassador Arria was thoroughly impressed by the narration of the priest and wanted to share it with all members of the Security Council. Arria invited all members for coffee in the delegates' lounge. That meeting was attended by many, and it was a great success, setting a standard for the years to come. Thus, the Arria formula originated from the creative ideas and movements Ambassador Arria stood for. The aforementioned formula was institutionalised between NGOs and the Council.[75]

The Arria Formula facilitated regular informal meetings between NGOs, Security Council members and other interested states. In these meetings, NGOs with expertise and experience on conflicts shared their views with the members of the Security Council. NGOs like Oxfam International, Medicins Sans Frontieres and Care International were already involved in humanitarian relief and assistance. NGOs' briefs pertaining to crises form an additional channel from the grassroots, apart from the existing United Nations and state channels. Hanifa Mezoni, Chief of the NGO Section of the DSEA, UN, highlights that the role of NGOs in conflict, prevention and peace-building is greatly appreciable.[76]

Early information presented to the Security Council provided an opportunity to quickly deploy forces and defuse crises. The quintessential examples of these are Macedonia, Central Africa and Haiti. The solution of crises and conflicts required multiple approaches, creative ideas and out-of-the-box thinking. Seeking the views and latest information from different sources, i.e. NGOs, scholars, religious practitioners, etc., put the Security Council in a better position so as to prevent human rights violations and armed conflicts.

---

[72] UN Charter, Articles 23 and 27.

[73] *Report of the Panel of Eminent Persons on United Nations—Civil Society Relations*, UN Doc. A/ 58/817 (June 11, 2004).

[74] The Secretary General, *Report of the Secretary General in response to the report of the Panel of Eminent Persons on UN-Civil Society Relations*, UN Doc. A/59/354 (September 13, 2004).

[75] *The Arria Formula*, http://www.globalpolicy.org.

[76] Mezoui (2004).

B. NGOs in Peace-Building

NGOs can work to promote peace through school curricula, public opinion mobilisation, conflict resolution through mediation, the rehabilitation of child soldiers, the disarmament of lethal weapons, national gun control laws and post-war peace building. For example, in Mozambique, the community of Saint Egidio offered an impartial environment for divided groups to communicate and negotiate, helping greatly to end a sixteen-year-old civil war.

The International Coalition to Ban Landmines launched a successful movement to stop land-mining, and won the Nobel Peace Prize in 1997. Similarly, International Alert, the Women's Centre for Peace and Development (WOPED), the Institute of Human Rights Commission (IHRICON), the Beyond Beijing Committee and Assist Yourself had constructive roles to defuse crisis situations in their respective areas.

NGOs' role in peace-building in post-conflict situations was experimented with successfully in Cambodia.[77] International NGOs created and supported local NGOs in the country. These NGOs worked for the less-privileged and deprived sections, garnering the help and technical experience of International NGOs. Their primary purpose was to build bottom-up peace or civic peace inspired by the conscience of the people.

The Security Council's peacekeeping operations in the Democratic Republic of the Congo (DRC), Liberia, Darfur in Sudan,[78] Haiti and Iraq, did not yield desired results within the expected time period. Similarly, Syria, Afghanistan and Rwanda were also in situations of turmoil.

Indeed, some states' infrastructure was fragile, particularly those in Africa. Any criminal groups or those with vested interests posed a threat to the security and integrity of the state. The World Summit, 2005, for Right to Protection (R2P), was unanimously adopted by the General Assembly in 2009. R2P created an obligation on the Security Council to protect the states through collective measures under the UN Charter. NGOs could be useful in providing eminent dangers information briefs to the Security Council for pre-emptive action.

NGOs entered into war-torn zones either to defuse the situation, make peace or for the purpose of post-war peace-building. The security and ground reality of war-affected nations must be of utmost importance. UN Peacekeeping Forces extend their protection to these countries in the aforesaid crisis areas. The UN Information Centre could be informed about the security perceptions and threats to NGOs. The Security Council and NGOs join hands in UN missions as partners to make it possible to restore peace and normalcy in conflict zones.

---

[77] Christie (2013).

[78] Kleinheisterkamp (2006).

8 Conclusion

Associating human life with a common cause became a reality with the founding of the UN in 1945. The UN framework is quite large, concerning all aspects of human existence, including the safety of subsequent generations. The United Nations has put noble ideas, principles and missions to practice for the past seventy-five years, with its journey continuing despite all hurdles and hindrances. In this journey of peace and betterment of human life, states were the prime movers and shakers. Nevertheless, conscience-keeper citizens or groups and NGOs joined them ever since inception. Subsequently, the private sector and businesses also embraced this human endeavour in 2004. To strengthen the UN's mission and vision, IGOs were also created, and they, in turn, went on to become partners in their specific issues areas.

States are the founders, IGOs are the integral parts, NGOs are the statutory partners and private sectors are the responsible contributors to the UN system. NGOs are endowed with consultative status under the ECOSOC and its subsidiaries. In the words of Professor Peter Willets, NGOs are "The Conscience of the World." Apart from the ECOSOC and its subsidiary agencies, NGOs are partners with IGOs, whereas the General Assembly and the Security Council are officially and formally inaccessible. Anyhow, NGOs developed leverage and good practices to intermingle with these organisations on an informal basis.

The need of the hour is that domesticating of NGOs should be discouraged. Procedure of accreditation of NGOs by the NGOs Committee should be revised, and the denial, deferral, warning, suspension and withdrawal of NGOs is to be used judiciously and not politicised by the member states.

The Cardoso Report, 2004, and the Secretary General's subsequent response, threw open the UN's gates to the private sector and business. The economic power and clout of corporations are unmatched when compared to NGOs, therefore, it is necessary to deal with them as per their orientation and capabilities.

The private sector and business play a significant role in value-creation, employment-generation and the provision of goods and services. The association of private sector and business enhances the realisation of the UN's purposes. The private sector and business possess the ability to mobilise funds for UN projects and plans. As humanity must exist at all costs, we owe much to the international community at large.

References

Bailey SD (1975) The procedure of UN security council. Clarendon Press, Oxford, p 346

Bowett DW (2009) Law of international institutions, Sands P, Klein P (eds). Sweet and Maxwell, London, pp 52–60

Burton JW (1972) World society. Cambridge University Press

Cassese A (1979) How could non-governmental organisations use UN bodies more effectively? Universal Hum Rights 1(4):73–80 at 74

Charter of the United Nations (UN Charter) (2014) Article 7. UN Department of Public Information, New York. https://www.un.org>uncharter>file

Chiang P-H (1981) Non-governmental organisations at the United Nations: identity, role and functions. Praeger, New York, p 132

Christie R (2013) Peacebuilding and NGOs. Routledge, London

Clarkson MBE (1998) The corporation and its stakeholders: classic and contemporary readings. University of Toronto, Canada

Claude I, Jr (1988) Swords into ploughshares: the problem and progress of international organisations. Random House, New York, p 54

de Frouville O (2008) Domesticating civil society at the United Nations. In: Dupuy PM, Vierucci L (eds) NGOs in international law—efficiency in flexibility? Edward Elgar, Chelteham, UK, p 85

Hanhimaki JM (2015) The United Nations: a very short introduction. Oxford University Press, p 13

Hougton RA (2014) A puzzle for international law: NGOs at the United Nations. North East Rev 2(2):1–24 at 2

Hutton W (1995) The state we are in. Jonathan Cape, London

Kaul I, Pedro C (2006) The new public finance: responding to global challenge. Oxford University Press

Kennedy P (2006) The parliament of man: the past, present and future of the United Nations. Vintage Books, New York, p 3

Kleinheisterkamp J (2006) The UN security council's incapacity of coping with conflict-related economic interests. In: Ala'l P (ed) Trade as a guarantor of peace and security? Studies in international legal policy, vol 37, Am Soc Int L. Washington, DC, pp108–123

Lagon R, Eleni M (2012) Article 71. In: Sima B, et al (eds) The charter of the United Nations: a commentary, 2nd edn, vol 2. Oxford University Press, p 1069

Leon G (2005) The UN secretary general and secretariat. Routledge, London

Malone D (2004) The UN security council: from the cold war to the 21st century. Lyme Reinner Publishers, Boulder, Colorado, USA

Marceau G, Pedersen PN (1999) Is WTO open and transparent? a discussion of the relationship of the WTO with non-governmental organisation and civil societies claims for more transparency and public participation. J World Trade 33(1):5–49

Martens K (2005) NGOs and the United Nations: institutionalization professionalization and adaptation. Palgrave Macmillan, New York, p 132

Martens J (2007) Multistakeholders partnership—future model of multilateralism. Dialogue on Globalization, Occasional Papers, No. 29, Friedrich Ebert, Berlin

Martens J, James P (2004) Comment on the report of Cardoso panel. Global Policy Forum, New York. http://www.globalpolicy.org/initiatives/panels/cardoso/08gpf.pdf

Mazower M (2012) Governing the world: the history of an idea. Penguin, New York

Mezoui H (2004) The United Nations' view on the role of NGOs with consultative status in the conflict prevention, peace building and development. Military L & L War Rev 43(1–2):155–164

Mingst K, Margaret K (2006) The United Nations in the 21st century. Westview Press, Boulder, Colorado, USA

Missoni E (2013) International non-governmental organisations. In: Missoni E, Alesani D (eds) Management of international institutions and NGOs: frameworks, practices and challenges. Routledge, UK, p 64

Peterson MJ (2005) The United Nations general assembly. Routledge, London

Sharp WR (1969) The UN economic and social council. Columbia University Press

Thakur R (2016) The United Nations, peace and security: from collective security to the responsibility to protect, 2nd edn. Cambridge University Press

Toussaint CE (1956) The trusteeship system of the United Nations. Stevens & Sons Ltd., London

United Nations (2017) Basic facts about the United Nations, 42nd edn. UN Department of Public Information, New York

Veromen S (2017) Eleanor open show and Madeleine Sinclair, handbook, Third Committee of the United Nations General Assembly, a practical guide for NGOs. ISHR Publications, Australia

Wapner P (2007) Civil society. In: Weiss TG, Daws S (eds) Oxford handbook on the United Nations. Oxford University Press, p 254

Willets P (1996) Consultative status for NGOs at the United Nations. In: Willets P (ed) The conscience of the world: the influence of non-governmental organisations in the UN system. The Brookings Institution, Washington, DC, p 32

Willetts P (2000) From consultative arrangements to partnership: the changing status of NGOs in diplomacy at the UN. Glob Gov 6(2):191–212

Willets P (2006) The Cardoso report on the UN and civil society: functionalism, global corporatism, or global democracy? Glob Gov 12(3):305–324

Woodward BK (2010) Global civil society in international law making and global governance. Martinus Nijhoff, Leiden, p 102

Part II
NGOs Relation with International Actors

Chapter 5
Operative Methods

1 Introduction

People attribute sensitivity, compassion and concern to humanity. Immanuel Kant greatly emphasised on humanity and peace. In his view, every person so has an obligation towards helping others. Neera Chandhoke observed:

> Why would activists and international NGOs spend much of their time and physical and mental energy struggling for justice for the worse off in remote parts of the world, unless their activism was inspired by a deep sense of obligation towards the impoverished, the oppressed and the marginalised?[1]

The concerns to humanity, deep sense of responsibility and rationality of the human mind, perhaps motivated conscious citizens to engage in activism and transnational advocacy. NGO activism is one of the ways in which to occupy civic space and to engage in the promotion and protection of peace, justice and humanity. This is very much visible in the protection of human rights, the environment, and business ethics. NGOs do their work within the framework of domestic and international law. Therefore, they employ peaceful means in transboundary advocacy.

NGOs' activism in the international arena was examined by Steve Charnovitz on the basis of state positivism, IGO functionalism and community deliberations.[2] State positivism or state absolute sovereignty is no more in practice. Thus, they are not exclusive actors in the international community. Democratic spaces are available for inter-governmental organisations (IGOs), NGOs and transnational corporations.[3] NGOs such as Amnesty International, Doctors Without Borders (MSF), Human Rights Watch, International Federation for Human Rights (FIDH), Greenpeace International, PEN International, International Commission of Jurists, Save the Children,

---

[1] Chandhoke (2007).

[2] Charnovitz (2011).

[3] Hobe (1997).

P. Rai, *Non-Governmental Organisations and International Law*,
https://doi.org/10.1007/978-981-97-5469-4_5

National Association for the Advancement of Colored People (NAACP), International Alliance for Women, Anti-Slavery International, and so on, have engaged in making and implementing international law.

In the international arena, civic space is available to NGOs for activism, advocacy and engagement. This available space is an opportunity for NGOs to participate in the public policy-making discourse, with the states and IGOs. The democratic space is closely related to the capacity for power-wielding.[4] NGOs' skill capacity, experience and strategy make them effective in their engagement and performance. They employ diverse methods of operation, as per available space and the need of the hour.

NGOs are engaged from the grass-roots level to the international stage and vice versa. Srilatha Batliwala conducted two case studies of grassroots-NGOs that became transnational actors in a very short span of time and had a great impact on the grassroots movements. These are—Women in Informal Employment: Globalizing and Organizing (WIEGO) and Slum Dwellers International (SDI). WIEGO and SDI have shown potential and power, making a case for grassroots movements to be given recognition at the international level.[5]

The precursor of WIEGO (1997) was the Self-Employed Women's Association (SEWA) in India during the 1970s. SEWA made strides in the international trade union movement. Domestic and home-based workers came to the forefront in the 1990s. WIEGO was eventually established in 1997. It engaged in the improvement of working conditions of poor women and the protection of their livelihood. Soon, it became an international advocacy network and collaborated with NGOs, cooperatives, trade unions, women's groups, the ILO and UN Women.[6]

SDI[7] is an initiative of SPARC—The Society for the Promotion of Area Resource Centres, 1984.[8] In addition to SDI, SPARC created organisations such as NSDF—The National Slum Dwellers Federation and Mahila Milan (Women Together) in India.[9] They have collaborated with NGOs like The Asian Coalition of Housing Rights, Bangkok[10] and The South African Homeless People's Federation, Cape Town.[11] They collectively became Slum Dwellers International (SDI) in 1996. Its headquarters is located in Cape Town, South Africa, having partnered with UN Habitat.

IEGO and SDI are international coalitions working for the livelihood of poor people and their housing, respectively. They have coordinated with multiple stakeholders and are engaged in the international advocacy network.

NGOs employ a series of diverse methods such as agenda-setting, fact-finding, naming and shaming, forming coalitions, campaigning and transnational networking,

[4] Gaventa (2006).

[5] Batliwala (2002).

[6] www.wiego.org; Chen et al. (2016).

[7] https://sdinet.org; Satterthwaite (2001).

[8] https://www.sparcindia.org.

[9] Patel and Mitlin (2001).

[10] http://www.achr.net.

[11] Baumann et al. (2001).

public protests and the participation in conferences and seminars. Whenever an NGO is engaged in work, it should adhere to the core values of transnational advocacy. The NGO's core values were adopted by the World Congress of NGOs, in Toronto, Canada, on 11 November, 2007. This is referred to as The Toronto Declaration of NGO Core Values. These values are: service beyond self, respect for human rights, maintaining a vision, responsibility to the public, cross-border cooperation, public-mindedness, accountability, truthfulness, transparency, non-profit integrity, a comprehensive viewpoint and volunteerism.[12]

2 Agenda-Setting

NGOs' engagement with agenda-setting in international law is a reflection of influence to raise the issue areas to the realm of public discourse. Agenda-setting is not well studied in international law.[13] It remains covered by public policy and media studies. Agenda-setting happens to also be called agenda-building. Primarily, the power of setting an agenda rests with law-making bodies and policy-making authorities.

The courts strictly set the agenda and list it as routine. Likewise, legislative bodies also set the calendars of business matters for proceeding in a legal action or making a legislation. Agenda-settings are of two kinds: formal agenda and public agenda. Informally, they are referred to as inside agenda or outside agenda, respectively. The inside or formal agenda is raised by the government and inter-governmental organisations (IGOs). Whereas, the outside or public agenda is raised by civic space or non-governmental entities, i.e. NGOs, civil society, media and interest groups.[14]

Roger Cobb, J K Ross and M H Ross have narrated four stages for agenda-setting: initiation; specification; expansion; and entrance. The agenda moves both ways; from the government to the people, and from the people to the government. At the IGO and state level, first, a policy decision is taken or the law is made or a plan of action is set out. Then the people are mobilised to successfully implement their agendas. For instance, peace-keeping or peace-building, conservation of natural resources, combating epidemics, etc. are framed by the Security Council or General Assembly or specialised agencies of the UN and subsequently, public grievances, issue areas and public support are sought. NGOs first identify community grievances, issue areas, build public movements and try to make them part of IGOs or the government's formal agendas. In the nineteenth century, abolition of slavery was the outside or public agenda raised by Anti-Slavery International and the civil society. Subsequently, it became a part of the formal state and IGO agenda, and the Anti-Slavery Law and International Convention was adopted.

---

12 www.wango.org; The Toronto Declaration of NGO Core Values (11 November 2007), https://www.wango.org>declaration; Yanacopulos (2015).

13 Livingston (1992) and Dearing and Rogers (1996).

14 Cobb et al. (1976).

NGOs' agenda-setting performance is interconnected to multiple factors like identifying issue areas and its characteristics, whether it is related to the public good, whether it has contemporary significance and potential to mobilise public opinion as well as the flexibility of the issue areas as per time and space.

NGOs' articulation, commitment, hard work, resources and continual hammer yield the desired results. Sometimes, they work behind the scenes and hand over their informal agenda to like-minded representatives of a state in order for them, in turn, to convert them into formal agendas.

NGOs' initial agendas are further modified and enlarged as per the need of the hour. They started a movement for the recognition of women's human rights in the nineteenth century.[15] The International Abolitionist Federation was established in 1875.[16] Abolitionists stressed on the abolition of prostitution and trafficking.[17] The International Council of Women (1888)[18] and the International Alliance of Women (1904)[19] added suffrage for women and it continued until Saudi Arabia confirmed women's suffrage in 2015. In our time, women's suffrage has been realised throughout the world.

The Inter-Parliamentary Union (1889)[20] established the Forum of Women Parliamentarians (1978) for increasing female representation in legislative bodies across the nations. WILPF -Women's International League for Peace and Freedom (1915)[21] emphasised on world peace and harmony because in situations of armed conflict and war, women suffered the most. Women for Women International (1993)[22] is engaged in the support of women survivors of wars and conflicts.

The Women's International Democratic Federation (1945)[23] has widened its scope of women's rights and has stressed on economic empowerment. Before the turn of the twentieth century, women's human rights agenda was enriched by encompassing the prohibition of domestic violence,[24] sexual harassment at work places,[25] reproductive rights and health,[26] and equality in all spheres of life.[27] NGOs' dynamic and flexible approach has led to women's issues becoming an ever-growing public agenda.

---

[15] Joachim (2007).

[16] Founded in 1875 in Liverpool, UK.

[17] Summers (2008).

[18] https://www.icw-cif.com.

[19] www.womenalliance.org.

[20] www.ipu.org.

[21] www.wilpf.org.

[22] www.womenforwomen.org.

[23] www.widf.org.

[24] www.globalfundforwomen.org; www.onebillionrising.org.

[25] http://genderatwork.org; Kantor and Twohey (2017) and Perkins (2017).

[26] https://reproductiverights.org; http://iwhc.org.

[27] www.equalitynow.org; www.ifrwh.com; www.unwomen.org.

The right to development is another example in which NGOs are engaged continuously with over the years. The aforementioned right as a human right was introduced by Kéba M'Baye in 1972.[28]

This was further conceptualised by Amartya Sen,[29] Arjun Sengupta,[30] Ronald Rich,[31] Mahbub ul Haq,[32] and Philip Alston.[33] The right to development was an outcome of the decolonisation process of Asian and African countries. These newly independent states were enthusiastic about their social progress and economic development. Their political independence could be sustained only when they were capable of giving pace to the trinity of social, economic and political development simultaneously.[34] The formation of the right to development agenda was collaboratively pursued by United Nations' specialised agencies, NGOs and third world nations.

There is an inherent relationship between human rights and development. NGOs are increasingly committed towards rights-based approaches to development.[35] NGOs like CARE International (1945),[36] World Vision International (1950),[37] Oxfam International (1942),[38] Plan International (1937),[39] ActionAid International (1972)[40] Amnesty International, Human Rights Watch, Save the Children and International Federation of Human Rights joined hands with African, Asian Nations and the UNDP and UNICEF to formulate the right to development agenda.[41]

The numerical strength of third world countries increased in the United Nations, therefore, they asserted adequate participation in the world economy. They raised their collective voice before the General Assembly, and in the first international human rights conference in Tehran in 1968, prepared the formal agenda on the right to development. The turning point came when the former UN Commission on Human Rights appointed a study group in 1977.[42] NGOs pursued the agenda of the right to development on the basis of their experience and expertise along with all stakeholders until its adoption. Henceforth, the Right to Development was adopted by the UN General Assembly in 1986.[43]

---

28 Barsh (1991).

29 Sen (2001).

30 Sengupta (1999) and Sengupta et al. (2005).

31 Nanda (1984).

32 Mahbub ul Haq led the establishment of the Human Development Report of the UNDP, published since 1990, www.hdr.undp.org.

33 Alston and Robinson (2005).

34 Arts and Tamo (2016).

35 Kindornay et al. (2011).

36 http://www.care-international.org.

37 http://www.wvi.org.

38 http://www.oxfam.org.

39 www.plan-international.org.

40 www.actionaid.org.

41 Nelson (2003).

42 UN Commission on Human Rights Resolution (XXXIII) (21 February 1977).

43 UN Document A/RES/41/128 (4 December 1986).

In the age of information, communication and technology, NGOs seize the opportunity to initiate, mobilise, and coordinate for the setting of the public agenda. Their preferred issue agendas are related to human rights, the environment and business ethics.[44] Traditionally, agenda-setting is initiated by the media and formulated by the concerned state. In international law, NGOs have space for the initiation of public agendas in collaboration with IGOs and like-minded representatives of the states. Online mobilisation of public opinion is available through social media, web pages, Facebook, Twitter, Instagram, blogs, etc. NGOs like Amnesty International, Human Rights Watch, and many others have successfully utilised online agenda-setting opportunities.[45]

3 Fact-Finding

NGO fact-finding is perhaps one of the most important methods in the field of human rights.[46] Fact-finding consists of the investigation, inquiry procedure and documentation. NGO fact-finding in the field of human rights differs from criminal investigation and the UN and IGOs' inquiry procedure because they have different objectives and purposes.

The main objective of criminal investigation is to find out evidence against the perpetrator of the offence, to prosecute and punish the accused before a competent court. They fix the individual's responsibility for the offence committed and investigate eyewitness testimony, sequence of events, the autopsy, the forensic report and any other relevant evidence which may prove the offence in the international courts and arbitral tribunals.[47]

UN and IGOs' inquiry commissions direct their fact-finding against states who are in conflict or contravention with the norms and standards of international law. Generally, UN inquiry commissions are politicised because states overshadow them for their diplomatic priorities and interests.[48] Inquiry commissions collect factual data and information from the realities on the ground. On this basis, the international tribunals and UN organs have used these factual situations as narrated by the inquiry commission in settlement of disputes between state parties.

Whereas, the mission of NGO fact-finding is to collect information and witness-testimony related to incidents and patterns of gross human rights violation. Reports produced by NGOs are released in the public domain. The main objective of the fact-finding reports is to promote and protect human rights infrastructure and to undertake transboundary advocacy. They focus on States' public policy, legislation, budget allocation and administrative actions. An NGO's fact-finding mission is closer

[44] Meriläinen and Vos (2011).

[45] Ibid., pp. 301–306.

[46] Ramcharan (2014), Alston and Knuckey (2016), and Thoolen and Verstappen (1986).

[47] Bassiouni (2012).

[48] Bassiouni (2001) and Thomas and Farley (1980).

to investigative journalism than that of criminal investigation or the UN and IGOs' inquiry commission.[49]

Criminal investigators and members of inquiry commissions are representatives of states or IGOs, while members of NGO fact-finding missions are private persons or their officials/volunteers. They have cross-learning of methodology and standards of investigation, inquiry and fact-finding procedures, but do not necessarily overlap.[50] The credibility of the fact-finding mission rests on their fairness, impartiality, methodology and observation of standards and quality of gathered information and evidence. NGOs have great experience when it comes to fact-finding missions in the field of human rights.[51]

The inquiry method was introduced in the Hague Peace Conference, 1907, for the settlement of international disputes.[52] Since then, it has become the corpus of international law.[53] The inquiry method is regularly employed by international tribunals and IGOs.[54] When compared to international tribunals and IGOs, NGOs' fact-finding traditions are older. It was a precursor of all inquiry procedures, as described by David Weissbrodt and James McCarthy. They enumerated the Anti-Slavery Society, Commission of the Churches on International Affairs, World Council of Churches, International Committee of the Red Cross, International Defence and Aid Fund, International Federation of Human Rights, International League for Human Rights, Minority Rights Group International, Survival International, World Peace Council, Amnesty International, International Commission of Jurists, International Association of Democratic Lawyers,[55] Human Rights Watch and others.

NGOs seek help from the families and friends of the victims of human rights violations, opposition political parties, released prisoners and other oppressed groups, for obtaining reliable information and material.[56] NGOs, particularly Amnesty International, Human Rights Watch and others, have introduced innovations and niceties to fact-finding.[57] Information Technology, computer facilitated networks and social media sites have increased speed, accessibility and scope with regard to human rights oversight. Human rights fact-finding has become an interdisciplinary issue area which is broadly connected to anthropology, information science, architecture, forensic science and statistics.[58]

---

[49] B.G. Ramcharan, *supra note* 46.

[50] Alessandra (2017).

[51] B.G. Ramcharan, *supra note* 49.

[52] Bar-Yaacov (1974).

[53] UN Charter, Article 33 para 1.

[54] International Commission of Inquiry, Fact-finding Missions, Chronologist list. https://libraryresources.unog.ch/factfinding/chronolist. visited on 31 March 2020.

[55] Weissbrodt and McCarthy (1981).

[56] Weissbrodt (1980).

[57] Alston (2013).

[58] Ibid., p. 62.

Thomas Franck and Scott Fairley have observed that "procedural due process" is employed in human rights fact-findings.[59] The high moral values and expectations are perhaps achieved by employing certain methods, techniques, standards and procedural safeguards. These are: "composition of fact-finding missions, methodology, imperative techniques and rigour of some fact-finding missions are in-depth examination".[60] Some authors have identified five key indicators of procedural probity: (1) selection of subject, (2) choice of fact-finders, (3) terms of reference, (4) procedures of investigation, and (5) utilisation of product.[61]

A. **Composition of Fact-Finding Missions**

Searching for a suitable person by NGOs for a fact-finding mission is not an easy task. Since NGOs have financial constraints, they are unable to pay a respectable honorarium to the fact-finders or the members of the mission. Unlike the UN and IGOs, members of a fact-finding mission do not enjoy diplomatic privileges and immunity from jurisdiction of the states concerned. In such a situation, a person committed towards the human rights movement comes forward and accepts a membership of an NGO's fact-finding mission.

Eminent persons or subject-matter experts certainly enhance the credibility of NGOs' fact-finding missions. Generally, an NGO's mission is delegated to three persons; among these, the first is an NGO official or volunteer, the second is either a lawyer or a professor of law, and the third is a member specialised in the issue areas or is well-known to the state concerned.[62]

NGOs' capability to appoint fact-finders comes through years of practice. They are not bound to follow the state's consent or mandate granted by the UN or IGOs. This is the NGOs' self-created mission. Therefore, it is necessary to lay down terms of reference for the mission and restrict itself only to the assigned work. NGOs like Amnesty International, International Commission of Jurists, International Federation of Human Rights (FIDH), Human Rights Watch, International League for Human Rights and others lay down terms of reference for their respective fact-finding missions.[63]

B. **Methodology of Fact-Finding Missions**

NGOs in their reports do not elaborate their methodology. They only mention briefly the methods and techniques used.[64] Fact-finding for human rights is also carried out by the UN special rapporteur, i.e. country or subject specific, human rights treaty bodies, international tribunals and commissions of inquiry. These have not adhered to any uniform methodology. They choose their methods and techniques according to

[59] Thomas M. Franck and Scott H. Fairley, *supra note* 48, pp. 308–345.

[60] P. Alston and S. Knuckey, *supra note* 46.

[61] Franck and Fairley, *supra note* 59, p. 311.

[62] D. Weissbrodt and J. McCarthy, *supra note* 55, pp. 45–46.

[63] Ibid., p. 43.

[64] Satterthwaite (2013).

their objectives. They focus on issue areas and remain restricted to gather information, facts and documentation.

NGO fact-finders interact primarily with the victims, their families, witnesses and all related persons during their on-site visits. They exhibit solidarity with the victims or survivors of human rights violations and influence positive change in state policy, patterns and the human rights landscape as a whole in the specific country.

D.F. Orentlicher analysed fact-finding methodology in the human rights areas of torture, extrajudicial execution, disappearances, arbitrary arrests and detention. She said that NGOs' country reports based on-site visits are known in their parlance as fact-finding missions.[65] NGOs collect direct evidence from the testimony of victims or eyewitnesses. It is better to seek their informed consent to provide testimony to use it in their fact-finding report. NGOs must avoid political prejudice and treat both the parties—ruling and opposition—on an equal footing. Victims or witnesses are selected for testimony from a broad range of sources and are confined only to the issue areas. NGOs conduct interviews covering a wide spectrum including activists, advocates, doctors, media persons, academics, attempting to build an overview on the long-term trends and patterns to the state concerned.

The collected testimony of witnesses and victims is corroborated from other sources such as autopsy reports, medical reports, police lock-up records and court records. The quality and credibility of sources are closely connected to the perception and memory of the witnesses and victims. The skill and impartiality of the fact-finder matters a great deal, in the same way as the employed methods and techniques. When fact-finders make an inquiry into the gross violation of human rights like torture, detention and sexual assault, the victim or survivor goes through trauma by recalling the difficult, unpleasant memories.

NGOs' mission on site visits provides them an opportunity to observe conditions prevailing after the incident. When the states concerned are unwilling to allow on-site visits, NGOs collect all the information sources available outside the country.[66] Fact-finders may seek the testimony from refugees. It is necessary that they have an overview on the human rights infrastructure of the visiting country.

C. **Outcome of Fact-Finding**

The time duration for the methodology of fact-finding has improved remarkably over the years. Networking and social media are popular modes of communication of late. They give pace to the availability of information sources and materials. Another significant change is, minimum standards, which are followed in the gathering of information and the collection of evidence. Now, writers have developed a benchmark and indicators[67] to map the compliance of human rights within their jurisdiction. Amnesty International and Human Rights Watch regularly use these

65 Orentlicher (1990).

66 Pillay (2010).

67 Fukuda-Parr et al. (2015).

recent technological advancements for the preparation of reports. NGOs like HURIDOCS[68] provide tools and techniques to gather information, analysis, report-writing and advocacy. It focuses on the NGOs of developing nations.

All collected information and material sources have to be used in report-writing. Reports must be produced as early as possible and displayed in the public domain. They should be impartial, credible and effective. The report is catalytic to the objective of human rights promotion. It makes suggestions for the improvement of human rights infrastructure in the related state. To redress the victim for their suffering owing to human rights violations, the perpetrator has to be identified and indicated for the purpose of accountability. The security for the life of the victim and the witness should not be undermined because of the report. The objective of the report, in turn, is to strengthen public advocacy and activism. NGOs employ various ways and means to strengthen human rights compliance, as per the need of the day.

4 Coalition, Campaigning and Networking

A. Coalition

NGOs unite themselves and pool their resources, time and activism for the cause of the people. Such a union is known as an NGO coalition. This is a temporary organisation. The NGO coalition works together for a common mission. Therefore, it differs from the Conference of Non-Governmental Organizations (CoNGO).[69] Coalition member NGOs have a separate identity and they remain autonomous organisations. Side by side, they are adjunct to the NGO coalition and they engage in collective activism and advocacy to influence the ongoing process of creation, development and enforcement of international law.

NGO coalitions have their own identity, status, logo, setup and statement of mission. NGO coalitions have resources, officials and volunteers at their disposal. They collectively march under a single banner on a shared agenda or common objective to be achieved. Some examples of these coalitions are as follows: The Coalition for the International Criminal Court, 1995,[70] International Coalition Against Enforced Disappearances, 2007,[71] Habitat International Coalition, 1976,[72] The

[68] https://huridocs.org (Geneva, 1982).

[69] www.ngocongo.org.

[70] www.coalitionfortheicc.org.

[71] www.icaed.org; The Latin American Federation of Associations for Relatives of the Detained-Disappeared (FEDEFAM) was founded in 1981, Lima, Peru. Subsequently, it was joined by Amnesty International, Human Rights Watch, International Commission of Jurists and other NGOs worldwide, and facilitated this coalition in 2007.

[72] www.hic-net.org.

Coalition for Food and Nutrition Security, 2007,[73] The Global Coalition on Migration, 2011,[74] International Alliance of Women for Suffrage, 1902,[75] Child Soldiers International, 1998,[76] International Disability Alliance, 1999,[77] World Organisation Against Torture, 1985,[78] International Coalition to End Torture, 2003,[79] International Detention Coalition, 1990,[80] Coalition for an Independent and Transparent Judiciary, 2011,[81] and the Coalition for Free and Open Elections, 1985.[82]

NGO coalitions are primarily a collective civil society, representing multiple nations, but sometimes they facilitate like-minded parliamentarians, representatives of states, businesses and professional associations. This inclusive nature strengthens the coalitions' voice, which, in turn, results in generating world public opinion for their mission. The coalition is a common cause, shared strategy, cross-learning tool and a broad world view on a particular issue area.[83]

NGO coalitions' success lies in establishing a coherence within the members of coalition, their activism and advocacy to popularise an undertaken agenda. The first step in the formation of a coalition is to identify the theme or issue area in which the coalition can be engaged. The issue area is contemporary, compelling and capable of seeking the attention of the people and decision-makers at large. The chosen issue area is built up through research and preparation of mission statements. Then, a wider network is created among NGOs and civil societies. In the early twentieth century, a coalition of women's NGOs was established for women's suffrage, and fighting continuously for the adequate representation of women in elected bodies.[84]

NGOs not only identify the problem but also propose workable solutions. The second important step is to set up infrastructure—venue, officials, leadership, volunteers, collective decisions—to bear the official expenses and funds for the campaign. Funds are available from the states, IGOs, transnational corporations, charities and foundations, and individual contributors. It is necessary to clarify which funds are to be accepted for their mission. The income or expenditure balance sheet is made available on the public domain, and a high standard of accountability and transparency is maintained to seek the trust of the donors, contributors, partner NGO volunteers, and

---

[73] www.nutritioncoalition.org.in, it was an initiative by MSS Research Foundation. It was founded in 1988, located in Chennai, India; https://www.mssrf.org.

[74] www.gcmigration.org.

[75] www.womenalliance.org.

[76] Child Soldiers International is a coalition of NGOs founded in 1998 located in London, UK. Formerly, it was known: Coalition to Stop the Use of Child Soldiers.

[77] www.internationaldisabilityalliance.org.

[78] http://www.omct.org.

[79] www.endtorture.org.

[80] https://idcoalition.org.

[81] http://coalition.ge; It is an independent and transparent judiciary organisation formed in 2011. Currently 40 NGOs are members of this coalition. It is located in Tbilisi, Georgia.

[82] www.cofoe.org.

[83] Ritchie (1995).

[84] Cox (2011); Helen Yanacopulos, *supra note* 12.

people. Some specific donors or partners could be sought out through conferences, campaigns and movements. Plans, strategies and a stipulated time frame are prepared well in advance with the mutual understanding of the NGO partners.

The coalition is a collective voice of all partner NGOs. Issues are resolved by consensus among the NGOs. They collectively engage on a single issue throughout the world—for instance, the International Disability Alliance. Such coalitions are represented by international NGOs—Amnesty International, HRW, FIDH, Oxfam, MSF, as well as national NGOs. They undertake joint efforts across the world. NGOs' coalition engagements have success stories in the fields of abolition of slavery, racism, torture, enforced disappearances, prolonged detention, and the protection of women, children, the disabled and migrants. In addition, coalitions are engaged with the promotion of climate action and business ethics.

NGOs establish interactions with states, IGOs and corporations at the national and international level. The resources and capacity of NGOs nowhere match up to the power-wielding of states, IGOs and corporations. Therefore, NGOs are forming coalitions as a means of collective strength, launching campaigns in favour of public interests and concerns.

B. **Campaigning**

In its broader sense, campaigning is synonymous with engagement, activism and movement. There is an interplay between them as they are closely connected. Coalition is a specific purpose vehicle and a collective forum to achieve laid-out objectives. Whereas, campaigning forms an NGO's activism and pace for coalition. Campaigns are a collective voice for NGOs. But a coalition is an institutionalised cooperation of NGOs in existence for a specific common cause. Most global issues are collectively pursued through campaigning under the aegis of coalition.

Sometimes, a coalition leads a campaign, and vice versa. Mothers and Relatives of Enforced Disappearance Victims marched against the dictatorship of Argentina.[85] FEDEFAM fought against repressive regimes of Latin America and the Caribbean.[86] It was acknowledged by the General Assembly and it resulted in the adoption of the International Convention for the Protection of All Persons from Enforced Disappearance (ICPPED). The convention was opened for signature on 6 February 2007. Simultaneously, NGOs such as Amnesty International, Human Rights Watch, International Commission of Jurists, Federation of International Human Rights, FIDH and FEDEFAM established the International Coalition Against Enforced Disappearances (ICAED) in 2007 to pursue ICPPED implementation. The Coalition is engaged with the member state to rectify the Convention and comply within their jurisdiction. The enforced disappearances campaign emerged first, and to sustain it, the coalition of NGOs was born.

Similarly, Transparency International[87] was founded in Berlin in 1993. Its main objective is to fight against corruption. Transparency International is engaged in more

[85] Finucane (2010).

[86] FEDEFAM an NGO of Latin America (1981); Vranckx (2006).

[87] www.transparency.org.

than 120 countries around the world. It has been publishing annual research reports, with the Corruption Perceptions Index being its key contribution.

The breakthrough came in 2003 when the campaign against corruption became an international community issue, with the UN Convention Against Corruption (UNCAC) being adopted in its footsteps.[88] At present, a country cannot easily ignore Transparency International and its annual report. Anne Peters said:

> Transparency obligations are especially important. Not coincidentally, the best-known anti-corruption NGO in the world is called Transparency International. Transparency is also a fundamental principle of the UNCAC.[89]

Corruption prevails everywhere, and in its narrow sense, it takes the form of bribery. In its broader connotation, corruption may refer to the misappropriation of property, abuse of public authority for personal gain, and it may also present itself in the form of political funding and business favour. Corruption is considered a violation of human rights.[90] Corruption is connected to economic, social and cultural rights, but nowhere in human rights treaties is there a reference to corruption.[91] In human rights law, corruption is a perception, and in criminal law, it is an offence, which requires proof and evidence. NGOs and civil society are engaged in combating corruption along with Transparency International in multiple ways.

C. **Networking**

The coalition and campaigning of NGOs received great momentum when the computer and the internet were used to network. Computers and the internet were introduced in the United States in the 1970s, expanding worldwide twenty-odd years later. In 2020, 4.5 billion people had easy access to the internet. Presently, the internet facilitates NGOs' transnational advocacy network across borders. Margaret E Keck and Kathryn Sikkink observed:

> A transnational advocacy network includes those actors working internationally on an issue, who are bound together by shared values, common discourse, and a healthy exchange of information and services.[92]

NGOs create and build up issue areas and mobilise people at large to pursue or pressurise the state, IGOs and corporations to influence their decision-making and actions in order to respect, protect, and observe human rights, the environment and business ethics.

NGOs' pressurising methods cover the mobilisation of shame[93] and the organisation of protest.[94] These methods are perhaps influencing the public policy of the state

---

[88] 2349 UNTS 41.

[89] Peters (2018).

[90] Rose (2016).

[91] Boersma (2012) and Kumar (2011).

[92] Keck and Sikkink (2002).

[93] Amanda and Davis (2012) and Katzenstein (2013).

[94] Hintjens (2006).

and the decision-making capabilities of IGOs. One of the more known public protests by NGOs is called the 'Battle in Seattle'.[95] That large-scale protest by NGOs and activists was a reflection of successfully utilising the transnational advocacy network.

NGOs pursue public interest and the common good by employing various methods. They are engaged in making people aware of the issues,[96] participation in conferences,[97] and garnering media attention for the purposes of public opinion and support. The information alone is not sufficient to get a grasp on the issue areas. Therefore, NGOs harness all the resources of art such as music, drama, painting, documentary filmmaking, cinema, exhibitions, and so on, for the issue areas to occupy a deeper layer in the public psyche. For instance, racism, apartheid, segregation, untouchability and the unequal treatment of women were rooted in culture and tradition. Abolishing these evils required the persistent and conscious efforts of all stakeholders including NGOs, activists, media, academia and the state machinery.

Networking is a dense wave of connections among NGOs. It is a cost-effective, time-saving and efficacious platform. This new avenue of shared values and ideas that enables NGOs to forge coalitions and successful organise campaigns. Such networking platforms are as follows:

The International Campaign to Ban Landmines, 1992 (ICBL),[98] Coalition for the International Criminal Court, 1995 (CICC),[99] Campaign Against Climate Change, 2001 (CACC),[100] Our World Is Not For Sale, 1999 (OWINFS).[101]

The transnational advocacy network is focused on the issue areas i.e. debt-relief, alleviation of poverty, combating corruption, arms trade, child labour, child soldiers, women empowerment, human rights, environment, climate change, genetic technology, medical treatment, business ethics, development, and so on.

In the beginning, some of the issues were a part of soft international law; for example, UDHR, 1948; Rio Declaration, 1992; Beijing Declaration, 1995; and UNFCCC, 1992. These declarations are the rallying points of the NGOs.[102] In other issue areas like torture, enforced disappearance and prolonged detention, NGOs are comparatively more successful in reducing physical violence perpetrated on individuals by repressive regimes.[103]

But these issues are required to be handled carefully because an individual's life is at stake. NGOs prefer diplomatic channels and persuasion methods even without disclosing information to the public domain. This practice was observed by the ICRC, keeping in mind the safety of victims and survivors. Amnesty International employs diplomatic channels for opponents of the ruling party in order to safeguard liberty.

---

[95] Kaldor (2000).

[96] Andreopoulos and Claude (1997).

[97] Clark (1998).

[98] Bower (2019); www.icbl.org.

[99] Struett (2008); www.coalitionfortheicc.org.

[100] www.campaigncc.org.

[101] https://ourworldisnotforsale.net.

[102] Clark (2001), Burgerman (2001), and Keck and Sikkink (2001).

[103] Price (2003).

Sometimes, it is better to bring it to the notice of higher authorities when it comes to the abduction of people, so as to get them released from local authorities. There may be fears that all types of testimony may be eliminated through extrajudicial execution.

NGOs' transnational networking is a shared value, collective voice, and common understanding based on the public interest and common good. NGOs are makers and shapers of human rights issues, and seek the attention of the public.[104] Regardless of the nature of injustice and repression prevailing in any state, social evils do not happen to stop on their own. Slavery was abolished in the nineteenth century through consistent persuasion by the Anti-Slavery Society, 1839.[105]

5 Protection of Human Rights Defenders

An individual who is engaged in the promotion and protection of human rights is known as a human rights defender. That individual can also be termed a human rights activist. The aforementioned definition is standardised in the UN Declaration on the Rights and Responsibilities, 1998.[106] Now, the protection of human rights defenders has become the concern of international law. This could be an individual or group or association which is contributing to the effective implementation of human rights and the fundamental freedom of people and individuals.[107] Human rights defenders are working in diverse capacities as volunteers or professionals or salaried employees with NGOs, IGOs and even within governments.

Preparing a catalogue of human rights defenders is not easy because they could be leaders of trade unions, journalists, teachers, lawyers, judges, police, whistle-blowers, politicians, architects, religious leaders, and so on. It depends on the nature of engagement at any given moment and the commitment towards human rights standards and environmental protection. They help others uphold the highest human values, inspiring courage to raise their voice against injustice, discrimination and repression.[108]

The protection of human rights defenders is the need of the hour as it involves "people's lives, freedom, physical and mental integrity. Besides, the survival of the organisation is at stake. Civil society operate as an essential break on absolute state powers."[109] There is a large number of unsung heroes who fought the peaceful

---

[104] Davis et al. (2012).

[105] www.antislavery.org.

[106] *Declaration on the Right and Responsibility of Individuals, Groups and Organs of Society to Promote and Protect Universally Recognized Human Rights and Fundamental Freedom*, 1998 (UN Declaration 1998) adopted by UN General Assembly, UNGA Res. 53/144 (9 December 1998); Clapham (2006).

[107] UN Declaration 1998, the Preamble para 4.

[108] OHCHR: Human Rights Defenders: Protecting the Right to Defend Human Rights, *Fact Sheet* No. 29, OHCHR, Geneva 2004.

[109] Wiseberg (1991).

battle against autocratic regimes, in the defence of life, liberty and people's property. The activism of human rights defenders must be peaceful, as laid out in the UN Declaration on Rights and Responsibilities, 1998.[110]

The human rights movement started in the later part of the twentieth century and has strengthened through the years. For instance, *Mothers of the Plaza de Mayo* originated in 1977, against enforced disappearances during the dictatorship in Argentina.[111] The human rights movements led by mothers, families and relatives have spread across the whole of Latin America, changing the said landscape of the southern hemisphere.

NGOs like Amnesty International, World Organisation Against Torture, Inter-Parliamentary Union, International Commission of Jurists, Lawyers' Committee for Human Rights (YUCOM), Federation of International Human Rights (FIDH), Survival International, Physicians for Human Rights, Committee to Protect Journalists, PEN International, Article 19, FEDEFAM, Peace Brigades International, and others, are actively engaged in the network for transnational advocacy. They work in collaboration with national and regional human rights NGOs for the protection of human rights defenders at the grassroots level. International NGOs introduce nuanced practices and innovative ideas to overcome repressive measures of autocratic regimes.

These regimes are involved in illegal arrests, prolonged detention, torture, enforced disappearances and extrajudicial killings of human rights defenders in order to silence their voices. In addition, autocratic states use despotic tactics against NGOs to push them back. They create obstacles such as denying their registration, stopping access to funds, abusing the income tax machinery, conducting raids and seizing their official documents, hindering the operation of bank accounts, branding them subversive and anti-national, denying passports, and subjecting them to excessive surveillance. In order to overcome the state's oppressive tactics, Laurie S. Wiseberg has suggested three methods: (1) public exposure and pressure, (2) quiet diplomacy and (3) technical and infrastructural support and solidarity.[112]

NGOs have employed these methods over the years as per the demands of the situation. They persistently ask the United Nations to take up the issues at the international level so that human rights defenders and NGOs may be protected across countries. In 1980, the UN Commission on Human Rights, the precursor of today's Human Rights Council, had adopted a resolution which appealed to all states to "encourage and support individuals and organs of society exercising their rights and responsibilities to promote the effective observation of human rights".[113] In following the mandate, the resolution commission established a working group to prepare a declaration on human rights defenders in 1984. NGOs took active part in this working group's deliberations and presented constructive suggestions to formulate the proposed draft declaration.

---

[110] UN Declaration 1998, *supra note* 107.

[111] Koepsel (2011).

[112] Laurie S. Wiseberg, *supra note* 109, pp. 531–540.

[113] Wille (2019).

The working group did not succeed in making substantive progress. But by the 1990s, the world scenario had changed remarkably. The Soviet Union disintegrated, military dictatorship in Latin America disappeared, the apartheid regime in South Africa vanished, and democracy spread throughout the world. This conducive atmosphere gave a new lease of life to the working group. Thus, they resumed their work on a preparatory draft and came out with a preliminary draft, which was, in turn, submitted to the UN Commission on Human Rights. Amnesty International, in its experience report with the working group brought the inside story to the public domain internationally. Consequently, opposing states of the Declaration on Protection of Human Rights Defenders have softened their stand and given way to furtherance of the cause of human rights.

The General Assembly took over the security issue of the human rights defender in 1993 and continuously worked to finalise it. Some of the states emphasised on giving recognition to individuals and NGOs as human rights defenders in international law. Whereas, others assumed that it is a threat against their sovereignty.[114] The General Assembly adopted draft Declaration by consensus in 1998. The title has now been changed from the Declaration on Human Rights Defenders to the Declaration on the Rights and Responsibilities of Individual Groups and Organs of Society to Promote and Protect Universally Recognized Human Rights and Fundamental Freedoms, 1998.[115] But it is popularly known as the Declaration on Human Rights Defenders.

The Declaration's longer name was not opposed by NGOs because it includes individuals, NGOs, the community and any private entity. The Declaration has nowhere defined defenders, meaning it is an inclusive term, and it has already been extended further and has encompassed a variety of activists and defenders. The bottom line is that their engagement in non-profit, non-violent activities and those in public interest and common good, is within the realm of law.

The Declaration is not a legally binding instrument but it is very much a part of soft international law. States are increasingly considering the adoption of the Declaration as binding national legislation.[116] It is most significant because it recognises the philanthropic work of individuals, groups and associations in the attempted elimination of the violation of human rights and fundamental freedoms.[117] The Declaration enumerates the rights of human rights defenders, the duties of the states and responsibilities of the community. Thus, each and every one has been included.[118] Article 1 states:

---

[114] Marcinkute (2012).

[115] UN GA Res. 53/144 (9 December 1998), Bennett et al. (2017).

[116] OHCHR: *Fact Sheet* No. 29, *supra note* 108, p. 19.

[117] Nah et al. (2013).

[118] UN Declaration of the Right and Responsibility, provide a catalogue of rights of the human rights defenders, and also corresponding duty of the state (Articles 2, 9, 12, 14 & 15). In addition, every individuals or organs responsibility to protect human rights defenders. (Articles 10, 11 & 18, Fact Sheet No. 29), *supra note* 116, pp. 20–22.

Everyone has a right, individually and in association with others, to promote and to strive for the protection and realisation of human rights and fundamental freedoms at the national and international level.

In 2000, the UN Commission on Human Rights mandated Hina Jilani as a UN Special Representative to appraise the situation of human rights defenders around the world.[119] The Special Representative mandate was upgraded to the UN Special Rapporteur in 2008, and Margaret Sekaggya was appointed the mandate holder.[120]

The UN Special Rapporteur seeks feedback from all stakeholders and concerned states visited to prepare an annual report on the protection of human rights defenders. The report is submitted to the General Assembly and the Human Rights Council for perusal at their end. The next mandate was assigned to Michel Forst in 2014.[121] As UN Special Rapporteur, he produced annual reports and enriched the idea of human rights defenders. He further extended the ambit of human rights defenders' protection to encompass business-human rights defenders.[122]

Two decades have elapsed since the adoption of the Declaration on Human Rights Defenders, 1998, but the states are still creating obstacles and using repressive measures to deal with human rights defenders. In this area, independent research, data and information find themselves lacking.[123] There are only NGO reports or state information. Both these entities lock horns in the human rights landscape while IGOs remain silent spectators because they are dependent on state funds and NGOs' information.

Life, liberty and the property of human rights defenders remain at stake. It imperative that a support system for Human Rights defenders be put in place, particularly in democratic-deficit countries and conflict zones. In emergency situations, a quick response should be arranged to save the life of human rights defenders from illegal arrest, prolonged detention, summary executions, torture and enforced disappearances. A comprehensive examination and analysis of each state's national legislations and institutions within the context of the international human rights regime is necessary.

Human rights defenders' capabilities to use information technology and digital security to establish coalitions and networking with NGOs, access to academics, media persons, lawyers, physicians, and any conscience-keeper citizens, further enhances the need for protection. The perception of danger to human rights defenders lacks an accurate assessment technique for timely action to be taken. It is not out of context to repeat that human rights defenders should strictly remain non-violent and peaceful, and maintain utmost political neutrality within conflict zones.

The 1998 Declaration is a new beginning with an aspiration and a hope. It has laid out minimum standards for the protection of human rights defenders. It gives

---

[119] UN Commission on Human Rights Resolution 2000/61 (26 April 2000).

[120] UN Human Rights Council Resolution 7/8 (27 March 2008).

[121] Human Rights Council Resolution 25/8 (2014), A/ HRC/RES/25/18.

[122] Annual Reports of UN Special Rapporteur are available at the http://www.ohchr.org/EN/I/SRHRDefenders/ Annual Report as visited on 15.4.2020.

[123] Alice M. Nah et al., *supra note* 117, pp. 416–417.

legitimacy, identity and recognition to human rights defenders, and their respective missions. To support them, multiple methods and techniques are used, namely honouring them with human rights awards to bring them to the limelight; inviting them to prestigious institutions or universities to deliver lectures or to become visiting fellows; appointing interns to accompany threatened human rights defenders; in critical times, making NGOs open silent, diplomatic channels to bring the matter to the notice of higher authorities to save the life of a human rights defenders. Sometimes, NGOs highlight the matter to the media, campaign via online petitions, get the appeal signed from eminent persons across the globe, and extend legal, financial and medical support to human rights defenders.

Peace Brigades International,[124] an NGO, deputes peace volunteers to accompany human rights defenders. They are allowed to carry only a digital camera and no weapons, whatsoever. Something such as this enhances the safety perception of human rights defenders.[125] Peace Brigades International has been practising Gandhian ideas of peace and non-violence[126] via its volunteers' contributions towards human rights defenders in Nicaragua (1983), Guatemala (1983–1999), Sri Lanka (1989–1998), Indonesia (2000–2011) and Kenya (2013). The NGO awards short-term study internships, but finding volunteers is no easy task as the job poses multiple risks.

6 Conclusion

NGOs' role in transnational advocacy is essentially non-violent and peaceful. They work within the bounds of resources and capabilities available to them. The prevailing states' repressive measures, unjustness and overall discrimination shocks the collective conscience of humanity. It is reiterated that injustice and repression do not automatically manifest a revolution and movement for a change in the society.

Some conscience-keeper citizens take initiatives and join hands with like-minded people. They occupy their time in meaningful ways to serve others even without the expectation of reciprocity. It is their inner voice that gives them motivation, joy and well-being.[127] NGOs employ multiple methods in their operations and missions. These are: agenda-setting, fact-finding, coalitions, campaigning and networking. Moreover, the protection of human rights defenders is intertwined with the transnational advocacy of NGOs.

NGOs' engagement requires funds from either individuals, states, IGOs, businesses or charities.[128] Their survival is dependent on these funds. NGOs' working nature is like the press. Print media is owned and controlled by a business house and it

---

[124] https://www.peacebrigades.org (founded in 1981).

[125] Coy (2001).

[126] Moser-Puangsuwan and Weber (2000).

[127] Oarga et al. (2014).

[128] Antrobus (1987).

also receives funds from the state and the market. Nevertheless, the media maintains free speech and functional autonomy in their news and views. That spirit is a must for NGO programmes, priorities and engagements. They cannot lose or divert their functional autonomy.

NGOs select issue areas that are contemporary, significant and have enough scope to engage and sustain. They build it as a pressing issue, find solutions, write mission statements, connect with like-minded NGOs, highlight things in the media, invite the attention of state, IGOs and people at large and try to make it a formal agenda. In the nineteenth century, NGOs laid down issue areas such as the abolition of slavery, prostitution and trafficking, prohibition of racism and the maintenance of peace among nations and ameliorated conditions of war victims and survivors.

In the twentieth century, NGOs successfully introduced the idea of human rights. They were international actors in the UN Charter, strived to proclaim the UDHR and gave it the shape of a binding treaty as an international covenant. NGOs further expanded the human rights agenda to include torture, disappearances, special group rights pertaining to women, children and disabled migrants, mining, and atomic weapons, as per need of the hour.

Another important NGO engagement is fact-finding. An NGO is the people's voice, and the voice must be based on factually correct and credible information, and sources and material that could be effective and can make a change in prevailing repressive and unjust situations. NGOs select fact-finding missions, visit countries, collect possible evidence and documents, employ modern technology to reach out to all concerned victims, witnesses, journalists, lawyers, physicians and academics, collect relevant and credible information, and produce reports as early as possible.

Coalitions, campaigns and networking are interconnected. The coalition is a collective endeavour of NGOs, campaigns sustain it in the long-run in order to achieve the laid-out objectives; networking is a modern form of coalitions and campaigning via the computer, internet, social media, etc. Transnational advocacy networking is organised beyond borders and connects all stakeholders. Coalition for an International Criminal Court, 1995, International Campaign to Ban Landmines, 1992, and Campaign Against Climate Change, 2001, are readily available examples. The internet is easily available throughout the world and it facilitates networking among NGOs.

NGOs also organise peaceful protests, demonstrations and conferences to educate, raise awareness and mobilise people.

Their advocacy and activism through various peaceful means annoys the state and its vested interests. This is an unwanted risk invitation to activists and NGOs. The life, liberty and property of human rights defenders are at stake.[129] NGO activities are riddled with obstacles, victimisation, false allegations and baseless prosecution. To overcome this undesirable situation, the UN General Assembly adopted the Declaration on Human Rights Defenders, 1998. It provides an identity and sense of security to human rights defenders as well as legitimacy to NGOs' engagement in the furtherance of public interest and common good. The Declaration has been expanded further

[129] Landman (2006).

by the UN Special Rapporteur to encompass activists in the field of environment and business ethics.[130]

References

Alessandra FD (2017) The accountability turn in third wave human rights fact-finding. Utrecht J Int Eur L 33(84):59–76

Alston P (2013) Introduction: third generation human rights fact-finding. Proc Am Soc Int L 107:61–62 at 61

Alston P, Robinson M (ed) (2005) Human rights and development: towards mutual reinforcement. Oxford University Press

Alston P, Knuckey S (2016) The transformation of human rights fact-finding. Oxford University Press

Amanda MM, Davis DR (2012) Shaming and blaming: using events data to assess the impact of human rights NGOs. Int Stud Q 56(1):1–16

Andreopoulos GJ, Claude RP (eds) (1997) Human rights education for the twenty-first century. University Pennsylvania Press, Philadelphia

Antrobus P (1987) Funding for NGOs: issues and options. World Dev 15(1):95–102

Arts K, Tamo A (2016) The right to development in international law: new momentum thirty years down the line. Netherlands Int L Rev 63:221–249 at 222–223

Barsh RL (1991) The right to development as a human right: results of the global consultation. Hum Rights Q 13(3):322–338

Bar-Yaacov N (1974) The handling of international disputes by means of inquiry. Oxford University Press

Bassiouni MC (2001) Appraising UN justice—related fact-finding missions. Washington Univ J L Pol 5(1):35–61

Bassiouni MC (2003) Introduction to international criminal law, 2nd edn. Martinus Nijhoff, Dordrecht (first edition, 2003)

Batliwala S (2002) Grassroots movements as transnational actors: implications for global civil society. Voluntas 13(4):393–409 at 400–404

Baumann T et al (2001) The age of cities and organisations of the urban poor: the work of the South African homeless peoples federation and the peoples dialogue on land and shelter. Working Paper, IIED, London, pp.1–43

Bennett K et al (eds) (2017) Critical perspectives on the security and protection of human rights defenders. Routledge, London

Boersma M (2012) Corruption: a violation of human rights and a crime under international law? Intersentia Publishing, London

Bower A (2019) Entrapping gulliver: the United States and the anti-personnel mine ban. Secur Stud 29(1):128–161

Burgerman S (2001) Moral victories: how activists provoke multilateral action. Cornell University Press, Ithaca

Chandhoke N (2007) Global civil society and global justice. Econ Polit Weekly 42(29):3016–3022 at 3017

Charnovitz S (2011) The illegitimacy of preventing NGO participation. Brooklyn J Int L 36(3):891–910

Chen M et al (2016) Editorial: urban livelihood: reframing theory and policy. Environ Urban 28(2):331–342

Clapham A (2006) Human rights obligations of non-state actors. Oxford University Press

[130] Ineichen (2018).

Clark AM (1998) The sovereign limits of global civil society: a comparison of NGOs participation in UN world conferences on the environment, human rights and women. World Polit 51(1):1–35
Clark AM (2001) Diplomacy of conscience: amnesty international and changing human rights norms. Princeton University Press, US
Cobb R, Ross JK, Ross MH (1976) Agenda building as a comparative political process. Am Polit Sci Rev 70(1):126–138
Cox B (2011) Campaigning for international justice. Bill and Milinda Gate Foundation, USA
Coy PG (2001) Shared risks and risk dilemmas on a peace brigades international team in Sri Lanka. J Contemp Ethnograph 30(5):575–606
Davis DR et al (2012) Makers and shapers: human rights INGOs and public opinion. Hum Rts Q 34(1):199–224
Dearing JW, Rogers EM (1996) Agenda-setting. Sage Publications, Thousand Oaks, California, USA
Finucane B (2010) Enforced disappearance as a crime under international law: a neglected origin in the laws of war. Yale J Int L 35:1–35
Fukuda-Parr S et al (2015) Fullfilling social and economic rights. Oxford University Press, Chapters 3 and 4
Gaventa J (2006) Finding the spaces for change: a power analysis. IDS Bull 37(16):23–33
Hintjens H (2006) Appreciating the movement of the movements. Dev Pract 16(6):628–643
Hobe S (1997) Global challenged to statehood: the increasingly important role of non-governmental organizations. Indiana J Global Legal Stud 5(1):191–210
Ineichen M (2018) Protecting human rights defenders: a critical step towards a more holistic implementation of the UNGPs. Business Hum Right J 3(1):97–104
Joachim JM (2007) Agenda setting, the UN and NGOs: gender violence and reproductive rights. Georgetown University Press, Washington, DC
Kaldor M (2000) Civilizing' globalisaiton? the implications of the 'battle of seattle.' Millennium: J Int Stud 29(1):105–114
Kantor J, Twohey M (2019) She said, Penguin, USA
Katzenstein S (2013) Reverse-rhetorical entrapment: naming and shaming as a two-way street. Vanderbilt J Trans L 46(4):1079–1100
Keck ME, Sikkink K (2001) Activists beyond borders: advocacy networking in international politics. Cornell University Press, Ithca
Keck ME, Sikkink K (2002) Transnational advocacy networks in international and regional politics. Int Social Sci J 51(159):89–101 at 89
Kindornay S et al (2011) Rights based approach to development: implications for NGOs. Hum Rights Q 34(2):472–506 at 472
Koepsel R (2011) Mother of the Plaza de Mayo: first responders for human rights. University of Denver, Colorado, USA, pp 1–13
Kumar CR (2011) Corruption and human rights in India: comparative perspectives on transparency and good governance. Oxford University Press, New Delhi
Landman T (2006) Holding the line: human rights defenders in the age of terror. British J Polit Int Relat 8:123–147
Livingston SG (1992) The politics of international agenda-setting: reagan and North South relations. Int Studies Q 36(3):313–329 at 313
Marcinkute L (2012) The role of human rights NGOs: human rights defenders or state sovereignty destroyers? Baltic J L Politics 4(2):53–77
Meriläińen N, Vos M (2011) Human rights organisations and online agenda setting. Corporate Comm—An Int J 16(4):293–310
Moser-Puangsuwan Y, Weber T (2000) Non-violent intervention across borders. University of Hawaii Press, USA
Nah AM et al (2013) A research agenda for the protection of human rights defenders. J Hum Rights Pract 5(3):401–420 at 417

Nanda VP (1984) Development as human right under international law. Denver J Int L Pol 13(2):161–179

Nelson P (2003) At the Nexus of human rights and development: new methods and strategies of global NGOs. World Develop 31(12):2013–2026

Oarga C, Stavrova O, Fetchenhauer D (2014) When and why is helping others good for well-being? Eur J Social Psychology 45(2):242–254

Orentlicher DF (1990) Bearing witness: the art and science of human rights fact-finding. Harv Hum Rights J 3:83–136 at 108. https://digitalcommons.wel.american.edu/facschlawrew/1725

Patel S, Mitlin D (2001) The work of SPARC, the national slum dwellers federation and Mahila Milan. Research Report, International Institute Envt and Devt, London, 1–44

Perkins L (2017) #MeToo: essays about how and why this happened, what it means and how to make sure it never happens again. Riverdale Avenue Books, New York

Peters A (2018) Corruption as a violation of international human rights. Eur J Int L 29(4):1251–1287 at 1261

Pillay N (2010) Lecture on human rights investigations and their methodology. OHCHR, Geneva, pp 1–8

Price R (2003) Transnational civil society and advocacy in world politics. World Politics 53(4):579–606

Ramcharan BG (2014) International law and fact-finding in the field of human rights, Revised edn. Brill, The Hague (first edition 1982)

Ritchie C (1995) Coordinate? cooperate? harmonise? NGO policy and operation coalitions. Third World Q 16(3):513–524

Rose C (2016) The limitations of a human rights approach to corruption. Int Comp L Q 65(2):405–438

Satterthwaite D (2001) From professionally driven to people—driven poverty reduction: reflection on the role of shack/slum dwellers international. Environ Urban 13(2):135–138

Satterthwaite M (2013) Finding, verifying, and curating human rights facts. Proc Am Soc Int L 107:62–65 at 64

Sen A (2001) Development as freedom, 2nd edn. Oxford University Press

Sengupta A (1999) Delivering the right to development: ESCR and NGOs. Econ Pol Wkly 34(41):2920–2922

Sengupta A et al (eds) (2005) Reflections on the right to development. Sage Publication, London

Struett MJ (2008) The politics of constructing the international criminal court: NGOs, discourse and agency. Springer, New York, Chapter 5

Summers A (2008) Introduction: the international abolitionist federation. Women's Hist Rev 17(2):149–152

Thomas F, Farley SH (1980) Procedural due process in human rights fact-finding by international agencies. Am J Int L 74(2):308–345

Thoolen H, Verstappen B (1986) Human rights mission: a study of the fact-finding practice of non-governmental organisations. Martinus Nijhoff, Dordrecht

Vranckx A (2006) A long road towards universal protection against enforced disappearance. UN Human Rights Council, Geneva. www.20070115-a-long-road-towards-universal-against-enforced-disapperace-2006PDF

Weissbrodt D (1980) Human rights implementation and fact-finding by international organisation. Proc Am Soc Int L 74:17–19 at 17

Weissbrodt D, McCarthy J (1981) Fact-finding by international non-governmental human rights organizations. Vargina J Int L 22(1):1–89 at 7–8

Wille P (2019) The history of the UN declaration on human rights defenders: its genesis, drafting and adoption. Blog Universal Rights Group, Geneva, 11 March

Wiseberg LS (1991) Protecting human rights activists and NGOs: what more can be done? Hum Rights Q 13(4):525–544 at 525

Yanacopulos H (2015) International NGO engagement, advocacy and activism: the faces and spaces of change non-governmental public action. Palgrave, Basingstoke, Chapter V

Chapter 6
NGO Relations with Inter-Governmental Organisations

1 Introduction

Organisations have co-existed with humanity since the dawn of civilisation. Primitive humans used to organise themselves for collecting food, finding shelter, protecting themselves against danger and raising their young. People lived in families, clans and tribes. These were the first organisations that came into existence on earth. Growth and development in the form of production and human relations have given a new shape to organisations. More sophisticated and modern organisations have originated as per the needs and circumstances prevalent in society. For instance, the state, market, community, IGOs, NGOs, corporations, religious and educational institutions[1] are the collective result of human endeavour.

'Organisation' is a Greek term which means a 'tool'.

Organisations represent the essence of associational life, embodying the collective efforts of individuals coming together to achieve a common purpose. One man alone can do little. And it is better that things are organised and done by a group of people.[2] Organisations do not just happen. They are created either by states, individuals or private citizens. These entities grow and develop, and from time to time, people intervene to enhance their functioning. Organisations have the inner dynamics of co-operation, competition and sometimes conflict too.

NGOs are created to serve humanity and to fulfil its envisaged goals. They were created to promote the social equality, the sustainable development, the protection of human rights and remove the barriers for the free flow of people, ideas and goods. NGOs and IGOs came into being in the nineteenth century, whereas the states, the markets and the community were already in existence. States and markets have enjoyed unbridled powers and influence over the centuries.

---

[1] Hatch (2011).

[2] Handy (1988).

P. Rai, *Non-Governmental Organisations and International Law*,
https://doi.org/10.1007/978-981-97-5469-4_6

The state is the main actor in world affairs. States extended their capacity and activities through their mutual associations—inter-governmental organisations (IGOs). Parallelly, markets increased their economic access through business associations and transnational corporations. In order to promote people's interest, freedom and happiness, individuals launched social movements and created religious charities, endowments and philanthropies. To extend their energy, action, influence, culture and capital, they created joint enterprises, viz. IGOs, NGOs, corporations, civil society and religious charities.

IGOs are inter-state entities, while NGOs are individuals or initiatives of private persons. Hence, their power, forum, origin, influence and capacities are different, because one is based on governmental powers and resources and the other on the commitment, expertise and donations of individuals. Both these distinct entities were visible in the nineteenth century and further increased their numbers, influence, activities and outreach down the ages. They have left their footprint on every nook and corner of the world.

The Vienna Congress, 1815, was the first event when European powers came to realise that problems could be sorted out through mutual co-operation. Earlier, they were confined to their national boundaries and relied upon their military prowess. The Vienna Congress was just a conference of European nations, and not an institution, in the modern sense of the term.[3] Apart from this, the Rhine River Commission for Navigation was also established. All Riparian States were members of the Rhine River commission. A similar commission was established for the Danube River in 1856.

European powers undertook issues in the Pan-European context. In addition to river navigations, they focussed on railways and communication facilities. They took initiatives to establish the International Union of Railways in 1890, International Telegraphic Union in 1865, Universal Postal Union in 1874, Permanent Court of Arbitration in 1899, the League of Nations in 1919 and the United Nations in 1945.[4] These conferences, bureaus and organisations were formulated in the nineteenth century and the early-twentieth century. The United States was there when the League of Nations was formed in 1919, but did not become a member. The United Nations is a universal body that's open to each and every member state around the world.

Alongside, non-governmental entities were established in Europe and the United States.[5] Inter-governmental and non-governmental actors were simultaneously working across nations. Their issue areas were overlapping and interplaying with each other. Earlier, IGOs' main concerns were to maintain peace, resolve disputes peacefully and promote co-operation among nations, whereas NGOs' objectives are to protect human rights, environment and business ethics and to raise the voice of the marginalised in society.

---

[3] Bowett (2009), Baldwin (1907).

[4] Mangone (2006).

[5] Charnovitz (1997); See this book, Chap. 2.

IGOs' objectives and activities are broadly governed by the principles and purposes of the United Nations, by international law and by their respective constitutions.[6] The UN mandate and international law are also applicable to both global civil society and NGOs. For obtaining consultative status in ECOSOC and maintaining relationships with IGOs, NGOs are hereby under an obligation to carry out the UN Charter mandate and the rules of international law.[7] D.W. Bowett has divided international organisations into two categories: first, private international unions, and second, public international unions. Private international unions cover non-governmental entities,[8] while the latter is not included within the realm of international organisations.[9]

However, it is a well-established fact that international organisations are broadly inter-governmental entities like the UN, World Bank, WTO, ILO, etc. Non-governmental entities have existed parallelly in this space as well, with the likes of the International Chamber of Commerce (ICC), Institute de Droit International, Union of International Associations, Amnesty International, MSF (Doctors Without Borders), etc.

2 Development of NGO-IGO Relationship

The relationship and co-operation between NGOs and IGOs is based on mutual understanding and interest. Both entities benefit from such an arrangement.[10] IGOs receive support from the grassroots and the realm of public opinion and legitimacy, whereas NGOs have the opportunity to participate in international events, which was earlier an exclusive domain of the diplomats. And NGOs are also in a position to influence the outcome of the IGOs' policy decisions through expression of their voices and submission of representations. NGOs' interaction with IGOs has expanded opportunities to contribute to the programmes and projects of global institutions. Certainly, it has enhanced the reputation of NGOs and enabled them to raise funds and volunteers.

Interaction between NGOs and IGOs originated and has developed, since the League of Nations, 1919.[11] The League of Nations covenant provided Article 24 and 25, which dealt with NGOs. Article 25 is exclusively related to Red Cross Societies. Reference for the remaining NGOs was implicitly given under Article 24 of the covenant. Instead of using the term NGO, Article 24 employed the term international bureaus or commissions, perhaps to include both IGOs and NGOs. Moreover, Article 24 provided that the financial expenses of the bureaus and commissions were partly

6 Amarsinghe (2005), Schermers and Blokker (2018).

7 U.N. Charter, Article 71 and ECOSCO Resolution 1996/31.

8 D. W. Bowett, *supra* note 3, pp. 4–8.

9 White (2016).

10 Rebasti (2008).

11 Seary (1996).

to be borne by the League of Nations. This was withdrawn in 1922 owing to the surge in NGOs.

A number of NGOs were accorded the 'Assessors' status by the committees of the League of Nations. According to Bill Seary: "These had the rights and privileges of a government representative, short of being able to vote."[12] Later on, this status was withdrawn, because it was nowhere mentioned in the covenant of the League of Nations, but NGOs' facilitation was continued. A number of prominent NGOs were associated with the League during its time (1919–1939). These NGOs included the International Chamber of Commerce (ICC); International Bureau for Suppression of the Traffic of Women and Children; International Federation for Aid to Young Women; International Federation of Trade Unions and the International Institute of Intellectual Co-Operation; etc.[13]

NGOs, visionary citizens and study groups emphasised to promote world peace in an organised manner. The allied powers—the USA, the UK, China and Russia—met during wartime at Dumbarton Oaks in 1944 to discuss the establishment of international institutions and associations. Religious groups and NGOs successfully persuaded these nations to incorporate the League of Nations' experiences of interaction with NGOs in the United Nations. This resulted in NGOs being accommodated under the UN Charter.

The UN Charter has institutionalised the relationship between NGOs and the ECOSOC and its subsidiaries. The provisions of the UN Charter are silent about the General Assembly, the Security Council, various specialised agencies, associated and attached institutions and remaining IGOs.[14] However, the relationship between NGOs and IGOs has been established on the basis of co-operation when it comes to programmes and policies on the one side and implementation in the field on the other. These relations are regulated on the broad guidelines of Article 71 of the UN Charter, followed by the Resolutions 1996/31, and also outside the existing consultative status. IGOs and NGOs have developed good practices since the era of the League of Nations (1919–1939) and its successor, the UN. The Conference of NGOs (CONGO) has formulated a self-regulations code of conduct for NGOs[15] to oversee mutual relationships with international governmental entities.

In the last quarter of the twentieth century, NGOs gained a prominent place in the international arena. The Cold War ended in 1990, and African, Asian and Latin American countries emerged on the global stage, raised their independent voices and emphasised on economic equality. A good number of NGOs and civil societies were visible in second and third world countries in addition to ones from the first world—i.e. Western Europe and the United States.

The numbers between NGOs and IGOs are uneven. NGOs' growth has surpassed IGOs and they have become visible participants at the international level. It is very

[12] Ibid., p. 22.

[13] Wheat (1951).

[14] UN Charter, Article 71, The Charter of the United Nations, UN Publications, New York 1945 and ECOSOC Res. 1996/31 (25 July, 1996).

[15] http://www.un-ngls.org.

challenging to make an accurate assessment of the number of NGOs and IGOs out there. There are nearly 250 IGOs and nearly 75,000 NGOs (Yearbook of International Organisations). According to Kerstin Martens:

> In the 1980s, the ratio of NGOs to IGOs stood at 15:1, whereas today, the ratio is 28:1.[16]

This data is based on the Union of International Association, 2004. Since then, the ratio of NGOs to IGOs might have further changed because the formulation of NGOs and IGOs is a continuous process. For instance, the International Solar Alliance (ISA) was established by states in 2015, in order to carry out the mandate of the Paris Climate Summit.[17] Likewise, NGOs are also created by individuals and private citizens. Since IGOs are inter-state entities, their creation and winding-up are noticed by the media at an international level. The League of Nations was wound up formally in 1946. The Trusteeship stopped working from 1994. NGOs' visibility spread across the international level thanks to their activism, engagement and their accreditation by the UN and the IGOs.

3 Institutionalisation of NGOs-IGOs Relationship

How is one to synchronise relations or interactions between NGOs and IGOs? Is legal formalisation a better way or do informal, traditional ways serve the purpose? Another option is to harmonise both in legal and traditional ways.[18] NGOs have a long experience of informal relations within the League of Nations and legal formal relations within the ECOSOC of the UN.

Legally, the institutionalisation of relations between NGOs and IGOs is neither easy nor is it taken in the right spirit by the member states. So far, legal relations of NGOs with ECOSOC and its subsidiaries are not extended to cover the General Assembly and the Security Council. However, there are possibilities to establish a relationship with UN specialised agencies and attached organisations like the International Atomic Energy Agency, World Bank, World Trade Organisation (WTO), and others international institutions.

[16] Martens (2005).

[17] The Economic Times, 14 March, 2018, p. 12.

[18] Emanuele Rebasti, *supra note* 10, p. 22.

It is interesting to note that regional organisations such as the Community of Europe (CoE),[19] Organisation of American States[20] (OAS) and the African Union (AU)[21] have legally formalised NGOs' relationships with them.

CoE, OAS and the AU are major regional organisations that have growing relationships with NGOs. This trend may be followed by other global, regional and inter-governmental organisations; for example, Black Sea Economic Corporation (BSEC) has institutionalised its partnership with NGOs.

The BSEC was created in 1998 for the purpose of maintaining peace and prosperity to the surrounding nations of the Black Sea region. Its charter contains a reference to NGOs for granting an observer status to them (Article 8, (2)). NGOs enjoy autonomy from government control. They discharge their functions without any intervention. NGOs do not prefer to indulge in any politics in the Black Sea area, and thus, they contribute a lot to BSEC policymaking and the implementation of rules. It is imperative for an NGO to carry on its international nature.[22]

A. **Tripartite System of ILO**

The International Labour Organisation (ILO) was the first IGO to institutionalise the relationship between the state, employers' association and employees' trade union. ILO was established in 1919 along with the League of Nations, and it is still working for social justice and welfare of the working classes. Institutionalised relations between governmental and non-governmental entities form the ILO tripartite system. In the said system, every member country is entitled to send four members including two governmental, one employer association and one workers' trade union to participate in the International Labour Conference.[23] This is a unique idea for establishing a social dialogue between governmental and non-governmental representatives.

It is institutionalised in ILO's constitution. The representatives of governmental and non-governmental entities also participate in the governing body of the ILO.[24] The International Labour Conference is the general house and the governing body is the executive council of the ILO.[25] Institutionalisation of relations between government and non-government and within the international institutional framework has been successful in the areas of labour, industry and employment generation. However,

---

[19] Committee of Ministers, Resolution (2003) 8, *Participatory Status for International Non-Governmental Organisations with the Council of Europe*, adopted on 19 November 2003; Resolution (2003) 9, *Status of Partnership for National Non-Governmental Organisations with the Council of Europe*, adopted on 19 November, 2003.

[20] The arrangements are regulated by CP/RES. 759(1217/99), *Guidelines for the Participation of Civil Society Organisations in OAS Activities*, 15 December, 1999.

[21] *Resolution on the Criteria for Granting and Enjoying Observer Status to Non-Governmental Organisations Working in the Field of Human Rights with the African Commission on Human and Peoples Rights*, adopted by the ACHPR at its 25 session, 26 April–5 May, 1999.

[22] Stribis (2005).

[23] ILO Constitution, Article 3.

[24] ILO Constitution, Article 7.

[25] http://www.ilo.org; Alston (2005).

the tripartite structure is replicated neither in the UN Charter nor in the specialised agencies or other inter-governmental entities.

B. **NGOs Conference**

The institutionalisation of NGOs-IGOs partnership was made possible through NGOs-active forum of the Conference of NGOs, rather than being mediated by government delegates. The ECOSOC has created two special forums: the first is the Permanent Forum of Indigenous Issues[26] and the second is the UNAIDS Coordination Board.[27] In these forums, both non-governmental members and governmental members are included and the non-governmental representatives are nominated by the Conference of NGOs.[28] ILO's pattern in which the member states are nominated by the representatives of non-governmental entities from the employees' association and trade unions has not been followed in the Permanent Forum on Indigenous Issues and the UNAIDS Coordination Board. The Permanent Forum on Indigenous Issues consists of 16 members, eight nominated by the states and eight nominated by the President of ECOSOC from indigenous people. The UNAIDS Coordination Board is constituted of 27 members, out of which 22 are from governments and the remaining five are from representatives of NGOs.

C. **NGOs and the African Economic, Social and Cultural Council**

The Organisation of African Unity came into existence in 1963 and it adopted the name of the African Union in 2002. The African Union (AU) has six organs, which are: the Assembly, the Executive Council, the Commission, the Pan-African Parliament, the Court of Justice and the Economic Social and Cultural Council (African ECOSOCC). The African ECOSOCC started functioning in 2005. It consists of NGOs or civil society organisations (CSOs) and is an advisory organ to the AU.

The African ECOSOCC has 150 members,[29] two from each member state, 10 regional, 8 continental, 20 from the African diaspora and 6 civil society organisations ex officio nominated by the AU commission on the basis of special knowledge. Presently, 55 members are entitled to be nominated out of a total of 110 members as per the statute of the African ECOSOCC. The remaining 40 members are adjusted in the aforesaid categories. There is also a rule to maintain diversity in the African ECOSOCC membership on the basis of age, gender, social groups, professionals, artists, social workers and the private sector. Their term is for four years and they can be re-elected.[30]

---

[26] *Establishment of a Permanent Forum on Indigenous Issues*, E/Res/2000/22 (28 July 2000).

[27] ECOSOC Res 1995/2, Joint and Co-sponsored United. Nations Programme on HIV/AIDs, Annex: *Arrangements for the participation on NGOs in the work of Programme Coordination Board of the Joint and Co-sponsored United Nations Programme on HIV/AIDS*: Report on the Informal Consultation of the ECOSOC, (3 July 1995).

[28] http://www.ngocongo.org.

[29] African Union Constitutive Act, Articles 5 and 22; Statute of the Economic, Social and Cultural Council of the African Union (ECOSOCC), ECOSOCC statute, Articles 3–4, http://au.int/about/ecosocc.

[30] Cowling (2002), Magliveras (2002), Udombana (2002).

Being an advisory body, the African ECOSOCC is working in partnership with the AU. It has designed programmes and projects as per the envisaged objectives of the AU charter and has enforced them, undertaking studies and making recommendations thereupon, promoting human rights, the rule of law, good governance, democracy and child rights. In addition, it strengthens the partnership between the AU and civil society organisations. The African ECOSOCC is engaging in the promotion of African culture and their way of life.

The African ECOSOCC takes decisions with a two third majority. Every member has an equal vote (Article 15–16). It allows the use of the commission's secretariat. There is a credential committee for NGOs and CSOs. There are nine members including two from the AU commission, five from CSOs and NGOs, one from the Diaspora and one from a specialist group. This committee is responsible for preparing the list of NGOs and CSOs for the purpose of African ECOSOCC's ready reference.[31]

D. **NGOs and the European Economic and Social Committee of the EU**

Like the African ECOSOCC, the European Economic and Social Committee (EESC) has formal relations with NGOs and the civil society. The EESC was established in 1957. It is a European Union (EU) advisory body which consist of Businesses, Trade Unions, Civil Society, NGOs and other interest groups across Europe. The EESC has three objectives: first, render advice to the European Parliament, Council and Commission; second, to strengthen civil society organisations in the EU to make a greater contribution to European development and third to promote the role of civil society organisations beyond the EU countries.[32] Meanwhile, the European Commission organises outreach efforts to beyond European nations. Hence, it created the external services to conduct EU foreign relations with other countries. This initiative of EU certainly is a way forward for European NGOs to carry out their transboundary activism.[33] NGOs participate in the EESC meetings and freely express their views on a regular basis.

E. **NGOs and the Council of Europe**

The Council of Europe (CoE) has developed a consensus among its members to partner with NGOs.[34] The relationship between the CoE and NGOs is based on self-regulation. This self-regulatory system attributes a specific role to the Liaison Committee and thematic groupings. The Liaison Committee and Thematic groupings have been established by an autonomous initiative of the NGOs participating in CoE programmes and activities. The main purpose of both the committees is to ensure a proper representation of their mutual interest. In this regard, the conference of NGOs plays a crucial role in bringing together every year on the platform, all CoE-accredited NGOs on a voluntary basis.

---

[31] Kithure (2003), Mutasa C (2004).

[32] https://www.eesc.europa.eu/about.

[33] Spence (2004).

[34] Participatory Status for International Non-Governmental Organisations with the Council of Europe, adopted by the CoE Committee of the Ministers on 19 November 2003, CoE Res (2003) 8; CoE Committee of Minister Resolution CM/Res (2016) 3.

The Liaison Committee consists of 36 members. Out of this, 25 are elected by the Conference of NGOs in their annual meetings and the remaining 11 (specialised in a particular field) are from thematic groupings. It enjoys the procedural power of accreditation of NGOs within the Council of Europe and its other related organs. At present, 400 NGOs possess participatory status with the Council of Europe.

F. **From Relationship to Partnership**

The relationship between IGOs and NGOs started off as an interaction and gradually acquired the status of a partnership. The interaction between them has been institutionalised in various ways. Some IGOs induct them in their organisational setup. The ILO (1919) introduced the tripartite structure to make non-governmental entities an integral part of their organisation. This is a rare occasion when governmental and non-governmental entities are partners on an equal footing. So far this has not been replicated by other IGOs. Some hybrid NGOs or IGOs have emerged over the course of time, for example, the International Union for Conservation of Nature (IUCN) and the International Chamber of Commerce (ICC). Both governmental and non-governmental members are present within hybrid international organisations.

The UN's ECOSOC's subsidiary bodies, Permanent Forum of Indigenous Issues, UNAIDS Co-ordination Board and African Union-ECOSOCC provide for NGOs' direct membership in their setup, whereas the Council of Europe allows NGOs to participate on the basis of self-regulation. NGOs' Liaison Services identify suitable NGOs through the Conference of NGOs and networking, and following that confirm their credentials. In areas where the formal system or legal framework is not in place, they extend the official facilities in an informal way. As a sample study, some relationships between IGOs and NGOs are highlighted hereby.

4 NGOs and the World Trade Organisation

A. **Background**

The World Trade Organisation (WTO) was formulated in 1995 by the member states.[35] The WTO charter envisaged its objectives: improved standards of living, full employment, expanded production of and trade in goods and services, sustainable development and an enhanced share of developing countries in world trade. The member states further committed to this agreement that they will contribute to achieving these objectives. The WTO charter lays down two principles for attaining these noble objectives: first, member states' substantial reduction in tariffs and other barriers to trade; and second, the elimination of discriminatory treatment in international trade relations.

Even though the WTO is not a specialised agency of the UN, it has associations with it. The WTO is fully committed to the liberalisation of trade and investment.

[35] The Uruguay Round Agreement Establishing the World Trade Organisation, 1993, 33 ILM 13 (1993); www.wto.org.

Therefore, as an international economic organisation, it is more like the Bretton Woods Organisations, i.e. the World Bank and International Monetary Fund (IMF).

The WTO is the successor to the General Agreement on Tariffs and Trade (GATT).[36] GATT (1947–1995) had non-binding rules, while the WTO has binding rules. GATT was a transitional arrangement mainly for tariffs and trade, while the WTO is a permanent IGO. Along with the World Bank and IMF, there was the idea to create the International Trade Organisation (ITO) in 1944. The World Bank and IMF became a reality, while the ITO remained unborn for the time being. The GATT, however, was created in 1947. The GATT was replaced by the WTO in 1995.

The main organs of the WTO are: the Ministerial Conference, General Council, Trade and Policy Review Body, Dispute Settlement Body, i.e. Appellate Body, Panels and Secretariat and the Secretary General. The administrative work is further divided between the committees. It is surprising to know that there is no committee on NGOs' accreditation. It is an exclusively inter-governmental entity and does not have any committee which can facilitate NGOs to participate in their international trade law-making, adjudicating process and enforcement. Amrita Narlikar pointed out that non-governmental organisations (NGOs) and interest groups have no direct entry into the WTO.[37]

However, Article V.2 of the WTO charter lays down:

> The General Council may make appropriate arrangements for consultation and co-operation with non-governmental organisations concerned with the matters related to those of the WTO.

In the beginning of the WTO, NGOs were not encouraged to participate in their conferences, negotiations and programmes. Jens Steffek observed:

> At first glance, the World Trade Organisation (WTO) appeared to be a relatively hostile environment for NGOs and social movements. The organisation continued to define itself as strictly member driven and, above all, a venue for confidential negotiation and the settlement of disputes among States.[38]

5 B. NGO's Strive for Hearing People's Voice

B. NGOs Strive for Hearing People's Voice

Despite the WTO's exclusive approach, NGOs have a very long and vast experience in establishing their relationship and interaction with such reluctant inter-governmental entities. Trade and investment cannot be ignored for long, neither can the burning issues of environment, sustainable development, human rights, consumer protection, good governance and democratic values. Without any specific provisions so far,

---

[36] 55 UNTS 187, GATT Agreement, 1947.

[37] Narlikar (2005).

[38] Steffek (2012).

NGOs have accessed the most significant universal institutions—the UN Security Council and General Assembly.

The workings of the WTO are quite a secret. The international trade law-making process in its ministerial conferences through agenda-setting, negotiation and the adoption of rules is exclusively dealt with by the trade ministers of member states. All the stakeholders—NGOs, global civil society, media and interest groups—are not informed to express their views on the outcome of these ministerial conferences.[39] Certainly, the ministerial conference decisions and rules impact the lives of people, and it results in discontentment among the people at large. Thus, the WTO wants to improve its global image by using NGOs as a link to the people.[40]

NGOs' relationship with the WTO is necessitated for many reasons, some of which are narrated by Jayati Srivastava—(1) NGOs have the technical expertise in their respective fields of operation; (2) NGOs have the advantage of grassroots reach and they stimulate community participation; (3) they are able to mobilise citizens for developmental efforts; (4) the expansion of participation of stakeholders and civil society; (5) they perform an effective advocacy and lobbying function and (6) the representation of marginalised people.[41]

The basic ideas of economic and business organisations like the World Bank, IMF and the WTO differ from security and social organisations like the UN Security Council, UNESCO, ILO and the WHO. The former prefer secrecy in dealing with inter-state business transactions, whereas the latter are open and accessible to NGOs and other stakeholders.

The close relations of IGOs and NGOs are mutually beneficial and imperative in the prevailing circumstances. When IGOs were created, they had limited resources and access, which were managed through co-operation with NGOs. NGOs' role is useful in drafting documents, providing inputs, technical knowledge, project implementation at the ground level and in the dissemination of information.[42] The WTO has an in-house capacity of technical knowledge, drafting skills and does not need any partners in order to implement projects at the grassroots level. But to redress democratic deficit and good governance, the WTO has to have an open relationship with NGOs, media, civil society, social movements and private sectors.

The WTO Ministerial Conference in Seattle in 1999 was a turning point for WTO-NGOs relations. In Seattle, 776 NGOs were accredited. Among them, 686 participated and the total number was in excess of 1500. NGOs' representatives employed various democratic means such as demonstration, street plays, parallel symposia, posters, songs and exhibitions to get the attention of the media, intelligentsia and people at large. This event was witnessed by 60,000 people on the streets of Seattle.

---

[39] Total twelve Ministerial Conferences were held: 1st Singapore, 1996; 2nd Geneva, 1998; 3rd Seattle, US, 1999; 4th Doha, 2001; 5th Cancun, 2003; 6th Hongkong 2005, 7th Geneva, 2009; 8th Geneva, 2011; 9th Bali, 2013; 10th Nairobi, 2015; 11th Buenos Aires, 2017, and 12th Geneva, 2022.

[40] Reichert (1996).

[41] Srivastava (2005), Clarke (1998).

[42] Jens Steffek, *supra note*, 38, p.303.

The WTO and government trade ministers of various countries did not envision the social movement and uprising of people in Seattle against WTO's secrecy and exclusive dealings.[43]

Protests and social movements by NGOs were well received by people across nations. NGOs' views were given full coverage by the media. The subsequent impact was the realisation of democratic deficit at the WTO, making it imperative to hear the voice of the people. Apart from business, environment, labour and human rights, the development gap between north and south came to be included in the WTO's trade framework.

C. **WTO's move towards Relationships with NGOs**

In 1996, the General Council of the WTO adopted a decision in persuasion of the WTO Charter, Article V.2, and laid down the guidelines for arrangements on relations with non-governmental organisations. WTO member states recognised the role that NGOs could play in increasing the public's awareness with respect to WTO activities and agreed to improve transparency and develop communication with NGOs in this regard.[44] The execution of the General Council decision about relationships with NGOs was assigned to the WTO secretariat.

In order to enhance this process, the secretariat will make available online the material which is accessible to the public, including derestricted documents. The secretariat should play a more active role in its contact with NGOs. It is necessary to form a meaningful interaction, for which the secretariat should extend more facilities to NGOs like, seminar halls, libraries, lounges, corridors, spaces and opportunities to express their views.

The guidelines laid down a certain set of criteria for NGOs' interaction with the WTO. First, an NGO is a valuable resource. And second, it can contribute to the accuracy and richness of the public debate. But how does the WTO secretariat measure these criteria? It can be understood by past practices, because the General Council decision was neither elaborated nor was it clarified by the secretariat. Samima Ahmed identified some factors such as size, resources, scope of operation, nature of the issue and the ability of the NGO community to speak in one voice, as important considerations.[45] The WTO's main issue area is international trade and investment among nations, and this is a specialised field of international economic law. Thus, NGOs' possession of knowledge and expertise in this issue area and operations globally is a prior requisition.

As per the guidelines of the General Council, the purpose of relations with NGOs is to increase public awareness about WTO's activities and related issues. In order to achieve the said purpose, the WTO has improved its transparency and communication with NGOs. NGOs are facilitated to organise symposia on WTO-related issues, and information is made available to interested government delegates along with briefings

---

[43] Paterson (2011), Joseph (2011).

[44] *Guideline for Arrangements on Relations with Non-Governmental Organisations*, Decision adopted by the General Council on 18 July, 1996, WT/L/162, 23 July, 1996.

[45] Ahmed (2011).

about WTO's forthcoming issues and their insights. But NGOs are not allowed in the WTO's negotiations and meetings of delegates. Moreover, NGOs are engaged at the national level to bring different elements of public interest on trade policy-making because the primary responsibility lies on the member states.

NGOs are meant to be a bridge between the WTO and the international community. They raise issues, submit briefs, make theme-specific presentations and help in drafting treaties.[46] Besides business, they raise the issue of human rights, labour, consumer protection, environment and social justice as well as the equitable share of developing countries in world trade.

D. **WTO's encounter with NGOs**

In 1996, the first Ministerial Conference of the WTO was held in Singapore. This was the first encounter between the WTO and NGOs. Afterwards, the legal framework of their interactions was laid down.[47] The WTO distinguishes itself as it has its own history and culture, so too its own language and mysterious practices. NGOs found themselves in a new and unfamiliar territory.[48] WTO meetings weren't within the reach of NGOs. Even a small state is discouraged from participating in the critical hours of decision-making during the conference of ministers. Nonetheless, NGOs have remained undeterred. Drawing upon their vast experience, they have adapted to the situation, learning various methods to expand the conference of ministers' agenda. Their primary focus lies in advocating for the public interest within the international trade regime, with a strong emphasis on reducing the north–south gap in world trade. Additionally, NGOs vociferously call for holding national governments accountable and not relying solely on the benevolence of transnational corporations.

In the Singapore Conference, 159 NGOs were accredited, with 108 participating in the meeting. It was difficult to tell how many public interest or specific NGOs—like business associations, trade unions, etc.—were present. The NGOs utilised this opportunity to interact, network and focus on the issues of trade. Only 15 NGOs participated regularly in the Ministerial Conferences that took place between 1996 and 2005,[49] owing to the fact that it was a technical area and developing countries' NGOs did not command the requisite resources to become proficient easily and quickly.

By its nature, the WTO is a government-centric organisation because it is not only a forum for discussions and deliberations, but it creates rights and liabilities of member states that matter a lot in their economic development. Presently, 164 member states are in the WTO, while the United Nations has 193. It has regulated world trade since 1995, managing trade competitions among nations and providing an opportunity to highlight public interests.

The objectives of NGOs are so broad that they cannot be achieved by merely participating in WTO conferences and seeking support from like-minded states. For

---

[46] Caceres (2012).

[47] WTO Charter, Article 4(2), 1867 UNTS 154, General Council Guidelines, WT/L/162, 1996.

[48] Halle (1997).

[49] Piwitt (2010).

instance, raising the standard of living, ensuring full employment and eliminating discriminatory treatment in international trade relations are some of the biggest global issues going around. Thus, the participation of NGOs at the WTO is to enhance resources, information and expertise, furthering the voices of the marginalised, being a watchdog over national governments, reviewing and critiquing the performance of the WTO and ensuring nations' compliance as far as their commitments go.[50]

> The Seattle Ministerial Conference of 1999 was attended by NGOs in large numbers, recalling the memory of the Rio Earth Summit of 1992. But the NGOs' street protest could not maintain its momentum. NGOs' interaction with the WTO has been gradually institutionalised. The WTO secretariat now has become more accommodative in the accreditation process of NGOs, but there are still issues like the reduced participation of NGOs from the South. In addition, the WTO overlooked the issues raised by NGOs, being least interested in the promotion of public good and community welfare.

Some issues were resolved; for instance, the dichotomy between development and the environment was harmonised in terms of sustainable development. Global Trade Watch, an NGO founded in 1972, played a central role in the successful derailing of the Multilateral Agreement on Investment in 1999, in the Seattle Conference, with the coalition of NGOs.[51] Apart from investment issues, NGOs have successfully handled health and the availability of medicines at reasonable prices.

The copyright regime of the WTO-TRIPS agreement resulted in raising the prices of generic medicines in developing countries. In 1999, NGOs established a coalition against the pharmaceutical companies and launched a campaign in favour of health and the availability of medicines. The corporations were forced to reduce the prices and allow the third world to produce its own medicine.[52] This led to two positive messages. Firstly, NGOs sought the confidence of developing countries because earlier they presumed that inducting labour, environment and human rights issues in WTO negotiations deprived them of an equal share in world trade and prosperity. Secondly, the message that despite the influence and wealth possessed by corporations, they could not deter NGOs from promoting matters of public interest.

World trade, investment and copyright are highly technical issues. Therefore, advocacy and campaigning at the WTO and at the site of Ministerial Conferences are primarily conducted by highly specialised NGOs that are based at the Geneva headquarters of the WTO, Europe and the United States. NGOs such as the International Institute of Sustainable Development (IISD), Centre for International Environmental Law (CIEL), International Centre for Trade and Sustainable Development (ICTSD), International Green Peace, Third World Network, Oxfam, World Wide Fund for Nature (WWF) and Friends of the Earth International have played active roles in ministerial conferences and have mobilised public opinion.

The Third World Network is based in Malaysia, providing a platform to developing countries. These aforesaid NGOs spread information, share their views, set up coalitions and network, publish magazines like '*Bridges*' and develop think tanks.

---

[50] Lin (2004).

[51] Sigfrido B. Caceres, *supra note* 46, p.84.

[52] He and Murphy (2007), Nathan (2004).

'*Bridges*' is published by ICTSD and is widely circulated, containing news and views of NGOs and the WTO.

The WTO felt the need of partnering with NGOs because that gave it more credibility in the eyes of the public, removing somehow, and its democratic deficit as well. International economic law is relatively a fresh area for NGOs, social movements and civil society. It is not anymore an exclusive domain of business sectors, with it having to be balanced with social sectors by NGOs engaging with the WTO and its respective national governments.

6 NGOs and the United Nations Educational, Scientific and Cultural Organisation

The WTO regulates and promotes the free flow of goods, services, money and the market, while the UNESCO promotes education, science, culture and information. The UNESCO's primary focus is on ideas, intellectuality, arts, architecture, free choices and diversity. The WTO's core idea is the material well-being of the people, whereas UNESCO's is on conscience and creativity.[53] NGOs' relationship with the WTO and UNESCO is quite diverse, with the latter having created and promoted innumerable NGOs.

A. **Origins of UNESCO**

In 1946, member states agreed to establish an international forum in the issues areas relating to science, education, culture and communication.[54] The UNESCO has the mandate to contribute to peace and security by promoting the collaboration among nations through education, science and culture. Moreover, UNESCO is also engaged in promoting the universal respect for justice, for the rule of law, human rights and basic freedom without discrimination. These wide and broad issue areas can be achieved through partnership with NGOs and intellectuals.

Since its inception in 1945, the UNESCO has engaged in standard-setting, sharing knowledge and information, creating NGOs and helping member states. The task that lay ahead of the UNESCO was difficult because the virtues and values it wanted to achieve might or might have been accepted by the member states. Its core was free expression, choices, creativity, conscience and intellectuality. The power of the day was in the hands of the member states and they were not pleased to promote these values in their respective countries.

UNESCO's headquarters were set up in Paris, and its first Director General (DG) was Huxley, from Britain. The Board of Directors and the General Conference are its apex bodies. Each member state and partner NGOs host secretariats under the D.G., National Commission of UNESCO. The General Conference comprised the representatives of member states, and the executive board had a certain proportion

[53] Voon (2006).

[54] Lacoste (1955).

of scholars, thinkers and great statesman from all over the globe. In the words of Richard Hoggart:

> they were the conscience of the organisation.[55]

These intellectuals, cultural personalities and creative minds were not appreciated and supported by the member states. Therefore, they changed the composition of the Executive Board in 1954, and free intellectuals were replaced by government representatives. But the ethos and values on which it was based have still prevailed.

B. **NGO-UNESCO Partnership**

The synergy of the UNESCO and NGOs was established to co-operate in design, draft and implementation of its policy and programmes worldwide. The constitution of the UNESCO has laid down certain provisions for its relationship with NGOs. As per Article XI clause 4 of UNESCO's constitution:

> The United Nations Educational, Scientific and Cultural Organization may make suitable arrangements for consultation and the co-operation with non-governmental international organisations concerned with matters within its competence, and may invite them to undertake specific tasks. Such co-operation may also include appropriate participation by representatives of such organisations on advisory committees set up by the General Conference.

Ever since it came into being, the UNESCO began its consultation and co-operation with NGOs. In fact, it took over the work and ideas of the International Institute of Intellectual Co-operation, founded in Paris in 1926. That international institute as an NGO played a key role in capacity-building of the newly founded UNESCO. Besides, the Conference of Allied Ministers of Education (CAME) had given shape to the basic ideas of the UNESCO and also its relations with NGOs. In the pursuit of UNESCO's constitutional mandate, background and nature, the UNESCO started informal relations with NGOs. It even took initiatives to create NGOs, relating to the specific issue areas of museums, music, theatre and so on. The UNESCO also extended financial support and secretarial facilities to NGOs.

In 1966, relations between NGOs and the UNESCO were formalised. The UNESCO adopted the "directives concerning UNESCO's relations with non-governmental organisations", something that set out the legal framework for the NGO-UNESCO relationship in a more systematic way.[56] These directives of 1966 were further amended in 1995[57] because there was a demand to reform the UNESCO's working, and in particular, the relations with NGOs.

---

[55] Richard Hoggart, "UNESCO and NGOs: A Memoir" in *The Conscience of World—The Influence of Non-Governmental Organisations in the UN System, supra note* 11, p.99.

[56] UNESCO Doc., Directives Concerning UNESCO's Relations with International Non-governmental Organisations (1966).

[57] UNESCO Doc., Directives Concerning UNESCO's Relations with Non-governmental Organisations (1995), UNESCO DOC, Directives concerning UNESCO's partnership with non-governmental organisations adopted by the General Conference at its 36th sessions (12 July 2022).

The United States withdrew from the UNESCO on 31 December 1984.[58] This was followed by Britain. The United States re-entered UNESCO on 29 September 2003, with Britain following suit. Both countries are prominent financial contributors to the UNESCO, though they halted their contribution during the period in which they weren't a part of the organisation. The UNESCO managed to overcome this very existential challenge, but the reforms within the organisation became inevitable from the 1980s.

Apart from the United States and United Kingdom resentment towards the workings of UNESCO, developing countries also wished for reforms in the system. The most contentious issues in the UNESCO were the accreditation and subvention to NGOs. Other pertinent issues included the proposal of new information and communication orders, recruitment of employees and UNESCO's budget and policy. The accreditation system or consultative status of NGOs[59] was amended by the directives of 1995. Therefore, the directives of 1966 were no longer applicable.

UNESCO's directives of 1995[60] laid down purposes, conditions, the withdrawal of consultative status and the organisation of conferences. Its purposes were as follows: advise the UNESCO, ensure UNESCO documentation, give technical assistance to UNESCO, express public opinion and promote the emergence of NGOs in the developing world.

C. **Conditions for Consultative Status in the UNESCO**

The conditions are laid down for accreditation of NGOs in the UNESCO. These are:

- NGO is international or national.
- Non-governmental in origin, purpose, function and operation.
- Non-profit in character.
- One or more activities in UNESCO's fields of competence.
- Able and willing to make effective contributions.
- Organisational structure (regular membership, recognised legal status, established headquarters and democratic status).
- Carrying out activities for at least four years.

There are also provisions for the withdrawal of consultative status of NGOs from the UNESCO. These are: downgrading possible; termination possible; also, automatic cessation of consultative status (after four years of continuous absence).

D. **Categories of NGOs under UNESCO**

The UNESCO directives of 1995 also divided NGOs into three categories, such as, Category 1: Formal Associate Relations (FAR); Category 2: Formal Consultative Relations (FCR) and Category 3: Operational Relations (OR). All three categories differ in admission, rights and duties.

---

[58] Wanner (2015).

[59] UNESCO Doc, *supra note*, 56.

[60] UNESCO Doc, *supra note*, 57.

Categories	Category 1 Formal Associate Relations (FAR)	Category 2 Formal Consultative Relations (FCR)	Category 3 Operational Relations (OR)
Admission	Only major international organisations	Only international organisations	Any organisation
Rights	Association as closely and regularly as possible with the various stages of the planning and execution of UNESCO activities. Provision of office accommodation	Invitation to meetings May address plenary session Submit written statements Receive documentation Consultation	May send observers to certain meetings Collective consultation
Duties	Expand activities in common with UNESCO, promote international co-ordination Maintain effective co-ordination with UNESCO	Advice, provide assistance, contribute to execution of UNESCO's programmes Enhance interests submit reports about activities	Exchange of information

The UNESCO directives of 1966 were changed in order to accommodate developing countries into the UNESCO system. The directives of 1995 have again categorised NGOs. Under the directives of 1966, NGOs were divided into categories A, B and C. These have now been replaced by the categories of first, second and third under the directives of 1995. NGOs are divided in Formal Associate Relations, Formal Consultative Relations and Operational Relations.[61] Formal relations NGOs might be invited by the Director General to send observers to the General Conferences and Commissions. They are allowed to submit written statements and receive documents. They are provided with secretarial assistance and also receive subvention or financial support from the UNESCO under the directives of 1966. The entitlement of financial support was abolished under the directives of 1995.

The second major change is the promotion of regional and national NGOs along with international NGOs. All three categories are encouraged to participate in conferences and to realise the UNESCO's programmes and activities. However, the first and second categories of NGOs are also involved in programmes and policymaking in addition to execution.[62]

An NGO is supposed to regularly participate in the UNESCO's programmes and activities, otherwise their absence for a long period, (say, for four years) may automatically lead to their consultative status being terminated. The relations with NGOs are not based on finance, but are rather intellectual in nature, as per the core of UNESCO system. In the directives of 1995, the UNESCO instituted international NGOs to either promote or create national NGOs and strengthen their capacities.

[61] Martens (2001).

[62] UNESCO Doc. 154 Ex/29, *Relations with Non-governmental Organizations, Foundations and Similar Institutions* (1998).

The UNESCO directives of 1995 had a definitive impact on NGOs and developing countries. The number of NGOs with consultative status has increased between the period of 1961 and 1995. In 1966, there were 187 NGOs, while in 1995, there were 588. The directives of 1995 provide opportunities to national NGOs to engage with UNESCO programmes and projects. The formal relations of NGOs' numbers have been stable, by and large, but the informal relations of NGOs' numbers have increased worldwide. NGOs' willingness, capacity and contribution towards the UNESCO have enabled them their first, second or third category, as the case may be. This is based completely on their performance and activities report.

Procedure of Accreditation of NGOs

The process of granting a consultative status is carried out by the NGO-UNESCO Liaison Committee. The NGOs international conference is held biennially. It brings together all NGOs who have statutory relations with the UNESCO. The conference elects members of the NGO-UNESCO Liaison Committee. The committee co-ordinates between NGOs, member states and the UNESCO. It is located at the UNESCO headquarters in Paris. Thus, it ensures permanent co-ordination and co-operation with UNESCO's policymaking and programme execution at the field level.[63] The final nod on consultative status is given by the Executive Board of the UNESCO.

NGOs can directly submit an application to the Director General for the purpose of accreditation to the UNESCO. The application contains: NGO statute, instrument of legal recognition, list of members, activity report and a brief discussion about activities implemented in co-operation with UNESCO. Thereupon, the Director General decides whether it deserves to be sent to the executive committee for the final decision. If an NGO applies for associate relations, i.e. Category 1, then it needs to have at least two years of experience in a consultative relationship in Category 2.

UNESCO's partnership with NGOs is essentially intellectual and moral. UNESCO is not a finance agency. It is meant to build peace in the mind of man. For more than 75 years, it continues to be a laboratory of ideas, creativity and standards for moral human beings. The organisation has maintained a valuable partnership with NGOs throughout its history.

7 NGOs and the World Bank

A. **Background**

The World Bank was established in 1944 at the Allied Powers meeting in Bretton Woods, New Hampshire, the United States. Its headquarters are located in Washington, D.C. The World Bank's purpose is to assist in the reconstruction and development of economies and raising productivity and the standard of living of member

---

[63] NGLS (2005).

states—particularly in the restoration of economies that were destroyed or disrupted by WW II. It also provides facilities and resources to less developed countries.[64]

The World Bank comprises: the International Bank for Reconstruction and Development (IBRD) and the International Development Association (IDA). Both are jointly referred to as the World Bank. The World Bank consists of three additional institutions: the International Finance Corporation (IFC), International Centre for the Settlement of Investment Disputes (ICSID) and the Multilateral Investment Guarantee Agency (MIGA). They are collectively known as the World Bank group.

The journey of the World Bank remained very slow and steady up until 1980. During that period, the bank staff learned the procedures, acquired confidence and sought the co-operation of NGOs and member states. The World Bank receives funds from member states and borrows from the market. Developed countries provide more funding so that they have voting and decision-making rights. In 1960, member states created the International Development Association (IDA) as a soft loan institute. Income of the World Bank and special funds are made available to the IDA for providing soft loans and grants to the least developed countries.

The highest authority of the World Bank is vested in the Board of Governors and execution powers are with the Board of Directors. These powers are exercised with the help of the bank staff. The representation of the member states is equal, but the voting capacity depends upon their share and financial contribution to the bank. In finance terms, this is known as the weighting vote.

The articles of agreement of IBRD and IDA do not explicitly provide the accreditation procedure of NGOs' relations with the World Bank, unlike the UN Charter Article 71 that provides consultative status to NGOs. However, Article V, section 8 of the IBRD's[65] articles of agreement, and Article V, section 4 of the IDA's[66] articles of agreement, indicate the World Bank's interaction with international organisations. These provisions authorise the World Bank to co-operate with general international organisations and public international organisations that have specialised responsibilities in fields relevant to the bank's work. In addition, IDA is mandated in the articles of agreement that it shall co-operate with public international organisations who provide financial and technical assistance to the less developed areas of the world.

The oil crisis and the western recession in the 1980s drastically curtailed the earning of developing countries, resulting in the debt crisis and the 'lost decade'.[67] It was a market failure, and with hollowness of the trickle the down effect, the capital flowed from rich countries to poor countries. It required a change in the

---

[64] Articles of Agreement, Article 1, International Bank for Reconstruction and Development (IBRD) popularly known as World Bank, World Bank Publication, Washington DC 1945; https://www.worldbank.org.

[65] Articles of Agreement, International Bank for Reconstruction and Development (IBRD: 1944); www.worldbank.org.

[66] Articles of Agreement, International Development Association (IDA: 1960) www.ida.worldbank.org.

[67] Seamus Cleary, "The World Bank and NGOs," in *Conscience of the World—The Influence of Non-Governmental Organisations in the UN System, supra note* 55, p.66.

World Bank's aid and advance policy. The World Bank's assumption was that the market was more efficient in comparison to the states. Therefore, the bank focussed on structural changes, reduction in subsidiary and social spending. This move manifested resentment and tension in the borrower states and was criticised by NGO community.

B. **World Bank-NGO Interaction**

The World Bank's relations with NGOs before 1980 were informal. Occasionally, the bank staff invited NGOs to have a dialogue about its financial activities. In 1981, the World Bank issued the Operational Policy Note (OPN) 10.05 and proceeded from informal relations with NGOs to formal relations.[68] The OPN 10.05 contains specific guidelines to assist the bank staff in making effective use of NGOs within the framework of bank-financed projects. NGOs could now play a specific role in financial activities and projects.

Recognising the relevance of NGOs, the World Bank established the NGO-World Bank Committee in 1982. This committee consisted of senior bank staff and 26 NGO representatives. The committee's initial objectives were: to strengthen relations and expand operational co-operation between the bank and NGOs.[69] Subsequently, the committee's mandate was expanded to include an in-depth discussion of the bank's development policy issues, such as structural adjustment and participatory development with NGOs.[70]

The World Bank has undertaken the policy of structural adjustment and over-emphasised the virtues of the private sector. In addition, the bank's programme is to reduce the state's role and intervention in productivity and the distributive sector of the economy. These policies and programmes of the World Bank have caused a great deal of inconvenience and resentment and have not yielded the desired results.

Over the years, the NGO community has earned the knowledge and experience of the bank's policy programmes and outcome. They criticised severely this restructuring plan, financial activities of the bank and their adverse effect on developing countries. When Barber Conable took over as the President of World Bank in 1986, he started with a constructive approach and had high hopes about the relations between NGOs and the World Bank. He expressed his opinion at the World Bank-IMF annual meeting in September 1988:

> NGOs in many developing countries have enormous potential for flexible and effective actions. I have encouraged the bank staff to initiate a broadened dialogue with NGOs.[71]

Despite this gesture on the part of the President of the World Bank, the collective resentment of the NGO community was expressed on the occasion of the Bretton

---

[68] *Involving Non-governmental Organisations (NGOs) in the Preparation and Implementation of Bank-Financed Projects.* Operation Policy Note 10.05, 31 December, 1981, and Annex-1, 13 May, 1981.

[69] *Terms of Reference of the NGO-World Bank Committee*, External Affairs Department, International Economic Relations Division, World Bank, May 13, 1981.

[70] Shihata (1992).

[71] The World Bank (1991).

Woods institutions in Berlin, 1988, when the IMF and World Bank organised an annual meeting. At the same time, NGOs held a popular trial through the temporary 'International Tribunal', set up as a special vehicle to expose the bank's misdeeds. Evidence was heard against the IMF and World Bank, relating to issues pertaining to poverty alleviation, environmental protection and human resources development. They generated evidence and debated to demand the accountability of the IMF and World Bank for the impact of their policy and programmes, particularly the structural adjustment programme.[72]

C. NGOs' Action in World Bank Projects

The World Bank wanted to improve its image and public perception, and thus, it adopted the Operational Directive (OD) 14.70 to involve NGOs in its financial activities.[73] The Operational Directive 14.70 of 1989 was in furtherance of NGOs' participation in the World Bank project cycle, including project identification, design, appraisal, financing, implementation, evolution and monitoring.

The involvement of NGOs in the World Bank was slow and steady. For instance, the NGO community was present in only 6% of projects cycles between 1973 and 1988. But within the short span of 1989 to 1991, NGOs were involved in more than 40% of bank projects.[74] This augured well for the NGOs-World Bank relationship.

From 1989 onwards, the relationship between the World Bank and NGOs was further extended from projects to bank policies. NGOs' campaign persuaded the World Bank to undertake environmental protection in its policy programmes and financial activities. The bank had included dams and reservoirs, indigenous people, displaced persons and their resettlement and environmental assessment in the Operational Directives from 1989 to 1991.[75]

Further to this, NGOs' initiatives helped to form the Global Environment Facility (GEF) in 1991. The GEF was a multilateral fund to promote the environment. It is implemented jointly by the World Bank, the United Nations Development Programme (UNDP) and the United Nations Environment Programme (UNEP). The environment is prominent on the policy agenda of the World Bank, in addition to the reduction of poverty and the advancement of developmental programmes.

NGOs and other stakeholders observe the World Bank's policy, programmes and financial activities. NGOs pursued for a permanent mechanism to monitor and review the bank policy on a regular basis. The concern exhibited by NGOs and developing economies led to the creation of the World Bank Inspection Panel in 1993.[76] The main objective of the panel is to receive representation from adversely affected communities within the bank's project purview. The Inspection Panel examines the project circle entirely and its adverse effects thereof on the local community or people at

---

[72] Nelson (1995), Goldman (2005).

[73] The World Bank Operational Manual, Operational Directive 14.70, August, 1989.

[74] The World Bank, External Affairs Department, International Economic Relations Division (EXTIE) Co-operation Between the World Bank and NGOs; 1991 Progress Report, 1 April 1992.

[75] The World Bank Operational Manual, Operational Directive, from 1989 to 1991.

[76] Shihato (1998).

large. The panel submits its findings to the bank's board of directors for the final decision. NGOs use this process in the prevention of harmful impact on environment, livelihood or natural habitat.

With the turn of the twentieth century, the World Bank became more accessible and open to NGOs, civil society, parliamentarians and private sectors. The World Bank-NGOs interaction is based on NGOs' competency, local knowledge, internal governance, legal status and institutional capacity. The Issues and Options for Improving Engagement Between the World Bank and Civil Society Organisations was adopted in 2005.[77] They recommended advisory services, a monitoring and evaluation system, review of the available NGO fund and learning and capacity-building programmes. NGOs can now be assigned research work. Governments hire NGO experts in order to implement the World Bank's projects. NGOs may seek the services of bank officials in their organisation.

NGOs' interaction with the World Bank works in three ways: facilitating, consultation or partnering in their programmes and projects. Over the years, the bank's agenda, scope and programmes have expanded as per the need of the day. At present, they are engaged in poverty reduction strategies (PRSPs), Heavily Indebted Poor Countries Initiatives (HIPC) and the World Development Report (WDR). The World Bank's interests in partnership offered new openings to NGOs; they have to undergo an often-lengthy process of learning the rules of the game for their capacity-building. Deborah A. Brautigam and Monique Segarra observed:

> NGOs learned relatively quickly that partnerships were in their interests. Participation and partnership offered new opportunities to increase their voice over and access to – State and international resources.[78]

The World Bank opened windows for global partnership and initiatives in its expanded programmes, activities and policies for NGOs. These include renewable energy, improving health and immunisation, millennium developmental goals and food security, apart from its regular financial activities. NGOs can utilise World Bank facilities such as the World Bank Training Institute (WBI), Global Development Learning Network (GDLN) and Justice Sector Peer Assisted Learning (JUSTPAL). The WBI was founded in 1955 as an Economic Development Institute with the support of the Rockefeller and Ford Foundations. It changed its name from EDI to WBI in 2000. GDLN holds events for learning and for conducting dialogue on development issues. It mainly focusses on small government agencies and NGOs. JUSTPAL was launched in 2011 to strengthen the justice delivery system.

---

[77] http://www.worldbank.org/WEBSITE/EXTERNAL/TOPICS/CSO.

[78] Brautigam and Segarra (2007).

8 Conclusion

Inter-governmental Organisations' (IGOs) numbers total to nearly 250, and hence, they deserve a full-fledged study. The case study of relations between IGOs and NGOs has been undertaken in a very compact manner. Both sets of organisations came into existence in the nineteenth century in a significant way, and over time, they have acquired a prominent role in the globalised world economy, i.e. information, ideas, culture and institutions.

NGO's relations with IGOs began at the time of the League of Nations, being institutionalised in the United Nations era. These relations further extended with specialised agencies, subsidiaries, programmes, funds and attached institutions of the UN and regional organisations. The relationship between IGOs and NGOs have their mutual benefits, as IGOs receive information, expertise and partners in their programmes, policies and democratic inputs, whereas NGOs receive global exposure, recognition and opportunities. In this complex world, the partnership between NGOs and IGOs certainly benefits to address the problems and challenges of our time, such as the reduction of poverty, preservation of environment, protection of human rights, gender justice and child rights, education, health, habitat, world peace and prosperity.

Three diverse relationships with NGOs have been examined, i.e. IGOs—WTO, World Bank and UNESCO. The World Bank and WTO deal with international finance, investment, trade and material prosperity, while the UNESCO deals with education, science, culture, information, intellectuality and peace of mind.

The UNESCO was a successor to international NGOs in the field of its command, so it welcomed the NGOs' partnership with respect to its purposes, programmes and intellectual activities. It started its journey with the creation and endowment of NGOs. The World Bank, along with Bretton Woods Institutions, was quite hesitant to establish partnerships with NGOs when it came to their economic activities. But it gradually opened its doors to NGOs, civil societies, parliamentarians and private sectors to respond to the ever-growing criticism regarding the deficit of transparency and democracy.

The WTO is a relatively young IGO; therefore, it started its journey alongside NGOs and other stakeholders in international trade, regulations and promotion. NGOs pushed for the inclusion of human rights, environment, labour and distributive justice in the WTO's trade regime, thus giving a human face to trade, market and business across nations.

References

Ahmed S (2011) The impact of NGOs on international organisations: complexities and considerations. Brooklyn J Int'l L 36(3):817–840 at 822

Alston P (ed) (2005) Labour rights as human rights. Oxford University Press

Amarsinghe CF (2005) Principles of the institutional law of international organisations, 2nd edn. Cambridge University Press (first edn 1996)

Baldwin SE (1907) International congress and conferences of the last century as forces working toward the solidarity of the world. Am J Int'l L 1(3):565–578

Bowett DW (2009) Law of international institutions. In: Sands P, Klein P (eds), 6th edn. Sweet & Maxwell, London, p 6

Brautigam DA, Segarra M (2007) Difficult partnerships: the world bank, states, and NGOs. Latin Am Polit Soc 49(4):149–181 at 150

Caceres SB (2012) NGOs, IGOs, and international law-gaining credibility and legitimacy through lobbying and results. Georgetown J Int'l Affairs 13(1):79–87 at 80–81. https://www.jstor.org?stable/4313421

Charnovitz S (1997) Two centuries of participation: NGOs and governance. Michigan Int'l L J 9(2):184–261

Clarke G (1998) NGOs and politics in the developing countries. Polit Stud 46(1):36–52 at 41

Cowling M (2002) The African union—an evolution. South African YB Int'l L 27:193–205

Goldman M (2005) Imperial nature: the world bank and struggle for social justice. Yale University Press, New Haven, CT, US

Halle M (1997) Non-governmental organisation's and the WTO. Bridges (Magzine) 1(1):1

Handy C (1988) Understanding voluntary organisations. Penguin, London, p 1

Hatch MJ (2011) Organisation – a very short introduction. Oxford University Press, p 2

He B, Murphy H (2007) Global social justice at the WTO? The role of NGOs in construction global social contrast. Int'l Affaires 83(4):707–727 at 719

Joseph S (2011) Blame it on the WTO?: a human right critique. Oxford University Press

Kithure K (2003) The normative and institutional framework of the African union relating to the protection of human right and the maintenance of peace and security: a critical appraisal. African Hum Rts L J 31(1):97–117

Lacoste MC (1955) The story of a grand design. UNESCO Publications, Paris, pp 29–30

Lin Z (2004) An analysis of the role of NGOs in WTO. Chin J Int'l L 3(2):485–497 at 492–493

Magliveras KD (2002) The African union—a new dawn for Africa? Int'l & Comp L Q 51(2):81–103

Mangone G (2006) A short history of international organisations. McGraw Hill, New York (first edn 1954)

Martens K (2005) NGOs and the united nations: institutionalization, professionalization and adaptation. Palgrave Macmillan, New York, p 2

Martens K (2001) Non-governmental organisations as corporatist mediator? An analysis of NGOs in the UNESCO system. Glob Soc 15(4):387–404 at 400

Mutasa C (2004) The African union—civil society contract: an act of democracy? Civil Soc Observer 1(5):1–2

Narlikar A (2005) The world trade organisation—a very short introduction. Oxford University Press, p 39

Nathan F (2004) Patents, access to medicines and role of non-governmental organisations. J Generic Med 1(2):137–145

Nelson PJ (1995) The world bank and NGOs: the limits of apolitical development. St. Martins, New York

NGLS (2005) UN system engagement with NGOs, civil society, the private sector and other actors. UN Publications, New York, p 120

Paterson WB (2011) The world trade organisation and protest movement: altering world order? Routledge, London

Piwitt M (2010) Participatory governance in the WTO: how inclusive is global civil society? J World Trade 44(2):467–488 at 478

Rebasti E (2008) Beyond consultative status: which legal framework for enhanced interaction between NGOs and inter-governmental organisations? In: Dupuy P-M, Vierucci L (eds) NGOs in international law: efficiency in flexibility? Edward Elgar, Cheltenham, UK, pp 21–22

Reichert WM (1996) Resolving the trade and environment conflict: the WTO and NGO consultative relations. Minnesota J Glob Trade 5:219–246 at 242

Schermers HG, Blokker NM (2018) International institutional law, 6th edn. Martnus Nijhoff, The Hague (first edn 1995)
Seary B (1996) The early history—from the congress of Vienna to the San Francisco conference. In: Willets P (ed) The conscience of the world—the influence of non-governmental organisations in the UN system. The Brookings Institution, Washington, DC, p 2224
Shihata IFI (1992) World bank and non-governmental organizations. Cornell Int'l L J 25(3):623–641 at 624
Shihato IFI (1998) World bank inspection panel, 2nd edn. Oxford University Press
Spence D (2004) European commission external service. Public Policy Admin 19(3):61–76
Srivastava J (2005) NGOs at world trade organisation—the 'democratic' dimension. Econ Polit Weekly 40(19):1952–1957 at 1953
Steffek J (2012) Awkward partners: NGOs and social movements at the WTO. In: Narlikar A et al (eds) Oxford handbook on the world trade organization. Oxford University Press, p 301
Stribis I (2005) Institutionalization of cooperation between inter-governmental organisations and NGOs: the BSEC experience. Non-State Actors & Int'l L 5(1):21–57
The World Bank (1991) The conable years at the world bank: major policy address of barber B. Conable 1986–1991:69
Udombana NJ (2002) The institutional structure of African Union: a legal analysis. Calif Western Int'l L J 33(1): 69–135; http://www.africa-union.org
Voon T (2006) UNESCO and the WTO: a clash of cultures? Int'l & Comp L Q 55(3):635–651
Wanner R (2015) UNESCO's origins, achievements, problems and promise: an inside/outside perspective from the US. University of Hong Kong, China, p 44
Wheat LC (1951) International non-governmental organisations. Rutgers University Press, New Brunswick, New Jersey, US
White ND (2016) The law of international organisations, 3rd edn. Machester University Press (first edn 1996)

Chapter 7
NGOs Before International Courts and Tribunals

1 Introduction

Co-operation and conflicts are an inevitable process in the international community. In the Mavrommatis case (1924), the word 'dispute' was explained by the Permanent Court of International Justice (PCIJ) as, "A disagreement on point of law or fact, a conflict of legal views or interest between two persons."[1]

Traditionally, there are two ways to settle a dispute, the first one is to use force, and the second is to use peaceful means. The United Nations has preferred peaceful means and prohibits the use of force and threat against any state.[2] The means for settlement of disputes is laid down in Article 33 clause 1 of the UN Charter. These are negotiation, inquiry, mediation, conciliation, arbitration, judicial settlement and regional agencies or arrangements. State parties can choose any of the means by mutual agreement, for settlement of disputes.[3]

The means of dispute settlement are divided into two categories, i.e. diplomatic and legal. Diplomatic methods include negotiation, inquiry, mediation and conciliation. NGOs have scope in the inquiry method only. The Commission of Inquiry clarifies the factual position of a dispute in order to facilitate a settlement.[4] NGOs have experience in fact-finding; therefore, they can also make a submission to the Inquiry Commission to reach an amicable solution between the parties on equitable basis.

---

[1] Mavrommatis Palestine Concessions (Greece v. UK), (1924), PCIJ, Ser. A. No. 2, p. 11.

[2] UN Charter, Article 2 para 4; www.un.org/charter/united-nation.

[3] Merrills (2017), Collier and Lowe (1999).

[4] Hyde (1929).

P. Rai, *Non-Governmental Organisations and International Law*,
https://doi.org/10.1007/978-981-97-5469-4_7

Legal methods are arbitration and judicial settlement. These include Permanent Court of Arbitration (PCA), International Court of Justice (ICJ), International Criminal Court (ICC), International Tribunal for the Law of the Sea (ITLOS), WTO Adjudicative Body, International Centre for Settlement of Investment Disputes (ICSID) and World Bank Inspection Panel (WB Inspection Panel).

The dispute settlement mechanism primarily resolves disputes among state parties. An individual or a private person does not have access to the international courts and tribunals. NGOs' participation in international courts and tribunals is as amicus curiae.[5] The international courts and tribunals cover a wide spectrum of disputes, i.e. territorial and maritime boundaries; crimes against humanity and controversies related to trade, investment and finance.

A. Development of International Adjudication[6]

Since long, the negotiation, conciliation and inquiry commission has been used by states to resolve their disputes. The origin of arbitration could be found in the Jay Treaty, 1794, between the United Kingdom and the United States. International arbitration practice was stimulated after the successful Alabama Claims Arbitration of 1872 between the United States and the United Kingdom.[7]

Disputes relating to land territory, maritime boundaries, navigational rights, economic claims or crimes against humanity have substantive interest, and sometimes, these are the causes of armed conflicts or war between states.[8] The peace societies across the Atlantic were engaged in discouraging war between states as a means of resolving their disputes. The London Peace Society was founded in 1816 and the American Peace Society in 1828.[9] There were 500 peace societies located in the United States and Europe. They fought for a century to promote world peace and resolve the disputes through amicable means. The peace societies held the International Peace Congress six times between 1843 and 1853.

The peace movement was interrupted by the Crimean War (1853–1856), American Civil War (1861–1865) and the subsequent wars of Europe.

In 1889, the Inter-Parliamentary Union[10] was established and contributed to the formation of PCA. James L. Tryon observed:

> The Inter-Parliamentary Union has had a profound influence upon the development of the arbitration and peace movement; its platform of resolutions has been influential in guiding the work of the Hague Conferences.[11]

The idea of arbitration as a substitute for war was put forward by the peace societies and Inter-Parliamentary Union. It was further enriched and given the legal framework

---

[5] Shelton (1994).

[6] O'Connell and VanderZee (2013).

[7] Moore (1898), Bingham (2005).

[8] Brownlie (2009).

[9] Tyrrell (1978).

[10] www.ipu.org; Lange (1932).

[11] Tryon (1911).

by the International Law Association[12] and Institute of International Law.[13] Non-profit publications: *Herald of Peace* (1851) and *Advocate of Peace* (1847–1884) had popularised the idea of arbitration. These ideas were taken well by the international community at the turn of the nineteenth century.

B. **Amicus Curiae**

In a dispute, there are two parties which have their claim, interest and rights to pursue in the courts. Both parties are entitled to participate in the judicial proceedings. In common law traditions, the third party, as a friend of the court or amicus curiae, has also been allowed to participate in the judicial proceedings.

Amicus curiae submits their knowledge on the point of fact and of law before the presiding officer of the court. According to Samuel Krislov:

> Inasmuch as permission to participate as a friend of the court has always been a matter of grace rather than right.[14]

Earlier, the participation of amicus curiae required the party's consent, but subsequently this was vested in the court rather than parties. The amicus curiae brief is permitted where the dispute is related to a larger number of people, and finding a solution to the dispute is not an easy task. The purpose of amicus curiae is to protect public interest and to assist the court.

Over the years, the nature of amicus curiae has been changed from neutrality to advocacy. The National Association for the Advancement of Coloured People (NAACP)[15] and American Civil Liberties Union (ACLU)[16] were the first who filed amicus curiae briefs.[17] The amicus curiae was spread in the civil law of countries, and subsequently, it became a part of international law. NGOs henceforth started submitting amicus curiae before the international courts and tribunals. This cultivates a sense of participation among NGOs in the dispensation of international justice. Moreover, this enhances transparency and acceptance of the decisions of international courts and tribunals. Participation of NGOs in dispute-resolution proceedings as amicus curiae has democratised international law.[18]

---

[12] www.ila-hq.org (1873, Brussels).

[13] www.idi-iil.org (1873, Ghent, Belgium).

[14] Krislov (1963).

[15] https://naacp.org, founded in 1909, Baltimore, US, Fighting for the Civil Rights of Coloured People.

[16] Www.aclu.org (formed in 1920, New York), Civil Liberties Advocacy.

[17] Guinn v. United States, 238 US 347 (1915); Samuel Krishlov, *supra note* 14, pp. 679, 707, 709.

[18] Crema (2012).

2 Permanent Court of Arbitration

NGOs such as the Institute of International Law and Inter-Parliamentary Union were instrumental in establishing a permanent court for the settlement of international disputes.[19] Thus, the Permanent Court of Arbitration (PCA) was created by the Hague Peace Conference in 1899.

PCA's nomenclature is misleading because it is neither permanent nor is it a court. Indeed, it is an institution with premises in the Peace Palace in the Hague, staffed with a Registrar and a panel of arbitrators. PCA is an inspiration for the international community to resolve disputes in peaceful ways instead of armed conflicts. The award by PCA is based on international law and is binding on the parties. It is a launching pad and the basis of proliferation of international courts and tribunals in different areas of international law.[20]

In the beginning of the twentieth century, NGOs did not make any mark as amicus curiae, but further to that they actively participated in the court proceedings. In a recent case of the South China Sea Arbitration (Philippines v. China) 2016, the Chinese (Taiwan) Society of International law submitted an amicus curiae brief in the PCA proceedings.[21]

3 International Court of Justice

The International Court of Justice (ICJ) is a principal organ of the United Nations. Its precursor was the Permanent Court of International Justice (PCIJ). The PCIJ was created in 1920 and was dissolved in 1946.[22] It had delivered 27 advisory opinions and 31 decisions on contentious cases.[23] Non-governmental groups participated in four advisory opinions. These four cases were related to labour issues, therefore trade unions participated as amicus curiae in the court proceedings.[23] The trade unions who participated as amicus curiae are: the International Association for the Legal Protection of Workers, International Federation of Trade Unions and International Federation of Christian Trade Unions. In the nineteenth century, Europe witnessed an industrial revolution. Trade unions were at the forefront in the protection of the working class as well as peoples' rights within the court and outside of it.

The PCIJ was the first-ever agency to entertain amicus curiae briefs from non-governmental groups. This was further carried on by the ICJ in the years to come.[24]

---

[19] Scott (1916).

[20] Alford (2000), Romano (1999).

[21] PCA Case No. 2013–19, decided on 12 July 2016; Chang (2017).

[22] Hudson (1943).

[23] De Brabandere (2018); UN, *Summaries of Judgements, Advisory Opinions and Orders of the Permanent Court of International Justice*, UN Publications, New York, available at: legal.un.org, uh.org/documents/english/PCJI_final Text.

[24] ICJ Statute, Article 34(1).

The ICJ has two kinds of jurisdiction, i.e. contentious and advisory.[25] Any state whose legal interest may be affected in the case could be allowed to participate as a third party in the court proceedings.[26] It is the purview of the ICJ to permit third party-participation in court proceedings, but it is not their right.[27]

The ICJ has no direct relations with non-governmental groups because it exclusively settles disputes between state parties only. As the ICJ Statute Article 34, clause 1 lays down: "Only states may be parties in cases before the Court."

A. **Contentious Proceedings**

The ICJ may request "public international organisations" to submit information related to the case. This power is used by the ICJ according to Rules of the Court.[28] In the Asylum case 1950,[29] an NGO-International League for Human Rights[30] requested to the ICJ for presenting information relating to the case. The Registrar of the ICJ had turned down the request for submission of amicus curiae brief because Article 34 clause 2 of the ICJ Statute did not include NGOs within 'public international organisations.' NGOs are private international organisations; therefore, they could not be included as public international organisations. The ICJ Rules of Court, Article 69 clause 4 lays down:

> the term public international organisation denotes an international organisation of States.[31]

As far as contentious cases are concerned, NGOs are not explicitly considered as public international organisations for the purpose of submitting amicus curiae as a matter of right. However, they can still request to the Registrar for submission of written and oral statement in the contentious proceedings under the ICJ Rules of Court 1978.[32]

In the *Gabčíkovo-Nagymaros Project* 1997[33] (Danube River case), the ICJ informally accepted submission from an NGO[34] and that was International Union for Conservation of Nature (IUCN).[35] The IUCN submitted amicus curiae by its own request and the court did not invoke Articles 20 and 50 in which it can ask NGOs or any competent groups to submit their facts about the case.[36]

---

[25] UN Charter, Article 96 and ICJ Statute, Articles 65–68.

[26] Chinkin (1993).

[27] ICJ Statute, Article 62.

[28] International Court of Justice, Rules of the Court Adopted on 14 April 1978 and entered into force on 1 July 1978, *Am J Int'l L*, vol. 73, no. 3 (1979) pp. 748–782.

[29] Asylum Case (Colombia v. Peru) ICJ Report 1950, p. 266.

[30] Founded in 1942, New York. Its name was International League for the Rights of Man until 1976.

[31] International Court of Justice, Rules of Court (1978) (ICJ Rule). www.icj-cij.org/rulesofcourt (1978); UN (2020).

[32] Shelton (2007).

[33] Galcikovo-Nagymaros Project (Hungary/Slovakia), Judgement, ICJ Reports 1997, p. 7, reprint in 3 ILM 1247 (1998).

[34] Bartholomeusz (2005a, b).

[35] www.iucn.org.

[36] Okowa and Evans (1998).

B. **Advisory Proceedings**

NGOs have indirect role in the advisory proceedings of ICJ.[37] In the *International Status of South-West Africa* case 1950,[38] the NGO: International League for Human Rights (ILHR) asked permission to submit their written or oral statements in the proceedings of the court. The court allowed amicus curiae of ILHR under ICJ statute, Article 66 clause 2. But it did not include ILHR submission in court proceedings because of its delayed submission.[39]

Legality of the Threat or Use of Nuclear Weapons in Armed Conflict 1996[40] is an important case related with NGOs' amicus curiae. A number of health NGOs such as International Physicians for Prevention of Nuclear War (IPPNW),[41] World Medical Association (WMA),[42] World Federation of Public Health Association (WFPHA),[43] and International Council of Nurses (ICN)[44] are deeply concerned with public health. They are worried about the danger of nuclear weapons. Health NGOs have successfully pursued the World Health Organisation (WHO) to take appropriate initiatives for banning and elimination of nuclear weapons.

The World Justice Project[45] has also joined the campaign. They all are collectively successful in pursuing the WHO. The WHO has approached the General Assembly to seek advisory opinion of ICJ about the legality of threat or use of nuclear weapons.[46]

In the meantime, a good number of NGOs, scientists, doctors, nurses and medical associations have submitted amicus briefs to the Registrar of the ICJ. NGOs coordinated with all stakeholders and highlighted the most sought out issues through media support. They collected the signatures and representation from scientists and eminent persons and incorporated them in the amicus briefs. These documents are kept in the library of the Peace Palace in the Hague by the Registry of the Court. However, the ICJ neither recorded, nor made any reference to these amicus curiae briefs in their advisory opinion.

In 2004, the ICJ had issued Practice Directions No. XII (2004) which provide inter-alia, that when an NGO submits a written statement and/or document in advisory proceedings on its own initiative, such statement and/or document is to be treated as a publication in the public domain, and may be referred to by the States and IGOs participating in proceedings.[47]

---

[37] UN Charter, Article 96 and ICJ Statute Articles 65 and 66.

[38] International Status of South-West Africa, Advisory Opinion, ICJ Report 1950, p. 128.

[39] Clark (1981).

[40] Legality of the Use by a State of Nuclear Weapons in Armed Conflict, Advisory Opinion, ICJ Report 1996, p. 226, 35 ILM 809 (1996).

[41] www.ippnw.org.

[42] www.wma.net.

[43] www.wfpha.org.

[44] www.icn.ch.

[45] https://worldjusticeproject.org.

[46] UNGA Res. A/RES/49/75K (15 December 1994).

[47] International Court of Justice (Basic documents) *Practice Directions* No. XII, Promulgated on 30 July 2004, https://www.icj-cij.org/practice-directions.

The Practice Directions do not bring an advancement in participation of NGOs in the proceedings of the court. It only facilitates them to send their documents, memorandums and written statements to the court. These documents are neither a part of the case file nor are they considered as amicus curiae briefs. According to Nicholas Leroux:

> The instruction ostensibly is a step forward towards more participation, while it is actually nothing but a standstill.[48]

The court rarely invites NGOs in framing its opinion or making decisions. It is an inherent power of the court to control proceedings or a litigation procedure. Hence, NGOs themselves come forward to submit their amicus briefs to the Registry of the Court.

4 International Criminal Court

The Rome Statute of International Criminal Court (Rome Statute) was concluded in 1998.[49] The Rome Statute received requisite ratification of sixty state parties in 2002. Thus, International Criminal Court (ICC) came into being. At present, there are 123 state parties of the Rome Statute.

Third-party settlement of disputes via PCIJ and ICJ between States has not fully succeeded to stop wars and armed conflicts. War and armed conflicts between states and non-state actors have been going on since times immemorial. Armed forces do not observe international humanitarian law within battle grounds. So far, victors appointed their ad hoc tribunal to punish the war criminals of opponents. A permanent tribunal was proposed to try war criminals of the First World War but it could not be materialised.[50]

A. **International Military Tribunals**

In 1945, allied powers had established the Nuremberg Tribunal to try Second World War criminals of Germany.[51] The Nuremberg Tribunal Judges and Prosecutors were appointed by four allied powers, i.e. the United States, the United Kingdom, Russia and France. The trial continued for ten months, and 19 war criminals were convicted to imprisonment or death and three of them were acquitted. Besides, three organisations were found guilty and another three organisations were cleared.[52]

Similarly, the United States established the International Military Tribunal for the Far East (IMTFE) that is known as the Tokyo Tribunal. The Tokyo Tribunal consisted

---

[48] Leroux (2006).

[49] *The Rome Statute of International Criminal Court* was adopted on 17 July 1998 and entered into force on 1 July 2002, (Rome Statute), 2187 UNTS 90; *The Rules of Procedure and Evidence of Crimes*, UNDoc. PCNICC/2000/1 Add.2 (30 June, 2002).

[50] Hall (1998).

[51] Bassiouni (1998).

[52] Wright (1947).

of 11 judges, which included one from India and one from the Philippines. The Tokyo Tribunal had conducted lengthy trial of 25 accused of war crimes and some of them were punished with death sentence and others were given imprisonment. The judges were not unanimous on the award of decision. It was indeed a victors' justice.[53]

Notwithstanding all lacunae of fair trial and procedural deficiencies, Nuremberg and Tokyo Trials had had a positive legacy for years to come.[54] The international humanitarian law (IHL) was developed on war crimes and crimes against humanity. The criminals could be prosecuted and punished for their misdeeds for conducting war. It laid down the foundation of international criminal justice for protection of the innocent and civilians from the war lords.

B. **International Criminal Tribunals for Former Yugoslavia and Rwanda**

The end of Cold War in 1990s provided opportunity to the Security Council to prosecute persons responsible for violation of international humanitarian law in the former Yugoslavia.[55] The Security Council took the decisions to set forth the International Criminal Tribunal for former Yugoslavia (ICTY).[56] The Security Council had primary responsibility to maintain international peace and security (UN Charter Article 24) and to take appropriate action under Chapter VII of the Charter.

It was deemed by the Security Council that in former Yugoslavia, violations of IHL constituted danger to the international peace and security. It was therefore necessitated to appoint War Crime Commission for fact-finding. In addition, it made an appeal to all stakeholders to transmit credible information of violation of IHL and prevailing situation in former Yugoslavia. NGOs provided credible information to the commission. An NGO, Physicians for Human Rights (PHR), was engaged in the fact-finding mission of about two mass graves in Croatia.[57]

International Criminal Tribunal for Rwanda (ICTR) was established in 1994[58] by the Security Council. In Rwanda, genocide was committed by Hutu group criminals on Tutsi group. This matter was highlighted by NGOs and human rights experts.[59] Therefore, the Security Council took initiative and appointed commission of experts for enquiry about ethnic cleansing incidents in Rwanda. On the basis of findings, the Security Council proceeded and established ICTR. Initially, it was welcomed by the Rwanda government, but due to some apprehensions, it opposed the Security Council Resolution. It is interesting to know particularly at that time, Rwanda was a non-permanent member of the Security Council.

In 1995, the ICTR resumed the work with immediate effect. The headquarters was located in Arusha, Tanzania, and its trial outcome was helpful in building peace in

[53] Minear (1971).

[54] Tomuschat (2006).

[55] O'Brien (1993).

[56] United Nations Security Council Resolution (UNSC Res) 827 (25 May 1993), 32 ILM 1203 (1993).

[57] *Supra note* 55 at 642; Kerr (2004).

[58] UNSC Res. 955 (8 November 1994), 33 ILM 1602 (1994).

[59] Akhavan (1996).

Rwanda and was a deterrent to any future ethnic cleansings. NGOs provided lawyers to the prosecution as well as to the defence.

ICTY and ICTR were ad hoc tribunals and a great improvement from Nuremberg and Tokyo Trials. These ad hoc tribunals enforced the IHL in a meaningful way,[60] and they deemed rape as war crime[61] and attack on civilians as crime against humanity.[62]

C. Formation of International Criminal Court

The legacy of ad hoc tribunals was further carried on by the ICC. NGOs were continuously campaigning for creation of ICC as a permanent institution. In 1995, NGOs established Coalition for the International Criminal Court (CICC). Now it is a global network of 2,500 NGOs of 150 countries around the world.

The CICC plays three kinds of role: first, the creation of ICC, second, adoption and ratification of the Rome Statute of ICC, and third, submission of information to the prosecutor and also amicus curiae in the court proceedings. The coalition has set up a steering committee and a secretariat in The Hague. It has been receiving funds from MacArthur Foundation, Ford Foundation, The European Union, Open Society Initiative and other philanthropists.

The creation of the Court was influenced by the activism of the NGO coalition for the ICC. The coalition advocacy succeeded in attaining sixty ratifications of the Rome Statute by 2002. NGOs participated in the making of the Rome Statute. They lobbied with state representatives and submitted legal documents and suggestions. Moreover, they were engaged in ratification campaign of the Rome Statute.[63]

CICC has organised conferences bi-annually at the ICC secretariat along with state parties of ICC. It oversees the working of the court upholding the principles of the Rome Statute. In addition, it helps in capacity-building of its coalition partners about IHL, international crime, courts, procedure and evidence. Internet facilitates NGOs to establish networks with their counterparts of the developing countries.[64] They seek worldwide support for the ICC.

NGOs broadened horizon of ICC for maintenance of international peace and security and to protect human rights and implement IHL. They emphasise on global justice as they campaign: 'No Peace without Justice' since 1995.[65]

ICC jurisdiction is limited to the most serious crimes which are concerned with the international community as a whole.[66] These crimes are: crimes of genocide, crimes against humanity, war crimes and crime of aggression.[67] The jurisdiction is applicable on crimes committed only after the establishment of ICC in 2002.

---

60 Akhavan et al (1998), Szpak (2013).

61 Adams (2018).

62 Sterio and Scharf (2019).

63 Haddad (2013), Lee (1999), Welch and Watkins (2011).

64 Pearson (2006), Struett (2008).

65 www.npwj.org.

66 Crawford (2019).

67 Rome Statute, Articles, 6–8.

The jurisdiction is applicable on state parties on the basis of territorial or personal level.[68] ICC is at work in The Hague with its judges, prosecutors and the registry office for smooth and efficient conduct of the court proceedings. The Preparatory Commission drafted the Rules of Procedure and Evidence[69] and also Elements of Crimes.[70]

D. The ICC Prosecutor

The office of the prosecutor takes initiative for investigation of international crimes. The office shall select the cases or situation for investigation and prosecution, if needed before the ICC. The Prosecutor shall be independent, impartial and mindful with the objectives and guided by legal criteria of the Rome Statute of ICC.[71] The Prosecutor shall receive information from Security Council, IGOs, NGOs or any other reliable sources related with crimes against humanity or war crimes.[72] The Prosecutor shall seek approval from Pre-Trail Chamber of ICC for carrying out investigation with the jurisdiction of the ICC.

The Prosecutor shall undertake the most serious criminal cases like genocide, crimes against humanity, destruction of the national, ethnic and religious groups and systematic attack directed against civilian population. In addition, there shall be compelling evidence to investigate and to prosecute alleged criminals. So far, prosecutor investigation of collateral damage to the civilian population has been conducted for former Yugoslavia and Iraq.

NGO's influence on humanatarian law has increased since 1990s. Their role in gathering information about collateral damage is acknowledged by the Prosecutor. NGOs parameter of zero tolerance of collateral damage of life and property of civilians is practically not workable in situations of armed conflicts,[73] because armed conflicts are bound to have civilian casualty and loss of property. The core issue is how to minimise and how to prevent civil casualty and destruction of property. Therefore, it is necessary to make plans and policy to save the lives of non-combatants.

E. ICC Proceedings

NGOs also appear as amicus curiae before ICC proceedings. The Rome Statute Article 44 clause 4 provides:

> The court may, in exceptional circumstances, employ the expertise of gratis personnel offered by State Parties, Inter-governmental Organisations or Non-governmental Organisations to assist with the work of any of the organs of the court. The Prosecutor may accept any such

---

[68] Schabas (2020).

[69] The Rules of Procedure and Evidence of Crime, *supra note*, 49.

[70] The Elements of Crimes, UNDOC/PCNICC/2000/1/Add.2 (30 June 2002), Available at https://www.refworld.org/docid/4ff5dd7d2.html.

[71] ICC: Office of the Prosecutor, Policy paper on case selection and prioritisation (ICC), 15 September 2016, available at: https://doi.org/10.1017/ilm.2018.49.

[72] Rome Statute, Article 15(2).

[73] Galvin (2005).

offer on behalf of the Office of the Prosecutor. Such gratis personnel shall be employed in accordance with guidelines to be established by the Assembly of State Parties.[74]

The Assembly of State Parties (ASP) adopted the Rules of Procedure and Evidence of ICC (2002) and further elaborated NGOs participation in the ICC proceedings as amicus curiae.[75] The Chambers of ICC invite NGOs to submit any observation, in oral and written form, on issues related with the case. NGOs amicus shall be filed before the Registry of the court within the stipulated time frame. The expedited proceedings of the court is an essential element of fair justice and economic prudence.

ICC Rules of Procedure and Evidence do not require clarification on content and interest in the case, unlike ICTY and ICTR proceedings. NGOs amicus curiae are made available to the Prosecutor and the defendant to respond to these observations. It is up to the discretion of the Chambers of ICC either to admit the NGOs amicus submission or to disregard it.[76]

The core idea of amicus curiae submission is the assistance in the determined case by an independent and impartial manner. Sarah Williams and Emma Palmer have identified certain limitations of NGOs amicus curiae submission before the chambers of ICC. These limitations are: (1) amicus is not a party of the case; (2) amicus curiae does not form part of the case unless accepted by the chamber; (3) if amicus curiae is rejected by the chamber of ICC then there are no records of who submitted the amicus and what the contents of it are.

An NGO's participation as amicus before ICC depends upon the discretionary nature of the international adjudication system. It provides an opportunity to NGOs to submit their legal observation. So far, they have been quite successful in their endeavour which highlighted gender justice and other issues as a war crime. Amicus based on the NGOs neutrality and field experience have stimulated the international criminal justice.[77] But their amicus submissions are determined by the chamber of the ICC.[78]

Judge Mauro Politi of the ICC has appreciated the role played by NGOs during its formation, its institutionalisation and the working of the court.[79] The ICC is a great hope of justice for international community. It deters, prosecutes and punishes the accused who committed crimes against humanity. At present, 123 countries are parties of ICC Rome Statute. But still major powers are least enthusiastic in associating and extending their support to the ICC.

In 2017, the word 'aggression' was dropped from ICC jurisdictions. NGO's Coalition for ICC has repeatedly stressed the importance of Rome Statute. They are

---

[74] *Rome Statute*, legal un.org/icc/ii_corr/estatute.

[75] Rule 103, *Rules of Procedure and Evidence of ICC*, Official Records of the Assembly of States Parties to the Rome Statute of International Criminal Court, First Session, New York, 3–10 September 2002, 2nd edn, ICC Publications, The Hague 2013; ICC-ASP/1/3 and Corr 1, part II.A (2002); Available at: www.icc.cpi.int/pids.

[76] Williams and Palmer (2016).

[77] Lohne (2019).

[78] Rules of Procedure and Evidence of ICC, Rule 103.

[79] Politi (2004).

engaged with the affected communities and established a Victim Rights Working Group to provide support to participate in the court proceedings.[80]

5 The International Tribunal for the Law of the Sea

The United Nations Convention on the Law of the Sea (UNCLOS) was adopted in 1982 and came into force in 1994. The UNCLOS has established legal regime over the oceans which covers all human activities, multiple uses of seas, delimitation of maritime boundaries, marine environment, freedom of shipping and settlement of maritime disputes.[81] The International Tribunal for the Law of the Sea (ITLOS) is an integral part of UNCLOS. It started functioning in 1996 in Hamburg, Germany.

Settlement of a dispute is prescribed under UNCLOS based on free choice of parties.[82] When parties are unable to choose a means for settlement of disputes freely, then, third-party dispute settlement procedure shall become mandatory. UNCLOS part XV, section 2 lays down outline of the compulsory dispute settlement procedure.[83] This procedure includes: (1) ITLOS, (2) ICJ, (3) Arbitration Tribunal and (4) Special Arbitration Tribunal. The UNCLOS provides an alternative choice for the parties, to settle sea disputes. It repeats the role of the ICJ and International Arbitration Tribunal as usual, apart from ITLOS and the Special Arbitral Tribunal. Perhaps, it would be better to present a single judicial institution—ITLOS instead of more confusing alternatives as provided under Part XV of the UNCLOS.[84]

A. **Jurisdiction**

The ITLOS has jurisdiction over sea disputes relating to fisheries, shipping, marine environment, marine scientific research, vessels-source pollution, dumping, mining and maritime boundary disputes. It has jurisdiction to the interpretation and application of the UNCLOS. State Parties have access to ITLOS. However, the Seabed Disputes Chamber (SBDC) of ITLOS is allowed to entertain the individuals and corporations in disputes related to deep seabed mining, beyond the limit of national jurisdiction under Part XI of the UNCLOS.

The limits and exceptions of ITLOS jurisdiction have been laid down under articles 297 and 298, with respect to military activities, historical bays and titles and situations in which Security Council exercises its powers. In addition, ITLOS jurisdiction is restricted to fisheries and marine scientific research in the 200 miles exclusive

[80] Evenson (2020).

[81] The *United Nations Convention on the Law of the Sea (UNCLOS): Official Text*, UN Publications, New York 1983, http://www.un.org/depts/los/convention-agreements/texts/unclos/unclos.pdf, signed on December 1982 and came into force on 16 November 1994.

[82] Klein (2005), United Nations (2007).

[83] UNCLOS, Article 286.

[84] Charney (1996), Boyle (1997).

economic zones (EEZ) because these matters lie in the coastal States discretionary powers.[85]

Jurisdiction of the ITLOS is extended primarily over the state parties of UNCLOS.[86] Any state party may accept ITLOSs jurisdiction by declaration or by an agreement. ITLOS enjoys mandatory jurisdiction in matters related to the prompt release of vessels and its crew which are detained by the coastal state.[87] Individuals on behalf of the flag of nation of the ship may make the application for prompt release of vessels and its crew.[88] An individual access to ITLOS is possible only though the flag of nation authorisation. There is a different approach, altogether, in SBDC beyond the limit of national jurisdiction cases related to the deep seabed mining.[89]

B. **NGO Participation**

The law of the sea is primarily state centric, but it cannot totally ignore non-state actors or NGOs. The International Seabed Authority (ISA) which governs the deep seabed has endowed observer status to 30 non-governmental organisations[90] under Rule 82 para 1(e) of its Rules of Procedure.[91] NGOs such as Greenpeace International, World Wide Fund for Nature (WWF), Centre for Seafarers' Rights, International Association of Drilling Contractors, International Ocean Institute and The Law of the Sea Institute and many more are closely associated with the authority. NGOs formed Deep Sea Conservation Coalition and are fighting for the protection of deep seabed from adverse mining activities.

In the beginning of ITLOS, since 1996, NGOs were not included in the judicial proceedings. ITLOS carried out its judicial functions through its four chambers: (1) Summary Procedure, (2) Fisheries Disputes, (3) Marine Environment Disputes and (4) Maritime Delimitation Disputes. Most of the cases have been related to the prompt release of vessels, its crew and provisional measures. Remaining few cases were of maritime boundary disputes, fisheries, marine environment, navigational rights and advisory opinions.

The Responsibilities and Obligations of States' Sponsoring Persons and Entities with Respect to Activities in the Area case, 2011, was the turning point of submission of NGO's amicus curiae.[92] ITLOS has adopted the Rules of Procedure persuading

---

[85] Noyes (1999).

[86] UNCLOS, Article 91 and Annex VI, and *Statute of the ITLOS*, Article 21(1).

[87] UNCLOS, Article 292(1) & (2).

[88] Adede (1987).

[89] Treves (2019).

[90] Guidelines for observer status of non-governmental organisations with the International Seabed Authority, ISBA/25/A/7/(4June2019).

[91] *Rules of Procedure of the Assembly of the International Sea Bed Authority*, adopted on 28 July 1994.

[92] *Responsibilities and Obligations of States Sponsoring Persons and Entities with Respect to Activities in the Area*, 1 February, 2011, Advisory Opinion of the Sea-bed Dispute Chamber for the ITLOS, available at https://www.itlos.org/fileadmin/itlos/documents/cases/case_no_17/17_adv_op_010211_en.pdf, last visited 22.04.2021; ITLOS, Case No.17 (2011) ITLOS Reports 10.

Article 16 of Annex VI of the UNCLOS. The ITLOS enjoys the jurisdiction in contentious as well as advisory cases.

Article 133 of the Rules of Procedure lays down advisory jurisdiction[93] of the SBDC which relate to deep seabed mining activities. The ISA requested the ITLOS for advisory opinion on responsibilities and liabilities for international seabed mining of the private entities and sponsored states. That issue was raised by Nauru and Tonga in the ISA to fix the responsibilities of private entities and sponsored states about the consequences of deep seabed mining near their maritime boundaries. This matter falls within the domain of the SBDC.

Seabed Disputes Chamber of the ITLOS, started the proceedings and called for opinion of all state parties and three IGOs-UNEP,[94] Interoceanmetal Joint Organisation (IOM)[95] and IUCN.[96] Seabed Chamber did not solicit NGOs to submit their briefs. However, Greenpeace International[97] and World Wild Fund for Nature[98] requested Seabed Chamber to submit amicus curiae briefs in advisory opinion case. The ITLOS Statutes and Rules of Procedure are silent whether they allow or not allow NGOs' amicus curiae briefs. ICJ did not encourage NGOs for amicus curiae brief in its case proceedings. While WTO-Dispute Panel and Human Rights monitoring Bodies welcome NGOs submission of amicus curiae briefs.

Responsibilities and *Obligations* case was a perfect occasion to deal with the potentiality of NGOs amicus curiae submission before the ITLOS proceedings. The aforesaid case is related with deep seabed mining activities.[99] Deep seabed is recognised as a common heritage of mankind.[100] It is not restricted with the interest of state parties, IGOs and corporations; moreover, it is concerned with the well-being of the international community. Therefore, Greenpeace International and WWF submitted amicus curiae brief to the Registry of the ITLOS in the *Responsibilities and Obligations* case proceedings before SBDC.

The President of the ITLOS has inherent rights to accept unsolicited amicus from the NGOs in order to check flood gate of private persons and corporations' briefs.

In this case, ITLOS accepted Greenpeace and WWF's amicus briefs. These NGOs were informed that their document contents were not part of case file. Hence, amicus documents were posted on a separate section of the Tribunal's website.[101] It served the purpose of NGOs, ITLOS and the related parties of the case. Scholars and activists

---

[93] ITLOS, Rules of the Tribunal, 25 March 2021, available at http://www.itlos.org/fileadmin/itlos/documents/basic_texts/ITLOS_8_25.03.21.pdf visited 23 April 2021.

[94] www.unep.org, UN special programme founded in 1972. It headquarter is located Nairobi, Kenya.

[95] https://iom.gov.pl, founded in 1987. Its headquarter is located in Poland. It is an inter governmental organisation of European nations.

[96] www.iucn.org, founded in 1948, Its headquarter in Gland, Switzerland. IUCN is a hybrid organisation consisting memberships of private citizens, states, NGOs and scientists.

[97] https://www.greenpeace.org.

[98] www.panda.org.

[99] UNCLOS, Part XI: The International Sea Bed Area, Responsibilities and Obligations of the States, ITLOS, Case No.17 (2011), *supra note* 92.

[100] Holmila (2005), Lodge (2012).

[101] Dolidze (2013).

made comments on the amicus briefs that enriched the ITLOS case proceedings and its decision-making. This opened the opportunity for NGOs to use their long experience and expertise in the proceedings within the ITLOS Chambers.

Another important occasion related to NGO's participation in ITLOS proceeding as amicus curiae was the *Sub-Regional Fisheries Commission* (SRFC) case 2015.[102] As per the past practice, NGOs are at liberty to submit amicus curiae on their own initiatives. In SRFC case, WWF submitted amicus curiae to the Registry of ITLOS. It was allowed but further oral statements in the proceedings of the case were discouraged.

Notwithstanding, WWF remained active and communicated their views and information to the ITLOS and other parties of the case.

The NGO, Greenpeace navigated the vessel named Arctic Sunrise, bearing the national flag of the Netherlands. It wanted information about marine environment from Russian EEZ in 2013. Russia detained the vessel and its crew. The Netherlands approached the tribunal for prompt release of the vessel and its crew under Article 292. The ITLOS ordered to release the vessel and its crew. ITLOS's decision relied on traditional tool of diplomatic protection rather than a human rights issue and it protected all crew members, irrespective of their nationality.[103]

6 WTO Adjudicative Body

The World Trade Organisation (WTO) provided a Dispute Settlement Understanding in the Final Act of Uruguay Round 1994.[104] WTO-Dispute Settlement Procedure consists of two tiers (1) Panels and (2) Appellate Body. The WTO Adjudicative Body is an inter-state system; therefore, NGOs have no locus standi. In other words, the NGOs cannot be a party in the case before the Panel or Appellate Body.

Since the days of General Agreement of Tariffs and Trade (GATT): 1947–1994, NGOs have been demanding transparency and information to people about the details of trade negotiations and adjudication.[105] Initially, WTO also followed secrecy protocols in their dispute settlement procedures and hence did not allow NGOs amicus curiae briefs.[106]

[102] Request for an Advisory Opinion submitted by Sub-Regional Fisheries Commission, Advisory Opinion, 2 April 2015, ITLOS Reports, p. 4 (Case No. 21); Freestone (2016), Gautier (2014).

[103] The Arctic Sunrise Case (Netherlands v. Russia), file 2013–2017. Case No. 22; Rieter (2014).

[104] Final Act of the Uruguay Round of Trade Negotiations, 33 ILM 1994 1125; 1867 UNTS 3; WTO (2017).

[105] Charnovitz (1996, 2000).

[106] WTO Adjudicating Body is working since 10 January 1995 and no amicus curiae briefs were submitted by NGOs, upto 1998.

In *US Shrimp-Turtle* case 1998, NGOs—Centre for International Environmental Law,[107] Centre for Marine Conservation,[108] The Environmental Foundation Ltd.,[109] The Philippine Ecological Network, Inc. (PENI),[110] Red Nacional de Acción Ecologista (RENACE),[111] World Wildlife Fund for Nature (WWF),[112] Greenpeace International[113] and Foundation for International Environmental Law and Development[114]—had submitted amicus curiae briefs. These briefs were rejected by the Panel because they had not 'sought' them.[115] The WTO-Dispute Settlement Understanding (DSU), Article 13 clause 1 provides:

> Each Panel shall have the right to seek information and technical advice from any individual or body which it deems appropriate.[116]

The Appellate Body had overruled the decision of the Panel regarding amicus briefs' admissibility. The Appellate Body observed:

> Authority to seek information is not properly equated with a prohibition on accepting information which has been submitted without having been requested by a panel. A panel has the discretionary authority either to accept and consider or to reject information and advice submitted to it, whether requested by a panel or not.[117]

Two business associations[118] had submitted briefs in *US-Lead & Bismuth II* case[119] to the Panel, after its second meeting. The Panel refused to admit amicus briefs on the basis that they were submitted untimely.

The Appellate Body has allowed business amicus briefs under Rule 16 para 1 of the Working Procedures for Appellate Review. DSU Article 17 clause 9 authorises the Appellate Body to lay down its own working procedure.[120] However, Appellate Body did not elaborately draw the Rules of Working Procedures.[121] Because Rules of

---

[107] https://www.ciel.org/about-us, founded in 1989 in the United States with offices in Washington DC and Geneva.

[108] http://www.cmc-ocean.org/

[109] https://www.efl.lk, founded in 1981 in the Sri Lanka, and office in Colombo, Sri Lanka.

[110] 33 1LM173 (1994).

[111] https://renace.net, founded in 1984 in Argentina.

[112] Www.panda.org founded in 1961, office in Gland, Switzerland.

[113] www.greenpeace.org/international, founded in 1969, in Canada. At present, office in Amsterdam, Netherlands.

[114] http://www.field.org.uk, established in 1989 in Britain with office in London.

[115] Marceau and Stilwell (2001).

[116] 33 ILM 1125 (1994) www.wto.org/dispute/dsu.

[117] US-Shrimp Case 1998, Appellate Body Report, WT/DS58/AB/R, paras 108–110.

[118] The American Iron and Steel Institute and Speciality Steel Industry of North America.

[119] Appellate Body Report, Panel Report on United States—Imposition of Countervailing Duties on certain Hot-Rolled Lead and Bismuth Carbon Steel Products Originating in the United Kingdom (US-Lead & Bismuth II), WT/DS138/R, para 6.2; WT/DS138/AB/R, (10 May 2000) paras 39–42.

[120] Working Procedure for Appellate Review, WTO, Geneva 2003, revised on 26 July 2010; https://unctad.org/docs.

[121] WTO-Dispute Settlement Understanding_Legal Text, https://www.wto.org/english/dsu_e.

Procedure shall be approved by the Chairman of Dispute Settlement Body, consisting of WTO Members and the Director General of WTO.

A. **State Discontentment against Amicus Curiae**

The Appellate Body overruled the decision of the panels in the *US Shrimp-Turtle* case (1998) and the *US-Lead & Bismuth II* case (1999) and allowed amicus. It sparked discontentment among WTO member states, particularly, developing nations. They were demanding the special sessions of the WTO General Council to discuss DSU and civil society and NGOs intervention in the Panel and Appellate Body proceedings.

In 2000, General Council's special session was held, in which members expressed their views on amicus curiae submissions.[122] The member's intention was to reaffirm the mandate of each constituent elements of the multilateral trading system.[123] The members emphasised Adjudicative Body's scope related to trade disputes between states to resolve their rights and obligations under the provisions of WTO regime.[124] Private persons, corporations and NGOs have little scope in the WTO's adjudicating proceedings.[125] The emphasis on extending standing to NGOs in the WTO Adjudicating Body's proceedings is due to writers and authors recognising their significant role in world affairs.

Overwhelming members of the WTO criticised the Panels and the Appellate Body for accepting and considering NGOs and civil society amicus briefs.[126] Developing nations—India, Egypt, Brazil, Uruguay, Mexico and Costa Rica[127]—have expressed their discontentment. On the other side, the United States supported the Appellate Body decision to entertain amicus briefs of NGOs within the ambit of Dispute Settlement Understanding.[128]

Earlier Dispute Settlement Body would be composed only of WTO state members. At the time of accepting Appellate Body Report on *US Shrimp-Turtle* case 1998, some states also objected to receiving NGOs' amicus briefs because those were in contravention of Article 19 clause 2 of the DSU.[129] The developing countries found that it was contrary to the DSU of the WTO, and it gave more rights to non-members in comparison to member states.

In addition, it overburdened the Adjudicative Body and disputed parties. The member state did not resolve the question of NGOs participation in WTO Adjudicative Body as an amicus curiae. Notwithstanding, NGO's participation as amicus curiae has continued.

---

[122] WTO General Council, *Minutes of General Council Meeting*, held on 22 November, 2000, WT/GC/M/60, 23 January 2001.

[123] El Khoury (2012).

[124] Dispute Settlement Understanding of WTO, Article 1 para 1; Reinisch and Irgel (2001).

[125] Shell (1995).

[126] Umbricht (2001).

[127] *Minutes of General Council Meeting*, supra note 122.

[128] Ibid., p. 74.

[129] Bartholomeusz (2005a, b).

In *Softwood Lumber* case,[130] NGOs submitted an amicus brief but neither the part in dispute nor a third-party state subscribed to their views or raised them in their arguments. Therefore, the Appellate Body ultimately did not admit these NGO's amicus briefs while rendering its decision. The Appellate Body was shy of explaining the reasons for not accepting unsolicited amicus brief.[131]

B. **State's Ambivalence about NGO's Participation as Amicus Curiae**[132]

International trade law cases are complicated in nature and thus require expert knowledge to pursue them in the Adjudicating Body. Especially, developing economies and small countries face deficiency of requisite knowledge, research, skills and resources.

DSU, Article 27 clause 2 provides that additional legal advice and assistance with respect to dispute settlement may be provided by the secretariat to members of developing countries. On the basis of a Venezuelan proposal,[133] an Advisory Centre on WTO Law (ACWL) was created in 2001. ACWL is an IGO and has far-reaching consequences in the working of Adjudicating Body,[134] because ACWL provides subsidised legal services to the developing countries. It has enhanced the access to the WTO Adjudicating Body. ACWL has provided support in 38 WTO Adjudicating Body proceedings between 2001 and 2011.[135] The WTO trade regime, possessing an in-built fair and balanced structure, received further reinforcement through the ACWL, which provides valuable legal advice. It has succeeded in addressing the deficiency of legal knowledge of the developing countries and hence raised their confidence.

State preference on NGO's access as amicus curiae is one of the reasons in the enhancement of developing countries' capacity. Theresa Squatrito has measured state preference of NGOs' access as amicus on the basis of four hypotheses, i.e. (1) sovereign costs, (2) commitment to democratic norms, (3) learning from IGOs and (4) legal capacity.[136] Based on the sensibility of states about its sovereign integrity, strong democratic traditions, cross learning between IGOs and NGOs and quality of legal personnel, their viewpoint was to tolerate and accept NGOs participation as amicus curiae before proceedings of the Adjudicating Body. Therefore, they never made any amendments to either the DSU or Rules of Procedure of Adjudicating Body. Over the years, they acquired legal capacity[137] and received requisite support from ACWL.

C. **Practice of Amicus Curiae before Panels and Appellate Body**

---

[130] United States—Final Countervailing Duty Determination with Respect to Certain Softwood Lumber from Canada (*Softwood Lumber-257 Case*) WT/DS257/AB/R (19 January 2004).

[131] Lim (2005).

[132] Squatrito (2012).

[133] Van der Borght (1999).

[134] Chad (2009), Shaffer and Melendez-Ortiz (2010).

[135] Shaffer (2011).

[136] Theresa Squatrito, *supra note* 132, pp. 179–182.

[137] De Carvalho and Canesin (2018).

A total number of 600 disputes have been brought before the panels and Appellate Body between 1995 and 2020. Out of these, 350 disputes have been decided so far and the remaining 250 are in the pipeline.[138]

There are 148 amicus-actors who participated in the proceedings before Panels and Appellate Body. Among them, there are 66 NGOs, 18 institutes, 13 individuals, 32 businesses, 8 labour representatives and 11 unknown actors.[139] NGOs are leading actors as amicus curiae and occupy more than half the space. Institutes are either of research or academia, individuals are either academic or scientists and trade unions having close proximity with NGOs because they are pursuing public interest, common good and welfare of the working class. Remaining 43 are representatives of corporations and business world who pursue value addition and profit.

There were total 98 amicus briefs submitted before the proceedings of Panels and Appellate Body during 1998–2014. NGOs submitted 38 amicus curiae briefs out of 98, remaining 60 were submitted by businesses and others. Amicus briefs submitted by NGOs are 21 before the Panel proceedings and remaining 17 are before the Appellate Body.[140] These amicus brief of NGOs are related to sustainable development,[141] protection of environment,[142] conservation of nature,[143] promotion of public health,[144] human rights[145] and morality[146] as a linkage with International trade regime.

There are some basic differences between NGOs and business associations' amicus submissions. NGOs are more concerned about human rights, public health, sustainable development, fairness and moral values, while business associations are concerned with anti-dumping, subsidies and countervailing measures.[147] The prime concerns of the WTO Adjudicating Body, i.e. states' interest and promotion of world trade, are perhaps balanced by NGOs perception of public interest.

D. Revamping the Adjudicating Body

The WTO Adjudicating Body has successfully completed 25 years of its journey, but at present it has virtually become defunct for want of Judges. The Appellate Body comprises seven members or judges, but lack of consensus among States has deprived it of selecting judges. Some writers suggested that the Appellate Body should revamp its procedure, keeping in mind the short deadlines, maximum length of amicus brief, restricting amicus brief to legal arguments only and right of state parties to respond

---

[138] www.wto.org.

[139] Squatrito (2018).

[140] Ibid., p. 89.

[141] Tanaka (2003).

[142] Appellate Body Report, Brazil-Retreated Tyres, WT/DS332/AB/R (3 December 2007).

[143] Appellate Body Report, EC-Sardines, WT/DS231/AB/R (26 September 2002).

[144] Appellate Body Report, EC-Asbestos, WT/DS/135/AB/R (12 March 2001).

[145] Appellate Body Report, EC-Seal Products, WT/DS401/AB/R (22 May 2014).

[146] Appellate Body Report, China-Publication and Audio Visual Report, WT/DS363/AB/R (21 December 2009).

[147] Charwat (2016).

to amicus briefs.[148] Moreover, Panels and Appellate Body are not, in a strict sense, a court of law but redressal fora to settle trade disputes.[149] In the WTO and outside of the WTO, dialogue is going on with the major world powers to build a consensus towards selection of Appellate Body judges for its smooth functioning.

7 International Centre for Settlement of Investment Disputes

Post-World War II, there was a pressing need to improve the climate of investment for reconstruction of Europe and to develop the newly independent states of Asia and Africa. The Convention on the Settlement of Investment Disputes between States and Nationals of Other States (ICSID convention) was concluded on 18 March 1965. It came into force in 1966.[150]

The ICSID convention established the International Centre for Settlement of Investment Disputes (ICSID). The World Bank President is a non-voting Chairman of ICSID, and it is governed by the administrative council. The Secretary General is elected by the administrative council for five years. Each member state has one representative in the administrative council.[151] ICSID has maintained the Panels of conciliators and arbitrators. Every member state has to nominate individuals for the Panels of conciliators and arbitrators, and the members are expert on international investment law.[152]

ICSID is an autonomous body in its adjudicating and conciliatory functions. The main objective of ICSID is to amicably settle investment disputes between states and nationals of other states. It facilitates conciliation and arbitration procedure for the settlement of investment disputes.

A. Jurisdiction

The ICSID convention mentions the jurisdiction under Article 25: *The Jurisdiction shall extend to any legal dispute arising directly out of an investment, between a Contracting State and a national of another contracting State.* Any contracting state at the time of ratification of the convention or any time thereafter can notify or accept jurisdiction of the Centre. There should be consent by both parties in writing. Parties to the disputes cannot withdraw or denounce unilaterally from this jurisdiction once they accept it.[153] ICSID shall apply the law of the contracting state party to the

[148] Lance Bartholomeusz, *supra note* 34, p. 261.

[149] Howse (2016).

[150] The Convention on the Settlement of Investment Disputes Between States and National of the Other States (ICSID Convention) Opened for signature 27 August 1965, entered into force 14 October 1966, 757 UNTS 159; 4 ILM 524 (1965).

[151] ICSID Convention, Articles 4–8.

[152] Parra (2012).

[153] Masood (1972).

dispute (including its rules on the conflict of laws) and such rules of international law as may be applicable.[154]

B. Evaluation of ICSID

In the beginning of ICSID, developing countries were suspicious of ratification of the convention. The hesitation of African, Asian and Latin American states resulted in the slow pace of functioning of the Centre.[155]

In the early years, only few cases were brought before the ICSID, and the first case was registered in 1972. Since then, nearly 600 cases have been concluded by the centre.[156] The ICSID arbitral tribunal's award is final and binding on the parties. The ICSID began well with three cases: *MINE v. Guinea*,[157] *B&B v. Congo*[158] and *LIAMCO v. Libya*.[159] These were decided by the ICSID and their decisions have been complied by the parties.[160] This was an encouragement to ICSID dispute settlement system and also a parameter of its effectiveness.[161]

The ICSID has acquired the worldwide acceptance. At present, there are 163 signatories. Out of these, 155 states have ratified the convention.[162] Ethiopia, Russia and Thailand have signed the convention, but their ratification is in awaited. Whereas Brazil, India and South Africa are reluctant in accepting the convention, Bolivia (2007), Ecuador (2010) and Venezuela (2012) have denunciated or withdrawn from the convention.[163] Denunciation of the ICSID convention does not produce immediate consequences except only for withdrawing states.[164]

C. Amicus Curiae Participation of NGOs

NGOs do not have direct access as a party to disputes in the ICSID. However, they are allowed to participate as non-dispute party before the ICSID arbitral tribunals' proceedings as amicus curiae. Some authors pursue protection of NGO funds in host state beyond their administrative and judicial mechanism.[165] The major portion of NGO funds is generated from private donors. Therefore, it is necessary to protect NGO funds like corporate funds in host States and at an international level.[166]

---

[154] ICSID Convention, Article 42(1); Mackenzie (1993).

[155] Gopal (1982).

[156] Icsid.worldbank.org/concludedcases.

[157] MINE v Guinea, 21 ILM 1355 (1982).

[158] B&B v Congo, 20 ILM 878 (1981).

[159] LIAMCO v. Libya, 62 ILR 140 (1982).

[160] ICSID Convention, Article 53(1).

[161] Delaume (1983).

[162] https://icsid.worldbank.org/database of ICSID Member States/list of contracting states and other signatories of the convention.

[163] ICSID Convention Articles 71 and 75, worldbank.org/denunciation.

[164] Lazo (2014)

[165] Büthe et al. (2012).

[166] G. W. MacKenzie, *supra note* 154, pp. 222–223.

International investment[167] has far-reaching impact on public interests, human rights, environment, public health, morality and labour. Therefore, it is directly connected with NGOs' concerns. However, only recently have NGOs become involved with international investment tribunals.

The *Methanex* case[168] was the first instance when NGOs participated before international investment arbitration as amicus curiae. The *Methanex* case was related to NAFTA Chap. 11 proceedings. The Arbitral Tribunal had decided that it had powers under Article 15 clause 1 subclause 3 of the UNCITRAL Rules and under NAFTA Chap. 11 section B to accept amicus curiae briefs submitted by non-governmental organisations.[169] NGOs[170] such as Communities for a Better Environment,[171] International Institute of Sustainable Development,[172] The Earth Island Institute,[173] The Center for International Environmental Law[174] and Bluewater Network[175] submitted amicus curiae briefs related to public concerns.

ICSID started working from 1972, but amicus curiae brief was allowed for the first time in the *Vivendi* case in 2005.[176] There were five NGOs—Associations Civil por la Igualdad y la Justicia (ACIJ),[177] Centro de Estudios Legales y Sociales (CELS),[178] Centre for International Environmental Law (CIEL),[179] Consumidores Libres Cooperativa Limitada de Provisión de Servicios de Acción Comunitarias/amparo (SAIJ)[180] and La Unión de Usuarios y Consumidores,[181] that submitted amicus curiae as non-dispute party. ICSID arbitral tribunal allowed an amicus brief in proceedings of the case under Article 44 of the ICSID convention. Courts and tribunals possess inherent power to regulate their procedures, thereby enabling the participation of NGOs as amicus curiae even without explicit authorization in a statute. In addition,

---

[167] Nature of cases in ICSID—Oil, gas & mining 25%, electrical power & energy 12%, transport 11%, finance services 7%, water, sanitation & flood protection 6% and others 39%; https://icsid.worldbank.org/icsidcaseload.

[168] Methanex v. US case (1999–2005), Filed 3 December 1999; Constitution of Tribunal 18 May 2000; accepting of amicus curiae 15 January 2001; partial award on jurisdiction 7 August 2002; Final award 3 August 2005. Available online: https://www.italaw.com/cases/683.

[169] Dumberry (2001).

[170] Methanex v. US case, Decision of the Tribunal on petitions from Third Persons to Intervene as "amicus curiae", Order on 15 January 2001, Washington DC, Para 3, https://www.itlaw.com/sites/default/files/case-documents/ita0517_0.pdf.

[171] www.cbecal.org, founded 1978, office in San Francisco, US.

[172] www.iisd.org, established 1990, office in Winnipeg, Canada.

[173] https://www.earthisland.org, founded 1982, office in San Francisco, US.

[174] https://www.ciel.org, founded 1989, offices in Washington DC and Geneva.

[175] https://foe.org, Bluewater Network have merged with the Friends of the Earth International.

[176] Vivendi case, ICSID case No. ARB/03/19 (2005) 19 May 2005, Award 30 July 2010, Order in response to a petition for transparency and participation as amicus curiae, pp. 342–350.

[177] https://acij.org.ar, founded in 2002, Argentina.

[178] https://www.cels.org.ar, established in 1979, Argentina.

[179] https://www.ciel.org, founded 1989, Washington DC, US.

[180] https://www.saij.gob.ar, founded in 1998, Argentina.

[181] https://www.launionuyc.org.ar, established in 1994, Argentina.

the tribunal explicitly referred to the *Methanex* case's interpretation of Article 15 of the UNCITRAL Rules in which participation of NGOs was allowed as amicus curiae.[182]

The ICSID Arbitration Rules were amended in 2006.[183] The new Rule 37 para 2 provides:

> After consulting both parties the tribunal may allow a person or entity that is not a party to the dispute (non-disputing party) to file written submission with the tribunal regarding a matter within the scope of the dispute.

In the *Biwater Gauff* case,[184] the ICSID tribunal had implemented the decision of *Vivendi* case and newly inserted Rule 37 para 2 of the ICSID Regulations and Rules.[185] Five NGOs: (1) The Lawyers' Environmental Action Team (LEAT),[186] (2) Legal and Human Rights Centre (LHRC),[187] (3) Tanzania Gender Networking Programme (TGNP),[188] (4) Center for International Environmental Law (CIEL)[189] and (5) International Institute for Sustainable Development (IISD)[190] submitted a petition to file amicus curiae brief in the proceedings of the case.

ICSID tribunal issued Procedural Order No.5, and granting opportunity to file a written submission in the arbitral proceedings, pursuant to ICSID Rule 37 para 2.[191] But they were not allowed to access arbitration documents,[192] not be present in the hearing[193] and submit only written briefs.[194]

The aforesaid five NGOs jointly filed their amicus curiae brief before the arbitral tribunal and highlighted human rights and sustainable development concerns.[195]The decision of the *Biwater* case reiterates the rule established in the *Vivendi* case, specifically Rule 17, para 2.[196] The decision also explained that NGOs as non-disputing party only have procedural rights to submit amicus and did not enjoy substantive rights unlike parties of dispute.

---

182 De Brabandere (2011); Rules of Procedure for Arbitration Proceedings (Arbitration Rules) available at: icsid.worldbank.org.

183 *ICSID Convention, Regulations and Rules*, Washington DC, ICSID/15, 2006, pp. 1–128, available online at https://icsid.worldbank.org.

184 Biwater Gauff (Tanzania) Ltd. v. United Republic of Tanzania, ICSID case No. ARB/05/22, Procedural order No. 5 (2 February 2007) 46 ILM 572 (2007).

185 Levine (2011).

186 https://leat.or.tz, established in 1994, office in Dar es Salaam, Tanzania.

187 https://www.humanrights.or.tz founded in 1995, office in Dares Salaam, Tanzania.

188 https://tgnp.or.tz established in 1993, office in Dar es Salaam, Tanzania.

189 https://www.ciel.org, founded in 1989, office in Washington DC, US.

190 www.iisd.org, founded in 1990, Winnipeg, Canada, Office in Toronto & Geneva.

191 Biwater Case, ICSID Case No. ARB/05/22 Procedural Order No.5 (2 February, 2007) Para 64, Arbitral Proceeding Order No.5.

192 Ibid., para 66,68.

193 Ibid., para 71.

194 Ibid., para 72.

195 Ibid., Para 12.

196 Eugenia Levine, *supra note* 185, p. 210.

Further in *Foresti* case,[197] four NGOs: (1) Centre for Applied Legal Studies (CALS),[198] (2) Legal Resources Centre (LRC),[199] (3) Centre for International Environmental Law (CIEL)[200] and (4) International Centre for the Legal Protection of Human Rights (INTERIGHTS)[201] jointly submitted amicus curiae before the arbitral proceedings. Besides, International Commission of Jurists (ICJ)[202] had also submitted their separate amicus brief.[203] Similarly, in *Philip Morris* case, NGOs participated as amicus curiae and supported public interest before the tribunal. That is an encouragement for NGOs participation in the proceeding of international arbitral tribunals as a non-dispute party.[204]

The ICSID tribunal allowed NGOs participation as amicus curiae in subsequent important cases. In *Bear Creek Mining v. Peru* case,[205] NGOs such as Civil Association of Human Rights and Environment (DHUMA), International Commission of Jurists and Columbia Centre on Sustainable Investment submitted amicus briefs. In their amicus briefs, they emphasised the indigenous peoples' rights of socio-environment protection. These NGOs also presented environment assessment reports as a part of their amicus.

In investment cases like *Infinito Gold v. Costa Rica*, *Lone Pine v. Canada* and *Gabriel Resources v. Romania*, amicus curiae were allowed by the tribunal.

ICSID tribunal has a five pages limit to the amicus briefs. It is also mandatory that a non-disputing party should explain its character by disclosing its legal status, financial source, membership, objectives, activities, non-profit status and its interest in the case.[206] The arbitral tribunal also introduced public hearing; it announced in advance about the date of public hearing for participation of people at large and submission of relevant information.[207] This would certainly enhance the transparency and credibility of international investment adjudicating system.

Gary Born and Stephanie Forrest have suggested certain ways for effective amicus curiae participation, i.e. ability of applicant, submission within the scope of dispute, public interest, fairness and efficiency of arbitral proceedings, independence and

---

[197] Piero Foresti, Laura de Carli & others v. Republic of South Africa, ICSID Case No. ARB(AF)/07/01 (25 September 2009); Friedman (2011).

[198] founded in 1978 as a research unit at WITS University, Johannesburg, South Africa.

[199] https://lrc.org.za, founded in 1979, office in Johannesburg, South Africa.

[200] https://www.ciel.org, founded in 1989, office in Washington DC, US.

[201] https://www.interights.org, founded in 1982, office in London, UK. It dissolved in 2014.

[202] www.icj.org, established in 1952, office in Geneva, Switzerland.

[203] Brickhill and du Plessis (2011).

[204] Philip Morris v. Uruguay, ICSID Case No. ARB/10/7 (8 July 2016), 56 ILM 1 (2017) available online at: https://www.italaw.com; Warren–Clem (2015).

[205] Bear Creek Mining v. Peru, ICSID Case No. ARB/14/21 (30 November 2017) available at: www.icsidfiles.worldbank.org, paras 57, 58 & 59; Annex of case file content Amicus brief, pp. 1–17; Paine (2018).

[206] https://icsid.worldbank.org/lone Pine Resources Inc. v. Canada (ICSID Case No. UNCT/15/2)-Public Hearing, News releases (17 November 2017).

[207] Gabriel Resources v. Romania, ICSID Case No. ARB/15/31, https://www.itlaw.com/cases/4721, Announcement: Public Hearing—28 September 2020.

impartiality of applicant.[208] These enhance the utility of amicus curiae participation of NGOs. Barnali Choudhary[209] focussed on human rights protection and referred to cases which protected the right to water,[210] right to health[211] and indigenous people's rights[212] in the decisions of the arbitral tribunals.

8 World Bank Inspection Panel

The Board of Executive Directors of the World Bank established an Inspection Panel in 1993. This is known as World Bank Inspection Panel. The Inspection Panel is an autonomous body and reports only to the Board of Directors. The Panel is composed of three members who are nominated by the President of the Bank with the approval of the Board. The Panel members' term is for five years which cannot be extended further. Members, after retirement, are not eligible for any post in the Bank. The Inspection Panel has its own secretariat. The main objective of the Panel is to bring transparency and accountability and redress grievances of the affected parties.[213]

A. **Genesis of the Inspection Panel**[214]

In the 1980s, NGOs raised their voice against World Bank's funded projects. NGOs continuously campaigned for transparency in the Bank policy, programmes and accountability to people. They insisted on issues related to protection of environment, rights of indigenous people and social cohesion. The first campaign on Polonoroeste, Brazil, in 1983–1987, was started by Brazilian NGOs such as National Indian Foundation (FUNAI)[215] and Brazilian Institute of Forest Development (IBDF). The campaign was actively supported by the United Nations-based NGOs, i.e. Cultural Survival, Environmental Defense Fund, National Wildlife Federation and Environmental Policy Institute. By effectively highlighting that the World Bank was the cause of harm to the people and failed to adequately address environmental and

---

208 Born and Forrest (2019).

209 Choudhary (2020).

210 Urbaser v. Argentina, ICSID Case No. ARB/07/26 (8 Dec. 2016); SAUR International v. Argentina, ICSID Case No. ARB/04/4 (6 June 2012); Vivendi I v. Argentina, ICSID Case No. ARB/97/3 (21 November 2000); Vivendi II v. Argentina, ICSID Case No. ARB/03/19 (30 July 2010).

211 Philip Morris v. Uruguay, ICSID Case No. ARB/10/7 (8 July 2016); Methanex v. US, UNCITRAL Rules & NAFTA Chap. 11 (3 August 2005).

212 Bear Creek Mining v. Peru, ICSID Case No. ARB/14/21 (30 November 2017).

213 Clark (1999).

214 Shihata (2000).

215 FUNAI was founded as Indian Protection Services in 1910. In 1967, it became Brazil Government Protective Agency for Welfare of Indigenous People: www.funai.gov.br; Non-governmental, Survival International, established in 1967, adopted FUNAI mission, www.survivalinternational.org.

social issues, they successfully created embarrassment for the Bank, branding it as both deceitful and negligent.

The Narmada River Project from India (1986–1996) was a seminal case. The World Bank funded the Narmada valley dam project in 1985. The Sardar Sarovar dam construction displaced more than two lakhs tribals because it submerged their land and rich forests. Medha Patkar, a firebrand leader, sustained a non-violent campaign against this project for nearly a decade. She established Narmada Bachao Andolan (save Narmada movement), an NGO that mobilised grassroots people, received support from Indian middle class and co-ordinated with the United States-based NGOs like Environmental Defence Fund (EDF), Natural Resources Defence Council (NRDC) and Bank Information Center. In addition, the United Kingdom-based Oxfam International also got associated with this movement.

World Media like the New York Times, Washington Post and Economic Times published news and views on the Narmada campaign.[216]

Thus, the Bank under the influence of the Narmada campaign appointed Morse Commission chaired by Bradford Morse, who had been the head of UNDP, on the environment and resettlement of displaced persons. Another member of the Commission was Thomas Berger, a Jurist of Canada. The commission issued a 363-page report that pressured the Government of India to decline advance payments from the Bank for the Narmada project. The World Bank President informally suggested this.

The Narmada campaign was a great success and it resulted in the dawn of the Inspection Panel of the World Bank.[217] In short, it was a new beginning for NGOs' engagement with the World Bank.

B. **The Operational Procedure**

Request for inspection or claims can be submitted by any of the adversely affected parties from the borrower states of the World Bank. Affected parties comprising more than two individuals, local representatives, in specific cases, non-resident representatives or any executive director of the Bank can file the complaint before the Inspection Panel. The Panel registers it and the management issues a detailed response within 21 days. The Panel then determines whether to recommend further investigation to the Board or not. The final decision needs the Board's approval. If the Board approves, then the Inspection Panel conducts fact-finding. During the fact-finding, the panel interacts with affected community, borrower government's officials, local Bank management and NGOs. Finally, the report is prepared and submitted to the Board for necessary decisions and actions, thereupon.[218]

The Bank did not explicitly mention NGOs as a requestor on behalf of the project-affected people. It was a deliberate attempt by the Bank, to limit the role of NGOs.[219]

[216] Lori Udall of EDF, Bruce Rich of NRDC and Medha Patkar of NBA took over leadership from Johan Clark's soft leadership. It was actively supported by Dutch Executive Director of Bank, Paul Arlman, US Secretary of Finance and US Congress.

[217] Lowenstein (2017).

[218] Weiss (2010), Carrasco and Guernsey (2008).

[219] Hunter (2003).

Despite which, NGOs were actively engaged on behalf of the affected communities of the World Bank projects and received written authorization from the affected parties. NGOs actively participated in preparing the complaints on behalf of the project affected people, supplied information, lobbying and advocacy in the Inspection Panel operation procedure.[220]

In an estimate, 150 complaints were registered before the Inspection Panel from 54 countries.[221] Apart from the project-affected people, 83 local NGOs, 75 national NGOs and 49 international NGOs are engaged with the World Bank Accountability Mechanism (AM).[222] As the Panel has only recommendatory powers, its main focus is fact-finding and maintaining its independence. Project-affected people of the Bank are hopeful to somehow seek redressal of their grievances through NGOs. Therefore, NGOs' role is crucial and they have to remain active in years to come.

9 Conclusion

In the latter part of the nineteenth century, a system of settlement of disputes among states was proposed by the peace societies and trade unions. It resulted in creation of Permanent Court of Arbitration (PCA) in 1899.[223] Since then, PCA is continuously at work. A breakthrough came when the Permanent Court of International Justice (PCIJ) was founded in 1920. The PCIJ was engaged in settlement of disputes until it was succeeded by the International Court of Justice (ICJ) in 1945. States are under obligation to settle their disputes by peaceful means.[224] The international courts and tribunals have proliferated in specific areas of international law such as International Criminal Court (ICC) 2002, The International Tribunal for the Law of the Sea (ITLOS) 1982, WTO Adjudicating Body 1994, International Centre for Settlement of Investment Disputes (ICSID) 1966 and World Bank Inspection Panel 1993.

The *Iran-United States Claims Tribunal*[225] was the first instance which allowed persons along with the state as a party of the international case. ICSID convention provides unique arbitral tribunals that resolve dispute between sand nationals of other states. ICC can prosecute individuals who are accused of crime against humanity and in violation of the law of armed struggle. The Inspection Panel allows affected individuals to file a request against the World Bank projects.

---

[220] Bradlow (1999).

[221] *Inspection Panel Cases from 1994 to 2020*, https://www.inspectionpanel.org/panel_cases.

[222] NGOs Participation in World Bank Accountability Mechanism available at: https://www.inspectionpanel.org/sites/www.inspectionpanel.org/files/publications/InspectionPanelAt10YearsEnglish.pdf.

[223] Grewe (2000).

[224] UN Charter, Article 2(4).

[225] Caron (1990).

The ICJ, ITLOS and WTO Adjudicating Body are means for peaceful settlement of disputes among state parties. However, the Seabed Disputes Chamber of ITLOS provides access to justice-seeking individuals, NGOs and corporations.

NGOs have access in International Courts and Tribunals' proceedings as amicus curiae. Only the WTO Adjudicating Body can explicitly allow NGO participation as amicus curiae. Remaining amicus curiae submissions are covered under procedural discretion of the courts and tribunals concerned. By practice, some space is available for non-dispute party as amicus curiae, because they are either allowed or left out for the court itself to decide for their amicus submissions.

The practice of Amicus curiae is well established in national judicial system worldwide. It enhances transparency, quality, efficiency and public voice in the decisions of the court. It is foregrounded in international law.

The proliferation of judicial institutions[226] at the international level is an undeniable reality. Since their inception, NGOs have engaged as amicus curiae or friends of the courts and tribunals. However NGOs have not been allowed to become parties in disputes before international courts. The scope of international law has expanded with globalisation, which has also facilitated NGOs' involvement in international court and tribunal proceedings as amicus curiae.[227]

References

Adams A (2018) The legacy of the international criminal tribunals for the former Yugoslavia and Rwanda and their contribution to the crime of rape. European J Int'l L 29(3):749–769

Adede AO (1987) The system for settlement of disputes under the united nations convention on the law of the sea: a drafting history and a commentary. Nijhoff Publishers, Leiden

Akhavan P et al (1998) Contribution of the Adhoc tribunals to international humanitarian law. Am Univ Int'l L Rev 13(6):1509–1539

Akhavan P (1996) The international criminal tribunal for Rwanda: the politics and pragmatics of punishment. Am J Int'l L 90(3):501–510 at 501

Alford RP (2000) The proliferation of international courts and tribunals: international adjudication in ascendance. Proc Am so'y Int'l L 94:160–165

Bartholomeusz L (2005a) The Amicus Curiae before international courts and tribunals. Non-State Actors & Int'l L 5(2):209–286 at 215

Bartholomeusz L (2005b) The Amicus Curiae before international courts and tribunals. NSA & Int'l L 5(2):209–286 at 257

Bassiouni MC (ed) (1998) The statute of the international criminal court: a documentary history. Transnational Publisher, New York

Bingham T (2005) The Alabama claims arbitration. Int'l & Comp L Q 54(1):1–25

Born G, Forrest S (2019) Amicus Curiae participation in investment arbitration. ICSID Rev 34(3):626–665

Boyle AE (1997) Dispute settlement and the law of the sea convention: problems of fragmentation and jurisdiction. Int'l & Comp LQ 46(1):37–54 at 40

[226] Eric De Brabandere, *supra note* 23, p. 466.

[227] Hakimi (2017).

De Brabandere (2011) NGOs and the public interest: the legality and rationale of Amicus Curiae interventions in internationals economic and investment disputes. Chicago J Int'l L 12(1):85–113 at 101

De Brabandere E (2018) International dispute settlement-from practice to legal discipline. Leiden J Int'l L 31(3):459–468 at 462

Bradlow DD (1999) Precedent-setting NGO campaign saves the world bank's inspection panel. HumRts Brief 6(3):23–27, online at: https://digitalcommons.wcl.american.edu/facsch_lawrev/932/

Brickhill J, du Plessis M (2011) Two's Company, three's a crowd: public interest intervention in investor-state arbitration (Piero Foresti v. South Africa). South African J Hum Rts 07(1):152–166

Brownlie I (2009) The peaceful settlement of international disputes. Chin J Int'l L 8(2):267–284 at 269

Büthe T et al (2012) The politics of private foreign aid : humanitarian principles, economic development objectives and organisational interests in NGO private aid allocation. Int'l Org 66(4):571–607 at 572

Caron DD (1990) The nature of the Iran-United States claims tribunal and the evolving structure of international dispute resolution. Am J Int'l L 84(1):104–156

Carrasco ER, Guernsey AK (2008) The world bank's inspection panel: promoting true accountability through arbitration. Cornell Int'l L J 41(3):578–629 at 585–594

de Carvalho IV M, Canesin CH (2018) The role of international-legal capacity and power in explaining the performance of developing countries in WTO disputes against the G2. Contex Int'l 40(1):161–183

Chad PB (2009) Self-enforcing trade. Brookings Institute Press, Washington DC, Chap. 6

Chang Y-C (2017) How does the Amicus Curiae submission affect a tribunal decision? Leiden J Int'l L 30(3):647–660

Charney JI (1996) The implications of expanding international dispute settlement systems: the 1982 convention on the law of the sea. Am J Int'l L 90(1):69–75 at 71

Charnovitz S (1996) Participation of non-governmental organisations in the world trade organisation. Univ Penn J Int'l Econ L 17(1):331–357

Charnovitz S (2000) Opening the WTO to non-governmental interests. Fordham Int'l LJ 24(1):173–216

Charwat N (2016) Who participates as Amicus Curiae in world trade organisation dispute settlement and why? New Zealand Univ L Rev 27(2):1–28 at 15

Chinkin C (1993) Third parties in international law. Clarendon Press, Oxford

Choudhary B (2020) Investor obligations for human rights. ICSID Rev 35(1–2):82–104

Clark RS (1981) The international league for human rights and South-West Africa 1947–1957: the human rights NGOs as catalyst in the international legal process. Hum Rts Q 3(4):101–136 at 116–119

Clark DL (1999) A citizen's guide to the world bank inspection panel, 2nd edn. CIEL, Washington DC, pp 1–24 at 3–4

Collier J, Lowe AV (1999) The settlement of disputes in international law. Oxford University Press

Crawford J (ed) (2019) Brownlie's principles of public international law, 9th edn, Oxford University Press, p 679.

Crema L (2012) Testing Amicus Curiae in international law: rules and practice. Italian YB Int'l L 22:91–132 at 95

Delaume GR (1983) ICSID arbitration and the courts. Am J Int'l L 77(4):784–803 at 803

Dolidze A (2013) Advisory opinion on responsibility and liability for international seabed mining (ITLOS Case No.17) and the future of NGO participation in the international legal process. ILSA J Int'l & Comp L 19(2):279–418 at 415

Dumberry P (2001) The admissibility of Amicus Curiae briefs by NGOs in investor-states arbitration: the precedent set by the methanex case in the context of NAFTA Chapter 11 proceedings. NSA & Int'l L 1(3):201–214 at 201

El Khoury M (2012) The role of environmentalist NGOs in the democratization of the WTO dispute settlement procedure," *Southern Cross Univ L Rev*, vol.15 (2012) pp.53–72 at 69.
Evenson E (2020) Too few trails, too many tribulations: the ICC's terrible year and where to go from here. Case Western Reserve J Int'l L 52(1):433–449 at 437–439
Freestone D (2016) Case 21: request for an advisory opinion submitted by the Sub-Regional Fisheries Commission (SRFC), international tribunal for the law of the sea. Asia-Pacific J Ocean L & Pol'y 1(1):131–138
Friedman A (2010) Flexible arbitration for the developing world: Piero Foresti and the future of bilateral investment treaties in the global south. Brigham Young Univ-Int'l L & Manage Rev 7(1):37–51
Galvin RJ (2005) The ICC prosecutor, collateral damage, and NGOs: evaluating the risk of a politisized prosecution. Univ Miami Int'l & Comp L Rev 13(1):2–103 at 47
Gautier P (2014) Standing of NGOs and third-party intervention before the international tribunal for the law of the sea. Belgian J Int'l L 47(1):205–224 at 213
Gopal G (1982) International centre for settlement of investment disputes. Case Western Reserve J Int'l L 14(3):591–611 at 602
Grewe WG (2000) The epoch of international law (revised & transl. by Michael Byers). Walter de Gruyter Publishers, Berlin, p 517 (first edn. 1984)
Haddad HN (2013)After the norm cascade: "NGO mission expansion and the coalition for the international criminal court. Glob Gov 19(2):187–206 at 191
Hakimi M (2017) Constructing an international community. Am J Int'l L 111(2):317–356 at 356
Hall CK (1998) The first proposal for a permanent international criminal court. Int'l Rev Red Cross 38(322):57–74 at 57
Holmila E (2005) Common heritage of mankind in the law of the sea. Acta Societatis Martensis 1:187–205
Howse R (2016) The world trade organisation 20 years on: global governance by judiciary. European J in'l L 27(1):9–77
Hudson MO (1943) The permanent court of international justice. Macmillan, New York
Hunter D (2003) Using the world bank inspection panel to defend the interests of project-affected people. Chicago J Int'l L 4(1):201–211 at 205
Hyde CC (1929) The place of commissions of inquiry and conciliation treaties in the peaceful settlement of international disputes. Proc Am Soc'y Int'l L 23:144–175
Kerr R (2004) International criminal tribunal for the former Yugoslavia—an exercise in law, politics and diplomacy. Oxford University Press, Oxford
Klein N (2005) Dispute settlement in the UN convention on the law of the sea. Cambridge University Press
Krislov S (1963) The Amicus Curiae brief: from friendship to advocacy. Yale L J 72(4):694–722 at 695
Lange C (1932) The inter-parliamentary union. Advocate Peace through Just 94(1):26–37
Lazo RP (2014) Is there a life for Latin American countries after denouncing the ICSID convention? Trans'l Dispute Manage 11(1):1–57 at 52
Lee RS (ed) (1999) The international criminal court: the making of the Rome statute. Kluwer Law International, The Hague
Leroux N (2006) NGOs at the world court: lessons from the past. Int'l Commun L Rev 8(2):203–221 at 219
Levine E (2011) Amicus Curiae in international investment arbitration: the implications of an increase in third-party participation. Berkeley J Int'l L 29(1):200–224 at 210
Lim CL (2005) The Amicus brief issue at the WTO. Chin J Int'l L 4(1):85–120 at 119
Lodge MW (2012) The common heritage of mankind. Int'l J Marine Coastal Law 27(4):733–742
Lohne K (2019) Advocates of humanity: human rights NGOs in international criminal justice. Oxford University Press

Lowenstein AK (2017) International human rights clinic. In: Deferring accountability: delays at the world bank's inspection panel. Yale Law School, US, pp 1–50 at 5–11. https://law.yale.edu/sites/default/files/area/center/schell/document/doferring_accountability_update.pdf
Mackenzie GW (1993) ICSID arbitration as a strategy for levelling the playing field between international non-governmental organisations and host states. Syracuse J Int'l Law Commerce 19:197–234 at 222
Marceau G, Stilwell M (2001) Practical suggestions for Amicus Curiae briefs before WTO adjucating bodies. J Int'l Econ L 4(1):155–187 at 159
Masood A (1972) Jurisdiction of international centre for settlement of investment disputes. J Indian L Inst 14(1):119–140 at 121
Merrills JG (2017) International dispute settlement, 6th edn. Cambridge University Press
Minear RH (1971) Victors' justice—Tokyo war crime trial. Princeton University Press, New Jersey, US
Moore JB (1898) History and digest of the international arbitrations to which the United States has been a party, vol 1. Govt. Print Office, Washington DC, pp 625–653
Noyes JE (1999) The international tribunal for the law of the sea. Cornell Int'l L J 32(1):109–182 at 122–123
O'Brien JC (1993) The international tribunal for violations of international humanitarian law in the former Yugoslavia. Am J Int'l L 87(4):639–659 at 639
O'Connell ME, VanderZee L (2013) The history of international adjudication. In: Romano CPR et al (eds), Oxford handbook of international adjudication. Oxford University Press, pp 40–61
Okowa PN, Evans MD (1998) Case concerning Galcikovo-Nagymaros project (Hungary/Slovakia). Int'l & Comp LQ 47(3):688–697 at 695
Paine J (2018) Bear creek mining corporation v Republic of Peru: judging the social license of foreign investments and applying new style investment treaties. ICSID Rev 33(2):340–348
Parra AR (2012) The history of ICSID. Oxford University Press
Pearson Z (2006) Non-governmental organisations and the international criminal court: changing landscapes of international law. Cornell Int'l L J 39(2):243–284 at 277
Politi M (2004) Some concluding remarks on the role of NGOs in the ICC. In: eds Treves T et al. (eds) Civil society, international courts and compliance bodies. TMC Asser Press, The Hague, pp 144–145
Reinisch A, Irgel C (2001) The participation of non-government organisations (NGOs) in the WTO dispute settlement system. NSA & Int'l L 1(2):127–151, at 135
Rieter E (2014) The Arctic sunrise case (Netherlands v Russia) (ITLOS). Int'l Legal Mater (ILM) 53(4):603–619 at 604
Romano CPR (1999) The proliferation of international judicial bodies: the pieces of the puzzle. NewYork Univ J Int'l L Polit 31(4):709–751
Scott JB (1916) The Haque court reports. Oxford University Press, pp XI–XII
Shaffer GC, Melendez-Ortiz R (eds) (2010) Dispute settlement at the WTO: the developing country experience. Cambridge University Press
Shaffer G (2011) Assessing the advisory centre on WTO law from a broader governance perspective. In: Minnesota Legal Studies Research Paper No. 11-46, pp 1–5 at 2
Shell RG (1995) Trade legalism and international relations theory: an analysis of the world trade organisation. Duke LJ 44(5):829–927 at 911
Shelton D (1994) The participation of non-governmental organisation in international judicial proceedings. Am J Int'l L 88(4):611–642
Shelton D (2007) The international court of justice and non-government organisations. Int'l Commun L Rev 9(2):139–155 at 150
Shihata IFI (ed) (2000) The world bank inspection panel. In: Practice, 2nd edn. Oxford University Press
Squatrito T (2012) Opening the doors to the WTO dispute settlement: state preference on NGO access as Amicus. Swiss Polit Sci Rev 18(2):175–198

Squatrito T (2018) Amicus Curiae briefs in the WTO DSM: good or bad news for non-state actor involvement? World Trade Rev 17(1):65–89, at 70, 72
Sterio M, Scharf M (eds) (2019) The legacy of the Adhoc tribunals in international criminal law: assessing the ICTYs and the ICTRs, most significant legal accomplishments. Cambridge University Press, Cambridge
Struett MJ (2008) The politics of constructing the international criminal court: NGOs, discourse, and agency. Palgrave Macmillan, London, Chap. 5
Szpak A (2013) Legacy of the Adhoc international criminal tribunals in implementing international humanitarian Law. Mediterranean J Social Sciences 4(9):525–531
Tanaka M (2003) Bridging the gap between northern NGOs and southern sovereigns in the trade-environment debate: the pursuit of democratic dispute settlements in the WTO under the Rio Principles. Ecology LQ 30(1):113–188 at 180
Tomuschat C (2006) Legacy of Nuremberg. J Int'l Criminal Just 4(4):830–844
Treves T (2019) Seabed disputes chamber: international tribunal for the law of the sea (ITLOS). In: Max Planck Encyclopedias of International Law (MPIL). Oxford University Press
Tryon JL (1911) The rise of the peace movement. Yale LJ 20(5):358–371 at 363
Tyrrell A (1979) Making the millennium: the mid-nineteenth century peace movement. Hist J 8(2):75–95 at 83
Umbricht GC (2001) An 'Amicus Curiae Brief' on Amicus Curiae briefs at the WTO. J Int'l Econ L 4(4):773–794.
UN (2020) Handbook of the international court of justice. ICJ Publications, The Hague, p 18; www.legal.un.org/manual_en.pdf
United Nations (2007) Digest of international cases on the law of the sea. UN Publications, New York; UNCLOS part XV, Articles 279–299
Van der Borght K (1999) The advisory centre on WTO law: advancing fiarness and equality. J Int'l Econ L 2(4):723–728
Warren-Clem K (2015) PMI v. Uruguay: public health and arbitration intertwinded and undermined. L & Bus Rev Am 21(4):395–410
Weiss EB (2010) On being accountable in kaleidoscopic world. Proc Am Soc'y Int'l L Proc 104:477–490 at 483
Welch Jr CE, Watkins AF (2011) Extending enforcement : the coalition for the international criminal court. Hum Rts Q 33(4):927–1031
Schabas WA (2020) An introduction to the international criminal court, 6th edn. Cambridge University Press
Williams S, Palmer E (2016) Civil society and Amicus Curiae interventions in the international criminal court. Acta Juridica 1:40–65 at 46
Wright Q (1947) The law of the Nuremberg trial. Am J Int'l L 41(1):38–72 at 38
WTO (2017) A handbook on the WTO dispute settlement system, 2nd edn. Cambridge University Press

Part III
Role of NGOs in Making of International Law

Chapter 8
NGOs in the Making of Human Rights

1 Introduction

The making of law is a legislative procedure. In international law, there is a lack of a central legislative body. However, the formation of law is not solely confined to the realm of the legislative body. This broad phenomenon encompasses all manifestations, creativity, traditions and the origin of rules, through which they acquire the force of law to regulate the conduct of states.[1]

The United Nations (UN) Charter mandates the General Assembly to initiate studies and make recommendations to encourage the progressive development of international law and its codification.[2] This task is carried out by the International Law Commission (ILC), the Sixth Committee of the General Assembly and International Conferences, specifically designated to address the issues assigned to them.

The making of International Human Rights Law (IHRL) involves the former UN Commission on Human Rights, the UN Human Rights Council, the Economic and Social Council (ECOSOC) and the Third and Sixth Committees of the General Assembly. Notably, non-governmental organisations (NGOs) have actively participated in the human rights law-making procedure within the UN system.[3]

The sources of international law are identified and listed in Article 38 Clause 1 of the statute of the International Court of Justice (ICJ). These are:

(a) International conventions.
(b) International custom, as evidence of a general practice accepted as a law.
(c) The general principles of law recognised by civilised nations.
(d) Judicial decisions.
(e) Opinions and writings of the scholars of international law.

---

[1] Jennings and Watts (1996).

[2] UN Charter, Article 13(1)(a).

[3] Woodward (2010).

P. Rai, *Non-Governmental Organisations and International Law*,
https://doi.org/10.1007/978-981-97-5469-4_8

These sources were first identified and catalogued in the statute of the Permanent Court of International Justice (PCIJ) in 1920 and in the statute of the ICJ in 1945. These sources serve two purposes: first, they provide information on the origin, process and material of international law; and second, they indicate the participants involved in the procedure of international law-making.

As per Article 38 Clause 1 of the ICJ statute, three participants are engaged in international law-making: states, courts and individuals. The statute of the ICJ does not explicitly envision the role of NGOs and intergovernmental organisations (IGOs). Under the auspices of the UN system, international law was developed progressively and codified by the member states. The judiciary, IGOs, NGOs and international law scholars have substantially contributed to this process.

Human rights law is a corpus of international law. Human rights first became a part of constitutional law in liberal democracies in the seventeenth, eighteenth and nineteenth centuries. Subsequently, in the twentieth century, it entered the international law lexicon when the Universal Declaration of Human Rights (UDHR) was adopted in 1948.[4] Traditionally, international law is based on the states' consent, and hence, the states are the only international lawmakers. Their explicit consent is known as a treaty or convention, and implied consent is customary international law. However, the sources of international law are not exclusively dependent on states' consent, as they primarily apply to inter-state relations.

Ian Brownlies describes sources of international human rights law (IHRL) as multilateral conventions and customary international law.[5] David Harris explains that human rights treaties, declarations and customary international law are key sources of IHRL.[6] Surya P. Subedi observed: currently, there are around 130 separate international human rights instruments (conventions, protocols, declarations, code of conduct and statements of standard and principles) that form the corpus of IHRL.[7]

IHRL sources are broadly divided into two categories: law-making treaties and soft laws.[8] Human rights treaties are the most significant sources of IHRL. They are governed under the Vienna Convention of Law of Treaties (VCLT), 1969.[9] Human rights treaties are universal in nature. Thereby, its application is broader than the signatories of the state. The objectives of these treaties are to strengthen human rights law and lay down the states' obligation for compliance thereupon. State parties are permitted to make reservations on some of the treaty obligations.[10] But the reservation must be compatible with the very purposes of the treaty thereto.[11]

[4] Universal Declaration of Human Rights, United Nations General Assembly Resolution (UNGA Res.) 217A(111), A/RES/3/217A (10 December 1948).

[5] Crawford (2019).

[6] Harris and Shivkumaran (2020).

[7] Subedi (2017).

[8] Van Hoof (1983), Schacter (1977), Baxter (1986), Bothe (1980).

[9] 1155 *UNTS* 331.

[10] Vienna Connection on the Law of Treaties (VCLT), Article 2(1)(d) and Articles 19–23.

[11] Reservation to the Convention on the Prevention and Punishment of Genocide, Advisory Opinion (1951) ICJ Reports 15.

Another important source of IHRL is soft law. It is not an independent source listed under Article 38 Clause1 of the ICJ statute. Rather, it is a human rights law-making process that establishes human rights standards and seeks consent through the participation of all stakeholders. The soft law of human rights is derived from customary international law, general principles of law, the decision of the courts, writers' opinions, General Assembly resolutions, declarations, jus cogens, rules of conduct and guidelines laid down by IGOs and NGOs. Soft law is non-binding in nature, but it has eminent legal value.[12]

States prefer soft law because the deviation from its obligations does not invoke sanctions under international law. The cumbersome procedure of ratification is easily avoided through soft law; it does not require ratification within a country's domestic law, like a law-making treaty, for instance.[13]

Soft law enables non-state entities to participate in the law-making process. Moreover, it is easy to seek the state's consent on the resolutions, declarations, guidelines, principles and rules compared to the process of treaty-making. For instance, UDHR was adopted instantly by all nations on the floor of the General Assembly, whereas concluding the human rights treaty took years together. Therefore, soft law is useful in bridging gaps within human rights law.

2 Precursor of International Human Rights Law

Anti-slavery and humanitarian laws were the precursors of human rights law. These laws were formulated in the later part of the nineteenth century. NGOs' Anti-slavery Society (1839[14]) and the International Committee of the Red Cross (ICRC) (1863)[15] were engaged in making anti-slavery[16] and humanitarian laws, respectively.

The practice of slavery existed in the ancient world. It was mentioned in Hammurabi's Code (1755–1750 BCE). Thracian Spartacus (111–71 BCE) headed a famous slave rebellion in the Roman Empire, fighting a war against slavery and sacrificing his life for the liberation of his fellow slaves. Numerous works of fiction, including films, television series and theatrical productions on the supreme tale of Spartacus, have inspired people of every nation.

The anti-slavery sentiment was kept alive, particularly in Britain and the United States. The Quakers, also known as the Society of Friends, a religious group that emerged during the seventeenth century in England, published a news magazine—*Philanthropist*[17] and emphasised the abolition of slavery and the slave trade. Another serious attempt was made by the Anti-Slavery Society, who continued their campaign

[12] Pronto (2008), Olitier (2002).

[13] Guzman and Meyer (2010).

[14] www.anti-slaveryinternational.

[15] www.icrc.org.

[16] Sinha (2017).

[17] Martin (1916).

to abolish slavery across the Atlantic Ocean.[18] The persistent campaign for the abolition of slavery resulted in the adoption of the Slavery Convention of 1926 under the auspices of the League of Nations.[19]

The objectives of this convention were to prevent and suppress the slave trade and slavery. The 1926 Slavery Convention was further refined by the Supplementary Convention on the Abolition of Slavery, the Slave Trade and Institutions and Practices Similar to Slavery on 7 September 1956. The convention came into force on 30 April 1957. The slavery abolition movement of NGOs in the nineteenth century was the first successful experiment in making international human rights law.

NGOs have played a pivotal role in shaping the formation of international humanitarian law. Humanitarian law and human rights are complementary to each other.[20] The creation, development and enforcement of international humanitarian law are inseparable from the ICRC. Henry Dunant, a Swiss businessman, philanthropist and humanitarian, took the initiative in establishing ICRC as an NGO in Geneva in 1863. The ICRC's objectives are ameliorating the condition of wounded, sick, prisoners of war and members of shipwrecked armed forces affected by armed conflict and war. The continuous efforts of the ICRC resulted in the adoption of the four Geneva Conventions of 1949.[21]

In addition to the Geneva Conventions of 1949, two protocols—one in 1977[22] and the other in 2005[23]—were adopted by the states as a corpus of international humanitarian law. Originally, ICRC was established as an NGO. Presently, it is more than an NGO, less than a state, but not exactly an IGO. It is governed by sue generis or a special legal regime under international law.

The UN Charter serves as a fountainhead for the establishment of IHRL. The UN Charter included seven articles plus a preamble with respect to human rights.[24] In addition, Charter Article 71 endowed consultative status to NGOs. It facilitated the progressive development and codification of IHRL and the participation of NGOs and IGOs in the law-making process. But states are still primary stakeholders, and their consent and acceptance are indispensable in the process of law-making.

---

[18] A.Y. Rassam, "Contemporary Form of Slavery and Evolution of the Prohibition of Slavery and Slave Trade under Customary International Law," *Vanderbilt J Transn'l L*, 39 (1998–1999) pp.304–329.

[19] The Slavery Convention signed on 25 September 1926 and entered in force on 9 March 1927, 60 *LNTS* 253.

[20] Ben-Noftali (2011).

[21] Geneva Convention for the Amelioration of the Condition of Wounded and Sick in Armed Forces in the Field, 12 August 1949, 75 UNTS 31; Geneva Convention for the Amelioration of the Condition of Wounded, Sick and Shipwrecked Members of Armed Forces at Sea, 12 August 1949, 75 UNTS 85; Geneva Convention Relation to the Protection of Civilian Persons in Time of War, 12 August 1949, 75 UNTS 287; Geneva Convention Relating to the Treatment of Prisnor of War, 12 August 1949, 75 UNTS 135.

[22] Additional Protocol I 1977 is related with the International Conflicts, Additional Protocol II 1977 is related with the Non-international conflicts, 16 ILM 1391 (1977).

[23] Additional Protocol III 2005 is created additional emblem, the Red Crystal, apart from Red Cross and Red Crescent, https://www.unorg/doc.36; Dormann and Maresca (2004), Bugnion (2004).

[24] UN Charter, the Preamble and Articles 1(3) 13(1)(b), 55, 56, 62, 68 and 76(c).

NGOs have successfully advocated the inclusion of human rights as a core objective of the UN. NGOs were involved in the negotiation and drafting process along with the state representatives. When the charter was adopted, 1200 NGOs and activists participated in this momentous event. At the time, NGOs were predominantly located in the United States and Western Europe.[25]

The participation of NGOs in the making of IHRL is based on: whether they take initiatives in agenda-framing, lobbying and networking to pursue the agenda; establish coalition and organise campaigns for framing of human rights; submit well-reasoned written and oral statements; give briefs to state representatives or become members of state delegations; mobilise public opinion; closely monitor treaty negotiations and attend international conferences. Finally, NGOs observe the outcomes to determine whether the issue areas of IHRL have accommodated their views and whether their engagement has resulted in positive outcomes.[26]

A breakthrough presented itself in the making of IHRL when the General Assembly adopted UDHR in 1948 and the two International Covenants in 1966. These instruments were signed and ratified by the member states of the UN. This troika was the cornerstone of the human rights infrastructure and is known as the International Bill of Rights.[27]

3 Universal Declaration of Human Rights (UDHR) 1948

One of the main objectives of the UN is the promotion and protection of human rights around the world. This is explicitly envisaged in the purposes of the UN Charter:

> to reaffirm faith in fundamental human rights, in the dignity and worth of the human person, in the equal rights of men and women and of nations large and small...

Further, Charter Article 1 Clause 3 lays down:

> to achieve international co-operation in solving international problems of an economic, social, cultural, or humanitarian character and in promoting and encouraging respect for human rights and fundamental freedom for all without distinction as to race, sex, language or religion.

During the World War II, the gross violation of human rights and the holocaust shattered the common consciousness of the international community.[28] Thus, the first task of the UN was to assign ECOSOC to engage in the promotion and protection of human rights and to set up the UN Commission on Human Rights to prepare an International Bill of Rights.[29] This was the first instance at the international level

[25] Robins (1971)

[26] Barbara K. Woodward, *supra note* 3, pp.3–4.

[27] http://www.ohchr.org/ Factsheet No.2 (Rev.1), The International Bill of Human Rights, UN Publications, Genevas, 1996, pp.1–10.

[28] Humphrey (1949, Lauterpacht (1948), Shabas (2013).

[29] Sohn (1967).

to proceed and create a universal standard of human rights. While in the nineteenth century, NGOs were engaged actively in the abolition of slavery and the formation of humanitarian law, the Covenant of League of Nations (1919) was silent on human rights issues.

The Covenant of the League of Nations primarily focussed on the protection of minorities in specific areas, which left out the pressing issue of human rights. However, the UN addressed this gap by addressing human rights concerns in its Charter. The UN swiftly established its Commission on Human Rights, emphasising the significance of safeguarding and promoting human rights globally. The UN Commission set up a committee under the Chairmanship of Ms. Eleanor Roosevelt.[30] It started its work in January 1947 and concluded in December 1948. Within this period, three sessions were held by the UN Commission, two sessions by the Drafting Committee and two sessions by the General Assembly, including its Third Committee and plenary session. The UDHR was adopted on 10 December 1948, as Resolution 217 in the third session of the General Assembly in Paris. Forty-eight members of the General Assembly voted in favour of the UDHR, while ten members were absent. Thus, the UDHR was unanimously adopted by the General Assembly.[31]

Ms. Eleanor Roosevelt of the United States, Rene Cassion of France, Charles Dukes of the United Kingdom, Charles Malik of Lebanon, Pang Chung Chang of China, Alexander Bogomolov of Russia, William Hodgson of Australia and Herman Santacruz of Chile were eminent persons associated with the drafting of the UDHR.

John P. Humphrey of Canada was the Director of the UN Human Rights Division. He prepared outlines of the UDHR draft. The NGOs, particularly the American Law Institute, submitted the background papers. Ms. Hansa Mehta of India, as a member of the UN Commission of Human Rights, proposed an amendment in Article 1 of the Draft of UDHR: "*All men are born free and equal*" was replaced by "*All human beings are born free and equal*". This amendment was positively received by the UN Commission and subsequently included in the final version of the UDHR. These prominent individuals, along with NGOs,[32] statesmen, intellectuals and conscience citizenry played a commendable role.

The UDHR is a monumental instrument of human rights. It provides impetus for the adoption of human rights treaties. As a Resolution of the General Assembly, it is not legally binding, in the strict sense, on UN member states.[33] The UDHR is not a treaty but a declaration. Therefore, it cannot create a legal obligation on the signatory states. However, it is considered a source of customary international law[34] and reflective of the general principles of law.[35] Ms. Roosevelt said: "The declaration was not a treaty or international agreement and did not impose legal obligations; it

---

[30] Glendon (2002).

[31] UN Doc A/810 (1948), digitallibrang. un.org/A_RES_217(111)AA_EN_PDF.

[32] Korey (1998)

[33] Oppenheim, *supra note* 1, pp.118–119.

[34] David Harris and S. Shivakumaran, *supra note* 7, p.557.

[35] Brownlie's, *supra note* 6, p.636.

was rather a statement of basic principles of inalienable human rights, setting up common standards of achievement for all people and all nations".[36]

NGOs are associated with the process of drafting, adoption and constant improvement of these standards set out by the UDHR.[37] At the time of UDHR's drafting, only 41 NGOs were accorded consultative status by the ECOSOC. Most NGOs are located in the United States and Western Europe. It is hard to ascertain their exact contribution because NGOs are not allowed to participate in debates on drafting texts, moving proposals or allowed to record their statements.

Rights related to marriage, family, children and motherhood are contributed specifically by women's human rights NGOs. William Korey reproduced the memoirs of the drafters—Rene Cessin and Charles Malik—highlighting the NGOs' role. Besides, the Chairman of the Third Committee of the General Assembly, the Secretary General of the UN and Ms. Eleanor Roosevelt, the Chairperson of the UN Commission on Human Rights,[38] provided significant insights and information during the development of the UDHR.

The UDHR is a non-binding instrument in international law, commonly referred to as "soft law" because it is not directly enforced by international courts or tribunals. The human rights council and treaty monitoring bodies have been taking 'views' on human rights violation cases and making recommendations to the states concerned. States, NGOs and scholars of international law hold the opinion that the UDHR manifested legal obligations to all stakeholders.[39]

In 2018, the World celebrated the seventieth anniversary of the UDHR. The declaration is the most visible legal document the world over. It has already been translated into 360 distinct languages across nations.[40] Through the years, it has been a source of several binding human rights treaties.[41] The UDHR, along with the International Covenant of Civil and Political Rights (ICCPR), 1966, the International Covenant of Economic, Social and Cultural Rights (ICESCR), 1966, and optional protocols (OPs) thereof are the cornerstone of the human rights infrastructure.

---

[36] Louis B. Sohn, *supra note* 30, p.20.

[37] William Korey, *supra note* 34, pp.45–46.

[38] Cessin (1968), Van Boven (1990).

[39] Statement of the Non-governmental Organisation Assembly for Human Rights at Montreal, 1968 reprint in *Int'l Commission Jurist Rev*, vol.9 (1968) p.94; Final Act of the International Conference on Human Rights, Tehran, 1968, UN Doc.A/Conf.32/41 (1968); Resolution of the International Law Institute, 1969, cited by Hurst Hannum, "The State of the Universal Declaration of Human Rights in National and International", *Georgia Int'l & Comp L*, vol.25 (1995–1996) pp.317–340 at 323.

[40] De Baets (2009).

[41] Brownlies and Goodwin-Gill (2010).

4 International Covenants 1966

When the General Assembly adopted UDHR on 10 December 1948, it requested the UN Commission on Human Rights to draft the covenant on human rights and devise the necessary measures for its implementation. The first draft prepared by the UN Commission was circulated among nations and IGOs for comments and suggestions to proceed further. Furthermore, the General Assembly asked the UN Commission to draft two separate covenants: civil and political rights and economic, social and cultural rights.[42] The Third Committee of the General Assembly examined the articles, word-by-word and sentence-by-sentence, to ensure the highest drafting standards.

NGOs also contributed significantly to this process. This was acknowledged by the members of the draft committee of the UN Commission and the Chairperson of the Third Committee of the UN General Assembly.[43] NGOs have long field experience and have acquired expert knowledge in areas of rights and freedoms. They possess the ways and means to submit their views and concerns, whether through states' representatives, IGOs or members of drafting committees. NGOs have been involved at every stage, except at the final one, when the General Assembly formally adopted the International Covenants of 1966.

The General Assembly adopted two covenants: the International Covenant on Civil and Political Rights (ICCPR),[44] 1966, and the International Covenant on Economic, Social and Cultural Rights (ICESCR),[45] 1966. ICCPR came into force on 23 March 1976, while the ICESCR on 3 January of the same year. Two Optional Protocols of ICCPR were adopted. OP-I, in which ICCPR deals with individual communications, allowing individuals to seek remedies from the Human Rights Committee or the Committee on the Civil and Political Rights. OP-II of the ICCPR relates to the abolition of the death penalty. OP-I of the ICCPR entered into force in 1976, with a total of 116 state parties joined it.[46] OP-II of the ICCPR came into force in 1991, with 109 state parties being associated with it.[47]

Likewise, Optional Protocol ICESCR was also adopted by the General Assembly on 10 December 2008 and entered into force on 5 May 2013.[48] There were only 24 state parties, and the remaining 149 states did not take any action to accede to it. OP-ICESCR dealt with individual communications, allowing individuals to seek remedy from the Committee on Economic, Social and Cultural Rights. NGOs have jointly

---

[42] Fact Sheet No.2 (Rev.1), *supra note* 28.

[43] Theo van Boven, *supra note* 39, 211.

[44] UNGA Res. 2200A (XXXI), UN Doc A/6316 (16 December 1966), 999 UNTS 171.

[45] UNGA Res. 2200A (XXXI) (16 December 1966); 993 UNTS 3.

[46] First Optional Protocol of ICCPR convention was adopted on 16 December 1966 and entered into force on 23 March 1976; Bair (2005).

[47] Second Optional Protocol of ICCPR convention was adopted on 15 December 1986 and entered into force on 11 July 1991.

[48] UNGA Res. A/RES/63/117 (2008); 'OHCHR Dashboard' (http://indicators.ohchr.org) 'status of ratification' visited 23 August 2019.

established the Centre for Economic and Social Rights and the NGOs Coalition on OP-ICESCR to build public opinion for states' accession to the OP.[49]

The ICCPR[50] and ICESCR have similar patterns as directed by the General Assembly to its Draft Committee. The preamble and Articles 1, 3 and 5 are identical within ICCPR and ICESCR.[51] In both Covenants, Article 1 provides that all people have the right to self-determination. The right to self-determination has three implications: (1) it is applicable for the colonial people to assert their right to sovereignty; (2) people freely choose their own form of government and also have full control of their natural resources; and (3) people prefer their own path of economic, social and cultural development through the market, state or mixed economy.

Both International Covenants hold equal legal status. All civil, political, economic, social and cultural rights are of equal footing in terms of their legal and moral standing around the world. However, their ways and means of implementation are different in nature, as outlined in Article 2 of the ICCPR and ICESCR.[52]

Article 2 of the ICCPR provides that the state shall implement civil and political rights and shall undertake the necessary steps to make them effective and to ensure remedial measures, while ICESCR Article 2 provides that the state shall undertake steps "to achieving progressively the full realisation of the economic, social and cultural rights".[53]

A. **Basic Human Rights**

Both ICCPR and ICESCR identified the basic human rights and provided a catalogue. ICCPR lists these rights in Articles 6 through 27, whereas ICESCR mentions them in Articles 6 through 15. ICCPR Article 28 mandates establishing the Human Rights Committee (Committee for Civil and Political Rights) for political and civil rights implementation. Similarly, the ICESCR establishes the Committee on Economic, Social and Cultural Rights to monitor the realisation of these rights (Articles 16 and 17). The monitoring system focusses mainly on overseeing the implementation of the covenants based on the states' reporting, information submitted by the IGOs and NGOs concerned and communication received from individuals and inter-state mechanisms.

Some NGOs specialise in specific areas of human rights. For instance, PEN International[54] and Article 19[55] specialise in the freedom of expression and opinion,

[49] www.cesr.org; Mahon (2008).

[50] Bossnyt (2013), Joseph et al. (2013).

[51] Craven (1995), Sinha (2006).

[52] Tomuschat (2014), Moren (1986).

[53] Senyonio (2011), Committee on Economic, Social and Cultural Rights, Comments No. 3, UNDOC E/1991/23 (1994); International Human Rights Reports, Nottingham UK (IHRR), p. 6.

[54] www.pen-international.org.

[55] www.article19.org.

while other NGOs such as the International Federation for Human Rights,[56] International League for Human Rights,[57] International Commission for Jurists,[58] Amnesty International,[59] and Human Rights Watch[60] are engaged in the creation and overall development of human rights law.

B. **Civil and Political Rights**

A catalogue of civil liberties is inserted in the ICCPR. These are the right to freedom of expression and opinion (Article 19); peaceful assembly (Article 21); association (Article 22) and thought, conscience and religion (Article 18). These rights to freedoms had already been pronounced by the British Bill of Rights, 1689, and the French Declaration of the Rights of Man and the Citizen, 1789. These were adopted by the United States in its constitution in 1791 and the General Assembly Declaration, UDHR 1948.

Individual freedom is central to the promotion of other freedoms. PEN International, a global association of writers founded in London in 1921 to promote friendship and intellectual co-operation between writers worldwide, has been fighting since its creation for the cause of poets, essayists, editors, novelists and playwrights. It is also engaged in human rights law-making under the auspices of the UN.[61]

(1) **Right to Freedom**

The right to freedom is the most fundamental aspect of human life. Freedom is the only way to attain the optimum development of human personality through which an individual makes life meaningful and creative. It includes reception and dissemination of information, holding and conveying thoughts and keeping the conscience flourishing. Individuals are free to choose any means, i.e. speech, print, electronic,[62] Internet, views and artistic mediums such as cinema, plays, novels, poetry, music,[63] storytelling, cartoons, mimicry, essays and sign language.

Any indication of probable and possible ways of expression that provide creative satisfaction to the mind enhances individual creativity, intellectuality and the humanisation of society. All this is possible only through the guarantee of the right to freedom.[64]

Freedom of opinion and its expression is not unlimited; therefore, it shall be subject to certain restrictions, as defined by laws, and is deemed necessary: (a) for

---

[56] Www.fidh.org (International Federation for Human Rights was established in 1922 in Paris).

[57] www.ilhr.org; Wiseberg and Sedale (1977).

[58] www.icj.org.

[59] www.amnesty.org.

[60] www.hrw.org.

[61] Howie (2018), UN Human Right Committee (2011) General Comment, Article 19, Freedom of Opinion and Expression, UN DOC CCPR/C/GC/34 (2011).

[62] Mukong v. Cameroon, Communication No.458/1991, UN Human Rights Committee (HRC) 21 July 1994, (1995) 2 IHRR 131; https://www.refworld.org/ cases,hrc,uae9acc1d.html.

[63] Eastrella v. Uruguay, Human Rights Committee (1983) 2 Selected Decisions HRC 93.

[64] Joseph et al. (2013).

respect or reputation of others, (b) for the protection of national security, public order, public health or morals." (Article 19(3)). Hate speech is not a part of freedom of speech (Article 20).[65]

Freedom of expression is the key to peaceful assembly (Article 21), association (Article 22), movement (Article 12) and religion (Article 18).[66] The enjoyment of these and their exercise thereof can be possible only through the bridge of freedom. By ensuring freedom of expression, people's right to assemble through conferences, protests and demonstrations is ensured. The right to freedom of association or union also receives meaning only based on freedom of expression. Likewise, conscience and religion are made functional in personal life and propagated in society at large through the root of freedom.

(2) **Political Rights**

Political rights, as stated in Article 25, and the freedom of opinion and expression, as outlined in Article 19, are closely intertwined. Free opinion and expression are crucial for the meaningful exercise of political rights. Without the freedom to express opinion and ideas, the purpose of exercising the right to vote, getting elected, participating in public discourse, and decision-making, is undermined. That's why both freedom and opinion are considered the lifeline of democracy.

(3) **Right to Life**

Article 6 of the ICCPR Covenant provides the right to life.[67] Life does not mean the mere physical existence of a human being, but its real spirit is dignified life, treated with humanity (Article 10(1)). It ensures the security of a person (Article 9), and it is an obligation of a state to extend it with all means. This is because all other freedoms depend on the existence and survival of an individual. Furthermore, the right to privacy[68] is an integral part of dignified life (Article 17). An individual needs to make choices about living and the autonomy to live alone and not be under constant surveillance in the age of information technology.

Life includes non-interference in matters such as marriage, family, children, home and correspondence (Articles 23–24). A person is recognised before the law (Article 16) based on their nationality and citizenship.

(4) **Personal Liberty**

Personal liberty[69] and security are protected under the ICCPR Covenant. It prohibits arbitrary arrest and prolonged detention and lays down certain procedural safeguards (Article 9). Whenever a person is arrested, detained or imprisoned, he shall be treated with humanity and dignity (Article 10). ICCPR protects against ex post facto law

---

[65] Mukong v. Cameroon, *supra note* 63.

[66] Wehrenfenning (2006).

[67] Etzioni (2010), Wicks (2012).

[68] Tene (2011), Yilma (2018).

[69] Macken (2005); ICCPR convention, Articles 9–11 and 14–15.

(Article 15), ensures a fair trial in courts and tribunals (Article 14)[70] and prevents imprisonment based on the inability to fulfil a contractual obligation (Article 11). Furthermore, it protects persons from slavery and forced labour (Article 8), genocide (Article 6(3)) and torture (Article 7) to ensure their life and liberty.

C. **Economic, Social, and Cultural Right**

Economic, social and cultural rights are second-generation collective rights. They are positive rights, and states are under obligation to realise these rights within their jurisdiction. ICESCR identifies economic, social and cultural rights listed in Articles 6 through 15 of the Covenant. These rights are further refined, authoritatively interpreted and precisely applied in a systematic manner by the Committee on Economic, Social and Cultural Rights (Committee on ESCR). Reports submitted by the UN special procedure mandate holders or the UN Special rapporteur further enrich these rights.

Presently, the right to food, housing, water, education, health and work are well taken by the Committee and other stakeholders.[71]

(1) **Right to Food**[72]

Food is a basic need for survival. It is an integral part of human dignity. Right to food means a person is free from hunger, food insecurity and malnutrition.[73] This implies the availability of food through purchase or production as provided by the state and market. The right to food talks about adequate food for everyday living. Food availability is related to production, distribution, import and export and easy reach to consumers.

NGOs like FIAN International,[74] Centre for Economic and Social Rights,[75] Right to Food & Nutrition,[76] Food First,[77] Heifer International[78] and others are actively engaged in formulating the right to food for all. IGOs such as Food and Agriculture Organisation (FAO), World Food Programme, United Nations Children's Fund (UNICEF) and United Nations Development Programme (UNDP) are also engaged in promoting the right to food. In fact, realising the right to food is a broad spectrum connected to the conservation of natural resources, progress in agricultural production and land reforms.

(2) **Right to Housing**

70 Zhang (2009).

71 Eide et al. (2001), Senyonjo (2011), General Comments of the Committee on Economic, Social and Cultural Rights and also Report of the UN Special Rapporteur are available at www.ohchr.org; https://www.refworld.org.

72 ICESCR convention, Article 11(1); Alston and Tomasevski (1984).

73 Frison and Claeys (2013).

74 www.fian.org.

75 www.cesr.org.

76 https://www.righttofoodandnutrition.org/.

77 www.foodfirst.org.

78 www.heifer.org.

Housing provides a person and his family space, privacy, security and identity. A house does not necessarily mean having a mansion with a big lawn or bungalow; it is not merely a shelter or roof over the head of a person but an adequate space to live with dignity.[79] The UN estimated over one hundred million homeless people worldwide and over one billion inadequately housed.[80] The homeless face constant harassment and denial of fundamental human rights.

In developing countries, people still suffer from an availability of adequate housing.[81] The right to housing is recognised in the UDHR (Article 25(1)) as well as the ICESCR (Article 11(1)). The UN Habitat, a global housing programme, and NGOs like the Centre on Housing Rights and Eviction (Cohre) and Habitat International Coalition, etc., are actively engaged in creating and developing the right to housing as a human right along with state parties, IGOs and the UN Special Rapporteur and Committee on ESCR, in particular.

(3) **Right to Health**[82]

The ICESCR Covenant, Article 12, defines the right to health in very broad terms. It contains "the right of everyone to the enjoyment of highest attainable standards of physical and mental health". It lays down state obligations to take steps to fully realise the right to health. Article 12 has two aspects—one is related to the prevention of diseases and the other is about states' responsibilities.

NGOs and foundations specifically work on the issue areas of the right to health for all. These are MSF (Doctors Without Borders), CARE International, Population Service International, Centre for Global Health, Global Health Network, Bill and Melinda Gates Foundation, Foundation for the National Institution of Health, Welcome Trust, Global Health Policy Centre, Global Alliance for Chronic Diseases and Global Health Technology Coalition, among others.

The UN Special Rapporteur, Paul Hunt (2002–2008), enriched the right to health through his intellectual produce literature. Paul Hunt's contribution was much appreciated and acknowledged globally.[83]

(4) **Right to Education**[84]

The ICESCR Covenant, Article 13, provides the right to education for everyone. Education is a vehicle for the optimum development of an individual's personality. The objective of education is to enhance the respect for human rights and fundamental freedom. Education cultivates mutual understanding, tolerance and friendship and works towards strengthening world peace and harmony too.

---

[79] S. Leckie, "The Right to Housing" in *Economic, Social and Cultural Rights: A Textbook (*eds.), A Eide C. Kraus and A. Rosas, *supra note* 73, pp.149–168.

[80] UNGA Official Records, 43rd Session Supplement No.8 addendum, A/43/8/Addl.1 (11 December, 1987).

[81] Speak and Tipple (2009); Ralf Wolf, "Participation in the Right to Access to Adequate Housing," *Tulsa J Comp & Int'l L*, vol.14, no.2 (2006–2007), pp.269–294.

[82] Tobin (2012), Marks (2013), Harrington and Stuttaford (2010).

[83] Hunt (2016).

[84] Beiter (2006).

States are under obligation to fully realise the right to education through free and compulsory primary education to all and endeavour for the realisation of secondary, technical and higher education for everyone. The realisation of the right to education for all is a big task. Hence, states shall seek co-operation from all stakeholders, i.e. UNESCO, World Bank, IMF, UNICEF, developed economies, NGOs, corporations, etc.

NGOs are involved in promoting the international right to education while prioritising key aspects such as the literature, quality of education, curriculum, pedagogy, education skill and the autonomy of educational institutions. While NGOs place a lot of emphasis on these issue areas, they pay relatively less attention to the international rights to education compared to other issue areas within the broader scope of international human rights. The UN Special Rapporteur on the Right to Education, Katrina Tomasevski (1998–2004), observed:

> a strong and vocal non-governmental organisations (NGOs) constituency, such as is found for freedom from torture or freedom, does not exist for the right to education.[85]

A good number of quality international NGOs and foundations are working in partnership with the United Nations Educational, Scientific and Cultural Organisation (UNESCO). According to UNESCO's official information, 370 international NGOs and more than 20 foundations are currently engaged with the UNESCOs on the right to education.[86]

(5) **Right to Work**

In the nineteenth century, technology was introduced to industrial production, where machinery replaced men at the workplace, and the demand for the right to work originated. Before this, the idea of the right to work was not articulated and mentioned within the catalogue of human rights.[87] Even the International Labour Organisation (ILO), 1919, did not mention the right to work as part of its constitution.

UDHR, Article 23, lays down the right to work, which was further adopted by the ICESCR Covenant, Articles 6, 7 and 8. The content and meaning of the right to work provide a broad spectrum, being inclusive in nature,

> The right to work, which includes the right for everyone and an opportunity to gain his living by work which he freely chooses or accepts....[88]

States realised the right to work through respect, protection and fulfilment of this aforementioned right by providing opportunities for work and employment. Right to work covers both public and private employments. The states make national policies on the right to work, formulate strategic action plans and seek expert knowledge from the ILO and co-operation from the IMF and World Bank, WTO and collaborate with

---

[85] Tomasevski (2005).

[86] Www.unesco.org > partnerships, non-governmental organisations and foundations.

[87] VanDerVen (1965).

[88] ICESCR convention, Article 6(1).

NGOs, corporations, the private sector, employer associations and trade unions, to expand employment opportunities.[89]

5 Specific Rights

The specific rights conventions are related to the elimination of racial discrimination, prevention of torture and protection against enforced disappearance. These conventions specifically protect individuals' life, liberty, dignity and equality. They address traditional prejudice against coloured people and the abuse of authoritarian powers.

A. **Racial Discrimination**[90]

Racial discrimination, prejudice and deprivation have traditionally been practised in their degraded form for centuries. However, conscience keeps people from raising their voices against these discriminatory practices of the feudal and imperial powers.

In 1909, the National Association for the Advancement of Coloured People (NAACP) was formed in New York. NAACP, an NGO, continuously fought against discrimination, deprivation and violence against people of African descent and other ethnic and coloured people. NAACP has made substantive contributions to the making of the International Convention on the Elimination of All Forms of Racial Discrimination (CERD).[91] Article 3 of the convention provides that the state shall prevent, prohibit and eradicate all practices of racial segregation and apartheid. It has limited itself to apartheid and does not explicitly mention other forms of discrimination.[92]

States are under obligation to amend laws and policies that are in contravention with the provisions of the CERD convention. Its basic idea of is equality before the law; therefore, the state shall combat racial hate and hate speech.

The Committee on CERD has been established under Article 8 of the CERD convention. The Committee has been monitoring the implementation of the convention's obligations by the state concerned.

The UN Special Rapporteur submitted its report on the Elimination of Racism and Racial Discrimination in 1994 to the Secretary General of the UN.[93] The Special Rapporteur acknowledged NGOs' contributions[94] in the provision of information.

The roles of NGOs such as Anti-Racism Information Service (ARIS), the International Association Against Torture (IAAT), the World Jewish Congress (WJC),

---

[89] Committee on ESCR, General Comment 18: Right to Work, 6 February 2006, para 19–30; Mundlak (2007).

[90] Adopted on 7 March 1966 and came into force on 4 April 1969. 660 UNTS 195; 5 ILM 352 (1966).

[91] Watson (1993), Rayan and Roy (2014).

[92] Moren (1985), Schwellonal (1966), Thormberry (2016).

[93] UNGA DOC A/49/677 (23 November 1994).

[94] The Report of the UN Special Rapporteur on Elimination of Race and Racism, 1999, para 39.

the RIGHTS, the World Council of Churches (WCC), the International Movement Against All Forms of Discrimination and Racism (IMADR), the International Women's Rights (IWR), Action Watch, the International Human Rights Association of American Minorities (IHRAAM), the Roma National Congress (RNC), the International Fellowship of Reconciliation (IFoR) and the Movement Against Racism and for the Friendship Among Peoples (MRAP)[95] are well appreciated in the eradication of racial discrimination.

B. **Torture**

Torture is a grave and serious danger to human life. It stands against individual dignity and security. It is also considered a crime against humanity. Prevention of torture is a pre-emption rule *jus cogens* of customary international law. The General Assembly adopted a Declaration on the Protection of All Persons from being Subjected to Torture and Other Cruel, Inhuman or Degrading Treatment or Punishment in 1975.[96]

NGOs such as the Association for the Prevention of Torture (APT),[97] International Rehabilitation Council for Torture Victims (IRCT),[98] Centre for Constitutional Rights (CCR),[99] Physicians for Human Rights (PHR),[100] Amnesty International,[101] International Commission of Jurists (ICJ),[102] International Federation of Human Rights (FIDH),[103] International League of Human Rights (ILHR)[104] have put their collective efforts into the formation of an international convention to stop torture and cruelty.[105]

The UN Committee Against Torture (UNCAT) has broadly interpreted state territory jurisdiction that encompasses ship, aircraft, national de jure and de facto control of the state,[106] emphasising the principle of "non-refoulement"—freedom from exclusion available to a refugee or an asylum seeker.

---

95 Ibid., para 44.

96 Declaration on the Protection of All Persons from being Subjected to Torture and Other Cruel, Inhuman or Degrading Treatment or Punishment, UNGA Res. 3452 (xxx) (9 December 1975).

97 http://www.opt.ch.

98 http://www.irct.org.

99 www.CCRJustice.org.

100 www.phr.org.

101 www.amnesty.org.

102 www.icj.org.

103 www.fidh.org.

104 www.ilhr.org.

105 Ackerman (1978).

106 UN Committee Against Torture, General Comment No.4 (2017) on the implementation of Article 3 of the Convention in Context of Article 22; UN Doc. CAT/C/GC/4 (4 September 2018) Para 10; UN CAT, General Comment No.2, Implementation by States, UN Doc. CAT/C/GC/2 (24 January 2008) Para 16.

NGOs[107] and UN Special Rapporteurs[108] have consistently reported incidents of torture being practised around the world. Arrested, detained and imprisoned persons deserve to be treated as human beings. States should facilitate the provision of information regarding the reasons for custody, grant access to a lawyer, impartial medical officer and legal aid, inform family members and friends, detain only on official premises, to not be put in confinement or solitude, stop degrading, inhuman and cruel behaviour, improve the conditions of prisons and lock-up facilities, avoid unnecessary handcuffs and chains and reform traditional and cruel interrogation methods to reveal information and extract confessions from victims.

States shall punish officials or non-officials who commit or inflict torture upon any individual or group. The state shall pay compensation to the victim who suffers and is left altogether to the mercy of officials committing the offence of torture.[109]

C. **Enforced Disappearance**

In the same way as torture, enforced disappearance is also a heinous crime. While a person's date of birth is known, the date of death remains unknown, leaving the victim's family and friends to suffer. Enforced disappearance was officially introduced in Germany in 1941 as a policy of "the Night and Fog Decree". This policy aimed to seize the persons and snuff them out without a trace. This practice was to later find its way to Latin America and spread across the globe.

NGOs such as Amnesty International, ICJ, IFHR, ILHR, Chatham House,[110] FEDEFAM,[111] International Coalition Against Disappearance (ICAD),[112] Family and NGOs Fighting for Victims' Rights, UN Watch, Civicus and Alkarama Foundation are actively engaged in the formation of convention and declaration on enforced disappearances.

The UN General Assembly adopted a Resolution on 20 December 1978 concerning disappeared persons, requesting the UN Commission on Human Rights to consider the issue of enforced disappearance and to make the appropriate recommendations.[113] In 1992, the General Assembly adopted the Declaration on the Protection of All Persons from Enforced Disappearance.[114]

Families of victims and NGOs consistently demand strengthened international law and mechanisms to combat the enforced disappearance of people. The UN General

---

[107] Amnesty International has published a report on state practice on Torture (1999); Nagan and Atkins (2001).

[108] UN Special Rapporteurs on Torture all in five, since 1985 to 2022. They have submitted regular reports to the UN. These Reports are invaluable documents because they prepared after spot visit in the countries and their scholarly submissions.

[109] Amnesty International (2001).

[110] www.chathamhouse.org.

[111] American Federation of Associations of Relatives of Disappeared Detaines.

[112] www.icaed.org.

[113] Sarkin (2012); UNGA Res. 33/173: Resolution on Disappeared Persons, UN Doc. A/Res/33/173 (20 December 1978).

[114] Declaration for the Protection of All Persons from Enforced Disappearance, UNGA Res 47/133, UN Doc. A/Res/47/133 (18 December 1992).

Assembly adopted the International Convention for the Protection of All Persons from Enforced Disappearance (ICPPED) on 20 December 2006. This was entered into force on 23 December 2010.[115]

States are under obligation to take necessary measures to declare enforced disappearance as an offence under their criminal law.[116] The state shall investigate the enforced disappearance cases and prosecute the responsible officials and punish them. This is an offence against humanity.[117] Victims are suitably rehabilitated and provided compensation for the violation of their rights and for being illegally deprived of their liberty. Individual communication may be submitted to the Committee on Enforced Disappearance (CED).[118] The CED was established under Article 32 and has been in operation since 2010.

NGOs and families of victims, along with all stakeholders, continue the campaign against enforced disappearance to eliminate this aforesaid crime against humanity.[119]

6 Groups Rights

Deprived groups like women, children, migrant workers and persons with disability (PwD) are protected under different UN Conventions.

A. **Women's Human Rights**

Half of the world's population comprises women and they ensure the continuity of humankind. Over the centuries, women have been treated unequally. They have been denied the equal enjoyment of freedoms and rights. They face discrimination, deprivation and violation in their existence. An NGO—International Abolitionist Federation (IAF)—was established in 1875 in Geneva,[120] engaged in the prohibition of trafficking and prostitution of women.

In the nineteenth century, women's suffrage was only officially recognised in New Zealand (1893). In 1904, the International Alliance for Women was formed in Berlin. This NGO fought for the women's vote and their political rights around the world.[121] Most countries conferred women's right to vote in the twentieth century.

NGOs have constantly struggled for women's equal rights and freedoms and the fight to end violations against them. The UN appointed the Commission on the

---

[115] 2716 UNTS 53; Lisa Qtt, *Enforced Disappearance in International Law*, Intersentia Publishers, UK 2011; Scovazzi and Citroni (2007), Solla and Fernanda (2005).

[116] ICPPED convention, Article 4.

[117] ICPPED convention, Article 5.

[118] ICPPED convention, Article 31.

[119] Committee on Enforce Disappearance, Third Session on 29 October – 9 November 2012, Geneva, paras 25 and 26.

[120] Summer (2006).

[121] O'Connor (1996).

Status of Women in 1946.[122] The breakthrough came when the Convention on the Elimination of All Forms of Discrimination Against Women (CEDAW) was adopted by the UN on 18 December 1979 and came into force on 3 September 1981.[123]

CEDAW has 30 Articles plus a Preamble that contains a definition and catalogue on women's rights and enforcement mechanism.

The CEDAW Committee was established to monitor the enforcement of the Convention across nations.[124] The Committee received states' reports on compliance with the Convention and progress made thereof. An optional protocol was added to the CEDAW in 2000, enabling women and NGOs to submit communications to the Committee in cases where the provisions of the Convention were violated.

The UN Special Rapporteur was appointed to visit countries, interact with all stakeholders, prepare a comprehensive report and submit it to the UN. In addition, the CEDAW Committee made a number of general recommendations to interpret, clarify and enlarge the Convention's mandate.[125] Martha C. Nussbaum, an American philosopher, elaborated on the contribution of the CEDAW convention that lays down international law for women and gives a purpose to NGOs to pursue women's causes worldwide.[126]

B. **Right of the Child**[127]

Stephen S. Wise, a prominent US Jewish leader, said:

> the child is not only the trusty of the past and the hope of the future, but it is the living present, entitled to every protection and security ...[128]

Children deserve care, protection, affection and optimum development. They face a lot of problems like child abuse, neglect, lack of education and skill, narcotic abuse, child labour, bonded labour and slavery, street life, child harassment, torture and disappearance, trafficking, prostitution, pornography, sale indenture, recruitment as child soldiers and victims of armed conflicts, juvenile justice, concerns regarding the well-being of unborn children and matters pertaining to child adoption. A child's life is for the enjoyment of childhood.

NGOs like Save the Children,[129] International Social Service (ISS),[130] the Friends World Committee for Consultation (Quakers),[131] the International Federation "Terre

---

[122] International Council of Women – an NGO established 1888, Washington DC. It fought for women's rights, gender justice and demanded for formation of Women Commission, www.icw.org.

[123] 1249 UNTS 13; Byrnes and Connors (2010), Rehof (1993), Nussbam (2016), Bayetskey (2000).

[124] CEDAW convention, Article 17.

[125] Www.reworld.org See the full text of Committee's recommendations.

[126] Martha C. Nussbaum, *supra note* 125, p.622.

[127] Adopted on 20 November 1989, entered into force on 2 September 1990, 1577 UNIT 53.

[128] Wise (2010).

[129] www.savethechildren.net.

[130] www.internationalsocialservice.net.

[131] www.quakersintheworld.org.

des Hommes,"[132] the International Abolitionist Federation (IAF),[133] CARE International,[134] Defence for Children International (DCI),[135] Child Fund,[136] Child Rights & You (CRY),[137] CIVICUS,[138] End Child Prostitution and Trafficking (ECPAT) International,[139] International Federation of Social Workers (IFSW),[140] EICE International,[141] Amnesty International[142] and Human Rights Watch (HRW)[143] have been continuously demanding the establishment of a convention outlining the rights of children.

The League of Nations in 1924 and the UN in 1959 adopted the Declarations on the Rights of the Child.[144] A substantive contribution was made in drafting the declarations by Save the Children and International Union for Child Welfare (IUCW).[145] In 1978, the Polish government submitted a proposal to the UN General Assembly to adopt the Convention on the Rights of the Child. The General Assembly authorised the UN Commission on Human Rights to prepare a Draft Convention on the Rights of the Child.

The UN Commission set up working groups to undertake the task of drafting the Convention. The Commission took ten years (1979–1989) to finalise the draft of the Convention. Meantime, NGOs were actively involved in the preparatory work of the Convention. They formed an NGO Group and collectively presented their recommendations to the working group or the representatives of the states to enhance the content of the draft convention and achieve maximum support.[146]

The Convention on the Rights of the Child (CRC), adopted on 20 November 1989, entered into force on 2 September 1990. The Committee on the Rights of the Child also received communication from NGOs, allowing them to submit alternative reports (Article 45).

NGOs formed the Children's Rights Information Network (CIRN), which collects and shares information related to the implementation of the CRC.[147] The CRC is a baseline of universal standards of children's rights. The remaining issues, such as

---

[132] www.terredeshomes.org.

[133] www.internationalabolitionist.org.

[134] www.care-international.org

[135] www.defenceforchildren.org.

[136] www.childfund.org.

[137] www.cry.org.

[138] www.civicus.org.

[139] www.ecpat.net.

[140] www.ifsw.org.

[141] Www.eiceinter.net

[142] www.amnesty.org.

[143] www.hrw.org.

[144] UNDOC A/4054 (1959).

[145] Cohen (1990).

[146] *United Nation: Legislative History of the Convention on the Rights of the Child*, UN Publications, Geneva (2007) 2 vol.; Le Blunce (1995).

[147] http://www.crin.org/ngogroupforcrc; Polonko and Lombardo (2015).

children in armed conflicts and the sale of children, child prostitution and child pornography, were addressed in the optional Protocols 2000.[148] These protocols were entered into force in 2002.

The UN Special Rapporteurs are appointed and assigned specific themes under child rights to visit countries, interact with all stakeholders and submit reports to the UN.

C. **Right of the Migrants**[149]

In the age of globalisation, the global economy has experienced a gradual process of integration. Developed economies of the world are facing low growth and an ageing population. They need an overseas workforce. When people cross their state boundaries in search of livelihood, they move from their country of origin to the host country.

In migration, three countries are involved: countries of origin, transit and destination. The flow of migrant workers increased from south to north. The migrants leave their homes, community and country for survival, better economic opportunities and employment. In other countries, these migrants generally face exploitation, abuse and expulsion. Sometimes resentment towards migrant workers manifests. Since 1975, the ILO, IOM, ECOSOC and NGOs have felt the need to form a convention under the auspices of the UN.

The International Organisation of Migration (IOM)[150] and NGOs were actively engaged in the formation of an international convention to protect migrant workers throughout the world. Earlier, the ILO had adopted a number of conventions and recommendations for the protection of migrant workers.[151] The General Assembly adopted a resolution in 1979 and established a working group to prepare an international convention on migrant workers.[152] It was obvious that the General Assembly convention was more effective than the triparty ILO convention.[153]

The International Convention on the Protection of the Rights of All Migrant Workers and Members of Their Families (ICPRMW) was adopted by UN General Assembly on 18 December 1990 and entered into force on 1 July 2003. Most destination countries and developed economies have not yet ratified the ICPRMW convention.

---

[148] Optional Protocol to the Convention on the Rights of the Child on the Involvement of the Children in Armed Conflicts, 2000, http://www.un.org/children/conflicts/english; Optional Protocol to the Convention on the Rights of the Child on the Sale of Children, Child Prostitution and Child Pornography 2000, UNGA Res., 54/263, 25 May 2000.

[149] International Convention on the Protection of the Rights of All Migrant Workers and Their Families 1990 (ICPR-MW), adopted on 18 December 1990, entered into force on 1 July 2003, UNGA Res. 45/158 (18 Dec. 1990); Cholewinski (1997).

[150] http://www.iom.int, UN Migration or International Organisation of Migrant is an IGO associated with the United Nations. It was established in 1951.

[151] Daway (2010).

[152] UNGA Res 34/172, December 1979.

[153] Hune (1985).

NGOs established the global campaign for the ratification of the ICPRMW convention on the rights of migrants[154] on 18 December 2010 in Geneva. NGOs from all over the world have been associated with this campaign. Thirteen NGOs plus one observer NGO formed a steering committee to carry on the campaign with the partnership of IOM.

The UN Special Rapporteur on the human rights of migrants was created in 1990. Special Rapporteurs did not require the ratification of the treaty to visit their country, interact with all stakeholders for the protection of migrant workers and provide assistance to the state. Special Rapporteurs submit annual reports to the UN with some scholarly submissions. Earlier, Trade Unions and NGOs fought for the formation of a convention for migrant workers and presently for its ratification and compliance.

D. **Rights of Persons with Disability**[155]

Approximately 15 per cent of the global population experiences some form of disability.[156] Disability is related to a bio-medical aspect such as difficulty in seeing, hearing or moving. Disability is a diversity in population with specific physical, intellectual or sensory impairments.

Disability rights have gradually developed since 1970 under the auspices of the UN. The General Assembly adopted the Declaration of the Rights of Disabled Persons, 1975[157], and the World Programme of Action (WPA), 1982,[158] for the protection and participation of persons with disability in social life.

The UN Special Rapporteur was appointed in 1994.[159] The Special Rapporteur and six international NGOs: Disabled People's International (DPI),[160] Inclusion International,[161] Rehabilitation International,[162] World Blind Union (WBU),[163] World Federation of the Deaf (WFD)[164] and World Federation of Psychiatric Users (WFPU),[165] have jointly emphasised the need for the formation of the UN Convention on Persons with Disability. This was a successful experiment of the partnership between NGOs and the UN in forming the Convention on the Rights of Persons with Disability (CRPD), 2006, a reality.

---

[154] www.migrantsrights.org.

[155] Adopted on 13 December 2006, entered into force on 3 May 2008, UNGA Res. 61/106; Megret (2008).

[156] www.worldbank.org, topic disability inclusion overview.

[157] UNGA Res. 3447/30 (9 December 1975), UN Doc. A/RES/3447.

[158] UN Doc A/RES/37/51 (1982).

[159] www.unorgdevelopmentdesadisabilities, A/52/56-Report of the first mandate of Special Rapporteur 1995.

[160] www.disablledpeoplesinternational.org.

[161] http://inclusioninternational.org.

[162] www.riglobal.org.

[163] www.worldblindunion.org.

[164] www.wfdeaf.org.

[165] www.wnusp.net.

The UN General Assembly adopted the CRPD on 13 December 2006, and it came into force on 3 May 2008, along with the optional protocol of CRPD.[166] This was a historical step because earlier, UDHR, 1948, and the International Covenants, 1966, had ignored disability rights.

NGOs established the International Disability Alliance (IDA)[167] for the implementation of the CRPD convention. Around 1,100 NGOs joined this Disability Alliance. NGOs were engaged collectively with other stakeholders in removing social barriers and promoting an enabling environment for disabled persons.

7 Conclusion

The stories of making international human rights law and non-governmental organisation (NGO) actions go side by side. In the nineteenth century, NGOs undertook the campaign for the abolition of slavery and the formulation of humanitarian law. A breakthrough came by adopting the Universal Declaration of Human Rights (UDHR) 1948, which was followed by nine core international human rights treaties. These are:

(1) The International Convention on the Elimination of All Forms of Racial Discrimination (ICERD), 1965.
(2) The International Covenant on Civil and Political Rights (ICCPR), 1966.
(3) The International Covenant on Economic Social and Cultural Rights (ICESCR), 1966.
(4) The Convention on Elimination of All Forms of Discrimination Against Women (CEDAW), 1979.
(5) The Convention Against Torture and Other Cruel Inhuman or Degrading Treatment or Punishment (CAT), 1984.
(6) The Convention on the Rights of Child (CRC), 1989.
(7) The International Convention on Protection of the Rights of All Migrant Workers and Members of Their Families (ICPRMW), 1990.
(8) The International Convention on Protection of All Persons from Enforced Disappearance (CPED), 2006.
(9) The Convention on the Rights of Persons with Disabilities (CRPD), 2006

The World Conference on Human Rights (WCHR) was held in Vienna in 1993, and it was declared that all human rights are available to one and all. Civil, political, economic, social and cultural rights are on an equal footing. They are indivisible, interrelated, interdependent and universal in their application.

Certain basic human rights like the right to life, right against torture, prohibition of slavery, imprisonment for debt, ex post facto law, recognition of persons before

[166] UNGA Res. 61/106 (13 December 2006); Kanter (2014).

[167] www.internationaldisabilityalliance.org.

the law and the freedom of religion are not derogatory; therefore, they cannot be suspended even at the time of public emergency.[168]

Human rights treaties have a humanitarian character and are based on the idea of international order and the promotion of human values. The treaties are based on the priority and mutual interests of state parties. Human rights treaties are based on the moral foundation of the international community. Reservation to human rights treaties is permitted only when they are compatible with the objectives and purposes[169] of the particular treaty, for instance, The Convention of Child Rights, 1987, etc.

A state cannot denunciate or withdraw its treaty obligations. This is permissible within the law of the treaty. The humanitarian character of the treaty is specifically protected under Article 60 Clause 5 of the Vienna Convention of the Law of Treaties (VCLT), 1969. Denunciation of the treaty is made by the executive branch of the government and is not necessarily endorsed by the parliament or judiciary. NGOs play a crucial role in the process of denouncing human rights violations by raising awareness among the public and advocating for transparency when states fail to fulfil their obligations under human rights treaties.

There is no uniformity in all nine core human rights treaties. But it is clear that withdrawal is only permissible on a procedural level, as opposed to a substantive one. The international norms of human rights must prevail globally.[170]

References

Ackerman S (1978) Torture and other form of cruel and unusual punishment in international law. Vanderbilt J Transn'l L 11:653–708 at 675–676

Alston P, Tomasevski K (eds) (1984) The right to food. Cambridge University Press, Cambridge

Amnesty International (2001) Putting an end to impunity: justice for torture victims. Int'l J Red Cross 87:123

Bair J (2005) The international covenant on civil and political rights and its (first) optional protocol. University of California Press, Berkley

Baxter RR (1986) International law in her infinite variety. Int'l Comp & LQ 29(4):549–566

Bayetskey AF (2000) The CEDAW convention: its contribution today. Proc Am Society Int'l 94:197–199

Beiter KD (2006) The protection of the right to education by international law. Martinus Nijhoff, Leiden

Ben-Noftali O (ed) (2011) International humanitarian law and international human rights law. Oxford University Press

Le Blunce LJ (1995) Rights of the child: united nations law making on human rights. University of Nebrarska Press, London

---

[168] Higgins (2011).

[169] Reservation to the Convention on the Prevention and Punishment of Genocide, Advisory Opinion (1951) ICJ Reports 15; Vienna Convention on the Law of Treaties 1969, Article 2(1)(d) and Articles 19–23; Ziemele and Liede (2013).

[170] Tyagi (2008).

Bothe M (1980) Legal and non-legal norms—a meaningful distinction in international relations. Netherlands YB Int'l 11:65–95
Bossnyt M (2013) Guide to the 'Travaux Preparatoires' of international covenant on civil and political rights. Martinus Nijhoff, Dordrecht
Brownlies I, Goodwin-Gill G (eds) (2010) Brownlie's documents on human rights, 6th edn. Oxford University Press, Oxford
Bugnion F (2004) The international committee of the red cross and the development of international humanitarian law. Chicago J Int'l L 5(1):191–215
Byrnes A, Connors J (2010) International bill of rights for women: the impact of the CEDAW convention. Oxford University Press
Cessin R (1968) Twenty years of NGOs efforts on behalf of human rights, in human rights: final report of the international NGOs conference. UNESCO Publications, Paris
Cholewinski R (1997) Migrant workers in international human rights law: their protection in countries of employment. Clarendon Press, Oxford
Cohen CP (1990) Role of non-governmental organisations in the drafting of convention on the rights of the child. Hum Rts Q, vol.12 (1990) 137–147 at 138
Craven M (1995) The international covenant on economic, social and cultural rights: a perspective on development. Clarendon Press, Oxford
Crawford J (ed) (2019) Brownlie's principles of public international law, 9th edn. Oxford University Press, pp 638–648
Daway P (2010) Migrant worker's rights and status under international law: Asian experience. J East Asia Int'l L 3(2):263–292 at 267–271
De Baets A (2009) Impact of the universal declaration of human rights on the study of history. Hist Theor 48:20–43 at 20
Dormann K, Maresca L (2004) The international committee of the red cross and its contribution to the development of international humanitarian law is specialized instruments. Chicago J Int'l L 5(1):1–17
Eide A, Krause C, Rosas A (eds) (2001) Economic, social and cultural rights: a textbook, 2nd edn. Martinus Nijhoff, The Hague
Etzioni A (2010) Life: the most basic rights. J Hum Rts 9(1):100–110
Frison C, Claeys P (2013) Right to food in international law. In: Encyclopedia of food & agriculture ethics, pp 1–8, at 1
Glendon MA (2002) A world made new: Eleanor Roosevelt and the universal declaration of human rights. Random House, New York
Guzman AT, Meyer TL (2010) International soft law. J Legal Anal 2(1):171–225
Harrington J, Stuttaford M (eds) (2010) Global health and human rights: legal and philosophical prospective. Routledge, London
Harris D, Shivkumaran S (2020) Cases and material of international law, 9th edn. Sweet & Maxwell, London, pp 59, 550 & 630.
Higgins R (2011) Derogation under human rights treaties. British YB Int'l L 48(1):281–319
Howie E (2018) Protecting the human right to freedom of expression in international law. Int'l J Speech-Language Pathol 20(1):12–15
Humphrey JP (1949) The universal declaration of human rights. Int'l J 4(4):351–361
Hunt P (2016) Interpreting the international right to health in a human right-based approach to health. Health Hum Rts J 18(2):109–130
Hune S (1985) Drafting an international convention on the protection of the rights of migrant workers and their families. Int'l Migrant Rev 19(3):570–615 at 571
Jennings R, Watts A (eds) (1996) Oppenheim's, International law, 9th edn, vol 1: Peace, part I. Longman, London, p 22
Joseph S et al (2013) International covenant on civil and political rights, 3rd edn. Oxford University Press, Oxford
Kanter AS (2014) The development of disability rights under international law from the charity to human rights. Routledge, London

Korey W (1998) NGOs and the universal declaration of human rights. Palgrave, New York
Lauterpacht H (1948) The universal declaration of human rights. British YB Int'l L 25:354–381
Macken C (2005) Preventive detention and the right of personal liberty and security under the international convention on civil and political rights 1966. Adelaide L Rev 26:1–28
Martin AE (1916) Pioneer anti-slavery press. Mississippi Valley Hist Rev 2(4):509–528
Marks S (ed) (2013) Health and human rights: basic international document, 3rd edn. Harvard University Press, Cambridge
Mahon C (2008) Progress the front: the craft optional protocol to the international covenant on economic, social and cultural rights. Hum Rts L Rev 8(4):617–646
Megret F (2008) The disability convention: human rights of persons' with disability or disability rights. Hum Rts Q 30(2):494–516
Moren T (1985) The meaning and reach of the international convention on the elimination of all forms of racial discrimination. Am J Int'l L 72(2):283–318 at 283
Moren T (1986) Human rights law-making in the united nations. Oxford University Press, Oxford
Mundlak G (2007) The right to work linking human rights and employment policy. Int'l Labour Rev 146(3–4):189–215
Nagan WP, Atkins L (2001) The international law of torture: from universal proscription to effective application and enforcement. Harvard Hum Rts J 14:87–122 at 89
Nussbam MC (2016) Women's progress and women's human rights. Hum Rts Q 38:589–622
O'Connor SD (1996) The history of the women's suffrage movement. Vanderbilt L Rev 44(3):657–676
Olitier M (2002) The relevance of soft law as source of international human rights. Comp & Intl'l L J Southern Africa 35(3):289–307
Polonko KA, Lombardo LX (2015) Non-governmental organisations and the UN convention on the rights of the child. Int'l J Child Rts 33:133–153 at 139
Pronto AN (2008) Some thoughts on making of international law. European J Int'l L 19(3):601–616
Rayan Y, Roy W (2014) The quiet revolutionary and NAACP. University Press Kentucky, Lexington K.Y.
Rehof LA (1993) Guide to the Travarx preparations of the united nations convention on the elimination of all forms of discrimination against women. Martinus Nijhoff, Leiden
Robins BD (1971) Experiment in democracy: the story of the US citizens organisations in framing the charter of the united nations. Parkside Press, New York
Sarkin J (2012) Why the prohibition of an enforced disappearance has attained Jus Cogens Status in international law. Nordic J Int'l L 81(4): 537–584 at 571
Schwellonal E (1966) Convention on the elimination of all forms of racial discrimination. Int'l & Comp L Q 15(4):996–1068
Scovazzi T, Citroni G (2007) The struggle against enforced disappearance and the 2007 united nations convention. Martinus Nijhoff, Leiden, p 007
Schacter O (1977) The twilight existence of non-binding international agreements. Am J Int'l L 71(2):296–306
Senyonio M (2011) Reflection on state obligation with respect to economic, social and cultural rights in international human rights law. Int'l J Hum Rts 15(6):969–1012
Senyonjo MS (ed) (2011) Economic, social and cultural rights in international law, 2nd edn. Hart Publishers, Oxford, UK
Shabas WA (ed) (2013) The universal declaration of human rights: the Travaux Preparatoaires. Cambridge University Press, Cambridge
Sinha MK (2006) Enforcement of economic, social and cultural rights: international and national perspectives. Manak Publishers, New Delhi
Sinha M (2017) The slaves cause: a history of abolition. Yale University Press
Solla P, Fernanda M (2005) Enforced disappearance in international human rights. McFarland Publishing Co., US
Speak S, Tipple G (2009) The hidden millions: homeless in developing countries. Routledge, London

Sohn LB (1967) The universal declaration of human rights. J Int'l Commission Jurists 8:17–26 at 17–18
Subedi SP (2017) The effectiveness of the UN human right system. Routledge, London, p 20
Summer A (2006) Which women? What Europe? Josephin Butter and international abolitionist federation. Hist Workshop J 62(1): 214–231; www.internationalabolitionist.org.
Tene O (2011) Privacy: the new generation. Int'l Data Privacy L 1:15–27
Thormberry P (2016) The international convention on the elimination of all forms of racial discrimination. Oxford University Press, Oxford
Tobin J (2012) Right to health in international law. Oxford University Press, Oxford
Tomasevski K (2005) Has the right to education a future within the united nations? A behind-the-scense account by the special rapporteur on the right to education 1998–2004. Hum Rts L Rev 5(2): 205–237 at 210
Tomuschat C (2014) Human rights between idealism and realism, 3rd edn. Oxford University Press, Oxford
Tyagi YK (2008) The denunciation of human rights treaties. British YB Int'l L 79(1):86–193
Van Boven T (1990) The role of non-governmental organisations in international human rights standard-setting: a pre-requisite of democracy. Calif Western Int'l J 20:207–225
van Hoof GJH (1983) Rethinking the sources of international law. Kluwar Law & Taxation Publishers, Netherlands
VanDerVen JJM (1965) The right to work as a human right. Howard LJ 11:397–412 at 398
Watson DL (1993) Assessing the role of NAACP in the civil rights movement. The Historian 55(3)
Wehrenfenning D (2006) The human right of religious freedom in international law. J Peace Rev 18(3):403–410
Wicks E (2012) Meaning of life: dignity and right to life in international human rights treaties. Hum Rts Rev 12(2):119–219
Wise SS (2010) Justice to the child. Ann Am Acad Polit Soc Sci 35:35–41 at 40
Wiseberg LS, Sedale HM (1977) The international league for human rights: the strategy of human rights NGO. Georgia J Int'l & Comp L 7:289–313
Woodward BK (2010) Global civil society in international law making and global governance. Martinus Nijhoff Publishers, Lieden
Yilma KM (2018) The right to privacy in the digital age: boundaries of the 'new' UN discourse. Nordic J Int'l L 87(4):485–503
Zhang J (2009) Fair trial in ICCPR. J Polit Law 4(2):39–43
Ziemele I, Liede L (2013) Reservation to human rights treaties: from draft guidelines 3.1.12 to guidelines 3.1.5.6. Eur J Int'l L 24(4):1135–1152

Chapter 9
Enforcement of Human Rights

1 Introduction

The enforcement mechanism of human rights is broadly divided in two categories, i.e. Charter-based system and Treaty-based system. The Charter-based system consists of former UN Human Rights Commission, UN Human Rights Council, Universal Periodical Review Mechanism and UN Special Rapperteurs, whereas treaty-based system is composed with UN Human Right Treaty Bodies. They are treated merely as monitoring bodies working at international and regional levels. Regional machineries are at work in the European, Inter-American and African continents.

As a precursor of the United Nations, the League of Nations had put monitoring mechanisms related to minorities' rights and mandated territories in its covenant.[1] The system of the League of Nations was applicable in some specific areas and countries. This was not as effective as the member states had expected.

The Charter emphasised the promotion and protection of human rights and fundamental freedom around the world.[2] Article 56 of the Charter obligates states to take joint and separate action with the UN human rights system. Human rights have universal application, and hence, no more exclusive domestic jurisdiction of a state is asserted.[3]

Apart from states, non-governmental organisations (NGOs) are also associated in the promotion, protection and realisation of human rights through consultative status arrangements under Article 71 of the UN Charter.[4]

General Assembly Declaration 1998 further clarified and invited individuals, groups and organs of society to promote and protect universally recognised human rights and fundamental freedoms across the nations. NGOs are on equal footing with

---

[1] Burgenthal (2006).

[2] UN Charter, Articles 1(3), 13(1)(b), 55(c) and 56.

[3] UN Charter, Article 2(7); Orakhelashvili (2019), Shaw (2019), pp. 199, 220.

[4] Wiseberg (2003), Goel and Tripathi (2010).

P. Rai, *Non-Governmental Organisations and International Law*,
https://doi.org/10.1007/978-981-97-5469-4_9

the governments and inter-governmental organisations (IGOs) in the realisation of human rights. Besides, the Declaration of 1998 lays down the rights and responsibilities of individuals, groups and organs of society being part of the human rights infrastructure.[5]

The UN Declaration 1998 confirms certain rights of NGOs to assemble peacefully and communicate with IGOs, receive and disclose information, carry out research studies, organise seminars and conferences, undertake advocacy, submit the petition, disclose alternative public policies and ask for redressal through fair and due process in the case of human right violation. Individuals, NGOs, groups and organs of society are free to engage for the realisation of human rights in every nook and corner of the world by employing aforesaid peaceful means.[6] The NGOs are responsible for making people aware, educated and trained to enjoy their human rights and fundamental freedoms.[7] The UN Declaration Rights and Responsibility, Article 18 Clause 2 says:

> Rights and Responsibility: Individuals, groups, institutions, and non-governmental organisations also have an important role to play and a responsibility in safeguarding democracy and promoting human rights and fundamental freedoms.

The United Nations Charter includes human rights, but it has "no word on implementing the aspirations or making it enforceable."[8] In the twentieth century, number of NGOs and their influence increased many folds.[9] Human rights NGOs and philanthropic foundations were more in number in comparison to independent states. Philanthropic Foundations such as Carnegie Foundation 1905, Rockefeller Foundation 1913 and Ford Foundation 1936 have extended financial support to human rights NGOs.[10]

After the World War II (1939–1945), the superpowers were busy in the cold war, European countries were preoccupied with their reconstruction, and Asian and African nations, which were newly independent, had limited resources and capacity, which naturally created space for private initiatives and NGO activism.[11]

NGOs are an integral part of the international human rights regime because human rights cannot be fully described and explained without recognising their role.[12] NGOs' engagement differs in methodology from the state, IGOs, corporations and other private actors.

---

[5] Declaration on the Right and Responsibility of Individuals, Groups and Organs of Society to Promote and Protect Universally Recognise Human Rights and Fundamental Freedoms 1998 (UN Declaration 1998) UN Doc Res. 33/141 (9 December, 1998); Brownlie's *Documents, supra note* 2, pp. 234–240.

[6] UN Declaration 1998, Article 13; Chap. 5 of this book.

[7] UN Declaration 1998, Article 16.

[8] Borchard (1946).

[9] Sinnar (1995).

[10] Parmar (2012).

[11] Iriye (1999).

[12] Henderson (1988).

Most international NGOs' headquarters are in Western Europe and the United States.[13] The international legal system was dominated by Western countries throughout the eighteenth, nineteenth and early-twentieth centuries. The Western powers had established their hegemony in the international regimes. NGOs activism cannot be allowed to replicate the Western countries' model. They have to accommodate and address the problems, needs and interests of the people of the southern hemisphere. NGOs should change their structure and decentralise their work to include developing countries adequately.[14]

Post the Cold War, a World Conference on Human Rights was held in Vienna in 1993. The Vienna Conference declared that human rights and fundamental freedoms are the birthright of all human beings; their protection and promotion are primarily the responsibility of all governments. In the follow-up, all NGOs like Amnesty International,[15] Human Rights Watch,[16] International Federation of Human Rights,[17] International Commission of Jurists[18] and Oxfam International[19] have reinvented their focus areas and have expanded their geographical reach. NGOs received financial contributions from philanthropic foundations[20] and individuals who signed to give pledges.[21] NGOs created large memberships, volunteers and individual donors because they did not prefer funding from states and the market. Human rights NGOs face ethical dilemmas regarding funding, operation and collaboration.[22] Despite these dilemmas, NGOs are continuously engaged with human rights bodies.

2 Charter-Based Bodies

Human rights are accumulated values of the global civilization.[23] It was visualised by Immanuel Kant in the early-eighteenth century that violation of human rights is concerned with all human beings.[24] When the United Nations was founded in 1945, it has envisaged human rights as one of its primary goals. Moreover, the UN has prescribed mechanism for their enforcement.

---

[13] Chandhoke (2005).

[14] Smith et al. (1978).

[15] Www.amnesty.org.

[16] Www.hrw.org.

[17] Www.fidh.org.

[18] Www.icj.org.

[19] Www.oxfam.org.

[20] Ford Foundation, www.fordfoundation.org; Rockfeller Foundation, www. rockfellerfoundation.org; Carnegie Foundation, www.carnegiefoundation.org; Oak Foundation, www.oaktnd.org.

[21] Warren Buffet, Bill Gates, Azim Premji, Sarah Blakely, Agakhan, Priscilla Chan, MacKenzie Bezos, Rohini Nilekini, see www.givingpledge.org.

[22] Bell (2004), Lamer (2005).

[23] McDougal and Bebr (1964).

[24] Kant (1903).

The Charter-based mechanisms are an integrated system consisting of two procedures and three institutions. The procedures are: Universal Periodic Review (UPR) Mechanism and UN Special Procedure, popularly known as the UN Rapporteur. There are institutions: (1) The former United Nations Commission on Human Rights (1946–2006); (2) The UN Human Rights Council (2006–) and (3) The Office of the High Commissioner of Human Rights (1993–). Their scope is outlined below.

A. **UN Commission on Human Rights**

In persuasion of the UN Charter Article 68, the ECOSOC established the United Nations Commission on Human Rights in 1946 for the promotion and protection of human rights.[25] The UN Commission was replaced by the United Nations Human Rights Council in 2006.

The former UN Commission did not exercise powers on violation of human rights from 1946 to 1966.[26] The Commission had received human rights violation complaints but did not act thereon.[27] The reason cited by the Commission was lack of power. Hersch Lauterpacht did not endorse the Commission's decision that it had no powers to take any action. The Commission had inherent powers, as per the Charter's mandate to protect human rights.[28]

In the evolving global landscape, Hersch Lauterpacht's perspectives gained prominence as the United Nations and its Commission witnessed an increase in membership from newly independent African and Asian nations.[29] In the *Namibia* case, the International Court of Justice (ICJ) held that discrimination based on colour, race, ethnicity and origin constitutes a denial of human rights and violate the purposes and principles of the Charter.[30]

In 1970, a significant breakthrough occurred with the adoption of ECOSOC's Procedure 1503. Although the Former Commission was replaced by the Council in 2006, the continuity of Procedure 1503 led to the establishment of the UN Special Procedure or the UN Special Rapporteur. The ECOSOC resolutions were authorised by the UN Commission to examine the following:

> "...situations in gross and consistence pattern of human rights violations." Out of these resolutions, two procedures - country-specific and thematic specific procedures came into existence. The Commission followed the three patterns in the human rights monitoring procedure i.e. first, gross and consistent violation of human rights; second, the confidentiality of the procedure, and third an exhaustion of local remedies.[31]

---

[25] United Nations Economic and Social Council Resolution (ECOSOC Res.) 5(1), (16 February, 1946).

[26] Rodely (2014), Shaw (2019), p 220; UN Commission on Human Rights took the position in it first session that it had no power to take action and send the report to the ECOSOC, UNDOC E/ 259 (Supp) (1947), para 22.

[27] Prasad (1975).

[28] Lauterpach (1950).

[29] Robertson and Merrils (1996).

[30] Namibia Case, Advisory Opinion, ICJ Report, 1971, p. 16; 49 ILR 2, p. 81.

[31] Rudolf (2000a).

The Former UN Commission utilised information supplied by NGOs.[32] NGOs are also involved in intensive lobbying for appointing country and thematic-specific procedures.[33]

In the first two decades, the religious NGOs—World Muslim Congress, World Council of Churches, Luthern World Federation, Pontifical Commission for Justice and Peace, Pax Romana, World Council of Religion and Peace and World Jews Congress—were actively engaged in the promotion of human rights. Besides, the International League for Human Rights, International Federation of Human Rights, International Commission of Jurists, Anti-Slavery International, PEN International, International Alliance for Women and International Trade Union were also engaged.

Aforesaid NGOs and many more were collecting information from newspapers, magazines, journals, UN publications, members and relatives of victims, whistle-blowers, travellers and many other possible sources.[34] They transmit this information to the UN Commission. Sometimes they directly contact the officials of the concerned state, victims, lawyers, friends and relatives to help the victims. Influential and impartial NGOs like ICRC and Amnesty International visit the concerned states.

B. **UN Human Rights Council**

United Nations Commission on Human Rights was replaced by Human Rights Council (HRC) in 2006.[35] NGOs community welcomed this replacement, hoping to remove the weakness of the former Commission with the advent of the new Human Rights Council.[36] The former UN Commission was a subsidiary of the ECOSOC, whereas HRC is a subsidiary of the General Assembly. In the Former UN Commission, there were 53 member states, while in HRC, there are 47 member states only.

NGOs with dubious membership and some countries with a poor record on human rights' protection were elected to the former UN Commission. These states tried to discourage NGOs' participation in the former UN Commission. Such a tendency could not be continued in the Human Rights Council for the years ahead. NGOs are pursuing their country's candidature on the basis of their voluntary commitments and responsibilities towards the protection of human rights.[37]

(1) **Composition**

The members are elected for three years and re-elected once only by the UN General Assembly. Systematic violation of human rights could lead to the suspension of membership from the Human Rights Council. Such resolutions are adopted by the General Assembly via two-thirds majority of members present and voting. The

---

[32] A. H. Robertson and J. G. Merrills, *supra note* 30, pp. 83–84.

[33] Wiessbrodt (1977).

[34] Ibid.

[35] UNGA, Res. 60/251 (15 March 2006).

[36] Ghanea (2006).

[37] Nader (2007).

membership of a nation as an elected member of the Human Rights Council is to be reviewed by the Universal Periodic Review Mechanism of human rights within each tenure. The composition of Human Rights Council consists of the majority of the global south, which is distributed based on equitable geographical regions.[38] The composition, representation and election process of Human Rights Council have significantly improved in comparison with the former UN Commission.[39]

The former UN Commission was accused of politicising the human rights issue. The Human Rights Council agenda is based on the principle of universality, impartiality, objectivity and non-selectivity.[40] HRC has been given the mandate to address situations of gross and systematic violation of human rights and to respond promptly to human rights emergencies.

NGOs are keeping a watch on the release of the agenda and the programme of work for the Human Rights Council sessions and establishing contact with the state representatives and other stakeholders. Human Rights Council holds three sessions annually for a minimum period of 10 weeks. Special sessions may be held whenever necessitated, with the request of one-third of the member states of the council. NGOs participate in these sessions.

NGOs with consultative status are entitled to submit their written or oral statements in a precise manner. Informally they have an opportunity at the Geneva headquarters of Human Rights Council to interact with all stakeholders of human rights. Apart from NGOs, UN specialised agencies, IGOs and the national human rights institutions (NHRIs) are also entitled to participate in the Human Rights Council sessions as an observer.[41]

The emphasis is on the procedural aspects of the Human Rights Council on dialogue and co-operation for the prevention of human rights violations.[42]

(2) The Human Rights Council Advisory Committee

The Advisory Committee was created with its members in 2008. The committee consists of 18 independent expert members—five African states; five Asian; three Latin American; three from Western Europe and other states and two from Eastern Europe. This is a think tank of the Human Rights Council.[43] The Human Rights Council Advisory Committee serves as the successor to the former subcommission of the UN Commission on Human Rights. The Advisory Committee's thrust is to conduct studies and research on human rights issues and to render advice to the Human Rights Council. The NGOs who bear the consultative status and also wishing to participate in the session of the Advisory Committee must send a letter of request

---

[38] Out of 47 Africa 13, Asia 13, Latin America and the Carribean 8, Eastern Europe 6 and Western Europe and others 7.

[39] Boyle (2009).

[40] Agenda and framework from the program of work, A/HRC/RES/5/1, 18 June 2007.

[41] UN Doc. A/60/251 (3 April 2006), Para 11.

[42] Ibid., para 5(f); Terlingen (2006).

[43] www.ohcher.org/aboutAC.

to the OHCHR. NGO Liaison Office also extends its services to NGOs' seeking accreditation for participation in the session of the HRC Advisory Committee.

(3) **The Human Rights Council Working Groups**

The Human Rights Council has two working groups for dealing with the complaint procedure. These working groups are known as Working Groups of Communication (WGC) and Working Groups on Situations (WGS). These working groups consist of five members each, representing all regional groups. They are independent experts selected from within the Advisory Committee. The WGC determines whether a complaint deserves to be admitted for investigation. The WGS receives the complaints forwarded by WGC, examines them and then presents them to the Human Rights Council. They meet twice a year for five working days for scrutinising the complaints. They can either drop it or forward it to the Human Rights Council for a final nod.

(4) **Sessions**

The Human Rights Council holds three regular sessions annually for at least ten weeks. A special session is to be held if one-third of the members request for it. Apart from 42 regular sessions, 28 special sessions were also held between 2006 and 2019. NGOs participated in regular and special sessions, interacting with representatives, non-member states, IGOs and NHRIs.

3 Communication Procedure

Human Rights Council's Communication Procedure is a tool for the effective implementation of human rights around the world. This was introduced in 1970 via ECOSOC Resolution 1503[44] and applied by the former UN Commission on Human Rights. The Human Rights Council as a successor of former UN Commission further improved procedure 1503. It has ensured that the procedure 1503 shall maintain impartiality, objectivity, efficiency, victim-friendly and time-bound disposal of complaints.[45] The communication procedure still maintains its confidentiality of procedure 1503. The complaints or communication is submitted to the OHCHR. The Office of the High Commissioner of Human Rights (OHCHR) is the secretariat of the Human Rights Council. The office organises the communication submitted by the states, NGOs, individuals or groups and forwards them to the working group of communication for further action.

The communication procedure is universal and available to every member state, i.e. 193 members of the United Nations. The communication of "a consistence pattern of gross and reliably attested violation of human rights and fundamental freedoms" are given serious consideration.

[44] ECOSOC Res. 1503 (27th May 1970) UN Doc. E/4832/Add.1.

[45] Human Rights Council Resolution (HRC Res.) 5/1.A/HRC/RES/5/1 (18 June 2007), For background of 1503 procedure, see Carey (1966), Tardu (1980), Lecpie (1988), Limon (2017).

The entire process is victim-oriented and based on technical co-operation, capacity-building and advisory service to the state concerned of the OHCHR. The communication procedure discourages politicising the human rights violation issues and to disclose communication and outcome to mass media. It is also necessary to exhaust available domestic remedies and matter that has not been pending before treaty monitoring bodies, regional machinery and any other procedure. The complaint should be appropriately worded in the UN official language (s), not abuse anybody, or personalise it, should be in a proper representative manner and be submitted to the OHCHR.[46]

Once a communication of human rights violation is received either from the victim, group or an NGO, then the chair of the working group of communication and OHCHR swings into action immediately, and the complaint is referred to the state concerned for comment. The WGC is determined whether a complaint deserves to be admitted for further investigation. Another Working Group of Situation (WGS) receives complaints forwarded by the WGC, and it takes action either to dismiss the complaint or to seek further information from the state concerned. If it finds a consistent pattern of reliably attested violation of human rights and fundamental freedom, it transmits the case to the HRC for further consideration.

NGOs play a significant role in communication procedure and its outcome; first, they submit the communication on behalf of victim groups of human rights violations to the OHCHR; in the second stage, they feed data, information and documents to prove the complaint of the gross and systematic pattern of human rights violation. The entire communication process before HRC is confidential, and secrecy is maintained. Therefore, Human Rights Council's working groups heavily depend on the NGO's grassroots connections, networking and reality check-up.[47]

Since 2007, OHCHR has improved records of the communication procedure, i.e. submission of communication, the role of NGOs, the state's response and outcomes. The primary outcome of this communication procedure is either discontinued or made public for capacity-building of the state concerned.

The NGOs welcomed procedure 1503 at the time of its creation in 1970. This procedure is universal in nature, and an individual or NGO can submit a complaint of human rights violation to the former UN Commission on Human Rights, now UN Human Rights Council. But procedure 1503 is slow, secretive, politicised and avoids public scrutiny. Therefore, NGOs demanded improvement in the confidential communication procedure (CCP), previously known as procedure 1503. This issue was addressed by the Human Rights Council by introducing measures in the CCP. The working group meets at least twice a year for five working days, and also HRC meets in three regular sessions and special sessions as per requirements thereon. The former UN Commission on Human Rights meets annually and conducts only one session. While the Human Rights Council holds three sessions in a year regularly, and

---

[46] Aloton (1992), Tomrisevski (2000), Ize-Cherrin (2001), OHCHR (2008).

[47] Marc Limon, *supra note* 47, p. 39.

if needed, it can hold a special session. The Human Rights Council has prescribed a two year time limit for resolving the human rights issues.[48]

4 Universal Periodic Review (UPR)

The UPR Mechanism of the Human Rights Council was created in 2006 by the UN General Assembly.[49] It is a unique mechanism that examines the fulfilment of human rights obligations and performance worldwide of all 193 nations. The cycle of review is in every four years, which covers 48 nations each year out of 193. The first cycle was started in 2008 and concluded in 2012. In the meantime, Human Rights Council amended the UPR cycle from four years to four and a half years and from 48 states to 42 member states.[50] This is a peer-group review of the member states that continuously work under the auspices of the Human Rights Council.[51] This is not only a peer review, but it is a periodic review. Therefore, apart from states, all stakeholders: specialised agencies of the UN, IGOs, NGOs, National Human Rights Institutions (NHRIs), and OHCHR, are also engaged in the Universal Periodic Review mechanism.[52]

The main purpose of the UPR mechanism is to improve human rights application in every country, to enhance capacity and co-operation among nations, provide technical assistance to each other, and replicate best practices in the field of human rights. It also addresses human rights violations in every nook and corner of the world.

The basis of the UPR mechanism is an obligation of states under the Charter of the United Nations, UDHR, human rights instruments, international humanitarian law and voluntary pledges and commitments made by the states.[53] The review is based on a twenty-page national report prepared by the State-under-Review (SuR) and ten pages by OHCHR on information received from special rapporteurs, treaty bodies and UN entities. The remaining ten pages were prepared by the NHRI and NGOs jointly. The report is strictly limited to 40 pages only, and the session's allotted time is also fixed, i.e. three hours and thirty minutes. These are interactive sessions based on dialogue and mutual co-operation.

The working group of HRC comprises 47 member states, and they meet thrice a year and adopt the final reports of the UPR mechanism. The state under review has the primary responsibility to implement these outcomes of the UPR mechanism. UPR is a continuous process, while Human Rights Council is an inter-governmental organisation. OHCHR, the High Commissioner for Human Rights and NGOs are an integral part of the UPR mechanism.

[48] Ibid., pp. 15–16.

[49] UNGA Res. 60/251 (2 April 2006).

[50] A/HRC/Res/16/21 (12 April 2011).

[51] Charlesworth and Larking (2015).

[52] UNGA Res. 60/251/Para 11 (3 April 2006).

[53] A/HRC/Resolution/5/1, Paras 1–2 (18 June 2007).

NGOs are engaged as information providers related to the compliance of human rights instruments and as participators in the sessions.[54] The role of NGOs in the UPR mechanism is not easy to be identified and to be established. Laura K. Landolt and Byungwon Woo have extensively surveyed literature related to human rights regimes. According to their findings, only five research articles directly and fifteen articles indirectly mentioned NGOs in their writings. Only two writers worked for grounded NGO activities in the human rights mechanism.[55]

However, the UPR mechanism offers NGOs unprecedented opportunities in its human rights monitoring procedure. The winds of change began with the UPR mechanism, including NGOs of the global south, and the national and regional NGOs' participation has been significantly increased in the human rights monitoring procedures.[56] The UPR mechanism would offer a unique opportunity for NGOs to bring human rights issues to the attention of the international community. NGOs are engaged in human rights advocacy at a national level with the association of international stakeholders.[57]

NGOs measure the landscape of human rights based on the position of non-derogable rights, availability of freedoms, level of development, working of the rule of law and vibrancy of democracy.

UPR mechanism is a "public audit ritual," that has turned out to be a productive institution. The UPR working group's three and a half hour review along with a one-hour adoption by the Human Rights Council together create a great public audit ritual.[58] NGOs are closely associated with the UPR procedures, which they enrich by providing information, facts, database and grass root realities.

NGOs like UPR-Info[59] and HURIDOCS[60] contributed remarkably in providing statistical data tools and techniques to NGOs to advocate human rights causes in a better way. It mainly focuses on developing countries' NGOs to enhance their capacity to gather credible information on human rights violations, analyse and hold accountable the responsible states or institutions. These two types of NGOs are just an example. Otherwise, there are many other NGOs having consultative status and engaged in the UPR mechanism.

UPR is a state-led review, where the state can discourage criticism and deny the alternate facts. But Human Rights Council, in its Resolution, ensured the inclusion of stakeholders, including NGOs, in the UPR process, from the beginning to the

---

[54] Alston (2006).

[55] Landolt and Woo (2016).

[56] Ibid., pp. 13, 19.

[57] McGaughey (2017).

[58] Jane Cowan, "The Universal Periodic Review as a Public Audit Ritual: An Anthropological Perspective on Emerging Practices in the Global Governance of Human Rights", in *Human Rights and Periodic Review*, *supra note*, 53, p.43.

[59] www.upr-info.org.

[60] www.huridocs.org.

adoption of outcomes.[61] NGOs participated in the national consultation, submitting information on the human rights situation to the OHCHR. A state that is under review engages in lobbying with the other members of the working group of the HRC. Working groups regularly attend the sessions of the HRC and participate at the time of adoption and oversight on the implementation of the recommendations of the UPR.[62]

The UPR mechanism is universal and treats all states equal in its processes. In every session, they review fourteen states, and yearly forty two states. The three state—troika is selected by lot, and representatives from each of the states work as rapporteurs along with the HRC members. They prepare the report, which contains recommendations for the state under review. These outcomes of the UPR process are adopted by consensus in the plenary session of HRC, and the expectations from the state under review are that they can be implemented by them. NGOs are engaged in their countries for the compliance of human rights recommendations along with other stakeholders.

5 United Nations Special Procedure

The Special Procedure includes a thematic rapporteur, a country-specific rapporteur, an independent expert and a five person working group for the promotion and protection of human rights. Among them the most visible is the UN Rapporteur or the UN mandate holders. The former UN Commission on Human Rights created the institution of the UN Rapporteur in 1970. The UN Rapporteur has preserved its successor—the new Human Rights Council. In the first decade, there were only four UN Special Rapporteurs. At the time of the replacement of the UN Commission by the UN Human Rights Council, there were forty UN Rapporteurs, including both thematic and country-specific ones.[63]

The pressure from NGOs is mainly responsible for the formation of the UN Rapporteurs.[64] The legal basis of the UN Rapporteur flows from Article 7 of the UN Charter.[65] They are not part of the United Nations political system.[66] In fact, they are independent, intellectual and impartial in their work and keep away from diplomatic manipulation. Whenever they visit the mandated country, they interact with the NGOs and other related persons and institutions to collect information.[67] In

[61] Institution-Building of the United Nations Human Rights Council, A/HRC/ RES/5/1, (18 June 2007) Para 3; Fiona McGaughey, *supra note* 59, pp. 423–426.

[62] www.upr-info.org/roleofNGOsintheUPR.

[63] Limon and Power (2014).

[64] Rudolf (2000c).

[65] Jaenicke (2012).

[66] Suvedi (2011).

[67] Ibid., at p. 215.

the visiting country, the UN Rapporteurs enjoy immunity and are hence not personally liable for any prosecution in their assigned duty.[68]

Besides, working groups were also established by the HRC in 2011 via résolution 17/4. Working groups are composed of five independent experts with equitable representation of all geographical regions. The working group has a mandate to promote, to disseminate and to implement the guiding principles on business and human rights.

A. **Origins of UN Special Procedures**

In the 1960s, the membership of the Asian-African nations increased in the UN system. Proportionately their influence is reflected in the UN Commission on Human Rights. They collectively demanded UN action against apartheid and the protection of human rights. The NGOs' demands were strengthened by the member states and collaborated with the representatives of the Asian-African nations, so the UN Commission had to take the appropriate action. Thus the UN Special Procedure came into existence. The UN Special Procedures are of two kinds, i.e. thematic or country specific. Those who carry out this task are known as UN Rapporteur. Generally, a UN Rapporteur is either an intellectual or human rights crusader.

Thematic Special Procedure was introduced in 1980.[69] This began with a working group on enforced disappearance. Since then, it embraced multiple issue areas, such as: African descent, arbitrary detention, business, cultural rights, development, disabilities, disappearance, education, environment, extra judiciary execution, food, foreign debt, freedom of opinion and expression, peaceful assembly and association, hazardous substances, health, housing, human rights defender, independence of judges and lawyers, indigenous people, internally displaced persons, leprosy, mercenaries, migrants, minority, older persons, poverty, privacy, racism, religion, sale of children, sexual orientation and gender identity, slavery, terrorism, human trafficking, truth, justice, reparation and guarantee of non-recurrence, unilateral coercive measures, violence against women, water and sanitation, women and girls facing discrimination, etc.

A country-specific procedure is appointed for a particular period. The country-specific procedures are constituted for Al Salvador, Afghanistan, Belarus, Bolivia, Burundi, Central Africa, Cambodia, Chile, Cuba, Congo, Chad, Cote d'Ivoire, Erteria, Equatorial Guinea, Guatemala, Haiti, Iran, Iraq, Liberia, Mali, New Guinea, North Korea, Palestine Territory, Poland, Papua Guinea, Romania, Rwanda, Somalia, Sudan, Syria, South Africa and former Yugoslavia.[70]

These thematic and countries specific procedures are covered under the UN Special Procedure mechanism. Special Procedure mechanism invokes only when the gross and constant violation of human rights appears in any country, for instance, enforced disappearance in 1980 in Argentina practised by arbitrary power and no

[68] Difference Relating to Immunity from Legal Process of a Special Rapporteur of the Commission on Human Rights, Advisory Opinion, ICJ Report 1999, p. 62. It is related to immunity of Special Rapporteur of the Commission on Human Right, visited in Malaysia and disclose information about independent of Judiciary.

[69] Gongales (1981), Tolley (1984).

[70] Marc Limon and Hilary Power, *supra note* 65; Franck (1984), Boeckle (1995), Bossuyt (1985).

adequate remedy is available to the victim; only then country-specific mandate was assigned by the United Nations. This procedure maintains confidentiality. Presently, the country mandate is engaged in Belarus, Cambodia, the Central African Republic, North Korea, Eritrea, Iran, Mali, Myanmar, Palestine Territory, Somalia, Syria, Sudan and South Sudan.

B. **NGOs Participation**

NGOs are closely engaged with the country-specific procedure and transmit credible information and grassroot reality to the UN Rapporteur. The special procedure mechanism is not bound to maintain confidentiality and disclose the issue in the public domain. It submits reports to the UN. But UN Rapporteur strictly maintains confidentiality about the source of information. Their primary focus is on the relief to victims and enhancing the respect and observe human rights in the state concerned.[71]

The UN Rapporteur visit states concerned via an invitation. The object of their mission is fact-finding, interacting with the stakeholders, providing relief to victims, and for improvement in human rights' infrastructure. The UN Rapporteur is an expert, impartial, and on mission, but this needs follow-up of the report's implementation. UN Rapporteur also renders technical advice to the states concerned. States that are not doing enough affected public opinion, international investment, trade and their image.

C. **Autonomy of the UN Rapporteur**

The UN Special procedure enjoys relatively higher autonomy. It is guided by the code of conduct adopted by the Human Rights Council on 18 June 2007.[72] Another guiding principle laid down by the HRC and adopted the *Manual of Operation* for the special procedure in June 2007.[73] The *Operation Manual* has established co-ordination between the special mandate holder and the HRC.

The UN Special Rapporteurs or mandate holders are accountable to the HRC for their assigned work. They are expected to examine, monitor, advise and prepare a report on the human rights situation prevailing in a specific country or on a major phenomenon of human rights violation worldwide.[74] The UN Special Rapporteur is like a human rights crusader taking along all stakeholders in its journey. Their role is appreciated throughout the world.

---

[71] Rudolf (2000b).

[72] Code of Conduct for Special Procedures Mandate-holders of Human Rights Council, HRC DOC 5/2, (18 June 2007).

[73] Available at www.ohchr.org.

[74] Supriya P. Subedi, *supra note* 68, p. 211.

6 Treaty-Based Bodies

There are nine core UN human rights treaties. Each of them has an expert committee. They are popularly known as treaty monitoring bodies or treaty-based bodies, or just simply treaty bodies. These are as follows:

(1) Committee on the Elimination of Racial Discrimination (CERD), International Convention on the Elimination of All Forms of Racial Discrimination 1966.[75]
(2) Human Rights Committee or Committee on Civil and Political Rights (CCPR), International Civil and Political Rights 1966.[76]
(3) Committee on Economic, Social and Cultural Rights (CESCR), International Covenant on Economic, Social and Cultural Rights 1966.[77]
(4) Committee on the Elimination of All Forms of Discrimination Against Women (CEDAW), Convention on the Elimination of All Forms of Discrimination Against Women 1979.[78]
(5) Committee Against Torture (CAT), Convention Against Torture, and Other Cruel, Inhuman or Degrading Treatment and Punishment 1984.[79]
(6) Committee on the Rights of the Child (CRC), Convention on the Rights of the Child, 1989.[80]
(7) Committee on Migrant Workers (CMW), Convention on the Protection of the Rights of All Migrant Workers and Their Families 1990.[81]
(8) Committee on the Rights of Persons with Disabilities (CRPD), Convention on the Rights of Persons with Disabilities 2006.[82]
(9) Committee on Enforced Disappearance (CED), International Convention for the Protection of All Persons from Enforced Disappearance 2006.[83]

Treaty bodies are independent expert committees that monitor the implementation of UN human rights treaties. The number of expert members in the committee is prescribed by the respective treaties. They carry out monitoring through a reporting procedure. The report is prepared by the state under review. The treaty monitoring body makes the concluding remarks and submits the report to the General Assembly for a final view.

---

[75] 660 UNTS 195; http://treaties.un.org. The Committee was established on the basis of treaty. Treaty was adopted on 7 March 1966 and entered into force on 4 January 1969.

[76] Human Rights Committee nomenclature is confusing with the Human Rights Council because both abbreviation is HRC. Therefore, UN now preferred term CCPR (Committee on Civil and Political Rights) instead of HRC, The CCPR entered into-force on 23 March 1976, 999 UNTS 171.

[77] 993 UNTS 3, Entered into force on 3 January, 1976.

[78] 1249 UNTS 13, Entered into force on 3 September 1981.

[79] 1465 UNTS 85, Entered into force on 26 June 1987.

[80] 1577 UNTS 3, Entered into force on 2 September 1990.

[81] 30 ILM 117 (1991), entered into force on 1 July 2003.

[82] Entered into force on 3 May 2008; Brownlie's Documents, *supra note*, 2, pp. 518–539.

[83] Entered into force on 2010; Harris and Shivkumaran (2015).

Along with the state's report, NGOs may also be allowed to prepare a shadow report and submit it to the treaty monitoring body.[84] The concluding remark of the treaty monitoring body is not legally binding. The treaty monitoring bodies sometimes follow-up through a Rapporteur.[85] All treaty monitoring bodies are established according to the provisions of the human rights treaty itself. The treaty monitoring body is described as the 'Committee' of the human rights treaty.

A. Functions of Treaty-Based Bodies

The treaty monitoring bodies' main functions are to carry out the observation of the treaty provisions by the state parties. In a duration of time, they devise procedures as they emerge through meetings of chairpersons of treaty bodies or their own experience. They perform the following functions: state reporting, general comments, individual communications, inter-state communications and inquiries.

(1) State Report

The UN human rights treaty signatory provides that the member states should prepare their periodic report about compliance of treaty obligations. The state report is submitted within a period of two to four years, regularly as per specific treaty provisions. The Committee prepares the 'list of issues' and transmits it to the reporting state before the session along with the concluding observations. Some treaty bodies also follow up for improvement in appearing deficiencies in compliance with treaty obligations.

The overall process is in a constructive dialogue manner. They may extend assistance from UN specialised agencies, subsidiary bodies, funds and programmes for better outcomes.[86] The state reports are not submitted timely, resulting in much pendency. It is a challenge to streamline the UN human rights treaty bodies system.

(2) NGOs' Input

The treaty bodies interpret treaty provisions and highlight state obligations and compliance of these provisions. Treaty bodies discuss the matter in its sessions and generally entertain the NGOs' views and written submissions before making general comments.[87] General comments are also known as concluding observations or treaty body recommendations.

B. Communication Procedure

The communication procedure of the nine treaty bodies is adequately designed. The committee or treaty body takes the view or comments based on communication and state reports. Treaty bodies receive communications either from an individual or inter-state basis. It should be noted here that no human rights treaty contains provisions

---

[84] Gaer (2003).

[85] 10th Inter-Committee Meeting of Human Rights Treaty Bodies was held on 13 November to 2 December, 2009.

[86] OHCHR: *Manual of Human Rights Reporting*, UN Publications, Geneva 1997; HR/PUB/91/1(REV.1).

[87] Felice D. Gaer, *supra note*, 85.

on NGOs participation in communication procedures.[88] NGOs' participation in the individual communication procedures was limited up to 1990 due to the Cold War between East and West.[89]

NGOs' participation in this communication procedure is useful in the collective nature of human rights. NGO's coalition submits the communication on behalf of the aggrieved persons or groups' alleged violation of human rights that could bring more constructive outcomes. Because this nature of rights is required to sustain the petition for factual and data support and redress only through policy initiative, allocation of budget and mobilisation of people, that can be more effective if the NGOs participate as one of the stakeholders, either through petitioner authorization or submission allowed by the treaty body.

Communication can be filed to a treaty body only after that treaty comes into force, and states concerned have ratified or acceded to it. In the case of violation of human rights, domestic remedies are to be exhausted first and no other forum of treaty body or regional machinery entertaining the matter that has been decided early.[90]

(1) **Inquiries**

A treaty body can initiate a confidential inquiry based on credible information on serious and systematic violations of human rights by a state party of the human rights treaty.[91] The enquiry procedure is generally used in matters related to torture and enforced disappearance.

The Treaty body arranges the visit to the site with the co-operation of the state concerned. This enquiry procedure is confidential. The report format is reasonably short.

(2) **General Comments**

General comments are not legally binding per se; however, they have great political and moral weightage. General comments are authoritative interpretations of treaty provisions. They initiate public debates and improve the treaty obligations in the domestic region. General comments are realised through parliament enactment, executive actions or domestic courts' reading in treaty bodies[92] for enlargement and enforcement of fundamental rights within their jurisdiction.

C. **Reform in Treaty Bodies**

Treaty bodies systems are opaque and not much effective as visualised. There are several weak points, such as delay in state reporting, backlog, overlapping, lack of compliance of concluding remarks and insufficient follow-up mechanism.[93]

---

[88] Sekowska-Kozlowska (2014).

[89] Lintel and Rynguert (2013).

[90] Collar V. Austria, Communication No.989/2001 CCPR/C/78/DR/989/2001 (30 July 2003).

[91] CAT, Article 20; OP-CEDAW Article 8; OP-CPD Article 6; CED Article 33; OP-CRC Article 13; OP-CESCR Article 11.

[92] Krommendijk (2015), Nimi (2003).

[93] Lhotsky (2017).

Proposals have been mooted for a single unified treaty body to remove the weakness in the current human rights treaty system. That unified body is proposed to be more rational, coherent, coordinated and effective.[94]

The High Commissioner for Human Rights initiated the Treaty Bodies reform process in 2006.[95] That was formally taken over by the General Assembly in 2014.[96] The Assembly emphasised strengthening and enhancing the effective functioning of the human rights treaty system.

It recommended additional meeting time, capacity-building, video conferencing, reducing the number of conferences and word limits and standardising the working procedure of different treaty bodies.[97] The General Assembly limit of words on NGOs submission is unnecessary because it is uncalled, as the cost is not borne by the OHCHR fund. The Assembly has ignored the qualifications and independence of the member of treaty bodies.

Human rights are becoming a worldwide concern because the ratification and accession of treaties have increased. Individual communications have also increased. The number of treaty bodies has also grown to nine and it could further increase in the field of elderly persons, corporations and businesses. The Committee on Political and Civil Rights (human rights committee) and the Committee Against Torture are most significant because two-thirds of the work of treaty bodies are discharged by these two committees.

M. Nowak put forward ideas to establish a World Human Rights Court to streamline the enforcement of human rights.[98] The proposal of the World Court of Human Rights does not inspire anyone. Similarly nine human rights treaty bodies unified in a single institution do not cater support of the member states.

7 Performance of NGOs in Treaty Bodies

The story of human rights development and the NGOs movement goes hand in hand. There are nine human rights treaties, and each treaty has a committee or monitoring body to ensure compliance for the human rights obligations of state parties. Every human rights treaty has its own rules and procedures to carry out its functions effectively. NGOs are engaged in every stage of the treaty monitoring process—state report, communication procedure, concluding observations, inquiry, visit and follow-up. NGOs' participation in the treaty bodies is based on an invitation from the Chairman of treaty bodies or the Office of the High Commission for Human Rights (OHCHR).

---

[94] O'Flaherty and O'Brian (2007), O'Flaherty (2010, 2014), Johnstone (2007).

[95] Concept Paper on the High Commissioner's Proposal for a Unified Standing Treaty Body, Report by the OHCHR HRI/MC/2006/2 (22 March 2006).

[96] UNGA Res. 68/268, UNDOC A/RES/68/268 (9 April 2014); Broecker (2014).

[97] Broecker and O'Flaherty (2014).

[98] Nowak (2007), Trechsel (2004).

The Committee on Elimination of Racial Discrimination (CERD), in its 78th session in 2011, had notified NGO participation, and they were allowed to submit written statements to the Committee at its sessions. NGOs can now submit their request in advance to participate in CERD sessions. The treaty body or Committee welcomes NGOs' written statements, but they should have direct nexus and be directly related to the treaty provision. Moreover, it should be based on authenticated data, and it should not be abusive and aggressive in nature.[99] This written statement submitted by NGOs to the treaty body is known as an 'alternative report' or 'shadow report' of the state party concerned.

Remaining treaty bodies—CCPR,[100] CESCR,[101] CEDAW,[102] CAT,[103] CRC,[104] CMW,[105] CRPD[106] and CED,[107] by and large, are allowed to collaborate with NGOs in the monitoring of compliance of treaty obligations by the state parties. The UN human rights system has multiple stakeholders—UN principal organs, specialised agencies, programmes, funds, treaty bodies, Human Rights Council, Rapporteurs, IGOs, NGOs, national human rights institutions (NHRIs), academic institutions, media and the states.

---

[99] NGO Information Note, CERD/C/78/1, 78th Session (14 February to 11 March 2011); ICERD (2015).

[100] Rule of Procedure of Human Rights Committee (24 May 1994), UN Doc. CCPR/C/3/Rev. 3(1994), UNCCPR/C/104/3, (1 June 2012). www.ccprcentre.org. The relation of Human Rights Committee with NGOs lays down and revised in its 104 session New York (12–30 March, 2012).

[101] Provisional Rules of Procedure of the OP-CESCR, adopted by the Committee at its 49th session (12–30 November, 2012), E/C, 12/49/13 (15 January, 2018), Rules of Procedure of the Committee on Economic, Social and Cultural Rights, E/C 12/1990/4/Rev.1 (1 September 1993), Participation Provision Rule 27 of the Rule of Procedure of CESCR.

[102] Rule of Procedure of the Committee on the Elimination of Discrimination Against Women, Rule 47, A/56/38 (SUPP), as Amended by A/62/38 (2007).

[103] Rule of Procedure of UN Committee Against Torchur, Rule 63, UN CAT/C/3/Rev./6 (1 September 2004) OP-UNCAT 2006: Sub-Committee, Inspection of Place of Detention and visit to the Country, General Assembly Resolution 57/199 (18 December 2002).

[104] Provisional Rule of Procedure of the Committee on Rights of Child, 1991, Rule 34 (2); CRC 1989, Article 45(A), CRC/C/4 (14 November 1991).

[105] Rule of Procedure of the Committee on the Protection of the Rights of All Migrant Workers and the Members of Their Families (CMW), Rule 30 and the Convention of the CMW Article 74(4) United Nations CMW/C/2 (8 February, 2019).

[106] Rules of Procedure of the Committee on the Rights of Persons with Disabilities (CRPD), Rule 30(3) vide CRPD Convention, Article 16(3) and 33(2) United Nations CRPD/C/1/Rev. (10 October 2016).

[107] Rule of Procedure of the Committee on Enforced Disappearances (CED) United Nations CED/C/1 (22 June 2012), Rule 44(2) vide Article 28 of the CED Convention.

NGO communities are actively engaged in the human rights movement. Their performance in human rights bodies depends on their expertise and commitment. NGOs establish networking at international, regional, national and grassroots level. NGOs such as PEN International,[108] Article 19,[109] Centre for Economic and Social Rights,[110] National Association for Advancement of Coloured People (NAACP),[111] International Alliance of Women,[112] Freedom from Torture,[113] Amnesty International,[114] Disabled Peoples' International,[115] and International Disability Alliance,[116] International Coalition Against Enforced Disappearance,[117] Global Worker's Justice Alliance,[118] and Save the Children International[119] are international NGOs engaged in their respective issue areas.

Participation of NGOs in the human rights bodies makes the entire process triangular.[120] The Committee oversees the compliance of treaty obligations, primarily on the state's reports. These official reports can be examined or countered by credible alternative information. The Committee or treaty body does not have independent or parallel sources except the NGOs. NGOs submit alternative or shadow reports of the state's reports. NGOs established coalitions worldwide on specific rights and freedoms.

The Treaty bodies, in their rule of procedure, provide space to NGOs for participating in Committee's mechanism. The Committee, in their general comment, has commended the role of NGOs in treaty bodies' procedures.[121]

---

[108] www.pen-international.org founded in 1921, London, PEN stands for Poets, Playwriters, Essayists, Editors and Novelists.

[109] www.article19.org, founded in 1989, London, defending freedom of information and expression worldwide. It's name has been derived from the Article 19 of UDHR.

[110] Www.cesr.org founded in 1993, New York, fight against poverty and in-equality and promoting for right to food, house, education, health and culture.

[111] http://www.naacp.org founded in 1909, Baltimor, Merryland, US, fight against racial discrimination.

[112] http://www.womenalliance.org founded in 1904, Geneva, fight for women's human rights, women suffrage, stop the violence against women and women empowerment.

[113] www.freedomfromtorture.org, founded in 1985, UK. It provides medical help and psychological counseling in rehabilitation to victims of torture.

[114] Amnesty International founded in 1965 UK (www.amnesty.org) is working for the prevention against torture and as defender of human rights.

[115] www.disabledpeoplesinternational.org founded in 1981, Canada. It is a Coalition of human right NGOs working as defender of disabled persons.

[116] www.internationaldisabilityalliance.org found 1999, New York, its goal is to enforce UNCRPD.

[117] www.icaed.org, founded in 2007. Total 58 NGOs are in coalition, engaged in the protection persons from enforced disappeared.

[118] www.globalworkers.org founded in 2012, New York. It is working migrant workers and their human right.

[119] www.savethechildren.org founded in 1922, London, work for children rights.

[120] De Schutler (2019).

[121] Committee on the Rights of Child, General Comment No. 5 (2003), General Measures of implementation of Convention on the Rights of Child, CRC/GC/2003/5 (27 November 2003).

8 Conclusion

Universal human rights bodies are of two kinds: Charter-Based Bodies and Treaty-Based Bodies. As per the Charter mandate, there is the Universal Periodic Review (UPR) of the Human Rights Council and the UN Special Procedure or UN Rapporteur of country-specific and thematic mandate holder.

At present, there are more than 60 UN Special Rapporteurs. They are independent experts who submit scholarly reports on an assigned issue areas or countries. They are complementary rather than duplicating human rights bodies with each other.[122]

Treaty Bodies or Committees are confined to nine specific issue areas; these are civil and political rights; economic, social and cultural rights; racial discrimination; torture; enforced disappearance; women; children; migrants and persons with disability. The maximum number of cases are dealt with by two human rights treaty bodies—Committee on Civil and Political Rights (CCPR) and Committee Against Torture (CAT).

The jurisdiction of the treaty bodies is limited to the treaty concerned. The Committee or treaty monitoring body oversees the compliance of treaty obligation by state-concerned parties only. At the same time, UPR covers every nation around the world in all human rights' concerns. It has a time-bound cycle of four and half years.[123] UPR procedure does not limit itself to human rights treaties but has an overview of the entire human rights landscape.

UN Special Procedures—Rapporteurs or mandate holders are independent experts. They oversight specific countries on human rights infrastructure and render invaluable advise on belief of the UN. Besides, they develop thematic areas of human rights in their applications. Their annual report and expert comments carry much weight and respect among nations.

NGOs are associated with the UPR mechanism, Treaty Monitoring Bodies and UN Special Rapporteurs in their functions and outcomes. Out of the 40 pages of the UPR reports, NGOs are allotted 10 pages to produce alternative or shadow reports along the side of the state reports. Whenever UN Special Rapporteurs visit a country, they organise interactive sessions with all stakeholders and give grassroots' feedback on human rights and compliance of the state concerned.

NGOs can communicate on behalf of victims of human rights violence. They help them in rehabilitation, render legal advice, draft petitions, disclose human rights violation issues in the media, coalition and network for advocacy to pursue the problems before the universal human rights bodies.

[122] Rodley (2003).

[123] Gaer (2007).

References

Aloton P (1992) The United Nations and human rights: a critical approach. Oxford University Press, Oxford

Alston (2006) Reconceiving the UN human rights regime: challenges confronting the new UN human rights council. Melbourne J Int'l L 7:185–224

Bell DA (2004) The ethical dilemmas of international human rights and humanitarian NGOs: reflections on a dialogue between practitioner and theorists. Hum Rts Q 26(2):300–329

Boeckle H (1995) Western states, the UN commission on human rights, and the 1235-procedure: the question of bias revisited. Netehrlands Q Hum Rts 13(4):367–402

Borchard E (1946) Historical background of international protection of human rights. Ann Am Acad Pol Soc Sci 243:112–117

Bossuyt M (1985) The development of special procedures of the united nations commission on human rights. Hum Rts L J 6:179–210

Boyle K (2009) New institutions for human rights. Oxford University Press, Oxford, pp 12–46

Broecker C (2014) The reform of the united nations human rights treaty bodies insights. Proc Am Soct'y Int'l L 18(16):1–6

Broecker C, O'Flaherty M (2014) The outcome of the general assembly's treaty body strengthening process. Universal Right Group, Geneva

Burgenthal T (2006) The evolving international human rights system. Am J Int'l L 100(4):783–807 at 784–785

Carey J (1966) The united nations double standards on human rights complaints. Am J Int'l L 60(4):792–803

Chandhoke N (2005) How global is global civil society? J World Syst Res 11(2):355–371 at 370

Charlesworth H, Larking E (eds) (2015) Human rights and the universal periodic review: rituals and ritualism. Cambridge University Press, Cambridge

De Schutler O (2019) International human rights law, 3rd edn. Cambridge University Press, New York, p 879

Franck TM (1984) Of gnats and camels: is there a double standard at the united nations? Am J Int'l L 78(4):811–825

Gaer FD (2003) Implementing international human rights norms: UN human rights treaty bodies and NGOs. J Hum Rts 2(3):339–357

Gaer FD (2007) A voice not an echo: universal periodic review and the human rights treaty body system. Hum Rts L Rev 7(1):109–139

Ghanea N (2006) From UN commission human rights to UN human rights council: one step forward or two steps sideways? Int'l & Comp L Q 55(3):695–705 at 696

Goel V, Tripathi MK (2010) The role of NGOs in enforcement of human rights: an overview. Indian J Polit Sci 41(3):769–793

Gongales T (1981) Political sources of procedural debate in the United Nations: structural impediments to implement human rights. NYU J Int'l L & Policy 13(3):427–472

Harris D, Shivkumaran S (2015) Cases and materials on international law, 8 edn. Sweet & Maxwell, UK, p 550

Henderson C (1988) Human rights and regimes: a bibliographical essay. Hum Rts Q 10(4):525–543

ICERD (2015) A guide for civil society actors. IMADR Publication, Geneva, pp 24–36

Iriye A (1999) A century of NGOs. Diplomatic Hist 23(3):421–435

Ize-Cherrin MF (2001) 1503: a serious procedure, international human rights monitoring mechanism. Martinus Sijhoff, Leiden

Jaenicke G (2012) On article 71. In Simma B et al (eds) Charter of the united nations: a commentary, 3rd edn, vol 1. Oxford University Press, Chap 10

Johnstone RL (2007) Cynical savings or reasonable reform reflection on a single unifications on a single unified UN human rights treaty body. Hum Rts Rev 7(1):173–200

Kant I (1903) Perpetual peace (trans. with introduction by Smith C). George Allen & Unwin, London (first edn. 1795)

Krommendijk J (2015) The domestic effectiveness of international human rights monitoring in established democracies: the case of UN human rights treaty bodies. Rev Int'l Org 10(4):489–512
Lamer M (2005) Representing poverty, impoverishing representation? A discourse analysis of a NGOs fund raising poster. Graduate J Soc Sci 2(1):37–59
Landolt LK, Woo B (2016) NGOs invite attention: from the united nations commission on human rights to the human rights council. J Hum Rts 16(4):407–427, at 412. https://doi.org/10.1080/14754835.2016.1153411
Lauterpach H (1950) International law and human rights. Frederic A. Prager, New York, p 470
Lecpie S (1988) The inter-state complaint procedure in international human rights law: hopeful prospects or wishful thinking. Hum Rts Q 10(2):249–303
Lhotsky J (2017) Human treaty body review 2020: towards an integrated treaty body system. European Inter-University, Centre for Human Rights and Democratisation, Venice, Italy, pp 4–9
Limon M (2017) Reform of the UN human rights petition system. Universal Rights Group publication, Switzerland, pp 8–18
Limon M, Power H (2014) History of the United Nations special procedures mechanism. Universal Rights Group publication, Switzerland, p 10. Available www.universal-rights.org
Lintel I, Rynguert C (2013) The interface between non-governmental organisations and the human rights committee. Int'l Community L Rev 15:359–379 at 362.
McDougal MS, Bebr G (1964) Human rights in United Nations. Am J Int'l L 58(3):603–641 at 613
McGaughey F (2017) The role and influence of non-governmental organisations in the universal periodic review—international context and Australian case study. Hum Rts L Rev 17(3):421–450 at 422
Nader L (2007) The role of NGOs in the UN human rights council. SUR-Int'l J Hum Rts Q 7:7–28 at 12
Nimi H (2003) National implementation of findings by united nations human rights treaty bodies. Avo Academy University, Turku, Finland, Institute for Human Rights, pp 1–65
Nowak M (2007) The need for world court of human rights. Hum Rts L Rev 7(1):251–259
O'Flaherty M (2010) Reform of the UN human rights treaty body system: location of Dublin statement. Hum Rts L Rev 10(2):328
O'Flaherty M (2014) The strengthen process of the human rights treaty bodies. Proc Am Society Int'l L 108:285–288
O'Flaherty M, O'Brian C (2007) Reform of UN human rights treaty monitoring bodies: a critique of the concept paper on the high commissioner's proposal for unified standing treaty bodies. Hum Rts & Rev 7(1):141–172
OHCHR (2008) Working with the United Nations Human Rights Programme: A Civil Society Handbook. UN Publications, New York. http://www.ohchr.org/EN/AboutUN/CivilSociety/Documents/ Handbooken.pdf.
Orakhelashvili A (ed) (2019) Akehurst's Modern introduction to international law, 8th edn. Routledge, London, p 351
Parmar I (2012) Foundation of the American Century: the Ford, Carnegie and Rockefeller foundations in the rise of American powers. Columbia University Press
Prasad M (1975) Role of non-governmental organisations into new united nations proceedings for human rights complaints. Denver J Int'l L Policy 5(2):441–462 at 445
Robertson AH, Merrils JG (1996) Human rights in the world, 4th edn. Manchester Universities Press, UK, pp 78–79
Rodely N (2014) International human rights law. In: Evan MD (ed) International law, 4th edn. Oxford University Press, p 805
Rodley N (2003) United Nations human rights treaty bodies and special procedure of the commission on human rights-complimentary or competition. Hum Rts Q 25(4):882–908
Rudolf B (2000a) The thematic rapporteurs and the working groups of the United Nations Commission on human rights. Max Planck UNYB 4:299

Rudolf B (2000b) The thematic rapporteurs and working groups of the united nations commission on human rights. In: Frowein JA, Wolfrum R (eds) Max Planck YB UN law. Kluwer International Law Books, Netherlands, pp 289–329
Rudolf B (2000c) The thematic rapporteurs and working groups of the United Nations Commission on human rights. Max Planck UNYB 4:289–329 at 293
Sekowska-Kozlowska K (2014) The role of non-governmental organisations in individual communication procedures before the UN human rights treaty bodies. Czeck YB Int'l L 4:367–388 at 369
Shaw MN (2019) International law, 8th edn. Cambridge University Press
Sinnar S (1995) Mixed blessings growing influence of NGOs. Havard Int'l Rev 18(1):54–79
Smith J, Pagnucco R, Lopez GA (1978) Globalizing human rights: the work of transnational human rights NGOs in the 1990s. Hum Rts Q 20(2):379–412
Suvedi SP (2011) Protection of human rights through the mechanism of UN special rapporteurs. Hum Rts Q 33(1):201–228 at 209
Tardu ME (1980) United nations response to gross violation of human rights: 1503 procedure. Santa Clara L Rev 20(3):559–601
Terlingen Y (2006) The human rights council: a new era in UN human rights work. Ethics Int'l Aff 21:167–171
Tolley H Jr (1984) The concealed crack in the citadel: the united nations commission on human rights' response to confidential communications. Hum Rts Q 6(4):420–462
Tomrisevski K (2000) Responding to human rights violation 1946–1999. Springer, Netherlands
Trechsel S (2004) A world court for human rights. North Western Uni J Int'l Hum Rts 1(3):1–19
Wiessbrodt D (1977) The role of non-governmental organisations in the implementation of human rights. Texas Int'l LJ 12:293–320 at 300
Wiseberg LS (2003) The role of non-governmental organisations (NGOs) in the protection and enforcement of human rights. In: Symonides U (ed) Human rights: international protection, monitoring, enforcement. UNESCO publications Paris, pp 247–368

Chapter 10
Regional Machinery

1 Introduction

Regional human rights are an essential part of the international human rights regime. The regional human rights system is well established in Europe, America (Inter-American) and the African continent. At the sub-regional level, South-East Asian nations,[1] South Asia[2] and Arab countries[3] are also trying to formulate the human rights system within their vicinity. The human rights machinery, at the regional level, is geographically connected closely sharing common culture, heritage, historical experience and aspirations.

The first step was taken by the Council of Europe (CoE)[4] in 1950 as Europe had suffered unprecedentedly in the Second World War and had to face fascist horror.[5] Europe witnessed gross violations of the inalienable right to life and freedom. They were encountered with the unimaginable Holocaust, which in turn awakened conscience and reason to overcome such a dark phase of history.

This gave birth to European human rights. Simultaneously, the Organisation of American States (OAS)[6] came out with the Inter-American human rights for the Americas—North America, South America and Caribbean countries. Later on,

---

[1] Mohamad (2002).

[2] Dhaliwal (2008).

[3] Abdullah (2001).

[4] Dowrick (1974).

[5] Robertson and Merrils (1996).

[6] The Original Charter of the Organisation of American States (OAS) was signed at Bogato, Columbia on 30 April 1948, and entered into force on 13 December 1951, 119 UNTS 48; Thomas and Thomas (1963).

P. Rai, *Non-Governmental Organisations and International Law*,
https://doi.org/10.1007/978-981-97-5469-4_10

African nations took initiatives for human and people's rights for their continent under the auspices of the African Union (AU).[7]

A. **Council of Europe**

The Council of Europe (CoE) was founded in 1949[8] and it had 47 member states of the European continent. CoE has two statutory bodies—the committee of ministers and the parliamentary assembly. Its headquarters are located in Strasbourg, France. The main purpose of the CoE is to uphold human rights, democracy and the rule of law in Europe. It is different from the European Union (EU) and has an observer status with the United Nations.[9] It has extended consultative status to NGOs since 1993, something that was converted later to participatory status by the CoE's committee of ministers.[10]

NGOs originated in Europe in the nineteenth century and have continuously been fighting for humanising of international law ever since. NGOs have persistently demanded the protection of human rights that was heeded by European states and adopted by the European convention on human rights 1950 under the aegis of the CoE.[11]

B. **Organisation of American States**

Across the Atlantic Ocean, the American nations founded the Organisation of American states (OAS) on 30 April 1948,[12] for the purposes of peace, justice, solidarity and collaboration among its members, and to defend territorial integrity and independence.[13] OAS, in its 9th international conference of American states at Bogota, Columbia, adopted the American Declaration of the Rights and Duties of Man 1948.[14] This is the first and foremost human rights instrument that was adopted by the Inter-American nations or America.

OAS has not laid down provisions for its relationship with NGOs. Instead, it has entered into an agreement of co-operation with the NGOs on a case-by-case basis[15] since 1971. Prior to that, NGOs who had consultative status in the UN and observer status in the CoE (and recognised by the member states) were engaged

---

[7] Brownlie and Godwin Gill (2010); The Charter of Organisation of African Unity (OAU) was adopted on 25 May 1963 and came into force in July 1964. OAU was replaced by its new name: African Union on 9 July 2002; Murray (2004).

[8] ETS No. 001 entered into force on 5 May 1949 (ETS later on replaced by term CETS).

[9] The Council of Europe's relation with United Nations, UNGA Res/Res/71/70 (17 October 1989).

[10] Committee of Ministers' Resolution (2016) 3.

[11] Kanunnikov (2017).

[12] http://www.refworld.org/docid/3ae6b3624.htm (accessed 10/2/2020), *Charter of the OAS* signed 30 April 1948, entered into force on 13 December 1951, 119 UNTS 48; https://perma.cc/LTP9A.

[13] OAS Charter, Article 1.

[14] The Declaration is to be found in the Final Act of 9th International Conference of OAS, Bogota, Columbia, held in March–May 1948, Reprint in Brownlie's Documents, *supra note* 7, pp. 949–954.

[15] Standards on Co-operative Relation between Organisation of American States and the United Nations, its specialized Agencies, and other National and International Organisations, AG/Res.57(I-O/71) OAS GA Proc., 1st Session, Vol. II (1971).

with the Inter-American Human Rights Commission (Inter-Am HR Comm) of the OAS. For instance, NGOs such as Amnesty International, International Commission of Jurists, FIDH, International Institute of Human Rights, International League of Human Rights and the Latin American Association of Human Rights are eminent names to be recalled.

NGOs could participate with OAS and its organs. For this purpose, they had to opt for registration with the secretariat of OAS. Otherwise, they had to seek permission to attend meetings and conferences or by signing co-operative agreements with the OAS secretariat.[16]

C. **African Union**

The Africans came forward to establish the Organisation of African Unity (OAU) on 25 May 1963 in Addis Ababa.[17] The old name of OAU was replaced by the African Union (AU) on 2 July 2002.[18] It represented the vast humanity of 1.25 billion within the African continent. AU's objectives are to encourage international co-operation in promoting and protecting human and peoples' rights in the light of the UN Charter, Universal Declaration of Human Rights (UDHR), African Charter of Human and Peoples' Rights (African Charter) and other relevant human rights instruments.

The Economic, Social and Cultural Council (ECOSOCC) is an advisory of AU which directly extends membership to NGOs and civil society in a limited capacity.[19] AU granted observer status to African-oriented international NGOs.[20] These NGOs participated in AU and its organs and have continuously increased their role since 2015 in the development of human and peoples' rights, therein.[21]

2 Evaluation of Regional Human Rights

The regional human rights system[22] has evolved in a different timeframe, having a diverse level of development as per the economy, legal institution and living standards. Regional human rights are greatly influenced by the UN Charter, UDHR and International Covenants.[23] It is to be observed here that the American Declaration was adopted seven months before the UDHR, 1948. The European Convention on

---

[16] *Guidelines for the participation of CSOs in OAS activities.* OEA/Ser.G CP/RES759 (1217/99) 15 December 1999 (OAS), https://www.oas.org/docs; Manual for Civil Society Participation in OAS Activities, Department of Int'l Affairs, Secretariat for External Relations, OAS Washington DC, 2010, pp. 1–19.

[17] OAU Charter Addis Ababa, 25 May 1963.

[18] http://www.au.int.

[19] Assembly/AU/Dec. 42 (III) (July 2004), Constitutive Act of the African Union, Article 22.

[20] Olz (1997), pp. 307–374 at 361.

[21] Www.un.org/office of the special advisor on Africa.

[22] Shalton and Karozza (2013).

[23] Burgenthal (1986).

Human Rights (European Convention), 1950, was adopted before the International Covenants, 1966.

However, the European Convention was heavily dependent on the UDHR. When the International Covenant on Civil and Political rights (ICCPR) and International Covenant on Economic, Social and Cultural Rights (ICESCR) came into being, the European Convention's catalogue of rights was seen to be very limited in number and scope. The CoE addressed this issue through the adoption of additional protocols and the European Charter of Social Rights (European Charter).

The American Convention of Human Rights, 1969 (American Convention), was adopted by the OAS. It is greatly influenced by ICCPR. An additional protocol to the American Convention was added in 1988, which pushed for economic, social and cultural rights. The Convention remained similar with the listed rights in the International Bill of Rights.

The African Charter of Human and Peoples Rights, 1981 (African Charter), was adopted by the AU. Among these three conventions, the African was the latest. In the Preamble of the African Charter, they mention UDHR, both International Covenants and other human rights instruments.[24]

There is a European Human Rights Court and European Committee on Social Rights in Europe, whereas in America they have the Inter-American Commission on Human Rights as well as the American Court on Human Rights. Similarly, the African Commission on Human and People's Rights and the African Court on Human and Peoples' Rights are present in Africa. American countries with the exception of the United States and Canada are developing economies, much like African nations. Therefore, economic, social and cultural rights carry a lot of weight in their everyday life. While in Europe, civil liberty is very near to their heart because they are mature democracies.

These regional conventions on human rights reaffirm the international human rights in their continents, which complement the international protection of human rights through their regional machinery. The core idea and philosophical foundations are, by and large, similar to international and regional human rights. Regional machinery is a bridge between national and international human rights infrastructure.[25]

Regional human rights are easily accommodated with their specific values, cultural realities and peculiar traditions within their continental level. Regional machinery has established a partnership with NGOs for the purposes of fact-finding, the protection of human rights defenders and to pursue reluctant states via diplomatic and collective measures.

Regional human rights originated and were accepted, first and foremost, in the European continent, followed in due course by American and African continents. They supplemented international human rights with their cultural heritage, development and specific needs in their particular regions. They guarantee human rights to the people within their continents and collaborate for their effective implementation.

---

[24] The Preamble and Article 60 of the African Charter of Human and Peoples' Rights.

[25] Wilner (1995).

They have also established regional machinery to make human rights a reality. They have similarities and differences[26] with each other but they have mutually benefitted and grown over the years. NGOs have made significant contributions to the creation, development and enforcement of regional human rights since their inception.[27]

3 European Machinery

The European human rights system is the most effective when compared to its counterparts. The roots of the European Convention for the Protection for Human Rights and Fundamental Freedoms (European Convention or ECHR),[28] 1950, were traced in the early twentieth century,[29] when Western Europe was assigned the task of promoting democracy, rule of law and human rights for the CoE. Their collective efforts resulted in the origin of the European Convention. The Convention was further expanded through additional protocols[30] thereof, and the European Social Charter, 1961 (European Charter).[31] The European Convention embraced the whole of Europe. It has 47 member states and 830 million people.

Enlightenment in Europe in the seventeenth century cultivated the idea of democracy, freedom, state and citizenry.[32] Western liberal democracies assimilated the rights of man in their basic law. Civil society and NGOs raised their voice for the abolition of slavery, protection of war victims and minorities. In the nineteenth century, NGOs such as Anti-Slavery Society 1839, ICRC 1863, FIDH 1922, PEN International 1921, International Alliance for Women 1904, Quakers seventeenth century, Plan International 1937 and Save the Children International 1919 were actively engaged in the promotion and protection of civil liberty and human dignity.

A. **European Convention on Human Rights**

The European Convention was drafted by the CoE's parliamentary assembly and approved by their committee of ministers. NGOs based out of Europe contributed remarkably in the framing of the European Convention, whereas the CoE succeeded in harmonising the tradition of common and civil law towards the rights and freedoms of individuals. In the beginning, only group rights like the abolition of slavery and servitude and protection of war victims, minorities, women and children were

[26] Burgenthal (1980).

[27] Welch (2001).

[28] European Convention for the Protection of Human Rights and Fundamental Freedoms 1950 (European Convention) adopted in 4 November 1950 and came into force on 3 September 1953, ETS No. 5; 213 UNTS 221.

[29] Robertson (1950).

[30] Protocols No. 11, 1, 4, 6, 7, 12, 13, 14 Bis, Reprint in *Brownlie's Documents, supra note* 14, pp. 681–716; Lemmes (2019).

[31] European Social Charter 1961 (European Charter) adopted 18 October 1961.

[32] Ishay (2008).

undertaken. During the course of time, individual rights took precedence over group rights.

The European Convention is consonant with the UDHR, and a number of rights are alike.[33] The UDHR under Articles 3 through 20 set out a catalogue of civil and political rights. The European Convention had opted out some of rights and freedoms. But they were added to the European Convention through Additional Protocols Numbers 1,[34] 4,[35] 6,[36] 7[37] and 11.[38] These added rights are: property (Article 1); education (Article 2); and free election (Article 3) under Protocol Number 1. Freedom from imprisonment for debt (Article 1); movement and residence (Article 2); nationality (Article 3); and asylum (Article 4) are added in Protocol Number 4. Protocol Number 6 further added prohibition of the death penalty (Articles 1–2), Protocol Number 7 guaranteed fair trial, due process and compensation for miscarriage of justice (Articles 1–4). It also ensured equality between spouses (Article 5). The enforcement of these Rights and freedoms is strengthened in Protocol Number 11.

Protocol Number 16[39] of the European Convention is empowered by the European Human Rights Court (EHRC). EHRC enjoys advisory jurisdiction, and it can render advisory opinion on human rights to the state concerned. This opinion is within the realm of the European Convention and Protocols. The advisory opinion is not binding, as usual, with seeking opinion rendering advice the liberty of the state and court. By and large, European civil and political rights are similar to the catalogue of UDHR and ICCPR. Notwithstanding, the European machinery is more effective in the implementation of human rights across the continent.

The European Convention has a decisive impact on its member states. It transformed domestic laws according to human rights standards as set out by the convention. Civil law countries deemed that envisaged rights and freedoms are part of their domestic laws, whereas common law countries also incorporated these rights in their national legislations.[40] Domestic courts reading the European Convention in their national laws applied them to their jurisdiction.[41] The European human rights system is the most effective model to uphold human rights in European countries.[42]

---

[33] Shindler (1962).

[34] Protocol No. 1 adopted on 20 March 1952 and entered into force on 18 May 1954, ETS No. 9.

[35] Protocol No. 4 adopted on 16 September 1963 and entered into force on 2 May 1968, ETS No. 46.

[36] Protocol No. 6 adopted on 24 April 1983 and entered into force on 1 March 1985, ETS No. 114.

[37] Protocol No. 7 adopted on 22 November 1984 and entered into force on 1 November 1988, ETS No. 117.

[38] Protocol No. 11 adopted on 11 May 1994 and entered into force on 1 November 1998, ETS No. 155; http://conventions.coe.int/; Brownlie's Documents, pp. 681–719, *supra note*, 30.

[39] Protocol No. 16 adopted on 18 June 2013 and entered into force on 2 October 2013 CETS No. 214 (ETS was replaced with the new name CETS, Council of European Treaty Series).

[40] Weil (1963).

[41] Drzemczerwski (1998).

[42] Buergenthal (2006).

It has succeeded because Europe is a fertile land of liberal democratic values. It has a sense of community and has fought against authoritarian governments.[43]

B. **European Social Charter**

The European Convention on Human Rights and Fundamental Freedoms is a regional variant of ICCPR, whereas the European Social Charter is a regional counterpart of ICESCR.[44] In the later part of nineteenth century, trade unions and social movements were usurped in Europe. First International, i.e. International Working Men's Association, was held in London on 28 September 1884.

The trade union movement was strengthened alongside with industrialisation. Europe had witnessed enlightenment and liberal ideas. This allowed women's education and employment. These liberal ideas and enlightenment had facilitated the origin of public space and growth of civil society. There were peoples' associations such as NGOs and trade unions. General Confederation of Labour 1895, Miners and Sea Men's Association 1851, Women's Trade Union League 1870, Federation of German Trade Unions 1949, along with NGOs—International Alliance of Women 1904, Zonto International 1919, Anti-Slavery Society 1839, Save the Children 1919, Oxfam 1942, etc. They demanded socio-economic rights of the people.

CoE began its work on the European Social Charter in 1954 and concluded in 1961. Most of the provisions of the European Social Charter (European Charter) are derived from the Labour Standards as laid down by the International Labour Organisation (ILO). The European Charter is primarily concerned with workers' rights. It provides right to work, decent working conditions, fair remuneration, right to organise and collective bargaining. In addition, right to child, women employment, vocational training, safety and medical assistance at the work place, social security right to persons with physical disability and the right to migrant workers and protection of family exist within it too.[45]

Social and economic rights are further extended by Additional Protocol 1988.[46] Again, it was thoroughly revised in 1996, increasing the catalogue of economic and social rights in a comprehensive way.[47] The European Charter is supplementary to the European Convention because it laid down economic and social rights as a counterpart to civil and political rights.[48] NGOs have provided quality input for the improvement of the Social Charter, and they are actively engaged in their compliance throughout Europe.

Additional Protocol 1995 of the European Social Charter[49] has allowed social partners and NGOs to submit their collective complaints to the European Committee

[43] Greer (2008a, b).

[44] Harris (1992), Harris and Darcy (2001); European Social Charter adopted on 18 October 1961 and came into force on 26 February 1965, ETS No. 35 http://conventions.coe.int.

[45] Betten (1988), Addison and Siebert (1991).

[46] ETS No. 128 (5 May 1988) Entered into force on 4 September 1992.

[47] The revised Social Charter was adopted on 3 May 1996 and entered force on 1999, ETS No. 160; Hendricks (1996), Vandamme (1994).

[48] Mikkola (2000).

[49] Adopted on 9 November 1995 and entered into force on 1 July 1998, ETS No. 158.

of Social Rights (European Committee) about the unsatisfactory performance of the state parties.[50]

ECHR guaranteed civil and political rights to the European people, whereas the Social Charter laid down economic and social rights for them. ECHR confirmed rights to individuals and ensured access to the European Court of Human Rights (ECHR) while the Social Charter provides group rights and a collective complaint system by NGOs and social partners.[51]

C. **NGOs Partnership**

NGOs were associated with the CoE since its inception. The International Committee of the Movements for European Unity[52] (ICMEU)—an NGO formed in 1947 in Paris—took initiatives to establish the Community of Europe. It organised the Congress of Europe for European unity at The Hague in 1948. That congress had conceived the idea of the European human rights charter.[53] It assisted greatly in the making of the ECHR.

NGOs' association with the CoE began in 1952 when the committee of ministers made the suitable arrangements. This was a consultative arrangement alike ECOSOC under Article 71 of the UN Charter.[54] The committee of ministers institutionalised the relationship between NGOs and the CoE and its organs by adopting resolutions in 1993.[55]

NGOs' consultative status was changed to participatory status in 2003.[56] More than 400 NGOs enjoyed participatory status, and they organised a conference. They regulated their collective efforts through a liaison committee and closely connected with the committee of ministers, parliamentary assembly and European Court of Human Rights. They are also closely connected with local and regional authorities. These four organs of the CoE, i.e. the committee of ministers, parliamentary assembly, European Court of Human Rights and Conference of NGOs oversee human rights affairs. The Conference of NGOS is now developed as one of the autonomous institutions of the CoE.

The European human rights compliance machinery consists of the European Commission on Human Rights, European Court of Human Rights and the Committee on Social Rights.[57] The European Court of Human Rights subsumed the European Commission, with two organs remaining in the European machinery presently, i.e. European Court of Human Rights and European Committee on Social Rights.

---

[50] Cullen (2009b).

[51] Amhlaigh and Nedelka (2003).

[52] ICMEU adopted new name European Movement International (EMI), https://europeanmovement.eu.

[53] Olz (1997), pp. 307–374 at 332, van Dijk Hoof et al. (2018).

[54] Committee of Ministers at its 8th Session adopted Statutory Resolution on 22 May 1951, ETS No. 8.

[55] Committee of Ministers, Resolution (1993) 38 adopted on 18 October 1993, at the 500th Meeting of the Ministers' Deputy.

[56] Committee of Ministers Resolution, Res. (2003) 8 Adopted on 19 November 2003.

[57] Harris et al. (2018).

D. **Former European Commission on Human Rights**

The European Commission on Rights (Europe Commission) was established in 1954 under the provisions laid down by the European Convention 1950.[58] The Commission's main objectives was to promote and protect rights and freedoms of the European people. These rights and freedoms are set out under Articles 2–18 of the ECHR and Articles 1 to 3 of its various protocols.[59]

The former Europe Commission received communications from individuals, interstate and NGOs with respect to the violation of human rights.[60] The Commission examined the admissibility of the communication as to whether it had already exhausted the local remedy or it deserved to be entertained or to be dropped. Admissibility of communication diverts further actions either through the committee of ministers or the European Court of Human Rights (ECHR) for final disposal. NGOs can appear before the Europe Commission as petitioner or amicus curiae.

Article 15 clause 1 of ECHR lays down that the Commission receives petitions from any person, non-governmental organisations or groups claiming to be the victim of human rights violation, but that person, group or NGO ought to be connected with any party of the European Convention. The petition or communication is addressed to the Secretary General of the CoE and received by the European Commission thereafter. The Commission decides the petition to be dropped or transmitted to the ECHR for final disposal.

The NGOs have various roles in the European Commission, i.e. they provide legal advice to the victims; inform victims about the possibilities of filing the petition; assist them to draft the petition; formulate arguments and provide necessary material for pursuing the case. NGOs' role becomes very crucial in the process of filing the petitions, engaging advocates and pursuing the case because the state is the opposing party that has command on the legal machinery and financial resources. In comparison, the victim is an individual, and the group is an unequal party with the state as opponent.[61] Therefore, rendering NGOs' support and help to victims, matters a lot when it comes to fighting the case against the state.

The European Commission was established in 1954, and it worked up to 1998. In this period, the Commission entertained more than ten thousand petitions. Protocol 11 of the European Convention restructured the European human rights bodies, and the European Commission was abolished in 1998.[62] Since then the Commission's functions have been taken over by the ECHR.

E. **European Court of Human Rights**

Now ECHR became an independent, full-time human rights court. It is the most effective human rights machinery of our time. Its jurisdiction covers the whole of Europe

---

[58] ECHR, Articles 20–37.

[59] Myers (1956).

[60] Nowicki (1996).

[61] Ibid., p. 296.

[62] Protocol No. 11 opened for signature on 11 May 1994, and entered into force on 1 November 1998, ETS No. 155 (1994) available at https://www.refworld.org/docid/42ef8c812.htm.

to interpret, to enforce human rights in their fullest sense, without any discrimination.[63] Earlier, the European Commission dropped most of the complaints at the admissible level, but after 1998 its admissibility and merit, both are decided by the ECHR's Chambers of the Seven Judges. There is an internal system to examine the admissibility of the case. The matter could be dropped at the admissibility level or it may be referred to the Chambers of ECHR for final disposal of the case on the basis of merit. There are 47 judges representing each member of the CoE. ECHR jurisdiction is limited up to civil and political rights as provided in the European Convention and subsequent protocols. Economic and social rights as listed in the European Charter are heard by the European Committee of Social Rights.

NGOs are closely associated with the ECHR proceedings through the amicus curiae briefs.[64] ECHR Article 36 provides third-party intervention in the proceedings of the court. NGOs can intervene in the court proceedings as a third party, based on the invitation of the President of the court. They may be allowed to take part in the hearing and submit a written brief to the court.[65]

NGOs submit amicus curiae briefs in important cases because it is not possible for them to be involved in all cases. They represent the public interest at large and are the watchdogs of human rights infrastructure in Europe. They are also representative of common good. NGOs emphasise on the teleology "to respect, to observe, to fulfil human rights". As a party of the case, NGOs can appear only when their rights are violated, otherwise they have no locus standi before the court (Article 34).

According to the findings of Laura B.D. Eynde, total briefs submitted were 300 cases (2012) to the grand chamber of the court.[66] The grand chamber decided cases on the bases of merit. How much outcome of the cases have direct nexus to the amicus brief of the NGOs is not found because nobody acknowledges this and credible statistical data is not available. But the utility of the NGOs' amicus curiae brief is very much relevant to the human rights infrastructure.

F. **European Committee of Social Rights**

In persuasion of the European Social Charter (European Charter), the CoE established the European Committee of Social Rights (European Committee) in 1991.[67] Previously, the Committee of the Independent Experts, under the supervision of the government committee on social rights, committee of ministers and parliamentary assembly of the CoE, had an oversight of the European Social Charter Expert from

---

[63] Council of Europe, *the European Court of Human Rights: Some Facts and Figures*, 1998–2008, CoE Publications, Strasbourge, France 2011.

[64] Van Den Eynde (2013).

[65] European Convention, Article, 36(2) and Rules of the Court, Article 44(2), *Rule of the European Court of Human Rights* adopted on 9 September 2019, registry of the court, CoE, Strasbourg, France, www.echr.coe.int.

[66] Laura B. D. Eynde, *supra note* 64, p. 293.

[67] The European Social Charter, Article 25, 529 UNTS 89, entered into force 26 February 1965, David J. Harris, *supra note* 44, pp. 659–676.

1960 to 1990. This mechanism was revitalised by the European Committee of Social Rights, and a system of collective complaints was introduced in 1995.[68]

Two major improvements were made in the European Charter of Social Rights; first, the government committee's role was eliminated and the role of the parliamentary assembly was limited up to annual discussions only; second, the collective complaint system was introduced within the European Committee of Social Rights. Now, social partners, i.e. employees' associations, trade unions and NGOs are allowed to collectively file complaints.

NGOs are entitled to file complaints before the European Committee in writing and on the basis of non-compliance of the Social Charter. They are required to have consultative status in the CoE, competency in the concerned area and objectives in its regulations for filing complaints. This is a collective complaint system, hence, individual cases cannot be submitted.[69] NGOs such as the International Federation of Human Rights League (IFHR), International Commission of Jurists (ICJ), Quaker Council for European Affairs and World Organisation Against Torture, etc. are some of the NGOs that filed complaints successfully in the European Committee.[70]

The European Committee is a quasi-judiciary body and its decisions lack binding force. NGOs are provided opportunities through this complaint procedure to engage in lobbying and networking for the improvement of law and practices, the allotment of budget and bring public policy within the gamut of social rights.

4 Inter-American Machinery

Human rights in Inter-America are inspired by the constitutional liberalism of the United States and Canada and the struggle against decolonisation in Latin America. Paolo G. Carozza focussed on:

> the ethical response to the Spanish conquest; the rights ideology of the continent's liberal republican revolution; the articulation of the social and economic rights in the Mexican Constitution of 1917; and the Latin American contributions to the genesis of the Universal Declaration of Human Rights.[71]

American heritage was well reflected in the American Declaration of Human Rights. By the Declaration of Rights of Men and of Citizens, Latin America made substantive contributions to the making of international human rights law, either through insisting to lay down human rights provisions within the UN Charter or the proclamation of America's Declaration of the Rights and Duties of Men. In addition,

---

[68] Additional Protocol to the European Social Charter providing for System of Collective Complaints, adopted in 9 November 1995 and entered into force in 1998, ETS no. 158; Cullen (2009a).

[69] 1995 Protocol, Article 1, 2 & 3; *ECSR's Rule of Procedures* 1999.

[70] Churchill and Khaliq (2004).

[71] Carozza (2003).

Latin American countries were vocal supporters of the UN General Assembly's adoption of the universal declaration of human rights in 1948.

When nations assembled at San Francisco in 1945 to adopt the UN Charter and to establish the United Nations, the largest groups of representatives belonged to Latin America. Out of 50 nations, 21 were from Latin America.[72] At that time, NGOs were mainly located and financed by the United States and Western Europe. They had cordial relations and mutual understanding with the Latin American delegates to collectively promote human rights around the world.

Columbus discovered America in 1492, and subsequently, the Spaniards led the conquest to newfound lands of the western hemisphere. Their barbaric behaviour towards the Native American Indians was protested by jurist Francisco Vitoria (1480–1546) and Francis Suarez (1548–1617), with emphasis to treat them as human beings.[73] They were inspired by the teachings of acclaimed theologist, Thomas Aquinas (1225–1274).

In sixteenth-century Latin America, Bartolone De Las Casas insisted on freeing native Indian slaves and stop the exploitation and atrocities on them.[74] These theologists and jurists prepared the philosophical foundation of human rights in America. Latin America encountered European colonisers in the sixteenth century, remaining in their grip till the early nineteenth century. Later on, they persistently faced US intervention in their domestic affairs for the next one hundred years, at least.[75] That gave them the sense to unite at a regional level and be prepared to develop a sense of unity, freedom and justice.

Since the beginning of the twentieth century, Latin American nations organised America's conferences and established regional judicial bodies. They continuously emphasised on the promotion of human rights, democracy and sovereignty at the continental level.[76] The Organisation of the American States[77] adopted the American Declaration of Rights and Duties of Man (American Declaration)[78] seven months before UDHR. The American Declaration of rights is based on natural law and attributes to human dignity and individual personality.

This matter was further assigned to the Inter-American Council of Jurists in 1953 for promoting human rights without determinant to national sovereignty and the Principle of non-intervention.[79] The Organisation of American States' foreign ministers in 1959 adopted two resolutions; first creating an Inter-American Commission on

[72] Humphrey (1984).

[73] Nusslaaum (1954).

[74] Paolo G. Karozzs, *supra note* 71, pp. 289–296.

[75] Goldman (2009).

[76] Cavranes (1968).

[77] The Charter of the Organisation of American States adopted 30 April 1948 and entered into force 13 December 1951, 199 UNTS 3; Le Blanc (2013).

[78] *American Declaration of the Rights and Duties of Man*, OAS Res. XXX, adopted 2 May 1948, reprint in *Basic Documents pertaining to Human Rights in Inter-American system*, OAS Doc. OEA/Ser. L V// II. 82 doc. 6 rev. 1 (1992) p. 17.

[79] Sandifer (1965).

Human Rights and second the Inter-American Council of Jurists. The Council of Jurists was assigned to prepare a draft convention on human rights and to prepare the groundwork for the human rights unit. The Council mandate rested on four Pillars *inter alia*: democratic institutions, individual liberty, social justice and respect for essential rights of man.[80]

NGOs' relationship with OAS has not been institutionalised, but they are there to engage in the making of Inter-American human rights.[81]

A. **American Convention on Human Rights**

The turning point came when the American Convention on Human Rights (American convention) was concluded in San Jose, Costa Rica, in 1969, and it entered into force in 1978.[82] The American Convention laid down a minimum standard of treatment for all individuals within their jurisdiction.[83] The American convention included civil and political rights, and subsequently, the Additional Protocol to this Convention inserted economic, social and cultural rights.[84] It emphasised on the right to marry and raise a family, and also on the right to vote and to be elected in genuine periodic elections. Apart from all civil and political rights, the Convention specifically mentioned that everyone has a right to simple and prompt recourse in case of human rights violations, either through court or commission.

B. **Inter-American Commission on Human Rights**

The Inter-American Commission on Human Rights (Inter-American Commission) was established in 1959 by the Resolution of ministers of foreign affairs of the OAS. There were seven independent members who occupied the position in the Inter-American Commission in their personal capacity. In 1960, the statute of the Inter-American Commission was approved by the OAS council and empowered the commission to examine the human rights situation in the Americas. The Commission used the Bogota Declaration 1948 till the adoption of the American Convention on Human Rights 1969 for monitoring human rights observation by OAS members.[85]

The Inter-American Commission's powers and functions were enhanced by the American convention 1969. Before it, the Commission focussed only on the promotional activities of human rights. Later on, the Inter-American Commission alongside the Inter-American Court monitored the compliance of human rights.[86] The Commission considered the individual, NGO and group petition of alleged violation

---

[80] Ibid., p. 513.

[81] Martin A. Olz, *supra note* 20, pp. 354–355.

[82] 1144 UNTS 123; OAS Treaty Series No. 36; Harris and Livingstone (1998), Engstrom and Hillebrech (2020).

[83] Burke (2004).

[84] *Additional Protocol to the American Convention on Human Right in the Area of Economic Social and Cultural Rights* adopted 17 November 1988, entered into force 16 November 1999, OAS Treaty Series No. 69 (1988).

[85] Engstrom and Hillebrecht (2018).

[86] American Convention, Article 33.

of human rights. It had compulsory jurisdiction throughout the Americas.[87] Its main focus was on the friendly settlement of the issue and to make the recommendations for remedy, visit to the troubled site, adoption of precautionary measures and publish a thematic and country-specific report.[88] The Commission responds to the human rights situation as per the demand of the time.[89]

NGOs actively participated in the Inter-American Commission from 1970 to 1980. In this decade, most of the countries of America encountered dictatorship and repressive regimes.[90] Amnesty International, Americas Watch, Washington office of the Latin America, CELS, FEDEFAM, Anti-Slavery League, Centre for Justice and International Law (CEJIL) are just a few examples among numerous NGOs. They employed multiple methods and techniques to promote and protect human rights. The American Convention, Article 44 and the Inter-American Commission Statute Article 20 provide NGOs participation with IACHR in the process of promotion and compliance of human rights.

C. Inter-American Court of Human Rights

The American Convention established the Inter-American Court of Human Rights (Inter-American court) on 22 May 1979 with seven members, elected by the states' parties of the convention.[91] The Inter-American court is located at San Jose, Costa Rica. The functions of the Court are described in three legal instruments[92]: (1) American convention,[93] (2) Statute of the Inter-American court[94] and (3) the Rule of Procedure.[95] The Inter-American court's functions are of two categories: adjudicatory or contentious and advisory jurisdiction.

(1) Adjudicatory Jurisdiction

Jurisdiction of the Inter-American courts on contentions cases is optional under the convention, and it requires the acceptance of the state concerned.[96] The court adjudicates cases related to interpretation and application of the provisions of the convention.[97] The Inter-American court has wide powers in comparison with the European court of human rights, its counterpart. Article 63 of the convention provides that the Inter-American court has power to issue interim measures "in cases of extreme seriousness and urgency, and when it is necessary to avoid irreparable damage." In

---

87 American Convention, Article 35.

88 American Convention, Articles 41–51; Inter-American Court of Human Rights (Inter-Am Ct Hum Rts) Statute, Articles 18–20.

89 Dulitzky (2011).

90 Padilla (1993).

91 American Convention, Article 52.

92 Buergenthal (1982).

93 American Convention, Articles 52–73.

94 19 IML 635 (1980).

95 20 IML 1289 (1981).

96 American Convention, Article 61(1).

97 American Convention, Article 63(3).

addition, the court directs to the state concerned to pay compensation to victims of human rights violence, as a remedial measure.

A petition can be submitted either by member states of the American Convention or Inter-American Commission to the Inter-American court. In the first instance, a person or group of persons or non-governmental entity recognised by one or more members of the OAS can submit their petition with the Inter-American Commission with regard to the violation of human rights against the state parties.[98] The commission decides the admissibility of the said petition. It is requisite that domestic remedy is exhausted, and within six months of the pronouncement of the decision, the petition should be filed. There are some exceptions like the lack of due process, denying the access of remedy and unwarranted delay in rendering the decision. But onus is laid on the petitioner because presumption is in favour of the state.[99]

After the admissibility stage, the Inter-American Commission proceeds towards the friendly settlement between parties. If that fails, then the commission examines the petition on the basis of merit and draws up a report of conclusion (Article 50). This report, with recommendations, is transmitted to the parties. If the recommendation is not complied then the commission submits it to the Inter-American court. The case moves in two phases—first, in the commission, and finally, in the court, in the event that the case is not settled at the commission level.

Enforcement of the judgement of the Inter-American court does not lay down an effective mechanism. The court highlights non-compliance of the judgement in its annual report that is submitted to the general assembly of the OAS within its work during the previous year (Article 65).

(2) **Advisory Jurisdiction**

The Inter-American court provides advisory jurisdiction under Article 64 of the convention. The member states of the OAS may consult the court regarding the interpretation of the American convention or other treaties concerning the protection of human rights. Moreover, states also seek the opinion of the court regarding the compatibility of any of its domestic laws with the convention and international human rights instruments.

The scope of advisory jurisdiction is broader than contentious jurisdiction because any member state of the OAS can seek the consultation from the court. It is not necessary to accept the jurisdiction of the court beyond the scope of Inter-American Convention. Generally, the court renders advice about its domestic laws under the Bogota Declaration of 1948 and the charter of OAS, apart from member states of the OAS. The Inter-American Commission and the General Assembly of the OAS also seek advisory opinion.[100]

Advisory opinion is not binding on member states and others but it has a great value in the development of human rights infrastructure in the Americas. Advisory

---

[98] American Convention, Article 44.

[99] American Convention, Article 46; Exception to the Exhaution of Domestic Remedies Inter-American Court of Human Rights, Advisory Opinion, OC-11/90 of 10 August 1990. The advisory opinion was requested by the Inter-Am Commission on Hum Rts.

[100] Pasqualucci (2012).

opinion is willingly followed by the states because it aids in the betterment of their legal system.

NGOs can submit an amicus curiae brief to advisory proceedings in the court, if permitted by the court's president. There is no specific provision for NGOs' participation in the Inter-American court proceedings. NGOs have been very adept at integrating the Inter-American court into their advocative strategy.

5 African Machinery

The African Union 2002 adopted the African Charter on Human and People's Rights (African charter) on 17 June 1981. The African Charter came into force on 21 October 1986,[101] and it is applicable on 55 member states located within the African continent—home to more than one billion people. The Africans fought a long battle against colonial powers to earn independence. To sustain their struggle for freedom, equality and social justice, they formulated a legal and political system on a national level to protect the core values of humanity.[102]

International NGOs such as the International Commission of Jurists, Amnesty International, Human Rights Watch, Lawyer's Committee for Human Rights and FIDH are working through their African chapters or branches. Recent African NGOs and legal societies are facilitated to organise conferences across Africa, playing a crucial role in the formation of the African charter.[103]

A. **The African Charter on Human and Peoples' Rights**

The African charter set out civil and political rights as well as social, economic and cultural rights.[104] These include equality, human dignity, liberty and security, fair trial, freedom of conscience, religion, information, expression, assembly, association, movement, right to property and political participation under Articles 3 to 16 of the charter. The African charter also guarantees right to work, health, education, cultural life, development and family.[105] Apart from rights, duties of the individual towards family, society and the state are also listed. Moreover, tolerance, harmony, contribution to national security and to pay taxes are present in the charter.[106]

There is absence of derogatory provisions under the African charter. Therefore, no state party is allowed to withdraw from attributed to regulating power on individual freedom within the law. A well-defined system of limitations is necessary

---

[101] 1520 UNTS 363; www.africa-union.org/root/au/documents/treaties.htm; Evans and Murray (2008).

[102] Heyns (2004).

[103] Martin A. Olz, *supra note* 20, pp. 632–370; Appilagiyei-Atua (2002).

[104] Umozurike (1983).

[105] African Charter, Article 17–18.

[106] African Charter, Article 27–29.

for reasonable restrictions for the implementation of the African charter; regional machinery is set forth, i.e. African Commission on Human and Peoples' Rights.

B. **African Commission on Human and Peoples' Rights**

The Article 30 of the African Charter has prescribed for the establishment of the African Commission on Human and Peoples' Rights. The African Commission came into existence in 1986 and starting operating in the following year.

The composition of the African commission is described in Articles 31–33. The African commission comprises 11 members, elected by the AU Assembly through secret ballots. The state parties of the African charter are entitled to nominate reputed African personalities as members of the African Commission. To become a member of the commission, one must possess qualifications equivalent to those of a judge of the Apex court of their respective countries. AU Assembly-elected members work for a six-year term. They serve the African commission in their personal capacity. All members of the African commission work on a part-time basis. That has obviously affected the efficiency of the commission. The African Commission meets twice a year for 15-day sessions to evaluate complaints.

The main functions of the African Commission are the promotion and protection of human and peoples' rights. Besides, it has the power to interpret the African charter. The African Commission employs various means including inter alia, to collect documents, undertake research, organise seminars and conferences, disseminate information and encourage national human rights institutions. It also makes recommendations on human and people' rights to the state concerned. Its attempt is to formulate the principles to lay down rules and regulations for African human rights institutions. (Article 45).

The African Commission receives communications from inter-state, individuals and NGOs (Article 55). Till 2017, only three inter-state communications were received by the African commission.[107] Communication received by the African Commission from individuals and NGOs related to the violation of human and peoples' rights. The commission, at the outset, decides the admissibility of the communications. If communications are found for further action, then the commission pursues the friendly settlement to concerned states. The commission is a quasi-judicial body that has only recommendatory powers.

The compliance of the findings of the African Commission does not meet expectations of human and peoples' rights.[108] The commission's findings are based on the interpretation of the African charter. That are created as the obligations of all state parties. The commission submits annual reports to the Assembly of the AU and highlights previous years' work and outcome of its findings.

C. **NGOs Participation**

NGOs are actively engaged in the commission's submission of communications and compliance of findings. Gina Bekker has studied the African Commission's remedial

[107] Ayeni (2019).

[108] Vil Joen and Lauw (2007).

performance since its inception. She cited a number of cases in which NGOs filed the communications. These NGOs are the Free Legal Assistance Group, Lawyers' Committee for Human Rights, Civil Liberty Organisation, Open Society Justice Initiative, Amnesty International, Forum of Conscience, Media Rights Agenda, Constitutional Rights Project, FIDH, Zimbabwe Lawyers for Human Rights, Associated Newspapers of Zimbabwe, INTER Rights, Association of Victims of Post Electoral Violence, Article 19, Advocates Sans Frontiers, Lawyers for Human Rights, Malawi African Association, International PEN, Centre for Economic and Social Rights, Sudan Human Rights Organisation, etc.[109]

D. **African Court on Human and Peoples' Rights**

The assembly of the heads of the state and government of the AU adopted a protocol establishing an African Court on human and Peoples' Rights in 1998 (Protocol on African Court).[110] The Protocol of African Court entered into force on 25 January 2004.[111] The African Court was created under Article 2 of the Protocol on the Statute of the African Court of Justice and Human and Peoples' Rights (African Court Statute). The African Court oversees and supervises the implementation of human and peoples' rights in Africa together with the African Commission. The African Court started its operations in 2008, with the first case being decided the following year.[112]

The court comprises 16 judges[113] elected by the member states of the AU. Diversity in composition of the African Court, on the basis of gender equality, representation of main regions and principle legal traditions, is assured.[114] The court judges elect a president from among them for a three-year-term as well as the appointment of a registrar, who assists the president in performing the court's functions. The president and vice-president are full-timers, with the remaining 14 judges offering assistance on a part-time basis. The term of all 16 judges is six years. The African Court has contentious and advisory jurisdiction. The court interprets and applies the African Charter and other human rights instruments.[115] The African Commission, African NGOs, state parties of the Protocol of Court are entitled to submit cases to the African Court (Protocol Article 5).

E. **NGOs Access to the African Court**

Individuals and NGOs also have access to the court if the state parties make explicit declaration in this regard.[116] The court first examines the requirement of admissibility

[109] Bekker (2013).

[110] OAU Doc OAU/LEG/EXP/AFCHPR/PROT(III); Reprint in Heyns and Killander (2013).

[111] Viljoen (2012), Naldi and Magliveras (1998).

[112] M. Chelot Yogogombaye v. Republic of Senegal, Appeal No. 001/2008 15 December 2009.

[113] Protocol on the Statute of the African Court of Justice and Human Rights, 2008, (African Court Protocol) Article 9 vide (Annex) Statute of the African Court of Justice and Human Rights (Statute of the African Court) came to force simultaneously, Article 3.

[114] African Court Statute, Article 3(7).

[115] African Court Statute, Articles 28, 31.

[116] African Court, Article 34(6).

of the case and, on the basis of merit, pronounces the decision. The African court's decision is final and binding.

Besides, the courts have advisory jurisdiction that is based on their discretion. It can render advisory opinion on any legal matter relating to the African Charter and other human rights instruments. AU and its organs and the African commission and African IGOs are able to seek the courts advisory opinion, but it is not binding on them. However, it is a way ahead for the dynamic and progressive interpretation of the African charter and human rights treaties. It has significant impact on the realisation of human rights in the African continent.[117]

NGOs have two ways to access the African court—either as a party of the case under the optional jurisdiction of the court[118] or as amicus curiae.[119] NGOs can submit the petition directly or communicate to the African Court. Its admissibility rests on the court's discretion. The onus of justification to direct access lays on the NGOs concerned. NGOs prove that a case brought to the court is urgent because it is related to "systematic, serious or massive human rights violation."[120] NGOs' communication fulfils the seven requirements laid down under Article 56 of the African Charter.[121] These condition are:

> (1) Author of the Petition, (2) Compatible with African Charter, (3) Written in proper language and not insulting, (4) Not exclusively based on media news, (5) Exhausted local remedies, (6) Submitted within reasonable period and (7) Case not settled earlier by any other adjudication fora.

That communication is subjected to the acceptance of the state concerned and declared thereof that such NGOs have consultative status accorded by the African Commission. The African Court Statute's Article 30 gives other organisations (non-governmental) permission to bring matter before the court. As Article 30 clause of 'f' prescribed that: individual or relevant non-governmental organisations those are having accreditation in the African Union or to its organs, subject to the provision of Article 8 of the Protocol may submit communication before the court. The Article 8, clause 3 of the Protocol of Statute of the African Court of Justice and Human Rights provide: any member state may, at the time of signature or when depositing its instrument of ratification or accession, or at anytime thereafter, make a declaration accepting the competence of the court to receive cases under Article 30 clause f involving a state which has not made such a declaration.

NGOs' direct access to the African Court is not feasible because the accused does not give their consent to NGOs filing the communication (complaint) in the African Court. Moreover, they does not prefer to stand before the court as NGOs to be an opponent party against states.[122] Therefore, it is better to opt for another way to access

---

117 Udombana (2000), Eno (2002).

118 African Court Protocol, Articles 5(1) and 5(3).

119 The Rule of the African Court on Human and Peoples' Rights (African Court Rule) Rule 3 g(f); Viligoen and Abebe (2014).

120 African Charter Article 58, African Court Rules, 61(2) and 84(2).

121 African Charter Article 56; African Court Protocol, Article 5(1); Gumedze (2003).

122 Mohamed (1999), Naldi (2014).

the court as amicus curiae[123] and make a contribution to the court's outcome. Their experience and expert knowledge in the human rights landscape certainly enrich the court's proceedings.

The African human rights system is based on the desire of African states to safeguard their own interests through effectively protecting human rights in Africa.[124] African states are more interested in the protection of their sovereignty and non-intervention of outsiders. They have a deficiency of democracy, rule of law and independent judiciary. In such a situation, NGOs have contributed a lot in the operationalisation of African regional machineries, i.e. African Commission and Court.

Human rights NGOs formulated in Africa are actively engaged in the promotion and protection of human rights. K. Appiagyei-Atua has enumerated NGOs such as Legal Resources Centre of Malavie (LRC); L'Association Mauritanienne des Droits de L'Home (AMDH), Mountania; Civil Liberty Organisations (CLO), Nigeria; Committee for the Defence of Human Rights (CHHR), Nigeria; Kituo Cha Sheria (Swahili) for Legal Advice Centre, Kenya; African Commission of Health and Human Rights Promoters (CADSDH), Congo and Ghana; Coalition Against Slavery in Muntania and Sudan.[125] These are Africa-based regional NGOs and have played a significant role in the promotion and protection of human and peoples' rights within the continent.

6 Conclusion

The regional human rights system is well placed at the European, American and African continents.[126] These three regional systems have different geneses and components, something needed by their contemporary societies. Europe witnessed the gross violation of human rights and the Holocaust in the Second World War, whereas Americans suffered conquest, atrocities and repeated intervention against their sovereign integrity. The African continent fought against colonialiam, apartheid and racial discrimination.

The European Convention focussed on civil and political rights and the Inter-American Convention emphasised on political and civil rights. The African Charter includes civil, political, economic, social and cultural rights. Europe and the Inter-American system subsequently added socio-economic and cultural rights to their respective conventions. The African Charter covered human and peoples' rights, encompassing the right to development and freedom within their social fabric.

The regional machinery is of a different variety. Initially, Europe had the European Human Rights Commission, European Human Rights Court and the CoE. Later

[123] Bekker (2007).

[124] African Charter, Article 25; African Court Statute, Article 46; African Court Rule 33.

[125] K. Appiagyei-Atua, *supra note* 103, pp. 279–282.

[126] Thomas Burgenthal, *supra note* 23, pp. 422–425.

on, the European Commission was abolished. The European Human Rights Court subsumed the jurisdiction of the commission, and its decisions are binding across Europe. Besides, the European Committee on Social Charter has a recommendatory role in the field of economic, social and cultural rights.

Commissions on human rights are working continuously in America and Africa. Their main role is to promote and protect human rights within their continent. The Inter-American Court is accessible only to the Inter-American Commission, and no individual is allowed to submit the case to the court.[127] The African Court, similar to the Inter-American Court, its counterpart, receives cases from the African Commission. The African and Inter-American Commissions, however, receive complaints through individuals and NGOs.

The European and African system is accepted by all countries within their continent, while the Inter-American system is not acceded to by the most prominent countries of the continent like the United States and Canada, although the headquarters are located in Washington, DC, and 75 per cent budgetary contribution comes from the US and Canada.

NGOs are associated with regional machinery, and they have contributed remarkably. In the early twentieth century, NGOs were located primarily in Western Europe and the United States. These NGOs promoted their counterpart organisations to open their chapter or branch offices in Latin America and Africa. They expanded cross-border funds and training to their counterparts in African and Latin American region.

NGOs are instruments to bring human rights violation complaints before African and Inter-American Commissions and to the European Human Rights Court. They provide legal aid, submit amicus curiae briefs, help in rehabilitation of victims and organise campaigns for the promotion of democracy, rule of law and independence of judiciary.

The European system is quite mature and firmly grounded on the roots of liberal democratic traditions and has a strong NGO support base. Their main concern is the individual's liberty, whereas the Inter-American and African systems are focussed on the rule of law, economic growth and social development.

References

Abdullah A (2001) Human rights in the Arab world: a regional perspective. Hum Rts Q 23(3):701–732

Addison JT, Stanley Siebert W (1991) Social charter of the European community: evolution and controversies. Industr Labour Relat Rev 44(4):597–625 at 597

Amhlaigh CM, Nedelka M (2003) Forty years of European social charter: celebration or commiseration. Univ College Dublin L Rev 1:67–91 at 79–82

Appilagiyei-Atua K (2002) Human right NGOs and their role in promotion and protection of right in Africa. Int J Minorities Group Rts 9(3):265–290

[127] Weston et al (1987), Thomas Burgenthal, *supra note*, 26, pp. 155–166.

Ayeni VO (2019)The African-human rights architecture: reflections on the instruments and mechanism within the African human rights system. Beijing L Rev 10(2):302–316 at 308
Bekker G (2007) The African court on human and peoples' rights: safeguarding the interest of African states. J African L 5(1):151–172
Bekker G (2013) The African commission on human and peoples' rights and remedies for human rights violations. Hum Rts L Rev 13(3):499–528
Betten L (1988) European social charter. Netherlands Q Hum Rts 6(2):69–82 at 69–70
Brownlie I, Godwin Gill GS (eds) (2010) Documents on human rights, 6th edn. Oxford University Press, pp 1017–1037
Buergenthal T (1982) The Inter-American court of human rights. Am J Int'l L 76(2):231–245 at 232
Buergenthal T (2006) The evolving international human rights system. Am J Int'l L 100(4):783–807 at 792
Burgenthal T (1980) The American and European conventions of human rights: similarities and differences. Am Univ L Rev 31:155–166
Burgenthal T (1986) The UN covenants and regional human rights system. Proc Am Soc'y Int'l L 80:422–424
Burke WW (2004) Human rights in the inter-American system. Int Stud J 1(2):33–56 at 36
Carozza PG (2003) From conquest to constitutions: retrieving a Latin American tradition of the idea of human rights. Hum Rts Q 25(2):281–313 at 281. https://scholarship.law.nd.edu/law_faculty_scholarship/581
Cavranes J (1968) Protection of human rights by the organisation of American States. Am J Int L 62(4):889–908
Churchill RR, Khaliq U (2004) Collective complaints system of the European social charte: an effective mechanism for ensuring compliance with economic and social rights? Eur J Int'l L 15(3):224–229
Council of Europe (2011) The European court of human rights: some facts and figures, 1998–2008. CoE Publications, Strasbourge, France
Cullen H (2009a) The collective complaint system of the European social charter: imperative methods of the European committee of social rights. Hum Rts L Rev 9(1):61–93
Cullen J (2009b) The collective complaint system of European social charter-interpretive methods of European committee of social rights. Hum Rts L Rev 9:61–93
Dhaliwal S (2008) Development of South Asian human rights culture: the role of South Asian Association for Regional Cooperation (SAARC). Indian J Polit Sci 63(3):565–675
Dowrick FE (1974) Juristic activity in the council of Europe-25th year. Int'l & Comp L Q 23(3):610–641
Drzemczerwski A (1998) The European human rights convention in domestic law: a comparative study. Oxford University Press
Dulitzky A (2011) The Inter-American human rights system fifty years later: time for change. Quebec J Int L (special edn), pp 127–164. https://id.erudit.org/idrudit/1068396ar
Engstrom P, Hillebrech C (eds) (2020) The Inter-American human rights system: the law and politics of institutional change. Routledge
Engstrom P, Hillebrecht C (2018) Institutional change and the inter-American human rights system. Int J Hum Rts 29(9):1111–1122 at 1112–1113
Eno RW (2002) The jurisdiction of the African court on human and peoples' rights. African Hum Rts LJ 2:223–233
Evans M, Murray R (eds) (2008) The African charter of human and peoples' rights. Cambridge University Press
Goldman RK (2009) History and action: the inter-American human rights system and of the role of the Inter-American commission on human rights. Hum Rts Q 31(4):856–887 at 857.
Greer S (2008a) What's wrong with European convention on human rights? Hum Rts Q 30(3):680–702 at 681

Greer S (2008b) The European convention on human rights: achievements, problems and prospects, 3rd edn. Cambridge University Press
Gumedze S (2003) Bringing communications before the African commission on human and people rights. African Hum Rts L I 3:118–148
Harris DJ (1992) A fresh imputes for the European social charter. Int Comp L Q 41(3):659–676 at 659
Harris DJ, Darcy J (2001) The European social charter, 2nd edn. Transnational Publisher, New York
Harris DJ, Livingstone S (1988) Inter-American system of human rights. Clarendon Press, Oxford
Harris DJ et al (2018) Law of the European convention on human rights, 4th edn. Oxford University Press
Hendricks A (1996) Revised European social charter. Netherlands Q Hum Rts 14(3):341–359
Heyns, Killander M (eds) (2013) Compendium of key human and peoples' rights documents of the African Union, 6th edn. Pritorial University Law Press, South Africa, p 41
Heyns C (2004) African regional human right system: the African charter. State L Rev 108(3):679–702 at 679–680
Humphrey JP (1984) Human. Rights and the United Nations: a great adventure. Transnational Publications, New York, p 13
Ishay MR (2008) The history of human rights. Black Swan University of California Press, Berkley, Chap. 2
Kanunnikov A (2017) International non-environment organisation in the council of Europe. imemo.ru 61(6):33–40. https://doi.org/10.20542/0131-2227_2017_61_6_33_40
Le Blanc LJ (2013) The OAS and the promotion and protection of human rights. Springer, New York
Lemmes K (2019) Protocol No.16 to the ECHR: managing backlog through complex judicial dialogue. Eur Const L Rev 15(4):691–713
Mikkola M (2000) Social rights as a human rights in Europe. Eur J Soc Secur 2(3):259–272
Mohamad M (2002) Towards a human rights regime in Southeast Asia: charting the course of state commitment. Contemp Southeast Asia 24(2):230–251
Mohamed AA (1999) Individual and NGO Participation in human rights litigation before court of human and peoples' rights. J Afr L 43(2):201–213
Murray R (2004) Human rights in Africa: from the OAU to the African Union. Cambridge University Press
Myers DP (1956) The European commission on human rights. Am J Int L 54(4):949–951
Naldi GJ (2014) Observations on the rules of the African court on human and peoples' rights. African Hum Rts L J 14:381
Naldi GL, Magliveras KD (1998) Reinforcing the African system of human rights: the protocol on the establishment of a regional court of human and peoples rights. Netherlands Q Hum Rts 16:1–35
Nowicki MA (1996) NGOs before the European commission and the court of human rights. Netherlands Q Hum Rts 14:289–302. http://localhost.8080/xmlvi/handle/1234566789/650
Nusslaaum A (1954) A concise history of the law of nations. Macmillan, New York, pp 58–72
Olz MA (1997) Non-governmental organisations in regional human rights system. Columbia Hum Rts L Rev 28(2):307–374
Padilla DJ (1993) The Inter-American commission of human rights of the organisation of American states: a case study. Am Univ Int L Rev 9(1):95–115 at 97
Pasqualucci JM (2012) The practice and procedure of the inter-American court of human rights. Cambridge University Press, pp 37–80
Robertson AH (1950) The European convention for the protection of human rights. Brit Y B Int'l L 27:145–163 at 146–147
Robertson AH, Merrils JG (1996) Human rights in the world, 4th edn. Manchester University Press, UK, pp 120–124
Sandifer DV (1965) Human right in the inter-American systems. Howard L J 11(2):508–528 at 512

Shalton DL, Karozza PG (2013) Regional protection of human rights, 2nd edn. Oxford University Press
Shindler D (1962) European convention on human rights in practice. Washington Univ L Q 2:152–165 at 154–157
Thomas AVW, Thomas AJ Jr (1963) The organisation of American States. Southern Methodist University Press Texas, US
Udombana NJ (2000) Towards the African court on human and peoples' rights: better late than never. Yale Hum Rts & Devt L J 3(2):45–67
Umozurike UO (1983) The African charter of human and peoples' rights. Am J Int L 77(4):896–914
Van Den Eynde L (2013) An empirical look at the Amicus Curaie practice of human rights NGOs before the European court of human rights. Netherlands Q Hum Rts 31:271–313
van Dijk Hoof P et al (2018) Theory and practice of the European convention of human rights, 5th edn. Intersentia Publishers, UK
Vandamme F (1994) The revision of European social charter. Int Labour Rev 133(5–6):635–656
Vil Joen F, Lauw L (2007) State compliance with recommendations of African commission on human and peoples' rights, 1994–2004. Am J Int'l L 101(1): 1–34
Viligoen F, Abebe AK (2014) Amicus curiae participation before regional human rights bodies in Africa. J African L 58(1):22–22
Viljoen F (2007) International human rights law in Africa, 2nd edn. Oxford University Press (first edn 2007)
Weil GL (1963) The evolution of European convention on human rights. Am J Int'l L 57(4):804–827
Welch CE Jr (ed) (2001) NGOs and human rights: promise and performance. University of Pennsylvania Press, Philadelphia
Weston BH et al (1987) Regional human rights regime: a comparison and appraisal. Vendervilt J Trans'l L 24:585–638
Wilner GM (1995) Reflections on regional human rights law. Georgia J Int'l & Comp L 25(2):407–426

Chapter 11
Protection of the Environment

1 Introduction

The term 'environment' is a broad concept that encompasses nature, culture and heritage. Nature constitutes biotic and abiotic components. Biotic constitutes human, animal, wildlife, birds, forest and all other living creature, whereas abiotic are land, air, water, etc. Thus the environment consists of all living and non-living things of our planet and their inter-relationship. The use of natural resources and human activities are within the ambit of environment.

The concept of environment protection is a worldwide phenomenon. In 1922, an NGO called the International Council of Birds Preservation was established. Presently, it is known as Birds Life International.[1] Its motto was to highlight the partnership of nature and people. Another milestone in the concept of environment protection came in the Trial Smelter dispute (1927–1941),[2] when the Arbitral Tribunal fixed the transboundary responsibility of a state.

The Trial Smelter dispute was between Canada and the United States with respect to use of territory and its effect thereof. The Canadian company Smelter caused injury to the State of Washington, United States. The Tribunal observed that every state had a right to use and exercise sovereignty over resources within their respective territories, in as much as that no one is allowed to harm other's territory, property and people.

Environment protection is a great cause for concern to humanity because acid rain, atmospheric pollution, climate change, extinction of species and depletion of natural resources have transnational effect. Therefore, protection of the environment requires international solidarity and collective action from every nook and corner of the world. The potentially irreversible damage done to the earth's environment

[1] www.birdslife.org.

[2] (1938) 3 RIAA 1905; *Am J Int'l L*, vol. 35, no. 4 (1941) pp. 684–736; Wirth (1996).

P. Rai, *Non-Governmental Organisations and International Law*,
https://doi.org/10.1007/978-981-97-5469-4_11

has led to the formation of an international environmental law so as to achieve legal control.[3]

The International Environmental Law (IEL) was developed after World War II, alongside domestic environmental laws. It acquired the shape and acceptability as a separate branch of international and domestic law in the 1960s. It assimilated customary law such as state practices, emergent legal principles, environmental treaty, declarations, court decisions, research and writings within its scope of application.[4] IEL is a joint venture of states, IGOs, NGOs, courts, academics, media, scientific community and environmentalists.

2 The Development of International Environmental Law

Wherever environmental problems have arisen, they have been addressed through international agreements among states. Thereby a number of international environment treaties related to ozone layer, hazardous waste, climate change, loss of biodiversity, desertification, marine pollution from ships, endangerment to life of whales, etc. have been concluded. This custom has remained an important source for IEL.[5]

The prohibition of transfrontier damage, precautionary principles, right to life of whales, protection of endangered species, engaged in consultation for the cause of transboundary harm are covered in customary international environmental law. Customs are reflected in state's behaviour towards environmental issues. Customs are observed by states themselves, if there is any dispute the state parties resolve it through negotiations or diplomatic methods.

A. Stockholm Conference

The turning point in the development of IEL came when the UN sponsored, Stockholm Conference on the Human Environment which was held from 5 to 16 June 1972, adopted a declaration and a comprehensive action plan.[6] Louis B. Sohn observed:

> "the Declaration contains a set of common principles to inspire and guide the people of the world in the preservation and enhancement of the human environment".[7] The Stockholm Declaration laid down 21 principles concerning the environment and development. In addition, an action plan with 109 recommendations and a resolution were also adopted.

Being a declaration it is not legally binding on the participant states of the Stockholm Conference, nonetheless it is considered a cornerstone to the infrastructure of international environmental law. The Conference established the United Nations

---

[3] Brownlie (2019).

[4] Sands et al. (2012); Birni et al. (2009); Bodansky et al. (2007).

[5] Bodansky (1995); Schachter (1991).

[6] Report of the United Nations Conference on Human Environment in Stockholm (1972) pp. 1–76; United Nations Conference on the Human Environment, UN DOC A/CONF.48/14/ Rev. 1 (1973); 11 ILM 1416 (1972).

[7] Sohn (1973).

Environment Programme (UNEP),[8] for creating a separate ministry of environment in each and every state, and celebrating World Environment Day on 5th June every year with a special theme.

B. **Rio Conference**

It was followed by the Rio Conference of 1992 on the United Nations Environment and Development. It stimulated the states, IGOs, NGOs, scientific community and individuals to engage in environment protection. It reaffirmed the 21 principles of the Stockholm Declaration. The Rio Conference emphasised the state's responsibility of transboundary damage to others.[9] This obligation was further endorsed by the International Court of Justice,[10] becoming a well-settled principle of IEL.

Apart from the states, IGOs, NGOs, corporations, scientists and environmentalists also participated at the Stockholm Conference in large numbers. The United Nations accredited 250 NGOs for the Conference.[11] It was for the first time that the United Nations officially invited NGOs on such a large scale to participate in an international conference and sought to make constructive contributions along with the states.

This was a noteworthy partnership between the states and NGOs for environment protection for years to come.[12] The Rio Conference also known as Earth Summit on Environment and Development was held from 3 to 14 June in 1992. There were 172 state representatives and 2400 accredited representatives from NGOs who participated in the Rio Conference. An additional 17,000 representatives of NGOs attended a parallel NGO conference at the same time, date and venue.

A large number of ecologists and scientists gathered there to provide authentic information and data on environmental problems of our planet. For media coverage of this monumental event, 9000 journalists from all over the world came to Rio to spread the news and views on the Earth Summit. In all, 40,000 participants assembled for the Rio Conference.[13]

NGOs, scientists, environmentalists and indigenous people among others organised a global forum or parallel Earth Summit in 35 big tents. This was a twelve-day event which was attended by a diverse spectrum of people from around the world. They remained outside, unofficially, and short of funds but they were enthusiastic, inspired and organised lectures, discussions on protection of environment and related issues. In the evenings, they organised and enjoyed vivid cultural programmes while networking with other NGOs. They become the 'soul and conscience' of the earth summit or Rio Conference 1992.[14]

---

[8] http://www.uneviron ment.org.

[9] *Report of the United Nations Conference on the Human Environment* (Stockholm, 5–16 June 1972), UN Publications, New York 1973; Principle 21 of the UN Conference in Environment and Development (1992); Grabb et al. (1993).

[10] *Legality of Threat or Use of Nuclear Weapon*, Advisory Opinion, ICJ Reports (1996) p. 226, and *Gabcikovo-Nagymaros Project (Hungary v. Slovakia)* Judgment, ICJ Reports (1997) p. 7.

[11] Weiss (2011).

[12] Betsill and Corell (2008).

[13] Reilly (1992).

[14] Getches (1993).

The Rio Conference 1992 adopted two legal instruments and three documents. The legal instruments were: The UN Framework Convention on Climate Change (UNFCCC)[15] and the Convention on Biological Diversity.[16] Besides, the three documents, i.e. Rio Declaration on Environment and Development[17]; Agenda 21[18] and Principles of Conservation of Forests[19] had also been adopted. In addition, the Rio Conference established the UN Commission on Sustainable Development (CSD)[20] and Global Environment Facility (GEF).[21]

The Rio Conference of 1992 was a unique event where developed nations met with developing countries, and official representatives with volunteers, cosmopolitans with indigenous people, free markets with sustainability, some focussed on population control and vast majority of people were inclined towards reduction of poverty.[22] But ultimately all agreed on the theme of environmental protection because of its indispensability. It was highlighted by the president of the United States. In the words of conservationist, Gifford Pinchot,

> a nation that has lost its liberty may win it... a nation divided may reunite ... but a nation whose natural resources are destroyed must inevitably pay the penalty of poverty, degradation and decay.[23]

The Rio Conference of 1992 became the roadmap for further development of international environment law. The scientific community is the first to find out problems through its research and laboratory experiments. NGOs like International Council for Scientific Union—ICSU, Paris (1931) had been mobilising knowledge and resources of the scientific community at the universal level.[24]

C. **NGOs Participation**

At present, the UNEP[25] has accredited a total of 594 environmental-based NGOs. In the twenty-first century a good number of NGOs were located in developing nations.

---

[15] UN Framework Convention on Climate Change (UNCCC), *United Nations Conference on Environment and Development*, 4 June 1992, 31 ILM 849 (1992).

[16] Convention on Biological Diversity, *United Nations Conference on Environment and Development*, 5 June 1992, 31 ILM 818 (1992).

[17] Rio Declaration on Environment and Development, *United Nations Conference on Environment and Development*, UN Doc. A/CONF./51/5/Rev. 1 (1992); 31 ILM 874 (1992).

[18] Agenda 21, *United Nations Conference on Environment and Development*, UN Doc.A/CONF.151/4 (1992).

[19] Statement of Principle for a Global Consensus of the Management, Conservation and Sustainable Development of All Types of Forests, *United Nations Conference on Environment and Development*, UN Doc. A/CONF. 151/6/ Rev. 1 (1992) 31 ILM 874 (1992).

[20] https://www.sustainbledevelopment.un.org.

[21] http://www.thegef.org.

[22] Goldman (1992).

[23] The President of United States, Address Before the UN Conference on Environment and Development (12 June 1992), William K. Reilly, *supra note* 13, p. 356.

[24] http://council.science, formerly known as International Council of Scientific Union (ICSU) now it is known as International Science Council.

[25] Www.unenvironment.org/list of accredited organisations (as on 25 February 2020).

NGOs such as Green Peace International,[26] International Union for Conservation of Nature (IUCN)[27] and World Wildlife Fund (WWF)[28] have contributed significantly in making and working of the international environmental law. The NGO—Fridays For Future (FFF)[29] also known as School Strike for Climate was formulated in Sweden in 2018. A NGOs coalition of International Campaign to Abolish Nuclear Weapon[30] and Climate Action Network International[31] were also established.

In addition to youth, indigenous people, women, workers and trade unions, business and industry, scientific and technological community, participated in the Rio Conference. They were specifically mentioned under Section III of Agenda 21, of the United Nations Conference on Environment and Development.[32]

NGOs' participation in environment protection was strengthen by the Aarhus Convention of 1998. The United Nations Economic Commission for Europe (UNECE) adopted the Convention on Access to Information, Public Participation in Decision Making and Access to Justice in Environment Matters on 25 June 1998 in Aarhus, Denmark. It came into force on 30 October 2001.[33] This convention later on came to be popularly known as the Aarhus Convention. It is a regional Conference for European Nations, sponsored by the United Nations and has acceptability throughout the world. The Aarhus Convention has enabled NGOs to seek environment information, participate in decision-making and to access judicial and administrative redressal in environmental matters.

NGOs can seek information from states, IGOs and corporations about their forthcoming project and sites and 'impact assessment reports' thereof.[34] NGOs have long experience, skill and resources to deploy in the international environmental cooperation[35] and stimulation. There are five major issue areas in international environmental law, these are: (1) Nature, (2) Atmosphere, (3) Marine life, (4) Nuclear and (5) Hazardous substances. NGOs are engaged in making and enforcing international environmental law through various ways and means.

[26] www.greenpeace.org.

[27] www.iucn.org.

[28] www.wwfinternational.org.

[29] http://www.worldwildlife.org; www.panda.org.

[30] http://www.icanw.org.

[31] www.climatenetwork.org.

[32] Www.sustainabledevelopment.un.org/contents/document/agenda 21-PDF visited on 21/4/2020.

[33] http://www.unece.org, 2161 UNTS 444; Karv-Chenko (2007).

[34] Mason (2010).

[35] Rautiala (1997).

3 Conservation of Nature

Conservation of nature is interwoven with human health, people's well-being and social justice. In the eighteen century, Europe found sophisticated fire power, which led to the industrial revolution and colonisation. The focus shifted to economic growth and gross domestic product (GDP).

But natural resources are limited in supply to bear such unprecedented human ambition.[36] In the later part of the twentieth century the idea of sustainable development emerged and was promoted through the concept of mitigation, carbon credit and green taxes.

E.F. Schumacher stated that the standard of living and well-being of people did not depend only on consumption but on simple and need-based life. He further stressed the need for a self-reliant economy based on eco-friendly technology.[37] Currently, economic growth overrides business ethics, social values and ecological balance. But conservation of nature is required for equilibrium of ecology, society and economics.[38] Moreover, an anthropocentric focus is required that encompasses all living creatures and natural surroundings.

Conservation of nature is synonymous to the protection of ecosystems and achieving sustainability through awareness, education and scientific research. The methods and techniques like protected areas,[39] community forest management,[40] payment for environment services,[41] sustainable certification[42] and eco-tourism[43] came into being for conservation of nature. These are to be applied to marine life, forests, species, natural landscapes and resources. Conservation of nature can sustain the well-being of people,[44] availability of wild food, fresh water, public health, traditional knowledge and the rights of indigenous people.

A. Wetlands and Water Fowl Habitat

The 1971 Ramsar Convention on Wetlands is the first international instrument for conservation of nature. The Ramsar Convention formally known as the Convention on Wetlands of International Importance, especially the Water Fowl Habitat was concluded on 2 February 1971 in Ramsar (Iran) and came into force on 21 December 1971.[45] It listed international privileged sites of important wetlands. At present, there are 2390 wetlands, covering a total surface area of 2.53 million hectares, around the world. In the beginning, there were 18 state parties of the Ramsar Convention, which

[36] Gean-Louis et al. (2016).

[37] Schumacher (1973).

[38] Giddings et al. (2002).

[39] Listte and Gaston (2010).

[40] Arts (2017).

[41] Mayrand and Paquin (2004).

[42] Gullison (2003).

[43] Wolf et al. (2019).

[44] Bottrill et al. (2014).

[45] 996 UNTS 245; 11 ILM 969 (1972); Bowman (1995).

now stands at 171 nations. State parties of the Convention have listed at least one site of their country or adjacent areas which has inherent international importance.

The Ramsar Treaty or Convention was led by the NGOs—International Union for Conservation Nature (1948),[46] Wetlands International (1954)[47] and World Wildlife Fund for Nature (WWF) 1961,[48] along with UNEP and state parties.[49] Many other NGOs—Society of Wetlands Scientists, SWS (1980),[50] Wild & Wetlands Trust WWT (1946),[51] The Nature Conservancy, TNC (1951),[52] Conservation International, CI (1997),[53] International Association of Impact Assessment, IAIA (1970),[54] and Birdslife International (1922)[55] were also engaged in the conservation of waterfowls and wetlands across the frontier. Besides, UNEP, UNDP, UNESCO and other IGOs, private organisation also participated in the promotion and protection of wetlands and waterfowls.

The Ramsar Convention broadly defined wetlands and encompassed fish as well as bird species and habitat.[56] The main purpose of the Ramsar Convention is conservation of wetlands and waterfowls.[57] It prescribes a protective obligation of state parties. They maintain ecological character and areas of wetlands and make management planning and monitoring systems. The early information about any change in wetlands due to technological development, pollution or human interference has to be resubmitted to the Ramsar Secretariat.[58] State parties were required to use wetlands in their territory wisely. The wise use[59] of wetlands is defined as, the maintenance of their ecological character, achieved through the implementation of ecosystem approaches within the context of sustainable development.[60] NGOs are supporting state parties in the compliance of the Ramsar Convention on conservation of wetlands.

According to Nick Davidson, wetlands are continuously disappearing. He estimated a 50% loss since the nineteenth century. This degradation of wetlands is still

---

[46] www.iucn.org.

[47] http://www.wetlands.org; Wetlands and its predecessor have engaged in protection of wetlands in 1937 known as International Wild Fowl Inquiry. In 1954 it become International Water Fowl and Wetland Research Bureau (IWRB) and in 1996, Wetlands International, located in Netherlands.

[48] www.worldwildlife.org; WWF precursor was conservation foundation 1948.

[49] Matthews (2013).

[50] http://www.sws.org, Society of Wetlands Scientists engaged with Convention, in restoration and scientific management and sustainability of Wetlands since 1980.

[51] http://www.wwt.org.uk.

[52] www.nature.org.

[53] http://www.conservation.org.

[54] http://www.iaia.org.

[55] www.Birdslife.org.

[56] Ramsar Convention 1971, Article 1; Bowman (1995).

[57] Ramsar Convention, 1971, Article 6 (1).

[58] Ramsar Convention, Article 3 (2).

[59] Ramsar Convention, Article 3 (1).

[60] Finlayson (2012).

on. Wetlands are invaluable for our ecosystem. The Ramsar Convention of Wetlands made a positive impact on North America and Europe, however Asia, deep flooded areas of Amazon and the Congo lack in data and information even now.[61]

The 1971 Ramsar Convention on Wetlands is a very precise legal instrument which contains 12 Articles in all. The convention of parties (COP) has held triennial sessions and revamped the Convention. State parties submit national reports to the Ramsar Secretariat. The Bureau of Scientists and Technologists assist states for conservation of wetland sites and offer some financial assistance to developing countries for their endeavours.

The Ramsar Convention has had a positive impact but then less than 19% of the global wetlands are in the Ramsar list. Therefore, it should be expanded to cover more wetlands around the world. Environmental NGOs and scientific community are best suited to strengthen public awareness about protection of wetlands. Ting Xu et al.[62] have recommended inter alia, management and policy, monitoring, knowledge and funding for conservation and restoration of global wetlands.[63]

B. **The World Heritage**

The World Heritage Convention, 1972,[64] is a significant legal instrument for the conservation of the cultural and natural heritage of mankind. Almost all the 193 states are parties to the convention. Many historical sites and cultural heritage were adversely affected during World War II. Architectural monuments like the Angkor Wat in Cambodia, Borobudur in Indonesia and Venice in Italy have degraded rapidly. Egypt's proposed construction of the Aswan Dam along the river Nile pose threats to their archaeological sites.[65] The United States and the IUCN (1948),[66] ICOMOS (1965)[67] and UNESCO jointly led a campaign to protect our cultural and natural heritage. It resulted in the formation of the World Heritage Convention 1972 at the General Conference of the UNESCO.[68]

The World Heritage Convention definition includes architectural monuments, art work, group of building connected by site, geographically unique places such as desert, forest, island, lake, wild areas and historically identifiable places like ancient remnants of civilisation and cultural landscapes. They have inherent beauty, aesthetic quality and outstanding universal value.

The Convention lays down the state's primary responsibility to conserve natural and cultural heritage.[69] The Convention established World Heritage Committee and

---

[61] Davidson (2014).

[62] Xu et al. (2019).

[63] Ibid., pp. 17–19.

[64] Convention Concerning the Protection of the World Cultural and Natural Heritage was adopted on 16 November 1972 by the General Conference of the UNESCO and entered into force on 27 December 1975, 1037 UNTS 151.

[65] Rodwell (2012).

[66] www.iucn.org.

[67] www.icomos.org.

[68] World Heritage Convention, Article 1.

[69] World Heritage Convention, Articles 4(7).

World Heritage Fund. The World Heritage Committee constitutes of 21 members elected by the General Conference of the UNESCO from the state parties of the Convention.[70] The World Heritage Committee has three international advisory members: (1) International Union for Conservation of Nature, 1948 (IUCN), (2) International Council on Monuments and Sites, 1965 (ICOMOS) and (3) International Centre for the Study of the Preservation and Restoration of Cultural Property, 1956 (ICCROM), an IGO located in Rome. They have experience in conservation of natural and cultural heritage and historical monuments.[71]

The World Heritage Committee has created a world heritage list, since 1978. The list is published, revised and updated regularly. The criteria for the inscription of the world heritage list are an important task of the World Heritage Committee. This is fulfilled with the help of three advisory bodies and consensus among the Committee members on the state proposal about any monument, site, area which carries eminent values of mankind and future generations.[72] The list is of aesthetic importance and a bridge between nature and culture, that is why the world heritage list is a single inscription of natural and cultural heritage.[73]

The World Heritage Committee constantly monitors the list of world heritage. It is empowered to publish the list of world heritage dangers for public attention and to mobilise the stake holders. The Committee can delist any inscriptions. So far Arabian Oryx Sanctuary in Oman and the Dresden Elve Valley in Germany have been delisted from the world heritage list in 2007 and 2009 respectively.

The World Heritage Fund was established under Article 15 of the Convention. The fund is utilised for the protection of world cultural and natural heritage of outstanding universal value. The Convention emphasises international assistance, educational programmes and prescribes states' obligation to submit the report on their inscription and listed sites to the UNESCO.

Apart from the World Heritage Fund, a Global Heritage Fund was founded in California, United States, in 2002. Charity is the main source of donation for the world heritage sites conservation.[74] Indian National Trust for Art and Cultural Heritage (INTACH)[75] is an NGO formed in 1984 and located in New Delhi. It stimulates and spreads heritage awareness and participates in conservation of monuments. It has been endowed consultative status by the UNESCO.

The protection of cultural heritage preserves human dignity, individual rights and collective interests of communities for future generations.[76] It promotes vivid imagination and cultural diversity. Total inscriptions in the world heritage list are 1121 including cultural, natural, mixed and transboundary; among them two are already

---

[70] The World Heritage Convention, Articles 8–10.

[71] Website of three advisor organisations. http://www.IUCN.org; www.icomos.org and www.iccrom.org.

[72] The World Heritage Convention, Article 11.

[73] Lixinski (2008), *European J Legal Studies*, vol. 2, no. 1 (2008) pp. 371–386.

[74] http://globalheritagefund.org.

[75] www.intach.org.

[76] Francioni (2004).

delisted as mentioned above and 53 are in the danger list.[77] The world heritage brand enhanced its attraction throughout world and attracted tourists and manifested economic gains. Sometimes it is difficult to manage and thus pose danger to the monuments, sites and natural beauty.[78]

Another threat to world heritage monuments is from armed opponent groups and armed conflicts. In spite of the Hague Convention for the Protection of Cultural Property 1954,[79] armed opponent groups destroyed the Buddha of Bamiyan (2001), the library in Bosnia & Herzegovina (1992), Churches in Kosovo (1991–1995), Palmyra in Syria (2015) and many other rare heritages.

C. **Endangered Species**

In the beginning of the nineteenth century, conservation of wildlife became a concern for the international community. An NGO for Preservation of Wild Fauna of the Empire (1903) in Cambridge, the United Kingdom, was formed for the conservation of wildlife.[80] Growth of population, colonial settlers[81] and human intentions were threatening the survival of wildlife. The problem was addressed by the London Convention Relative to the Preservation of Fauna and Flora in their Natural Status, 1933.[82] This convention was concluded by the colonial powers to save hunting grounds and revenue for wildlife resources.

This is applicable in the colonies such as Africa, South Asia and Indonesia.[83] The IUCN took an initiative in 1963 for the conservation of wildlife and to save the endangered species. The first draft of the convention was prepared in 1964 by IUCN. It was sent to all member states of the UN and the NGOs. A number of suggestions and improvements were made by 39 states and 18 NGOs.[84]

The substantive progress was made after Stockholm Conference 1972. The United States hosted the Conference in Washington DC in 1973 where the Convention on International Trade in Endangered Species in 1973 (CITES) was set up.[85] CITES is a universal treaty, and at present there are 183 state parties to it.

It is a significant treaty for conservation of wildlife, sustainable use and viable international trade of flora and fauna.[86] CITES has protected 7875 fauna and 30,034

[77] www.whc.unesco.org; World Heritage List, visited on 2 May 2020.

[78] D. Rodwell, *supra note* 65, pp. 64–85.

[79] The Hague Convention for the Protection of Cultural Property in the Event of Armed Conflicts adopted in the Hague, 14 May 1954, entered into force, 7 August 1954; 249 UNTS 215; Keefe (2006).

[80] https://www.fauna-flora.org>about us; Prendergast and Adam (2003).

[81] Griffiths and Robin (1997).

[82] Signed on 8 November 1933, entered into force 1936, 172 LNTs (1936) pp. 241–272.

[83] Sand (1997).

[84] CITIES World official news latter of the parties, special edition, 3 March 2003 on it 30th Anniversary, p. 2. www.cites.org/sites/default/files/eng/news/world/30special. PDF.

[85] The Convention on International Trade in Endangered Species (CITES) signed on 3 March 1973, entered into force 1 July 1977, 993 UNTS 243; (1973) 12 ILM 1085.

[86] Oldfield (2003); Hill (1990).

flora species.[87] As per an estimate, in 2007 the value of international wildlife trade has been US $ 3325 billion annually.[88]

The CITES Secretariat worked with the IUCN for some time, and subsequently it was taken over by the UNEP. The Secretariat is located at Geneva, Switzerland. Conference of parties (COP) is a supreme body. It meets triennially and adopts resolutions and takes decisions and monitors state reports of compliance of the convention. It can also revise list of the appendix and improve the convention.[89] COP created Standing Committee of 21 elected members which work in interval of three years.[90] Another two Scientific Committees one for animals and other for plants were established.[91]

The COP endowed observer status to NGOs—IUCN, WWF and TRAFFIC under Article XI clause 7 of CITES. These NGOs are allowed to participate, make submissions and express their views but do not have rights to vote. Besides NGOs, IGOs and representatives of education institutions, business and private entities are also allowed to participate. In 2004, COP-12 was attended by a total of 1164 participants, among them were 37 national NGOs, 55 international NGOs and 13 IGOs. Remaining were representatives of state, academic, science and business sectors.[92]

The primary objective of CITES is to ensure that international trade in wild animals and plants does not threaten their survival.[93] There are three appendixes in the convention. First is known as blacklist of species endangered with extinction because commercial trade is prohibited, with exception for academic and scientific purposes.[94] Second is a grey list of wild species where international trade is permitted. Third is open for the treaty party to enlist any species for protection and co-operation in their preservation.

The compliance of CITES rests with the state parties of the treaty. They have to take steps in establishing the scientific authority, frame the national legislation to prosecute the violators of CITES and confiscate illegal possession of species. State parties are required to submit their compliance report to the Secretariat.

The International Consortium on Combating Wildlife Crime (ICCWC) established for a global collaboration was to fight against wildlife and forest crimes.[95] It is an IGO consisting of representatives of CITES, Interpol, UNODC, World Bank and World Customs Organisation (WCO). In addition to it, the UNODC has developed: World Wide Life Crime Report 2016 to highlight the poaching and illegal trade of thousands of species across the globe.

---

[87] http://www.cites.org/eng/disc/species.php, visited 4/5/2020.

[88] Engler (2008).

[89] CITES, Articles XI (3).

[90] COP Resolution 2.2/1979.

[91] COP Resolution 11.1/2000 and further revised in 2016.

[92] CITES World, Official Newsletter of the Parties, Geneva, 2004.

[93] Reeve (2006); Chalakkal (2014); Sand (2017).

[94] Reeve (2002).

[95] Resolution Conf. 11. 3 (Rev). COP 17.

The CITES is a success story of expending wildlife conservation mission to international trade and joining hands with NGOs, IGOs, scientists and business to save the world's wildlife.

D. **Migratory Species**

Migratory species travel from their habitat to other places. Migration is cyclical, occurring seasonally and therefore a predictable phenomenon. The migratory species migrate to take advantage of sunlight, weather and food while breeding and nursing their young ones.[96] Migratory species' routes and destinations are fixed, and they impart this knowledge to their future generations. Transboundary migration is a matter of international law. There are terrestrial, aquatic as well as avian migratory species on this planet and their movements are diverse, i.e. animal migration is annual, birds travel seasonally and fish migrate regularly.

Migratory species are facing problems of hunting, habitat destruction, pollution, degradation of feeding grounds, making international protection of migratory wildlife necessary. The Stockholm Conference of 1972, Resolution 32 recommended to the states to convince the international conference for the protection of migratory species.[97] NGOs too demanded protection of migratory birds, fish and animals.[98] It resulted in the Convention on the Conservation of Migratory Species of Wild Animals, 1979. It was concluded in Bonn on 23 June 1979 and came into force on 1 November 1983. The convention is also known as CMS or Bonn Convention.[99]

In 1979 there were 29 state parties to the Bonn Convention, and their number has now increased to 129. The main objective of the Bonn Convention is to conserve, use wisely and safely transfer this legacy to future generations.[100] Primary responsibility is vested with the state parties and world community. Bonn convention has two appendixes. Appendix I includes endangered migratory species, those on the verge of extinction of a significant portion of its range.[101] In this situation, State shall strictly protect their habitat and endeavour to restore the habitat. There are 1080 entire listed in Appendix I as of 24 February 2020.

Appendix II relates to migratory species with an unfavourable conservation status. These species have maintained themselves, and their numbers are not reducing. They maintain their population on a long-term basis when a suitable ecosystem exists, and a wise and efficient management is at place.[102] The Appendixes are amended and updated from time to time by the conference of parties (COP) of the Bonn Convention on the basis of scientific research and evidence.

[96] De Klemm (1989).

[97] Caddell (2005).

[98] Prideaux (2014a, b).

[99] 1651 UNTS 28394; 19 ILM 15 (1979).

[100] Bonn Convention Preamble.

[101] Bonn Convention, Article I (1) (e).

[102] Bonn Convention, Article I (1) (c).

Bonn Convention is an umbrella international treaty. Under its auspices, 106 action plans, 19 memorandum of understandings (MOU) and 7 major conservation agreements have been concluded.[103]

The CMS includes state parties, UN agencies, NGOs, scientific community, media and non-party states. The Bonn convention COP-13 (2020) held at Gandhinagar, India, was attended by 263 delegates, among them 197 were NGOs. Developed economies like the United States, Russia, some Asian nations like China have not so far become a party to the Bonn Convention. This has resulted in fund scarcity for the conservation of migratory species. Scientists provide credible data, NGOs stimulate it and state parties endeavour to conserve, but it needs more support and funding[104] because population of most migratory species covered under the CMS are declining.

E. **Biodiversity**

NGOs and scientists in the 1960s made efforts to highlight environmental issues. In 1962 Rachel Carson published her book *Silent Spring*[105] and explained the adverse impact of pesticides and chemicals on the ecosystem. Paul Ehrlich who wrote the *Population Bomb* in 1968 highlighted the consequences of unprecedented growth of human population. The demographic surge has disturbed the natural balance of species.[106] Growing population density and pace of development expose the limit of growth,[107] technology and natural resources.[108]

The seminal works of scientists, Rachel Curson, Paul Ehrlich, D.H. Meadows and Berry Commoner are well taken by NGOs. They educate people against the excess use of pesticides and synthetic chemicals in agriculture and their adverse effect on human health and global ecosystems.

Industrialisation, urban dwelling and pattern of consumption have resulted in displacement of indigenous people, deforestation, erosion of soil, destruction of wildlife habitat and unsustainable exploitation of natural resources. In the United States and Western European countries, NGOs created environmental awareness in the 1960s. In due course of time, environment movements embraced the entire world.[109]

NGOs are well connected with scientists and journalists. Scientists have identified and named 1.8 million species, out of 10s of millions of living species. Therefore, scientists are also willing to collaborate with NGOs to rapidly identify extinct species and to conserve them with the help of the community.[110]

---

[103] Hensz and Soberon (2018).

[104] Mason et al. (2020).

[105] Carson (2000) (first edition 1962).

[106] Ehrlich (1968).

[107] Meadow et al. (2006) (first edition 1972).

[108] Commoner (1971).

[109] Yap (1989–1990).

[110] Bock and Human (2002).

NGO's access to journalists helps highlight the environmental issues in the media. They strengthen environmental advocacy among the nations and demand their proactive role in conservation of living species globally. A United Nations report has estimated that one million species are now at risk of extinction around the world.[111]

The inter-governmental negotiation committee (INC) on biodiversity started its work in 1989 under the auspices of UNEP and the Convention on Biological Diversity (CBD), and it was concluded on 22 May 1992 at Nairobi. CBD convention came into force on 29 December 1993.[112] The process of negotiation of CBD was not addressed adequately by state parties and also did not receive inputs from outside.[113] CBD has been covering wide issue areas, principles, jurisdictions, protected areas and indigenous people, federal system environment impact assessment, intellectual property rights (IPR), biotechnology and finance.[114] Biodivcrsity convention is a legal framework. That can further create the binding rights and duties of the parties. At present there are 196 state parties to the CBD.

The Biodiversity convention covers the genetic material of plants, animals and micro-organisms. The purpose of the convention is to conserve biodiversity, sustainable use of the ecosystem and to share fair and equitable benefits from genetic diversity.[115] The Biodiversity convention reaffirmed the State sovereign rights over their natural resources and common concerns for human kind. The convention reconciled these cordial principles so that the State can use biodiversity within the realm of common heritage.[116] Beyond the limit of national jurisdiction, states are under obligation to co-operate with parties of the treaty and the IGOs.[117]

The Biodiversity convention coexists with other international agreements particularly in the field of trade, fisheries, wildlife, etc.[118] The state parties have a right to establish the protected areas[119] but they cannot ignore the rights of indigenous people and their traditional knowledge.

NGOs play a significant role in protection of life, culture and habitat of indigenous people. These NGOs are: International Indian Treaty Council 1974 (iitc.org), World Council of Indigenous Peoples 1974 (cwis.org), Survival International 1969 (survivalinternational.org), Cultural Survival 1972 (authoredsurvival.org), Green Peace International 1971 (greenpeace.org) and The Nature Conservancy 1951

[111] UN Reports: *Nature's dangerous decline and unprecedented spacies extinction rate accelerating*. http://www.un.org/substainabledevelopment/belo/2019/05/nature_decline_unprecedent_report/. Accessed 10 May 2020.

[112] 1760 UNTS 79; 31 ILM 818 (1992).

[113] Koester (1997).

[114] Chandler (1993).

[115] CBD Preamble; Guruswamy and Mc-Neely (1998); CBD *Hand Book*, 3rd edn 2007. http://www.cbd.int/hanbook.

[116] CBD Convention, Article 3; 1972 Stockholm Conference, Principle 21; Brownlie (2019).

[117] CBD Convention, Articles 5.

[118] CBD Convention, Article 22(1).

[119] Korson et al. (2014); CBD Convention, Article 8.

(nature.org). State parties are expected to introduce 'environmental impact assessment' procedures and allow NGOs and public participation wherever appropriate.[120] The IPR deals with access of genetic resources, transfer of biotechnology and distribution of benefits.

Biodiversity convention, COP-10 adopted Nagoya Protocol[121] in 2010 (Nagoya, Japan) that come into force in 2014 with a total of 79 states as parties. The Nagoya Protocol allows countries to conclude agreements on bilateral contracts for access to and usage of resources and sharing of benefits. The Conservation International, a United States based NGO has published a list of 17 mega diverse countries which are storehouses of genetic diversity. Global South is nature rich, whereas the North has biotechnology, finance and the house of corporations. The spirit of Nagoya Protocol is equitable and fair sharing of resources, process and benefits. So far it has not yet met the acceptances.[122]

4 Protection of the Atmosphere

Atmosphere means the gas cover surrounding the earth. Atmosphere influences environment of the earth. It is the largest resource to our planet extended over earth and ocean. Global atmosphere is a common heritage of mankind. These resources are used and shared by the international community.

Atmospheric pollution is caused by human activities, directly or indirectly releasing substances into the atmosphere. These substances include energy, light, noise and chemicals. Whenever these are released in the air, it results in atmospheric pollution. Traditionally, atmospheric pollution is related to aircraft. Over the years, it has been established that it is further polluted by satellite communication, pollutant emissions and diffusion.[123]

In 2013, International Law Commission (ILC) in its 65th session included protection of the atmosphere topic in its agenda. Shinya Murase of Japan was appointed as Special Rapporteur by the ILC. The Special Repporteur submitted his final report on 'Protection of the Atmosphere' to the Commission,[124] along with comments received from the states on earlier report. The outcome of the report was to highlight gaps in the law of the atmosphere rather than propose a comprehensive treaty draft on this topic.

There are three main areas related to the protection of atmosphere: (1) transboundary air pollution, (2) ozone depletion and (3) climate change.

A. **Transboundary Air Pollution**

---

[120] CBD Convention, Article 14.

[121] http://www.cbd.int/abs/text.

[122] Pauchard (2017); Muller (2018); Overthii and Rogendel (2014).

[123] Sand and Wiener (2015).

[124] Shinya Murase, Special Repporteurs', *Report*, UN General Assembly A/C N. 4/735 (11 February 2020).

Air is an important part of our life, without air we cannot survive. It is a source of food for every living creature on earth. Air is a means of radio communication. It saves the lives on earth from the harmful ultraviolet rays of the sun. Therefore, protection from the transboundary air pollution is indispensable for terrestrial and aquatic life.[125]

Transboundary air pollution originates through natural operation and human activities. Air pollution is obviously transboundary phenomenon. It crosses geo-political and maritime boundaries. Air current and winds carry pollutants to either water or land and vice versa. Air mass temperatures are as per the characteristic of the earth's surface, i.e. humid, hot and cold according to their sources of origin. Smog, acid rain, acid deposition, particulate matter, mercury, haze and persistent organic pollutants are the major emissions and substances discharged into the air.[126] They adversely affect public health. One-third of deaths from stroke, lung cancer and heart disease are due to air pollution.[127]

Scientists have affirmed that transboundary air pollution has increased day by day. NGOs are engaged in combating transboundary air pollution. In 1892, an NGO–Sierra Club[128] was founded in Oakland, United States. It has been working towards protection of the planet and sustainable use of energy. Sierra Club is opposing the use of fossil along with other NGOs. International Association of Meteorology and Atmospheric Science (IAMAS)[129] was established in 1922 in Rome, to promote research in atmospheric sciences and focussed on international coordination of scientists. International Union of Air Pollution Prevention and Environmental Protection Associations (IUAPPA)[130] was established in Britain, 1964, for protection of air pollution. It emphasises the implementation of a policy for clean air with coalition of scientists, policy-makers, business and citizen's group. Furthermore, Earth Justice,[131] Union of Concerned Scientist,[132] Mom's Clean Air Force[133] and many more NGOs are working for clean and healthy air for all.[134] NGOs, advocacy is desperately needed in protecting the transboundary air pollution, although it is lacking international legal regime.

However, regional level multilateral agreements, declarations and guidelines are at place. The most significant is the Convention on Long-Range Transboundary Air

[125] Walker (2007).

[126] Fellin and Digiovanni (2006).

[127] http://www.who.int>airpollution, How air pollution is destroying our health; Dominiciatal (2010).

[128] www.sierraclub.org.

[129] www.iamas.org.

[130] www.iuappa.org.

[131] www.earthjustice.org.

[132] www.ucsusa.org.

[133] http://www.momscleanairforce.org.

[134] Trazyna et al. (1996).

Pollution 1979[135] (CLRTAP), and its Gothenburg Protocol 1999 was adopted by the European nations.[136] Subsequently, Central Asia, United States and Canada acceded to the convention. CLRTAP Protocol does not rectify beyond Western Europe.[137]

Similarly, the United States-Canada Air Quality Agreement was adopted in 1991.[138] These Convention and Agreements deal with acid rain. Another major step was taken by the South East Asian nations when they adopted the ASEAN-Agreement on Transboundary Haze Pollution 2002.[139] ASEAN agreement is related to haze pollution resulting from land and forest fire. These three regional instruments have limited application within their specific areas and issues of acid rain and haze pollution.[140]

Apart from North America and South East Asia, initiatives have been taken by North East-Asia,[141] South Asia,[142] Latin America, Caribbean[143] and African nations.[144] However, they have not yet concluded either into a convention or an agreement but have adopted the guidelines, declaration and action plan. The legal landscape of transboundary air pollution is facilitated only at regional level. Co-operation and understanding among the nations are needed for clean air which is vital to sustain life on earth. Bad air quality could result in further depletion of the ozone layer.

B. **Ozone Depletion**

Ozone (O_3) is a gas which is present within the earth's atmosphere. The ozone layer is a thin sheet of O_3 molecules in lower atmosphere (atmospheric ozone) and upper atmosphere (stratospheric ozone). Stratospheric ozone completely covers the earth and protects it from harmful ultraviolet radiation. In 1974, three scientists—Paul Crutzen, Mario Molina and F. Sherwood Rowland[145] demonstrated that chlorofluorocarbons (CFC) would break down stratosphere and allow ultraviolet radiation (UV-B). The depleting ozone layer has exposed the planet to harmful ultraviolet radiations. This has caused adverse effect on public health like skin cancer, eye

---

135 CLRTAP signed on 14 November 1979 and came into force on 16 March 1983, 1302 UNTS 217; 18 ILM 1442 (1979).

136 Gothenburg Protocol to Abate Acidification, Eutrophication and Ground—Level Ozone, Gothenburg, Sweden 30 November 1999, came into force 15 May 2005. https://www.unece.org/environment_policy_air?protocol_abate_audification_eutrophication_and_ground_level_ozon&ved=2ahUKEwil_8arudD; Byrne (2015).

137 Kuklinska and Nomiesnik (2015).

138 30 ILM 676 (1991); Roelofs (1993).

139 http://haze.org>asean-agreement on transboundary haze pollution; Chen (2018).

140 Yamineva and Romppamen (2017).

141 Inkyong (2007).

142 Kumar et al. (2018).

143 Riojas-Rodriguez et al. (2016).

144 Alberick and Nsompi (2018).

145 Molina and Rowland (1974); Paul J. Crutzen, Ozone production rates in an oxygen-hydrogen–nitrogen oxide atmosphere. J Geophys Res 76(30):7311–7327.

damage, immune system damage and difficulty in breathing. Additionally, there are adverse effects on air quality, terrestrial plants, aquatic ecosystem and climate.[146]

DuPont, one of the world's largest producers of chemicals and science-based products indicated the development of chlorofluorocarbons (CFC)[147] used in refrigeration units, production of computer chips, aerosol sprays, styrofoam and other products. Their usage accelerated after World War II, in the developed economies. The accumulated CFC and other ozone depleting substances have caused damage to the stratosphere or the upper atmosphere.

The world community led by scientists and supported by NGOs emphasised on regulation of ozone depletion. UNEP convened a meeting in 1977 of all the stakeholders for environmental education. In 1985, an ozone hole had appeared in the Antarctica.[148] After successful negotiation UN Convention finalised the UN-Vienna Convention for the protection of ozone layer by state parties in 1985.[149] This is a legal framework for parties to protect ozone layer.

In order to operationalise, the Vienna Ozone Layer Convention, the Montreal Protocol on Substances that deplete ozone layer was adopted in 1987.[150] Vienna Convention 1983 and Montreal Protocol 1987 were too little and too late. Emerging economies like China, India, Brazil, South Africa, Mexico, etc. were not parties to the Vienna Convention and Montreal Protocol.[151]

Vienna Convention laid emphasis on international co-operation and the Montreal protocol assigned responsibilities to eliminate the use and production of CFC and ozone depleting substances (ODS).[152] Protocol Article 19 provides that state parties should respect research outcomes, development, exchange of information and public awareness. NGOs role of advocacy for protection of the ozone layer was visualised in this Article. All nations rectified or acceded to both the Convention and the Protocol. The Convention and the Protocol mandated state parties (COP) to submit reports of compliance every four years and to further improve and amend the Montreal Protocol.

London COP 1990 deliberated[153] on the adjustment and amendment to the Montreal Protocol on substances that deplete the ozone layer. China and India participated and became a party to the Vienna convention and the Montreal protocol. Arrangements for funds and transfer of technology to developing countries were also made by the London COP of Montreal protocol, under fair and favourable conditions.[154] London COP of 1990 was attended by 53 member countries, 31 non-member

---

146 Adeoyee and Aina (2019).

147 Caron (1991).

148 Tortell (2020).

149 *Vienna Convention for the Protection of Ozone Layer* signed on 22 March 1985 and came into force on 22 September 1988, 1513 UNTS 29; 26 ILM 1516 (1987).

150 *Montreal Protocol* opened for signature on 22 September 1987 and entered into force on 1 January 1989, 1522 UNTS 29; 26 ILM 1550 (1987); Anderson and Sarma (2004).

151 Handl (1990).

152 Montreal Protocol, the Preamble.

153 30 ILM 537 (1991); Haas (1992).

154 London Amendment, Article 10A; Victor (1994–1995).

countries and 28 NGOs.[155] Green Peace,[156] Friends of Earth and other environmental NGOs raised the voice of the people in this meeting.

CFC was replaced by another less harmful ozone depleting substance but scientists did not appreciate these measures. Because these gases when accumulated and concentrated were posing problems in the near future.[157] States never reported accurately about the production, use and transport of ODS. However, Montreal Protocol in the world of international agreements is most successful in collaborating scientific discoveries, national regulation, international instruments, industry products, NGOs advocacy, IGOs and states concerns.[158]

C. **Climate Change**

Climate change is a long-term alteration to our planet. Climate change has occurred as a result of human activities. The earth has been warming since 1850 which was scientifically proven in 1960, through computer modelling, NASA scientists' findings and laboratory observations, as atmosphere and ocean warmed, snow and ice melted, sea levels rose and concentration of greenhouse gases like water vapour, ozone, carbon dioxide, methane and nitrous oxide increased. It adversely affected the climate and ecosystem by raising temperatures up to 2 °C. Therefore, world community should collectively strive for reducing greenhouse gases.[159]

The UN General Assembly established an international negotiating committee for climate in 1990.[160] After two years of negotiations, the United Nations Framework Convention on Climate Change 1992 (UNFCCC) came into force.[161] The UNFCCC has 197 state parties and thus has acquired universal status. The objectives of UNFCCC are to prevent dangerous anthropogenic interference with the earth's climate and to reduce atmospheric concentration of greenhouse gases.[162] Another principle under UNFCCC is the common but differentiated responsibilities of the state,[163] as per their capabilities. Developing countries are more interested in reduction of poverty rather than emission of substances. Therefore commitment to mitigation of emission depends on transfer of funds and technology by the developed countries.[164] This is imperative for developing countries to harmonise both the things side by side to fulfil their domestic and international commitments.

---

[155] Lawrence (1992).

[156] Mate (2001).

[157] Montzka et al. (2018).

[158] Birmpile (2018).

[159] Cinnamon (2016).

[160] *Protection of Global Climate for Present and Future Generations of Mankind*, UN GA Res 45/212, UNDOC. A/Res/45/212 (21 December 1990).

[161] UNFCCC opened for signature 9 May 1992 came into force 21 March 1994, 1771 UNTS 107.

[162] UNFCCC Article 2.

[163] UNFCCC Article 3.

[164] UNFCCC Article 4.

The UNFCCC, COP-3 adopted the Kyoto Protocol 1997, to reduce global warming and greenhouse gas (GHG) concentration in the atmosphere.[165] Developing countries were required to reduce their aggregate GHG emissions by 5% that of 1990 levels by early twenty-first century.[166]

D. **NGOs Activism**

Activism by NGOs has increased in protecting the environment since the Rio Conference 1992. Michele Betsill has minutely observed role and influence of NGOs in the Kyoto Protocol Negotiations.[167] It is a matter of international co-operation that states adhere to sovereignty, engage in treaty negotiations, make the rule of procedure and finally sign the treaty. How NGOs influence the outcome of the treaty negotiations, can be seen in UNFCCC, COP-3, Kyoto Protocol 1997. On the occasion of COP-3 (1997), and there were 1000 representatives of 40 NGOs present in Kyoto, Japan. Among them, were the Green Peace, Friends of Earth and WWF.

The most significant was the NGO coalition—Climate Action Network International 1989 (www.climatenetwork.org). At that time, there were 280 NGO members of the Climate Action Network, across borders. This was a collective voice of NGOs at Kyoto. They published the newsletter 'Eco' and covered day to day progress of the outgoing negotiations. The Climate Action Network rendered technical advice to the representatives of the state, organised workshops, gathered information, lobbied and spread awareness among people about the consequences of climate change. NGOs employed distinct methods at Kyoto, i.e. demonstration, sit in, exhibition, symposium and so on that are vividly described by Michele Betsill.[168]

NGOs became observers and made statements in open sessions. They succeeded in exposing rigid positions of certain state representatives in the media. NGOs made their presence felt in the negotiations at Kyoto to some degree but more was desired.

In Kyoto, emerging economies like China, India, Brazil and Indonesia did not participate. Kyoto protocol introduced principles of trading of right to emit greenhouse gases and to get credit for carbon sink via changes in land use and forestry practices.[169] The report of the Intergovernmental Panel on Climate Change (IPCC) of 1995 indicated human influence on climate change. The IPCC is a worldwide scientists' group, and they regularly produce research outcomes on climate change.[170]

Al Gore, former Vice-President of the United State and the IPCC were jointly awarded Nobel Peace Prize 2007 for their efforts to generate and disseminate greater knowledge about man-made climate change and listed measures that are needed to counteract such change.[171]

---

[165] *Kyoto Protocol to the United Nations Framework Convention on Climate Change* 1997, opened for signature 16 March 1998, entered into force 16 February 2005; 37 ILM 22 (1998); Boom (1998).

[166] Kyoto Protocol, Article 3(1).

[167] Betsill (2002).

[168] Ibid., pp. 53–55.

[169] Jacoby et al. (1998).

[170] Parry et al. (2007).

[171] The Nobel Peace Prize 2007.NobelPrize.org. Nobel Prize Outreach AB 2021. Saturday 31 July 2021. https://www.nobelprize.org/prizes/peace/2007/summary/.

In 2015, COP-21 adopted the climate agreement[172] which laid down 'nationally determined contribution' (NDC) that was based on voluntary measures taken by state parties. This is known as the Paris Agreement. To limit global warming, it rescheduled target from 2 to 1.5 °C. Large number of NGOs assembled and organised a massive demonstrations in Paris for a strong international climate agreement.[173] NASA in 2016 and the IPCC report of 2018 emphasised on reducing GHG emissions that caused global warming.

Students under the leadership of Greta Thunberg and the NGO-Friday for Future[174] have been actively demanding strong action on climate change. Friday for Future has pictorially revised Earth Day when students upraised themselves to celebrate and raise their voice for protection of environment. All stakeholders such as state IGOs, NGOs, businesses and scientists contributed to save the earth from climate change.

NGOs and businesses should be more active at the domestic and international levels. Pro-active investments from businesses and NGOs' advocacy are highly warranted in international policy space.[175] The core idea of UNFCCC and subsequent Kyoto protocol and Paris agreement are to enhance international co-operation in mitigating emission. There is a need to get every country involved in decision-making and submit oversight report on climate change. They can learn from each other and share their experience.[176]

5 Protection of the Marine Environment

The sea around us covers 71% of the earth's surface and 90% of biospace.[177] Ocean is a treasure house of renewable and non-renewable resources. Over the centuries, ocean has been used for fishing, shipping and occasionally as battle ground. During the onset of the fifteenth century, new maritime routes were discovered across the Atlantic Ocean and around the Indian Ocean. Power engine was introduced in navigation in the beginning of nineteenth century. That increased speed, frequency and volume in shipping and fishing. Thus human activities spread across the oceans. The exploitation of the oceans caused danger to the marine environment.[178]

In order to regulate the multiple exploits of oceans, expanded claims of coastal states, freedom of navigation and prevention of marine pollution, the United Nations

172 *Paris Agreement*, 2015, United Nations FCCC/cp/201510/Add.l (29 January 2016).

173 Christoff (2016).

174 http://www.fridayfuture.org; Wahlstrom et al. (2019).

175 De Sepibus and Holzer (2014).

176 Moncel and Van Assetl (2012).

177 Carson (1951).

178 Clark (2001).

Convention on the Law of the Sea (UNCLOS) was adopted in 1982.[179] UNCLOS is an outcome of nine years of negotiations (1973–1982) of the representatives of states and supported by NGOs[180] and the scientific community.[181] The UNCLOS is a comprehensive constitution of World Ocean.[182] The UNCLOS, Part XII deals with the protection and preservation of the marine environment. UNCLOS Article 1 clause 4 defines, 'pollution of the marine environment' as follows:

> the introduction by man, directly or indirectly of substances or energy into the marine environment, including estuaries, which results or is likely to result in such deleterious effects as cause harm to living resources and marine life, hazards to human health, hindrance to marine activities, including fishing and other legitimate uses of the sea, impairment of quality for use of sea water and reduction of amenities.

The sources of marine pollution are land-based activities, marine atmospheric pollution, dumping, seabed activities and shipping. These pollutants adversely affect marine environment, marine life, fish stock and human health. Land-based activities[183] and marine atmospheric pollutants are the major causes of marine pollution, which accounts for about 80% of total pollutants. Remaining 20% is due to dumping, shipping and seabed activities.

A. **Land-Based Sources**

Land-based sources of marine pollution spread from national territories. These include sewage, industrial waste, fertilisers and pesticides, chemicals, warm water, fumes, plastic,[184] debris,[185] marine litter,[186] estuaries and outfall of polluted rivers in the ocean.

B. **Marine Atmospheric Pollution**

Marine atmospheric pollution is a further extension of land-based sources, i.e. chemicals, nitrogen, iron, phosphorus, lead mercury and carbon dioxide which are transferred into the marine atmosphere then deposited in marine ecosystem and climate.[187] UNCLOS Article 212 clause 1 provides that states shall control atmospheric pollution from their vessels and aircrafts. Marine atmospheric pollution is an anthropogenic interference, and it is increasing with increased demographic pace and consumption.

C. **Seabed Activities**

---

[179] UNCLOS was signed Montego Bay, Jamaica on 10 December 1982, enforced 6 November 1994; 1833 UNTS 3; 21 ILM 1261 (1982).

[180] Parmentier (2012).

[181] UN Group of Experts on Scientific Aspect of Marine Environment Protection (GESAMP), www.gesamp.org>about>history.

[182] Boyle (1985).

[183] Kwiatkowska (1984); Qing-Nan (1992).

[184] Howard (2008).

[185] Derrack (2002).

[186] Lohr et al. (2017).

[187] Duce et al. (2009).

Besides territorial boundaries, coastal states are engaged in seabed activities in their territorial sea and continental shelf. They explore gas, oil, minerals, chemicals and generate energy. This causes marine pollution in the adjacent sea. Beyond the limit of national jurisdiction of the coastal state, the sea is known as the 'Area' or deep seabed. It is a common heritage of mankind.[188] Presently states acquire technological and investment capabilities to exploit mineral-nodules from the deep seabed. UNCLOS regulates the state activities in their territorial seabed[189] as well as deep seabed outside the limit of national maritime zones.[190]

D. **Dumping at Sea**

Ocean is a vast area, and hence it is more convenient to dump the waste therein. Dumping is a deliberate disposal of waste or matter from vessels, aircrafts, platforms or other man-made structures into the sea. The London Convention 1972[191] and later on London Protocol 1996[192] were adopted, to regulate dumping at sea. London Convention 1972 was eventually replaced by London Protocol 1996.

UNCLOS and London Protocol 1996 have similar definitions of dumping that focus on the deliberate disposal at sea of waste or other matter.[193] Dumping does not include "placement of matter for a purpose other than mere disposal thereof".[194] London Protocol 1996 kept the original definition of dumping and updated list of dumping waste matter. There were originally seven items in the list, i.e. dredged spoil, sewage sludge, industrial fish waste, shipping vessels, offshore platforms and other man-made structures. Certain bulky items have been added newly to London Protocol 1996.[195]

In 2006, carbon dioxide stream from carbon sequestration process inserted in ocean waters became permissible waste to dump in the sea. The growth of plankton may be promoted which absorbs carbon dioxide. The process is popularly known as ocean fertilisation.[196] In 2009, Article 6 of the London Protocol, was amended that allowed parties to export carbon dioxide stream for disposal.[197]

Ocean fertlisation and export of carbon are not yet scientifically and legally well-settled principles; therefore precautionary measures are applicable thereon.

E. **Pollution from Vessels**

---

[188] UNCLOS, Article 136.

[189] UNCLOS, Article 193; Evan (1986).

[190] UNCLOS, Article 209(2); de Mestral (1979).

[191] The Convention on the Prevention of Marine Pollution by Dumping of Wastage and Other Matter 1972 (London Convention) signed 29 December 1972, entered into force 13 August 1975, 1046 UNTS 120; 11 ILM 1294 (1972).

[192] London Protocol, Signed 7 November 1996 entered into force 24 March 2006, 36 ILM 1 (1997).

[193] UNCLOS, Article 1(5)(1)(a); London Protocol, Article 1(4) (1–4).

[194] UNCLOS, Article 1(5)(1)(b); London Protocol, Article 1(4).

[195] Verlaan (2009).

[196] Schiermeier (2009).

[197] Meeting of Parties of the London Protocol, Resolution L P 3(4) 30 October 2009; Dixon (2014).

Maritime transportation is another major source of marine pollution. Vessels cause pollution in the oceans by oil spills, carbon dioxide, sulphur waste, wastage, ship scraping, wrecking, ballast water, sound, collision at sea and air pollution. These are usually pollutants from operational vessels but sometimes accidental pollution like the Titanic disaster of 1912, Torrey Canyon 1967,[198] Amoco Cadiz 1987, Exxon Valdez 1989, Erika 1999, Prestige 2002 and the recent Iranian oil tanker ablaze in 2018 have also occurred.

The regulation of vessel-source pollution is done in two ways—one is according to International Maritime Organisation (IMO) conventions and another is UNCLOS.[199] IMO adopted two conventions—The International Convention for the Prevention of Pollution from Ships 1973 (MARPOL)[200] and The International Convention for the Safety of Life at Sea 1974 (SOLAS).[201] The objective of MARPOL is the prevention of vessel–source pollution and focus on construction, design, equipment and manning (CDEM) measures of ships and assign the primary responsibility to the flag of nations,[202] whereas the main purpose of SOLAS is the safety of merchant navy and of cargo at sea. It enhances maritime security and port facility for global shipping.[203]

UNCLOS, Article 211 established jurisdiction framework for flag state, port state and coastal states, to prevent, reduce and control marine pollution from vessels.[204] It is necessary that a ship should bear the national flag whenever it wants to enjoy the freedom of navigation.[205]

Flag states are under obligation to ensure international standards over ships which bear their flags.[206] A flag state has exclusive jurisdiction over its ships. Coastal states have the power and responsibility to prevent marine pollution from vessels in the territorial sea and exclusive economic zones but it is the duty of a coastal state not to hamper or create hindrance to innocent passengers of foreign vessels.[207]

Similarly port states also enjoy extended powers over foreign vessels, especially those that visit their maritime ports and seek facilities. Ports are located within the internal waters of coastal states and in an emergency or distress, access to a port cannot be denied. Port states are not required to impose unnecessary national laws.[208] Regulation to vessel-source pollution and jurisdiction thereon shall be compatible with mobility of shipping around the world oceans.

---

[198] Nanda (1967).

[199] Khee and Tan (2006).

[200] MARPOL, adopted on 2 November 1973 and modified by the Protocol of 1978, entered into force 2 October 1983, 1340 UNTS 184.

[201] SOLAS, adopted on 1 November 1974, entered into force 25 May 1980, 1184 UNTS 277.

[202] Nengye (2010); Kopela (2017).

[203] Hesse and Charbambous (2004).

[204] O'Conell (1984).

[205] UNCLOS, Article 92.

[206] Zwinge (2011).

[207] Molenaar (1998).

[208] Molenaar (2007).

F. **Marine Life**

Marine resources include plants, animals and ecosystem of the ocean.[209] Fish resources are essential components of food security. Sea food intake has doubled from 1960 to 2014, increasing fish harvesting. Sea food provides at least 20% of the protein intake to more than three billion people.[210] Currently, the population of the world is 8 billion and is projected to be 9 billion by 2030.[211]

Aquaculture supplements the food demand of the burgeoning population and it surpassed marine fishing in 2016. But over-exploitation of fishing is increasing day by day, and some of the species of fish and aquatic mammals are on the verge of extinction.[212] Marine protected areas are established in the ocean for conservation of living resources.[213] There are 15,000 marine protected areas which cover roughly 70% of the world's marine environment. The success of Marine Protected Areas (MPA) is measured on the basis of fish bio-mass and well-being of people. Sylvaine Gaikoumi et al. in their book suggest holders' engagement in the Marine Protected Areas for feedback, social auditing and promoting co-operation in marine conservation.[214]

Apart from the state, coastal communities, NGOs and businesses, scientists, marine ecologists and oceanographers are considered stakeholders. A large number of NGOs are engaged in conservation and protection of marine living resources.[215] NGOs play an important role as advocate, expert, manager, watch dog and enablers in the conservation of marine resources.[216] NGOs are persistently fighting for conservation of marine life. Anthropogenic interference through over-catching of fish and mammals, release of marine pollutants, destruction and disturbance of marine habitats via marine transit and impact of climate change are gradually destroying marine resources.

The UNCLOS laid down a comprehensive framework for the protection and preservation of marine living resources.[217] Coastal states are under obligation to not harm marine living resources when they exercise sovereign rights in their territorial seas,[218] contiguous zone[219] continental shelf[220] and exclusive economic zones.[221]

[209] Chrishty and Scott (1965).

[210] Guillen et al. (2019).

[211] Gerland et al. (2014).

[212] Gewin (2004).

[213] Gaines et al. (2010).

[214] Giakoumi et al. (2018).

[215] www.imo.org <consultativengo; www.marinebio.org <list of ngos.

[216] Crosman (2013).

[217] Chatzand and Honnball (2020); Oda (1983).

[218] UNCLOS, Article 2(3).

[219] UNCLOS, Article 33(1)(a).

[220] UNCLOS, Article 77(4).

[221] UNCLOS, Article 61–69; Dahmani (1987).

States, either coastal or land locked, have the freedom to fish,[222] subject to conservation and management of living resources of the high seas.[223] High seas cover 64% of ocean surface, and it is a shared area for fishing benefits to all.[224] There is a lack of exclusively dedicated organisations to monitor overfishing, illegal fishing or polluting high seas. The UN in 2019 sought the consent of all stakeholders, to establish a robust legal regime for conservation of marine living resources in consultation with the IMO, FAO, International Seabed Authority, marine scientists and NGOs.

6 Nuclear Risk

Nuclear energy is the only source of power that could be used for civil, military and industrial purposes. Conventional resources could be exhausted in supplementing the ever-growing energy needs and human ambition.[225] Nuclear energy was used for military purposes in 1945, when the nuclear bomb was dropped on people in World War II. It shattered the human conscience and posed a danger against security and survivability of humankind.

NGOs since then have been fighting to stop the abuse and misuse of nuclear power.[226] A number of NGOs and physicians, individually and collectively, have mobilised public opinion against the threat and use of atom bombs. In comparison to other issue areas, the nuclear risk issue is at a nascent phase in terms of NGO activities. There are three NGOs—Ballona Foundation,[227] European Environmental Bureau[228] and Green Peace.[229] Along with three media outlets: World Nuclear News (WNN), NucNet and Nuclear.Ru, which are partners of the International Atomic Energy Agency (IAEA).

They are engaged in technological solutions and to protect nuclear installations of nuclear plants. They want to improve the environment and side by side, and they are involved in transboundary advocacy, media update on nuclear information from all over the world for the purposes of imposing nuclear safety and environment.[230] The world witnessed the Chernobyl nuclear disaster in 1986. It resulted in the loss of human lives and spread transboundary nuclear pollution.[231]

---

[222] UNCLOS, Article 87(e).

[223] UNCLOS, Article 116–120; Vicuna (1999).

[224] Sala et al. (2018).

[225] Hardy (1961).

[226] Dalaqua (2013); Swittner (2009).

[227] http://ballona.org.

[228] http://www.eeb.org.

[229] http://greenpeace.org>international.

[230] http://gnsn.iaea.org>pages>.

[231] Melon (1987).

The international community has adopted two conventions for early notification[232] and assistance[233] in case of a nuclear accident or radiation emergency. Moreover, to strengthen the nuclear safety regime, the convention on nuclear safety (CNS)[234] was set up as a first step in the formation of international nuclear law under the IAEA. The objective of CNS is the safe operation of nuclear power plants.[235]

States are under obligation to report about the safety measures of their nuclear plants. The IAEA secretariat oversees the Convention compliance. State reports are reviewed by IAEA and also by state parties of the Convention. NGOs can submit feedback of the country's performance to the IAEA secretariat. The CNS is a broad framework and parties are required to mutually benefit from sharing and learning about the installation, operation and management of nuclear plants.[236]

Another nuclear incident occurred in Fukushima in 2011. The media and internet spread information all over the world in seconds.[237] People became directly aware about the information and the nuclear risk. Nuclear risk is a transboundary consequence, and therefore states are under obligation to pay damages for loss of public health and property. The case can be constituted for the recovery within the jurisdiction of that country.[238]

7 Conclusion

International environmental law is a very broad area, and more than 747 international environmental agreements have been concluded from 1875 to 2012.[239] The environment is not just related to the present generation but it is also concerned with future generations. Environment encompasses nature, air, water and entire ecosystem. It is a global issue with transboundary impact. Unlike human rights, UN Charter does not mention the protection of the environment. Environment became the corpus of international law in later part of twentieth century after the conclusion of the Stockholm Conference on human environment in 1972.

NGOs raised the issue of environment in the beginning of the twentieth century when Bird Life International was formed in 1922 and engaged in the conservation of nature. The formation of international environmental NGOs such as Friday For

---

[232] Convention on Early Notification of a Nuclear Accident or Radiological Emergency, 26 September 1986, 1439 UNTS 275.

[233] Convention on Assistance in the case of a Nuclear Accident or Radiological Emergency, 26 September 1986, 1457 UNTS 133.

[234] Convention on Nuclear Safety, adopted 20 September 1994, came into force 24 October 1996, 1963 UNTS 293; Stoiber (2003).

[235] CNS, Article 1.

[236] Hanschel (2012).

[237] Kus (2011).

[238] Vienna Convention on Civil Liabilities for Nuclear Damage, 21 May, 1963, 2241 UNTS 265.

[239] Kim (2013).

Future established in 2018 is a continuous process. These are mainly fighting against climate change. NGOs are engaged in the formation of international environmental conventions and declaration and also for enforcement thereof.

Clean environment is a human rights issue.[240] Human rights such as right to life, privacy, health and property can be interpreted in the light of the protection of environment.[241] Protection of environment is also related to world trade, investment and finance, for instance, CITES 1973 prohibits the trade of endangered species.[242]

IGOs such as—UNEP, IMO, IAEA, FAO and GEF are engaged in governance of environment with the active support of NGOs, corporations and civil society.[243] State attributes the notion of sovereignty in international law and possess sovereign rights over its natural resources within its territory. Notwithstanding, states are the bearer of responsibility to do no harm to others or cause the loss of life and property.[244] International environmental law strikes a balance between a state's sovereignty and its responsibility.

States are distinct in their unique viewpoints and priorities. Developing states are more interested in alleviation of poverty and enhancement of economic growth rather than environment issues.[245] That can be sorted out by making funds and technology available to them and adopting the principle of "common but different responsibilities."

NGOs are engaged in creation, development and enforcement of international environmental law. First of all, they choose pressing issues in public interest, mobilise people, seek media attention and subsequently pressurise their states to come forward in support of making of the international environmental law. NGOs influence the negotiation process and its outcome.[246] IEL is not a strictly state obligation but rather a commitment. Environmental conventions are broad legal framework for a way forward; examples are UNFCCC and CBD. Conference of parties (COP) further developed law in their subsequent meetings as per prevailing situations.

NGOs collectively present their view point in COP and engage in advocacy with states' representatives for a positive outcome. IEL does not have a unified IGO or a UN specialised agency for monitoring of the environment. Also, it has a lack of adjudicating body. NGOs have two options; first, they file a public interest litigation (PIL) before their national courts for enforcement of international environmental law (IEL).[247] Secondly, they participate in International Court of Justice (ICJ), European Court of Justice (ECJ), International Criminal Court (ICC), Permanent Court of Arbitration (PCA) and International Tribunal for the Law of the Sea (ITLOS)

---

240 Boyle (2012); Shelton (2008).

241 Bondansky et al. (2012).

242 Neumayer (2001).

243 Raustiala (1997).

244 Schroeder (1986).

245 World Commission on Environment and Development (1987).

246 Betsill (2001).

247 Cumming (2013).

proceedings.[248] NGOs may explore innovative methods for effective implementation of the IEL in their respective issue areas with all stakeholders.[249]

References

Adeoyee OJ, Aina SA (2019) An appraisal of ozone layer depletion and its implication on the human environment. J L Pol Global 83:6–10

Alberick T, Nsompi F (2018) State of atmosphere pollution in West Africa health impact. Int Curr Res 10(9):73970–73975

Anderson SO, Sarma KM (2004) Protection of the ozone layer. In: Sinclair L (ed), Earthscan Publications, London

Arts B (2017) Community, forest management: a assessment and explanation of its performance through QCA—science direct-science Direct. Com. World Devt 96:315–325

Betsill M (2001) NGO influence in environment negotiation: a framework for analysis. Global Envt Polit 1(4):65–85

Betsill M (2002) Environmental NGOs meet the Sovereign State: the Kyoto protocol negotiations on global climate change. Colorado J Int Envt L Pol 13(1):49–64

Betsill MM, Corell E (eds) (2008) NGOs diplomacy: the influence of nongovernmental organisations in international environmental negotiations. MIT Press, London, p 8

Birmpile T (2018) Montreal protocol at 30: the governance structure, the evolution and the Kigali amendment. Compt Rend Geosci 350(70):425–451

Birni P, Boyle A, Ridgwell C (2009) International law and environmental, 3rd edn. Oxford University Press, Oxford

Bock JH, Human K (2002) NGOs and the protection of bio-diversity: the ecologist's views. Colorado J Int Ent L Poc 13(1):167–181

Bodansky D (1995) Customary international environmental law. Indiana J Global Legal Stud 3(1):105–120

Bodansky D (2011) Implementation of international environmental law. Jpn YB Int 54:62–96

Bodansky D et al (eds) (2007) Oxford handbook of international environmental law. Oxford University Press, Oxford

Bondansky D et al (2012) International environmental law: mapping the field. Oxford University Press, p 15

Boom FK (1998) The third session of the parties to the United Nations framework convention on climate change-Kyoto. Singapore J Int Comp L 2(1):191–202

Bottrill M et al (2014) What are the impacts of nature conservation interventions on human well-being: a systematic map protocol. Envt Evid 16(3):1–11

Bowman MJ (1995) Ramsar convention. Int J Mar Cosatal L 10(4):547–555

Boyle A (1985) Marine pollution under the law of the sea convention. Am J Int L 79(2):347–372

Boyle A (2012) Human rights and the environment: where next? Eur J Int L 23(3):613–642

Brownlie S (2019) Principles of public international law. In: Crawford J (ed), 9th edn. Oxford University Press, Oxford, p 352

Byrne A (2015) The 1979 convention on long-range transboundary air pollution: assessing its effectiveness as a multilateral environmental regime after 35 years. Trans Envn L 4(1):37–67

Caddell R (2005) International law and the protection of migratory wild life: an appraisal of twenty-five years of the Bonn convention. Colorado J Int Evnt L Pol 16(1):113–156

Caron DD (1991) Protection of the stratospheric ozone layer and the structure of international environment law making. Hast Int Comp L Q 14:755–780

[248] Rest (2004).

[249] Bodansky (2011).

Carson R (1951) The sea around us. Oxford University Press

Carson R (2000) Silent spring. Penguin, London

Chalakkal K (2014) Trade in endangered species. YB Int Envt L 25(1):283–304

Chandler M (1993) The bio-diversity convention: selected issues of interest to the international lawyer. Colorado J Int Envt L Pol 4(1):141–176

Chatzand VJ, Honnball AN (2020) International fisheries law. Oxford University Press

Chen Q (2018) Transboundary atmosphereic pollution in South East Asia: current methods, limitations and future developments. J Crit Rev Int Sci Tech 48(16):997–1029

Chrishty FT, Scott A (1965) Commonwealth in ocean fisheries. John Hopkins Press, Baltimore

Christoff P (2016) The promissory note: COP 21 and Paris climate agreement. J Envt Polit 25(5):1–23

Cinnamon P (eds) (2016) Oxford handbook of international climate change law. Oxford University Press

Clark RB (2001) Marine pollution, 5th edn. Oxford University Press

Commoner B (1971) The closing circle: nature, man and technology. Knopf, New York

Crosman KM (2013) The role of non-governmental organisations in marine conservation (PhD Thesis). University of Michigan, pp 1–86

Cumming FJ (2013) The role of NGOs in multi-lateral environmental agreement compliance. J N Zeal Environ L 17:41–80

Dahmani M (1987) The fisheries regime of the exclusive economic zone. Nijhoff Publications, Dordrecht

Dalaqua RH (2013) Securing our survival (SOS): non-state actors and the campaign for nuclear weapons convention through the prism of securitisation theory. Brazil Pol Sc Rev 7(3):1–28

Davidson N (2014) How much wetland has the world lost? Long term and recent trend in global wetlands area. Mar Fresh Water Res 65:935–941

De Klemm C (1989) Migratory species in international law. Natl Resour J 29(4):935–978

de Mestral ALC (1979) The prevention of pollution of the marine environment arising from offshore mining and drilling. Harvard Int L J 20:469–518

de Sepibus J, Holzer K (2014) The UNFCCC at crossroads: can increased involvement of business and industry help rescue the multilateral climate regime? Carbon Clim L Rev 1:23–34

Derrack JGB (2002) The pollution of marine environment by plastic debris: a review. Mar Pollut Bullet 44(9):842–852

Dixon T (2014) Update on the London protocol: development on transboundary CCS and geo-engineering. Energy Proced 63:6623–6628

Dominiciatal F (2010) Protection of human health from air pollution: shifting from a single pollution to a multi-pollutant approach. Epidemiology 21(2):187–194

Duce RA et al (2009) The impact of atmospheric disposition to the ocean on marine ecosystem and climate. WMO Bull 58(1):61–66

Ehrlich P (1968) Population bomb. Bulletined Books

Engler M (2008) The value of international wildlife trade. TRAFFIC Bull 22:4–5

Evan SM (1986) Control of marine pollution generated by offshore oil and gas exploration and exploitation. Mar Policy 10:258–270

Fellin P, Digiovanni F (2006) Transboundary air pollution. Encyclopedia of Life Support System, Oxford, pp 1–30

Finlayson CM (2012) Forty years of wetlands conservation and wise use. Aquat Conser 22:139–143

Francioni F (2004) Beyond state sovereignty: the protection of cultural heritage as a shared interest of humanity. Michigan J Int L 25(4):1209–1212

Gaines SD et al (2010) Designing marine reserve network for both conservation and fisheries management. PNAS 107(43):18286–18293

Gean-Louis S et al (2016) The need to respect nature and its limits challenges society and conservation science. PNAS 113(22):6105–6112

Gerland P et al (2014) World population stabilization unlikely this century. Science 346:234–237

Getches DH (1993) The challenge of rio. Colorado J Int Envt L Pol 4(1):1–20

Gewin V (2004) Troubled waters: the future of global fisheries. PLoS Biol 2(4):422–427
Giakoumi S et al (2018) Revisiting 'success' and 'failure' of marine protected areas: conservation scientists perspective. Front Mar Sci 5(223):1–5
Giddings B et al (2002) Environment, economy and society: fitting them together into sustainable development. Sustain Devt 10(4):187–196
Goldman BA (1992) Equity and the 1992 rio summit. Fortham Envt L Rev 4(1):1–8
Grabb M et al (1993) The earth summit agreements: a guide and assessment. Routledge, Abingdon
Griffiths T, Robin L (1997) Ecology and empire: environmental history of settler. Edinburg University Press
Guillen J et al (2019) Global sea food consumption foot-print. Ambio 48:111–122
Gullison RE (2003) Does forest certification conserve bio-diversity: UN convention on bio-diversity. Oryx 37(2):153–165
Guruswamy L, Mc-Neely J (eds) (1998) Protection of global biodiversity: converging strategy. Duke University Press, Durham
Haas PM (1992) Vanning chlorofluorocarbons: epistemic community efforts to protect stratospheric ozone. Int Org 46(1):187–224
Handl G (1990) International efforts to protect global atmosphere: a case of too little, too late. Eur J Int L 1(1):250–257
Hanschel D (2012) Prevention, preparedness and assistance concerning nuclear accidents-effective international legal framework or patchwork. German Y B Int L 55:217–252
Hardy MJL (1961) International protection against risks. Int Comp L Q 10(4):739–759
Hensz CM, Soberon J (2018) Participation of the convention on migratory species: bio-geographical assessment. Ambia 47:739–746
Hesse H, Charbambous NL (2004) New security measures for the international shipping community. WMU J Maritime Aff 3:123–138
Hill K (1990) The convention of international trade in endangered species: fifty years later. Loyeda Los Angeles Int Comp L J 13(2):231–380
Howard M (2008) Plastic pollution of the world seas and oceans as a contemporary challenge in ocean governance. Nat Commun 9:67–69
Inkyong K (2007) Environmental cooperation of north East Asia: transboundary air pollution. Int Relat Asia-Pacif 7(38):439–462
Jacoby HD et al (1998) Kyoto's unfinished business. For Aff 77(4):1–8
Karv-Chenko S (2007) The Aarhus convention and innovations in compliance with multilateral environmental law and policy. Colorado J Int Envt Pol 48(1):1–50
Keefe RO (2006) The protection of cultural property in armed conflicts. Cambridge University Press
Khee A, Tan J (2006) Vessel: source marine pollution: the law and politics of international regulation. Cambridge University Press
Kim RE (2013) The emergent network structure of the multilateral environmental agreement system. Global Envt Change 23(5):1–12
Koester V (1997) The bio-diversity covention negotiation process and some comments on the outcome. Envtl Pol L 27(3):175–192
Kopela S (2017) Making ships cleaner: reducing air pollution from international shipping. RECIEL 26(3):231–242
Korson K et al (2014) Everyone solution? Defining and redefining protected areas at the convention of biodiversity. Conser Soc 12(4):190–202
Kuklinska K, Nomiesnik J (2015) Air quality policy in US and the EU: a review. Atmos Pollut Res 6(1):129–137
Kumar R et al (2018) How will air quality change in South Asia by 2050. Adv Earth Space Sci 123(3):1840–1864
Kus S (2011) International nuclear law in the 25 years between Chernobyl and Fukushima and beyond. Nucl Bull 87:7–26
Kwiatkowska B (1984) Marine pollution from land based sources: current problems and prospects. Ocean Devt Int L 14:315–335

Lawrence P (1992) Technology transfer fund and the law: recent amendment to the Montreal protocol on substances that deplete the ozone layer. J Envt L 4(1):15–28

Leysters S (2010) International wild life law. In: Bowman MC et al (eds) Cambridge University Press

Listte CS, Gaston KJ (2010) Very large protected areas and their contribution to terrestrial biological conservation. Bio-Science 60(10):808–818

Lixinski L (2008) World heritage and the heritage of the word. In: Francioni F, Lenzerini L (eds) The 1972 world heritage convention: a commentary. Oxford University Press

Lohr A et al (2017) Solution for global marine litter pollution. Curr Opin Envt Substain 28:90–99

Mason M (2010) Information discloser and environment rights: the Aarhus convention. Global Envt Polit 10(3):10–31

Mason N et al (2020) Global opportunities and challenges for transboundary conservation. Nat Eco Envt 4:694–701

Mate J (2001) Making a difference: a case study of the green peace ozone campaign. RECIEL 10(2):190–198

Matthews GVT (2013) The Ramsar convention of wetlands: its history and development. Ramsar Convention Bureau Publications, Gland, p 7

Mayrand K, Paquin M (2004) Payment for environment services: a survey and assessment of current schemes. Unisfera International Centre, Montreal, pp 1–41

Meadow DH et al (2006) The limit of growth. Earthscan Publications, London

Melon L (1987) The chernobyl accident: a case study in international law regulating state responsibility for transboundary nuclear pollution. Columbia J Envt L 12:203–241

Molenaar EJ (2007) Port state jurisdiction: towards comprehensive mandatory and global coverage. Ocean Devt Int L 38(1–2):225–257

Molenaar EJ (1998) Coastal state jurisdiction over vessel-source pollution. Kulwer Law Int'l, The Hugue

Molina M, Rowland FS (1974) Stratospheric sink for cholorfloromethanes: chlorine atom-catalysed destruction of ozone. Nature 249:810–812

Moncel R, Van Assetl H (2012) All hands on deck: mobilizing climate change action beyond the UNFCCC. RECIEL 21(3):163–176

Montzka SA et al (2018) An unexpected and persistent increase in global emission of ozone depleting CFC-11. Nature 557:1–9

Muller RM (2018) Access to genetic resources and benefit sharing 25 years on: progress and challenges. ICTSD, Geneva, pp 1–24

Nanda VP (1967) The torrey canyon disaster: some legal aspects. Denver L J 44:400–425

Nengye L (2010) International legal framework on the prevention of vessel sourced pollution. China Oceans L Rev 12:238–263

Neumayer E (2001) Trade and environment: a critical assessment and some suggestions of reconciliation. J Envt Devt 9(2):138–159

O'Conell DP (1984) International law of the sea. In: Shearer IA (ed) Clarendon Press, Oxford

Oda S (1983) Fisheries under United Nations convention on law of the sea. Am J Int L 77(4):739–755

Oldfield S (ed) (2003) The trade in wildlife: regulation for conservation. Earthscan Publication

Overthii S, Rogendel GK (eds) (2014) Global governance of genetic resources: access and benefit sharing after nogoya protocol. Routledge, Abindon, pp 11–24

Parmentier R (2012) Role and impact of international NGOs in global ocean governance. Ocean YB 26:209–230

Parry ML et al (eds) (2007) Impact, adaptation and vulnerability, contribution of Working Group II to the fourth assessment report of the IPCC. Cambridge University Press

Pauchard N (2017) Access and benefit sharing under the convention on biological diversity and its protocol: what can some numbers tell us about the effectiveness of the regulatory regime? Resources 6(11):1–14

Prendergast DK, Adam WM (2003) Colonial wildlife conservation and origin of the society for the preservation of wild fauna of the empire (1903–2014). Oryx 37(2):251–260

Prideaux M (2014a) A nature affiliation: developing the role of NGOs in the convention on migratory species family, wild migration Australia, Parndana, South Australia, p 20
Prideaux M (2014b) Wild life NGOs and the CMS family: untapped potential for collaborative governance. J Int Wild Life L Pol 17(4):254–264
Qing-Nan M (1992) Land based marine pollution. Mar Pol 12:3–72
Raustiala K (1997) State, NGOs and international environmental institutions. Int Stud Q 41(4):719–740
Rautiala K (1997) State, NGOs and international environmental institutions. Int Stud 41(4):719–740
Reeve R (2002) Policing international trade in endangered species: CITES treaty and compliance. Earthscan Publications, London
Reeve R (2006) Wild life, sanctions and compliance: lessons from CITES regime. Int Aff 82(5):881–897
Reilly WK (1992) Reflections on rio. J Nat Resour Envt L 8(2):353–356
Rest A (2004) Enhanced implementation of international environmental treaties by judiciary—access to justice in international environmental law for individual and NGOs: efficacious enforcement by the permanent court of arbitration. Macquaire J Int Comp Entl L 1:1–28
Riojas-Rodriguez H et al (2016) Air pollution management and control in Latin American and Caribbean: implication climate change. Rev Panansalud Publ 40(3):1–10
Rodwell D (2012) The UNESCO world heritage convention 1972–2012: reflections and directions. Hist Envt 3(1):64–85
Roelofs JL (1993) United States-Canada air quality agreement: a framework for addressing transboundary air pollution problems. Connell Int L J 26(2):421–454
Sala E et al (2018) The economy of fishing of the high seas. Sci Adv 4:1–13
Sand PH (1997) Whither CITES? The evolution of a treaty regime in borderland of trade and environment. Eur J Int L 1:29–58
Sand PH (2017) International protection of endangered species in the face of wild life trade: whither conservation diplomacy? Asia Pacif J Envt L 20:5–27
Sand PH, Wiener JB (2015) Towards a new international law of the atmosphere? Goettingen J Int L 7(2):1–25
Sands P et al (2012) Principles of international environment law, 3rd edn. Cambridge University Press, Cambridge
Schachter O (1991) The emergence of international law. J Int Aff 44(2):457–493
Schiermeier Q (2009) Ocean fertilization: dead in the water. Nature 457:521–523
Schroeder CH (1986) Rights against risks. Columbia L Rev 86(3):495–562
Schumacher EF (1973) Small is beautiful: economics as if people mattered. Harper & Row, New York
Shelton D (2008) Human rights and environment: problems and possibilities. Envt'l Pol'y 38:41–49
Sohn LB (1973) Stockholm declaration on the human environment. Harv Int L J 3:423–515
Stoiber C (2003) Handbook on nuclear law. IAEA Publications, Vienna
Swittner L (2009) Confronting the bomb: a short history of world nuclear disarmament movement. Stanford University Press, California
Tortell PD (2020) Earth 2020: science, society and sustainability in the anthropcene. PNAS 117(16):8683–8691
Trazyna TC et al (eds) (1996) World dictionary of environmental organisations, 5th edn. Earthscan Publications, London
Verlaan S (2009) Geo-engineering, the law of the sea, and climate change. Carbon Clim L Rev, 446–458
Victor W (1994–1995) Ozone depletion, developing countries, human rights: seeking better grounds on which to fight for protection ozone layer. J Nat Resour Envt L 10: 3–112.
Vicuna FO (1999) Changing international law of high seas fisheries. Cambridge University Press
Wahlstrom M et al (eds) (2019) Protest for future: composition, mobilization and motives of the participants in Friday for future climate protests on 15 March 2019 in 15 European cities, Saunders, Clare and Brian Doherty

Walker G (2007) A ocean of air: a natural history of the atmosphere. Bloomsbury, London

Weiss EB (2011) The evolution of international environmental law. Jpn Y B Int L 54:1–27

Wirth JD (1996) Trial smelter dispute: Canadian and American confront transboundary pollution. Environ Hist 1(2):34–51

Wolf ID et al (2019) Nature conservation and nature based tourism: a paradox. Environments 6(9):104–127

World Commission on Environment and Development (1987) Our common future. Oxford University Press

Xu T et al (2019) Wetlands of international importance: states threats and future protection. Int J Envt Res Public Health 16(10):1–23

Yamineva Y, Romppamen S (2017) Is law failing to address air pollution? Reflections on international and European development. RECIEL 26(3):189–200

Yap N (1989–1990) NGOs and sustainable development. Int J 45, 75–105

Zwinge T (2011) Duties of flag state to implement and enforce international standards and regulations: and measures to counter their failure to do so. J Int Bus L 10(2):291–323

Chapter 12
Business Ethics

1 Introduction

"Do good and forget it," is the broad motive of an NGO. An NGO is not a profit-oriented organisation. It is for public good. It is not a business organisation. Generally, NGOs are engaged in the public interest and common cause, whereas business enterprises are engaged in commercial activities. According to C.K. Prahalad,

> Larger businesses can bring efficiency. NGOs can bring creativity to solve problems that are faced by us.[1]

Business operates through markets, corporates, manufacturing, distribution of goods and services. Business prefers, generally, upper strata with deep pockets. However, low-income groups cannot be ignored because four billion of the world population is still living in poverty. These groups are potential producers and consumers of goods and services.

Market is a public place where buyers and sellers can meet to facilitate the transaction of goals and services. It could be a traditional shop or retailer in local area or virtual global marketing like Amazon.

Priority of NGOs is the poor, marginalised and weaker sections of society. NGOs engage for their overall development and empowerment. In comparison to business, NGOs have a more diverse approach to reach out to the people. Businesses want to expand their activities and enlarge the market in new areas for profits. Since the poor are also the stakeholders in the world, it is a social imperative for businesses to collaborate with the state, NGOs and IGOs, to get involved in poverty-reduction.

All business are market focused. Market is a great institution for operationalising the business and it only understands the language of money. In the long run, markets flourish when integrated with moral values and commercial interests.[2]

---

[1] Prahalad (2019).

[2] Brenan and Jaworski (2016).

P. Rai, *Non-Governmental Organisations and International Law*,
https://doi.org/10.1007/978-981-97-5469-4_12

A. Business Ethics

Business ethics entered into the discourse in the 1960s and became a part of the curriculum from the next decade onwards. Business ethics are derived from religious tenets and moral philosophy. For example, the Buddha enlightened life and living by moral practices.[3] Confucius emphasised on moral values to maintain social stability.[4] Aristotle described trade and commercial activities to pursue wealth-creation with fair treatment and justice for all.[5] The primary concern of these philosophers was morality, virtue, fairness and justice in personal interactions with society.

Perhaps this sagacious prescription may have inspired the business community. The age-old idea of ethics was further enriched and enlightened by G.W.F. Hegel, John Stuart Mill, John Locke, Immanuel Kant, J.G. Hamann, Adam Smith, Karl Marx and Mahatma Gandhi.[6] They emphasised that every individual concerned with common good and prosperity should keep human values in mind while creating wealth.

John Rawls' theory of justice continues to influence contemporary business ethics. He proposed the democratic regulation of the market by state and governance of ownership and corporations.[7] Amartya Sen says that ethics is integral to business in the eastern and western thoughts.[8] These philosophers and economic thinkers primarily focused on individual virtues, moral values, honesty, character traits, and responsive behaviour in the business world. These human qualities are further strengthened by literary works like novels, poetry, cinema and cultural activities.[9]

Individual behaviour has its own importance in the business practices. Ethical values are successfully applied to the medical and legal professions. But it is not an easy task in the business world since it is a competitive market place where everyone is under constant pressure to make profits. Personal virtues and moral values have their own limitations when applied to the profession of business.[10] Therefore, business ethics are applicable to business organisations as well as to individuals.[11]

Moreover, business ethics are greatly influenced by the ethical and moral values of their owners and senior executives. Since profits and competition drive business, it is not always easy to apply these values. Thereby NGOs encounter to business world.

Today, businesses have expanded largely and society appears like a bazaar. Economies have globalised and corporations have presence in many countries with

---

[3] Gould (1995).

[4] Wood (2011).

[5] Solomon (2004).

[6] Luetge (2013).

[7] Norman (2015).

[8] Sen (1993).

[9] Freeman (1990).

[10] Norman (2021).

[11] Solomon (1999).

larger budgets. There are many complex scenarios in the world of contracts, stockholders, profits, taxation and record keeping.[12] Business is not just a contract between two parties or the production of services and goods or the maximisation of profit and creation of capital, it is much more than that. It also has a social responsibility towards people at large. Corporates and market cannot ignore issues such as environmental pollution, human right violation, employment-generation, the distribution of justice and public health.

NGOs have provided inputs to implement business ethics. They fight against corruption, illegal action and anti-social activities of corporations and the market place.[13] They demand transparency and responsive behaviour of the business sector. Thus, it is necessary for the business world to accept ethical values in their daily commercial transactions. It is also important that states lay down an ethical code and framework for business. The ethical code is voluntary for corporates and the market, whereas a legal framework is mandatory to observe them all. NGOs' activism influences both business and state to accept and implement ethical values as an integral part of business.

B. **Market Place for Small Farmers**

NGOs promote access to small stakeholders to the market place.[14] In Uganda, NGOs intervene in favour of poor farming communities. These communities face problems due to poor road infrastructure and the non-availability of credit facilities.[15] The small producers need timely reach to the market to earn a sufficient living. Local Ugandan farmers collectively demand from the state authority for all-weather feeder roads and nearby bank branches. Similarly, in Tanzania, seven NGOs are engaged in the advocacy for access of small farmers' products to the market place. They have demanded credit facilities for small farmers from cooperative societies. Small farmers need ready access to the markets for their own sustainability.[16]

C. **Value-Added Collaboration**

NGOs' intervention in markets and collaboration with business is a new phenomenon. Traditionally, business-NGO relations were based on either philanthropy or adversity.[17] Notwithstanding, business donates to NGOs, and thus NGOs carry on service, relief and welfare missions. NGOs' advocacy for the promotion of human rights, environment, sustainable development and inclusive economic growth has manifested the situation of collaboration between NGOs and business. NGOs' strategy and innovation have opened the window of collaboration between profit and non-profit organisations.

---

[12] Brenkert and Beauchap (2009).

[13] Remisova and Lasakoya (2018).

[14] Grieg-Gren and Wilson (2007).

[15] Marter and Wandscheider (2002).

[16] Kimaro (2013).

[17] dt_rs_chapter3.pdf. "*Collaboration Between NGOs and Business*," 1997, pp. 38–68 at 41. www.bath.ac.uk/carpp/publications/doc_thesis_links_shah.html.

In collaboration, business and NGOs can create value in the economy, ecology and the realm of human rights. The creation of value benefits the international community.[18] First and foremost, collaborative value-creation is mutually beneficial to NGOs and businesses.[19] But NGOs are more mindful about their reputational perception because their sustainability and influence are based only on trustworthiness and non-profit orientation. In the NGO-business collaboration model, they share information, skill, experience and pool their resources together for a common cause—for instance, climate change and sustainable development. NGOs may receive funds from business to engage in awareness, advocacy and watchdog operations in return for businesses getting legitimacy and reputation to expand their market and network.[20]

D. **Economic Globalisation**

The advancement of technology and inexpensive means of transportation and communication facilitate people, capital, goods and services, worldwide. This process is known as globalisation, and it affects the sovereignty of nations.[21] Globalisation has increased space for inter-governmental organisations (IGOs), NGOs, corporations, business and private sectors. Economic globalisation started in 1820 in the western world and it expanded throughout the globe in the 1990s. The process of globalisation encompasses world economy, polity, law, society and culture.[22]

Globalisation has substantively contributed to world economic growth since the 1850s and, for the next 100 years, Western Europe and the United States enjoyed its fruits. With the exception of the West, the rest of the World—Asia, Africa and Latin America—is used only for raw materials and market.[23] On the other side, discontents of economic globalisation[24] have been witnessed in terms of income and wealth inequality.[25] The winds of change blew in the later part of the twentieth century when developing economies such as China, India, Indonesia, South Korea, Brazil, South Africa[26] and others set to integrate the world economy on an equal footing with the developed world.

Integrated economy is operationalised under the realm of international economic law.[27] The world trade law and international investment law are already well-developed courtesy multilateral and bilateral treaties. Moreover, the settlement mechanisms of trade, investment, and disputes are well-placed. International economic law is possibly applicable in three phenomena: (1) rules between the states, (2) rules between the state and the individual and (3) also between persons, either natural

---

[18] . Austin and Seitanidi (2012).

[19] Mironska and Zaborek (2019).

[20] Darko (2014).

[21] Ku and Yoo (2013).

[22] Friedman (1999).

[23] Boldizzoni (2015).

[24] Stiglitz (2002).

[25] Piketty (2014).

[26] Martin et al. (2018).

[27] Lowenfel (2002).

or juridical.[28] It contains trade and finance agreements, customary rules[29] and soft law.[30] Besides trade and investment, other areas like international taxation and finance remain formative stage.[31]

There are four main players in the global economy, namely, states, corporations, IGOs and NGOs. Integration of the world economy puts constraints on state capabilities in taxation, capital markets, finance and also the ability of redistribution of justice, reduction of disparity and social spending.[32] Whenever states impose more taxation on capital markets then the capital is moved to another country where the taxation is lower.

The IMF provides funding to a nation with some suggestions to curtail state expenditure, spending and stimulate foreign direct investment (FDI). State power wielding has remained relevant in international economic law and its enforcement within its jurisdiction. IGOs such as the World Bank, IMF, WTO and the United Nations Conference on Trade and Development (UNCTAD) are playing regulatory and suggestive roles in the world economy.

Corporations are instruments of the business sector, and they earn profit. It is therefore, expected from them, to fulfil their social obligations as it is an intrinsic part of the business world. NGOs are not-for-profit, primarily representing social sectors. But they are not silent spectators to the discontents of the world economy. NGOs are catalysts for change in the global economy as well as for inclusive growth and distributive justice.[33]

NGOs—business interface is a vast area but the present study sheds light mainly on world trade, international investment, and NGOs' cross-border funding. NGOs are engaged in the formation of international trade and investment law. They also oversee the enforcement and outcomes. World trade law is about the free flow of goods and services across the borders, while international investment law is related to importing capital to the country.[34]

2 International Trade Law

International trade law is based on bilateral and multilateral agreements between parties on the reciprocal exchange of benefit and advantage. Freedom of trade is endowed to every state under international law. International trade raises the income, employment and prosperity among nations. In addition, it stimulates economic

[28] Charnovitz (2011).

[29] Zamora (1989).

[30] Seidl-Hohenveldern (1999).

[31] Brummer (2010).

[32] Stiglitz (2003).

[33] Eden (2004).

[34] Akehursts (2019).

growth and provides opportunities for the better use of land, labour and capital.[35] International trade could be carried out by maritime, air, rail, road and online connectivity. The International Court of Justice (ICJ) in the *Nicaragua* case held that no state shall create hindrance to others in the engagement of lawful trading around the world.[36]

International trade law is derived from *lex mercatoria* or the law of merchant, which was used throughout Europe in the Middle Ages.[37] The law of merchant is beyond the state, within the state and among the states, therefore, it contributed to the idea of freedom of contract, arbitration settlement of trade disputes and observance of contractual obligations.

International trade law has its roots in the nineteenth century. IGOs such as the Hague Conference on Private International Law (HCCH) 1893[38] and International Institute for the Unification of Private Law (UNIDROIT) 1926[39] were associated with the League of Nations. They had assigned the task of unification of the rule of private international law or conflict of laws to the realm of business.

Besides, NGOs like the International Chamber of Commerce (ICC) 1919[40] International Chamber of Shipping (ICS) 1921[41] and Comite Maritime International (CMI) 1897,[42] were also actively engaged in the formation of international commercial and maritime law. ICC has substantively contributed to the establishment of the ICC-Arbitral Tribunals[43] and ICC Advertising and Marketing Communications Code. Since 1923, the ICC-Arbitral Tribunals have resolved 24,000 commercial disputes between parties. ICC is a specific NGO that was accorded observer status by the General Assembly of the United Nations. ICC's forum, World Chambers Federation (WCF), has extensive chamber membership connecting ICC to small and medium sized enterprises (SMEs), worldwide. At present, 12,000 commercial chambers across the world have joined it. Apart from this, more than one hundred states are also associated with the ICC.

The International Maritime Committee (CIM or IMC) is a prior NGO of maritime affairs, engaged in the promotion and unification of international maritime law and practices. It assimilated the views of ship owners, freighters, insurances, arbitrators and bankers for improved sea-borne trade.[44] IMC has facilitated to develop international maritime law and international carriage of goods by sea. It has consultative status with the UN and is closely associated with the WTO, UNCTAD, IMO, UNCITRAL, and office of the Law of the Sea and Legal Affairs of the UN. Another

---

[35] Thompson et al. (2007).

[36] Nicaragua (Nicaragua v. United States) Merits, ICJ Report 1986, p. 14 at 129.

[37] Michaels (2007).

[38] www.hcch.net; Droz (1994).

[39] www.unidroit.org.

[40] www.iccwbo.org.

[41] http://www.ics-shipping.org.

[42] https://comitemaritime.org.

[43] Gaudet (1982).

[44] Bekiashev and Serebriakov (1981).

maritime NGO is the International Chamber of Shipping,[45] which commands 80% merchant navy memberships. It has been engaged in the formation of international shipping law and sea-borne trade.

There are three legal academic NGOs, i.e. the Institute of International Law (IIL) 1873,[46] International Law Association (ILA) 1873[47] and International Association of Legal Science (IALS) 1950.[48] They have undertaken legal research in contemporary issues and tried to build consensus among states on international trade law. In particular, IALS has made a substantive contribution to the field of international comparative law and in finding out common elements of international commercial law.[49]

So far, developing countries have not benefitted from the international trade regime. But they are numerically in a better position in the UN system. Therefore, they raised their concerns before the General Assembly. In response, the General Assembly has adopted a number of Declarations, i.e. Permanent Sovereignty over Natural Resources 1962;[50] The Principle of Sovereign Equality of States 1963[51]; and Charter of Economic Rights and Duties of States 1974.[52]

The 1974 Charter, Article 4, laid down that the state should promote international trade and economic co-operation through multilateral and bilateral agreements among the parties. These trade agreements are based on free choice of the states concerned. The charter further emphasises on a more rational and equitable world economy.[53]

United Nations Conference on Trade and Development (UNCTAD) 1964[54] is a UN organ specifically working for the interests of developing economies and their participation in international trade.[55] The UNCTAD promotes financial aid for trade.[56] The financial aid from developed nations comes with certain conditions, which directly or indirectly affect the independence of developing countries.[57] Financial aid is also not a long-term solution. Therefore, investment in developing

---

[45] Ibid., pp. 123–133; Nersesian (2009).

[46] www.idi-iil.org.

[47] www.ila-hq.org; Olmstead (1974).

[48] https://aisj-ials.net.

[49] Zajtay (1978).

[50] *Permanent Sovereignty over Natural Resources*, United Nations General Assembly Resolution (UNGA Res) 1803 (XVII) (14 December 1962).

[51] *The Principle of Sovereign Equality of States*, UNGA Res 1966 (XVIII) (6 December 1963).

[52] *Charter of Economic Rights and Duties of States, 1974*, UNGA Res 3281 (XXIV) (12 December 1974); ILM 251 (1975); Chatterjee (1991).

[53] Charter of Rights and Duties of State, Articles 8,9,11,13.

[54] www.unctad.org.

[55] Temu (1974).

[56] Suwa-Eisemamm and Verdier (2007).

[57] Koul (1977).

countries is a better option. It can result in a possibility of sustainable growth and development in the said economies.[58]

UNCTAD relentlessly emphasises on equity in international trade law. Many NGOs also have participated in the UNCTAD endeavour. There are 241 NGOs working with UNCTAD. Among them, 148 belong to the general category, with 93 in the special category.[59] UNCTAD-NGO partnerships relate to the sharing of information, advocacy support and raising public awareness about international trade and development.

A. **General Agreement of Tariffs and Trade (GATT)**

World trade flourished in industrial countries between 1870 and 1913. It was affected by the First World War (1914–1918) and the Great Depression of the 1930s. It was further affected by state-imposed trade barriers and protectionism. In consequence, 30% of imports exports of industrialised nations decreased.[60] In order to revive international trade, the United States and the United Kingdom prepared the groundwork in the early 1940s, and expedited it post World War II.[61] They proposed the establishment of the International Trade Organisation (ITO) for the liberalisation of the world economy and the increase of employment opportunities.

A Preparatory Committee was established to prepare the charter of the ITO. It formulated Rules of Procedure to carry out the assigned task.[62] Initially, there were four NGOs associated with the Preparatory Committee—the International Chamber of Commerce (ICC), World Federation of Trade Unions (WFTU), International Cooperative Alliance (ICA) and American Federation of Labour (AFL). They submitted their views to the committee, and emphasised on the transparency and openness in trade negotiations.[63]

GATT completed this task in 1947[64] because the proposed ITO never saw the light of day. GATT was simply a body of multilateral trade rules and agreements that also functioned as an ad hoc international trade institution. GATT came into force on 1 January, 1948.[65] It carries out responsibilities with the help of a small secretariat located in Geneva. Its purpose is to establish a legal mechanism for tariff negotiations on reciprocal benefits, and also to discourage protectionism amongst nations. GATT has carried out seven multilateral trade negotiations in its 47-year

---

58 Bhattarai (2016).

59 UNCTAD-NGOs Relationship Governed under Article 15, Rule 77. Rules of Procedure of the Trade and Development Board, New York 1989.

60 Madsen (2001).

61 Iwin (1995).

62 Rules of Procedure of the Preparatory Committee of the International Conference on Trade and Employment, 16 December 1946, UN Doc. E/PC/T/2/Rev. 1 Rule 46.

63 De Souza Farias (2013).

64 Winham (2009), Chap. 2; Dam (1970).

65 Protocol of Provisional Application of the General Agreement on Tariffs and Trade, 30 October 1947; 55 UNTS 308.

journey (1948–1995). During this impressive period, it has attempted to sort out the economic problems of the developing world.[66]

The GATT secretariat maintained a list of NGOs that consisted of the ICC, International Co-operative Alliance, International Organisation of Employers, International Federation of Agricultural Producers, The International Association for Protection of Intellectual Property, The International Transport Workers' Federation and International Co-operative Women's Guild.[67] NGOs' relations with the international trade regime were well placed under the Havana Charter of the proposed ITO. Their experience and expertise at this the formative stage of development of international trade law was well-known within the community of world trade.[68]

B. **Final Act of the Uruguay Round**

The GATT conducted eight rounds, with its last round of multilateral trade negotiations known as the Uruguay Round. It commenced on 20 September 1986, and concluded on 15 April 1994. The Uruguay Round adopted legal texts or the Final Act by 123 countries.[69] The Final Act is a comprehensive legal document which includes agriculture, trade in services, intellectual property rights (IPR), investment, subsidies, dumping, textiles and clothing. Besides Dispute Settlement Understanding, the World Trade Organisation (WTO) was established. GATT 1947, which dealt with the trade of goods, was now revised and updated thoroughly. This also became a part of the Final Act of the Uruguay Round 1994 or the international trade regime.[70]

Many NGOs were involved in the Uruguay Round, organising a Shadow GATT Conference in Montreal in 1988 to discuss the issues. They formed the NGO-GATT steering committee, comprising NGOs and the international trade network. In addition, NGOs with UNCTAD organised a summit and held a shadow GATT talk. NGOs co-ordinated their activities for monitoring negotiations, analysing specific issues, formulating common viewpoints and engaging in lobbying and advocacy.

A Shadow Conference on GATT issues was held once again from 28 November to 2 December 1990 in Brussels. In fact, NGOs were latecomers to the Uruguay Round, when they were intensifying their campaign as well as during the conference in November 1992 in Hamburg, Germany. The Uruguay Round negotiations were the finishing touches.[71] The outcome of the Hamburg Conference had a little space for accommodation of the Uruguay Round negotiations.

---

[66] Protocol Amending the GATT to introduce Part IV on Trade and Development, 1965. It came into force in 1966. http://wto.org >party_e PDF.

[67] Chrnovitz and Wickham (1995).

[68] Ibid., 121.

[69] Hudec (1995).

[70] General Agreement on Tariffs and Trade: Multilateral Trade Negotiations Final Act Embodying the Results of the Uruguay Round of Trade Negotiations signed at Marrakesh, Morocco, 15 April 1994, entered into force on 1 January 1995, 33 IL M 1125 (1994); 55 UNTS 1994.

[71] Wilkinson (1996).

The final act of the Uruguay Round established a rule-based international trade system.[72] It was a unified package deal, with a single dispute settlement mechanism[73] and a newly created World Trade Organisation (WTO).[74] The Uruguay Round accommodated developing countries' interests in a better way.[75] Its main focus was on the growth rate of the world economy. NGOs have access to the trade dispute understanding as amicus curiae[76] and to participate in the WTO activities.[77]

NGOs' participation in international trade law is essential for the flourishing of free trade and the elimination of trade barriers.

3 Trade Linkages

Some issue areas are inherent to the international trade regime. They are linked in a straight line, and having deep, common roots. Initially, multilateral agreements were related to trade issues. The linkage issues came into force either through official negotiations or by street protests. NGOs influenced the multilateral trade policy during the Uruguay Round (1986–1994) negotiations; they intensified their activism for transparency and openness in the WTO activities.[78] NGOs did not hesitate to organise street protests during the ministerial conference or at the headquarters of the WTO for highlighting trade linkage issues.[79]

Trade linkage issues are of two kinds: (1) coherence and (2) consequential.[80] Coherent issues are trade-related. These refer to services, intellectual property rights, investment, etc. GATT started its journey with the trade of goods and encompassed all trade themes in the Uruguay Round. Consequential issues are not part of international trade law. They have their own regimes; for instance, human rights, environmental protection and labour standards. According to David W. Leebron,

> Linkage of issues can also be achieved through the participation of NGOs that effectively constitute special interest groups for particular issue areas.[81]

A. **Trade and Health**

---

[72] Jackson et al. (1992).

[73] Martin (2013); Pauwelyn (2019).

[74] Gallagher (2005).

[75] Wilkinson and Scott (2008).

[76] Reinisch and Irgel (2001).

[77] WTO Relations with Non-Governmental Organisations, Legal Text-Marrakesh Agreement or Final Act of Uruguay Round, Articles V: 2, Guidelines for arrangement of relations with non-governmental organisations was adopted by General Council of WTO, WT/L/162, 18 July, 1996.

[78] Leebron (2002).

[79] Esteve (2011); Bayne (2000); Aslton (1980).

[80] David W. Leebron, "Linkage", *supra note* 78 at 11.

[81] Ibid., p. 23.

The liberalisation of trade increased prosperity and living standards of people around the world.[82] The linkage between trade and human rights is desirable as per Articles XX (a) and (b) of GATT 1994.[83] GATT Articles XX (a) and (b) require that necessary measures are to be taken in the protection of public morals or health, respectively. These are exception clauses of the GATT 1994. It is accepted that weighing and balancing measures are required between free trade and trade restrictiveness in the context of public morals and health.[84] In addition, it is also necessary that women shall be specifically protected under the public morals exceptions clause,[85] because women are more vulnerable, facing discrimination and sexual harassment.

Economic globalisation is related to health because it promotes high standards of living and wellness. On the flip side, globalisation is one of the reasons for the spread of disease worldwide; Covid-19 is a perfect example. Free trade has increased the availability of fast food and tobacco. Simultaneously, it has created opportunities to access medicines and physicians' services globally.[86] The access of health services and medicines is intrinsic to human rights.

NGOs such as the Global Health Network[87] are engaged in the framing of health policy and its subsequent enforcement.[88] NGOs are successfully engaged in the advocacy network of the WHO Framework Convention on Tobacco Control (FCTC), 2005.[89] In addition, they are also involved in the access to essential medicines,[90] addressing malnutrition,[91] maternal and child health[92] and the prevention of HIV/ AIDS.[93]

NGOs intervene in the medicine market to make it accessible to the poor and needy. Maureen Mackintosh and Co. conducted a study of African and Indian NGOs found that the said market is comparatively unregulated. Therefore, NGOs' role is desirable to complement state action.[94] In India, NGOs like LOCOST[95] (Low-cost Standard Therapeutics) and CDMU[96] (Community Development Medicinal Unit) are involved in manufacturing drugs for sale to other NGOs. CDMU is a wholesale

---

82 Sykes (2003); Cottier et al. (2012).

83 GATT, Articles, XX (a) and (b), 55 UNTS 194.

84 Harris and Moon (2005).

85 Jarvis (2001).

86 Smith (2006).

87 https://tghn.org.

88 Gomez (2018).

89 Adopted by World Health Assembly on 21 May 2003, entered into force on 27 February 2005. https://www.who.int/fctc/about.

90 Chapman (2009); Murphy (2012).

91 Kraak et al. (2011).

92 Smith and Shiffman (2016).

93 Desouza and Dutta (2008).

94 Mackintosh et al. (2011).

95 http://www.locostindia.in/.

96 http://www.cdmuindia.org.

distributor, distributing medicines to other NGOs. They are successful in medicine market intervention owing to the control of price and maintenance of quality.

Similarly, in Tanzania and Kenya, NGOs intervene in the medicine market with the help of Donors—Global Fund for HIV, TB and Malaria,[97] PEPFAR,[98] Global TB Drug Facility,[99] and Action Medeor,[100] etc. Health NGOs have added value to the medicine supply market via manufacturing and distribution. Besides, NGOs are engaged in advocacy, awareness and research to ensure better health care to all. NGOs have established networks such as Health Action International (HAI),[101] International Dispensary Association Foundation[102] and the Global Fund for HIV, TB and Malaria. Medicines Sans Frontiers (MSF),[103] making doctors and paramedicos available around the world.

B. **Trade and Food**

The Uruguay Round incorporated agriculture under the international trade regime. It resulted in the insertion of the Agreement on Agriculture (AoA)[104] within the Final Act of the Uruguay Round 1994. The AoA dealt with the liberalisation of the agriculture market, reduction of tariffs, agriculture subsidy, prohibition of export dumping, trade-distorting, and support measures. Food security is a non-trading concern of the WTO Agreement on Agriculture (AoA). But the availability of adequate food is a part of human rights under Article 25, clause 1 of UDHR 1948.

The main purpose of AoA is to increase global food trade. However, the related Articles of AoA were not only poorly constructed but internally contradictory as well.[105] Therefore, the WTO-ministerial conference further improved the provisions of the AoA, which were related to the open trading system of agricultural products and food security. They emphasised that the agricultural trading system should change as per the need of food security.[106]

Oxfam International, in collaboration with other NGOs, organised the 'Make Trade Fair' campaign. They demanded market access to poor countries, thus ending agricultural dumping between 2002 and 2006.[107] In addition to it, there are several issues such as the support for poor farmers, public stock holding for food security purposes,[108] food aid not to be tied to commercial sale, and financial and technical aid, etc., which require an adequate response by the WTO-ministerial conference.

---

[97] http://www.theglobalfund.org.

[98] http://www.pepfar .gov (The US President's Emergency Plan for AIDS Relief).

[99] http://www.stoptb.org/.

[100] https://medeor.de/ (German medical aid organisation founded in 1964).

[101] http://haiweb.org/.

[102] https://idafoundation.org/.

[103] https://www.msf.org/ (MSF in English: Doctors Without Borders).

[104] 33 I.L.M. 1125 (1994).

[105] Ritchie and Dawkins (2000).

[106] Ibid., p. 29.

[107] Murphy and Hansen-Kuhn (2017).

[108] Margulis (2018).

Agriculture is a source of living, food and culture, in addition to global trade.[109] The NGOs' collective voice for food security is based on sustainable agricultural development at the local level so that this can be further supplemented by the international food market. According to Alan Matthews, "There can be a temptation to dismiss or ignore these voices but this would be a mistake."[110]

NGOs such as the Institute for Agriculture and Trade Policy,[111] Friends of the Earth International,[112] Oxfam International[113] and many more, are engaged in food security and reform in the WTO—Agreement on Agriculture. They have highlighted special interest of the developing countries that must be focused on in WTO-ministerial conferences.[114]

C. Trade and Environment

Free trade and the protection of the environment are different but mutually supportive when it comes to the subject of sustainable development.[115] Environmental issues did not get highlighted in GATT 1947.[116] Article XX of the Final Act of the Uruguay Round incorporated environmental measures as an exception clause. In addition, production and process were also linked to the environment under Sanitary and Phytosanitary measures (SPS) and Technical Barriers to Trade (TBT) Agreements within the Final Act. The international trade regime is a multilateral agreement by which a state cannot impose environmental measures that aren't mentioned within this regime unilaterally. The WTO-Dispute Settlement Panel in Tuna-I[117] and Tuna-II[118] cases found that unilateral restrictions on imports contravened to the provisions of the Final Act of the Uruguay Round.

Environmental NGOs are engaged in the linkage between the environment and free trade regime. So far, three multilateral environment agreements—(1) Convention on International Trade in Endangered Species of Wild Fauna and Flora (CITES) 1973, (2) Convention on Control of Transboundary Movement of Hazardous Wastes and their Disposal 1989 (The Basel Convention), and (3) Protocol on Substances that Deplete the Ozone Layer 1989 (The Montreal Protocol)—are directly linked to free trade and environmental protection.[119]

---

[109] Margulis (2017).

[110] Mathews (2014).

[111] https://www.iatp.org.

[112] https://www.foei.org/.

[113] https://www.oxfam.org/.

[114] Rorden et al. (2016).

[115] Ward (1996); Copeland and Taylor (2003); Najam et al. (2007).

[116] Bodansky and Lawrence (2009).

[117] United States—Restrictions on Imports of Tuna, DS 21/R, 3 September, 1991.

[118] United States—Restrictions on Imports of Tuna, DS 29/R June 1994.

[119] Chapter 11 of this Book.

Initially, there was no formal role visualised for NGOs, either in the GATT or WTO international regimes. Subsequently, environmental NGOs got engaged in the development of international trade law and dispute settlement procedures. They were eventually allowed to submit their briefs as amici curiae before the WTO dispute settlement understanding. In addition, NGOs participated in WTO-ministerial conferences in order to influence their decisions and harmonise business interests with environmental issues.

According to Daniel Esty,

> NGO participation in international trade debates, specifically in the context of the WTO, is beneficial for reasons such as reduction of the risk of market failure and enhancement of conservation of natural resources and public good.

He further observed that state representatives have their own limitations because business and industry interests are very strong and enjoy economic power wielding. Therefore, they representatives hesitate to take appropriate decisions when it comes to the conservation of environment in the trade realm.[120] Environmental NGOs are free to balance business interests with environmental concerns without the interference of vested interests.

The WTO set up the Committee on Trade and Environment (CTE) in 1994.[121] The committee was required to make appropriate recommendations for the integration of trade and environment. NGOs are contributing to the CTE with fresh ideas, results of scientific and research findings, and highlighting the issues of developing countries. Environmental NGOs participated, observed and influenced trade policy decisions of the WTO-ministerial conference.[122]

The relationship between the North American Free Trade Agreement (NAFTA) 1994 and NGOs is well-placed. NGOs' role is appreciated in the formation and enforcement of the trade agreement between the United States, Canada and Mexico.[123] Change is also visible in the WTO trade regime, with importance given to NGOs' participation at the CTE, ministerial conference and dispute settlement understanding (DSU) within the WTO trade framework.[124]

D. **Trade and Labour**

Liberalisation of trade and labour standards are not just solitary ideas, but they express and operate coherently with each other.[125] Both of these have common objectives, with different paths to improve the quality of life. GATT 1947 does not consider labour issues within its established international trade regime.[126] The Final Act of

---

[120] Esty (2000).

[121] Sinha (2013).

[122] Mason (2003).

[123] Hogenboom et al. (2003).

[124] Sampson (2005); Bernascom-Osterwalder et al. (2006); Sanchez (2006).

[125] Langille (1997).

[126] Chernovitz (1987).

the Uruguay Round 1994 just made a passing reference: "ensure the full employment" under its preamble, and "protection of the prisoner labour" within its general exception clause.[127]

Trade unions are considered the voice of labour and hence they are engaged in the protection of labour rights. The international trade union movement became weak between 1920 and 1990 owing to the World Cold war. The World Federation of Trade Unions (WFTU) was founded in 1945. The labour agenda was further weakened due to globalisation, economic liberalisation, decline of labour NGOs[128] and the trade union movement.

There are two prominent trade union federations at the international level, i.e. (1) World Confederation of Labour (WCL) and (2) International Confederation of Free Trade Unions (ICFTU).[129] They joined hands with NGOs to pursue labour issues within the WTO trade regime.

The international trade regime is a broad framework that was further developed by WTO's ministerial conference. The WTO-Ministerial Conference of member states was held every two years. It discussed the trade linkage issues such as human rights, environment and labour, and how to accommodate them within the international trade regime. The WTO-Ministerial Conference in Singapore in 1996 established that consensus to core labour standards should be upheld.[130]

The WTO did not come forward to tackle labour issues as they remained the responsibility of the ILO. The core labour standards were already identified by the ILO.[131] These are as follows: (a) freedom of association and right to collective bargaining; (b) the elimination of all forms of forced labour; (c) abolition of child labour; and (d) elimination of discrimination in respect of employment and occupation.

With respect to the implementation of core labour standards, NGOs and trade unions organised a public protest in Seattle where the Ministerial Conference was held in 1999. In consequence, the Conference agreed to examine a possible link between trade and labour.[132] As core labour standards should have a minimum effect on labour wages, developing countries easily agreed on them.[133] They have had a competitive edge in labour intensive exports when compared to developed countries. And the race to the bottom can easily be arrested due to standardised minimum wages.

Labour rights are subsumed by UDHR 1948 and the International Covenants on Civil and Political Rights, and on Economic, Social and Cultural Rights, 1966. With

---

[127] Final Act of Uruguay Round 1994, Article XX(e).

[128] Gallin (2000).

[129] Hale (2004); Spooner (2004).

[130] McCrudden and Davies (2000).

[131] ILO Declaration on Fundamental Principles and Rights at Work 1998, International Labour Conference, Eighty-Sixth Session, Geneva (18 June 1998) (Annex revised 15 June 2010); Kellerson (1998).

[132] Summers (2001).

[133] Polaska (2003).

the collaboration of NGOs and IGOs, the human rights bodies are monitoring the implementation of labour rights. Simultaneously, the WTO has effective enforcement mechanism as well, i.e. dispute settlement understanding,[134] but it is highly restricted in trade disputes. So far, the ILO does not have any adjudication system. Therefore, trade and labour issues are dealt with by either their tripartite system or human rights bodies.

An empirical study found that observing core labour standards does not affect trade export. This study related the manufacturing of soccer balls in Sialkot, Pakistan, by Nike. The Silver Star manufacturing firm from Pakistan implemented core labour standards, as set out by ILO. Despite this, Silver Star maintained momentum and expanded its business. As this is a single empirical study, its findings require to be compared to other developing countries.[135]

4 International Investment Law

Investment refers to the pumping of money into an undertaking with the intention of deriving benefit out of it. The International Investment Law (IIL) governs the relationship between foreign investors (including states as) and transnational corporations.[136] Foreign investment was dealt with under customary international law, with investment disputes being resolved through diplomatic channels.[137] There was no universal convention prevalent to deal with foreign investment issues. Thus, bilateral investment treaties (BITs) occupied this area, and they started regulating international investment transactions in the 1960s. International investment regimes are still waiting for a nod from the international community. Multilateral Agreements on Investment (MAI) may well see the light to day in the near future.

A. **Origins of Foreign Investment**

By the sixteenth century, the Europeans had reached the shores of Asia, Africa and the Americas. Businessmen, missionaries and military regimes entered these continents, and the rest is a history of encounters, exploitation, resistance and decolonisation. Being foreigners, they asked the native rulers to protect their life and property within their territory. Thus, international investment law was born, originating from the protection of foreign investment within the host state.[138] It is a narrative of capital, export and import, and financial transactions among states. Modern international investment law is not solely based on the protection of foreign investment, but also on

[134] Eric Verhoogen, "How Labor Standards Can be Good for Growth," *Harvard Business Rev* (online), April 27, 2016 (pdf), verhoogenHBR Apr 2016.pdf.

[135] Subedi (2020); Dolzer and Schrever (2012).

[136] Eichengreen (2019).

[137] Lipson (1985).

[138] Miles (2015).

the protection of the legitimate rights of the host state, and to address environmental, labour and human rights issues.[139]

Protection of investment in foreign countries is claimed on the principle of International Minimum Standard of Treatment (MST).[140] The minimum standard of treatment is a part of customary international law which is reflected in BITs and decisions of the International Centre for Settlement of International Disputes (ICSID).[141] The application of minimum standards required fair justice and non-discriminatory treatment to alien property by the host state. In situations of appropriation or nationalisation of foreign property, they can ask for reasonable compensation to be considered.

Sometimes, investor countries emphasise on a diplomatic settlement of investment disputes arising out of appropriation. Even investor countries intervene with armed forces to protect the property of their nationals. Developing countries opposed any kind of similar intervention by foreign investors in the host country in the name of minimum standard of treatment.

Latin American jurist Carlos Calvo of Argentina articulated the doctrine of economic sovereignty of state in 1868. Calvo re-opened the window of fresh air for peoples of the third world, as he argued that the foreign investors would not be entitled to superior rights and claims in comparison to their own nationals. In the case of appropriation or nationalisation of property, they are at liberty to approach the court of the host country for reasonable compensation.[142]

B. **Regulation of Foreign Investment**

After World War II, a new era began in the political economy of the world. The process of decolonisation strengthened the voice of Asia, Africa and Latin America. They collectively put their efforts in the United Nations and other international fora for the regulation of foreign investment and world trade. In 1962, the General Assembly adopted a resolution on the permanent sovereignty over natural resources.[143] Another resolution was adopted by the General Assembly on the charter of economic rights and duties.[144] These resolutions strike a balance between state sovereignty and appropriation of foreign investment. The host state does not enjoy a free hand when it comes to the nationalisation of foreign property. There must be compelling reasons, public interest or common good for nationalisation. In addition, the host state cannot be deprived of redressal and compensation. In other words, the investor country has no overriding power over the host country's sovereignty, their natural resources or

[139] Jennings and Watts (1996); Crawford (2019); Paparinskis (2013); Blandford (2017).

[140] Tudor (2008).

[141] Shea (1955); Freeman (1946).

[142] UNGA Res. 1803 (XVII) (14 December 1962).

[143] UNGA Res. 3281 (XXIX) (12 December 1974).

[144] Texaco Overseas Petroleum Co. v. The Government of the Libyan Arab Republic, Arbitral Award, 9 January 1977, 17 ILM 2 (1978).

the process of decision-making. The General Assembly resolutions constitute soft international law, which reflect the customs and practice of the state.[145]

Apart from General Assembly resolutions, the World Bank established the International Centre on the Settlement of Investment Disputes (ICSID) in 1965.[146] It provided access to the state and corporations in matters related to investment disputes. NGOs were also allowed to submit amicus curiae briefs to ICSID. The World Bank further created the Multilateral Investment Guarantee Agency (MIGA) 1985 for the protection of investment in developing countries. Objectives of MIGA are to promote investment and capital flow into developing economies.

C. **Bilateral Investment Treaties**

The 1960s proved to be a turning point in the annals of international investment law. In 1959, Germany concluded two bilateral investment treaties (BITs)—one with Pakistan and the other with the Dominican Republic.[147] Eventually, the movement of BITs expedited and spread throughout the world. At present, there are 3000 BITs. They are improved versions of the bilateral treaties of friendship, commerce and navigation (FCN) of the eighteenth and nineteenth centuries. BITs have protected the investments of the state, corporations and individuals. For this purpose, they have included dispute settlement provisions in their bilateral treaties.

BITs are core legal documents of the international investment regime. These are concluded between the developed and the developing economies. BITs' contents are the same, irrespective of parties. They are guided by the principles of international investment law.[148] BITs are concluded from the free will of parties. Developing economies are motivated to attract foreign direct investment (FDI). They agree to pay adequate and prompt compensation in case of appropriation of foreign property. Moreover, both the parties of BITs agree to resolve their dispute through ICSID or ICJ. The existence of BITs fills the gap of international investment law because there is no comprehensive multilateral framework for the regulation of foreign investment.[149]

D. **TRIMs Agreement**

International investment was a major issue during the Uruguay Round negotiation.[150] The Final Act of the Uruguay Round adopted an agreement on Trade Related Investment Measures (TRIMs agreement) along with GATT 1994. The TRIMs agreement was just a retract of the GATT 1947 and did not elaborate the international investment framework. The agreement was not to liberalise investment around the world, even though the FDI flow has increased on an unprecedented basis since the 1980s.

---

[145] Schreuer and Malintoppi (2001).

[146] Vandevelde (2005–2006).

[147] R. Dolzer and C. Schreves, *supra note* 135; Vandevelde et al. (1998).

[148] Mosoti (2005).

[149] Mashayekhi and Gibbs (1999).

[150] Low and Subramanian (1995).

The United States, European Union, Canada and Japan perused a separate investment agenda at the Uruguay Round negotiations. But developing countries did not subscribe to the developed worlds' viewpoint.[151] Developing countries want full autonomy in their decision-making so that they can deal with corporations and developed economies as per their investment needs.[152]

The purpose of the TRIMs agreement is:

> to promote liberalisation and to facilitate investment across international frontiers, so as to increase the economic growth of all trading partners, particularly developing countries. All members while ensuring free competition[153]

Article 2 clause 1 of the TRIMs agreement lays down that all TRIMs agreements be consistent with GATT Article III: national treatment; and Article XI: prohibition of quantitative restriction on imports and exports. An illustrative list of inconsistent investment measures to the GATT Articles III and XI are appended as Annexure to the TRIMs agreement.[154]

GATT provisions deal with exceptions,[155] transparency[156] and the settlement of disputes.[157] These provisions are applicable to the TRIMs agreements. A Committee on TRIMs was also established to monitor its implementation.[158] The Committee has extended an opportunity to the members to consult investment matters with each other.

The TRIMs agreement covered only goods and left the services part out. Similarly, TRIMs limited itself to states and leftover corporations and NGOs. Corporations are major players in international trade and the investment system, while NGOs monitor the outcome of international investment within the context of human rights, environment and labour standards.

E. **Towards Multilateral Agreement on Investment**

The TRIMs agreement neither laid down investment policy nor did it provide regulatory framework for international investment. This space was occupied by BITs. The Organisation for Economic Co-operation and Development (OECD) made an attempt to prepare a Multilateral Agreement on Investment (MAI) in May, 1995.[159] The negotiations for MAI were conducted between members of the OECD, and it was expected that in due course developing countries would accede to it. But that never ended up happening because it lacked political support in Europe and beyond.

---

151 Kwaw (1991).

152 Morosini et al. (2018); Preamble of the Agreement on Trade Related Investment Measures, TRIM agreement, *Final Act of the Uruguay Round of Multilateral Trade Negotiations*, Annex 1A, 15 April 1994, 1867 UNTS 14; 33 ILM 1143 (1994).

153 Ibid., Article 2(1).

154 TRIMs agreement, Article 3 vide GATT, Articles XX and XXI.

155 TRIMs agreement, Article 6 vide GATT, Articles X.

156 TRIMs agreement, Article 8 vide GATT, Articles XXII and XXIII.

157 TRIMs agreement, Article 7.

158 Fitz Gerald et al. (1999).

159 Kobrin (1998); Mabey (1999).

It was only in the 1990s when NGOs actively engaged with international investment. There were 30 NGOs who participated in the OECD negotiation. They succeeded in mobilising people against the MAI as a threat to state sovereignty, environment, core labour standards and human rights.[160]

NGOs such as AFL-CIO, Amnesty International, Australian Conservation Foundation, Friends of the Earth International, Oxfam International, Public Citizen, Sierra Club, Third World Network, United Steel Workers of America, Western Governors Association and World Development Movement collectively called a halt to OCED negotiation on MAI, consequently deferring it to October, 1998.[161] OCED never revived MAI negotiations in the end.

Thus, the MAI framework task was undertaken by the WTO. NGOs continuously opposed the framework because they held that "government policies and negotiating strategies have been captured by the big corporate lobbies of the major countries".[162]

In 2001, the WTO ministerial conference was held in Doha, Qatar. This initiated the Doha Round on the formation of MAI, following the ministerial conference. The Doha Round covered international trade, investment, competition, labour standards, environment, transparency and other related issues, but that had not been concluded so far. The WTO remains the preferable venue for the MAI framework negotiations.

In the meantime, International Investment Agreements (IIAs) proliferated in the form of bilateral BITs, region specific-NAFTA, Trans-Pacific Partnership (TTP), Regional Comprehensive Economic Partnership (RCEP), and subject-specific International Energy Charter and others. In addition, FDI stocks increased in the global GDP from 6 to 34% between 1970 and 2013.[163] International investment is a driving force behind world economic development. Therefore, a multilateral investment agreement is required for an equilibrium between investment, protection and regulation.

There is a need to learn from OECD's failure of MAI negotiations,[164] to get rid of them, and to pursue the Doha Round on international investment law. NGOs' campaign to 'Stop MAI' was launched in 1997 after the OECD negotiation draft was posted on the internet by NGOs for public disclosure. As estimated, 600 NGOs from nearly 70 countries were involved in the 'Stop MAI' campaign. This was a larger collision of civil societies, human rights NGOs, environmental NGOs, developmental NGOs, faith-based NGOs—Quakers and Churches, trade unions and even some political parties.[165]

---

[160] www.Aflcio.org, American Federation of Labor and Congress of Industrial Organizations is the largest trade union of the United States, which are affiliated with ITUC.

[161] Walter (2001); Graham (1998).

[162] Shan (2015).

[163] WTO-Ministerial Conference, first was held in Singapore, 9–13 December 1996 (Singapore MC I/1996) followed by Geneva MC11/1998; Seattle MCIII/1999; Doha MCIV/2001; Cancun MCV/2003; Hong Kong MCVI/2005; Geneva MCVII/2009; Geneva MCVIII/2011; Bali MCIX/2013; Nairobi MCX/2015; Buenos Aires MCXI/2017; Geneva XII/2022.

[164] Kurtz (2002); UNCTAD (1999).

[165] Gallus and Peterson (2006); Evered (1996).

The OECD finally stopped preparatory work on MAI. In the age of internet and social media, secrecy does not pay. Only transparency had the power to win over public support. Thereby, the Doha Round addressed the concerns of host states as well as that of FDI states, which are related to investment liberalisation. They narrate the benefits and consequences of economic globalisation in such a way that it could match with NGOs' narratives and field experience. Allowing NGO activism does not mean that they occupy a high place at the negotiating tables. These high tables are already occupied by state representatives. At most, NGOs provide them information and grassroots feedback. State representatives, in turn, can accommodate NGOs' concerns in the international investment regime.

5 Protection of NGOs Cross-Border Funding

In the international investment regime, corporations are the main actors. Their investment in foreign countries is protected under the international investment law, either directly or through their nationality.

There is no need to say that corporations are legally entitled to profit-making whilst NGOs are not-for-profit. Both are engaged in economic activities but with vastly different objectives. But NGOs are not explicitly covered under international investment law. According to Lloyd H. Mayer,

> NGOs' cross-border funding is needed for the protection of business under international investment treaties.[166]

NGOs receive cross-border funding to meet the expenses of their projects and humanitarian work. Some countries do not have traditions of philanthropy or public charity. NGOs located in the developing world are burdened with the paucity of resources and funds. This forces them to accept overseas funding.[167] The protection of their limited funds is a prerequisite to freely pursue their non-profit objectives.

NGOs' activities are broadly classified into two categories, i.e. advocacy and service providing. As far as service, humanitarian action and relief are concerned, there are no hurdles from state authorities. But when NGOs engage in advocacy to hold the government accountable or protest against public policy and decisions, then the state blocks their funding, sinks civic space and crushes their endeavours.

The sinking of civic space, blocking of cross-border funding, and the discouragement of non-profit activism is the life story of an NGO. This is more visible in authoritative states. Most regions including China, Russia, India, Central Asia, Eastern Europe, Latin America and Africa are involved in the pushback of NGOs within their jurisdiction.[168] India passed the Foreign Contribution Regulation Act (FCRA)

---

[166] Mayer (2018).

[167] Roth (2016).

[168] FCRA Act, No.42/2010, and FCRA Rule 2010 as amended in 2015, Minister of State for Home Affairs of India, *made the statement in the Council of State* (Upper House of Parliament) dated 25 July 2018; Times of India, 26/07/2018, p. 9.

2010 for controlling cross-border funding. Since then, over 13,000 NGOs have been deprived of overseas funding. The Indian Government felt the move necessary for national security and combating terrorism.[169] Being the world's largest democracy, India's non-profit cross-country funding was pushed back appreciably. Furthermore, there is no need to say anything about countries like Russia, China, Turkey, Egypt, Hungary, Belarus, Kazakhstan, Brazil, Ethiopia, Venezuela and many more.

A. **NGOs in Investment Treaties**

The international investment regime has successfully protected transnational business so far. Whether NGOs can avail themselves of the same for their protection of cross border-funding, is the question?[170] This issue has two dimensions. The first is related to the concept and prescription of international investment law, and the second to the investment dispute settlement mechanism. The infrastructure of international investment is inclusive, and NGOs have their standing within this investment regime.

Traditionally, the protection and regulation of foreign funding has been done through the Treaty of Friendship, Commerce and Navigation (FCN) from 1778 to 1960. The United States concluded that the FCN treaties on bilateral basis with other countries. FCN provided the nationals of the United States the right to engage in all types of commercial, industrial, and financial activities to gain from another country or treaty party.[171] NGOs are also protected within these FCN treaty provisions.[172]

Presently, BITs provide protection to FDIs and the cross-border funding of NGOs. BITs also cover private persons in addition to states and facilitate NGOs and corporations to access international investment arbitration tribunals. Historically, BITs have given a broad meaning to investment that encompasses property, companies, industrial property rights, business, etc. They adopted the concept of investment in all-inclusive ways.[173] The term investment has not been explicitly defined within international investment treaties because it is a sensitive matter which has a direct nexus with the jurisdiction of the ICSID. Another reason is the diversion of view-points among developed and developing economies.[174]

B. **The Concept of Investment and Inclusion of NGOs**

The definition of investment is derived from multiple sources such as Article 25 of the ICSID convention,[175] provisions of BITs' drafting history of investment treaties and arbitral decisions of investment tribunals. The concept of investment has a direct bearing on its application in the protection of cross-border funding of NGOs. The ICSID convention Article 25, clause 4 provides:

---

[169] Nick Gallus and Luke E. Peterson, *supra note* 165 p. 528.

[170] Coyle (2013).

[171] Ibid., pp. 343–344; Lloyd H. Mayer, *supra note* 166, p. 1224.

[172] Salacuse (1990); Salacuse (2015).

[173] Mortenson (2010a, b).

[174] *The Convention on the Settlement of Investment Disputes Between States and Nationals of Other States* (ICSID) signed on 18 March 1965, entered into force on 14 October 1966, 575 UNTS 159.

[175] ICSID Convention, Article 25(4).

> Any contracting state may, at the time of ratification, acceptance or approval of this Convention or at any time thereafter, notify the Centre (ICSID) of the class or classes of disputes which it would or would not consider submitting to the jurisdiction of the Centre.[176]

In the *Salini v. Morocco* case[177] 2001, the ICSID tribunal identified four characteristics of investment, i.e. (1) contribution must be made in the host country; (2) a certain duration of performance of the contract; (3) participation in the risk of transaction; and (4) contribution to economic development of the host state. These were further refined in subsequent cases[178] by the ICSID tribunal. The investment disputes are scrutinised by arbitrary tribunals on the criteria laid down in the *Salini* case because simple commercial transactions like the sale of goods cannot be entertained by the ICSID tribunal. ICSID is meant only for investment disputes between states and nationals of other states.

BITs define investment in a broad sense to encompass every kind of asset. These assets include traditional property rights, intellectual and industrial property rights, and concession or similar rights. The basic idea of the BITs' definition of investment is to promote freedom of trade, receive foreign funds and provide protection to it. The risk is an intrinsic part of profit or gain, thereby connecting it to investment law.

The ICSID convention focused on the consent of the parties to entertain investment disputes. It did not feel the need to define investment. The purpose of the convention was to resolve investment disputes amicably.

BITs treaties go as far as to include all kinds of assets, economic activities and commercial transactions, even. But the ICSID tribunal restricted up to financial commitment, risk, duration and significant contribution to the host state's development. Profit, gain and return are not the indispensable criteria to determine investment. The preamble of the ICSID envisaged the role of private investment in the host state's economic development. According to C.H. Schreuer,

Economic development does not limit itself to the GDP alone, but it includes overall development encompassing human resources, political and social development, and environmental protection.[179]

There are various kinds of approaches towards investment. Developed countries want a wide scope of application while developing countries prefer to limit the scope and narrow down the definition of investment.[180] The contemporary model of BITs also explores the definition and scope of application of the international investment law. This is reflected in the United States model of BIT 2012[181] and

---

[176] Salini Costruttori S.P.A. and Italstrade S.P.A. v. Kingdom of Morocco, 23 July 2001, ICSID case No.ARB/00/4, 42 ILM 609 (2004).

[177] Phoenix Action Ltd. v. The Czech Republic, award on 15 April 2009, ICSID case No. ARB/06/5; Joy Mining Machinery Ltd. v. Arab Republic of Egypt award on 6 August 2004, ICSID Case No. ARB/03/11; Saba Fakes v. Republic of Turkey, award on 14 July 2010, ICSID case No. ARB/07/20.

[178] Hwang and Chang (2011).

[179] Schreuer (2009).

[180] Mortenson (2010a, b); Sattorova (2012).

[181] 2012 US Model of BIT, the text available at 2009–2017.state.gov/e/eb/ ifd/bit/index.htm, press release April 2012.

the Indian model of BIT 2016. The United States has revised the 2004 BIT model but it has not changed substantively.[182] However in the present, text transparency, public participation, environmental protection and labour have been added. In the formation of BIT model 2012, the United States government received extensive inputs from NGOs. Other stakeholders, i.e. the Congress, companies, academics, etc., also rendered their suggestions. NGOs welcomed the added linkages of investment in the 2012 model.[183]

The Indian model of BIT 2016[184] covered only the enterprises which carry out a real and substantive business in the host state. It is a narrow definition, and it is moving away from an asset-based definition of investment.[185] It required exhausting local remedy or waiting up to at least five years for a move to ICSID.

NGOs encounter several hurdles in their international operations. The host state pushes them back from their economic activities.[186] A special study was conducted on NGO-CARE International. CARE was engaged in food distribution and relief work in Haiti, Ethiopia and Somalia, and in Mexico 1970, 1980 and 1985, respectively. It was found that host states created hurdles by diverting relief material and funds.[187] These are not isolated cases, and there are many more to be found in other parts of the globe.

NGOs channelise funds which are received from donors of their home countries to improve public health and living standards of people in the host state. Business investment in the host state runs parallelly to NGO funding, except that the later does not engage in profit-making.[188] Therefore, they deserve equal treatment and protection of their assets. NGOs should be recognised in international investment law and provided access to the ICSID.[189]

C. **NGOs' Access to the ICSID**

The arbitral tribunal has three kinds of jurisdiction—temporal, personal and material. BITs are generally implemented in a perceptive way, therefore, they cover disputes arising after a treaty comes into force. ICSID entertains disputes between the state and nationals of other states. This means it entertains individuals, corporations and NGOs in addition to states. Material jurisdiction relates to investment disputes. The ICSID or arbitral tribunal deals with investment disputes between parties. The parties are known as investors and host states. An investment case can be brought either to ICSID or the tribunal under UNCITRAL Rules or the International Chamber of Commerce—arbitral tribunal laid down as per provisions under BITs and other investment treaties. The consent of parties is necessary for filing the case.

---

[182] Kantor (2012).

[183] De Rosa (2012).

[184] Ranjan et al. (2018).

[185] Thadikkaran (2015).

[186] Nick Gallus and L. E. Peterson, *supra note* 169, p. 527.

[187] MacKenzie (1993).

[188] Timothy C. Evered, Ibid., pp. 153–179.

[189] Nick Gallus and L.E. Peterson, *supra note* 186, p. 529.

Traditionally, investment has had connotations of commercial activities. Thus, it does not encompass economic development of the host state. NGOs' cross-border funding certainly contributes to economic development, social progress, protection of the environment and the promotion of labour standards. Therefore, they are entitled to fair and equal treatment.[190]

There are significant hurdles for NGOs to bring claims before the arbitral tribunals as arbitrating such cases against the host state ends up angering the later. This creates problems in the performance of their humanitarian duties. Pursuing litigation is a costly affair for NGOs. There are certain ways to avert this expensive affair. Firstly, the tribunal can waive charges or reduce the fees. Secondly, advocates can do pro bono work or arrange for third-party funding. In the *Philip Morris v. Uruguay* case in 2016,[191] the US-based Campaign for Tobacco-Free Kids provided funds to Uruguay to pursue the case. This third-party financial mechanism may replicate some other instances as well.

There are three options available to NGOs to protect their cross- border funding and humanitarian activities. One, they can opt for the court of the host state, wherever the judicial system is independent and effective. Two, they can choose a diplomatic route through their home state and, three, they can reach out to the ICSID and other arbitral tribunals, as a final option. It is necessary for NGOs to be aware of available redressal mechanisms and seek justice within the international investment regime.

BITs explicitly extended ICSID jurisdiction for NGOs. The Norwegian model of BIT included profit and non-profit activities and assets within the realm of investment so that the NGOs could access the arbitral tribunal.[192] Corporations are already making their claims before the ICSID, with this route being open to NGOs as well.

6 Conclusion

NGOs have been actively engaging with the business world since the 1990s. They emphasise on business ethics in this era of globalisation. The world economy has rapidly integrated. Parallelly, the internet has greatly assisted NGOs in establishing connectivity with their counterparts around the world. In this globalised structure, there are four major actors, i.e. states, corporations, NGOs, and IGOs like the World Bank, IMF, WTO, UNCTAD.

International economic law emerged as a separate corpus of international law. World trade and international investment law are two prominent areas of this discipline. Their primary task is the development and regulation of the world economy.

[190] Lloyd H. Mayer, *supra note* 166, pp. 1240–1241.

[191] Philip Morris Brand Sarl, Philip Morris Products S.A. (Switzerland) and Abal Hermanos S.A. v. Oriental Republic of Uruguay, ICSID case No. ARB/10/7 file requested for arbitration on 19 February 2010 and decision awarded on 26 September 2016.

[192] Norway Model BIT 2015, Article 2(1), https://investmentpolicyhub.unctad.org/.

This task was furthered by the United Nations Conference on Trade and Employment 1946–1948. It was created by the General Assembly. Its preparatory committee consulted with NGOs when it came to the formation of international trade law. The first global step was taken up by the Conference of Trade and Development, as it recommended to remove tariffs and trade barriers from exports and imports. This General Agreement on Tariffs and Trade (GATT) 1947 was adopted and embraced worldwide.

NGOs learned from this experience and used it in the Uruguay Round 1987–1994. The Uruguay Round adopted the Final Act as a package deal, establishing the WTO and Dispute Settlement Understanding. NGOs associated with the WTO-highlighted trade linkage issues such as human rights, environment and labour standards.

International investment law is developed by BITs, ICSID, and the TRIMs agreement of the Uruguay Round, but it is still waiting for a comprehensive and packaged deal of the MAI framework. The international regimes of trade and investment are based on the principle of fair and equal treatment but the two areas are separate and distinct in their history, objectives and context.[193] Trade and investment are closely connected to the liberal economy and free market. Trade law deals with the reduction of tariffs and other barriers of exports and imports, whereas investment law is focused on economic development. Investment has a greater effect on society in comparison to trade. Investment is employed in the production process of large projects, and is done for long durations.[194] World trade linkage with respect to human rights, environment, public health, morality and business behaviour is also applicable on international investment.

Investment is protected by international investment law, which already covers corporations and needs further extension to encompass cross-border funding of NGOs. States are attracted to Foreign Direct Investment (FDI) for their economic development and job-creation. Thereby, they adopt the route of BITs and protect investments within the host states. That attraction of NGOs' cross-border funding is not visible.

In Latin America, Andean countries such as Bolivia, Chile, Ecuador and Peru made a decision, i.e. 24/1970, which discouraged foreign funding. But later on, they realised that foreign investments are imperative for their national development and prosperity. Therefore, they adopted a subsequent resolution, i.e. 220/1987, relaxing 24/1970 to welcome foreign funds.[195]

NGOs must learn from the foregoing instance and they should highlight and sustain their contribution based on credibility, data and research. Only then, will they be able to mobilise cross-border funding in the host state and receive the guarantee of

---

[193] DiMascio and Pauwelyn (2008).

[194] Ibid., p. 81.

[195] Murphy (1990).

protection within their jurisdiction. States welcome service NGOs engaged in humanitarian action and relief work. Generally, they are partners of government development projects. But advocacy NGOs are unwelcome everywhere because they highlight public policy issues and hold governments accountable to their people. Therefore, the cross-border funding of NGOs should be protected under the international legal regime explicitly.

References

Akehursts L (2019) Modern introduction to international law. In: Orakhelashvili A (eds) Routlege, New York, p 407

Aslton P (1980) Linking trade and human. German YB Int L 23:126–158

Austin JE, Seitanidi MM (2012) Collaborative value creation: a review of partnering between non-profit and business: part-I: value creation spectrum and collaborative stage. Non-Profit Volunt Sect Q 41(5):726–758

Bayne N (2000) Why did Seattle fail? Globalisation and politics of trade. Govt Oppos 35(2):131–151

Bekiashev KA, Serebriakov V (eds) (1981) International marine organization. Springer, New York, pp 140–148

Bernascom-Osterwalder N et al (2006) Environment and trade: a guide to WTO jurisprudence. Earthscan Publications, London

Bhattarai K (2016) Impact of foreign aid on growth and trade. J Econ Devt Stud 4(3):41–55

Blandford AC (2017) The history of fair and equitable treatment before the second world war. ICSID Rev 32(2):287–303

Bodansky D, Lawrence JC (2009) Trade and environment. In: Bethlehem D et al (eds) Oxford handbook of international law. Oxford University Press, Oxford, pp 7–8

Boldizzoni F (2015) Routledge handbook of global economic history. Routledge, New York

Brenan J, Jaworski PM (2016) Market without limits: moral values and commercial interests. Routledge, New York

Brenkert GG, Beauchap TL (eds) (2009) Oxford handbook of business ethics. Oxford University Press, Oxford, p 4

Brummer C (2010) Why soft law dominates international finance and not trade. J Int Econ L 13(3):623–643

Chapman A (2009) Globalization, human rights and the social determinants of health. Bioethics 82(2):97–111

Charnovitz S (2011) What is international economic law? J Int Econ L 14(3):3–22

Chatterjee SK (1991) The charter of economic rights and duties of the states: an evolution after 15 years. Int Comp L Q 40(3):669–684

Chernovitz S (1987) The influence of international labour standards on the trading regime: a historical review. Int Lab Rev 126(5):565–584

Chrnovitz S, Wickham J (1995) Non-governmental organisations and the original international trade regime. J World Trade 29(5):111–122

Copeland BR, Taylor MS (2003) Trade and the environment: theory and evidence. Princeton University Press

Cottier T et al (2012) Human rights and international trade. Oxford University Press, Oxford

Coyle JF (2013) The treaty of friendship, commerce, and navigation in the modern era. Columbia J Trans L 51:302–359

Crawford J (ed) (2019) Brownlie's principles of public international law, 9th edn. Oxford University Press, pp 613–626

Dam K (1970) The GATT: law and international economic organization. University Chicago Press, Chicago
Darko E (2014) Private actors and NGO engagement. Overseas Development Institute, pp 1–15
De Rosa P (2012) The new 2012 U.S. model BITs staying the course. Kluwer Arbitration Blog
Desouza R, Dutta M (2008) Global and local networking for HIV/AIDS prevention: the case of the Saathii e-forum. J Health Commun 13(4):326–344
DiMascio N, Pauwelyn J (2008) Non-discrimination in trade and investment treaties: worlds apart or two sides of the same coin? Am J Int L 102(1):48–98
Dolzer R, Schrever C (2012) Principles of international investment law, 2nd edn. Oxford University Press, Oxford
Droz GAL (1994) A comment on the role of the hague conference on private international law. Law Contemp Probl 57(3):3–11
Eden L (2004) Globalization and NGOs: transforming business, government and society. J Int Bus Stud 33:564–566
Eichengreen B (2019) Globalizing capital: a history of the international monetary system, 3rd edn. Princeton University Press
Esteve MP (2011) WTO rules and practices for transparency and engagement with civil society organisations. In: Working Paper, IISD, Geneva, pp 1–22
Esty DC (2000) Why the world trade organisation needs environmental NGOs. ICTSD, Geneva, pp 1–24
Evered TC (1996) Foreign investment issues for international non-governmental oranisations: international health projects in China and the former soviet union. Buffalo J Int L 3:153–179
Farias RDS (2013) Mr GATT: Eric Wyndham white and the quest for trade liberalization. World Trade Rev 12(3):463–486
Freeman AV (1946) Recent aspects of the calvo doctrine and the challenge to international law. Am J Int L 40(1):121–147
Freeman RE (1990) Business ethics: a literary view. Soc Respon 16:5–13
Friedman TL (1999) The Lexus and olive tree: understanding globalization, forrar. Straus and Giroux Publishing House, New York
Gallagher P (2005) The first ten years of the WTO: 1995–2005. Cambridge University Press, Cambridge
Gallin D (2000) Trade Unions and NGOs: a necessary partnership for social development. UNRISD, New York, pp 1–33
Gallus N, Peterson LE (2006) International investment treaty protection of NGOs. Arbitration Int 22(4):527–548
Gaudet M (1982) The international chamber of commerce: court of arbitration. Proc Am Soc Int 76:172–175
Gerald F et al (1999) The development implications on the multilateral agreement on investment. OECD Publications, Paris, pp 1–55
Gomez EJ (2018) Civil society in global health policy making: a critical review. Global Health 14:1–11
Gould SJ (1995) The Buddhist perspective on business ethics: experiential exercises for exploration and practice. J Bus Ethics 14(1):63–70
Graham EM (1998) Regulatory takings, supernational treatment and the multilateral agreement on investment: issues raised by non-governmental organizations. Cornell Int L J 33(3):599–614
Grieg-Gren M, Wilson E (2007) NGOs as market actors. IIED, London, pp 1–7
Hale A (2004) Beyond the barriers: new forms of labour internationalism. Devt Pract 14(1–2):158–162
Harris R, Moon G (2005) GATT article XX and human rights: what do we know from the first 20 years? Melbourne J Int L 16:1–52
Hogenboom B et al (2003) Cross-border activism and its limits: Maxican environmental organisations and the United States. Centre for Latin American Research and Documentation, Amsterdam, pp 1–32

Hudec RE (1995) The GATT legal system and world trade diplomacy. Praeger, New York
Hwang M, Chang JFL (2011) Definition of 'investment': a voice from the eye of the storm. Asian J Int L 1:99–129
Iwin DA (1995) The GATT in historical perspective. Am Econ Rev 85(2):323–328
Jackson JH et al (1992) What's needed for the GATT after Uruguay round? Proc Am so'ty Int L 86:69–87
Jarvis LM (2001) Women's rights and the public morals exception of GATT Article 20. Michigan J Int L 22(1):219–238
Jennings SR, Watts SA (1996) Oppenhum's international law, 9th edn. Pearson, pp 911–927
Kantor M (2012) Little has changed in the new US model bilateral investment treaty. ICSID Rev 27(2):335–378
Kellerson H (1998) The ILO declaration of 1998 on fundamental principles and rights: a challenge for the future. Int Lab Rev 137(2):223–228
Kimaro AE (2013) The role of NGOs in lobbying and advocacy for market access by smallholder farmers: a case of Mkuranga District. Sokoin University of Agriculture, Tanzania, pp 1–81
Kobrin SJ (1998) The MAI and the clash of globalizations. For Policy 112:97–109
Koul AK (1977) The legal framework of United Nations conference on trade and development in world trade. Springer, Netherland
Kraak V et al (2011) Balancing the benefits and risks of public-private partnerships to address the global double burden of malnutrition. Public Health Nutr 15(3):503–517
Ku J, Yoo J (2013) Globalisation and sovereignty. Berkeley J Int L 31(1):210–235
Kurtz J (2002) NGOs, the internet and international economic policy making: the failure of the OECD multilateral agreement on investment. Melbourne J Int L 3(2):213–246
Kwaw EMA (1991) Trade related investment measures in the Uruguay round: towards a GATT for investment. NCJ Int L Com Reg 16(2):309–349
Langille BA (1997) Eight ways to think about international labour standards. J World Trade 31:27–53
Leebron DW (2002) Linkages. Am J Intl L 96(1):5–27
Lipson C (1985) Standing guard: protecting foreign capital in the nineteenth and twentieth centuries. University of California Press
Low P, Subramanian A (1995) TRIMs in the Uruguay round: an unfinished business. In: Vandevelde K et al (eds) The Uruguay round and the developing economies. World Bank Publications, Washington DC, pp 413–434
Lowenfel AF (2002) International economic law. Oxford University Press, Oxford
Luetge C (ed) (2013) Handbook of the philosophical foundations of business ethics. Springer, New York
Mabey N (1999) Defending the legacy of rio: the civil society campaign against the MAI. In: Mayne R, Picciotto S (eds) Regulating international business: beyond the MAI. Palgrave Macmillan, London, pp 60–81
MacKenzie GW (1993) ICSID arbitration as a strategy for levelling the playing field between international non-governmental organisations and host states. Syracuse J Int L Com 19:177–234
Mackintosh M et al (2011) Can NGOs regulate medicines markets? Social enterprise in wholesaling, and access to essential medicines. Global Health 7(4):1–13
Madsen JB (2001) Trade barriers and collapse of world trade during the great depression. South Econ J 67(4):84–88
Margulis ME (2017) The forgotten history of food security in multilateral trade negotiations. World Trade Rev 16(1):25–57
Margulis ME (2018) The world trade organisation between law and politics: negotiating a solution for public stock holding for food security purposes. Trans Legal Theory 9(3–4):343–360
Marter A, Wandscheider T (2002) Role of NGOs and CBOs in markets in Uganda. Natural Resources Institute, New York, pp 1–36
Martin R et al (2018) Globalisation at a critical conjuncture? Cambridge J Relig Econ Soc 11:3–16
Martin M (2013) WTO dispute settlement understanding and development. Brill, Leiden

Mashayekhi M, Gibbs M (1999) Lessons from the Uruguay round negotiations on investment. J World Trade 33(6):1–26
Mason M (2003) The world trade regime and non-governmental organisations: addressing transnational environmental concerns. In: LSE Research Online Documents on Economics, London, 1–35
Mathews A (2014) Trade rules, food security and the multilateral trade negotiations. Eur Rev Agric Econ 41(3):511–535
Mayer LH (2018) Globalization without a safety net: the challenge of protecting cross-border funding of NGOs. Minnesota L Rev 102:1205–1271
McCrudden C, Davies A (2000) A perspective on trade and labour rights. J Int Econ L 3(1):43–62
Michaels R (2007) The true Lex Mercatoria: law beyond the state. Indiana J Global Legal Stud 14(2):447–468
Miles K (2015) The origin of international investment law: empire environment and the safeguarding of capital. Cambridge University Press
Mironska D, Zaborek P (2019) NGO-business collaboration: a comparison of organisational, social and reputation value from the NGO perspective in Poland. Non-Profit Volunt Sect Q 48(3):532–551
Morosini F et al (eds) (2018) Reconceptualizing international investment law from the global south. Cambridge University Press
Mortenson JD (2010a) The meaning of investment: ICSID's travaux and the domain of international investment law. Harvard Int L J 51(1):257–318
Mortenson JD (2010b) The meaning of 'investment': ICSID's Travaux and the domain of international investment law. Harvard Int L J 51(1):257–318
Mosoti V (2005) Bilateral investment treaties and the possibility of a multilateral framework on investment at the WTO: are poor economies caught in between. North West J Int L Bus 26(1):95–138
Murphy EE (1990) The andean decisions on foreign investment: an international matrix of national law. Int Law 24(3):643–654
Murphy H (2012) Rethinking the roles of non-governmental organisations at the world trade organization. Aust J Int Aff 66(4):468–485
Murphy S, Hansen-Kuhn K (2017) Counting the costs of agricultural dumping. IATP, Geneva, pp 1–14
Najam A et al (eds) (2007) Trade and environment: a resource book. IISD, Geneva
Nersesian RL (2009) International chamber of shipping and international shipping federation, pp 1–9
Norman W (2015) Rawls on markets and corporate governance. Bus Ethics Q 25(1):29–64
Norman W (2021) Business ethics. In: LaFallette H (ed) International encyclopedia of ethics. Wiley, New Jersey, pp 652–668
Olmstead CJ (1974) The international law association: a worldwide organisation for development and promotion of international law. In: Bos M (ed) Present state of international law and other essays. Spinger, New York, pp 3–9
Paparinskis M (2013) The international minimum standard and fair and equitable treatment. Oxford University Press
Pauwelyn J (2019) WTO dispute settlement post 2019: what to expect? What choice to make? J Int Econ L 22(3):297–321
Piketty T (2014) Capital in the twenty first century. Harvard University Press, Cambridge MA
Polaska S (2003) Trade and labor standards: a strategy for developing countries. Carnegie Endowment for International Peace
Prahalad CK (2019) The fortune at the bottom of the pyramid: eradicating poverty through profit (revised and, updated. Pearson, New Jersey
Ranjan P et al (2018) India's model bilateral investment treaty: are we too risk averse? Brookings Institute India Centre, New Delhi, 1–60

Reinisch A, Irgel C (2001) The participation of non-governmental organisations (NGOs) in the WTO dispute settlement system. Non-State Act Int 1(2):127–151
Remisova A, Lasakoya A (2018) On NGOs role in the development of business ethics in Slovakia. Ethics J Bus Econ 4(4):389–403
Ritchie M, Dawkins K (2000) WTO food and agricultural rules: sustainable agriculture and the human right to food. Minnesota J Int L 9(9):9–37
Rorden W et al (2016) The WTO in Narobi: the demise of the Doha development agenda and the future of the multilateral trading system. Global Pol 7(2):247–255
Roth K (2016) The great civil society choke-out. For Policy 12:1–6
Salacuse JW (1990) BIT by BIT: the growth of bilateral investment treaties and their impact on foreign investment in developing countries. Int Lawyer 24(3):655–675
Salacuse JW (2015) The law of investment treaties, 2nd edn. Oxford University Press
Sampson G (2005) The WTO and sustainable development. UN University Press, Tokyo
Sanchez MR (2006) Brief observations on the mechanism, for NGO participation in the WTO. SUR Int J Hum Rts 4:103–126. https://doi.org/10.1590/S1806-64452006000100007
Sattorova M (2012) Defining investment under the ICSID convention and BITs: of ordinary meaning, telos, and beyond. Asian J Int L 2:267–290
Schreuer CH, Malintoppi L (2001) The ICSID convention: a commentary. Cambridge University Press
Schreuer CH (2009) The ICSID convention: a commentary, 2nd edn. Cambridge University Press, p 14
Seidl-Hohenveldern S (1999) International economic law, 3rd edn. Kluwer Law International, The Hague, pp 39–42
Sen A (1993) Does business ethics make economic sense? Bus Ethics Q 3(1):45–54
Shan W (2015) Toward a multilateral or plurilateral framework on investment. ICTSD, Geneva, pp 1–15
Shea DR (1955) The calvo clause, a problem of inter-American and international law and diplomacy. University of Minnesota Press
Sinha M (2013) An evaluation of the WTO committee on trade and environment. J World Trade 47(6):1285–1322
Smith RD (2006) Trade and public health: facing the challenges of globalization. J Epidemiol Commun Health 60(8):650–651
Smith S, Shiffman J (2016) Setting the global health agenda: the influence of advocates and ideas on political priority for maternal and newborn survival. Soc Sci Med 166:86–93
Solomon R (1999) A better way to think about business: how personal integrity leads to corporate success. Oxford University Press, Oxford
Solomon RC (2004) Aristotle, ethics and business organisations. Organ Stud 25:1021–2043
Spooner D (2004) Trade Unions and NGOs: the need for cooperation. Devt Pract 14(1–2):19–33
Stiglitz J (2002) Globalisation and its discontents. W.W. Northon Publishing Co., New York
Stiglitz J (2003) Globalization and the economic role of state in the new millennium. Ind Corp Change 2(1):3–26
Subedi SP (2020) International investment law: reconciling policy and principle, 4th edn. Hart Publishing
Summers C (2001) The battle in Seattle: free trade, labor rights, and societal values. U Pa J Int Econ L 22(1):61–90
Suwa-Eisemamm A, Verdier T (2007) Aid and trade. Oxford Rev Econ Pol 23(3):481–507
Sykes AO (2003) International trade and human rights: an economic perspective. In: Working paper no. 188. University of Chicago, pp 1–34
Temu PE (1974) UNCTAD: its role and prospects. J Develop Areas 8(3):355–362
Thadikkaran M (2015) Model text for the Indian bilateral investment treaty: an analysis. National Univ Jurid Sci L Rev 8(1):31–42
Thompson RL et al (2007) Globalisation and benefit of trade. Chicago Fed Lett 236:1–4

Tudor I (2008) The fair and equitable treatment standard in the international law of foreign investment. Oxford University Press
UNCTAD (1999) Lesson from the MAI, UNDAC-UNCTAD/ITE/IIT/MISC
Vandevelde K et al (1998) UNCTAD: bilateral investment treaties in the mid-1990s. UN Publications, Geneva
Vandevelde KJ (2005–2006) A brief history of international investment agreements. J Int L Pol 12, 157–194
Walter A (2001) NGOs, business, and international investment: the multilateral agreement on investment. Seattle and beyond. Global Gover 7(1):51–73
Ward H (1996) Common but differentiated debates: environment, labour and the world trade organization. Int Camp LQ 45(3):592–632
Wilkinson MD (1996) Lobbying for fair trade: northern NGDOs, the European community and the GATT Uruguay round. Third World Quart 17(2):251–267
Wilkinson R, Scott J (2008) Developing countries participation in GATT: a reassessment. World Trade Rev 7(2):473–570
Winham GR (2009) The evolution of the world trading system: the economic and policy context. In: Bethlehem D et al (eds) Oxford handbook of international trade law. Oxford University Press, Oxford
Wood PR (2011) Junzi' and Rushang: a Confucian approach in business ethics in a contemporary Chinese context. Victoria University Melbourne, pp 1–17
Zajtay I (1978) The international association of legal science: its contribution to comparative law. Am J Comp L 26(3):441–445
Zamora S (1989) Is there customary international economic law? German YB Int'l L 32:9–42

Part IV
Recent Developments

Chapter 13
NGO Accountability

1 Introduction

The development and influence of the NGOs had some repercussions as their demand for accountability arose at the forefront. The role of NGOs in the making of law, setting of standards and global governance was more predominant in the 1990s. The demand for NGOs' accountability was made clear by the states, IGOs, corporations, academics and media, parallelly. In the beginning of the twentieth century, the media highlighted this urgent need through famous newspapers, magazines and research journals, carrying out the necessary news and views surrounding it.

The Economist carried out stories about NGO accountabilities, with titles such as: "Sins of the secular missionaries", "NGOs can get into bad ways because they are not accountable to anyone,"[1] Who guards the guardians?"[2] Other similar stories were carried out in the New York Times, with one title reading, "Holding Civic Groups Accountable", in its editorial:

> ... non-governmental organisations, or NGOs, are now part of the power structure too. They receive donations from the public and advocate policies that each group claims are in the public interest. As they become part of the established political landscape worldwide, the groups owe it to the public to be accountable and transparent themselves.[3]

Foreign Policy narrated the NGO campaign against the World Bank-funded dam project at Bujagali Falls, Uganda. The International River Network (IRN) NGO, based at Berkeley, California, opposed this dam project, and in co-ordination with the local NGOs, alleged that it caused the displacement of persons and harmed the environment. In keeping with the view of IRN and local NGOs, thus, the World Bank stopped donating funds for the project. Journalist Sebastian Mallaby visited the site

---

[1] The Economist, 29 January, 2009.

[2] The Economist, 20 September, 2003.

[3] The New York Times, 21 July, 2003.

P. Rai, *Non-Governmental Organisations and International Law*,
https://doi.org/10.1007/978-981-97-5469-4_13

and found that the claim of campaigns about environmental harm and displacement of persons were not sustainable.[4]

This report damaged the advocacy of NGOs' credibility. However, a response to this report was given by Peter Brosshard, International River Network (IRN); Mark Halle, European representative of IRN; International Institute of Sustainable Development; and Juliette Majot, former executive director of IRN, where they focused on the international advocacy network to project the voices of voiceless local people.[5]

Apart from the media highlights and academic queries, the states, IGOs and corporations had also raised questions pertaining to NGO accountabilities, because NGOs frequently demanded accountability from them. Obviously, these international actors also demanded the same of those who kept them in check.[6] NGOs are engaged either in advocacy or service-providing. When they engage in advocacy work they focus on standards, democratic values, people-participation and transparency. But NGOs primarily undertake accountability towards donors, they hardly engage with beneficiaries in their decision-making process.[7] This issue also highlighted NGO's responsible behaviour and accountability.

The NGOs engaged in service-providing are not substitutes to either governments or corporations. They are comparatively more resilient by nature and work easily in adverse situations. These organisations are mainly preoccupied with remaining accountable to donors and fundraisers, but they hardly pay proper attention to *downward* accountability and learning and improvement.[8]

Accountability players have taken voluntary initiatives to extend NGOs' accountability services. These accountability institutions are One World Trust,[9] Accountability,[10] the Global Rating Initiative,[11] Humanitarian Accountability Partnership International,[12] Charity Navigator,[13] Guidestar,[14] and NGO's Watch.[15] These have put their efforts to bring transparency and accountability to the network of NGOs. Such factors have brought clarity to the NGOs' mission, vision and fund-raising initiatives.

The issue of accountability intensified in the beginning of the twenty-first century, along with the growing numbers, influence and participation of NGOs in international law-making, setting of standards, implementation and the involvement in global

---

[4] Sebastian (2004).

[5] Ibid.

[6] Baur and Schmitz (2012); Zadex (2003), This article are drawn from the authors book, *The Civil Corporate Citizenship*, Earthscan Publishers, London 2001; www.accountability.org.uk.

[7] Slim (2002).

[8] Ebrahim (2005).

[9] www.oneworldtrust.org.

[10] www.accountability.org.

[11] www.globalratinginstitute.org.

[12] www.humanterianaccountabilitypartnership.in.

[13] www.charitynavigator.org.

[14] www.guidstar.org.

[15] www.ngowatch.org.

governance. Steve Charnovitz referred to *Rerum Novarum*, 1891, an official letter of the Pope written to the Bishops, that the private associations were far more common than before with respect to NGO accountability.[16] The Pope's official letter further stated that the states should thrust themselves into their peculiar concerns and their organisations, for things move and live by the spirit inspiring them, and may be killed by the rough grasp of a hand from without.[17]

NGOs' accountability is a noble idea but it should be designed, standardised and implemented in a spout of early guidelines and mandate as expressed in the Pope's letter written to Bishops for private associations or NGOs. The accountability of NGOs does not undermine the spirit, initiative and creative ideas to inculcate the democratic values, transparency and participation of people at large.

2 Concept of Accountability

The term accountability is used in the context of states, organisations, corporations and NGOs to denote their powers, activities and responsibilities to the people. The Merriam-Webster dictionary defines accountability as:

> the quality or state of being accountable; especially an obligation or willingness to accept responsibility or to account for one's actions.[18]

As per the ancient roots of accountability, it means record-keeping activities of government or related institutions. Accountability is—to be answerable to somebody who exercises power, assigns duties and delegates work. Accountability, in a narrow sense, is the maintenance of the accounts or records, and to carry out audit. Presently, it has acquired a broad connotation and encompasses ethics, values, transparency, responsibility, legitimacy and participation. In the context of NGOs' accountability, it has been understood by writers in a broader sense. Ruth W. Grant and Robert O. Keohane, have described accountability in the context of power-wielders' accountability and have examined its application with the states, multilateral organisations or IGOs, multi-national enterprises or corporations, NGOs and the trans-governmental network.[19]

> Accountability, as we use the term, implies that some actors have the right to hold other actors to a set of standards, to judge whether they have fulfilled their responsibility in light of these standards and to impose sanctions if they determined that these responsibilities have not been met.[20]

Grant and Koehane define the term accountability in the realm of power in world politics. It is more commonly used in business and private sectors, and they define

[16] Charnovitz (2005).

[17] Rerum novarum, 15 May 1891, available online.

[18] www.merriam-webster.com.

[19] Grant and Keohane (2005).

[20] Ibid., p. 29.

accountability with a set of stakeholders. In a corporation, accountability rests on a number of stakeholders including promoters, board members, shareholders, management, workers, consumers and communities. NGOs are neither a political institution nor a business organisation. They are perhaps, at the core, a social movement or civil society. Thereby, NGOs' accountabilities can be defined as a contractual way and are to be designed for implementing the mechanism accordingly.

There are four essential queries of accountability, that are to be addressed in an effective manner. These are as follows:

(1) Who is accountable?
(2) To whom?
(3) For what?
(4) And how?[21]

Who is accountable? Any person, group or institute who affects others, are certainly responsible. NGOs neither enjoy political powers nor economic resources but despite this, they have influence in world politics and community life. They are responsible and accountable for their activities and initiatives. NGO accountability is altogether different from the accountability of states, IGOs, corporations and business organisations'.[22] NGOs themselves face increasing scrutiny for their actions by a new set of watchdogs and donors.[23]

The accountability of NGOs has not been such a priority area thus far, with its emergence a recent phenomenon. The question of accountability is already applicable in the corporate segment on the basis of stakeholders and democratic values. It is an essential query pushed by the states, businesses, media, academia and community. This is the need of the hour and NGOs should respond to this with creative ideas.

NGOs' accountability is related to four questions, and they are: Who is accountable? To whom? For what? And how? The first question—who is accountable? Have they already been settled because NGOs similar to other international actors, states, IGOs, corporations, are also accountable to the world community. An academic study of 152 NGOs was conducted by Hans Peter Schmitz, Paloma Raggo and Tosca Brunovon Vijfeijken from 2006 to 2008.[24] These NGOs were working in five issue areas: peace and conflict-resolution, human rights, environmental protection, humanitarian relief and development.

The writers made queries to the representatives of these 152 NGOs about NGO accountability. They categorically asked their opinion on the following:

(1) What is accountability?
(2) Accountable to whom?
(3) Accountable how?

---

[21] Bendell (2006), Bendell et al. (2010).

[22] Wapner (2002).

[23] Dorthea Baur and Hans Peter Schmitz, *supra note* 6, pp. 9–21.

[24] Schmitz et al. (2011).

NGOs' representatives most frequently answer questions pertaining to finance-management, followed by the mission of the organisation, transparency and legal obligations, according to their understanding. This, per se, is the definition of accountability. Smaller NGOs gave priority to financial management, whilst larger NGOs preferred to give value to the mission statement of their organisation. Smaller NGOs did not have space and resources to think more broadly and encompass all essential elements with the exception of financial management.

Another query made is: accountable to whom? The representatives of the NGOs frequently mentioned donors, followed by the board and beneficiaries, to be accountable to. Smaller NGOs restricted their accountability to these three stakeholders: donors, board members and beneficiaries. Larger NGOs are more aware about the complex regime of accountability, and that various other stakeholders exist apart from donors, board members and beneficiaries.

The next query related to accountability is how. In other words, how does your organisation manage and strengthen accountability, what sort of measures and strategy do you prefer to be employed with? The representatives of an NGO most frequently mentioned audit: external and internal, followed by evaluation, outcomes of activities, policies, public disclosure of report and consultations; They felt this is how they are accountable to the stakeholders.

This was a comprehensive study that collected views, understanding and practices of accountability of NGOs, both small and large. This sample study's outcome firmly established that NGOs are well-prepared and willing to adopt strategy, standards, parameters and management practices to strengthen their accountability.

3 NGOs' Accountability Discourse

NGOs' accountability discourse is a very broad area. Hereby, some glimpses of conceptual aspects, practical methods and practices of NGOs are put forward. The question of NGOs' accountability arose in the discourse in the 1990s and intensified at the beginning of the twenty-first century. As the number of NGOs increased manifold for instance, in the beginning of the nineteenth century, there were 176 NGOs, and with the turn of the twentieth, there were nearly 38,000 NGOs. Along with the numbers, their influence and involvement increased in international law and global governance.[25]

The major actors of international law and global governance are states, IGOs, corporations and NGOs. From their very nature, powers and influence differ from each other substantively. For instance: states are power-wielders; IGOs also enjoy full delegated powers issued by the states; corporations have enormous economic power while NGOs do not command either political powers or economic resources, they only have influence, networking, social movement and last but not the least,

[25] Held and McGrew (2002).

they thrive with the support of public opinion. Thus, the discourses of accountability studied in political science, states and IGOs, economics and management, corporations are already well established.

The NGOs' accountability study is carried out in law and sociology. These are neither strict compartments nor altogether distinct entities. There are strong possibilities for the cross-learning of the accountability mechanism, strategy, standards and processes within its realm.[26] Paul Wapner said:

> That the questions of accountability are relevant at both the domestic and international level. When considering the questions of accountability, critics most often compare NGOs to states and then criticise NGOs for being unable to mimic state accountability in a democratic context.[27]

Paul Wapner reflects on the overstepping of state accountability. There are 60% of democratic governments across the world. For the remaining 40%, the question of state accountability does not arise. Even within democracies, however, there is no reason to question the depth and effectiveness of accountability. The state accountability in liberal democracies is based on elected representation, the constitution and an independent judiciary. As per Wapner's opinion, the gap between citizen concerns and government is so wide, that all major theories of the democratic state either highlight or have been taken to task for ignoring an accountability deficit. States' accountability is mainly visible within the domestic sphere, and, in limited way, in the international arena.

NGOs' accountability is more reflected at the international scale because they have international orientation and are focused on the areas of issue-based work. NGOs are very much responsible to their members, donors and the board. These are the internal layers on which NGOs are accountable. Besides, NGOs are responsible to their peer groups for collaborating and networking.

Ruth W. Grant and Robert O. Keohane examined the accountability of international actors, particularly states in global politics.[28] States exercise the power that is democratically accountable to the people. Those persons who are affected by the state's actions are entitled to be held accountable. Accountability of powers could be made either by democratic responsibility or business ethics and moral values. In democracy, people entrust power to the state and expect that power should be exercised on the basis of a set of standards and within the legal framework.

Grant and Keohane provide the two basic models—participation and delegation—which leads to different strategies and a mechanism of accountability. The delegate model is applicable in the case of IGOs because states explicitly authorise them to act on their behalf in the international arena. Therefore, states are the accountability holders of IGOs. For example, IMF, World Bank and WTO. States are themselves responsible through the system of participation and representation model, but that is workable only in a constitutional democracy, where an election process directly

[26] Jordan and Van Tuijl (2006); Edwards and Hulme (1996a, b); Ebrahim (2003a, b); Scholte (2011).

[27] Paul Wapner, *supra note* 22, p. 199.

[28] Ruth W. Grant and Robert O. Keohane, *supra note* 19, pp. 30–31.

facilitates citizens participation. For example United States, Britain, India and a number of other democracies.

Steve Charnovitz observed:

> Grant and Keohane offer some important insights regarding NGOs' accountability, a problem that they see arising because NGOs are among the powerful entities. in "World Politics".[29]

Therefore, unlike IGOs, NGOs have acquired their power without delegation or authorisation. They articulated standards by which other power-wielders may be held accountable. For instance, the International Organization for Standardization (ISO) and Social Accountability International (SAI)[30] are non-governmental entities that determined the norms of accountability for state and market. If NGOs' global accountability is examined at an international level then these yardsticks should be applied upon them.

The NGOs' accountability is limited to the donors and members, and only larger NGOs lay down procedures to define accountability in a broader context. NGOs' accountability is indeed a reputational accountability to the public and peer accountability.

Peter J. Spiro so expressed his views on the inner dynamics between power and accountability of NGOs. He said that whenever power is exercised, the questions of accountability are posed.[31] According to Paul Wapner: They (NGOs) have no armies, police or other coercive tools at their disposal. In many cases, the only thing they have is their reputation, and this rests on their credibility.[32] Historically, power is enjoyed by the states, but according to Jessica T. Mathew, a "power shift" occurs in a small way from state to non-state actors since NGOs are more prompt than governments who respond to new demands and situations. This is made possible through high technological information and communication facilities. Those are available easily to the non-state entities.[33]

Peter J. Spiro lays down two kinds of processes for NGOs' accountability. These are: (1) Internal Accountability and (2) External Accountability. Internal Accountability is related to members and staff, and board members are the lifeline of the NGOs, hence, management is accountable to them. Members support the NGOs' mission, contributing time and money. They have an easy passage to exit from NGOs when compared to the state, because members of the state, as citizens, cannot leave the state. When it comes to the state, there is a strong framework of accountability for its members or citizens, like vote rights, free speech, periodical elections, parliament and independent judiciary.[34]

External accountability is related to the system, whereas they work on international standards where they are part of standard settings. For example, Green Peace

---

[29] Steve Charnovitz, *supra note* 16, p. 14.

[30] Jem Bendell et al., "These Pages Have Been Regulated for You: Issues Arising from the Governance of Market by NGOs" *supra note* 21, pp. 129–156.

[31] Spiro (1995), (1996), (2002).

[32] Paul Wapner, "Defending Accountability in NGOs", *supra note* 27, at 203.

[33] Mathew (1997).

[34] Mulgan (2003).

International cannot accept funds from those donors who are involved in deforestation, the construction of dams or in the chemical and pesticide business. NGOs engaged in campaigning, networking and coalition for advocacy are accountable to NGOs' liaison committees and peer groups.

Benedict Kingsbury enquired about the legal framework of NGOs in which they are accountable, like other international actors. He made his queries with respect to "First Amendment Liberalism" or the First Amendment of the Constitution of United States (1787, 1791) in which freedom of association is guaranteed to the citizens of United States and followed subsequently, worldwide.

NGOs are responsible within the constitutional framework and in international rules, practices and understanding.[35] The problems of NGOs' accountability have minimum conceptual resources, except when it comes to First Amendment Liberalism.[36] He explained his views through NGOs' accountability to indigenous people. For instance, Green Peace led a campaign against seal-hunting that resulted in the loss of livelihood of indigenous people. Hence, Green Peace dropped this campaign. This is a special type of accountability of NGOs towards indigenous people.

Accountability of NGOs is necessary but it should not be overstepped. Debora Spar and James Dail observed that too much accountability could hinder NGOs from performing their duties.[37] Lisa Jordan discussed the mechanism for NGO accountability on the basis of three parameters. First, who is asking questions of accountability and why are they asking now? Second, the mechanism of NGO accountability in which they explain their response, evaluate and improve their work against attacks to their credibility. The third one analyses the ways to strengthen NGOs' accountability.[38]

Lisa Jorden referred to the American Enterprises Institute, a Washington-based NGO, which organised a conference on NGO Accountability in 2003, with collaboration of the American government. This seminar attempted to discredit NGOs and erode their standing in international fora.[39] NGOs pursue to make state and market players quite uncomfortable by asking their responsibilities about broad public interest, resulting in the state and market forces, in turn, asking NGOs about their efficiency, organisational structure and legitimacy.

Indeed, the questions of accountability arise on various sides, therefore, it is necessary to know who is asking the question and for what purpose. Donors, academia, media and beneficiaries' questions are obvious, and as per usual. These queries may be responded to by NGOs for their credibility and trustworthiness. But the question of accountability came forth through government and market forces. These certainly eroded the working and mission of NGOs.

---

[35] Kingsbury (2002).

[36] Ibid., p. 186.

[37] Spar and Dail (2002).

[38] Jordan (2003).

[39] Ibid., p. 5.

4 Accountability Mechanisms

NGOs have used various mechanisms of accountability over the years. The query NGOs' accountability was intensified along with the growth of NGO influence in the international arena. Writers suggest various measures and mechanisms for improving and learning NGOs' accountability. Jan Aart Schotte identified four aspects of accountability, viz. (1) transparency, (2) consultation, (4) evaluation and (4) correction.[40]

Transparency

Transparency is the first essential step towards accountability, because without transparency there can be no accountability.

Consultation

The second aspect is consultation; incorporating the views of affected people into deliberations and thus, providing the opportunity to shape the outcome of any decision-making process. The affected or beneficiaries' identification, and to establish a meaningful dialogue with them in the decision-making process, enhance the quality of accountability.

Evaluation

The third aspect is evaluation, that is carried out by independent assessment impacts of the projects, policies and campaigns of the NGOs by other agencies.

Correction

The fourth aspect of accountability is correction, which means to ensure that there are mechanisms whereby affecting actors take responsibility for their actions for any harmful consequences, and learn from their mistakes. Scholte's main focus is on transparency and consultation with affected parties or beneficiaries. NGOs' own accountability, responsibility and continued learning is suggested for improvement.

Ruth W. Grant and Robert O. Keohane have narrated seven accountability measures that operate in world politics on the basis of which improved practices of accountability could be built.[41] These seven accountability measures are: (1) hierarchical, (2) supervisory, (3) fiscal, (4) legal, (5) market, (6) peer groups and (7) public reputation. These seven mechanisms are broadly applicable to all actors of world politics. However, all may not be applicable for NGO accountability. As Grant and Keohane said:

> In practice, few NGOs have a well-defined procedure for accountability to anyone other than financial contributors and members—quite a small set of people.[42]

[40] Jan Aart Scholte, *supra note* 26, pp. 217–222.

[41] Ruth W. Grant and Robert O. Keohane, *supra note* 28, pp. 35–37.

[42] Ibid., p. 38.

Michael Edwards and David Hulme lay down certain measures for the effective accountability of NGOs. These measures are inter alia, including statement of goals, transparency of decision-making and relationships, honest reporting of what resources have been used and what has been achieved, an appraisal process for overseeing of authority to judge whether results are satisfactory, and concrete mechanism for holding to account those responsible for performance.[43] The duo emphasises the statement of goals, transparency, reporting, appraisal and performance measures for NGOs' accountability.

J. Avina divided accountability into short-term and strategic accountability.[44] Strategic accountability is a process for improvement of the credibility and effectiveness of NGOs through these measures.

Alnoor Ebrahim illustrates accountability through five broad mechanisms. They are: (1) reports and disclosure statements, (2) performance assessment and evaluation, (3) participation, (4) self- regulation and (5) social audits. Besides these, he identified three dimensions of accountability: upward-downward, internal–external, and functional-strategic.[45] In addition, the accountability mechanism is divided into tools and processes. Traditionally, NGOs prepare statements and reports of their accounts and activities. These accounts statements and reports are disclosed to the donors. This is the requirement for funds and it is known as upward accountability.[46]

The upward goal of accountability is sometimes a legal requirement, i.e. to submit annual reports of activities and audited financial statements. This is needed to maintain the not-for-profit status and tax exemption where the NGO is located. The downward accountability practice is not undertaken by NGOs so far, because generally it is neither required by the donor nor the law. This type of accountability is related to beneficiaries or community. It depends on NGO's initiatives because unlike donors, they are not fundraisers. But the participation of beneficiaries or community enhances the credibility of NGOs and effectiveness of projects or campaigns.

The accountability mechanism is also divided into internal and external process. Internal process is related to themselves—NGOs' vision and mission, members, volunteers and staff. External process is related to donors and legal requirements. The accountability mechanism is further divided into tools and processes. Tools include disclosure of reports and evaluation of performance. Whereas, process includes participation and self-regulation. Social auditing includes both the tools and processes mechanism.

Writers also divided accountability into functional and strategical mechanism. Functional mechanism is a short-term accountability which includes account audit reports and project outcomes while strategic mechanism is a long-term accountability which affects NGOs' stakeholder interaction and promoters' long-term NGO planning.[47] Social auditing is a long-term strategy of the auditing mechanism of NGOs.

---

[43] Edwards and Hulme (1996a, b).

[44] Avina (1993).

[45] Ebrahim (2003a, b).

[46] Najam (1996).

[47] J. Avina, *supra note* 44; A Najam, *supra note* 46, p. 351.

It has been recently introduced for NGO accountability and shall become effective in the years to come.

A. **Donors' Accountability**

A donor is anyone who dedicates resources to an NGO without monetary compensation. Thus, it includes volunteers and various donors—governments, IGOs, corporations, funds, charitable trusts and individuals. The term 'donor' includes all kinds of monetary and human resources given to NGOs for their objectives and activities. Accountability towards donors has been well established over the years, and this is practised by small as well as large NGOs.

Accountability of NGOs is not only a legal and public requirement but it is necessary for NGOs' trustworthiness towards donors too.[48] Donors have genuine expectations that their time and money will be used wisely during the course of the NGOs' mission. Public perceptions of NGOs' trustworthiness will attract donors, as they give donors an idea for promoting NGOs that fulfil their expectations. Thereby, credibility, reputation and high public perception are a pre-requisite for the flow of funds and volunteers. In order to carry out their missions, campaigns, advocacy and service delivery, funds and volunteers are an absolute must for every NGO.

The donors' trustworthiness to an NGO is ensured by transparency and external accountability of the NGOs. But the accountability process should not be cumbersome and cost-oriented. Regulations should not hinder the achievement of the aim.[49] Donors are not homogenous groups; they are more complex since NGOs' funding comes from various sources like the government, corporates, foundations, and individuals. There are broadly two types of donors with varied requirements. Some donors give priority to feedback, legal bonds, monitoring, transaction and transparency. Others prefer shared identities, common values, group membership and working with the mission.

The social trust theory denotes that those who feel the need to share identity and common purposes do not give much emphasis to formal evidence and disclosure of public information. They are generally individual givers. But the government, corporates and public donors do require evidential performance and reports from NGOs.[50]

Donors' financial resources are made available to the NGOs, which need a closer inspection, whether they are purely for charity and missions or quid pro quo or to enhance profile.[51] Sometimes, government grants and funds are provided on preferential political ideology. They expect, in return, a support for political process. Even humanitarian aid is driven by political interests rather than in accordance with real-time needs.

Government aid agencies such as British DFID or USAID and others are major donors from developed countries. Their involvement is, at times suspect, as the

---

48 Keating and Thrandardottir (2017).

49 Cordery (2013); Hind (2011).

50 Sloan (2009).

51 Jem Bendell, Debating NGO Accountability, *supra note* 21, p. 67.

donation received may interfere in the nation's domestic politics. The governmental funds of developed countries such as in Latin America were studied by writers, who in turn, described the politicisation of NGOs in Central America in the 1980s by USAID.[52] Right-wing NGOs were funded by USAID whilst other NGOs based out of the developed world supported a range of left-wing groups.[53]

The flow of funds is channelised by developed countries through NGOs. This is reflected in USAID and British DFID, Canadian, Dutch and Scandinavian governments' aid and donations to the NGOs of developing countries. Between 1975 and 1995, the Organisation for Economic Co-operation and Development (OECD) indicated a sharp rise of donations from the northern side of developed countries or NGOs of the southern side of developing countries NGOs. During this period, the origin and growth of NGOs was witnessed in Asia, Africa and Latin America.[54]

The funding of NGOs has increased, and side by side, their acceptance and accountability has also grown, wherein NGOs successfully adhered to their vision and mission and raised their voice for marginalised people.

Jay S. Ovsiovitch conducted a specific study of three major foundations—Ford, Carnegie and MacArthur—indicating how philanthropic funds are able to influence the agenda for human rights organisations. On the other side, three NGOs—Human Rights Watch (HRW), Lawyers Committee for Human Rights (LCHR) and International Commission of Jurists—co-ordinated with the United States foreign policy.[55]

Governments of developed countries provided grants to their country-based foundations, then these foundations further extended the grants to NGOs based in their country. The official aid agencies of USAID and DFID grant allocations exhibited as they are accountable to their own nations. These official aid agencies are connected with foundations and NGOs on the other side. To know the real purpose of foundations and official aid agencies, a closer look is necessary because funds and donors are meddling with national policies and missions of NGOs.

Another major donation is through corporate funding, something that has grown recently. In India, there is a legal provision for companies to transfer donations to NGOs under the umbrella of corporate social responsibility (CSR).[56] A company's primary concern is marketing, advertisement, profiteering and to be accountable to all stakeholders. Corporates, particularly multi-national enterprises, are regular donors to NGOs, with funds coming out of its profit.[57] Here, the NGOs' accountability does not arise towards the corporates' explicit interests such as marketing, advertising, and so on.

NGOs must adhere to their mission statement, advocacy and service delivery activities in an effective manner. The corporate funding to NGOs is entitled to receive

---

[52] Beggington et al. (1993).

[53] Michael Edwards and David Hulme, *supra note* 43, at 961.

[54] Hulme and Edwards (1996); Smith and Lipsky (1993).

[55] Ovsiovitch (1998).

[56] The Companies Act, 2013, Act No.18, Section 135, Schedule VII (India).

[57] Yaziji and Doh (2009).

tax exemption. Through this type of funding, corporates enhance their standing in society. Corporations cannot directly be involved in social activities because they are not entitled for tax exemption like non-profit sectors.

NGOs must be careful while receiving funds and donations from corporations. This is an issue which was raised for debate. For instance, the World Social Forum (WSF) 2004 did not accept donations from corporations and the Ford Foundation. However, WSF accepted grants from Oxfam and Action Aid.[58] NGOs do not prefer to receive funds from corporations, something that contradicts their mission and values. For example, health sector NGOs cannot accept funds from Tobacco companies.

NGO accountability towards donors is related to fiscal accountability, which means accounting, auditing and filing tax returns. Another aspect is transparency or the disclosure of information and the observation of national law, international standards and security concerns. Donors' accountability could be promoted through the participation of all stakeholders when it comes to decision-making, transparency and social auditing practices.

In addition, the short-term frames for most of the donor-funded projects encouraged NGOs to focus on the outcome of all projects. The overemphasis on donors to ignore accountability of other stakeholders may create the problem for long-term sustainability of NGOs and their mission in the community.[59] Sometimes, NGOs operate in hostile situations like Afghanistan and Iraq-Syria, requiring flexibility in the utilisation of donors' funds. So, it is better to promote accountability on their own. NGO accountability is beneficial to them because it enhances transparency, participation, trustworthiness and credibility. But the question arises as to who regulates the system of accountability? Marck Havrda and Peter Kutilek have suggested three methods, namely: state regulation, self- regulation and multi-party regulation.[60]

B. **State Regulations**

NGOs—local, national or international have headquarters within a national boundary to carry out activities therein. They are registered within a country for taxation exemptions being not-for-profit and receiving and managing foreign donations and funds. For example, the International Committee for Red Cross (ICRC) is registered under Swiss law, with headquarters based in Switzerland. NGOs work under the existing legal framework and institutions of that country.

Every country is not like Switzerland and every NGO is not like ICRC. Therefore, NGOs cannot claim full liberty and autonomy to create, activate and operationalise their organisations as per their mission, vision, ideas and human concerns. Sometimes, they face lack of legal enabling environments for smooth and effective working. Government officials deliberately push NGOs back because they are engaged in advocacy, suggesting public policies and alternate development. NGOs also get into trouble because they have ideas that differ from the government of

---

[58] Jem Bendell, Debating NGO Accountability, *supra note* 51.

[59] Szporluk (2009).

[60] Marek Havrda and Peter Kutilek, "Accountability 2.0—in search of new approach to international organisation's accountability", *supra note* 21, p. 166.

the day as they pursue transparency, the demanding for human rights compliance, environment obligations and so on.

The state is there to provide the legal framework to the institutions in which NGOs can operate. It has the authority to oversee the statement of mission, utilisation of funds, tax exemption and national security. The state genuinely expects from NGOs to fulfil minimum standards required for governance. The state is one of the stakeholders of NGOs as it provides not-for-profit status, thus tax exemption and legal status of an entity to adhered rights, duties and capacity to interact at national as well as at international level.[61]

In addition, the state also provides grant-in-aid and facilitates service delivery activities to NGOs. The regulatory power of the state is of a plenary nature. It is a legal exception that the state uses these powers in a judicious and a wise manner with respect to the NGOs. NGOs' advocacy role emphasises on the compliance of international commitment, sometimes manifesting unpleasant situations before the state. Sometimes, state regulations fail to visualise the failure of non-governmental entities. In 2008, the market regulation system did not perform effectively, resulting in the financial crisis. Since then, states' intervention increased in the functions of non-state actors, i.e., corporations and NGOs.

NGOs perform the role of advocacy, raising the voice against the states and market. Powerful government officials and corporate captains lobby for strict regulations towards NGOs' accountability. It results in the unreasonable restrictions upon freedom of association and workings of NGOs.[62] The people have every right to actively participate in decision-making and governance. These are the essential ingredients of democracy that people have franchised and freely exercised, demonstrated for, raised their voices for, done advocacy for and marched in protest for numerous public issues. According to Alecis de Tocqueville:

> the right of association is closely related to the right of liberty, and democracy is endangered if this right is unprotected.[63]

State regulations at work are reflected only in some case studies of nations. In a liberal democracy, the working of NGOs is generally not hampered, but in democratic-deficit societies, NGOs are generally pushed back through a strict regulatory regime. A case study of Egyptian NGOs was conducted by James G. McGram, reflecting on the state regulations of NGOs at work.[64] Egypt is a developing country with a democratic government. NGOs began to gather steam in Egypt since 1973, with their growth spiking in the 1990s. There are five categories of NGOs in the country dealing with development, religion, scientific, cultural and private associations. They have received donations and *zakat* from foreign contributions and the local population.

---

[61] Ibid., pp. 166–167.

[62] Scholte (2004); Armstrong (2006).

[63] De Tocqueville (2004).

[64] Mcgann (2008).

The Egyptian government gave a push back to the NGO community through employees' legal and extra-legal measures. Legal measures include registration limitations, funding restrictions, strict monitoring and restrictions of NGOs' activities, especially in discouraging NGOs through non-registration, stopping their funds and activities. The government also employed extra-legal measures such as state control of the media, suppression of key leaders, threats of armed forces and an underdeveloped legal framework.[65] This remedied only the fair legal framework and independence of the judiciary as well as NGOs' efforts to restore their trustworthiness and public perception.

Another study of state regulation conducted by Magda Hornemann is of China's religious NGOs.[66] The obtaining of registration as a non-profit is a tough task. Moreover, funding and the state's grant-in-aid is a big challenge before NGOs. Likewise, in Egypt and China, the three main hurdles that exist are with respect to obtaining registration, seeking tax exemption under not-for-profit status and receiving funds from the state, corporates and overseas.[67] In addition, public perception and support from the media are also worthwhile for the NGO community.

There is an urgent need for the constitutional guarantee of freedom of association, independent judiciary, fair law of registration, taxation and foreign funds, besides NGOs' credibility and trustworthiness through transparency and accountability.

C. **Self-Regulation**

Self-regulation is an emerging measure in the subject of NGOs' accountability. It was introduced to the corporate sectors in the 1980s. In the nineteenth and twentieth centuries, the economic and social sectors grew enormously, therefore, the state's human and economic resources were not sufficiently at a place which could regulate all activities of business and non-profit sectors. In this situation, corporations and NGOs had to opt for self-regulation.

Ever since the last quarter of the twentieth century, in the era of globalisation, the state's role willingly or unwillingly was limited to economic and social sectors, so much so that corporates and NGOs enjoyed the autonomy to carry out their activities with minimal intervention from state regulation. This facilitated incorporates and NGOs regulating themselves.

NGOs' influence has increased since the 1990s; they moved focus from relief and welfare to advocacy and policy. The media and people generally supported NGOs. Questions then arose from the market and state as to their accountability. They found a way to respond to this accountability and transparency question through self-regulation. In 1971, the Philippines took initiative and formed the caucus of Development of NGOs and laid down the code of conduct for NGOs. The certification system of NGOs was also introduced,[68] with the trend being replicated worldwide.[69]

---

[65] Ibid., pp. 29–30.

[66] Hornemann (2012).

[67] Ibid., pp. 31–32.

[68] Constantino-David (1992).

[69] Lloyd (2005).

State regulation is limited up to registration, tax exemption and control of foreign contribution of NGOs. The remaining questions of accountability, trustworthiness and credibility are open to be addressed. Mobilisation of funds, public support, media coverage, and ethics and values of NGOs are put in place, and the concerns of beneficiaries are met. The unoccupied space was filled by a coalition of NGOs at both the national and international level.

The retention of public trust and confidence is a prerequisite for the sustainability of NGOs and the successful operation of missions and projects.[70] Public trust in NGOs is comparatively better than that of corporates and other actors as NGOs raise the voice of the un-heard as well as un-address public issues related to human rights, environment, gender justice and equality. To continue this high esteem, support and participation, NGOs voluntarily opted for self-regulation in the domain of accountability and transparency. This, in turn, facilitated the further flow of donations to their varied activities.

The self-regulation system is based on the NGOs' voluntary adoption and enforcement. There are no clearly defined international mechanisms accepted for accreditation by the UN, IGOs and NGOs' coalition and network. The self-regulation model was first adopted by the corporates in order to avoid strict state regulations. This path was introduced by the NGOs later on. Many sectors in business are self-regulated, for instance, the code on pharmaceutical marketing practices.[71] The aforementioned system is needed, hence its emergence, but the primary challenge remains its effective implementation. However, the national and international NGOs' coalition network, some watchdogs and independent initiatives are taking appropriate steps to tackle the situation.

Marek Havrda and Peter Kutilek observed that government regulation would not work, therefore they looked forward to a multi-party system for a way forward. They explored the available writings, practices and standards towards effective enforcement of NGO accountability.[72] For instance, the corporate accountability practice of stakeholders could be replicated in the case of NGO accountability. This aforesaid practice expanded NGO accountability from the state and donors to beneficiaries, volunteers, members, staff, the governing board and peer groups.

The practice of social auditing is another measure of accountability. It is effective in the disclosure of information, participation of all stakeholders, evaluation of projects, response of queries and learning and improvement. The certification and rating of NGOs (like the Philippines Council for NGOs' Certification) by Charity Navigator are other measures to ensure accountability in an effective manner.

P. F. Drucker ensured NGOs' accountability by asking them five questions.[73] These are: (1) What is our mission? (2) Who are our beneficiaries? (3) What do the beneficiaries consider valuable? (4) What have been our results? and (5) What is our plan?

---

[70] Thrandardottir and Keating (2018).

[71] Marek Havrda and Peter Kutilek, *supra note* 61, p. 168.

[72] Ibid., pp. 166–175.

[73] Drucker (1993).

But the crucial thing is, who is asking these questions and why are they asking them? NGOs are not nearly as powerful as the state, IGOs, corporations and others. There are numerous private universities and hospitals, religious organisations, think tanks and research institutes, and professional organisations in the private domain. Why should NGOs alone be questioned, and not others? There are a number of foundations and trusts; why not question them about their accountability?[74]

5 Codes, Standards and Watchdogs

In order to strengthen accountability of NGOs, certain codes, standards and certification procedures are laid down by various institutions and academia. NGOs' accountability practice of self-regulation does not have in place the enforcement mechanism. It is totally dependent on the inherent ethics and values of NGOs because oversight is lacking. Accountability is tilted to the side of strong stakeholders—the state and donors—and thus ignoring beneficiaries and the populace.[75] Academia calls for the improvement in NGO accountability, transparency and governance. This has given rise to certain criteria, processes and tools, with two institutes being referred to, namely, the Hauser Center for Non-Profit Organisation at Harvard[76] and the Centre for Studies of Global Governance at the London School of Economics.[77]

Besides, certain not-for-profit organisations such as Civicus,[78] Humanitarian Accountability Partnership International,[79] One World Trust,[80] INGO Accountability Charter,[81] Global Policy Forum,[82] GRI,[83] Charity Navigator,[84] UN Non-Governmental Liaison Service (NGLS),[85] KPMG,[86] CHS Alliance[87] and HAP International, People In Aid and Sphere Project, and Joint Standard Initiative (JSI)[88] have laid down standards, codes, certification and rating procedures for NGO accountability.

---

74 Jem Bendell, *supra note* 58, pp. 75–79.

75 Lloyd and de Las Casas (2005).

76 www.hausercenter.harvard.edu.

77 www.centreforstudiesofglobalgovernance (London School of Economics, UK).

78 www.civicus.org.

79 www.hapinternational.org.

80 www.oneworldtrust.org.

81 www.ingoaccountabilitycharter.org.

82 www.globalpolicy.org.

83 www.globalreporting.org.

84 www.charitynavigator.org.

85 www.un-ngls.org.

86 www.rpmg.com.

87 www.chsalliance.org.

88 www.jointstandardinitiative.

A number of voluntary networks for standard settings, clarification and procedures working at the national level have been in place. For instance, Guide Star in the United States, the Philippines Council for NGO Certification (PCNC), South African NGO Coalition Code of Ethics, InterAction's Standards, NGO Code of Conduct for Ethiopia, Nigeria Draft Code of Standards Practice for NGOs, Pakistan Centre for Philanthropy's Non-Profit Organisation Certification Programme, VANI (India) and International Centre for Not-for-Profit Law. Almost all countries across the world have a self-regulation or peer regulation mechanism for NGO accountability.[89] They employ and design multiple measures like codes, certification, guidelines and ratings for this purpose. The national mechanism for NGOs accountability is beyond this study.

Oxford Analytica expressed its concerns about holding NGOs accountable after post-tsunami relief work. The existing mechanism of accountability to donors, state, self-regulation and peer regulation. The UN accreditation systems are not effective for NGOs' growth, influence and role at the international level. To enhance the accountability of NGOs, the private sectors' tools could be introduced for efficient and timely financial and non-financial reporting.

In addition, it suggests that "board members and managers will need to be held accountable for their actions against objective criteria communicated to the stakeholders of the organisation."[90] Oxford Analytica's suggested measures of NGO accountability are mainly based on private sector practices and sanctions, but the idea of the sanction to make accountable to board members and managers is a bizarre suggestion.

Charity Navigator denoted NGOs' accountability and obligation as well as the willingness of NGOs to disclose the financial status and performance of its stakeholders.[91] It uses the information about their audited accounts, income and expenditure and NGOs' website information. After analysis of this information, Navigator accords them ratings. Apart from financial statements and website disclosures, it gives weightage to the documentation of board meetings, provisions of whistle blowers, policy, chief executive officer's salary and loaning to the staff. But ratings and stars akin to the hospitality sector would not be adequate measures to enhance NGO accountabilities.

'Accountable Now' has laid down 12 accountability commitments:

(1) mainly focused on people's participation and to encourage women's participation;
(2) collaboration with people to develop, innovate and systematic solution for environment issues;
(3) focuses on long results through evaluation, learning, adoption and innovation;
(4) beneficiary involvement in decision-making, partnership with organisations to share goals;

---

[89] Robert Lloyd and Lucy de Las Casas, *supra note* 75.

[90] Oxford Analytica, Holding NGOs Accountable, *Forbes*, 5 April, 2005, pp. 1–4.

[91] Charity Navigator: How do we rate charitie's accountability and transparency? https://www.charitynavigator.org.

(5) information, resources and experience;
(6) advocacy work carried out with support of affected people;
(7) transparency about who we are? What we do? How decisions are made? And impact of work;
(8) staff fairly recruited and skilled, volunteer-adhered values and professional standards;
(9) donations received with values and goals;
(10) use responsive ways and accounts audited;
(11) received feedback and decision-making through public involvement; and
(12) governing body and management accountability.

These twelve accountability commitments are as per usual, but its innovative idea is Accountable Now's website; they disclose all information in the public domain and receive feedback, which is, undoubtedly, a creative approach.[92]

Accountability now is a global non-profit network working since 1995 to promote accountability innovations. It published the AA1000 series comprising accountability principle standards related to stakeholders' engagement (2005) and sustainability assurance (2008). It laid down three foundational principles: (1) inclusivity, (2) materiality and (3) responsiveness.

Inclusivity refers to affected people or beneficiaries who participated as stakeholders of the NGOs' activities, sources and performance. Materiality refers to what matters most to the beneficiaries as stakeholders and NGOs. This should be determined on the basis of information sharing, concerns and acceptance of both. Responsiveness means NGOs are responsible for the stakeholders as to their decisions, actions, performance and communication. Only then can stakeholders take informed decisions. The sustainability assurance could be achieved through active participation of the stakeholders.[93]

Core humanitarian standards have been laid down jointly by the 'HAP International', 'People In Aid and the Sphere Project for humanitarian'. These core humanitarian standards are to be followed by workers and volunteers in their relief and assistance work.[94] People work at the heart of humanitarianism. The primary motivation of any response to crises is to save lives, alleviate human suffering and to support the right to life with dignity.[95]

Humanitarian action is guided by four universal principles accepted by the International Red Cross and Red Crescent Movement[96] and the General Assembly of

[92] Accountable Now founded in 2008 in Berlin, Germany, Global Standard Local Trust: 12 Accountability Commitments, www.accountablenow.org.

[93] http://www.accountability21.net.

[94] www.corehumanitarianstandards.org.

[95] Core Humanitarian Standard, 2014, p. 8.

[96] The fundamental principles of the international red cross and red cresent movement. https://www.icre.org>4046_th_fundamental_principles_of_the_international_red_cross_and_crescent_movement.pdf.

the United Nations.[97] These principles are humanity, impartiality, independence and neutrality. The aforesaid principles are the foundations on which humanitarian actions yield positive results. Humanitarian action is undertaken promptly to safeguard lives and health, and to ensure that human beings are protected at all costs.

The human crisis response should be done with impartiality and humility. It must be attended to with priority, without any discrimination on the basis of nationality, race, gender, religion, class or political leaning. These humanitarian actions must be independent from political, economic and military objectives. This is confined to only humanitarian actions relating to relief and assistance. Humanitarian agencies and volunteers must be neutral, and should not indulge to take any sides during hostilities or engage in any controversy of a political, racial, religious or ideological nature. These four humanitarian principles are at the core of all humanitarian actions. They maintain the said action's distinguished role in any human suffering and crisis, thereby conveying the vastness of the human spirit and heart.

The core humanitarian standards on quality and accountability are as follows:

(1) Humanitarian response is appropriate and relevant.
(2) Humanitarian response is effective and timely.
(3) Humanitarian response strengthens local capacities and avoids negative effects.
(4) Humanitarian response is based on communication, participation and feedback.
(5) Complaints are welcomed and addressed.
(6) Humanitarian response is coordinated and is complementary.
(7) Humanitarian actors continuously learn and improve.
(8) Staff is supported in order to do its job effectively, in addition to fair and equitable treatment.
(9) Resources are managed and used responsibly for their intended purpose.[98]

Core humanitarian standards are a voluntary international yardstick on quality and accountability for non-governmental humanitarian agencies (NGHAs). The NGHAs include the ICRC, National Societies of the Red Cross, Red Crescent and NGOs. Core humanitarian standard ideas created a simple set of standards that could be easily understood by NGOs and humanitarian volunteers, which in turn, could be adopted towards humanitarian action.[99]

Core humanitarian standards followed the principles of the International Red Cross Code of Conduct, 1994. It is also a voluntary code, enforced by the will of non-governmental humanitarian agencies. The main objectives of the code of conduct are to seek standards of behaviour of aid agencies, and to facilitate effective delivery of human assistance. The code of conduct laid down ten standards for the Red Cross and NGOs in disaster response programmes.

---

[97] United Nations General Assembly Resolution (UNGA Res) 46/182 (19 December, 1991), and UNGA Res 58/114 (5 February, 2004).

[98] Core Humanitarian Standard 2014, pp. 1–24 at 9. https://www.chsalliance.org/get_support?resource/core_humanitarian_standard/.

[99] Pruvis (2015).

These aforementioned standards are: humanitarian assistance in the response of disaster is our shared obligation and is needed to alleviate human suffering; aid is given without any discrimination on equitable access to all disaster victims; aid delivery is above any consideration of politics, religion and creed; NGHAs act independently from governments and are guided by voluntary motivations; respect culture and customs of the communities; to strengthen capacity of local people; to involve beneficiaries in the design, management and implementation of assistance relief programmes; the relief programmes are implemented keeping long-term sustainability in mind so that dependency is reduced on external aid; NGHAs and volunteers are responsible towards donors as well as beneficiaries for the impact of disaster assistance and management; and the disclosure of information about aid assistance and relief to the media and public.[100]

Some NGOs, academia and media suggest the idea of creating a humanitarian ombudsman in the wake of recent adverse news pertaining to humanitarian assistance.[101] This idea was explored two decades ago but was dropped later on. Humanitarian assistance and relief were not up to the mark in Rwanda, Kosovo, Afghanistan and Sierra Leone, but the solution does not lie in the humanitarian ombudsman. It is better to mobilise non-governmental humanitarian assistance, donors and volunteers to strictly observe the core humanitarian standards to maintain the quality and responsibility of their mission. It should be remembered that humanitarian action is facing numerous challenges in the face of current hostilities and disasters.

6 Conclusion

In the 1990s, NGOs' numbers, influence and activities grew in a significant way in the field of human rights, humanitarian assistance, and environmental protection through advocacy and service delivery. The accountability of NGOs is demanded by the media, academia, charitable foundations, governments and corporations. NGOs are campaigning for governmental responsibility and corporate accountability for the sake of all stakeholders. The same demand was put forward by corporations and governments before NGOs. NGOs are less powerful in comparison to the state, IGOs and corporations because they possess neither political power nor economic power; they are just a voice of the poor and marginalised.

Therefore, NGOs are primarily responsible for those whose voices they claim to represent. Accountability of NGOs is a four-way query: Accountable to whom? Accountability for what? Accountability how? What does accountability mean? Accountability of NGOs is further identified via four components: transparency, answerability, compliance and enforcement. The said accountability is upward to

[100] Code of Conduct for the International Red Cross and Red Crescent Movement and NGOs in Disaster Relief (12 December 1994) Publication Ref. 1067. https://www.icrc.org?en?doc/resources/documents/publication/p.1067.htm.

[101] ALNAP: A Humanitarian Ombudsman Revisited? www.alnap.org.

state and donor, and downward to beneficiaries, internal-staff, members, board of directors. In addition, NGOs are responsible towards their peers and counterparts.

NGOs, in practice, follow the audited accounts procedure in order to submit the same to the government for income tax exemption and to donors for the flow of funds. Now, this is required to be disclosed to the public. Apart from transparency, the participation of beneficiaries through all stages of the project, especially during design and enforcement, is a must. This move will certainly enhance NGO accountability.

The most important question that arises is how to ensure NGO accountability without discouraging and pushing them back? There are three measures employed so far. First, self-regulation, second, state regulations, and third, multiple regulations. The states and donors are already enjoying enormous power. The state have capacity to impose sanctions in the field of NGO registration, regulations of foreign funds and tax exemption. Donors, charitable foundations and resource providers extend financial support to NGOs, which can be withdrawn at any time. Hence, there is no need to further strengthen their positions for a holistic and conducive environment for NGOs.

The beneficiaries' accountability, on the other hand, needs to be strengthened more. In spite of short-term outcomes of projects, the long-term sustainability needs to be strengthened as well. NGO accountability can be understood in the context of transparency, participation, efficiency and learning. There is no scope for overemphasis of sanctions. NGOs' principles are akin to the first amendment liberation of the United States, the human rights covenant and a part of the whole democratic fabric. Some democratic-deficit countries push back the advocacy work of NGOs because the latter emphasises compliance of the state's international obligations.

References

Armstrong P (2006) The limits and risks of regulations. In: Jordan L, Van Tuil P (eds) NGO accountability: politics, principles and innovations. Earthscan Publications, London, pp 61–80

Avina A (1993) The evolutionary life cycle of non-governmental development organisations. Public Admin Devt 13(5):453–474

Baur D, Schmitz HP (2012) Corporations and NGOs: when accountability leads to co-optation. J Business Ethics 106(1):9–21

Beggington A, Thiele G et al (1993) NGOs and the state in Latin America: rethinking roles in sustainable agriculture development. Routledge, Abingdon, p 182

Bendell J et al (2010) These pages have been regulated for you: issues arising from the governance of markets by NGOs. In: Steffek J, Hann K (eds) Evaluating transnational NGOs. Palgrave Macmillan, New York, p 132

Bendell J (2006) Debating NGO accountability, UN-NGLS development dossier. UN Non-Governmental Liason Services, Geneva, p 5

Charnovitz S (2005) Accountability of nongovernmental organisations (NGOs) in global governance. In: GWU legal studies research paper No. 145, pp 1–39. https://scholarship.law.gurc.edu/faculty_publications

Constantino-David K (1992) The Philippines experience in scaling-up. In: Edward M, Hulme D (eds) Making a difference: NGOs and development in changing world. Earthscan Publications, London, pp 137–147

Cordery C (2013) Regulating small and medium charity: does it improve transparency and accountability? Voluntas 24(4):831–851
Drucker PF (1993) The five most important questions you will ever ask about your non-profit organisation: participants handbook. Drucker Foundation, San Francisco
Ebrahim A (2003a) NGOs and organisational change: discourse, reporting and learning. Cambridge University Press, Cambridge
Ebrahim A (2003b) Accountability in practice: mechanisms for NGOs. World Devt 31(5):813–829
Ebrahim A (2005) Accountability myopia: losing sight of organisational learning. Non-Profit Volunt Sect Q 34(1):56–87
Edwards M, Hulme D (1996a) Beyond the magic bullet: NGOs performance and accountability in the post-cold war. Kumarian Press, Hartford
Edwards M, Hulme D (1996b) Too close for comfort? The impact of official aid on nongovernmental organisations. World Devt 24(6):961–973
Grant RW, Keohane RO (2005) Accountability and abuses of power in world politics. Am Polit Sci Rev 99(1):29–43
Held D, McGrew A (2002) Governing globalization: power, authority and global governance. Polity Press, New York, pp 1–21
Hind A (2011) New development: increasing public trust and confidence in charities: on the side of angels. Public Money Manag 31(3):201–205
Hornemann M (2012) China: changing climate for religious NGOs? Int J Civil Soc Law 10(3):27–35
Hulme D, Edwards M (eds) (1996) Too close for comfort? NGOs, states and donors. Martins Press, London, St
Jordan L (2003) Mechanisms for NGO accountability. Global Policy Res Paper Ser 3:1–20
Jordan L, Van Tuijl P (2006) NGO accountability: politicis, principles, innovations. Earthscan Publications, London
Keating VC, Thrandardottir E (2017) NGOs, trust and the accountability agenda. Br J Polit Int Relat 19(1):134–151
Kingsbury B (2002) First amendment liberalism as global legal architecture: ascriptive groups and the problems of the liberal NGOs model of international civil society. Chicago J Int Law 3(1):183–195
Lloyd R, de Las Casas L (2005) NGO self-regulation: enforcing and balancing accountability. One World Trust, pp 1–8
Lloyd R (2005) The role of NGO self-regulation in increasing stakeholder accountability. One World Trust, pp 1–15
Mathew JT (1997) Power shift. For Aff 76(1):50–66
Mcgann JG (2008) Pushback against NGOs in Egypt. Int J Not-for-Profit Law 10(4):29–42
Mulgan R (2003) Holding power to account: accountability in modern democracies. Palgrave Macmillan, Basingstoke
Najam A (1996) NGOs accountability: a conceptual framework. Devt Policy Rev 14(4):339–353
Ovsiovitch JS (1998) Feeding the watchdogs: philanthropic support for human rights NGOs. Buffalo Hum Rts Law Rev 4:341–363
Pruvis K (2015) Core humanitarian standard: do NGOs need another set of standards? The Guardian
Schmitz HP et al (2011) Accountability of transnational NGOs: aspirations versus practice. Nonprofit Volunt Sect Q 41(6):1175–1194
Scholte JA (2004) Civil society and democratically accountable global governance. Govern Oppos 32(2):211–233
Scholte JA (ed) (2011) Building global democracy? Civil society and accountable global governance, Cambridge University Press, Cambridge
Sebastian M (2004) NGOs: fighting poverty, harting the poor. For Policy 144:50–58
Slim H (2002) By what authority? The legitimacy and accountability of non-government organisations. J Humanitarian Assistance
Sloan MF (2009) The effects of non-profit accountability ratings on donor behaviour. Non-Profit Volut Sect Q 38(2):220–236

Smith S, Lipsky M (1993) Non-profits for hire: the welfare state in the age of contracting. Harvard University Press

Spar D, Dail J (2002) Of measurement and mission: accounting for performance in nongovernmental organisations. Chicago J Int Law 3(1):171–181

Spiro PJ (1995) New global communities: nongovernmental organizations in international decision-making institutions. Washington Quart 18(1):45–46

Spiro PJ (1996) New global potentates: nongovernmental organisations and the unregulated marketplace. Cardozo Law Rev 18:957–970

Spiro PJ (2002) Accounting for NGOs. Chicago J Int Law 3(1):161–169

Szporluk M (2009) A framework for understanding accountability of international NGOs and good governance. Indiana J Global Legal Stud 16(1):339–361

Thrandardottir E, Keating VC (2018) Building trust in NGOs, pp 1–4. https://www.e-ir.info/2018/08/10/building_trust_in_ngos/

de Tocqueville A (2004) Democracy in America trans. by Arthur Goldhammer, Penguin Classics, New York, pp 220–596

Wapner P (2002) Defending accountability in NGOs. Chicago J Int Law 3(1):197–205

Yaziji M, Doh J (2009) NGOs and corporations: conflicts and collaboration. Cambridge University Press, Cambridge

Zadex S (2003) In defence of non-profit accountability. Ethical Corporation Magazine, pp 34–36

Chapter 14
Case Study

1 Introduction

NGOs has acquired a significant status in international legal system. They have participated for more than two centuries in global governance, international law development and in the enforcement of rules. Civil society organisations have encompassed all kinds of non-governmental entities, private initiatives and actors.

The United Nations data based on civil society organisations includes associations, foundations, institutions, IGOs, local government, NGOs, media, private sector, trade unions, academics, indigenous people's organisations, the disability sector, development and human rights organisations, open-ended working groups on ageing, co-operatives and others. In their total strength, NGOs cover the maximum numbers working in various fields: economic and social, trade and finance, gender issues and empowerment of women, population, public administration, statistics, sustainable development, peace and conflict resolution.[1]

NGOs are operating globally, encompassing regions such as Africa, Asia, Europe, North America, Oceania, Latin America and the Caribbean. In Africa, a significant number of NGOs have been established and have engaged in the overall development of the continent during the last century. For example, out of 13,335 NGOs in collaboration with the UN system, 6680 NGOs are located in the African continent.

It is not easy to identify the exact number, growth and engagement of NGOs in the international arena. But there are two credible sources: the Yearbook of Union of International Association (UIA)[2] and the United Nations Department of Economic and Social Affairs' NGO branch.[3] According to the Yearbook of Union of International Association, there are 75,700 NGOs in the world. Among them, 37,700 actively

[1] www.esango.un.org.

[2] www.uia.org.

[3] www.undesa.ngobranch; www.csonet.org.

P. Rai, *Non-Governmental Organisations and International Law*,
https://doi.org/10.1007/978-981-97-5469-4_14

participate in world affairs, while the remaining 38,000 are dormant. The formation, engagement and disengagement of NGOs is a continuous process throughout world.

Another most credible source of NGOs is their participation at the international level. Their consultative status with the United Nations Economic and Social Council (ECOSOC) under Article 71 of the UN Charter is of high significance. There are more than 6000 NGOs that are endowed with consultative status by the ECOSOC.[4] They are divided into three categories, i.e. General, Special, and Roster. Their status is accorded as per their contribution and performance in the UN purposes, principles and programmes.

Besides, NGOs are accredited by UN specialised agencies, subsidiaries, programmes and funds as per the Integrated Civil Society Organisation (ICSO) system developed by the UN Department of Economic and Social Affairs (DESA), which facilitate interaction between NGOs and DESA. A total number of 11,413 NGOs are working in association with the UN system.[5]

There enters a glorious moment in NGO community life when they are honoured by the Nobel Peace Prize. Thereby, they become Nobel Laureates, in the same vein as path-breaking statesmen, eminent personalities and institutions. Some NGOs who are Nobel Laureates include:

- Institute of International Law, 1904
- Permanent International Peace Bureau, 1910
- Friends Service Council and Friends Service Committee (The Quakers), 1947
- Amnesty International, 1977
- International Physicians for Prevention of Nuclear War, 1985.
- International Campaign to Ban Landmines (ICBL), 1997
- Mėdicines Sans Frontiėrs (MSF), 1999
- National Dialogue Quartet, 2015
- International Campaign to Abolish Nuclear Weapons (ICAN), 2017
- Ales Bialiatski, Memorial and the Centre for Civil Liberties, 2022

Apart from Nobel Laureate NGOs, there are a good number of NGOs that have been endowed with consultative status by the ECOSOC. They are making significant contributions in the areas of development, human rights, environment, business ethics, humanitarian assistance, global governance and in the making of international law and enforcement of rules.

---

[4] List of Non-governmental Organisations in Consultative States with the Economic and Social Council, as of 31 December 2022, 6343 NGOs enjoy active consultative status with ECOSOC, see *basic Fact about ECOSOC Status, NGO Branch, Department of Economic and Social Affairs of the United Nations*.

[5] Official website of Nobelprize.org; Abrams Irwin, *The Nobel Peace Prize and the Laureates: An Illustrated Biographical History, 1901–2001*, Massachusetts Science History Publications, US 2001.

2 The Institute of International Law

The Institute of International Law (Institute de Droiet International, in French) was founded in 1873 in the Netherlands.[6] The Institute of International Law is a legal body conscious of the world community. It is a non-governmental initiative instituted by eminent scholars of the last quarter of nineteenth century. Initially, its founder members were European and American, with membership expanding worldwide, subsequently. It consists of three categories of members: lifetime members, associates and honorary members. The membership is still strictly restricted to the demonstration of scholarly attainment and to those who are likely to be free from political pressure. Membership is distributed in such a way that it covers all continents, legal systems and stages of development.

The Institute of International Law is purely scientific and private, which is fully dedicated to the creation, development and enforcement of international law. It promotes maintenance of peace and the amicable settlement of international disputes. Its motto is 'Justice and Peace'. This is an intellectual collective that was awarded the Nobel Peace Prize in 1904. The Nobel Peace Prize enhanced the reputation of its legal thinking on global issues and also facilitated its financial resources.

The Nobel Peace Prize committee acclaimed the institute's contribution to the field of international arbitration and law of armed conflicts. The Institute's contribution was reflected in the establishment of the Permanent Court of Arbitration in 1899 and 1907.[7]

Ever since its inception, the Institute of International Law has undertaken legal issues of that time independently, as it was commissioned by no individual or government. It took initiatives on its own but its work could be used by the states. For example, the League of Nations (1919) and the United Nations (1945) legal foundations were built up on the legal work and creative ideas of eminent jurists belonging to the International Law Institute.

The Institute of International Law undertook contemporary legal issues and tried to build up consensus between different viewpoints of scholars and adopted resolutions. The resolutions do not have legal binding, but they carry a lot of weight and influence because they were prepared by the great legal luminaries of the day and were supported by global public opinion.

The Institute of International Law published yearbooks containing their intellectual activities and contributions. That yearbook is a major source of their performance in the field of development of international law, principles, ideas and institutions. The institute has an illustrated history of more than a century. Recently, the ECOSOC council has been endowed with general consultative status under Article 71 of the UN Charter and via para 22 of the ECOSOC Resolution 1996/31. Earlier, the institute had special consultative status which was upgraded to general status in 2017.

[6] www.idi-iil.org; Editorial Comment (1907).

[7] Abrams (1957).

3 Permanent International Peace Bureau

The Permanent International Peace Bureau (IPB) was founded in 1891 in Rome by the Third World Peace Congress. Its main objectives were to co-ordinate the *peace society* and *peace movements* across the nations. After 1870, the peace movement spread across the Atlantic, and peace societies were established in Europe and the United States. It was deemed necessary that an institute must be developed to co-ordinate among peace societies and peace movements in order to strengthen peace, disarmament and the amicable settlement of disputes. Fredrik Bajer was the main architect of IPB as well as its first President.[8]

The Permanent International Peace Bureau was in its time synonymous with the peace movement, which co-ordinated activities of peace societies through its executive body. IPB had promoted the concept of peaceful settlement of international disputes; that idea was realised in 1899 and 1907 through the Permanent Court of Arbitration. The bureau had arranged the annual congress of peace societies to strengthen the peace movement and exchange of ideas to further their objectives. It established close co-ordination with the Inter-Parliamentary Union and also published a yearbook. The International Peace Bureau's contribution was well recognised, and thus, it was bestowed the Nobel Peace Prize in 1910.

The outbreak of the First World War in 1914 adversely affected IPB's work, and after the end of the war in 1919, it could not be revived fully. IPB's ideas of peaceful settlement of disputes were adopted by the national and inter-governmental community at their end. At the international level, the Permanent Court of Arbitration (PCA) and Permanent Court of International Justice (PCIJ) came into existence. Over the years, IPB has lost its eminent position in the international arena.

Another reason for this was the peace, disarmament and adjudication of disputes that had become more complex and diversified. Therefore, one single NGO–IPB could not stand in the years to come. Also, this issue area was occupied by inter-governmental organisations (IGOs).[9]

The Permanent International Peace Bureau dropped the 'Permanent' affix in 1912, and thus, it became just the International Peace Bureau. In 1924, the IPB moved its headquarters to Geneva because at the time, the League of Nations was also located there. The IPB continued its work from Geneva to organise conferences, build a library and publish a periodical. Again, IPB's work came to a halt during the Second World War (1939–1945), and it resumed operations in 1961 under the new name of the International Liaison Committee of Organisation for Peace (ILCOP). Legal complications arose under Swiss law with the shift from the International Peace Bureau to the ILCOP. Then, in 1968, it reverted to its old name; since then, it has been continuously engaged in peace and disarmament movements through research, publication, campaigning and networking with other NGOs. Presently, the peace movement is focused on peace education, campaigns against military spending, disarmament and people's harmony.

---

[8] www.ipb.org.

[9] Herz (1969).

4 The Quakers

A Quaker is a member of 'the society of friends', a Christian religious group that meets without any formal ceremony and is strongly opposed to violence and war.[10] The Quaker movement was founded in England in the 1640s by George Fox. They believed strongly in the humanistic doctrine that the presence of God exists in every person. Therefore, spiritually, every man and woman is equal.

The Quaker movement arrived in the American continent in the 1650s. The Friends Service Council in the United Kingdom and Friends Service Committee in the United States were established to support and promote the missionary activities of the Quakers. In 1758, Quakers in Philadelphia were ordered to stop buying, selling and owning slaves by all Quakers. The Government was hostile towards the Quakers' beliefs and mission on both sides of the Atlantic Ocean.

The missionary efforts were focused on organising and maintaining schools and hospitals, and gradually involved the natives in their mission. In the nineteenth century, they expanded their mission to India, China, Ceylon, Syria, Madagascar and Africa. They had assumed relief work during war time and sent their Quaker groups to hostile zones. Since 1870, the Quakers have been actively engaged in providing relief work during times of war. Their relief work and humanitarian assistance during the Franco-Prussian War and the First and Second World War were widely acclaimed by the global community, resulting in the Nobel Peace Prize in 1947.[11]

The Nobel Peace Prize 1947 was jointly awarded to the Friends Service Council, Britain (FSC) and American Friends Service Committee (AFSC). Quakers believed that every man and woman have worth and equal values, they are fundamentally good and deserve affection and equal treatment. Therefore, they were dead against slavery and violence. Quakers are actively engaged in social reforms as well. They pursue their work at a personal level and are motivated by their strong religious feelings to help the humanity's suffering. In the Spanish civil war of 1939, Bengal famine of 1943 and two world wars, their commitment of humanity was illustrated vividly. The Quakers' humanitarian action, thus, was acclaimed worldwide.

They established the Quaker United Nations Office (QUNO) in 1948 in New York and Geneva. They have the consultative status in the ECOSOC. The Quakers' UN office headquarters co-ordinates with their members of organisations such as the Friends World Committee for Consultation (FWCC), Quaker Peace and Social Witness (OPSW) (earlier known as British Friends Service Council), American Friends Service Committee (AFSC) and Quaker Council for European Affairs (QCEA).[12] FWCC is an apex organ of these three Quakers organisations that co-ordinate with the UN, and it has consultative status via QUNO.

Presently, there are more than 4,00,000 Quakers around the world. They expanded their reach to the last corners of the earth and have also broadened their issue areas.

---

[10] *Oxford Advanced Learners Dictionary*, Oxford University Press, Oxford, 10th edn., 2020.

[11] Milligan (1968); Bacon (1969); Official Website: www.NobelPeacePrize.

[12] www.quno.org; www.fwcc.world; www.quaker.org.uk; www.afsc.org; www.qcea.org.

Initially, they worked only to ameliorate the suffering of humanity. Now, they are engaged in justice, human rights, refugees, peace, climate change, food security and sustainability. Human rights have been the concern of Quakers ever since its origin. So, it is but natural that they have been consistently pursuing anti-slavery campaigns, the plight of women in prison, rights of indigenous people, refugees and migrant workers through research, advocacy and diplomacy.

Peace and disarmament, non-violence and harmony are their primary concerns. They have been vehemently against child soldiers and military conscription. In September 2013, the UN Human Rights Council adopted Resolution 24/17 without a vote. The Council Resolution says:

> Recognises that the right to conscientious objection to military service can be derived from the right to freedom of thought, conscience and religion.[13]

5 Amnesty International

Amnesty International known as Amnesty or AI in short was founded in 1961 in London. Amnesty is working for the cause of human rights, mainly for the protection of prisoners of conscience. In 1977, Amnesty International was awarded the Nobel Peace Prize for its defence of human dignity against torture.[14] In 1978, Amnesty was awarded the United Nations Prize in the field of Human Rights.[15] It is independent of all governments, financial players, political conviction and religious faith.

Amnesty International was founded by the initiation of British human rights advocate, Peter Benenson. The idea of the organisation came to Benenson after reading a newspaper report about two Portuguese students in Lisbon during the dark days of Antonio Salazar's dictatorship. These two students who toasted to freedom were arrested and sentenced to seven years imprisonment for this offence.

Benenson had approached Luis Blom-Cooper, the legal correspondent at the London Observer, and Eric Baker, a prominent Quaker, about his ideas to defend human rights and to promote justice. They published an article in the Observer about political prisoners, whom they termed "prisoners of conscience". The article contained information about "forgotten prisoners" across the nations. Jonathan Power said:

> the reaction was overwhelming; a flood of letters and donations powered in, together with a great amount of information on thousands of other prisoners of conscience.[16]

The objectives of Amnesty International were limited but clear-cut, as Linda Rabbens said:

---

[13] Human Rights Council Resolution 24/17 of September, 2013; A/HRC/24/17.

[14] www.nobelpeaceprize.org (1977).

[15] www.listoftheunitednationsprizeinthefieldofhumanrights1978.

[16] Power (1981).

> the appeal for Amnesty had four aims: to work impartially for the release of those imprisoned for their opinions; to seek for them a fair and public trial; to enlarge the right to asylum for political refugees; and to advocate for effective international machinery to guarantee freedom of opinion.[17]

Amnesty International began its journey in the London headquarters, and in a very short span of time it transformed into an international centre in 1963. Amnesty expanded its membership and outreach worldwide. When it received the Nobel Peace Prize in 1977, there were more than 1000 voluntary groups across the nations. This is a remarkable milestone in the human rights movement. Amnesty started its journey with three members. Since then, it marched tirelessly on. At the turn of twentieth century, Amnesty's membership increased to approximately two million members.

The day-to-day work of the organisation is carried out by the Secretary General, with the assistance of London-based secretariat. Apart from staff and the Secretary General, Amnesty is constituted by its members, the international council (IC) and the Chairman. The international council consists of the representatives of sections or branches. The country branch is referred to as section or structures. The section is well-established, with a sizeable number of members. In national branches comprising fewer members, it is known as structures. The sections have more members in the international council when compared to structures.

Every 2 years, the international council holds meetings, lays down policy framework and elects the international board. The international board is a small body consisting of one chairperson, treasurer and eight members. It meets twice a year, being answerable to the international council. It takes decisions on behalf of Amnesty International; these decisions are executed by the Secretary General, with the help of secretariat staff, members and volunteers.

Being a charitable organisation, Amnesty International is financed largely by fees and donations from its worldwide memberships. It does not accept donations from either governments or governmental organisations as it wishes to maintain its independence from any political ideology. However, Amnesty has accepted funds from corporations with careful weightage. It is expected that Amnesty International utilise its available funds or financial resources for its purposes and functions, rather than administrative overhead charges.

Once there was a controversy with respect to payments and expenditures. The said matter was raised by conservative parliamentarians and others in Britain. Amnesty settled this issue judiciously and as per the acceptance of the people. Besides, members, staff and funds, there are performing artists, cultural groups, musicians, bands, drama troops, and media persons associated with Amnesty International. These groups are very effective in spreading education and awareness among people at large about the global human rights movement.

Amnesty's principles and purposes strictly adhere to non-violence. It has undertaken the cause of non-violence activists, reformists and opposition leaders. There

[17] Rabbens (2002).

was controversy surrounding Nelson Mandela in 1964, whether or not he was a prisoner of conscience.[18] However, Mandela's cause (of release from imprisonment) was continuously pursued.

Amnesty first began its work primarily on "forgotten prisoners" and later expanded its principles and purposes to the implementation of human rights, opposition of capital punishment, cessation of torture, and the rights of prisoners and refugees. The organisation also focused on forcefully disappeared persons and migrant workers. Child soldiers and LGBT rights are issue-based areas for Amnesty. It also tries to find work for political refugees and where they can seek asylum.

Amnesty International employs various techniques to achieve its objectives, purposes and carry out its activities. It does not assign work to its activists in its own country for prisoners' release and also does not expect to provide information about its own country. Moreover, they are not responsible to the international headquarters for Amnesty activities in their country.

To identify prisoners of conscience and to adopt them for their release and help, Amnesty conducts research to verify the information and facts in order for it to take necessary steps for their release, fair trial, and to stop torture and degraded treatment. The research department is based in London, and it prepares a dossier on prisoners of conscience full of relevant information.

Amnesty deploys multiple techniques such as letter writing, appeal to the media, publicity work, demonstration, lobbying, campaigning and fund raising. It also sends mission delegates of qualified and experienced personnel with the permission of the country where prisoners of conscience are located. They present their case to the host government, but sometimes missions witness governmental harassment. For example, in 1966, Nils Groth, a Danish lawyer sent to Guinea to enquire about prisoners of conscience, was arrested shortly after his arrival, and was detained for two months and later released. Similarly, such unwelcome gestures by the government have been witnessed in Iran, Argentina and others.[19]

Amnesty's work has already been acclaimed by the world community and it has had a great impact in generating hope for prisoners of conscience and their families. Jonathan Power has narrated number of such stories in a very impressive way. It is difficult to assess the emotional support it has received from long-forgotten prisoners confined in isolation and the family members of disappeared persons.

When someone receives letters from remote countries, organisations and individuals, the hope of survival is manifested in the individual. Sometimes, it leads to the release of arrested prisoners, detained persons, the cessation of torture, and inhuman and degraded treatments in custody. For instance, Shahid Nadeem's case in Pakistan, in 1978, received several letters from all over the world. That campaign succeeded in changing his plight along with other fellow inmates.

The case of Archana Guha (in India, 1976) was also mentioned by Jonathan Power. Archana Guha, aged 38 at the time, was the Head Mistress of a school during the Emergency in India. She was tortured mercilessly by the Kolkata police of on

[18] Williams (2010), Chap. 1.

[19] Jonathan Power, *supra note* 16, pp. 27–28.

suspicion of her alleged association with the Naxalite movement. Archana's body was paralysed from the torture The Amnesty International Danish medical group brought her to Copenhagen, and fortunately she recovered to some extent. In Archana's words:

> You (Amnesty International Mission) have given me a new life—you have caused my rebirth.[20]

Amnesty International has with dealt several cases like these aforementioned ones. In Eastern Europe, alone, 12,000 political prisoners were released. Apart from East European countries, the Middle Eastern, Latin American, Asian and even the United States and other Western European democracies were not fully immune from the violations of human rights dignity.

Amnesty uses multiple methods and techniques, such as research for fact-finding and to check the reality of episodes, writing of letters on behalf of victim-prisoners and initiating missions on the spot. These methods and techniques have been quite successful, yielding positive results.

There was a debate in Amnesty International, whether it should limit its mandate to prisoners' conscience, fair trial, the stopping of torture, abolishment of the death penalty and to end extra judicial execution and coercive disappearances of persons. The organisation began with prisoners of conscience in 1961, and over the years, expanded its purview, according to Jonathan Power, in four specific areas, i.e.—against capital punishment, against torture, to save the children and against the arms trade.[21] These areas come under Amnesty's work for its two early decades (1961–1981). Furthermore, its objectives and mandate were extended in the 20th International Council meeting in Yokohama in 1991.[22]

There are two approaches within Amnesty International. The first is to observe self-imposed limits up to prisoners' conscience and related issues, and the second is Amnesty's expansion of its purview up to the protection of human rights. Members' support of Amnesty's purview includes all kinds of human rights violation cases. Whereas, the staff of Amnesty wants to limit its scope, objectives and mandate to the context of available financial resources, manpower and time constraints. This issue has been settled by experience and mutual understanding over time.

Amnesty International's two basic principles are: impartiality and non-violence.[23] When they began operations in 1961, they selected three prisoners of conscience, one each from the western, eastern and third world, without discrimination. This concept was appreciated and time-tested, and ever since, they have followed this as one of their core principles.

Another primary principle is non-violence, with regard to the realm of prisoners' conscience.[24] Amnesty selected cases only when the prisoners were not involved in violent activities. The organisation also does not get involved in their political

---

[20] Ibid., pp. 25–30.

[21] Ibid., pp. 32–43.

[22] Kaufaman (1991).

[23] Larsen (1978).

[24] Baehr (1994).

ideology and movement; they are only concerned with their release, fair trial and a check on cruelty, death sentence and disappearance.

Amnesty International has been on an onward march since the 1960s. In its more than 60-year journey, it has expanded worldwide with approximately 10 million members, supporters and sympathisers, who actively support its vision and mission.

The institution has clear-cut ideas to protect opposing views and alternative ideologies of governments of the day. Every human being has their own worth, therefore, they should be treated equally. Every person is entitled to enjoy human rights without any discrimination on the basis of political opinion, race, sex, religion and economic standard. Amnesty is committed to protect primarily prisoners of conscience, ensuring their fair trial, and the cessation of torture, death and disappearance of persons.

Amnesty moved further and focused on the human rights framework without compromising its core objectives and principles. On the specific occasion of the Nobel Peace Prize Lecture in 1977 in Oslo, Mumtaz Soysal spoke on behalf of Amnesty International:

> Human Rights are ends rather than means, Human Rights are indivisible, Human Rights are concrete and specific, Human Rights are universal and Human Rights will not be protected if left solely to the governments.[25]

It goes without saying that Amnesty International is one of the pioneer NGOs in the issue area of human rights. It has saved dissidents, opponents and ultimately promoted democracy, human rights and the rule of law.

6 International Physicians for the Prevention of Nuclear War

International Physicians for the Prevention of Nuclear War (IPPNW) was founded in Boston in 1980 by physicians from the United States and the Russia. Its main objectives were to mobilise doctors, medical students, health workers and people against the threat and use of nuclear weapons. IPPNW has expanded worldwide. Presently, it has reached 63 countries with national groups of doctors, medical students and health workers assisting in the anti-nuclear, peace and disarmament movement. This movement has been joined by more than 1,50,000 physicians and health professionals from across the world.

In the 1960s, cardiologists of the United States and the Russia established co-operation in research, sharing experience in their chosen field of medical science. Two leading cardiologists in Dr. Bernard Lown of the Harvard School of Public Health and Dr. Yevgeny Chazov of the Russia Cardiological Institute took the initiative in the formation of IPPNW in Geneva in 1980, meeting with one another and their fellow physicians.

[25] www.nobelpeaceprize.org (1977).

IPPNW organised the annual World Congress to discuss the published reports and studies on the effect of nuclear war and its prevention, the protection of life and the preservation of health. In addition, they drew up plans to involve the physicians across the world to strengthen their movement. They do not take positions on specific policies of any government, remaining neutral in the process. In a very short span, the IPPNW gained popularity and united global physicians. In the words of former New Zealand Prime Minister, David Lange, "The IPPNW made medical reality a part of political reality."

IPPNW's work has led to the conferring of the UNESCO Peace Education Prize in 1984 and the Nobel Peace Prize in 1989. It has succeeded in mobilising two hundred thousand physicians, health workers and citizens, establishing a network of 500 NGOs and from approximately 100 countries in the prevention of nuclear war. The organisation conveys the message of dangers involved in nuclear war, something that threatens human existence. Japanese physicians collected all the information and data of the bombs dropped in Hiroshima and Nagasaki, and its adverse effects to the life and ecology of the people in these cities. In comparison to 1945, the threat of nuclear war and the rise of terrorists and rug regimes have spawned even more dangerous situations.

The IPPNW has emphasised the complete abolition of nuclear arsenal, i.e. the production, trading, mining, processing, export and import of nuclear weapons. It should be used for peaceful purposes only. The idea of nuclear deterrence is not a workable solution as it promotes the nuclear weapons race among nations. Nuclear weapons are an unprecedented threat to our very existence. The idea of war first comes to the fore through political decisions, being eventually carried out by the armed forces. Scientists are involved in the making of weapons which result in death and destruction. In order to continue our existence on earth, the worldwide call of physicians' movement and initiatives generates great hope. Nuclear war cannot be easily stopped because it is a man-made catastrophe. Bernard Lown recited a Langston Hughes poem on the occasion of his Noble Lecture in 1985:

Hold fast to dreams

For if dreams die,

Life is a broken-winged bird

That cannot fly.[26]

7 International Campaign to Ban Landmines

International Campaign to Ban Landmines (ICBL) is a coalition of NGOs to campaign for anti-personnel mines and cluster munitions.[27] ICBL was formed in 1992, initially by six NGOs including Human Rights Watch, Medico International,

---

[26] www.nobelpeaceprize.org; (1985).

[27] www.icbl.org.

Handicap International, Physicians for Human Rights, Vietnam Veterans of America Foundation and the Mines Advisory Group. They had common objectives to free the world from the dangers of land mines. Jady Williams was co-ordinator, playing a significant role in the networking of NGOs for this campaign.

The ICBL movement has succeeded in pushing political leaders to agree to ban anti-personnel mines. The Mine Ban Treaty—the Convention on the Prohibition, Use, Stockpiling, Production and Transfer of Anti-personnel Mines and on Destruction was concluded in 1997. This international legal instrument is also known as the Ottawa Convention or Treaty.[28] It entered into force on 1 March, 1999, and presently there are 164 state parties of the Ottawa Treaty.

The treaty was the outcome of the successful advocacy of ICBL and networking of 1200 NGOs connected to human rights, humanitarian assistance, children, peace, veterans, physicians, development, disarmament, religious, and environmental and women rights groups across the nations. NGOs lobbied individually and collectively for this at the both the national and international level. The International Campaign to Ban Landmines or ICBL and its co-ordinator, Jody Williams, were awarded the Nobel Peace Prize in 1997.

ICBL's role on the ban of anti-personnel landmines was recorded in the Cameron, Lawson and Tomlin-edited book: *To Walk Without Fear: The Global Movement to Ban Landmines* (1998).[29] The story of NGOs in making coalitions, establishing networking and collaborating with like-minded states, IGOs and sympathisers for the cause of disarmament in anti-personnel mines, is a painstaking one. In Kenneth Anderson's view:[30]

> The ban on anti-personnel mines was initiated by the International Committee of the Red Cross (ICRC) in the 1980s, but ICRC was not involved directly in this coalition because of its basic nature and statutory limits, although they generated awareness and helped the land mining victims.

Kenneth Anderson has drawn seven lessons from the campaign banning landmines. These are: coalition experience of NGOs; networking with sympathiser states and IGOs; simple and clear-cut messaging about the comprehensive ban on anti-personnel mines; mining ban was a small part of military arsenal; armed manufacturing and marketing; systematic pressure on treaty-making on ban of land mining; it gives a risk-free opportunity to small and mid-level states to counter the hegemony of big powers; and finally, the UN and IGOs had extended their full support.[31] This opened a new gateway in the field of international law and global governance.

Anti-personnel land mining is different from other weapons because it remains located where it is installed. The war is over but it can cause danger at any time. Therefore, removing of land mines is necessary besides the ban on its use, production, transfer and stockpiling. Funds and technical assistance are required to remove mines in addition to the provision of medical care to victims of anti-personnel land mines.

---

[28] 36 ILM 1507 (1997).

[29] Cameron et al. (1998).

[30] Anderson (2000).

[31] Ibid., pp. 104–108.

The major powers of the United States, Russia, China, India, North Korea, Pakistan, Israel, Syria and Egypt were reluctant in so far as to put a signature and rectify the Ottawa treaty of 1997. The ICBL's national and international NGOs are lobbying to governments of the day and mobilising public opinion for the Ottawa Treaty, to ensure the safety of future generations.

8 Mėdicines Sans Frontiėrs (MSF)

Mėdicines Sans Frontiėrs (MSF) is also known as Doctors Without Borders in English. It was founded in Paris in 1971,[32] being a non-governmental organisation engaged in humanitarian action and healthcare. MSF began with the association of mainly doctors, nurses, health workers and journalists. Later on, it was joined by other professionals and volunteers. MSF is based on the principles of neutrality, impartiality and independence. It provides assistance to populations in distress such as victims of natural and man-made disasters, armed conflicts, etc. They serve the people on an equal footing, irrespective of race, religion, creed, or political opinions.

MSF is primarily a medical aid NGO, therefore, it observes universal medical health ethics during humanitarian assistance and the treatment of patients and victims. It maintains principles of independence, impartiality and neutrality, so that it cannot be alleged to support any party of an armed conflict. The Code of Medical Ethics is necessary to be observed by any doctor, nurse and health worker with respect to patients, to maintain dignity, and integrity. Patients have the right to be informed about their consent and confidentiality. The patient's religious belief and cultural orientation is to be respected by doctors, nurses and health workers of MSF. The principles and medical ethics are indispensable in its endeavour in order for MSF to provide health care, treatment, surgery and counselling to patients and victims.

Since its origin in 1971, MSF has succeeded remarkably in providing health assistance around the world in adverse conditions with the support of local doctors, nurses, health workers and volunteers. It has received the overwhelming support of donors and volunteers worldwide. According to the disclosure of information in the public domain:

> In 2014, the MSF medical team carried out more than 8 million out-patient consultations, delivered 194,400 babies, treated more than 2.1 million people for malaria, provided over 2,00,000 mental health consultations, registered 2,29,900 HIV patients under care, conducted more than 81,700 surgeries, treated 46,900 people for cholera and vaccinated almost 1.5 million against measles, and more than 75,100 for meningitis.[33]

Medicinės Sans Frontiėrs (MSF) has general consultative status with the UN Economic and Social Council.[34] It received the Nobel Peace Prize in 1999[35] in

---

[32] www.msf.org.

[33] www.doctorswithoutborders.org.

[34] www.esango.un.org.

[35] www.nobelpeaceprize.org (1999).

recognition of its humanitarian action by doctors, nurses, health workers, logisticians, volunteers and supporters. It is continuously endeavoured to provide medical care in acute crises, as well as to raise international awareness of potential humanitarian disasters.

MSF also received the Laskar-Bloomberg Public Service Award in 2015. MSF's name in English, 'Doctors Without Borders', has inspired a number of NGOs to adopt similar names (for example, Reporters Without Borders). A documentary film, Living in Emergency, by Mark N. Hopkins was made on MSF doctors' challenging medical services in the hostile environments of Liberia and the Congo. This film premiered at the Venice Film Festival in 2008 and released theatrically worldwide in 2010. Besides this, academicians and journalists have also produced books and articles on MSFs remarkable contributions to the field of health care and humanitarian actions.[36]

The origin of MSF could be traced to the Nigerian Civil War of 1967–1970. Nigeria's south eastern province of Biafra, blocked by the Nigerian military, had caused painful situations for their people decimated by famine. French Red Cross volunteer doctors and nurses rendered their services during this time of great need. The Nigerian army attacked voluntary health camps and murdered civilians and also blocked of Biafrans who were facing starvation. French volunteer doctors criticised the Nigerian government for blocking of the Biafra region and stopping medical care and food supply from reaching the people. Moreover, ICRC relief work limitation also came to light, because there was a shortage of doctors and nurses. The ICRC's hesitation to become witness to the misdeeds of Nigerian government was also a problem.

Two French doctors, Dr. Max Recamier and Dr. Bernard Kouchner, were also working as volunteers in Biafra. They strongly believed that the world should know about the plight of civilians being murdered and starved to death, as they were being blocked by the Nigerian army. They openly criticised the Nigerian government and the Red Cross. The Nigerian government had misused their power, being responsible for the murder of civilians and starvation while the Red Cross remained silence, choosing not to utter a single word on the grave situation of Biafran people.

In 1971, journalist Raymond Borel, the editor of the French medical journal *Tonus*, issued an appeal to start the group "French Medical Relief" to help people suffering from armed conflicts and natural disasters the world over. Dr. Recamier and Dr. Kouchner, with experience from Biafra, joined this initiative. Initially, 13 persons including 9 doctors and 4 journalists were part of this movement. Thus, Mėdicines Sans Frontiẻrs (MSF) or Doctors Without Borders, came into existence on 22 December, 1971. Their motto was, "doctors would go where the patients are and the national boundaries do not exist for humanitarian action and medical relief."

The response was increasing as 300 doctors, nurses, health workers and volunteers joined this movement immediately. MSF has a firm belief that every human being deserves medical care and humanitarian assistance across the world regardless of gender, race, caste, religion or political opinion.

---

[36] Fox (2014); Haffman and Au (2017); Bortolotti (2004).

Within a year, in 1972, MSF had started its first mission in Nicaragua's capital, Managua, where an earthquake in 1972 had destroyed the city and killed people in the range of 10,000 and 13,000.[37] Since then, Doctors Without Borders marched on with its humanitarian mission of medical care and saved human life. In 1974, it set up a relief mission to help the people of Honduras, after hurricane Fifi caused major flooding, killing thousands. This was a long-term health care mission set up by MSF.

MSF undertook a large-scale mission in the Cambodia refugee crisis between 1975 and 1979. The Cambodian people, forced by the Pol Pot government, left their country for the neighbouring states of Vietnam and Thailand as refugees. These refugee camps in Vietnam and Thailand were in desperate need of health care, food and medicine. MSF had to meet the large-scale and long-term availability of doctors, nurses, health workers, volunteers and donors.

This experience led MSF to run a well-structured, organisational setup. There were two approaches—some wanted a need-based group of doctors, nurses and volunteers while others wanted a permanent official structure. This was resolved through voting, with a permanent official structure being preferred in 1979. Since then, MSF has transformed into a professional organisation. MSF has expanded worldwide and opened its sections in 28 countries with 30,000 employees including doctors, nurses, health workers, staff, logisticians and volunteers. They have treated millions of people around the world, as and when needed, on a short and long-term basis.

Between 1970 to 1980, MSF became a larger health care organisation. To meet the financial requirements, it focused on fund-raising issues. This was also necessitated to maintain the independent working of the organisation. President Rony Brauman introduced fund-raising by mail to maintain a better collection of donations. MSF has large base and support of thousands of regular individual donors from around the world. In emergencies like the Indian Ocean Tsunami of 2004, MSF found itself very quickly overfunded for all the extensive relief work. This reflects the credibility of its mission in the public perception. The mission also enhanced the accountability of MSF in general.

That is why MSF immediately issued an appeal to for the cessation of funds as it had more than met its requirement. The organisation learned to assess and estimate the expenditures, receive requisite funds, and immediately withdraw the public appeal. The 2010 Haiti earthquake is a perfect case in point.

MSF's purpose of humanitarian action is to save the lives and ease the suffering of people caught in acute crises, and thereby, restore their ability to rebuild their lives and community.[38] Its work focuses on terrible situations that have occurred due to armed conflicts, epidemics, natural disasters, malnutrition and waterborne diseases, and the exclusion from health care. Armed conflicts—either conventional or civil war—cause people grave suffering. People are injured by weapons, bounded, displaced, lose properties and means of survival, sexually exploited, beaten and lose

[37] Bortolotti (1974).

[38] www.doctorswithoutborders.org.

their lives. In such a situation, MSF responds with humanitarian action, medical care, relief and assistance in a speedy manner.

In the armed conflicts in the Congo, Yemen, Iraq, Syria, Sri Lanka, Haiti, Nigeria, Somalia, Kosovo, Sierra Leone and others, MSF was always there to provide medical care and relief. Sometimes MSF doctors, nurses, health workers, logisticians and volunteers work with local medical staff and workers in dangerous situations. In Afghanistan, the situation was so dangerous that it forced them to evacuate in 2004. Five volunteers were killed in Afghanistan by unidentified militia. Two MSF staff were killed in the Central African Republic in 2008. Also, in Somalia, Yemen and Syria, a number of MSF staff had lost their lives during the mission.

Natural disaster is another scenario in which MSF has responded promptly and effectively. Calamities such as the Indian Ocean Tsunami of 2004, the earthquake in Kashmir on both sides of India and Pakistan in 2005, the cyclones in Bangladesh and Myanmar in 2007 and 2008, respectively, the earthquake in Haiti in 2010. The Pakistan flood of 2013, Typhoon Haiyan in Philippines in 2013, and the Nepal earthquake of 2015, are instances where MSF successfully mobilised doctors, nurses, volunteers, health workers, medicines, food, blankets and other necessary items to help the victims and devastated communities in their darkest hour.

MSF provides medical care in grave situations like armed conflicts, natural disasters and the outbreak of epidemics. Cholera, meningitis, measles, malaria, tuberculosis, HIV/AIDS, kala-azar, sleeping sickness, chagas diseases and other communicable infections require a timely medical response, otherwise they spread rapidly and can be fatal. MSF diagnoses patients, writes prescriptions and makes treatment and medicines available in the time of these epidemics. They also campaign to make drugs available at affordable prices in the third world. The organisation has pursued multinational pharmaceutical companies to produce generic medicines as per their corporate social responsibility (CSR) programmes.

In order to make health care effective, MSF undertook the issues of malnutrition and sanitation. In the African sub-Sahara and South Asian countries, children and adults face problems of malnutrition. Treatment can be a success only when malnutrition and hunger are erased, with proper dietary requirements being restored. In 2014, MSF introduced therapeutic food or RUTF (ready-to-use therapeutic food) in response to malnutrition. It contains minerals, vitamins, nutrients and proteins for patients with malnutrition.

Another key component of medical care is clean water, hygiene and sanitation. Availability of potable water is necessary in the fight against water-borne diseases. MSF has put in concerted efforts for the proper storage of water, digging wells and the filtration and chlorination of water resources. Personal hygiene and sanitation, sewage treatments, waste-management and the sterilisation of medical instruments are other essential components added by MSF. Immunisation and vaccination are also practised by the organisation to promote health and prevent the spread of various diseases.

MSF has taken some new initiatives to spread awareness through photo exhibits, data and statistics on display in the public domain, as well as study material the consistent documentation of situations. Sometimes, these manifested problems and challenges before the MSF as governments, militias and multinational pharmaceutical companies preferred not to disclose the said sensitive information to the public at large.

On the specific occasion of receiving the Nobel Peace Prize in 1999, James Orvinski, on behalf of MSF, delivered the Nobel Lecture. It highlighted the contribution made by the organisation in the areas of health care and humanitarian assistance as well as during times of distress and natural or man-made disasters. However, MSF's work is supplementary and it cannot work as a replacement to the state, corporations and community. Their primary role is taking care of the regular health and medical well-being of the people.

Public health care is a political responsibility that cannot be carried out by health NGOs and volunteers alone. Doctors cannot stop war, armed conflicts, genocides and disasters. They can only undertake humanitarian actions and support people in need. MSF gives new orientations of health missions by simply reaching out to patients and sufferers in times of grave need.

9 Tunisian National Dialogue Quartet

The Tunisian National Dialogue Quartet was formed in the summer of 2013. The Tunisian National Dialogue Quartet consists of four Tunisian civil society organisations:

(1) The Tunisian General Labour Union
(2) The Tunisian Confederation of Industry, Trade and Handicrafts
(3) The Tunisian Human Rights League
(4) The Tunisian Order of Lawyers[39]

The Tunisian National Dialogue Quartet played a central role in the build-up to constitutional democracy in Tunisia. It was awarded the Nobel Peace Prize in 2015.

In 2011, Tunisia was in the throes of the Jasmine Revolution. This spread throughout northern Africa and the Arab world, coming to be known as the Arab Spring. The Arab Spring posed a serious challenge before the established governments in the Middle East. The Tunisian Constituent Assembly was assigned responsibility to draft a new constitution for the country. But the Constituent Assembly was unsuccessful in completing its task of producing a constitution on the basis of asserting consensus on certain values from political parties and civil societies.

The Jasmine Revolution aimed to remove the government of the day for unfulfillment of its promise and lax attitude. The government refused to resign as they had assumed power through democratic means and had the legitimacy to govern. The dialogue between the government and opposition eventually collapsed, and the stability and security of the country was considerably compromised. A situation of lawlessness took hold of the country. The opposition leader, Chokri Velaid, was

[39] www.nationaldiaglogue quartet.com.

assassinated on 6 February, 2013, with Mohamad Brahmi also being assassinated on 25 July, 2013. The country was on the brink of civil war. In this situation, the National Dialogue Quartet was framed to resume dialogue among all the stakeholders.

The Jasmine Revolution of 2011 spread far and wide, leading to the Arab Spring, which in turn, resulted in the collapse of a number of governments in the Middle East and Northern Africa. At this critical juncture, the Tunisian General Labour Union took initiatives and approached the Tunisian Confederation of Industry, Trade and Handicrafts. Labour and industry had had a historic rivalry, but despite differences, they were united in the larger interest of their country. Subsequently, they were joined by the Tunisian Human Rights League and Tunisian Order of Lawyers. The Labour Union of Tunisia thought beyond the interests of the working-class and demonstrated commitment to the constitutional democracy and human rights.[40]

These four organisations had approached the ruling party and the opposition to resume dialogue and overcome the crisis. Tunisians wanted democracy to succeed but not at the expense of security and progressive reforms. The aforementioned civil societies approached both the parties to resolve the deadlock through dialogue and consensus. These four organisations laid down the road map and agreed on the formula and prerequisite agreement for further negotiations.

This draft road map had four main points:

(1) Acceptance to form a technocrat government of professional experts headed by an independent national figure. The members of the government could not run in the upcoming elections. Moreover, the existing government had to pledge to step down as soon as the new technocrat government was appointed.
(2) The National Constituents Assembly was to resume its functions and determine its mandate and the ending of its proceedings.
(3) Commencement of consultations on the independent figure who would be entrusted to form the government.
(4) Agreement on a road map for completion of the transition process that would set the timetable for presidential and legislative elections. The timetable was to be announced to the general public after being signed by all parties. The roadmap agreement was to be issued under an act adopted by the National Constituent Assembly in a special meeting. Besides, there should be a provisional organisation and review of the public authorities.[41]

Twenty-one political parties of Tunisia had accepted this road map to ensure that national dialogue was possible. However, one of the ruling parties—the Congress for the Republic—had missed the opportunity and made itself unavailable to participate in this historic event. The Transnational Ministry of Human Rights and Justice was responsible for facilitating this dialogue. The said dialogue session was started on 5 October 2013 and concluded on 24 January 2014 with ratification of the new constitution.

---

[40] Omri (2015).

[41] www.nobelpeaceprize.org 2015.

The Quartet had not just provided its good offices but also played an active role in the success of the important task at hand. The National Dialogue Quartet was awarded the Nobel Peace Prize on 9 October 2015 for its significant contribution in building a pluralistic democracy in Tunisia in the wake of the Jasmine Revolution of 2011.[42]

The 2015 Nobel Lecture was delivered by the representatives of National Dialogue Quartet, providing insight into this monumental success of civil society in the promotion of constitutional democracy, protection of human rights and rule of law in Tunisia. This made it explicitly clear that political parties were indispensable to democracy and the government. Apart from political parties, the role of academia, trade unions, media, law professionals, human rights' defenders and industrial associates, civil society and NGOs cannot be stressed enough. The Jasmine Revolution of 2011 and Arab Spring of 2013 had successfully achieved its objectives by peaceful means in Tunisia.

The role of the National Dialogue Quartet in the peaceful transformation from social upheaval to constitutional democracy was highly appreciated around the world. The United State President Barack Obama said that the Quartet is an inspiring reminder that lasting peace and security can only be achieved through dialogue and non-violence when citizens are empowered to forge their own future. He further stated that democracy is possible and necessary in North Africa and the Middle East.[43]

German Chancellor Angela Markel also appreciated the National Dialogue Quartet for their contribution, and praising their choice as Noble Peace Prize laureates. She said:

> They deserved the award for working on Democracy, for sticking to the ideas that people, that have shaken off dictatorship, deserve something better than a new dictatorship.[44]

The Secretary General of the UN, Ban Ki-moon, also acclaimed the Quartet's role in the Arab Spring for peacefully resolving the issue between the ruling party and opposition and "to avoid the disappointment and the dashed hopes that have tragically emerged elsewhere." He also paid tributes to those who sacrificed their lives in the revolution for the sake of peace, progress and democracy.[45]

10 International Campaign to Abolish Nuclear Weapons

The International Campaign to Abolish Nuclear Weapons (ICAN) is an international coalition of NGOs. ICAN was formulated in 2007, with 468 NGOs as its partners around the world. These NGOs are located in more than 100 countries. ICAN's

---

[42] Ibid.

[43] Washington Times, 9 October 2015.

[44] New York Times, 9 October 2015.

[45] The Observer, 8 October 2015.

headquarters are based in Geneva, from where it co-ordinates with partner NGOs and has launched campaigns against nuclear weapons.[46] The Nobel Peace Prize 2017 was awarded to the International Campaign to Abolish Nuclear Weapons.[47] The Nobel Peace Committee observed:

> For its work to draw attention to the catastrophic humanitarian consequences of any use of nuclear weapons and for its ground-breaking efforts to achieve a treaty-based prohibition of such weapons.[48]

Disarmament and peace were the long-standing issues before NGOs and peace makers worldwide. At the turn of the twentieth century, the Nobel Peace Prize was awarded to the Institute of International Law (1904), for their contributions in the promotion of disarmament and peace. Permanent International Peace Bureau (1910) and International Campaign to Ban Landmines (ICBL) (1997). The coalition of NGOs to campaign for the prohibition of Nuclear Weapons treaty is a continuous endeavour of ICAN when it comes to world peace and security.

ICAN began its campaign during the non-proliferation of the nuclear weapons preparatory committee meeting in Vienna. It intensified its worldwide campaign at the Non-Proliferation Treaty (NPT) Review Conference in New York in 2010. It called all states to support a nuclear weapons convention. ICAN moved further towards a new treaty for banning nuclear weapons. This strategy received support of non-nuclear weapons states within the UN General Assembly and outside.

Eminent global citizens and Nobel Peace Prize Laureates Desmond Tutu, Dalai Lama and Judi Williams, the musician Herbie Hancock, legendary cricketer and journalist Ian Chappell, actors Martin Sheen and Michael Douglas, and artist Yoko Ono, also extended their support to the movement.

In 2012, ICAN launched "Do Not Bank on the Bomb" movement and organised three major conferences in 2013 and 2014, emphasising on the humanitarian impact of a nuclear weapons explosion. These conferences garnered support from 127 nations, IGOs, academic institutions and civil societies. ICAN successfully lobbied for the UN General Assembly; a landmark resolution in December 2016 to launch negotiations on a legally binding treaty to prohibit nuclear weapons.[49] Around two-third of the world nations voted in favour of adopting this agreement.

The UN Treaty on the Prohibition of Nuclear Weapons was adopted on 7 July 2017 by 122 UN members.[50] This treaty is also known as the BAN Treaty. Already, 58 nations have become signatories, with and 10 nations ratifying the BAN Treaty. In order for it to come into force, signatures and ratification by at least 50 countries is required. The remaining 40 UN member states' ratification is needed because 10 members have already deposited at the UN headquarters.

---

[46] www.icanw.org.

[47] www.nobelpeaceprize.org (2017).

[48] Ibid.

[49] www.icanw.org.campaign overview.

[50] www.news.un.org UN Conference adopts treaty banning nuclear weapons, 7 July, 2017; www.treaties.un.org, United Nations Treaty Collections.

The BAN Treaty 2017 is a comprehensive legal instrument towards the "common inspiration of a world without nuclear weapons." As Professor Richard Falk observed:

> The BAN Treaty prohibition extends to the developing, testing, producing, manufacturing, possessing, stockpiling and deploying of nuclear weapons, transferring or receiving them from others, using or threatening to use them, or allowing any stationing or deployment of nuclear weapons or national territories of signatories, and assisting, increasing, or including any of these prohibited acts.[51]

He also observed that it should be understood that the prohibition contributes further to the de-legitimisation of nuclear weapons, but it does nothing by way of disarmament.

The overwhelming majority of nations supported the BAN Treaty but nuclear powers like the United States, Russia, Britain, France, and China (P-5 of Security Council) did not agree to sign the treaty. Remaining unofficial nuclear powers, i.e. India, Pakistan, Israel and North Korea also did not sign the BAN Treaty 2017. These countries still believed in the traditional theory of deterrence and geo-political strategies of their security and influence. The nuclear powers are not interested in the world to be free from nuclear weapons thus far.

In spite of the reluctance of nuclear powers, the adoption of the BAN Treaty 2017 is a monumental step taken by ICAN and supported by NGOs, civil society, Nobel Laureates, overwhelming nations, academic institutions, media and the people at large. With the collective human endeavour against nuclear weapons, the Nobel Peace Committee conferred the Nobel Peace Prize 2017 to the International Campaign to Abolish Nuclear Weapons (ICAN).

The Nobel Peace Prize 2017 selection was not appreciated by one of the world's most influential and popular media houses—The *Economist*, London. The Economist stated that, "The Nobel Committee, no doubt regards the nuclear—BAN Treaty as a good deal in a bad world. Whether it will do anything to advance peace is, however, doubtful."[52] The rest of the media around the world appreciated the Nobel Peace Committee's selection of ICAN for the Nobel Peace Prize in 2017.[53] The world 'without nuclear weapons' would almost certainly be a safer, saner, more humane place than the one we now inhabit.

On the occasion of the Nobel Peace Prize ceremony on 10 December 2017 in Oslo, Setsuko Thurlo, one of the surviving members of the Hivakusha family, who survived the atomic bombing of Hiroshima and Nagasaki, delivered the Nobel Lecture. Thurlo's lecture was a testimony in front of the distinguished participants of the global committee.

Thurlo was just a school-going child of 13 when she witnessed the devastating atomic bombing of Hiroshima and Nagasaki. She lost just about everything worth living for in the tragedy. In Thurlo's opinion, that was the biggest war crime

---

[51] Falk (2017).

[52] The Economist, October 2017, The 2017 Nobel Peace Prizes: This Year's Nobel Peace Prize Rewards a Nice But Pointless Idea.

[53] Worldwide media reports 6 October 2017 and 7 October 2017.

committed by the United States. The UN Treaty on the Prohibition of Nuclear Weapons 2017 is "the beginning of the end of Nuclear Weapons." She went on to say:

> Tonight, as we march through the streets of Oslo with a torch flame, let us follow each other out of the dark night of nuclear terror. No matter what obstacles we face, we will keep moving and keep pushing and keep sharing this light with others. This is our passion and commitment for our precious world to survive.[54]

Beatrice Finn also gave a Nobel Lecture along with Thurlo on behalf of ICAN. Finn presented her discourse, highlighting three things: fear, freedom and the future. The prohibition of nuclear weapons ensured freedom from fear of nuclear devastation. Nuclear weapons posed an existential threat, a threat all too real in the age of nationalism, terrorism and cyber warfare. The prohibition of nuclear weapons is rational and consonant with humanity and humanitarian law. It is for democracy. It is for freedom from fear. It is freedom of choice. Beatrice Finn concluded:

> The treaty on Prohibition of Nuclear Weapons provides the pathway forward from a moment of great global crisis. It is light in a dark time. And more than that, it provides a choice.[55]

11 Ales Bialiatski, and Memorial, and Centre for Civil Liberties

Recently, the Nobel Peace Prize 2022 was awarded to human rights advocate, Ales Bialiatski, from Belarus, the Russian human rights organisation Memorial and the Ukrainian human rights organisation Centre for Civil Liberties.[56]

A. The Memorial

The Russian civil society organisation or non-governmental organisation, Memorial, was founded in 1987 in Moscow. Later on, it was expended in other cities, towns and provinces of the Russian Federation.[57] Memorial represented the post-communist phenomenon, as independent political action was taking shape. That was the time of Gorbachev, who promoted reform within the communist party of the Soviet Union and openness in Russian society (glasnost).

The primary objectives of Memorial were to carry out research about victims of political repression, and to set up a memorial complex in the form of a museum and archives as mark of their remembrance. Memorial would also like to create a supportive system for the welfare of survivors and their close relatives. Moreover, Memorial was fighting for democracy, rule of law and the protection of human rights.[58]

---

[54] www.nobelpeaceprize.org (2017).

[55] Ibid.

[56] www.nobelprize.org/prizes/peace2022/summary/.

[57] White (1995).

[58] Orlova (2019).

Memorial succeeded in receiving support from the intelligentsia, theatre personalities, journalists, researchers, teachers, writers and cultural visionaries. It exposed the reality of forced labour camps (gulag) and prison cells. Memorial established that most of the victims were poor and needy, therefore, they were deserving of empathy, rehabilitation, medical care and housing.

In the initial phase, the state bureaucracy welcomed Memorial's engagement with the survivors and their dependents as well as the remembrance of victims. But very soon, larger questions arose; who was responsible for the repression, for instance? What was the time frame? And whether the Memorial campaign affected the image of the present-day Russian government?[59]

In 2012, the Russian government enacted the Foreign Agent Law. The law requires NGOs who receive foreign funding as well as those engaged in political activities within Russia, to register and declare their status as foreign agents.[60] Memorial was the first NGO to be targeted and branded a foreign agent in 2013.[61]

The Memorial office was raided and shut down by the Russian authorities, who alleged that it violated provisions of the Foreign Agent Law. It made further accusations that the NGO was involved in anti-national activities in contravention to the sovereignty of the state. Memorial approached the court to defend itself but lost its case. The Russian Prosecutor General succeeded to prove in court that Memorial, Human Rights Centre protected terrorists and anti-national elements. Simultaneously, the Russian prosecutor highlighted a number of Nazi collaborators' names that appeared in the database prepared the Memorial Research Centre. Finally, both of Memorial's institutes—the Human Rights Centre and Research Centre—were closed down by the order of the Russian Supreme Court on December 28 and 29, respectively.[62]

The setback, notwithstanding, Memorial has contributed a lot in the promotion of human rights and the rule of law in Russia, and it has also succeeded in collecting credible information and data about victims of the totalitarian regime. Their track record has been appreciated the Russian people. All these factors contributed to them winning the 2022 Nobel Peace Prize.

On the occasion of the Nobel Peace Prize Ceremony, Jan Rachinsky, on behalf of Memorial, said:

> Two hundred years ago, the Russian writer, Pushkin wrote that a 'person's' sovereign is anchored in dignity, personal freedom, sense of belonging to the past and to love 'for his native ashes' and 'paternal coffin'. This indivisible link between memory and freedom is the foundation of Memorial's work.

Memorial, in its 35-year journey, has enriched human understanding about the ideas of 'freedom', that freedom is not only an issue of the present day but past memory is equally indispensable too, and therefore, it is worthy to be preserved for the succeeding generations.

[59] Gersen (2022).

[60] Alexandra V. Orlova, *supra note* 58, p. 384.

[61] Masha Gersen, *supra note* 59, p. 3.

[62] Ibid., p. 5.

B. **Centre for Civil Liberties**

The Centre for Civil Liberties was founded in 2007 in Kyiv.[63] The Centre for Civil Liberties (CCL) is an NGO working for human rights, democracy and solidarity in Ukraine and countries of the Organisation for Security and Co-operation in Europe (OSCE) 1992. It was actively engaged in the formation of public opinion, public policy and supporting civil society activism in Ukraine and other European countries. CCL has established networking with international NGOs around the world for the promotion of human rights, rule of law, democracy and solidarity within the Ukraine.[64]

CCL has been active for the past 16 years, carrying out its mission. It has documented Russian Troops' crimes of 2014 in Crimea, Donetsk and Luhansk. And it continued to collect information and data about war victims during the Russia-Ukraine conflict that began on 24 February 2022. The purpose of collecting information and data is to prove the crimes that were committed by the Russian armed forces on Ukrainian civilians. CCL is insisting for the restoration of justice for all victims of war crimes and placing the responsibility firmly on the wrongdoers, because without justice it is near to impossible to sustain international peace and security.

The Centre for Civil Liberty of the Ukraine created an institute and a map of disappeared people resulting from the violent actions of state authorities on human rights defenders, journalists and activists. Another institute called the Kyiv School of Human Rights and Democracy was also established. The said institute was set up for people's education and awareness, and to motivate them to participate in the ongoing campaign for human rights, rule of law and democracy.[65] CCL has received support from the Ukrainian people. Its contribution was well taken by the international community and was awarded the Nobel Peace Prize in 2022. During the prize ceremony, the Chairperson of the Centre for Civil Liberties observed:

> Ukraine wants peace more than anyone else in the world.[66]

12 Conclusion

The members of NGOS are very large, as listed by the yearbook of the Union of International Association (UIA). Even the NGOs endowed with consultative status by the United Nations ECOSOC form a catalogue of six thousand plus. That was the main reason which limited the scope of this, study to eleven NGOs.

The Institute of International Law was an international NGO of legal conscience that strengthened the peaceful settlement of disputes and development of international law in the very beginning of the nineteenth century. World peace and disarmament was one of the early areas of issue which was undertaken by NGOs. The

---

[63] ccl.org.na/en/.

[64] ccl.org.na>about_the_ccl.

[65] Ibid., ccl.org.ua/en/.

[66] www.nobelprize.org, nobel peace prize ceremony 20,022.

Permanent International Peace Bureau co-ordinated with NGOs to strengthen world peace and also emphasised on stopping the arms race. This mission was further carried out by International Physicians for Prevention of Nuclear War, the International Campaign for Ban on Land Mines and International Campaign for Abolition of Nuclear Weapons. These are some the collaborations of NGOs worldwide, ably supported by eminent persons, institutions, academia, media, like-minded governments and corporations. They succeeded in getting anti-personnel mines banned in 1997 and continuously made endeavours to ban nuclear weapons. They succeeded in the creation of legal obligations of states towards a complete ban on the use, threat and storage of nuclear weapons.

The Quakers started doing humanitarian work which expanded in the mid-seventeenth century throughout the United Kingdom, the United States and other parts of the world. They have a firm belief that every person is worthwhile and deserves love and compassion. They played a significant role during both world wars and have been continuously engaged in their mission.

NGOs have done monumental work in the field of promoting and protecting human rights and providing health care. Prominent health NGO, MSF, has reached out to patients and victims at their doorstep in their hour of need, in times of crises and distress. These crises and distress may be global disasters that are natural, man-made or both. Another human rights NGO, Amnesty International, is a pioneer organisation that deals with the protection of prisoners of conscience, forgotten people and opposing voices against the government of the day. It has saved numerous lives by bringing these issues to light on a global stage as well as raising awareness of world public opinion.

The Arab Spring mainly succeeded in Tunisia due to the contribution made by the National Dialogue Quartet. These four civil societies—labour, industry, human rights and the legal profession collaborated to prepare a road map for constructive dialogue between all the stakeholders towards adopting a constitution and promoting human rights and establishing democracy in their country.

Memorial—a Russian NGO, has preserved memories of victims of political repression, creating a support system for survivors and their close relatives. The Ukrainian NGO, Centre for Civil Liberties, has been collecting information and data relating to war crimes committed on civilians by the Russian troops. In addition, they are involved in the promotion of human rights and the free choice of people in their respective nations.

References

Abrams I (1957) The emergence of international law societies. Rev Polit 19:361–380

Anderson K (2000) The Ottawa convention banning landmines, the role of international non-governmental organisations and the idea of international civil society. Eur J Int Law 11(1):92–120

Bacon MH (1969) The quiet rebels: the story of the Quakers in America. Basic Books, New York

Baehr PR (1994) Amnesty international and its self-imposed limited mandate. Netherlands Q Hum Rts 12:21–25

Bortolotti D (1974) The earthquake in Managua. Lancet 303:25–26
Bortolotti D (2004) Hope in hell: insides the world of doctors without borders. Firefly Books, Canada
Cameron MA et al (eds) (1998) To walk without fear: the global movement to ban landmines. Cambridge University Press, Cambridge
Editorial Comment (1907) Societies of international law. Am J Int L 1(1):135–137
Falk R (2017) Nobel peace prize 2017: international campaign to abolish nuclear weapons (ICAN). www.foreignpolicyjournal. Accessed 1 Oct 2017
Fox RC (2014) Doctor without borders: humanterian quests, impossible dreams of medicins sans frontiers. Johns Hopkins University Press, Baltimore
Gersen M (2022) The Russian memory project that become enemy of the state. New Yorker (daily newspaper of US), pp 1–5
Haffman M, Au S (eds) (2017) The politics of fear. New York University, School of Medicine
Herz U (1969) The international peace Bureau: history, aims, activities. IPB Publications, Geneva
Kaufaman E (1991) Prisoners of conscience: the shaping of a new human rights concept. Hum Rts Q 13(3):339–367
Larsen E (1978) A flame in barbed wire: the story of amnesty international. Frederick Muller Ltd., London
Milligan EH (1968) The past is Prologue: 100 years of Quaker service overseas. Friends Service Council Publications, London
Omri MS (2015) No ordinary union: UGTT and the Tunisian path to revolution and transition. Worker World 1(7):14–29
Orlova AV (2019) Foreign agent, sovereignty and political pluralism: how the Russian foreign agent law is shaping civil society. Pan State J L Int Aff 7(2):332–417
Power J (1981) Amnesty international: the human rights story. McGraw-Hill Book Company, New York, p 11
Rabbens L (2002) Fierce legion of friends: a history of human rights campaign and campaigners. Brentwood, Maryland, p 272
White A (1995) The memorial society in the Russian province. Europe Asian Stud 47(8):1343–1366
Williams R (2010) The divided world: human rights and its violence. University of Minnesota Press

GPSR Compliance

The European Union's (EU) General Product Safety Regulation (GPSR) is a set of rules that requires consumer products to be safe and our obligations to ensure this.

If you have any concerns about our products, you can contact us on ProductSafety@springernature.com

In case Publisher is established outside the EU, the EU authorized representative is:

Springer Nature Customer Service Center GmbH
Europaplatz 3
69115 Heidelberg, Germany

The manufacturer's authorised representative in the EU is Springer Nature Customer Service Centre GmbH, Europaplatz 3, 69115 Heidelberg, Germany. If you have any concerns regarding our products, please contact ProductSafety@springernature.com

Printed and bound by CPI Group (UK) Ltd, Croydon, CR0 4YY
01/10/2026
02225853-0010